916
St2a

100720

DATE DUE			
April '80			

Africa: A Study in Tropical Development

Africa: A Study in Tropical Development

THIRD EDITION

Sir L. Dudley Stamp
Late Professor Emeritus of Social Geography
University of London

W.T.W. Morgan
University of Durham
Formerly Joint Professor of Geography
University College, Nairobi

John Wiley and Sons, Inc. New York, London, Sydney, Toronto

Copyright © 1953, 1964, 1972 by John Wiley & Sons, Inc.

All rights reserved. Published simultaneously in Canada.

No part of this book may be reproduced by any means, nor transmitted, nor translated into a machine language without the written permission of the publisher.

Library of Congress Catalogue Card Number: 75-178152

ISBN 0-471-82008-3

Printed in the United States of America.

10 9 8 7 6 5 4 3

Preface

Sir Dudley Stamp was a wise man and a great geographer. His lucid interpretation of Africa and its potential for development should clearly remain available, yet the rapid pace of change, which he foresaw, required an extensive revision within the overall structure of this book. This it has been a labor of love to make: in the memory of my great mentor and recalling with pleasure time spent in that vast and fascinating continent, my home for many years and in which I hope always to feel at home.

This book exemplifies two of the essential aspects of Sir Dudley's viewpoint. First, that man is a part of this world, not apart from it. From this it follows that in order to improve himself, man must understand his environmental setting and his relationship to it. Secondly, that geographical studies are concerned with very real, everyday problems, and the relevance of their conclusions to those problems that arise during the process of economic advancement is a good test of their validity.

The aim of this book is therefore a comprehension of Africa, rather than the provision of the latest information. The volume of such information has been expanding greatly and in making use of it in this way, I trust the authors whose works and maps have been referred to will find the acknowledgements as full as they deserve—as was my sincere intention. Unfortunately it is a practical impossibility to list the host of people in many parts of Africa who have shared with me their first-hand knowledge of specific areas or specialized topics. The entire manuscript however, has been read by Professor Benjamin E. Thomas and has benefited from his advice and courteous comments, especially on matters of transport and the region of the Maghreb. The timely guidance and encouragement of Audrey N. Clark, who also provided the invaluable statistical summary, is gratefully acknowledged. The numerous new and revised figures owe their clarity and style to the draftsmanship of Mr. H. R. Harvey.

W. T. W. MORGAN

July, 1971

List of Figures

Contents

CONTENTS

Africa: A Study in Tropical Development

PART **I**

The African Continent

CHAPTER 1

African Highlights

Africa is unique among the continents. Although each of the great continental masses of the earth's land surface has its own distinctive features, there are points of comparison among some of them. North and South America, for example, are broadly alike in build, with a great complex of mountain ranges trending from north to south in the west, vast plains in the center, and old mountain remnants and plateaus in the east. Australia repeats some of these features, though reversed — plateau in the west, central plains and mountains in the east. Asia with its huge arid mountainous heart is quite distinctive, but most mountain ranges in Asia trend from east to west, cutting off northern lands very sharply from southern. The same is true of Europe; the east–west central mountains, such as the Alps, cut off the north and northwestern European lands from the Mediterranean.

But Africa in all its major features stands alone. In the first place it lies fairly and squarely athwart the equator and projects almost equally into both the northern and southern hemispheres (Figure 1.1). It is very roughly the same distance [2580 miles (4152 km)] from the equator to its northernmost point (Ras ben Sakka just west of Cap Blanc near Bizerte in Tunisia), which is in latitude 37°21′ North, as from the equator to its southernmost point in South Africa (Cape Agulhas), which is in latitude 34°51′ South [2400 miles (3862 km)]. True, the continent is much broader in the north than in the south, so that two-thirds of its area is situated in the northern hemisphere and only one-third in the southern.

The bulk of its 11,700,000 square miles (30.3 million km²) lies within the tropics — over 9,000,000 square miles (23.3 million km²), in fact — so that Africa is essentially the world's problem continent where development under tropical conditions is concerned. Africa's northern lands, cut off by the great waste of Sahara from the tropical parts, form worlds apart, fascinating in their own special problems and so different in their historical backgrounds from the rest of the continent. In the extreme south of the continent the milder climatic conditions of lands again outside the tropics have combined with historical circumstances to give South Africa over the last 400 years a history

3

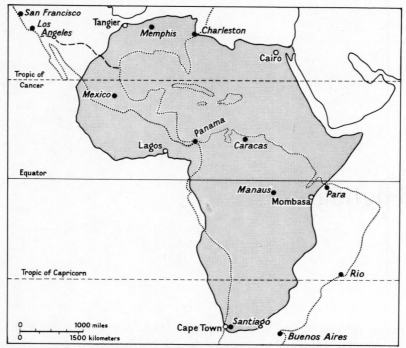

1.1 The position of Africa. An outline of the Americas superimposed on that of Africa to illustrate the scale and the latitudes involved.

very different from the history of the main mass.

Africa is a remarkably compact land mass with no great gulf of the sea penetrating towards its heart. Figure 1.2 shows all those parts which are more than 250, 500, 750, or 1000 miles from the salt water of the oceans. This is in marked contrast to the North American continent. Yet the African continent has never really been a unit. The Mediterranean shoreland and the Barbary States of the northwest have always been part of the Mediterranean world, cut off from what may be called Africa proper by the great desert of Sahara. Egypt has been linked throughout its history with either its Asian neighbors or the Mediterranean world. Similarly the beginnings of the ancient polity of Ethiopia can be traced back to the migration of Sabeans from Southen Arabia into the Ethiopian highlands. Off the west coasts, the Azores and Cape Verde Islands are stepping stones along transatlantic routes rather than African islands. The eastern

shorelands of Africa have long been part of the Indian Ocean basin, indeed since the Hovas, allied racially with the peoples of Southeast Asia, crossed the ocean and settled in Madagascar. The Arab traders and slavers for centuries ranged the East African coasts and penetrated considerable distances inland; they maintained the link with the other shores of the Indian Ocean and even imparted a veneer of Islam over the once extensive sultanate of Zanzibar. Thus the "core" of Africa is intertropical Africa, south of the great deserts and away from the coasts. This, the true *Afrique noire,* does have a considerable unity, even monotony, of pattern. The absence of mountain barriers means that peoples and their cultures have flowed back and forth over its gently rolling plateau surfaces, and there is much to be said which remains true of all parts of the tropical zone.

Africa is not quite an island. Its link with Asia in the northeast is a narrow neck of flat desert land, less than 150 miles (240 km) across, between the Mediterranean Sea and the Gulf of Aqaba, which joins the Red Sea. West of Sinai, between the Mediterranean and the Gulf of Suez, the isthmus of Suez is even narrower, less than 100 miles. Yet this isthmus of Suez has played a role throughout Africa's history out of all proportion to its inconspicuous appearance on the map. In the great days of world exploration in the fifteenth and sixteenth centuries, it forced the explorers' ships that were seeking passage to the Indies to circumnavigate Africa, and incidentally to discover America. When the isthmus was cut by the Suez Canal in 1869, it focused a world spotlight on the essential link in a new world trade chain. Its strategic significance still makes dispute in this area a problem of international rather than of purely local concern.

Although, beginning with the voyage of Vasco da Gama from Portugal to India in 1497–1498, the continent of Africa had been continually circumnavigated, almost until the end of the nineteenth century Africa remained the unknown, the Dark Continent. Books with such titles as *In Darkest Africa* served by those very titles to underline the remoteness and the isolation of lands which so long remained unknown and unexplored by Europeans.

That the whole vast extent of Africa south of the Sahara should thus have remained unknown to Europeans for more than three centuries after its shores were charted is due to an interesting and fundamentally important combination of circumstances. Inhospitable desert coasts are succeeded quite abruptly by almost equally forbidding swamps and forested shores. Except for temporary use as ports of call for running repairs, water supplies, and the like on the route to India and the Far East, there was little to attract the European voyager. The scantily clad black inhabitants were all regarded simply as savages, and there were no fabulous

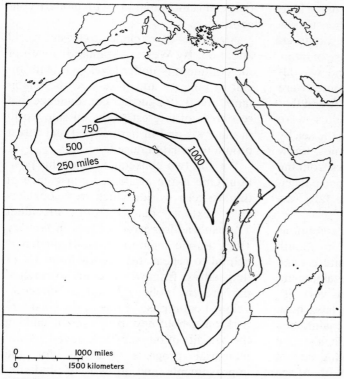

1.2 Distances from the heart of the continent to the coasts.

cities with gold and silver treasure to attract *conquistadores* as in South America. Nor was there any reason why the native peoples should receive voyagers from afar with joy. For countless generations the foreigner had been identified with slave raiding; never had the stranger brought other than sorrow. Where, as on the east coast, alien traders (the Arabs) were established, they were far from friendly towards possible rivals.

The prevalence of various tropical fevers added to the unattractiveness of tropical Africa, and where the adventurous sought to penetrate inland, natural obstacles presented themselves. In the first place, the coastline of Africa is almost devoid of any major opening permitting penetration by sea into the heart of the land; indeed, on some coasts even harbors affording reasonable shelter are few. Along great stretches of the coast there are onshore winds, and the great waves which break some distance out in a line of surf presented another formidable hazard. With no roads, often no tracks other than footpaths wandering from village to village, and only human porters afraid to go far from their own village because of intertribal feuds, penetration by land was almost impossible. The obvious routes were up the few major rivers. It was found that in nearly all cases these routes were barred at no great distance from the sea by rapids and waterfalls which we now know to mark the descent of the rivers from the great African plateau. That great navigable stretches lay beyond these falls was not realized until much later.

Where the hinterland offered conditions more physically attractive in South Africa, the story of European interest and subsequent settlement and development, as we shall see later, has been very different. In tropical Africa there have been coastal trading posts and forts maintained by European nationals for the last five hundred years, but the "opening up" of the interior and the partition of Africa among the European nations took place almost entirely within the last century. It was in 1855 that Livingstone reached the Victoria Falls on the Zambezi, and it was as recently as 1871 that H. M. Stanley set out to look for the missing Livingstone and found him lying ill at Ujiji on the shores of Lake Tanganyika.

The story of the development of Africa in the last hundred years is a complex one. It is sometimes depicted as one of exploitation of the African by the white man, but, although there are elements of exploitation to be found, a more dominant motive was the suppression of the age-old slave trade.

The opening up of tropical Africa has brought a crop of problems, perhaps best described as the results of a clash of cultures. African tribal organizations and systems of law and justice have been brought up against Western concepts of democracy and European law. Jungle law (the survival of the fittest and "might is right") may have been reflected in some aspects of the earlier European penetration, but is incompatible with modern concepts.

Africa has other claims to urgent world attention. By Western standards much of the continent is underdeveloped, with resulting poverty and misery to its inhabitants, and with a further consequence that resources of interest to the outside world in minerals and in agricultural and forest products remain unused.

We find two consequences of this position. One is the awakened conscience of the Western world, which to a considerable extent dates from President Truman's address to Congress in January 1949. Public memory is short, and it is helpful to repeat the famous Point IV of that address from which stems so much of the present policy of aid to underdeveloped countries: "Fourth, we must embark on a bold new program for making the benefits of our scientific advances and industrial progress available for the improvements and growth of underdeveloped areas." Such a flow of financial and technical assistance is now an established feature of the world economy.

The second consequence of the long-continued stagnation of African economy is the dramatic awakening and growth of political consciousness. It was inevitable that as Africans seeking higher education should come into contact with the Western world they should return dissatisfied with the conditions in their homeland. In the period since the end of World War II, Africa has become a collection of independent nations.

When the first edition of this book was published in 1953, Africa could be described as the last remaining great colonial domain of the European powers, where Britain, France, Belgium, Portugal, and Spain had their chief colonial dependencies. Although each of the European powers may be said to have envisaged the eventual independence of these African territories, there were marked contrasts in the mode and pace of progress toward that goal. There seemed then to be a three-cornered contest among nationalism, communism, and Western interests. Few could then have foreseen the rapidity with which nationalism would sweep through Africa, but many might have prophesied that the attainment of independence would bring unhappiness and chaos in place of order, which has, alas, proved to be the case in some areas, although fortunately not in others.

Anyone who has a concern for his fellow man must look long and hard at Africa today. Here is by far the largest agglomeration of new nations which are demonstrating that the problems of political unity, of the legitimate exercise of authority and dissent, and of the maintenance of impartial law and order are painfully real. The rest of the world has to accommodate itself to a vociferous, although not always unanimous, bloc of voices and votes in the United Nations. The numerous disparate social groups in Africa are struggling to reconcile deeply felt codes of social behavior and moral beliefs which are sometimes highly antagonistic. Unfortunately the least diversity is found in material standards of living, and the low incomes per head prevailing over so much of tropical Africa is activating the consciences — and frequently even the generosity — of the more prosperous parts of the world. All these problems have made postcolonial Africa a laboratory for the social sciences. While we shall here seek to understand more of these problems, we should never forget that the vital need is to solve them.

Although in parts of Africa there is considerable pressure of population on land resources, the continent as a whole is still sparsely peopled. In 1900, the population of the continent is estimated to have been 120 million; in 1920, 141 million; in 1930, 157 million; in 1940, 176 million; and in 1950, 206 million. By mid-1960 the Statistical Office of the United Nations gave a total of 254 million out of a world total of 2995 million, and by mid-1970 it was probably about 350 million. If, however, one excludes the Moslems of the Atlas lands, Libya, and Egypt and the whites of South Africa, the population of Negro Africa is about two-thirds of this total — about 240 million in 1970. The growth is now rapid: until recently Africa has been steadily losing ground in its relative world position. If an estimate of 100 million is accepted as the population in 1650, that figure would represent over 18 percent of the world's population. By 1850, using Carr-Saunders' figures, an estimated population of 95 million would represent only 8 percent of the world total.[1] Today Africa as a whole has about 9 percent of the world's people, and Negro Africa over 6 percent.

Although in some areas the population density may be the maximum supportable under existing conditions and existing economic systems, potential changes are enormous. The spread of the knowledge

[1] A. M. Carr-Saunders, *World Population* (London, 1936).

de la Nougerede

"Tarzan, can't you understand—Africa's changing!"
1.A (From *Punch* May 13, 1970.)

of medicine and hygiene means greatly increased survival rates and greater longevity. The conquest of such pests and diseases (so often described as the real rulers of Africa) as tsetse fly, locusts, yellow fever, malaria, and hookworm means that enormous areas which are at present unusable may be opened to settlement and development. Increased control of water supplies will mean a maintenance of crop yields as well as an extension of irrigated areas; the spread of agricultural knowledge can only result in greater productivity. When cattle come to be regarded as sources of human sustenance rather than symbols of wealth, the carrying capacity of the lands in terms of people will be still further increased.

Some writers place the control of water as the foundation for all development, but others would echo the words of Lord Lugard: "The material development of Africa may be summed up in one word—transport."

All the signs indicate that Africa is on the threshold of a period of great population expansion coupled with economic and political development. Over and over again the lesson of Africa, however, has been to "make haste slowly." The failure of some recent large schemes has served to emphasize this lesson.

The emphasis in this book is on Africa between the tropics. The monotony of the physical pattern over much of this vast area is matched by the sameness of human response. From the far west to the east coasts, the traditional African system of shifting cultivation is found with little variation. Yet there are contrasts, and Africa today may be divided into four regions: Mediterranean Africa, which is part of the Moslem world; western Atlantic Africa, which is tropical Africa *par excellence;* eastern Africa, affected by large-scale immigration of non-African peoples, notably Arabs, Indians, and Europeans; and South Africa, the white man's stronghold. (The cultural and environmental individuality of Ethiopia make it a further special case.) Each has its own problems; each reacts upon the others. Not least among the problems is the contrast between the white settlers' outlook in South Africa and the attitude of the rest of the Western world.

Further Reading

The survey made for the Twentieth Century Fund by George H. T. Kimble, *Tropical Africa* (New York, 2 vol., 2nd Ed., 1962), provides a comprehensive point of reference for more detailed or more recent studies. Although subtitled *A Survey of Social Research,* a wider range of topics than might be expected is covered by the authorities who contributed to *The African World* (New York: Praeger, 1965), edited by Robert A. Lystad for the African Studies Association. The growth of studies in the natural sciences is described by E. B. Worthington in *Science in the Development of Africa* (London: C.C.T.A., 1958). United Nations publications provide useful occasional summaries on a continental level of which one of particularly practical relevance is *A Review of the Natural Resources of the African Continent* (Paris: UNESCO, 1963).

There are two atlases which provide maps of various topics and statistics covering the whole of Africa. These are the *Oxford Regional Economic Atlas* and *Africa Maps and Statistics* published by the Africa Institute in South Africa.

CHAPTER 2

Unrolling the Map of Africa:

Exploration, Partition, and Independence

The sea in the midst of the lands, the Mediterranean, if not the cradle of mankind, has seen around its shores the birth, growth, and decay of many great civilizations. Its Asian, African, and European shorelands have all shared in this early history — Babylonia, Assyria, Phoenicia, Israel, and later the Ottoman Turks in Asian lands; Greece and Rome in Europe; and Minos on the island of Crete. But perhaps the greatest of all these early civilizations was in Egypt, on African soil. Egyptian civilization flourished for some four millennia before the birth of Jesus Christ. In the great days of Rome, Carthage, founded by the Phoenicians in the ninth century before Christ in North Africa, was more than once a serious contender for "world" supremacy. In the eighth and ninth centuries of the Christian era, when Islam swept across North Africa, Moorish or Arab domains extended from Egypt across to Morocco and thence into Iberia.

Thus the long, well-documented history of North African lands is in complete contrast to that of most of the rest of the continent. What was the barrier which separated two worlds so utterly in contrast? It was, as it still is, the greatest arid waste on the earth's surface, the great desert known as the Sahara, stretching unbroken from the Atlantic coasts to the shores of the Red Sea, and nowhere less than a thousand miles wide (Figures 2.1 and 2.2).

The one natural route across the desert waste would appear to be the River Nile. But sailing up the Nile beyond Upper Egypt is impossible, for no less than six series of cataracts obstruct navigation between Asswan and Khartoum. Above Khartoum another obstacle exists in the form of great masses of floating vegetation, or sudd.

Thus, for thousands of years, those who dwelt within reach of the Mediterranean had no direct knowledge of the lands which lay to the south of the great wastes. The nomadic tribesmen who knew the secrets of its waterholes took care to keep their knowledge to themselves, for their livelihood depended upon the transport of a few rare commodities cheaply obtained in the south which the northerners valued.

In the Christian era the spread of Islam only intensified the division; the Christian who attempted to penetrate the barrier took his life in his hands. Cut off from the rest of Christendom lay Ethiopia, knowledge of which persisted in stories of the Empire of Prester John.

For many centuries, indeed millennia, Negro Africa, as we may call those parts of the continent south of the Sahara, yielded but one product of major interest to the outside world: slaves. Slavery would seem to be indigenous in Negro Africa itself. There were Negro slaves in ancient Egypt; Ethiopian and Negro slaves were by no means unknown in Greece and Imperial Rome—slave traders brought them across the northern deserts; Arab slave ships called in at ports down the east coast. The mistaken idea is widely held that Europeans introduced slavery into Africa. Nothing could be farther from the truth. Indeed, its suppression within Africa remained a problem long after it had been abolished elsewhere. About 1442 the first Negroes were brought from West Africa by the Portuguese to work in Spain and Portugal,

and from there they were introduced into the New World—some to Haiti as early as 1502. In 1517 Bartolome de las Casas, the celebrated Bishop of Chiapa, sought to relieve the sufferings of the native Indians of Haiti working in the mines by securing a license to import slaves. This was really the beginning of the systematic slave trade between Africa and America.

When the Portuguese were alloted by the Pope's Line the Brazilian shores of South America, they did not find there the sophisticated Inca cities with stores of gold and silver that had lured the Spaniards in the western parts of the continent. They found instead land which could yield abundantly if only labor were available. This constituted another large demand for slave labor in the New World. Though the English Admiral John Hawkins, at war with Spain and Portugal, captured slaving ships and then sold the slaves to the Spanish settlements as early as 1562, it was not until 1620 that a Dutch ship sailed for Jamestown in Virginia and sold the first slaves to a British American settlement. As sugar plantations became established in the West Indies and cotton

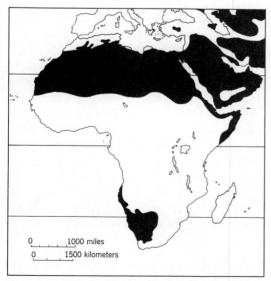

2.1 The arid lands of Africa. Areas in black receive less than an average of 10 inches (250 mm) of rain a year.

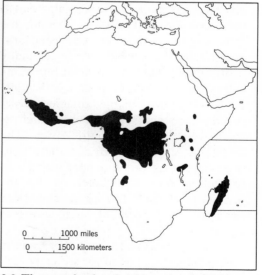

2.2 The wet lands of Africa. Areas in black receive more than an average of 60 inches (1500 mm) of rain a year.

plantations in the American South, Britain developed the notorious "triangular traffic." Ships left Liverpool, Bristol, or Lancaster in Britain with cotton goods, cheap jewelry, and other merchandise, or gold as the price of slaves. They took on their human cargo along the "Slave Coast," as parts of West Africa were long known, sailed across the Atlantic, sold the slaves, and returned to Britain with cargoes of sugar and raw cotton. Bad as the conditions were on the slave ships, the hardly won cargo was too valuable to lose, and the survival rate was high, about 85 percent. On the coasts of East Africa conditions in the slave trade were infinitely worse; it has been said that sometimes only 10 percent of the cargo of some Arab slave ships survived. The West African trade reached its height just before the War of American Independence when 192 slave ships, with a capacity of 47,000 Negroes, were sailing from these British ports. In 1790, during the revival of the slave trade after the war, 75,000 slaves were landed in America by the British, French, Portuguese, Dutch, and Danes.

The slave trade conferred one lasting benefit on Africa. For the purpose of feeding the slaves herded together in the coastal barracoons awaiting shipment to the Americas and also for feeding the same slaves en route, the Europeans, especially the Portuguese, introduced many exotic food plants, since local foodstuffs were either too scarce or too perishable. In this way corn, peanuts, manioc, sweet potatoes, coconuts, bananas, and citrus fruits were introduced into Africa. The long-term results on African diets have been almost as revolutionary as the introduction into the Americas by the Spaniards of such European animals as the horse and cattle or such grains as wheat.

It may seem strange that this trade in Negro slaves continued for so many centuries. Why, for example, did not the Africans band themselves together to prevent it? It is necessary to form a picture of a continent inhabited by competitive tribes. The hunters who depended for their existence on the chase wanted vast tracts of land in which to hunt; they resented any intruders. The nomadic cattle keepers and herdsmen needed vast open grasslands for their animals and resented any enclosures, though their animals appreciated succulent crops stolen from sedentary cultivators. Those who had adopted the settled life and systems of shifting cultivation were at pains to keep off the cattlemen. Almost any one of these groups would view the selling of an enemy as a slave a more profitable solution to his problem than killing him. Over this continent-wide pattern of incompatible economic elements were the ambitious empire builders, gaining wealth and power by selling their captives or betraying enemies. Although it seems that the number of slaves exported was not as great as the calculations of the abolitionists suggested, careful study by Philip Curtin concluded that up to eleven million people were transported in the Atlantic slave trade during the four centuries of its existence.[1]

Mention of the early Portuguese participants in the slave trade brings us to consider the European exploration of African coastlands. The Carthaginian Hanno claims to have made a voyage about 470 B.C. through the Pillars of Hercules (Strait of Gibraltar) and along the west coast of Africa, with the object of founding colonies. He probably reached south of the Gambia River, but for many centuries his discoveries were forgotten. Early commercial contacts along the coasts of the Red Sea and the Indian Ocean are reflected by the *Periplus of the Erythrean Sea,* a Greek handbook of the late first or early second century A.D. It was only after the decline of the Moorish power in

[1] Philip D. Curtin, *The Dimensions of the Atlantic Slave Trade* (Madison: Wisconsin University Press, 1969). See also J. D. Fage, "Slavery and the Slave Trade in the Context of West African History," *J. African History,* X, 3 (1969) pp. 393–404.

Spain and the rise of Spain and Portugal to front rank among the nations that European exploration by sea of the African coasts was undertaken in earnest.

Prince Henry the Navigator (1394–1460) was the fourth son of King John (João) I of Portugal and his French bride Philippa the daughter of John of Gaunt. He established a school for navigation and an observatory, and one of his captains discovered the fertile island of Madeira. His ships were delayed for decades by navigation difficulties along the Moroccan and Saharan coasts before reaching the green lands beyond; hence the name Cape Verde ("Green Cape") and Cape Verde Islands.

Before the voyages of Columbus, the Portuguese had sailed along the coasts of Guinea, and Bartholomeu Diaz (1455–1500), without realizing it, had rounded the south of Africa into the Indian Ocean in 1486. It was the strong easterly winds which drove him back to the Cape of Storms, afterwards renamed by the king of Portugal the Cape of Good Hope.

These probing voyages of the Portuguese were prompted by a desire to reach the spice lands of the Far East by an all-water route instead of having to rely on the uncertain and expensive supplies brought to Europe overland.

Although the shores of Greenland, Labrador, and other parts of North America were undoubtedly known to early Norse voyagers and others from northwestern Europe, the discovery of America is usually understood to mean the first sighting of land by Christopher Columbus in the Bahama group in 1492. The voyage of Columbus the Genoese, financed by Spain, had been undertaken, it is generally believed, to find a westward route to the Spice Islands of the East Indies. There are, however, those scholars who consider that the North American continent had been discovered some years earlier by Portuguese sailors and that when Columbus sailed he already knew

that his way to the west would be barred by a great continent. At a time when there was intense rivalry, indeed mortal enmity, between Spain and Portugal, it is difficult to understand why Columbus on his return voyage called at the Azores — Portuguese territory — and then went straight to Lisbon. It is difficult to believe that he was such a bad navigator that he struck Lisbon in Portugal accidently instead of Cadiz or some other part of Spain. In Lisbon he was certainly granted an interview with the king of Portugal and then allowed to depart unhindered for Spain, instead (as one might have thought) of being imprisoned or even executed. Was King John of Portugal his secret master? Was the object of the intrigue to draw the attention of Spain to the opportunities of the New World while Portugal consolidated her interests in India and the Far East by seeking the Cape route? If so, it succeeded to an amazing degree, and we have fully explained the lack of Spanish interest in the early exploration and development of Africa.

If those who believe the Portuguese knew of the existence of the American continent before Columbus sailed on his first voyage are right, we have a reason for the ready acceptance by the Portuguese of the Treaty of Tordesillas in 1493. It will be recalled that this treaty gave lands discovered west of 60° West to Spain; lands east of that line to Portugal. Although this treaty is normally considered as applying to the Americas (it gave Brazil to Portugal before land in that area was even discovered), it clearly gave authority to Portuguese claims to *any* lands east of the 60° West meridian, that is, to all Africa. While Columbus and the Spaniards were concentrating on the New World, Portugal was certainly active in the search for the sea route to India. Vasco da Gama rounded the Cape of Good Hope in 1497 and landed on the well-watered, forested coasts farther to the northeast on Christmas Day; hence the name Natal which he gave to the area, and which has

2.A Fort Jesus, Mombasa, Kenya, built by the Portugese in 1593. It was sited at the entrance to a natural harbor, on an island of raised coral reef. After two centuries of Portuguese rule, it became an Arab stronghold. (Photo: Camera Press.)

remained to this day. He reached what is now Lourenço Marques on Delagoa Bay on March 1, 1498, but farther north he was not welcomed by the Arab traders and settlers in the coastal towns. As it turned out, this was fortunate, for he secured a pilot who directed him across to India and he landed at Calicut, previously visited by Cavilhão traveling via Egypt in 1486. The way to India was won. The great spice trade was soon firmly in Portuguese hands and the Spaniards could have America. A settlement was established at Mozambique in 1505; a fortified factory was built at Calicut in 1510 and established as a Portuguese settlement and trading post; Goa was occupied in 1510; the coasts of Ceylon were settled in the next few years, and Malacca on the coast of Malaya was captured in 1511. A little later, in 1557, Portuguese settled on the island of Macao off the south of China.

While the Spanish *conquistadores* were busy with the northern coastlands of South America, the Portuguese Cabral, taking advantage of the northeast Trades on his way to India, found himself carried too far westward and off the coasts of Brazil. This was in 1500, and the land was promptly claimed by Portugal. In the following year, 1501, the King of Portugal sent out Amerigo Vespucci to follow up Cabral's discovery. He probably (though there is some doubt about his achievements) traversed the whole coast of South America from Cape San Roque to the Plate estuary, and then sailed on to South Georgia. Portugal thus gained interests on both sides of the South Atlantic, but it was the sea route to India which was of immediate importance. It is said that Algoa Bay (on which Port Elizabeth now stands) was the resting place "on the way to Goa," while Delagoa Bay in what later became Portuguese East Africa was the most convenient port of call "on the way from Goa."

In the meantime the Portuguese had penetrated well into the Gulf of Guinea. They observed the frequent thunderstorms around the norite mass which forms the Peak in what is now Sierra Leone and likened the noise to the constant roaring of lions, hence the name Lion Mountains or Sierra Leone. They founded their first permanent station at Almina on the Gold Coast as early as 1481. The small quantities of alluvial gold brought down from the interior and exchanged for manufactures by the tribes of the coast originally made these lands of interest to Europeans. African ivory had long been famous, but it was slave trading that soon became most important. The Portuguese established a string of forts to guard their interests in the trade. British traders visited the West African coasts from 1530 onwards, and it was as early as 1554 that the famous Captain Thomas Wyndham died in the creeks of the Oil Rivers, or Niger delta. It was not until the early seventeenth century that the British established their first trading post, a fort on the Gambia River. That century witnessed the ousting of the Portuguese by

the Dutch; but the Dutch found themselves sharing interests with the British, while Denmark and Brandenburg also had forts along the coast. France was also interested in the Far Eastern trade. French interests in Senegal (West Africa) date from 1637, and the capital, Saint-Louis, was founded in 1658. In the Indian Ocean the French have held Reunion since 1643 and were masters of Mauritius (Ile de France) from 1715 to 1810; Pondicherry, the oldest French Indian settlement, was founded in 1674.

It was not until toward the end of the eighteenth century that a profound change took place in the European (and by this time American) attitude towards Africa. On one hand was the growth of the movement for the abolition of slavery; on the other hand, was the urge toward exploration of the unknown African interior.

In Britain the abolitionists found a champion in William Wilberforce. Born in 1759, he was elected to Parliament at the age of 21 and was soon known for his

2.B A slave raid in central Africa. This nineteenth century illustration exemplifies the way in which small parties of raiders were able to penetrate far inland because of superior weapons, more efficient organization, and, in this case, the use of an imported mule. (From Radio Times Hulton Picture Library.)

2.C Slavery was never permitted in the British Isles and, despite British involvement in the earlier days of the slave trade, the Royal Navy was used in an effort to suppress the traffic, especially after the 1840's. This is a romantic portrayal of an incident in 1887. (From Radio Times Hulton Picture Library.)

forceful advocacy of many philanthropic causes. In 1787 he took on the leadership of the abolitionists and fought doggedly for 20 years before his dreams were realized. In 1807 the British Parliament passed a measure for the abolition of the slave trade. This was, of course, an entirely different matter from the abolition of slavery and the emancipation of slaves, but Wilberforce lived to see this ideal realized too. He died in 1833, the year in which slavery was abolished throughout the British Empire. Even in the early days the abolitionists were not inactive. In 1787 they formed the Sierra Leone Company, with a trading charter from the British crown, but with the avowed object of resettling freed slaves in Africa. It was impossible to return slaves to their native places because these places were unknown. A tract of land, therefore, was ceded to the company by its native ruler in Sierra Leone. The task was a difficult one, but after early troubles progress was made, especially after the founding of Freetown in 1792. However, the company was glad to transfer its responsi-

bilities to the British Crown in 1808. Though it was not the oldest of the British Colonies in Africa, the origin of Sierra Leone, one of the oldest, as a home for freed slaves, deserves not to be forgotten.

American interests in tropical Africa have a similar origin. In 1812 the American Colonization Society selected Cape Mesurado (now Monrovia) as an area to which freed slaves could be sent, and the American–Negro colony was founded between 1822 and 1828 by the white American Jehudi Ashmun, some 30 years after the founding of Freetown. The name Liberia was given to the settlement in 1824 by the Reverend R. R. Gurley. Another settlement (a republic, like Liberia) named Maryland, existed until the two were joined in 1857. Curiously enough, the United States did not recognize the new republic until 1862.

The early years of the nineteenth century were the days of Britain's struggle with Napoleon of France, a struggle which did not cease until the decisive victory at Waterloo in Belgium in 1815 and Napoleon's exile to St. Helena. Even then, the traditional British–French rivalry persisted. The abolition of slavery in 1807 rendered the West African forts of little value. By 1821 the number of British stations was reduced from twelve to four, despite some requests from Africans that Britain should take over the whole coast from Gambia to the Congo. By 1820 the forts assumed a new importance as bases from which the British navy could operate against the remaining slave traders. The handful of traders who refused to leave the coast when Britain proposed to evacuate the whole area turned the scales towards a new growth of real trade.

Turning to exploration, we have an important name in the Scottish doctor, Mungo Park, who set out from the mouth of the Gambia in 1795 to find the great river known to exist inland and called the Niger. He traveled almost due east, and passed through country where he found strong, well-built Negroes engaged in cattle rearing and in burning the grass of the savanna lands in the dry season, which they believed improved the growth of succulent shoots later. When he entered the country of the Islamic emirates, he found hostility but persisted — as a Christian in danger of his life — northeastwards to the Saharan margins, where wandering pastoralists were still unfriendly. He reached the Niger at Segu and traveled down it some fifty miles before he decided to return. Despite great hardships (it was the rainy season), he had, on his return, a burning desire to solve the riddle of the Niger. In 1805 he set out again on a similar route. He was never again seen alive by white men; he was drowned at the falls of Bussa (now in the heart of Nigeria) after an attack by local tribesmen. So the outlet of the Niger remained a mystery until 1830, when R. L. Lander proved the "Oil Rivers" to be the delta of the Niger (Figure 2.3).

In the same portion of the continent, the famous town of Timbuktu (Tombouktou) was reached by Major Gordon Laing in 1826 but he was murdered on his return journey; the Frenchman, Réné Auguste Caillie, passed through it in 1828 on a route from Guinea and survived to cross the Sahara and reach Fez in Morocco. One of the earliest and most scientific of travelers in the region was Heinrich Barth, a German employed by the British government, who from 1850 to 1855 crossed the Sahara and traveled and studied throughout an area from Timbuktu to Cameroon, including much of what is now northern Nigeria. He subsequently became Professor of Geography at the University of Berlin.

It is interesting to turn for comparison to South Africa, where the story of European interest and penetration was very different. In general terms the climatic conditions around the Cape of Good Hope are comparable to those in the pleasantest parts of California. The winters are milder, and the summers are less scorching than in Mediterranean Europe, but there is abundant sunshine in the well-watered coastal plains and valleys. Furthermore, there are some reasonably good natural harbors, especially the harbor of Cape Town under the shelter of Table Mountain. Though known to and used by the Portuguese ships en route to the Indian Ocean, Cape Town came into being as a regular halfway house when the Dutch ousted the Portuguese in the Far Eastern trade and established a settlement on the site of Cape Town in 1652. Although the Dutch East India Company was sternly against setting up a colony, it was convenient to allow old servants of the Company to retire there and grow produce and rear cattle for the benefit of ships which called to rewater and revictual. Naturally farms were established at increasing distances from the coast, and the settlers came into collision with the native Hottentots against whom the Dutch company had neither men nor materials to defend Dutch nationals.

The British occupied the Cape during the Napoleonic Wars to protect the sea

2.3 Reproduction of a map of Africa, 1821. This map shows the large areas of
the interior then remaining unknown to the outside world, including the Congo
and Zambezi rivers, the true course of the Niger and the source of the Nile.
(From *A New and Comprehensive System of Modern Geography,* by Thomas
Myers, London, 1822.)

2.D Groot Constantia. This beautiful example of Dutch traditional architecture was built in South Africa in the seventeenth century by Governor Simon van der Stel. (Courtesy of South Africa Department of Information.)

route to India, and by the Peace Treaty of 1814 they retained the territory. By this time the Dutch farmers or "Boers" (boer = farmer) had become well established, but, as they expanded farther into the interior, they met increasing resistance not only from the Hottentots but also from the Kaffirs, as the Boers called the Negro peoples they found in Southeast Africa. The Kaffirs were being pressed southward by other and warlike Bantu tribes sweeping southward from central Africa. The Boer farmers had in the past relied on slave labor, and tended to take the frontiersman's view that when there were signs of trouble a dead Kaffir was safer than a live one.

The British, on the other hand, had abolished slave trading and were seeking to abolish slavery altogether. They sought to replace the frontiersman's methods by peaceful settlements. Disagreement between the Boer farmers and the British government came to a head in 1833 when slavery was abolished and the Boers received eventually somewhat inadequate compensation for the loss of their slaves. In 1836 the Great Trek began; the Boer settlers set off with their great lumbering ox wagons, each with a "span" of sixteen

oxen, into the interior. They crossed the Orange River and later set up the Orange Free State (Orange Vrij Staat). Others crossed the Vaal River, fought the Matabele, and established what later became the Transvaal Republic. In 1837 Piet Retief crossed the scarp of the Drakensburg into country occupied by the Zulus, but he and other leaders were murdered by the Zulu king in February 1838. Though the Zulus were defeated later the same year, the Boers found a British colony already established at Fort Natal. After a period of friction Natal was declared a British colony (1843), and the Boers left.

The British government was in a difficult position when the Great Trek took place. Should it try to follow the trekkers and attempt both to control and protect them, thus involving itself in a possibly endless war? Or should it let them go and risk their being overcome by the hostile Kaffir tribes? In 1852 the decision was made by recognizing the Transvaal as an independent republic, provided there should be no slavery. The trekkers of the Orange Free State were more doubtful about accepting independence if it involved losing protection. Nevertheless, the Orange Free State was declared formally independent in 1854. Thus in broad lines the four countries which eventually became provinces of the Republic of South Africa were established by 1854.

It should be stressed however that nation building was not exclusively a prerogative of the whites. The plundering activities of Shaka and subsequently of Dingane did not leave behind an established order, but the more constructive abilities of Sobhuza and Mswazi led to the creation of Swaziland, while the great Sotho king Moshesh founded the Basuto kingdom, now Lesotho.

By this time the work of exploration from South Africa associated with the name of Dr. David Livingstone was already well advanced. David Livingstone, the son of a poor Scot, was born in 1813. Though he was working in a cotton mill at the age of 10, he had a burning desire to become a medical missionary to China. The London Missionary Society sent him instead to South Africa. He arrived at Cape Town early in 1841, proceeding at once to the mission station established by Robert Moffat at Kuruman in southern Bechuanaland. In 1844 he married Mary Moffat, who (sometimes with young children) accompanied him on many of his journeys until her death at Shupanja in 1862. In 1849 he discovered Lake Ngami, which has since partly dried up. In 1850 he reached the Upper Zambezi with his wife and children, but they fell sick and he sent them back to Cape Town (incidentally, they took nearly two years on the journey). From the Upper Zambezi he went north and west up the Liba to Lake Dilolo, arriving, exhausted from fever and ill nourished, at Loanda, on the west coast, on May 31, 1854. Undaunted, he returned in 1855 to the interior, determined to follow the Zambezi to its mouth. On this journey he discovered the great falls, which he named in honor of Queen Vicotria, in 1855, and reached the mouth of the Zambezi the following May. After a sojourn in England he set off in 1858 on a second journey to Africa with

his brother Charles and John Kirk. The expedition started up the Zambezi and its tributary the Shire, but met the inevitable rapids; on a second attempt, light canoes were carried to the navigable upper reaches. The party had many other troubles, but when he returned in July 1864 Livingstone had explored the Shire River, discovered Lakes Shirwa and Nyasa, and opened the eyes of the world to the horrors of the slave trade which still existed.

Although Livingstone declared that he found exploring easier than writing, his diary[2] is fascinating reading. On his 1849 journey to Lake Ngami he spent some time among the Bushmen. By showing them how to irrigate their crops in this dry Kalahari country from wells in the dry season and streams in the precarious wet season he did much to ameliorate their hard life. In his 1855 journey he met with suspicion as well as demands for bribes from the native chiefs. He learned also of the many plagues of Africa: heat and drought; mosquitoes which were sometimes only annoying, at other times dangerous carriers of fever; the tsetse fly, which caused havoc among his cattle and pack animals and was capable also of bringing the dread sleeping sickness to man. Travel by canoe involved the hazards of attack by crocodiles and by the floating logs which resolved on approach into hippopotami capable of capsizing the canoes if only in play. Living entirely on the country meant killing antelopes in the savanna lands and subsisting on nuts and fruits in the forests.

In 1865 he started on his last journey, with the object of finding the source of the Nile, an old problem. It cannot be said that he was treated overgenerously. The British government granted him £500 (then about $2500), and the Royal Geo-

---

[2] *Missionary Travels and Researches in South Africa* (London, 1857). See also *Livingstone's Private Journals, 1851–1853,* edited by I. Schapera (London: Chatto and Windus, 1960).

graphical Society a like amount. While he wandered over vast tracts of country from Lake Nyasa to Lake Tanganyika he was lost to the world, and his fate for five years was unknown.

The explorations of Dr. Livingstone and his revelations of the horrors of the slave trade which still existed had aroused intense interest in the United States, where slavery had been finally abolished in 1864. Mr. Gordon Bennett of the *New York Herald* translated into deeds the popular demand by sending Henry Morton Stanley with a well-equipped expedition to search for Livingstone. Stanley was an Englishman born in North Wales in 1841, who emigrated to New Orleans at the age of fifteen and sought adventure as a roaming journalist. Having already accompanied Lord Napier's Abyssinian expedition in 1867–1868 as a special correspondent for the *New York Herald,* he was the obvious person to send in search of Livingstone. Reaching Zanzibar in 1871, later in the year he came upon Livingstone, ill with fever but indomitable as ever, at Ujiji on the shores of Lake Tanganyika. Livingstone refused to return, and, partly recovered in health, he and Stanley explored the northern end of Lake Tanganyika together. When Stanley reluctantly left him, Livingstone set off once again to seek the source of the Nile. His health deteriorated, and on May 1, 1873, his followers found him dead. He was at Chitambo's village on the Moli-lamo, actually one of the headstreams of the Congo. The love and confidence he had inspired in his African followers were well shown in the devotion with which they carried his body a thousand miles to Zanzibar; from there it was conveyed to England and buried in Westminster Abbey.

Before we review the later work of Stanley we must look at some of the earlier exploration in East Africa (Figure 2.4). Little is known of the early contacts between Egypt and the peoples to the south, including the ancient Empire of Ethiopia or Abyssinia. The Ethiopians proper, or Amharas, were converted to Christianity in the fourth century, and connection was maintained continuously with the Coptic Church of Alexandria, since the Abuna or Chief Bishop of Ethiopia had (until World War II) always been a Copt and appointed by the Coptic Patriarch of Alexandria. This did not, however, result in any direct contacts between Europe and Ethiopia. The first written record of a land exploration by a European is that of the Portuguese missionary, Father Lobo, who reached Ethiopia in 1622. Although he saw the deep valleys whose waters feed the Blue Nile he did not realize the connection, and it was not until 1770 that the Scottish explorer James Bruce (1730–1794), in the course of five years' journeying in Ethiopia, solved the riddle by following the Blue Nile down until it joined the main river, the White Nile, at Kahrtoum. Nearly a century was to pass before Speke solved the riddle of the source of the White Nile.

Exploration in East Africa was hindered, even along the coastlands, by Arab seamen and traders. Richard Francis Burton, born in England, educated in France, Italy, and at the University of Oxford, served as a young man in the Indian Army and as a surveyor before he made his famous journey to Mecca in 1853 disguised as an Indian Pathan. He then turned his attention to Africa and was the first white man to enter the Somali capital of Harrar. He had time to serve in the British army, though never actually reaching the front, in Crimea before joining John Hanning Speke (1827–1864). They set off in June 1857 from Zanzibar westward. They crossed the high grassy plateau abounding in game in what is now Tanzania until they overlooked that great rift in the earth's crust, the East African rift valley, with the long narrow Lake Tanganyika at their feet. This was in 1858, and they reached the settlement of Ujiji where thirteen years later Stanley

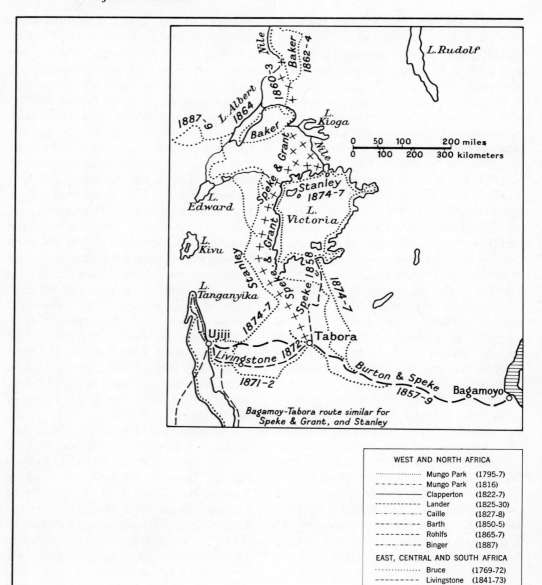

2.4 The routes of some leading explorers of Africa. The routes shown are those followed by the explorers whose work is mentioned in the text, together with those who added greatly to the knowledge of the interior of the continent prior to 1850.

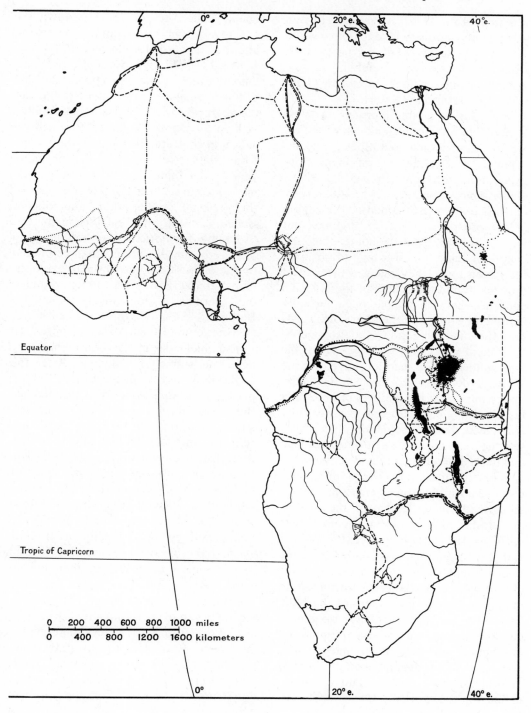

Equator

Tropic of Capricorn

0°   20°   400   600   800   1000 miles
0°   400   800   1200   1600 kilometers

was to find the sick Livingstone. Burton was already seriously ill, and, leaving him at Tabora, Speke went on northwards alone. He discovered the great inland sea, which he named in honor of Queen Victoria, before returning to Burton.

With Burton's later journeys in West Africa, South America, and elsewhere we are little concerned, but Speke, accompanied by J. A. Grant, set off on a second expedition with the help of the Royal Geographical Society in 1860. They reached and were detained in the capital of the prosperous land of Buganda but were later released. Finding that the waters of Lake Victoria poured out over the Ripon Falls, they realized that at last they had found the source of the Nile. To confirm what must have been virtually certain they followed the river northwards until they had the good fortune to meet S. W. Baker (1863) who, accompanied by his long-suffering wife, had journeyed up the White Nile through the Sudd region. Speke published his findings in 1863, but his old companion Burton was not fully convinced. Speke accidentally shot himself the very day he was to meet Burton and defend his momentous discoveries.

Samuel White Baker (1821–1893), after eight years in Ceylon attempting to form an agricultural settlement on the English model, started his explorations of the Nile basin in 1861. He explored the Atbara and Ea tributaries and, after meeting Speke, went on to find Albert Nyanza (1864), which he showed contributed an important part of the waters of the Nile. In 1870 he was actually appointed governor-general of the Nile Equatorial Districts by the Khedive Ismael to suppress the slave trade and open up the area to trade. In this post he laid the foundation for the work of General Charles George Gordon, his successor.

We must now return to H. M. Stanley, who set out on his second journey in 1874 with the main object of solving some of the great problems which the death of Livingstone had left unsolved. He circumnav-

igated Lake Victoria, passed down the Lualaba to where it becomes the Congo and then down that great river to the sea. It was Leopold II, king of the Belgians, who realized the enormous potential value of this navigable highway penetrating into the heart of Africa. On his behalf Stanley headed an expedition in 1879 which resulted in the establishment of the Congo Free State five years later. For many years, indeed until 1907–1908, this enormous area in the heart of Africa remained the personal possession of the king of Belgium. With its establishment the "scramble for Africa" may be fairly said to have begun. Partition was precipitated by the activities of the German explorer, Karl Peters (1856–1918). Peters founded the German Colonization Society at Berlin in 1884 and in the same year made an expedition to East Africa. (Figure 2.5.)

The chief ruler in East Africa had long been the sultan of Zanzibar. After the abolition of slavery in the British Empire in 1833, Britain's policy was to influence this powerful ruler against slavery, to persuade him to undertake the necessary reforms, and to help him to do so. The first British consul at Zanzibar was appointed in 1840, but it was not until Sir John Kirk was appointed in 1873 and occupied himself with great skill for fifteen years that slavery was actually brought to an end and replaced by legitimate trading. At first the closing of ports to the Arab slavers drove them inland; then Britain supported the Zanzibar Sultan Barghash with arms and ammunition, and the sultanate began to grow into a real state (Figure 2.6). But Karl Peters had gained access to East Africa with three companions, all in disguise and using false names. They traveled around the country, obtaining concessions for the German Colonization Society from chieftains who were in fact under the sultan of Zanzibar's suzerainty. In 1855 the German government backed up the claims based on these treaties with local chieftains and sent a fleet to anchor off Zanzibar, which they

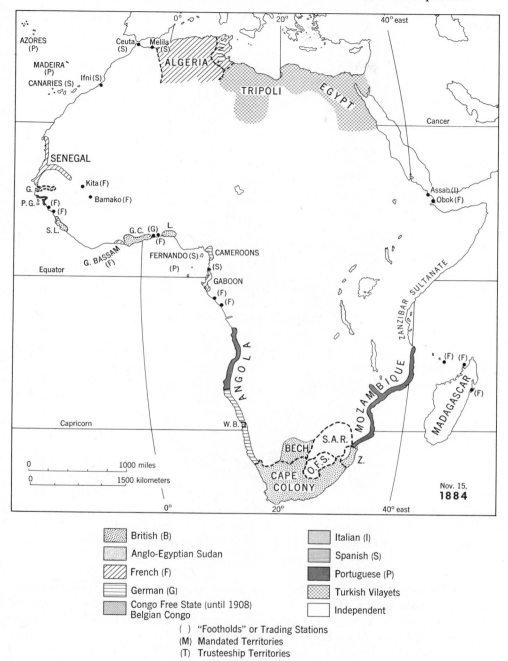

British (B)	Italian (I)
Anglo-Egyptian Sudan	Spanish (S)
French (F)	Portuguese (P)
German (G)	Turkish Vilayets
Congo Free State (until 1908) Belgian Congo	Independent

( ) "Footholds" or Trading Stations
(M) Mandated Territories
(T) Trusteeship Territories

2.5 Africa, November 15, 1884. This map shows the spheres of influence of the various European powers prior to the Berlin Conference. It indicates also the footholds or trading stations. With the exception of two French trading stations in Senegal, European influences were entirely restricted to the coast. *Note.* Figures 2.5 to 2.13 show the partition of Africa among European and other powers. Each of these maps has been drawn on the same scale and with the same key. They demonstrate the rapid partition of Africa and the very small part of the continent (indicated by unshaded areas) which remained under African control until after World War II.

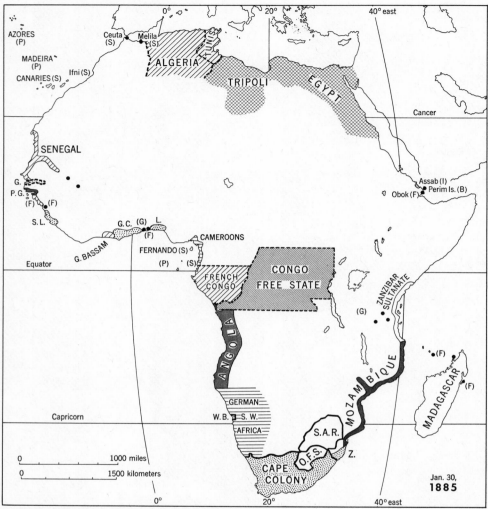

2.6 Africa at the end of January, 1885, after the Berlin Conference. The broad claims of the French to the French Congo is indicated by broken lines and the approximate area laid down for the Congo Free State.

threatened to bombard. The British government weakly instructed Kirk to advise the Sultan to submit, with the result that he lost the bulk of his mainland territory, and German East Africa came into existence.

But for two circumstances the whole of East Africa might have become German. One was an Arab revolt which, though suppressed in 1889, occupied the attention of the German administration. The other was the formation of the British East Africa Company in 1888 with the primary aim of rousing British public opinion to a realization of the importance of East Africa and to act as an agent of civilization and good government in the regions entrusted to it. The company successfully contested the claim of Peters to Uganda until the British Prime Minister, Gladstone, was forced by public opinion against his own will to take over responsibility in 1893. The company similarly looked after the destiny of the territory later known as Kenya, until it surrendered its charter in 1895 (Figure 2.7). British East Africa became a protectorate under the British crown, and the construction of the Kenya–Uganda railway dealt a final blow to the slave trade. Zanzibar became a British protectorate in 1890.

The revival of French interest in West Africa was an indirect result of France's defeat by Germany in 1870–1871 and the loss of Alsace–Lorraine. To restore her prestige and self-esteem she turned her attention to West Africa, and had secured a firm hold by the time Germany became active in the same area. Various British trading interests had consolidated themselves as the United African Company in 1879, which became the Royal Niger Company in 1886. The vigorous policy of the company's chief, George Taubman Goldie, secured trading places and agreements with Negro authorities, thus forestalling the activities of Herr Flegel, who attempted the same methods that Karl

Peters was using in East Africa. By the Berlin Conference of 1884–1885 (the "General Act" was signed on February 26, 1885) Great Britain's paramount interest in Nigeria was confirmed. German claims were restricted to the Cameroons and Togoland, both of which may be regarded as becoming German in 1884. It was also in 1884 that Germany annexed Southwest Africa.

Both Germany, from the west, and Portugal, occupying Mozambique on the east and Angola on the west, had plans for stretching inland across the whole of the southern part of the continent, which Portugal claimed but had neither explored nor annexed. But a strong man arose in the person of the British Cecil John Rhodes. In 1887 Portugal attempted to close the Zambezi, announcing that the interior be-

2.E The Garrison of Witu, 1892 (now part of Kenya). Colonial administration was established by such small groups of representatives of European powers, aided by such technological advantages as the maxim gun. (From J. W. Gregory, *The Great Rift Valley*, 1896.)

longed to her. Rhodes retaliated by securing in 1888 from Lobengula, the king
of the Matabele, exclusive rights to work
minerals in his territories, which lay north
of the Transvaal. In 1889 he formed the
British South Africa Company for the
purpose. In 1891, the limits of the Portuguese and British spheres of influence
being agreed upon, Nyasaland became a
British Protectorate (now Malawi),
whereas the bulk of the heart of the
country was handed over to Rhodes' company, afterwards becoming Northern and
Southern Rhodesia (subsequently Zambia
and Rhodesia).

In the meantime French interests in
West and Equatorial Africa had been consolidated. In Equatorial Africa (long
called French Congo) acquisition began
on the Gabun River in 1841, and Libreville was founded in 1849. The coastal
possessions extended along the coast for
200 miles to include Cape Lopez. Everywhere the story is the same: coastal settlements followed much later by extension
inland. In West Africa, the British had
failed to respond to requests—a natural
result of the British Anti-Slavery Law of
1807—to take the whole coast under protection, and so had left the field open to
the French. However, there was little
activity by France until she recovered
from the Napoleonic Wars. The French
obtained rights on the Ivory Coast about
1842 but did not actively and continuously occupy the territory until 1882. In
Dahomey the footing on the coast dates
from 1851, but not until 1894 was the
whole Kingdom of Dahomey annexed.

Along the Guinea Coast fragments remained to Portugal (Portuguese Guinea
and the islands of São Tomé and Principe)
and to Spain (Spanish Guinea and the
islands of Fernado Poó and Annobón).
Although many boundaries were not defined until much later, it may be said that
by 1891 practically the whole of tropical
and South Africa had been parceled out
between Britain, France, Belgium, Germany, Portugal, and Spain. Even the Re-

public of Liberia was alien, not African
(Figures 2.7 and 2.8).

The story over the north of the continent was somewhat different. The Atlas
lands of the northwest, long called the
Barbary States from their Berber inhabitants, had formed part of the dominion of
Carthage. Carthage itself was near the
modern Tunis. After the fall of Carthage
in 146 B.C. the Atlas lands continued to
flourish under Roman rule; many cities
were built and the land provided much
food for the Roman Empire as a whole.
The Roman Empire fell and later there
were Moorish or Arab Empires over
North Africa, and in turn most of the Barbary States became nominally part of the
Turkish or Ottoman Empire, which extended from Egypt to Algeria. Conditions
were least settled in Algeria, where Turks
and other renegades terrorized both
inhabitants and traders along the coasts,
and became notorious as the Barbary
Pirates from 1650 onward. English,
Dutch, French, Spaniards, and Americans all failed successively to check
piracy until in 1830 the French bombarded Algiers into submission. This was
the begining of the French regime in
Algeria. Abd al Kadir inspired a tena-
cious resistance which survived his cap-
ture and exile in 1847 and lasted until
1883. It was based on the highland
massifs, the strategic significance of which
reemerged during the fighting of
1954–1962. In due course, however,
Algeria came to be administered with but
few differences as an integral part of
France and the home of a million and a
quarter Frenchmen, mostly born there
and representing an eighth of the total
population. Tunis or Tunisia was a
kingdom whose ruler, the Bey, was descended from one who, a native of Crete,
made himself master of the country in
1705 while acknowledging the suzerainty
of the sultan of Turkey. The desire of the
French to protect their role recently established in neighboring Algeria led to invasion in 1881 and the placing of Tunisia

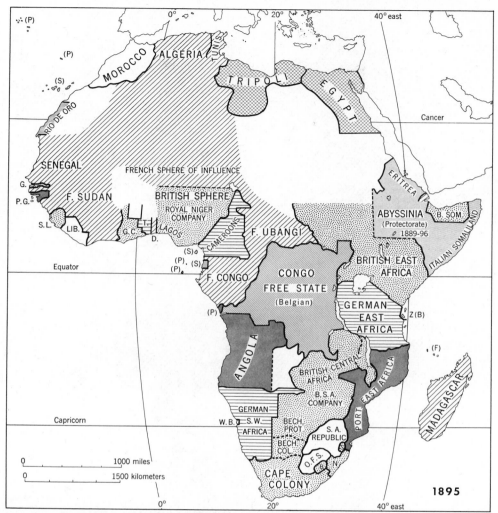

2.7 Africa at the end of 1895. This map contrasts very sharply indeed with the preceding ones and indicates that within the short space of ten years from 1885 to 1895, practically the whole of Africa had been partitioned among the leading European powers. 1895 was before the outbreak of the war between the British and the Boer settlers, whose two independent republics, the Orange Free State and the South Africa Republic, are shown unshaded.

under the protection of France. This lasted until 1955–1956, when France recognized the independence of Tunisia. The monarchy was abolished in 1957 and the country became a republic.

Although Morocco remained nominally an absolute monarchy in which the reigning sultan exercised both supreme religious and civil authority, the threat of German interference led to the establishment of "zones" of protection by France

(the bulk) and Spain in 1912 and the subsequent recognition of the "International Zone" of Tangier by agreement with Britain in 1923. Unity and independence were restored to the country in 1956.

With independent Morocco to the west and independent Tunisia to the east, it was scarcely to be expected that the Moslem majority in Algeria would remain content for the country to continue as

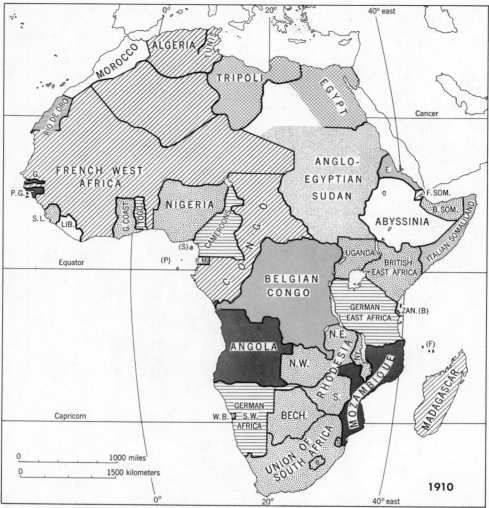

2.8 Africa in 1910. This was the year in which the four South African colonies united to form the Union of South Africa. The Congo Free State had been annexed to the Belgian Crown as the Belgian Congo and the Anglo-Egyptian Sudan had been established for more than ten years.

French territory. An unhappy period of internal strife culminated under the regime of de Gaulle in a referendum of which the result was a foregone conclusion. Algeria became an independent republic on July 4, 1962. The majority of the French (who had never had any other home) fled the country. It was estimated that in July 1963 fewer than 100,000 remained.

Between the Atlas lands and Egypt lies the country, largely desert, known as a whole as Libya. This area, part of the Turkish or Ottoman Empire, despite a certain measure of Arab autonomy was a Turkish vilayet from 1835 to 1911. In the latter year a quarrel between Italy and Turkey, then the "Sick Man of Europe," led to Italian annexation.

The story of Egypt is much more complex. For a long time part of the Turkish Empire, Egypt was at least nominally a vassal state of Turkey until the outbreak of World War I. From the latter part of the eighteenth century Great Britain had had special interests in Egypt. The old route from Britain to India was by ship to Egypt, then up the Nile to a point where the desert was crossed to the Red Sea, and so by ship again to Indian ports. Egypt was thus a vital link in a chain of Empire, and the strategic importance of Egypt's position was emphasized rather than diminished when the Suez Canal was opened in 1869.[3] The protection of the Canal became of first importance to Britain. In 1882 internal disorders led to British military intervention and the stationing of British troops in the country. When World War I broke out in 1914, with Turkey ranged among the enemies, a British protectorate over Egypt was declared, thus ending its status as a Turkish vassal. The protectorate ended in 1922 when Egypt became an independent kingdom, later a republic.

We turn now to the vexed and complicated question of the Sudan and northeast Africa. Between Khartoum and Aswan the Nile follows a long course interrupted by successive rapids across 500 miles of waterless desert, effectively dividing the habitable parts of Egypt from the Sudan. The Nile water is the life blood of Egypt, so that there is an obvious importance in considering the water problems of the Nile basin as a whole. From about 1820 onward, the Egyptians began to extend their control over the Sudanese peoples and to claim the newly discovered equatorial lands. The Khedive Ismael of Egypt relied largely on collaboration with the British, and in 1870, as we have already seen, S. W. Baker was appointed governor of the Equatorial Provinces to deal with the suppression of the slave trade. The British General Charles George Gordon (1833–1885) was governor of the Sudan

from 1873 to 1880, when he resigned after dealing successfully with the slave trade. Two years later came the great revolt of the Sudanese under Mohammed Ahmed, who declared himself the Mahdi. It was decided to abandon the Sudan, and General Gordon was sent in 1884 to undertake the difficult task of evacuating the Egyptian population. With only one English officer he and his faithful Egyptian Moslem band were surrounded and besieged in Khartoum for five months. There was fatal delay in sending a relief party, which reached Khartoum eventually on January 28, 1885, two days after Gordon had been put to death. There followed thirteen years of despotic rule by the Mahdi and his successor, the Khalifa. In 1896 an Anglo-Egyptian army commenced operations for the recovery of the lost provinces, culminating in the overthrow of the Khalifa in 1898 and his death in 1899. The convention between the British and Egyptian governments signed at Cairo on January 19, 1899, provided for the administration of the territory jointly by Egypt and Britain as a condominium, and lasted until December 3, 1955.

Among other foreigners in the service of the Egyptian government in the expansionist days of the seventies was a German, Eduard Schnitzer, who had been a medical officer under General Gordon, and who was appointed governor of the Upper Nile provinces (Equatoria). Known as Emin Pasha, he was isolated by the rebellion in which Gordon was killed, and the lack of news of him caused anxiety. So Stanley, having founded the Congo Free State, was sent to search for him. Because access via Egypt was impossible, Stanley determined to travel up the Congo, and had a very difficult journey both by river and through the forest. He discovered Emin Pasha at Lake Albert in April 1888, happy and comfortable with his men and disinclined to leave Uganda for Europe. Emin's real object

[3] See below, Chap. 10. Incidentally, the strategic value of Aden, the islands of the Red Sea such as Perim, and the ports opposite, on African shores, were also enhanced.

was to remain and to claim Uganda for his fatherland, Germany. A little later, while exploring, he was killed by Arab slave traders; otherwise the story of East Africa might have been very different.

Lying east of the great knot of Ethiopian mountains are the arid plains of Somalia occupying the "Horn of Africa," with shores along the Indian Ocean, Gulf of Aden, and Red Sea. Near the entrance to the Red Sea the French acquired the port of Obok in 1862 but did not undertake its active occupation until 1884, when the territory was extended. In 1888 the French created the port of Jibuti and later constructed the Jibuti–Addis Ababa railway, for a long time the main outlet of Ethiopia. The Somali Coast farther east was administered by Egypt until 1884, when their control collapsed and the British Indian government administered the territory as a protectorate. Italian interest in these coastlands dates from the establishment of a colony in Eritrea whose boundaries were defined in 1889–1891. In 1892 the sultan of Zanzibar leased certain Somali ports to Italy, selling them outright in 1905 when Italy assumed control of Italian Somaliland.

Between the momentous decade of 1880–1890 and the outbreak of World War I in 1914, changes in Africa were mostly of the character of consolidation of interests (as of the French in North Africa); further exploration; definition of boundaries; organization of administration and administrative units; construction of railways, roads, ports, and administrative centers; and the development of agriculture, commerce, and trade. There were inevitable clashes and minor wars. The attempt of Italy to extend its hold from the Red Sea colony of Eritrea into the heartland of Ethiopia was foiled by a significant defeat at the battle of Adowa in 1895. By this time the local ruler, Emperor Menelik, had been able to obtain European arms. The one serious conflict involving two peoples of European stock was the Anglo–Boer War of

1899–1902, which will be considered under South Africa. The political map of Africa as it was in 1914 is shown in Figure 2.9.

With the outbreak of hostilities in August 1914 between Britain and Germany, things began to happen in Africa. German Southwest Africa surrendered to the forces of the Union of South Africa on July 9, 1915. Togoland surrendered unconditionally to British and French forces in August 1914; the Cameroons, in February 1916. German East Africa was conquered in 1918. Britain, France, Belgium, and South Africa all accepted the jurisdiction of the League of Nations. Southwest Africa was entrusted under mandate to the Union of South Africa. This was a Class C mandate, which laid down that territory should be administered as an integral part of the territory of the mandatory power, but made the mandatory power responsible for promoting the moral and material welfare of the peoples. Togoland and the Cameroons were divided between Britain and France as a Class B mandate. An important though small strip of German East Africa (Ruanda-Urundi) passed to Belgium, also under Class B mandate, and was added to the Belgian Congo; the main part became a Class B mandate under Britain as Tanganyika. It was laid down that Class B mandates should be separately administered, but again making the mandatory power responsible for promoting the moral and material welfare of the peoples. After World War II all these mandated territories passed under the trusteeship scheme of the United Nations.

Figure 2.10 shows the political map of Africa as it appeared shortly after the end of World War I.

The period between the world wars was marked by much economic activity—the building of railways and roads, the opening up of mineral deposits, especially in the Katanga, and the development of air transport, which has made such a tremendous difference to the accessibility of

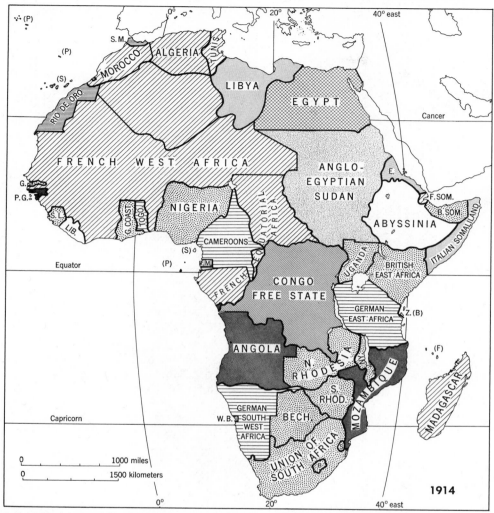

2.9 Africa in 1914. This was at the outbreak of World War I, and it will be noticed that the Germans had so far extended their territory of the Cameroons as to split French Equatorial Africa into two separated portions.

the heart of Africa. The British Colonial Office, following the tenets laid down especially by Lord Lugard after his experience in Nigeria, did much to develop indirect rule, that is, it encouraged the Africans to perfect their own administration based on tribal customs and laws under British guidance, so that the British officers interfered only when African customs were found to be directly opposed to Western ideas of right and justice.

To this interwar period belongs the story of Italian expansion. With a restricted and overpopulated homeland, Italy's need was for land suitable for settlement; and imperial adventures were politically attractive to the fascist government. Libya, acquired in 1911, though large, was mainly desert; Somalia was no better. Eritrea had some good land but had nothing compared with the undeveloped resources of the ancient kingdom of Ethiopia. So Ethiopia, or Abyssinia, was invaded and conquered in 1935–1936. With Eritrea and Somalia it was reorganized to form Italian East Africa (Africa Orientale Italiana) by the

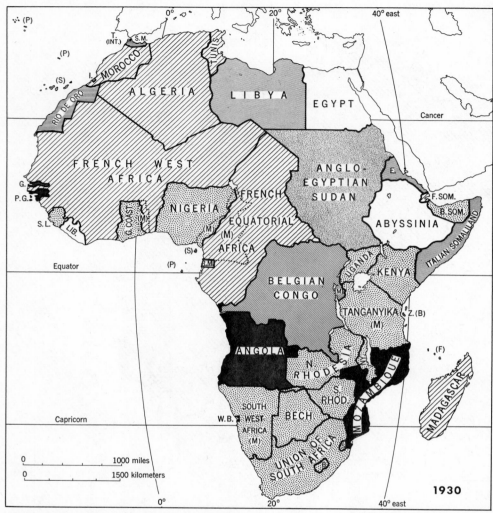

2.10 Africa in 1930. With the defeat of Germany in World War I, German territory in Africa disappeared. Former German territory is shown as held under mandate from the League of Nations by Britain, France, Belgium, and South Africa. As a reward for Italian efforts, Italian Somaliland was increased in area by the addition of the country round the Juba river. (M = Mandated Territories.)

Act of June 1, 1936, under the dictatorship of Benito Mussolini (Figure 2.11). Italy declared war on Britain on June 11, 1940. British Imperial forces invaded Ethiopia, and by November 1941 the country was cleared of Italian forces and Emperor Haile Selassie restored to his throne.

After World War II Libya, Eritrea, and Somalia were governed under British Military Administration, replaced later by a British Civil Administration until 1950. Libya was then granted independence, taking effect formally on January 1, 1952. Eritrea became an autonomous state under the Ethiopian crown, until 1962, when it was incorporated as a province of Ethiopia. Somalia was returned to Italy as a United Nations Trusteeship Territory for the period 1950–1960 when it joined with the British Somaliland Protectorate to form the independent Somali Republic.

The decolonization of Africa was almost as precipitate as had been the original "scramble." Although much of the coastline was already under European control or within "spheres of influence" it was the years between 1885 (the conclusion of the Berlin Conference) and 1891 that saw the parceling out of the greater part of the interior of the continent. Between 1956 and 1966, most of these colonial regimes were ended. In 1956 the French protectorates over Tunisia and Morocco were terminated as was the curious control, nominally by Egypt as well as Britain, over the Sudan. The first British colony to be independent was the former Gold Coast which became Ghana

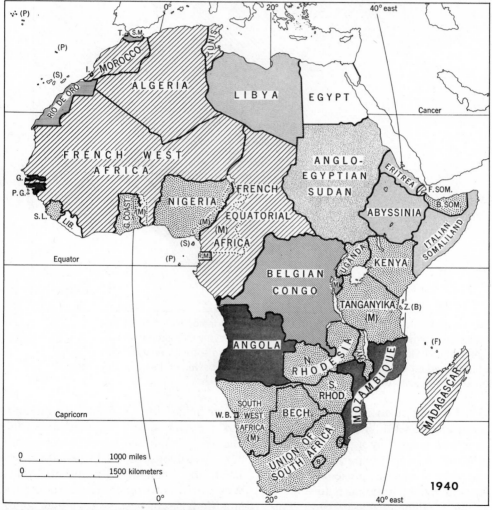

2.11 Africa in 1939–1940. At the outbreak of World War II, the Italian Empire had come to include Abyssinia as well as Eritrea and Italian Somaliland, together with the enlarged and redefined Libya. Only two countries in the whole of Africa (other than the Union of South Africa) are shown as independent, Egypt and Liberia.

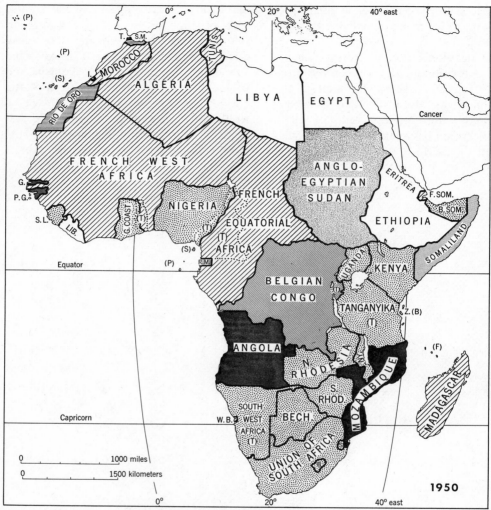

2.12 Africa in 1950. At the end of World War II the former mandated territories became trusteeships under the United Nations. An independent Ethiopian Empire, including Eritrea, had now appeared, as had Libya, together with the old independent countries of Egypt and Liberia. Africa was still essentially a colonial continent however. (T = Trusteeship Territories.)

in 1957. In addition to its reputation for education and general "advancement," it had benefited greatly by a period of high prices for its principal export, cocoa. Its "big brother" Nigeria presented more problems of a constitutional nature but it was granted independence in 1960. This year saw a virtual "clean sweep" of the tropical colonies of France. The new constitution of the Fifth Republic introduced by General Charles de Gaulle in 1958 had replaced the French Union by a choice of looser links within a French Community (*La Communauté*). At that time only Guinea became completely independent, but by a constitutional amendment in 1960, the component parts of French West Africa, of French Equatorial Africa, and Madagascar became sovereign states. Thus were born the republics of Senegal, Mauritania, Mali, Upper Volta, Ivory Coast, Dahomey, Niger, Chad, Congo (Brazzaville), Gabon, the Central African Republic, and the Malagasy Republic.

2.F The Supreme Court at Accra, Ghana: typical of the physical and cultural legacy of the European powers to the independent states of Africa. (Official photograph.)

The former French Trusteeship territories of Togo and Cameroun also became independent.

This remarkably orderly process of transfer of authority was unhappily interrupted by the chaos which followed the abrupt departure of the colonial administration from the Belgian Congo in the same year. The actual transfer of power in the Belgian trusteeship territories of Ruanda and Burundi in the following year was relatively peaceful and the subsequent slaughter of the Tutsi people in Ruanda attracted little attention.

Meanwhile the agony of Algeria continued. This had less relevance to the rest of the continent, however, because of the large numbers of settlers involved, and it became eventually a three-cornered civil war among the independence movement, the settlers, and the government of France. Open warfare broke out in 1954 and continued until independence in 1962.

In British East Africa an uneventful timetable was followed with a by now almost traditional independence ceremony in Tanganyika in 1961, Uganda in 1962, Zanzibar and Kenya in 1963, Malawi and Zambia in 1964. Following a revolution Zanzibar joined with Tanganyika to form the United Republic of Tanzania in 1964. In West Africa, Sierra Leone became independent in 1961, and tiny Gambia in 1964. Following a United Nations plebiscite, the British trusteeship territory of Cameroon was divided, and the southern portion joined the French-speaking Cameroun Republic while the northern section joined Nigeria.

British authority over Rhodesia (formerly Southern Rhodesia) had been limited by the granting of responsible self-government in 1923, and attempts by the United Kingdom Government to force a greater legislative representation by the black African majority led to a unilateral declaration of independence ("U.D.I.") in 1965. By contrast, the three protectorates which formed the British "High Commission Territories" adjacent to or within the Republic of South Africa became independent, namely Botswana (1966), Lesotho (1966), and Swaziland (1968). The only remaining French territory, Somaliland, voted to remain a French territory in a controversial plebiscite held in 1967 and the name has been changed to "The French Territory of the Afars and Issas."

In the Indian Ocean, the islands of the Comoro Archipelago have the same status while Réunion is an Overseas *Département* of France.

The Spanish territories of Rio Muni and Fernando Poó became the sovereign state of Equatorial Guinea in 1968, and in 1969 the enclave of Ifni was transferred to Morocco. The status of the large Portuguese colonies of Angola and Mozambique, and the smaller territories of Guinea and the islands of São Tomé and Principe remains unchanged but in a condition of unrest.

The Union of South Africa insisted on following the policy of *apartheid* so out of line with development elsewhere, and especially with the views of other members of the British Commonwealth. This led to the inevitable break and in 1961 the Union became the Republic of South Africa and withdrew from the Commonwealth — the first major self-governing country to do so. The Republic insisted it held Southwest Africa under the conditions of the fomer League of Nations mandate and refused to let the United Nations take over its administration. The territory is also referred to as Namibia. This contrast with events in tropical Africa has led to the concept of a white *laager* in South Africa, so named from the defense camp of wagons placed in a circle during the "Great Trek" of the Boers. It includes the Republic of South Africa, Southwest Africa, Rhodesia, Mozambique, and Angola.

In retrospect, the episode of African colonization is beginning to appear as an inevitable process of restructuring the pattern of political authority to enable the continent to become part of the world society and economy. The innumerable small tribal units have been replaced by nation states with membership of the United Nations (Figure 2.15).

The resulting political boundaries are more a reflection of European history than of local conditions but in general African states have wisely recognized that attempts to correct them could lead to mutually destructive international bickering. Thus the attempt to found a greater Somalia based on ethnic principles has received little support from other African nations.

Nevertheless, the sense of national identity often remains weak and many new countries face problems of separatism based on tribalism and differences in language, religion, and regional economic interest. By contrast, there is a widely expressed political desire for larger grouping as expressed in the organization for African Unity. Fortunately some of the larger groupings of the colonial powers still have some validity. Thus the former French Equatorial Africa is replaced by the Customs and Economic Union of Central Africa consisting of the Central African Republic, Congo (Brazzaville), Gabon, Chad, and including the former trusteeship territories now forming Cameroun. Similarly, the customs union of Senegal, Mali, Ivory Coast, Dahomey, Upper Volta, Niger, and Mauritania reflects the former French West Africa. Valiant efforts have been made to maintain cooperation in East Africa among Kenya, Tanzania, and Uganda through what is now known as the East African Community. Another inheritance of colonialism has been the language of the ruling power. This has had a unifying effect by providing a *lingua franca* above the babel of tribal languages (and one which Europe could well do with). Yet "francophone" and "anglophone" Africa still find it literally difficult to talk to each other and tend to go their own ways.

Resistance to colonial rule was often heroic although usually unsuccessful. In a conscious search for their origins, African countries are bringing into their rightful place in national histories the record of these endeavors and the lives of the leaders who were involved, only some of whom could be described above. The birth of the independent states of Africa was associated with a number of statesmen who, whatever their subsequent fates, will be remembered by future generations. Among these key figures are such very different personalities as Kwame Nkrumah, Leopold Senghor, Mohammed Ben Bella, King Mohammed V, and Jomo Kenyatta.

The rise and fall of the colonial empires in Africa is demonstrated by Figure 2.14. The decolonization is effectively shown by comparing Figures 2.12 and 2.13 which show the position in 1950 and 1970.

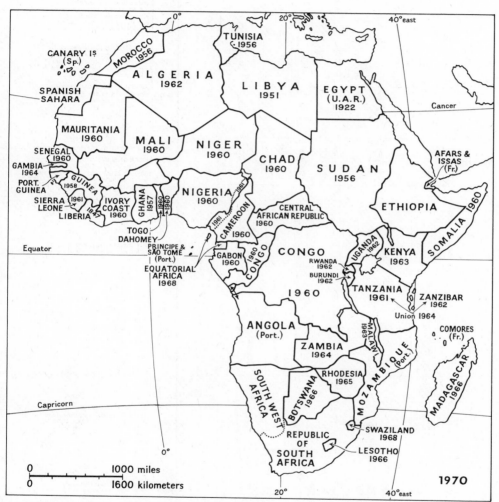

2.13 Africa in 1970. Africa has been transformed into a continent of independent sovereign states. Only the Portugese territories and Spanish Sahara remain of the former European empires. Dates of independence are shown.

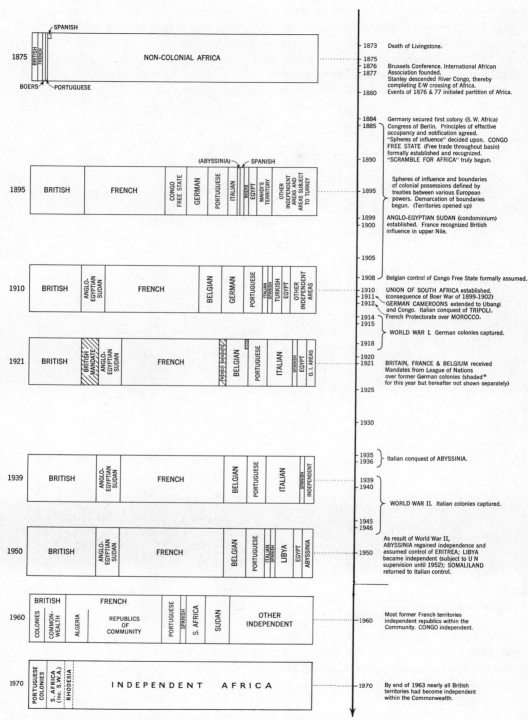

2.14 A diagram to show the partition of the continent from 1875 to 1970.

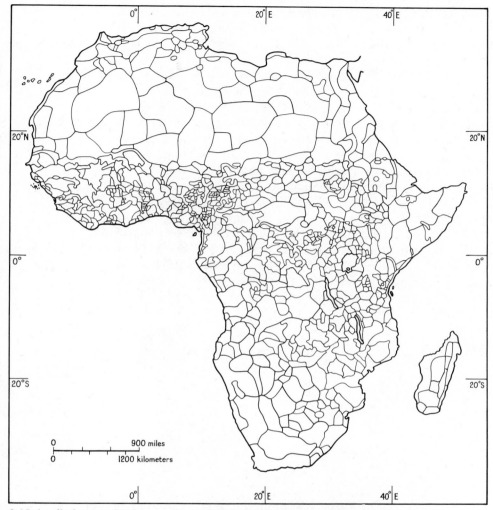

2.15 A tribal map of Africa. The complexity and number of these indigenous socio-political territories contrast with the map of national boundaries, Fig. 2.13. (After G. P. Murdock.)

Further Reading

Africa is necessarily prominent in a number of works on European exploration such as J. N. L. Baker's *A History of Geographical Exploration* (London: Harrap, 1st Ed., 1931) or Percy Syke's *A History of Exploration* (London: Routledge, 1st Ed., 1934). The account of the explorers themselves, however, provides vivid reading, and a convenient anthology from British sources covering the period 1769 to 1873 is provided by Margery Perham and J. Simmons in *African Discovery* (London: Faber and Faber, 1st Ed., 1942).

The partition of Africa as it took place in the crucial years 1880–1895 is well shown and clearly illustrated by maps in *The Partition of Africa* by J. Scott Keltie (London: Stanford, 1st Ed., 1893) and relevant documents are provided in *The Map of Africa by Treaty* by

Sir E. Hertslet (London: HMSO, 1909 three volumes and an atlas). A modern study of the partition, more particularly in the British areas, is *Africa and the Victorians* by Ronald Robinson and John Gallagher (London: Macmillan, 1961).

The literature of "decolonization" is rapidly growing and is cluttered with ephemera and the reader must make his own selection, but we may note *Unscrambling an Empire* by W. P. Kirkman (London: Chatto and Windus, 1966) and *The Changing Map of Africa* by R. D. Hodgson and E. A. Stoneman (Princeton: Van Nostrand, 2nd Ed., 1968). The changing picture may be followed in *The Statesman's Yearbook* (New York: Macmillan, annually about August).

Broad historical works on Africa include the handy paperback by Roland Oliver and J. D. Fage, *A Short History of Africa* (Penguin, 1st Ed., 1962) and Robert Rotberg: *Political History of Tropical Africa* (New York: Harcourt, Brace and World, 1965). Recent research, particularly that reconstructing the history of "Black Africa" before European records are available, has been popularized by Basil Davidson, beginning with his well-known *Old Africa Rediscovered* (London: Gollancz, 1959). Important scholarly articles appear in *The Journal of African History*.

CHAPTER 3

The Build of Africa

GEOGRAPHY AND MAN

Throughout much of Africa, especially tropical Africa, the course of man's life is still in large measure an elaborate accomodation to the physical environment. Even where the weapons of modern Western science have been introduced, the physical factors are so strong that their influence is everywhere clearly seen in the pattern of population distribution. The focal points of modern Africa's industrial development are clearly associated with sources of minerals and power and are thus related to the age-old geological structure of the continent. That population density in rural areas is primarily related to climatic conditions, especially rainfall, has long been clear, but the subtle and intimate relationships between the form of the land surface, drainage, soils, and land use are only now being slowly appreciated. It is because of the paramount influence which they exert that the various physical features of Africa will now be examined in detail.

GONDWANALAND

Throughout the many millions of years of the earth's geological history there have

always been areas of relative stability separated by belts of instability. Although at the present time the earth is enjoying in the geological sense one of its quiet periods, so that earthquakes disturb the surface but rarely and volcanic activity is at a minimum, it is still true that there are certain earthquake belts and certain lines of crustal weakness with which volcanoes are associated. In times past the belts or regions of orogenic, or mountain-building, movement have fluctuated in position, and so have the position and the shape of the stable blocks between. Those stable blocks are sometimes referred to as the great "unfolded" masses of the earth's surface — an entirely false concept, because they usually consist of rocks which have been most intensely folded, broken, recemented, and worn down by long glaciations so that ancient boulder clays or tills of glacial origin exist. But the *Glossopteris* flora of the swamp forests of Gondwanaland flourished over 200 million years ago. What has happened in the meantime?

Evidence has been adduced to show that the specific gravity of the rocks underlying the continents is lower than the specific gravity of rocks found beneath the

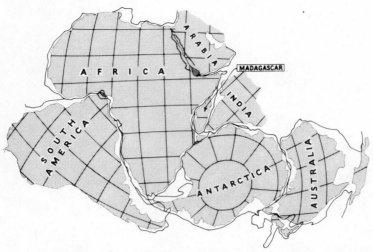

3.1 Gondwanaland. The southern continents aligned to fit at the 500 fathom contour, except for Antarctica, fitted at the 1000 meter bathymetric contour. Geophysical and geological evidence support such a reconstruction. (After A. G. Smith and A. Hallam *Nature* **225,** Jan. 10, 1970, p. 140.)

great ocean basins. On this evidence it has been postulated that the continental masses may be regarded as blocks having the approximate composition of granite resting on a lower layer having the approximate composition of basalt. The lighter continental rock material has been given the name sial from the dominant silicon and aluminium, while the heavier layers have been given the name sima from the dominant elements silicon and magnesium. It is of course known that there is a rapid rise in temperature as the earth's crust is penetrated and that at no great distance from the surface extremely high temperatures occur, so that if it were not for extreme pressure the rocks would be molten. It is quite possible that these lower layers of the earth's crust are at least in a plastic condition. Having gone this far, we find that it is not difficult to go further and to believe that the continental masses of sial, floating, as it were, on a plastic layer of sima, are able to move, to split into sections, to drift apart or to be pushed closer together.

The general concept of the lateral movement of continental masses is by no means new, but worked out in detail it has become associated with the name of Alfred Wegener, as Wegener's Hypothesis of Continental Drift. Thus the position may have been that the South American, African, Indian, and Australian sections of Gondwanaland formed one whole continent which has split up, and the constituent sections drifted apart (Figure 3.1).

It would seem to be quite clear that the great continental mass of Africa drifted, or was pushed, northwards, for it is on this basis and almost on this basis alone that we can explain the intense folding of the Alps and associated Alpine ranges in Europe, including the Atlas ranges of North Africa. These movements were at their height in Miocene times, approximately 20 million years ago.

Virtually conclusive evidence of the movement of continents has been provided by studies of paleomagnetism. Igneous rocks are endowed with a very weak but persistent magnetism in the direction of the Earth's magnetic field at the time of their solidification. By comparing the orientation of this magnetism with that of the present field, the original location of the rocks can be determined—and thus of the continents of which they are part. At the same time, exploration of the mid-oceanic ridges, including more paleomagnetic work, suggests that they may mark lines of upwelling of material away from which the continents are "drifting." The volcanic material of which they are composed becomes progressively older in parallel zones away from the center of the ridge, suggesting that the upwelling of new material is pushing apart the continental masses.

THE GEOLOGICAL SEQUENCE

In broad outline, both the geological structure and the geological history of the African continent are relatively simple, but very much remains to be investigated in detail (Figure 3.2).

The ancient crystalline basal complex is exposed over very large areas. In some sections the dominant rocks are granites,

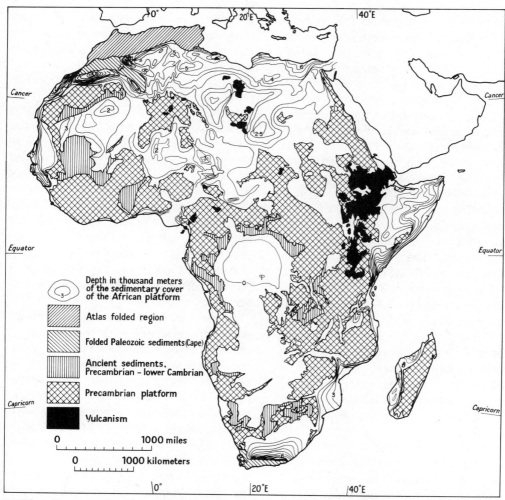

3.2 The structural elements of the African continent. (Simplified from the Tectonic Map of Africa, C.C.G.M./Unesco, 1968.)

or granitic rocks, which show varying degrees of alteration, and fall into the groups known as orthogneisses (metamorphosed granites) and paragneisses (metamorphosed sediments). Elsewhere the dominant rocks are also very highly metamorphosed, not only gneisses but schists of varied character which may originally have been sediments and volcanic rocks.

Consisting of these two main groups, the African Platform resembles in general the other ancient earth masses, such as the Canadian Shield or the Brazilian Plateau. Certain parts of the complex are highly mineralized, and Africa is of course a repository of a number of extremely valuable mineral deposits. For reasons which will appear later there are considerable possibilities of new discoveries. Resting on these very ancient metamorphosed rocks, often with basal conglomerates, are sedimentary rocks, for the most part comparatively little altered, some of which are also believed to be Precambrian in age; others are early Paleozoic. These too may be economically very important, because of the association of gold and other metallic ores with them. The gold of the Rand comes from Precambrian conglomerates; the copper of the Katanga from rocks of early Paleozoic age.

The ancient earth block, from its establishment in earliest times to the present day, has been subjected to vertical movements of elevation and depression, but only to relatively slight subsequent folding. Consequently there are considerable areas of its surface covered by older Paleozoic rocks of marine origin, little altered, for the most part nearly horizontal, though sometimes gently folded. Where these Paleozoic rocks are folded it is claimed that the folds can be termed broadly Hercynian, and in West Africa, for example, the gentle Hercynian folds trend from northeast to southwest. It should be noted that the older marine Paleozoic sediments are succeeded by rocks of Carboniferous and Permian ages, with which are associated the coal seams

of Africa's one important coal field, in South Africa.

The post-Paleozoic sedimentary rocks in Africa were either deposited in shallow seas which locally invaded the continental mass and occupied extensive gulfs, as in parts of West Africa, or were laid down in broad, shallow basins on the surface under fresh or brackish water conditions. The large stretches of sandstone and other sediments, so important in North Africa, called broadly Nubian sandstones, are of later Mesozoic or early Tertiary age.

With the absence of folding and the long-continued exposure of huge tracts to atmospheric weathering, the surface of Africa was reduced to an almost level surface, referred to below as the Miocene Peneplain. This ancient surface has since been raised many thousand feet above sea level, and in the process three important things have happened.

In the first place, the great rigid block of Africa gave way under the strain, and great fractures developed from north to south on the eastern side of the continent and locally elsewhere. Thus from the Red Sea in the north, almost to the borders of the Transvaal in the south, were formed those gigantic troughs, or *graben,* the famous rift valleys of East Africa, since occupied in part by the East African lake system. The general position of the East African rift valley system is shown in Figure 3.3.

In the second place, volcanic activity was also associated with this faulting or cracking of the rigid mass. There are enormous areas covered with flows of lava in Ethiopia; there are other lava-covered areas in East Africa, and a number of magnificent volcanic cones are reminders of this volcanic activity. Mount Kenya, Kilimanjaro, and Mount Elgon are three outstanding examples. More localized fracturing in the west is associated with the great volcanic peak of Cameroun Mountain. Incidentally, it may be noted that the rift valley area of East Africa is still an area of relative instability and

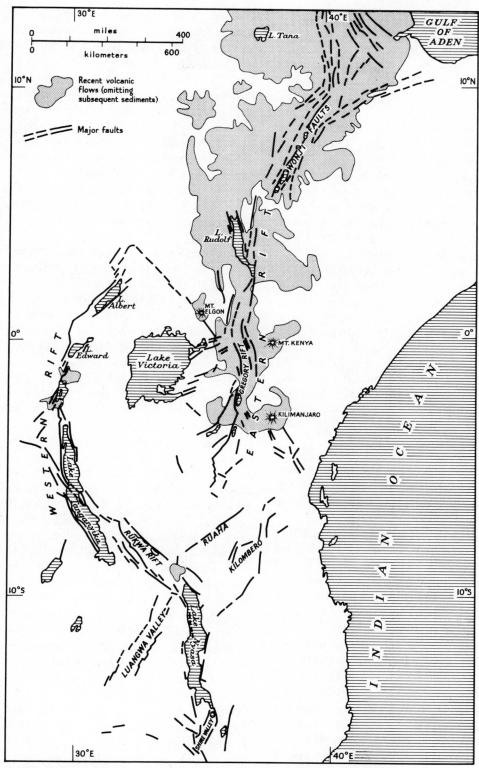

3.3 Rift valleys and volcanic areas of eastern Africa. (Largely after the International Tectonic Map of Africa.)

hence appears as one of the earthquake belts of the world of today. In both southern and eastern Africa, old volcanic necks or pipes became plugged with a consolidated lava of very basic composition which is the source rock of most of Africa's diamonds.

In the third place, broad, shallow basins in the uplifted surface gave rise to vast inland seas or lakes which have since disappeared or have left but small remnants. In them were deposited huge stretches of Quaternary and Recent alluvium; hence the Quaternary lake basins of the Upper Niger, of the Lake Chad region, and of the Central Congo. The rivers of today meander across these old basins before tumbling over the edge of the plateau to reach the present sea coast. Lake Victoria affords an example of a large lake of this character on the plateau surface.

Elsewhere the older rocks are still hidden by a mantle of aeolian deposits, the wind-borne sands of the Great Sahara and other wastes.

EROSION SURFACES

From the foregoing description we see that the interest of the geographer lies often in the geomorphology rather than the geology of Africa.

One of the most striking features of the African landscape is the vast extent of level or gently undulating surfaces. At high levels on the plateau we have the illusion of traveling over a lowland plain, often monotonous in the extreme. Such plains occur at different levels and are erosion surfaces which may be found up to heights of 8600 feet (2620 m) (as in the Basuto Highlands) above the present sea level. The great task of correlating these and placing them in a coherent sequence was begun by F. Dixey and has been carried forward into a comprehensive synthesis by Lester King. Dixey[1] points out that, since the widespread movements

[1] "African Landscapes," *Geog. Rev.*, XXXIV (July 1944) pp. 457–467.

of the late Karoo or post-Karoo times (Permo-Carboniferous), central and southern Africa have been a stable land mass subject to periodical uplift. The main periods of uplift have been separated by intervals long enough for possibly three important erosion cycles to have run their course and for resulting peneplains to have developed, There are also certain incompleted cycles, whereas the whole has been modified at a late stage by the rift faulting of East Africa, accompanied by volcanic activity, and the related gentle warping of regions to the south and southwest.

One well-marked, high-level erosion surface is found in a number of widely separated plateau remnants: at 7000–8000 feet (2130–2440 m) on the Cape ranges, where it is quite independent of the folding of the rocks; at 8000 feet (2440 m) in southwest Africa, and rather higher in the Basuto Highlands; at 7000–7500 feet (2130–2290 m) in the Nyika Plateau. This peneplanation is ascribed to the late Jurassic and indicates that the rise of the African continental mass has been of the order of 7000–8000 feet (2130–2440 m) since that time.

At lower levels there are remnants of other surfaces. In early Cretaceous times troughs were opened and later filled with sediments (as in the Nyasa trough), but a really well-marked erosion surface is one at about 4500 feet (1370 m), ascribed to the Miocene or mid-Tertiary. It may seem surprising that so much of this surface is preserved, but the major rivers such as the Congo, Zambezi (with the Luangwa, Shire, and Lake Nyasa), Limpopo, and Orange have carved out for themselves great valleys in troughs floored by the Karoo sediments of low resistance. It is on the weaker sediments and on Cretaceous beds filling the Nyasa and Luangwa troughs that the Pliocene or late Tertiary erosion surface at 2500–4000 feet (760–1220 m) has been developed.

Dixey finds it unnecessary to postulate warping of the Miocene surface or block faulting to explain the higher plateau sur-

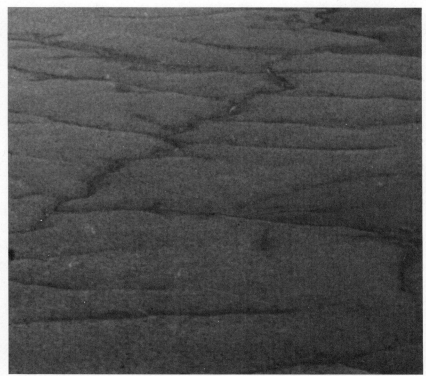

3.A The peneplain of northern Uganda. Long sustained erosion has reduced the ancient rocks to a near-plain with only ridges of more resistant strata standing out. (Copyright W. T. W. Morgan.)

faces as others have done. He considers that the low divides between the great river basins, such as the one between the Congo and Zambezi, are features of the old Miocene peneplained surface — legacies from the past.

It is almost certain that vast areas of Africa have been exposed to atmospheric weathering for many millions of years. On the old Miocene peneplain surfaces, therefore, the solid rocks may have been disintegrated to a very considerable depth, but the soils which have been formed have been formed *in situ,* and their mineral particles consist of comminuted fragments of underlying rocks. Not infrequently it is possible to trace a vein of quartz from the underlying rock through into the subsoil and to find an abundance of fragments of the shattered quartz in the surface soil, a feature of the utmost significance in determining the nature and usability of African soils.

MINERAL POTENTIALITIES

We are now in a position to make some economic interpretation of the geological map of Africa. The continent is far from mapped in detail, but the broad lines of its rock formations are now known.

Rocks of the ancient Precambrian mass, the whole comparable in character to the Canadian Shield except for the weathering of the surface, reach the surface and so are "exposed" (that is, they are not covered by later rocks) over approximately a third of the whole of Africa. It must be remembered that large parts have been subjected to the action of the atmospheric elements for many millions of years, so that the solid rocks themselves may be obscured by many feet of laterite and other products of weathering. This superficial mantle makes the search for ore bodies particularly difficult, and there is little wonder that spectacular finds are still being made and are almost certain to be made far into the future, especially as modern methods of prospecting, such as geophysical methods, are applied. Mineralization of the rocks and consequent occurrence of metallic ores are always irregular, but deposits are widely distributed in Africa.

It must be borne in mind that the rocks of the ancient complex underlie nearly the whole of Africa and that metalliferous deposits may lie buried (but not too deeply for future exploitation) where sediments cover the old mass. The sands of the deserts, the alluvium of the old lake basins, perhaps some of the flows of lava, may one day be penetrated to reach ore bodies hidden below.

The older sedimentary rocks, especially the shales and sandstones of Karoo (Permo-Carboniferous) Age, are important in two ways. First, they have their seams of coal in South Africa, Zambia, Rhodesia, and Tanzania. In the second place, the beds are usually almost horizontal, and weathering has given rise to those mountains of circumdenudation, the flat-topped mesas, which are such a characteristic feature of the landscape in so many parts of Africa. This is especially true in South Africa, where resistant volcanic rocks are interbedded with the sediments.

There are huge areas like those of the Congo with its great stretches of soft sandstone (see Chapter 16) and the middle Niger and Chad basins (Chapter 13) with sediments of continental origin. There are also sediments of marine and brackish-water origin, representing incursions of the sea at times when the whole continental surface was lower than at present, and which are largely confined to basins along the seaward margins of the continent. In 1950 the American Geographical Society published a map of such basins where it was considered oil might occur (*World Geography of Petroleum*) but that was before the spectacular discoveries of oil and natural gas which have so transformed the economic geography of the Sahara (Chapter 12). Prior to the first major strike in Saharan Algeria in 1956 it could be said, as it was in the first edition of this book, that Africa had no oil apart from the small fields along the shores of the Gulf of Suez in Egypt, and seven tiny fields in Morocco and Algeria. The picture is now very different, in large measure owing to modern methods of geological prospecting which enable investigation of what exists beneath the superficial sands, gravels, and alluvia occupying vast areas. Subsequent to the discoveries in the Sahara, oil and gas fields have been found more widely, including some in Nigeria and Cabinda, and the expectation of further discoveries is widespread. Many of these prospecting areas are in coastal situations, onshore or offshore. The discovery of underground sources of water has been scarcely less important in suggesting an agricultural utilization of previously useless desert areas.

THE RELIEF MAP OF AFRICA

The common generalization that Africa consists of a gigantic plateau bordered, except on the northwest where the Atlas ranges occur, by narrow coastal plains may now be stated more exactly. In fact, Africa consists of a succession of plateau surfaces at varying elevations, generally higher in the south and lower in the north, often with abrupt edges. On the surface of the plateaus are shallow depressions, some forming basins of inland drainage, others drained by rivers which pass over cataracts or through gorges as they leave the plateau surfaces to reach the coastal plains (Figure 3.4). It is common to distinguish between High Africa, in the south and east of the continent, a large proportion of which is over 3000 feet, and the remainder of the continent, Low Africa, where, although including such mountainous regions as the Atlas, Ahaggar, Tibesti, and Cameroun, lower elevations are the rule.

Thus, in the south of the continent the average elevation is over 3000 feet (915

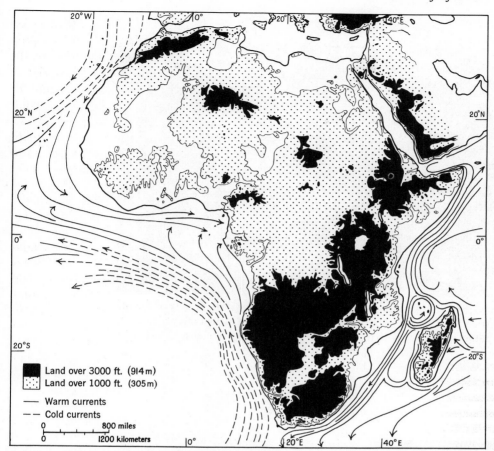

3.4 The relief of Africa. This map indicates the general plateau character of the continent. The ocean currents influencing climatic conditions are also indicated.

m), and the magnificent scarp of the southeastern edge known as the Drakensberg exceeds 10,000 feet (3050 m) in most places. Rising from the plateau surfaces, flat-topped mesas are common features; rocky hills with "tors" are features of the old rocks where granites occur. The divides between the broad, open river basins are usually inconspicuous, and the ridges between tributary valleys are so little developed that the water partings can be detected only by careful leveling.

The lofty plateau of East Africa is complicated in several ways. The great north–south trenches of the rift valleys (Figure 3.3) are deeply incised in its surface, and the section between the two main rifts has sagged in the center, which is occupied by the huge but shallow Lake Victoria, over

26,200 square miles in area and the world's third largest lake (after the Caspian Sea and Lake Superior). From the surface of the plateau rise the great volcanic piles of Kilimanjaro [19,340 feet (5895 m)], Elgon [14,172 feet (4320 m)], and many others. Different in character is the lofty horst of Ruwenzori, rising to 16,794 feet (5,119 m). Northward a large part of the mountain complex of Ethiopia is over 4000 feet (1220 m) in elevation.

The great basin in the heart of equatorial Africa is that of the Congo and its tributaries. From an average elevation of rather over 1000 feet (305 m) in the center of the basin, the land rises gently to 3000 and 4000 feet (915 and 1220 m) around the rim. The whole is indeed like a shallow saucer.

3.B The edge of the African plateau in the Drakensberg Mountains of Natal, South Africa. This shows clearly the horizontal beds of sandstone which here make up the plateau. (Copyright Aircraft Operating Company of Africa.)

3.C Flying over the highest point of the African continent. Snow capped Kilimanjaro in Tanzania reaches 19,340 feet (5895 m) and is an extinct volcano. This picture shows the view looking into the old crater. (Courtesy British Overseas Airways Corporation.)

The plateau surfaces and basins to the north of the Congo are at generally lower elevations, and parts of the Sahara actually sink below sea level. There are areas characterized by mesas; there are some rock-edged highlands, notably the Futa-Jallon-Liberian massif, and the Tibesti Mountains tower to snow-covered heights in the midst of the Sahara. The volcanic pile of Cameroun Mountain [13,350 feet (4069 m)] repeats in the west some of the features of East Africa, being associated with fault lines trending northeast to southwest.

Utterly in contrast are the Tertiary fold ranges of the Atlas and Anti-Atlas ranges,

with the elevated plateaus of the Shotts which lie between.

The coastal plains between the edge of the main plateau and the sea vary in character, as well as in width. Sometimes there are steps up to the plateau, sometimes a belt of foothills between a coastal plain and the plateau edge. Only in parts of northern Africa does the plateau edge tend to disappear or become inconspicuous.

AFRICAN RIVERS AND RIVER BASINS

It may be said that two-thirds of the surface of Africa is drained by seven or eight

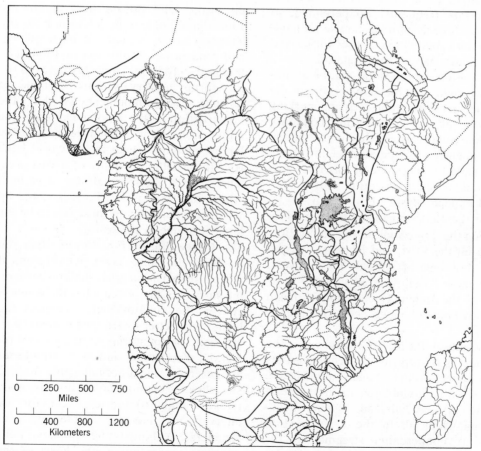

3.5 The rivers and river basins of the heart of Africa. This map shows that the great river basins have little relation to political units, the boundaries of which are indicated by fine dotted lines. Note the extensive areas of inland drainage, especially associated with the Rift Valley in eastern Africa.

major rivers; much of the remainder is occupied by basins of inland drainage with no outlet to the sea (Figure 3.5).

The Orange River Basin. In southern Africa the plateau slopes in general from the high eastern edge (the Drakensberg) to the west. Nearly all the surface is drained by the Orange River, the chief tributary of which is the Vaal. The southern half of the Kalahari "Desert" in Botswana lies in the same basin, but the watercourses are nearly always dry. True to the African type, the Orange passes over the Great Falls on its way to the Atlantic Ocean, but its bed is usually dry before the ocean is reached through the coastal desert belt of the Namib. Even in the damper parts of the High Veld the streams are frequently nonperennial, so that the whole system has no use for navigation and but limited use (discussed under South Africa) for irrigation.

Yet the Orange in flood can be an impressive sight, and the same is true of the Cunene, a considerable stream marking for part of its course the boundary between Southwest Africa and Angola. Consequently, exaggerated claims have been made for the value of this river as a potential source of irrigation water.

The Limpopo Basin. For much of its course the Limpopo forms the boundary between the Transvaal on the south, Botswana on the west, and Rhodesia on the north. It is one of Africa's lesser rivers, but it drains well-watered country eastward to the Indian Ocean, and its basin includes lands of much economic importance.

The Zambezi Basin. In many ways the Zambezi is a "typical" African river. Its upper course drains a huge shallow basin, floored with alluvial deposits, in the heart of the African plateau. Those headstreams which drain the drier western lands are nonperennial streams, but the main river is constant and navigable by traditional craft over much of its plateau course. Then the great river cascades over the world-famed Victoria Falls [343 feet

(105 m) high, compared with 165 feet (50 m) of Niagara] and passes through a narrow zigzag gorge excavated in the crushed rock of successive fault lines. There are long navigable stretches in the lower courses before the river is joined by the Shire, draining the waters of Lake Nyasa to the sea. Thus, like the greater African rivers, the headstreams of the Zambezi could be used for local irrigation, but little such use is made of them. The plateau courses are navigable over large stretches; the various falls and changes in level provide an enormous potential source of power; the lower reaches are valuable for navigation, though interrupted by gorges and rapids; but only a relatively minor port (Chinde) has grown up on the delta, not on the main stream. Immediately below the Victoria Falls the Zambezi gorge is spanned by a railway and road bridge completed in 1904. The 900 miles (1450 m) from this point to the sea forms a very serious obstacle to north–south communications, but the construction of the Kariba Dam and the conversion of the Kariba gorge into the largest manmade lake in the world have transformed the economy of a vast area. The Lower Zambezi Bridge was built where the river is 3775 yards (3452 m) wide and can claim on this basis to be the longest bridge in the world.

The Congo Basin. Even more than the Zambezi, the Congo is the river of tropical Africa. It also has a great shallow basin on the surface of the plateau, but the whole is cut by the equator and so enjoys the higher and better-distributed rainfall characteristic of equatorial latitudes. As a result, its mainstream and all its tributaries are perennial, most are navigable for long stretches by country boats, and the main river and major tributaries, except for rare interruptions, are naviagable by river steamers. Although the Stanley Falls interrupt navigation in the heart of the basin, the main drop from the plateau to the Atlantic Ocean occurs through a succession of rapids and falls below the lake, known as Stanley Pool [800 feet (245 m) above sea level], only 250 (320 km) miles in a direct line from the open sea. Such a great drop of so large and constant a volume of water makes this the site of Africa's, and perhaps the world's, greatest potential source of water power, and the first steps to harness it are now being taken. Together with local mineral resources, this provides a possible basis for future industrialization on a large scale. The deep, sheltered mouth of the Congo has proved more useful than those of other rivers. The port of Matadi has grown up at the head of ocean navigation [85 miles (137 km) from the sea], Boma lower down on the opposite (northern) side, and Banana on a delta distributary.

The Niger Basin. The Niger repeats some of the main features of the Zambezi. It has a long plateau course with many "tributaries" from the northern side which are normally dry watercourses. Its mainstream is valuable for navigation until the chief rapids and falls, a long way from the ocean, are reached. Below the falls there are again long navigable stretches; the important tributary, the Benue, invites comparison with the Shire. The main headwaters of the Niger are in the very wet Futa-Jallon highlands of the Sierra Leone border, less than 200 miles (320 km) from the Atlantic Ocean, but the river transports this water 2600 miles (4180 km) before discharging it into the ocean. In so doing, it swings in a great loop into the arid Sahara lands and so confers an immensely valuable gift of irrigation water on land well suited to receive it, in the neighborhood of the so-called inland Niger delta above Timbuktu.

The Nile Basin. With a total length of about 4000 miles (6500 km) the Nile rivals the Mississippi and Amazon for its sheer length, but in other ways it has features which are unique. The mainstream, the White Nile, is a relatively constant river, because it receives the well-distributed equatorial rainfall collected in the natural reservoir of Lake Victoria, from which it spills over at Owen Falls. Uniting with the Albert Nile draining Lake Albert, its main navigable course begins below the Fola Rapids when it enters the great Bahr-el-Ghazal basin. It may be said to pass out of that saucer-shaped hollow shortly before it is joined by the Blue Nile at Khartoum. Since the Blue Nile receives the monsoon rain of the Ethiopian mountains, it is a fluctuating stream and so responsible for the annual rise of the united Nile as it passes over its six cataracts and enters its amazing 10-mile-wide (16 km), cliff-bound trench through Egypt. Below Cairo the Nile delta is the prototype of all deltas, its triangular shape resembling the Greek capital letter inverted, establishing the term for all time. To the Nile and its floods the thirty million inhabitants of Egypt owe their prosperity and very survival, and it provided the basis for its ancient civilization through millenia.

The Lake Chad Basin. This may be noted as one, indeed the largest, of the inland drainage basins of the great Saharan region. The diminution in the size of the lake after it was first seen by Europeans supported the hypothesis of "dessication" in Africa, but subsequent fluctuations in level have suggested a more variable regime.

THE AFRICAN COASTLINE

Large parts of the long coastline present difficulties to the development of ports. The Atlantic coast has long stretches of dune and sandbar coasts continually pounded by surf driving in from the great fetch of the ocean. Here were surfports, some being still in use, by which ships stand out to sea and laboriously load and unload through surfboats. Today the major ports have been developed either by improving the natural entrances to the lagoons behind the bars and dredging across shallow sand banks as at Lagos, or by cutting a completely new channel into the lagoon, as at Abidjan. Elsewhere the problem is boldly met by flinging long breakwaters out to sea to enclose an entirely artificial harbor. Thus Takoradi was built to replace the surfport of Sekondi, and Tema that of Accra.

Surf is less of a hindrance on the East Coast and a sand bar coastline is largely restricted to the east coast of Malagasy and Somalia. Much of the coastline is formed of coral but there are many entrances across the reefs (although they may be narrow and difficult) and the geological evolution of the coast has provided many drowned creeks, e.g., Mombasa, Tanga, Dar es Salaam, and Mtwara. The growth of ports on this coast is limited by lack of commerce rather than by lack of harbor sites.

The Mediterranean coast is again more favorable and the traditional folktale of the general absence of good harbor sites around Africa is greatly exaggerated. It reflects the long historical preoccupation of British and French commerce with the Guinea Coast for which it is a valid generalization. Certainly, if one thinks of such ports as Dakar, Freetown, Matadi, Lobito Bay, Durban, Lourenço Marques, Mombasa, and many others, it must be conceded that many of the major ports of the continent have perfectly adequate, and some have excellent, sites.

THE CONTINENTAL SHELF

Except for the Mediterranean and the Red Sea basins, the continental shelf around Africa is everywhere narrow. The shelving shores on which the oceanic rollers break extend but a short distance from the coastline before the gentle submarine slope gives place to the abrupt edge of the continental shelf and the drop to oceanic depths of 2000–3000 fathoms (3700–5500 m). In the Atlantic, Ascension, St. Helena, and Tristan da Cunha are true oceanic islands — the tops of volcanic piles rising from great ocean deeps — and the same is true of Mauritius and Reunion in the Indian Ocean.

This fact has several important results. Where winds are offshore, the main surface waters are replaced by cold oceanic waters welling up from those depths where temperatures remain about 34°F (1°C). The cold currents which lave the African shores — the Canaries and Benguela — not only flow from colder to warmer areas but also have their waters replenished in this way, with a correspondingly increased effect on the temperature of the air masses above them, and so on neighboring lands.

Because the shallow waters overlying the continental shelf around the Japanese and British islands are particularly favorable to breeding and growth of fish, these islands have great fishing industries. In Africa, where such favorable conditions are absent over long stretches, commercial fishing has been slow to develop. Off South Africa the fishing industry which has been developed is associated with certain offshore "banks," but both here and off Angola, the great possibilities of onshore fisheries are now being realized.

Further Reading

The geomorphology of Africa is comprehensively treated in Chapter IX of *The Morphology of the Earth* (Edinburgh: Oliver and Boyd, 1962), the masterwork of Lester King, Professor of Geology in the University of Natal. He places the continent and its physical features within the concept of continental drift, of which the classic account is given in Alfred Wegener (translated by John Biram) *The Origin of Continents and Oceans* (London: Methuen, 1967). In this edition, an introduction by B. C. King summarizes the more recent evidence derived from paleomagnetism and mid-oceanic ridges. Important original papers are contained in *A Symposium on Continental Drift,* organized by the Royal Society by P. M. S. Blackett, Sir Edward Bullard, and S. K. Runcorn, Phil. Trans. Royal Soc., **258,** No. 1088 (1965). More recent is D. H. Tarling and M. P. Tarling, *Continental Drift* (London: Bell, 1971). A geological summary, largely stratigraphical, is provided by R. Furon (trans. A. Hallam and L. A. Stevens), *Geology of Africa* (Edinburgh: Oliver and Boyd, 1963). A. K. Lobeck's *Physiographic Diagram of Africa* (New York: Columbia University, 1946), with its accompanying test, provides a helpful and remarkably detailed account.

The Association of African Geological Surveys in Paris publishes, in conjunction with Unesco, an *International Geological Map of Africa* (1963) and an *International Tectonic Map of Africa* (1969). Both are at a scale of 1:5 million on nine sheets, accompanied by a small explanatory brochure.

CHAPTER 4

African Climates and the Water Problem

Africa lies between 35° North and 35° South, with the result that, excluding the lands associated with the lofty Atlas ranges in the north, the high plateau in the south, and isolated mountainous areas elsewhere, the whole continent has average temperatures over the crucial figure for plant growth of 42°F (5.6°C) throughout the year. Despite the elevation of the plateau in East Africa, frost is practically unknown throughout humid intertropical Africa. Furthermore, violent fluctuations of temperature which are associated with the movements of fronts in the North American continent are absent. Thus plant life is assured of temperatures which permit growth throughout the year, and the farmer is assured of a regular temperature regime which, though it may scorch, is unlikely to wither by unexpected cold. In Africa climatic interest centers on rainfall rather than on temperature. For rainfall the story is very different. Viewed over the averages of a span of years the rainfall regimes may appear regular enough, but few places enjoy an "average" rainfall. Instead there are violent fluctuations from year to year, serious differences in the dates when the rains come, and violent spasmodic downpours rather than steady falls.

The key to the whole of Africa's development is control of water. Drainage and flood control are needed where rainfall is regularly or occasionally excessive; storage and irrigation are needed where rainfall is normally moderate, both to guard against bad years and to extend the growing period; irrigation is essential where rainfall is low, despite the fact that in a majority of years the rainfall may be sufficient for dry zone crops. Unless there is elaborate provision for the storage of food produced in excess in good years (which there is not in Africa) without irrigation the land can support only the population which it can support in the *bad* years.

Being situated in low latitudes and almost entirely surrounded by water, there is no immediate source of cold continental air to affect the continent. South Africa is separated by 2000 miles of ocean from Antarctica and, unlike South America, has few invasions of cold polar air from that direction. Though northern parts of Africa are affected by conditions in Eurasia and are more "continental" in the wide range of temperature, there is an approximately symmetrical distribution of climatic types north and south of the equator. The greatest differences are between the northeastern and southeastern segments of the continent. In the northeast the great African hot desert area continues across the Red Sea into Arabia, and Ethiopia comes within the ambit of the great Asiatic monsoon. In the southeast, on the other hand, Africa is open to the influences from over the open south Indian Ocean.

Gradual transitions from one type of climate to another are the general rule over the whole of Africa. There are no great mountain chains to act as climatic divides as in America or Asia, though the Atlas mountains in the north restrict good winter rains associated with Mediterranean cyclones to the coastlands. The elevation of the great African plateau, especially since its higher parts are in the east towards the windward, modifies both temperature and rainfall. The July temperatures of the East African plateau, actually on the equator, are 20°F lower than they would be at sea level and actually 10° lower than those of the coastlands of the southeast, outside the tropics, at the same season. The heavy equatorial rainfall and equatorial climate of the Congo Basin does not extend across to the East African Plateau. Although on the equator, the East African Plateau is thus suited to European crops and farm animals and the equatorial rainforest is virtually absent.

Climatic conditions around the African coasts are considerably influenced by oceanic currents. Along the west coast of northern Africa the cold Canaries current flows southward. The low sea temperatures are due partly to the northern origin of the water, partly to the upwelling of cold bottom water to replace the surface waters constantly propelled towards the southwest by the dominant northeasterly winds. Coastal fogs are frequent, but summer temperatures are relatively low. With offshore winds, the coastlands

are very arid. Similar effects are associated with the cold northward-flowing Benguela current off the shores of southwest Africa, where conditions resemble those of northern Chile. The Canaries and Benguela currents both swing westwards, while between them the eastward-flowing equatorial countercurrent or Guinea current brings very warm water to the Guinea or West African coast. Because the air currents are onshore, the coastlands are constantly bathed by very warm and moist air masses, with a resultant heavy rainfall almost from Dakar to Libreville.

The east coast of Africa with its onshore winds driving warm surface currents towards the land is entirely different. South of the equator the island of Madagascar splits the main South Equatorial current of the Indian Ocean, and the Mozambique current flows southward from off Mombasa to about Lourenço Marques, where it merges into the Agulhas current. The presence of these warm surface currents results in sea-surface temperatures 15–20°F. higher than on the west coast, and the warm moist air masses associated with* them afford a moderate to good rainfall along the coastlands. In the north Indian Ocean, circulation of waters is reversed according to the Asiatic monsoon. In the season of the northeast monsoon (November to April), the drift of water is from northeast to southwest along the coast—a cool current flowing *towards* the equator; in the season of the southwest monsoon, the air movement is offshore, the current is alongshore from southwest to northeast, and there is localized upwelling of cold water from the depths. Because neither condition favors precipitation, the coast is arid from the equator northward.

The principal cause of rainfall or aridity on a continental scale, however, is the pattern of the atmospheric circulation. If we view Africa in relation to the world system, we see that it is dominated by the two subtropical high-pressure belts and

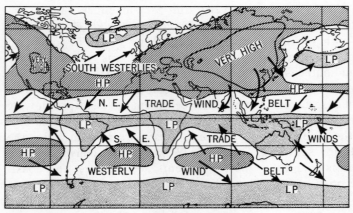

4.1 Theoretical arrangement of world pressure belts and winds in relation to Africa in January. LP = Low Pressure; HP = High Pressure.

the equatorial low-pressure belt between (Fig. 4.1). These so-called permanent belts move northward in the northern summer, lagging behind the overhead sun, and southward in the southern summer. On the poleward side of the high-pressure belts, rainfall is mostly associated with the progression from west to east of alternating depressions (cyclones) and wedges of high pressure. These circular movements, with their rain-inducing "fronts," are largely absent from the tropics where the most widespread cause of rainfall is a relatively broad uplift of air leading to cooling of the air mass to saturation point. This is most commonly the result of *convergence* of air, by which more is entering an area at the surface than is leaving it, so that some air must ascend (Figure 4.2). Conversely, *divergence* will bring about a subsiding air mass, likely to result in aridity. The high-pressure belts are areas of descending air and lie over some of the major deserts, including the Sahara and the Namib of South West Africa. Between the high-pressure belts, however, the movement of air tends to be convergent (ideally the northeast and the southeast trade winds).

It should be realized that it is temperature and pressure conditions throughout a column of air that counts, and that the weather will therefore not reflect precisely

the pressure and winds observed at the surface.

For the month of January (northern winter, southern summer) the position is shown in Figure 4.3. The Azores High-Pressure Cell lies over the Sahara, and to the north of it cyclones move in from the Atlantic, following the path of the Mediterranean and bringing winter rains to North Africa and the northern fringe of the Sahara. On the west side of the conti-

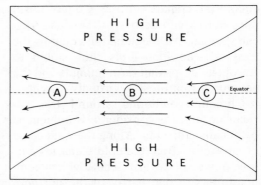

4.2 A diagram to illustrate atmospheric convergence by the confluence of airflows between two high-pressure cells on either side of the equator. Convergence is taking place at C and divergence at A, with the likelihood of rainy and dry conditions, respectively. Convergence may also be caused by decreasing speed of the airflow.

nent, the South Atlantic High is almost stationary and the equatorial trough of low pressure lies in the vicinity of the West African coast. The very dry *harmattan* winds cover most of the Guinea lands. On the east side, the low pressure lies far to the south of the equator and rains are received in the zone of convergence between air from the northern and the southern hemispheres.

In July, as shown in Figure 4.4, the picture is largely reversed. The Azores High has moved north, blocking the entry of the cyclonic system from the Atlantic and bringing dry summers. This permits the deep penetration of southwesterly winds from the south Atlantic. Southern Africa is now dry beneath a strong high-pressure system and air from both the Indian Ocean and the south Atlantic penetrates as far as the Ethiopian highlands, which is experiencing heavy rain. Most of East Africa (Kenya, Tanzania, and Uganda), however, is dry. Rain would have been received during the transition period but in July the region is covered by a flow of air curving round to flow towards the intense low pressure over India—the Monsoon. This is a diffluent pattern, bringing

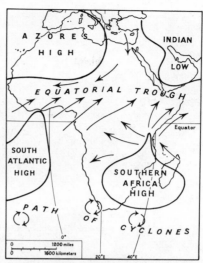

4.4 Idealized atmospheric pressure and airflow over Africa during July. (In part after B. W. Thompson.)

stable atmospheric conditions and great aridity to the Horn of Africa. A more northerly location of the South Atlantic High-Pressure Cell permits the depressions to follow a more northerly path, bringing winter rain to the vicinity of the Cape of Good Hope.

By analogy with the cold and warm fronts of temperate depressions, the concept of an intertropical front (ITF), associated with rainfall, was proposed. It has subsequently been realized that convergence may take place over a wide or a narrow band or may not take place at all, depending largely upon the alignment and the relative strengths of the pressure cells at any one time. It is this irregular and rapidly changing behavior which is responsible for Africa's greatest curse, irregularity of rainfall. The term "front" also implies a temperature discontinuity involving air masses of very different characteristics, whereas the converging air is often very similar. Thus the term intertropical convergence zone (ITCZ) has become preferred. The pressure system concerned is the equatorial trough, and the old seaman's expression "the Doldrums" obviously refers to this zone.

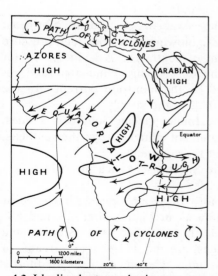

4.3 Idealized atmospheric pressure and airflow over Africa during January. (In part after B. W. Thompson.)

4.A A pair of giraffes silhoutted against a heavy evening sky above the East African Plateau. Over the extensive plains and plateaus of Africa, climatic divides are formed by the fluctuating boundaries of extensive air masses and the vertical structure of temperature and humidity within them. (Courtesy British Overseas Airways Corporation.)

Brooks and Mirrlees[1] distinguished seven air streams, as shown by arrows, lettered *a, b, c, d, e, f,* and *g* in Figures 4.5, 4.6, and 4.7. They may be compared with the theoretical arrangement of winds shown in Figure 4.1. Two other air streams affect the extreme northwest and southeast of the continent. The air streams are:

(a) the Atlantic Northeast Trades, blowing toward the southwest from the Azores high-pressure system;

(b) the Harmattan, the air stream blowing from the Saharan high-pressure belt across the Sudan and toward West Africa;

(c) the Egyptian air stream, blowing up the Nile valley as a northerly wind and reaching as far south as Botswana;

(d) the Atlantic Southeast Trades, blowing toward the equatorial low-pressure belt over the South Atlantic. On

crossing the equator, which they do especially during the northern summer, these winds become southwesterly and produce a monsoon effect in West Africa, but penetrate in January only a short distance inland;

(e) the Arabian or Indian Northeast Trades, blowing from the high-pressure system of southwest Asia in the winter months only, being eliminated and reversed by the monsoon currents for the other half of the year;

(f) the Indian Ocean Southeast Trades, the dominant influence over the southeast part of the continent;

(g) the Southeast Africa air, which is a dry mass;

(h) and**(i)** these air streams, indicated as "cyclones," in Figures 4.5, 4.6, and 4.7, though not studied by Brooks and Mirrlees, are the westerly air streams of midlatitudes. The one over the Mediterranean is a cyclonic belt of alternating depressions and wedges of high pressure, responsible for the winter rainfall from

[1] C. E. P. Brooks and S. T. A. Mirrlees, "A Study of the Atmospheric Circulation over Tropical Africa," London, Meteorological Office, *Geophysical Memoirs,* VI, No. 55 (1932).

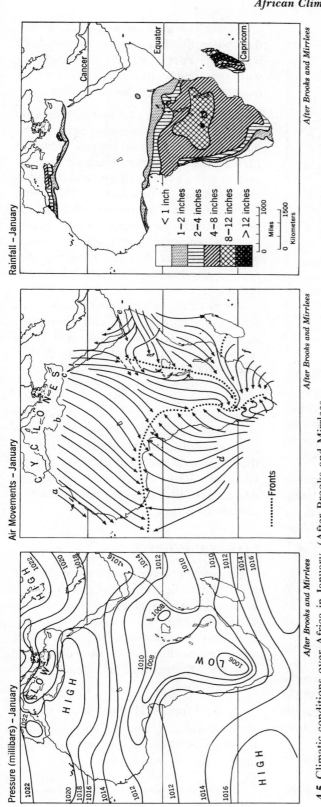

4.5 Climatic conditions over Africa in January. (After Brooks and Mirrlees, "A Study of the Atmospheric Conditions over Tropical Africa." *Geophysical Memoirs*, VI, No. 55, 1932, London, Meteoroligical Office.)

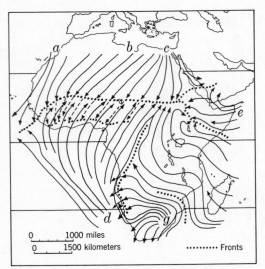

4.6 Wind conditions in April, showing the variable conditions of the main intertropical front or convergence zone (ITCZ). (After Brooks and Mirrlees.)

Morocco to Egypt. The one over the southern ocean is associated with strong, more regular winds, the Roaring Forties (named from their prevalence in the forties of south latitude), and is responsible for the winter rainfall of the Cape.

Since Brooks and Mirrlees prepared this classic analysis of the air circulation over Africa, climatologists have become accustomed to thinking in terms of air masses. Thus Haurwitz and Austin[2] distinguish the following:

(a) *Tropical Maritime Air* (mT): warm, moist air, originating over the ocean north and south of the equator.
(b) *Tropical Continental Air* (cT): warm, dry air originating over the vast, dry Sahara and also over the Kalahari.
(c) *Polar Maritime Air* (mP): invading the extreme northwest of the continent in the northern winter; a similar type invading the extreme southwest in the southern winter.
(d) *Polar Continental Air* (cP): as already

noted, such air does not reach Africa from the Antarctic, but during the southern winter the continental cooling tends toward the creation of a mild type of cP air over the highlands of South Africa.

The maps (Figures 4.5 and 4.7) leave no doubt of the close association between the main air streams and rainfall. Thus in January the Northeast Trades (the Harmattan and Egyptian air streams, *b* and *c*) blow from colder to warmer latitudes and are dry winds. The air stream from the South Atlantic (*d*) brings a small rainfall to the Guinea coast, but farther south it blows from over the cold Benguela current to the heated land and no rainfall results.

The destructive hurricanes which are so serious in parts of tropical and subtropical America are less numerous and more restricted in their incidence in Africa. They originate in the southern Indian Ocean (where they are known as cyclones) and affect Madagascar, Mozambique, and occasionally the very southern portion of the Tanzanian coast. With such great quantities of moisture involved in the hot and humid equatorial air masses, however, very heavy and sometimes destructive falls of rain are not uncommon elsewhere.

CLIMATIC REGIONS

Despite the several systems of climatic classification in common use, the general picture in Africa is clear. The scheme shown in Figure 4.8 is derived from that of Glenn T. Trewartha.[3] This is a classification modified and simplified from that of W. Köppen and the categories consist of:

A. Tropical Humid Climates

(1) Tropical wet climate, also known as the tropical rainforest or equatorial climate (Köppen: Af, Am)

[2] B. Haurwitz and J. M. Austin, *Climatology* (New York, 1944) pp. 332–336.

[3] *The Earth's Problem Climates* (Madison: University of Wisconsin Press, 1962).

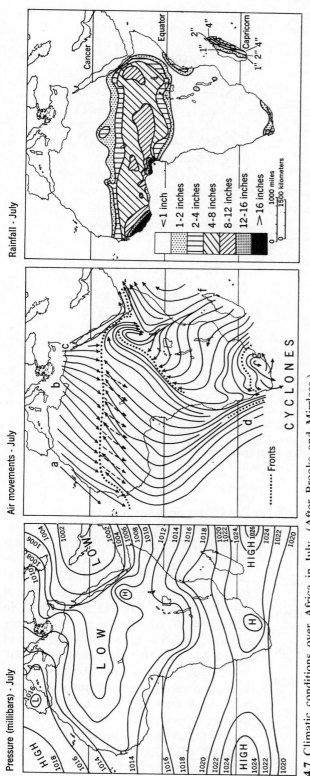

Pressure (millibars) - July

Air movements - July

Rainfall - July

CYCLONES

·········· Fronts

<1 inch
1-2 inches
2-4 inches
4-8 inches
8-12 inches
12-16 inches
>16 inches

0   1000 miles
0   1500 kilometers

4.7 Climatic conditions over Africa in July. (After Brooks and Mirrlees.)

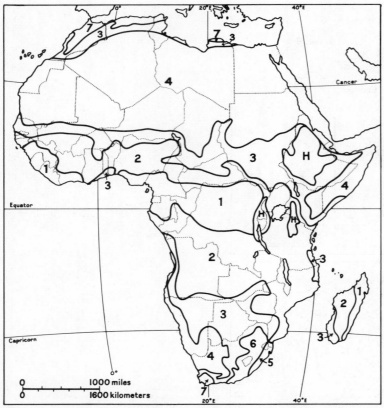

4.8 The climates of Africa. 1: Tropical wet; 2: tropical wet-and-dry or savanna; 3: semi-arid or steppe; 4: arid or desert; 5: humid subtropical; 6: middle
latitude steppe or high veld; 7: dry-summer subtropical or mediterranean; 8:
undifferentiated highland. (After Glenn T. Trewartha.)

(2) Tropical wet-and-dry or savanna climate, covering more than a third of all
Africa (Köppen: Aw)

B. Dry Climates

(3) Semi-arid or tropical steppe climate
(Köppen: BSh)

(4) Arid or desert climate (Köppen: BW)

C. Humid Mesothermal Climates

(5) Humid subtropical climate (Köppen:
Ca)

(6) Middle latitude steppe or high veld
climate (Köppen: BSk)

(7) Dry-summer subtropical or Mediterranean climate (Köppen: Cs)

H. Highland Climates

(8) Undifferentiated highland climates
(Köppen: H)

As has been explained, it is rainfall
that is the key differentiating climatic element in Africa, and the average annual
rainfall is shown in Figure 4.9. As important as the amount of rainfall, however, is
its duration and the length and severity of
the dry season, and this is indicated in
Figure 4.10 by the number of rainy
months, which is taken to be a month in
which 2 inches (50 mm) or more of rainfall
is received. Most of Africa is seen to have
a regime of a rainy season during the
period of high sun followed by a dry
season (Figure 4.11). The area with no
month receiving less than 2 inches is relatively small. The two rainy seasons and
two dry seasons in each year found over
the Horn of Africa are related to its posi-

tion on the edge of the monsoonal circulation and to the large seasonal displacement of the Intertropical Convergence Zone, and its accompanying rain, on this side of the continent.

THE EQUATORIAL OR TROPICAL RAINFOREST CLIMATE (1)

The keynote of the equatorial climate is monotony: constant heat, constant humidity, and constant rainfall. There is little or no seasonal rhythm and little relief at night from the heat of the day. Yet there are no great extremes: in lowland stations the thermometer remains around 80°F, on the hottest day it rarely rises to much above 90°, and in the coolest night it rarely sinks below 70°. With early morning mist there may be a feeling of chill, more apparent than real. As the sun climbs high at midday there is a sense of great heat, often dispelled by afternoon cloud and rain, giving place to clear starlit nights. Plant growth takes place throughout the year, so that luxuriant vegetation is the rule. It is the absence of seasonal rhythm which constitutes the

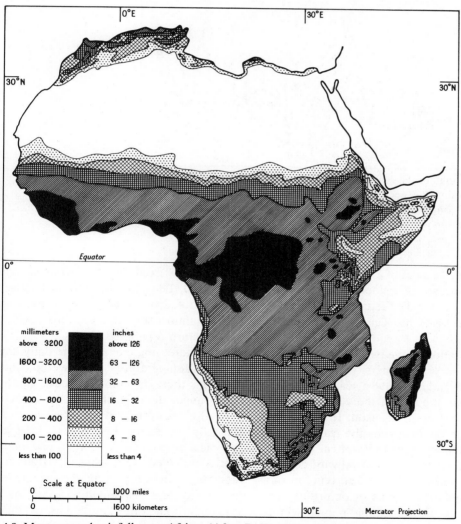

4.9 Mean annual rainfall over Africa. (After B. W. Thompson.)

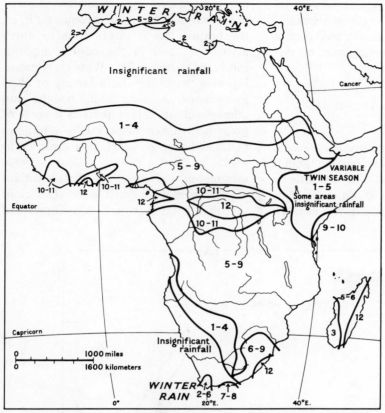

4.10 The length of the rainy season. The number of months in each year when the mean rainfall exceeds 2 inches (50 mm). Over most of Africa the rainy season is during the summer (the period of high sun). (After B. W. Thompson, *The Climate of Africa*.)

"unhealthy" aspect of a climate which has been described as a good servant but a bad master. H. J. Fleure characterized equatorial lands as regions of "constant endeavor."

Some stations have two rainfall maxima during the year; others (especially towards the margins) have a season which is rainier than the rest of the year, but typically there is no dry season. It is this feature which distinguishes the truly "equatorial" climate from the wettest parts of the tropical savanna or windward coasts. In many parts of the region, lying in the belt of equatorial calms or doldrums, the rainfall is convectional, and regular winds are absent. The heat of the sun causes

evaporation from water surfaces and damp land. The heated, saturated air rises and is cooled by convection so that rain falls on almost the same area from which the moisture originated.

With increasing elevation the daily and monthly temperatures are lowered, and, although there is some increase in the daily range, there is little in the annual.

In the western part of West Africa, typically in Sierra Leone and Liberia, there is a marked dry season, but so much rain is received from what is virtually a monsoonal indraft during the remainder of the year (e.g., Freetown: 157 inches a year) that it must be classified as an equatorial climate. Koppen uses the index

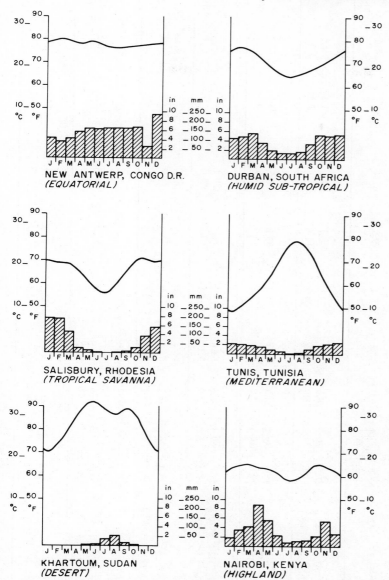

4.11 Some African temperature and rainfall graphs. Over the vast bulk of Africa a rainfall, whether heavy or light, well distributed throughout the year is unknown.

Am rather than Af. Another curiosity is that the east coast of Madagascar receives heavy rain in all months so that, although nearly outside the tropics, it must be regarded as receiving an essentially equatorial-type climate. The rain derives from the southeast trade winds but the movement of the convergence zone to the south during the southern summer brings more rain to the north of the island at that time. This type of climate has been described as that of the "windward coasts."

In Table 4.1, New Antwerp may be called typically equatorial, with Freetown and Tamatave typical of the monsoonal influence and the tropical windward coast.

Table 4.1 Temperature and Rainfall according to Climatic Classification.

Station	January	February	March	April	May	June	July	August	September	October	November	December	Range	Year
						The Equatorial or Tropical Rainforest Climate (1)								
New Antwerp, Zaire [Congo (Kin.)] (1230 ft.) °F	79.2	80.1	79.2	78.1	79.2	78.4	76.5	76.3	77.0	77.4	77.9	78.1	3.8	
Rainfall (in.)	4.1	3.5	4.1	5.6	6.2	6.1	6.3	6.3	6.3	6.6	2.6	9.3		67.0
Lagos, Nigeria (25 ft.) °F	80.9	82.2	83.3	82.5	81.8	79.3	78.0	77.7	78.4	79.5	81.4	81.5	5.6	
Rainfall (in.)	1.1	2.1	3.7	5.7	10.5	18.7	10.7	2.8	5.3	7.8	2.6	0.8		71.8
Freetown, Sierra Leone (223 ft.) °F	81.3	82.3	82.4	82.4	81.5	80.3	78.6	77.9	79.1	80.1	81.2	81.4	4.5	
Rainfall (in.)	0.4	0.3	1.2	4.1	11.5	20.0	35.6	36.6	28.5	12.6	5.1	1.4		157.3
Tamatave, Madagascar (16 ft.) °F	79.3	80.6	78.3	76.5	72.5	69.3	68.4	69.3	71.2	73.8	76.5	78.6	12.2	
Rainfall (in.)	15.0	14.3	17.8	12.0	9.8	14.4	13.2	8.5	7.1	5.3	3.9	9.6		130.9
Entebbe, Uganda (3863 ft.) °F	71.1	71.1	71.3	70.3	69.8	69.4	68.4	68.6	69.4	70.1	70.1	70.2	2.7	
Rainfall (in.)	2.6	3.6	5.8	9.7	8.5	5.1	2.9	3.1	3.1	3.5	5.0	5.1		58.0
Debundja, Cameroun (39 ft.) °F	79.3	79.9	79.2	78.8	78.3	76.8	74.7	74.5	75.6	75.9	77.9	87.6	5.4	
Rainfall (in.)	8.0	10.9	17.1	17.3	24.8	59.7	64.4	57.7	65.2	45.2	26.6	15.1		412.0
						The Tropical Savanna (2)								
Gorée (Dakar), Senegal (20 ft.) °F	68.5	66.2	68.2	68.9	71.6	78.3	81.1	81.5	82.4	82.0	78.3	72.0	16.2	
Rainfall (in.)	0	0	0	0	0	0.9	3.6	9.9	5.2	0.7	0.1	0		20.4
Kayes, Mali (197 ft.) °F	77.2	80.8	88.7	94.1	96.4	90.5	83.7	81.7	82.2	84.5	83.1	77.2	19.2	
Rainfall (in.)	0	0	0	0	0.6	3.9	8.3	8.3	5.6	1.9	0.3	0.2		29.1

Station	January	February	March	April	May	June	July	August	September	October	November	December	Range	Year
Mongalla, Sudan (1440 ft.) °F	80.4	81.7	82.6	81.0	79.0	77.4	75.9	75.7	77.2	78.1	79.0	79.2	6.9	
Rainfall (in.)	0.1	0.7	1.5	4.2	5.4	4.6	5.2	5.8	4.9	4.3	1.8	0.3		38.8
Luluabourg, Zaire [Congo (Kin.)] (2034 ft.) °F	76.1	75.7	76.3	77.0	76.6	76.3	76.5	76.3	75.9	76.3	76.6	77.2	1.5	
Rainfall (in.)	7.2	5.4	7.9	6.1	3.1	0.2	0.1	2.5	6.5	6.6	9.1	6.6		61.3
Salisbury, Rhodesia (4880 ft.) °F	69.7	68.8	68.2	65.7	60.6	56.9	56.1	60.2	66.4	70.7	70.7	69.6	14.6	
Rainfall (in.)	7.5	7.4	4.5	1.0	0.5	0.1	0.1	0.1	0.3	1.1	3.7	5.8		32.0

Arid and Semi-arid Climates or Desert and Tropical Steppe (4 and 3)

Station	January	February	March	April	May	June	July	August	September	October	November	December	Range	Year
Alexandria, Egypt (105 ft.) °F	56.1	57.2	60.1	63.7	68.5	73.4	77.0	78.1	76.3	73.0	66.4	59.4	22.0	
Rainfall (in.)	2.1	0.9	0.5	0.2	0	0	0	0	0	0.3	1.3	2.6		7.9
Khartoum, Sudan (1280 ft.) °F	70.3	73.4	79.2	86.0	90.7	91.4	88.5	86.5	88.2	87.4	80.2	72.1	21.1	
Rainfall (in.)	0	0	0	0	0.1	0.3	1.6	2.2	0.7	0.2	0	0		5.1
In-Salah (Sahara), Southern Algeria (919 ft.) °F	54.7	59.4	67.8	76.1	85.6	94.3	99.3	97.0	91.6	80.1	68.2	57.7	44.6	
Rainfall (in.)	0	0	0	0	0	0	0.1	0.4	0.3	0	0	0		0.8
Swakopmund, S. W. Africa (Namibia) (20 ft.) °F	62.6	63.1	63.3	59.9	60.6	58.5	56.5	54.9	56.1	58.1	58.6	61.5	8.4	
Rainfall (in.)	0	0.1	0.2	0	0	1.2	1.2	1.7	0	0.1	0	0.2		0.6

The Humid Subtropical Climate (5)

Station	January	February	March	April	May	June	July	August	September	October	November	December	Range	Year
Durban, Natal, South Africa (260 ft.) °F	76.3	76.8	74.9	71.8	67.8	64.8	64.3	65.8	67.6	69.5	72.0	74.6	12.5	
Rainfall (in.)	4.6	4.9	5.4	3.4	1.9	1.2	1.2	1.7	3.2	5.1	5.0	5.1		42.7

Station	January	February	March	April	May	June	July	August	September	October	November	December	Range	Year
Pietermaritzburg, Natal, South Africa														
(2225 ft.) °F	73.3	73.4	71.4	67.8	61.9	57.6	58.6	62.4	65.2	67.4	69.1	71.8	15.8	
Rainfall (in.)	5.1	6.2	5.1	2.6	1.1	0.3	0.1	0.8	1.8	2.5	5.3	5.0		35.9

Middle Latitude Steppe or High Veld Climate (6)

Station	January	February	March	April	May	June	July	August	September	October	November	December	Range	Year
Graaf Reinet, Cape Province, South Africa														
(2500 ft.) °F	71.8	72.3	68.2	61.8	56.5	53.0	51.0	53.8	59.0	63.8	68.5	71.5	2.13	
Rainfall (in.)	1.7	1.4	2.7	0.9	1.2	0.4	0.2	0.7	1.3	0.9	2.5	1.4		15.3

The Mediterranean Climate (7)

Station	January	February	March	April	May	June	July	August	September	October	November	December	Range	Year
Funchal, Madeira														
(82 ft.) °F	59.4	59.2	59.7	61.2	63.5	67.1	70.2	72.1	71.4	68.4	64.4	61.2	12.9	
Rainfall (in.)	3.4	3.6	3.4	1.9	1.1	0.4	0.1	0.1	1.2	4.0	4.7	3.2		27.1
Algiers, Algeria														
(72 ft.) °F	49.3	50.4	52.5	55.8	61.0	67.8	73.4	74.7	70.3	63.7	56.8	51.8	25.4	
Rainfall (in.)	4.0	2.6	3.3	2.0	1.7	0.7	0.1	0.1	1.2	3.4	4.1	4.0		27.2
Tunis, Tunisia														
(141 ft.) °F	48.4	51.3	54.3	58.3	64.4	72.0	77.7	78.6	74.5	66.7	58.8	52.3	30.2	
Rainfall (in.)	2.1	2.0	1.9	1.5	0.9	0.5	0.1	0.2	1.0	1.9	2.1	2.4		16.6
Cape Town, Cape Province, South Africa														
(40 ft.) °F	69.9	70.3	68.1	63.2	58.9	55.7	54.7	55.6	57.9	61.2	64.6	67.9	15.6	
Rainfall (in.)	0.7	0.6	0.9	1.9	3.8	4.5	3.7	3.4	2.3	1.6	1.1	0.8		25.3

Highland Climates (H)

Station	January	February	March	April	May	June	July	August	September	October	November	December	Range	Year
Nairobi, Kenya														
(5450 ft.) °F	63.8	64.7	65.2	63.9	63.4	61.6	58.5	59.3	61.6	64.8	64.0	62.3	6.7	
Rainfall (in.)	1.9	3.6	4.2	8.9	5.6	2.2	0.9	1.1	1.2	2.3	5.3	2.8		40.0
Addis Ababa, Ethiopia														
(18,005 ft.) °F	60.1	62.4	64.8	64.4	65.7	63.5	61.7	61.0	61.3	61.7	59.2	58.6	7.1	
Rainfall (in.)	0.6	1.9	2.8	3.4	3.0	5.7	11.0	12.1	7.6	0.8	0.6	0.2		49.6

Entebbe shows a station modified by elevation, and Debundja demonstrates the amount of moisture that is available in the equatorial air masses to fall as rain, given suitable local conditions. (See Table 4.2 for conversion of °F to °C and inches to millimeters.)

THE TROPICAL SAVANNA (2)

This is *par excellence* the climate of tropical Africa, just as the varied forms of savanna which result are the dominant natural vegetation of the vast intertropical plateaus. Since the savanna stretches from the equatorial rainforest on the one

Table 4.2 Conversion Table.

Conversion: °F to °C

°F	°C	°F	°C	°F	°C	°F	°C
48	8.9	66	18.9	84	28.9		
49	9.4	67	19.4	85	29.4	0.1	0.1
50	10.0	68	20.0	86	30.0	0.1	0.1
51	10.6	69	20.6	87	30.6	0.2	0.1
52	11.1	70	21.1	88	31.1	0.3	0.2
53	11.7	71	21.7	89	31.7	0.4	0.2
54	12.2	72	22.2	90	32.2	0.5	0.3
55	12.8	73	22.8	91	32.8	0.6	0.3
56	13.3	74	23.3	92	33.3	0.7	0.4
57	13.9	75	23.9	93	33.9	0.8	0.4
58	14.4	76	24.4	94	34.4	0.9	0.5
59	15.0	77	25.0	95	35.0		
60	15.6	78	25.6	96	35.6		
61	16.1	79	26.1	97	36.1		
62	16.7	80	26.7	98	36.7		
63	17.2	81	27.2	99	37.2		
64	17.8	82	27.8	100	37.8		
65	18.3	83	28.3				

Conversion: in. to mm.

in.	mm.	in.	mm.	in.	mm.	in.	mm.
100	2540.0	10	254.0	1	25.4	0.1	2.5
200	5080.0	20	508.0	2	50.8	0.2	5.1
300	7620.0	30	762.0	3	76.2	0.3	7.6
400	10160.0	40	1016.0	4	101.6	0.4	10.2
		50	1270.0	5	127.0	0.5	12.7
		60	1524.0	6	152.4	0.6	15.2
		70	1778.0	7	177.8	0.7	17.8
		80	2032.0	8	203.2	0.8	20.3
		90	2286.0	9	228.6	0.9	22.9

hand to the desert margins on the other, the savanna climate must clearly vary greatly also. In fact the variation is primarily in the total amount of precipitation, commonly from 80 inches on the equatorial margins (but greatly exceeding this on exposed slopes) to 16 inches where it merges into the semi-arid or tropical steppe climate. There is a consequent effect on temperature, but the rhythm of the seasons is constant throughout. A cool or at least relatively cool dry season (November to February in the northern hemisphere) gives place to a hot dry season, so that in the northern hemisphere the hottest month is early in the year, commonly in April or May. The coming of the rains causes a lowering of the temperature, except where the falls are too small to have this effect, and the rainy season is thus equivalent to a midlatitude summer.

For reasons already indicated as related to the movement of air masses and the associated fronts over a continent where there are few physical barriers to air movement, the break of the rainy season may be early in some years, greatly delayed in others. Annual totals show a wide variation from year to year, whereas in any given year the incidence may show remarkable irregularities since the rain falls almost entirely as heavy showers or thundershowers. The irregularities between one month and another, as well as from year to year, increase as the average total fall decreases. Thus in one year a place with an "average" fall of 40 inches may have abundant moisture for a good harvest; the next year the fall may only total 20 inches, and famine conditions result. This is in addition to the "hungry season," which occurs after all the crops of one harvest have been consumed and before the first crops from the new harvest are ready for consumption. A good example of the climatic vagaries is afforded by a station in Gambia, where the rainfall totals for 18 successive years were as follows:

Year	Inches	Year	Inches
1901	45	1910	44
1902	29	1911	28
1903	57	1912	34
1904	38	1913	24
1905	66	1914	49
1906	64	1915	48
1907	34	1916	38
1908	44	1917	38
1909	57	1918	54

Taking individual months in the same place, we find that June showed a range from 2.24 inches in one year to 12.32 in another. Over the same period May ranged from nil to 1.90 inches, and October from 0.24 to 9.08 inches.

The figures for temperature show that plant growth is normally possible throughout the year. Though the day temperatures, especially in drier regions, greatly exceed those in the equatorial belt, they do not reach the extremes found in the great deserts. There is everywhere close correlation between daily and annual temperature ranges and the situation relative to the sea and to moist air masses. Bathurst on the coast in Gambia (13° North) has a range from 74°F in January to 80°F in July (when rainfall is 12 inches), but October, when the rains have almost ceased (average 4 inches), is one degree hotter than July. Inland stations such as Kayes show a range from 77°F in January to 96° in May.

ARID AND SEMI-ARID CLIMATE OR DESERT AND STEPPE (4 and 3)

Deserts are defined by low precipitation but on the margins towards the equator it is difficult to say where "desert" fades into what Trewartha records as "steppe," and where the steppe gives place to tropical "savanna." For the savanna limit many would follow Gourou, using the 16-inch (400 mm) isohyet.[4] On the pole-

ward margins a low rainfall limit may be taken to indicate where the steppelands fade into the Mediterranean. In the heart of the Sahara such rain as falls (as at Tamanrasset) comes in storms at irregular intervals; along the southern margins the "rainy season" is the hot season or summer; along the Mediterranean margins it is the winter – well exemplified by Alexandria.

Like all deserts, the African regions have great temperature extremes. The daily range in the heart of the desert is as much as 50–60°F; the highest recorded temperatures on the surface of the earth are claimed by the Sahara. Shade recordings of 136°F (58°C) are said to have been made; the surface of the ground frequently exceeds 170°F. Most of the heart of the Sahara has a July mean exceeding 95°F. The annual range is between 30 and 40°F; in the north the coldest month has a mean of 50°F, so that frost is quite usual.

The mean annual cloudiness is normally less than 10 percent, so that cloudless skies are the rule – bright sunshine by day, starlight by night. The atmosphere is so dry that the wet-bulb thermometer may be 40 degrees lower than the dry. The air may be so dry as to inhibit plant life, and it has been claimed that a man needs to drink a minimum of 10 pints of liquid a day to maintain his health.

Conditions in the corresponding area in southern Africa are much less severe. There the most arid strip is along the coast (the Namib); the so-called Kalahari Desert has in fact sufficient vegetation to be classed at worst as semidesert only.

HUMID SUBTROPICAL CLIMATE (5)

In Africa this is the climate of Natal and neighboring parts of the southeastern coasts of the continent at about latitude 30 degrees. Durban shows the small range of temperature near the coast, increasing slightly inland as indicated in Pieter-

[4] Pierre Gourou, *The Tropical World,* 3rd Ed., trans. E. D. Laborde (London: Longman, 1961).

have characteristically lower winter averages.

MEDITERRANEAN CLIMATE (7)

The Mediterranean climate, deriving its name from the fact that it is characteristic of so many countries around the Mediterranean Sea, is one of the most distinctive of all climatic types. It shares its hot dry summers with the neighboring desert lands; its cool moist winters derive their rainfall from the westerly air streams which bring the rain through a succession of depressions or lows to lands nearer the poles. The rainfall may show a fall maximum (the "former rains" of the Bible) and a spring maximum ("latter rains") rather than a single winter maximum, but the fact that the supply of moisture coincides with the cool season results both in a slow formation of soil and a slow vegetative growth. In the long, hot summer, plants need to conserve their moisture, and, unless they tap deep-seated supplies by very long roots, they have reduced leaf surfaces with such protective devices as hairs (for example, olive trees) and waxed or leathery surfaces (laurels, evergreen oak, pines). The thick "cork" bark of the cork oak is another protection against loss of moisture. Cultivation of grain and herbaceous crops necessitates an early harvest before the scorching heat of late summer, or a dependence on irrigation.

The Mediterranean climate is found in the northwest and extreme southwest of the continent, where mountain ranges, deep valleys, and coastal strips of varying exposure give marked and rapid local variations in temperature and rainfall. Rainfall generally increases with elevation. Though rare at sea level, frost and even snow occur at comparatively low elevations and are usual at greater heights.

The examples given in Table 4.1 include the island site of Funchal (Madeira) and the coastal stations of Algiers and Tunis in the north and Cape Town in the south. Marrakesh, inland at a height of

4.B The Drakensberg above the coastal plain of South Africa. Great relief can raise parts of Africa above the adjacent climate and here the plateau can be seen above an inversion layer. (Copyright Geographical Publications Limited.)

maritzburg. In neither place is the range as great as in areas like the southeastern United States.

MIDDLE LATITUDE STEPPE OR HIGH VELD CLIMATE (6)

In Africa this is the climate of the damper parts of the South African High Veld. It owes its character in large measure to elevation which results in a lower temperature throughout the year. Although snow is not unknown and winter frosts occur for 3 to 6 months, the area is too near the moderating influence of the ocean to suffer from the climatic extremes of northern steppelands and prairies. Graaff Reinet shows a spring or early summer rainfall maximum and also one in the fall. This station is only 2500 feet above sea level; places like Bloemfontein

1542 feet, though dry, shows a fall and a spring maximum.

UNDIFFERENTIATED HIGHLANDS (H)

The whole of the African plateau exhibits climatic modifications due to elevation. In Nairobi, on the equator, the modification is profound and is shared by the large area of highland in East Africa. There remain, however, parts of the continent, notably the mountain knot of Ethiopia, where rugged or varied relief results in a vertical zonation of climatic types; the same is true of the great volcanoes of East Africa. This is the reason for the inclusion of "undifferentiated highlands" on the map—where parts rise to the snowline.

CLIMATE AND LAND USE

No influence upon life in tropical Africa exceeds rain in importance. This can be seen in the way in which inumerable ceremonies and customs still widely remembered have sprung from the vital necessity of an adequate fall of rain in an area marked by violent fluctuations from year to year. The most striking and institutionalized of these involved a traditional "rain maker."

Customary practices however also provide more practical methods of coping with the problem of insufficient and unreliable rainfall. Nomadism is the principal adaption of pastoral peoples, and this should not be interpreted as aimless wondering. Study of any such people reveals an intricate and highly adaptable system of movement designed in the light of immense local knowledge and accumulated experience to maximize the carrying capacity of the land. It represents the application of critical path analysis to a complex of grazing and browse areas and

4.C Turkana (Kenya) tribeswomen obtaining water from a dry river bed. In such arid and semi-arid areas, most rivers only flow for a few days in the year and water must be obtained from that percolating in the deep sands of the river bed. (Photo: Monitor.)

4.D The "hungry season" in northern Ghana. This is during the dry period of the "winter" solstice. (Official photograph.)

watering points, all in a state of change from season to season. This enables regions of great environmental difficulty to support surprisingly large numbers of peoples and stock with a minimum of technology. Development funds and efforts have generally been channeled to the areas of more densely settled peasant cultivation, but if the knowledge of the traditional herders can be utilized, the commercialization of the rangelands of Africa offers considerable opportunities in the future.

Seasonal rainfall also presents grave problems for the peasant cultivator. Over vast areas that have marked wet and dry seasons, life during the rains is not difficult. Heat and moisture combine to encourage plant growth, and a varied assortment of vegetables becomes available for human food. This is the time for sowing. The months which follow are the months for harvesting the various grains — corn, millets, peanuts, and rice — but harvesting of all crops is over two months before the next rains break. Thus the months of March and April north of the equator, September and October to the south, are slack months

in the cultivation year. If the harvest has been poor, so that food does not last over this period or later, until other food is available, this is the "hungry season," often one of great distress. This problem is made much worse by inadequate storage methods so that a large proportion of the crop is lost to rats and to infestation with insects. One solution is to grow one crop, such as cassava, which will survive and can be harvested in the dry season. Similarly the variability of the main rains is met in some measure by growing a wide range of crops so that some will bring a harvest even if others fail — whether the rains are too small or too great for the main crop.

Where there are reliable river floods this "hunger period" is absent. This is clearly seen in the Central Barotse plain of Zambia, where the Zambezi floods annually with a maximum in March and April. The people, the Lozi, live on mounds in the plain free from floods (the ownership of which is very important) and cultivate the soil as gardens, at the same time keeping cattle and fishing, so that they enjoy a varied diet.

CLIMATE AND THE "WHITE MAN"

The high death rate among Europeans serving in the tropics, and perhaps especially the disastrous mortality among British soldiers serving in India and compelled to march and fight in close-fitting cloth uniforms and small caps, gave rise to beliefs about the influence of climate on the white man which persisted, with very little foundation, for more than a century. The direct effects of climate have been confused with the serious effects of disease, especially insect-borne and water-borne. Among the myths was the danger of sunstroke, which was believed to affect particularly the spine (hence the wearing of spine pads) through the head, which accordingly needed protection by a sun helmet or solar topee (without which no self-respecting Britisher would venture abroad in sunlight or even with the sun lurking behind clouds). Medical men had been denying the existence of "sunstroke" in the old accepted sense for a decade or more before the experience of troops in New Guinea, Burma, and Africa in World War II finally dispelled the myth. Heat-stroke apoplexy is real enough, and is best countered by all those measures which encourage the body to "breathe": loose, light clothing and abundant water to encourage perspiration. Light rays received through the eyes may be dangerous; hence the wearing of dark glasses.

As exact evidence based on controlled experiments accumulates, the trend of the evidence indicates that there is nothing in the tropical climate to inhibit hard manual labor for white as well as colored men, though temperature and humidity conditions may be above the optimum for both physical and mental energy. Certainly some who have lived for any time in the tropics and then returned to experience a so-called temperate climate find it hard to be convinced of its reputed advantages.

The absence of seasonal rhythm in the equatorial lands has already been cited as a deleterious climatic factor. In addition, high humidity as well as exceptionally high temperatures may be noted as having a directly enervating effect. That high temperatures have a direct effect is instanced by the relatively harmless but very annoying condition known as "prickly heat," an intense irritation which may or may not show on the surface of the skin.

Tropical climates have of course many indirect effects on the white man. Since the intake of a large part of our food is required for the maintenance of bodily temperature in cold latitudes, it follows that there is less need for energy-giving carbohydrates or "fuel." Yet the white man is reluctant to change his eating habits, and therefore often accumulates too much fatty tissue. The need for a large intake of moisture often leads to excessive intake of alcohol. In short, the feeding and drinking habits among whites in many parts of the tropics are, or have been, such that the survival of the individual becomes a daily miracle.

The long-assumed superiority of the white man has given rise consciously or unconsciously to the concept that manual labor is not for him in a country where there are others to do such work; this then leads to the idea that such work is physically impossible.

If we thus destroy some of the old shibboleths, we do not prove that white settlers can be at home anywhere in the tropics. The harmful effects of certain high temperatures have been admitted, but when the "white man's grave," as West Africa was once called, gained its notoriety it was not primarily the climate which was responsible. Disease is another matter.

Interest in the effects of tropical climates on the white man has widened from the influence of heat and humidity to include more subtle considerations. On the supposedly "healthy" highlands there seems to be some undue stimulation of the nervous system. There is often an increased irritability in the individual, and there is some evidence of decreasing mental stability, especially in the second or third generation of white settlers. Could it be the influence of cosmic rays, the increased reception of radiation, the slowness of adjustment to lower atmospheric pressure, or are there other factors? The answers are still lacking.

In recent years the whole position has greatly changed with the widespread use of airconditioning, rapidly becoming as common as central heating in cold lands. Not only can temperature and humidity (but not pressure) be adapted to human needs and varied at will, but similar controls make possible delicate manufacturing processes, notably fine-quality printing, previously impossible in the humid tropics.

THE AFRICAN WATER PROBLEM

So much of Africa suffers from aridity—permanent, seasonal, or occasional—that some writers have gone so far as to say that no rain falling on the surface of the continent ought ever to be allowed to reach the sea. We may perhaps modify this by adding "until it has fulfilled some function of benefit to mankind." Primarily the water is needed to ensure food production, though Africa, because of its plateau character, has more potential water power than any other continent. In the south the Orange River does not normally reach the sea, drying up before it disgorges into the Atlantic. But the aim that no river should reach the sea is scarcely compatible with the development of power at the falls which mark the main drop from the plateau and are usually near, or relatively near, the mouth.

In contrast to the peoples, for example, of southeast Asia and also of northern Africa and northern Sudan, where wells, shadoof, water wheels, Persian wheels, flumes, "tanks" with irrigation ditches, terracing, and many other devices for reaching, storing, and using water are almost universal, the Africans of the tropics are to a surprising degree not "water-minded." With certain exceptions, their crops depend upon the rains when they come, and their domestic supplies are laboriously carried from stream or lake. Although wells are not uncommon, they are the exception rather than the rule, and streams are rarely dammed to maintain a supply either for domestic use or for watering crops.

It is with this position in mind that we suggest that the solution of the African water problem should begin with the education of the African peasant and the development of small schemes which he himself can construct and maintain, the so-called "middle level technology." The position is changing, but in the early stages a pump is often discarded as soon as it fails to work, while anything which "belong him government" is something quite apart. The higher up a stream conservation takes place, the better, and the first need is instruction in building a dam or weir of any local material—soil, rubble, or stone. Of course it is better still if laterite blocks or precast porous concrete is available. The next stage is to teach the advantages of keeping the supply as free as possible from contamination and of saving labor by conducting a gravity supply by pipe or flume to the villages. Since this is largely a saving of woman's work, it is unlikely to rank as first priority among African men.

Knowledge of the water cycle is fundamental to the planning of land use of much of Africa and it forms a major item of research in such centers as the East African Agriculture and Forestry Research Organization. The components of the cycle vary in proportion from region to region but runoff may be between 2 and 12 percent of rainfall, percolation between 2 and 40 percent, while evapotranspiration may be anything between 40 and 96 percent. In the dry northeast of Kenya, potential evapotranspiration averages more than 100 inches (2600 mm) a year and over very large areas of Tanzania it lies between 80 and 85 inches (2000 and 2200

4.E A water-wheel in the Sudan. An ancient form of irrigation which has here made use of old metal drums and of wire. (Photo: J. Allan Cash.)

mm). These estimates of potential evapotranspiration are calculated from records of temperature, radiation, air flow, humidity, etc. by the Penman method.[5] By a less complex method, Davies and Robinson[6] have produced a more generalized map of potential water-loss for the whole of Africa and compared it with the average annual rainfall [Figures 4.12(a) and 4.12(b)]. It will be seen that over most of Africa, the potential evapotranspiration is much higher than the rainfall. The only area where this is not so is largely coincident with the distribution of the rainforest. Elsewhere, this loss of moisture back into the atmosphere means that, except at the height of the rainy season, the amount of water available for surface runoff and for irrigation is likely to be limited.

With such high rates of evaporation, the best place for water storage, provided it can again be made available, is underground. Where there are natural water-

[5] East African Agriculture and Forestry Research Organization Record of Research, 1967, pp. 14–17.

[6] J. A. Davies and P. J. Robinson. "A Simple Energy Balance Approach to the Moisture Balance Climatology of Africa" *in* M. F. Thomas and G. W. Whittington, *Environment and Land Use in Africa* (London: Methuen, 1969).

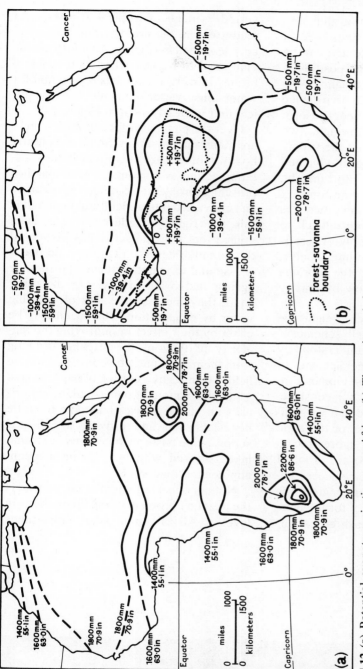

4.12 (a) Potential evapotranspiration over Africa. (b) The moisture balance over Africa (the difference between precipitation and potential evapotranspiration). Note that for most of Africa this is negative, and its relationship with the forest boundary. (After J. A. Davies and P. J. Robinson.)

holding beds, such as gravel or alluvium, in which underground water finds its level in the permanent water table and can be reached by shallow wells, the position is excellent. Peasants can be taught to dig and line wells, and such a primitive device as an endless porous rope of fibers absorbing water and passing through two wooden rollers to squeeze out the supply is within the power of the least educated to make and maintain. Unfortunately, over much of Africa's underlying complex of ancient rocks the water table behaves irregularly, and a well is both difficult to dig and uncertain of its supply. There is much to be said, in hilly or rolling country, for horizontal "wells" into the hillsides from which water would flow by gravity as an artificial spring.

Undoubtedly very much might be achieved in Africa by small schemes—dams and wells—made and understood by the people themselves. Larger schemes of water control and power development, involving capital and experts for construction and maintenance, stand in a very different position. The success of the great Gezira scheme and the more recent Kariba dam (see Chap. 18) are proof of what can be done, but their success depends on much more than engineering alone. They require a market for the electricity generated and the cash crops har-

vested. Not all of tropical Africa is yet ready for the big project. The Nile projects described in Chapter 10, illustrate the vital need to regard Africa as a series of basins. How rarely the basin, as a unit for water conservation, coincides with a political unit is clearly seen in Figure 3.5.

Over the plateau surface of Africa there are many marshy areas. Some are natural hollows; others are due primarily to vegetation acting as a sponge. These marshes present a problem: Some can be drained and converted into agricultural land, but is this the right procedure? It has been argued that their presence has prevented the spread of desert conditions, and that it is essential to maintain them as insurance against increasing aridity. On the other hand, they increase the loss of valuable water by evaporation. This again may be offset by their effect in improving the regularity of flow of the streams draining from them. Can parts be converted to rice fields? Can regular cutting of papyrus give a valuable source of paper-making material? Can marsh grasses palatable to cattle be established and provide an all-year supply? Can pastures be improved around lakes stocked with fish, giving a much-appreciated food supply?

Not unconnected with the marsh land is the puzzling problem of the fluctuations in level of Africa's great lakes. Sometimes

4.F The Sennar Dam, across the Blue Nile in the Sudan. Built in 1925, the dam was the key to developing the vast Gezira irrigation scheme. (Photo: J. Allen Cash.)

this fluctuation is certainly due to accumulation of vegetation (with silt) at the outlets. An interesting case study is afforded by Lake Nyasa and its outlet, the Shire River. The lake fluctuates in level as much as 20 feet, and the upper part of the Shire River has such a shallow gradient that water may flow upstream after a heavy rainstorm. Lower down, the river flows over a rocky ridge through a gorge with facilities for a power dam site before reaching a flood plain often invaded by water from the Zambezi. Lake Victoria is also subject to fluctuating levels, following a sequence of exceptionally heavy rains over its catchment. This can lead to flooding of cultivated land—and of port facilities.

It is, of course, impossible to separate the water problem from many of Africa's other major problems. Africa has little coal; therefore the chief source of domestic fuel is wood. This means constant cutting of woodland, and a depletion of timber reserves introduces the danger of soil erosion. If water power could be harnessed to provide electricity at a low cost to the peasant consumer, this danger would disappear and more land would be released for other purposes.

Further Reading

By far the best account of the synoptic features and the seasonal synoptic situation over Africa is provided by the succinct introduction to *The Climate of Africa* by B. W. Thompson (Nairobi: Oxford University Press, 1965). The remainder of the book forms an atlas unusual because it includes conditions at isobaric levels up to the 200-mb surface (about 40,000 feet above ground level). More detailed maps at ground level are provided in S. P. Jackson's *Climatological Atlas of Africa* (Pretoria, 1961). The relevant chapters (7–10 and 15–16) of Glenn T. Trewartha's *The Earth's Problem Climates* (Madison: University of Wisconsin Press, 1962) provides an explanatory account of the climates of the major regions of Africa while his climatic classification is most conveniently consulted in *An Introduction to Climate* (New York: McGraw-Hill).

The complex question of the influence of climate on human beings has given rise to a large but still often inconclusive literature. Important summary works include C. E. P. Brooks, *Climate in Everyday Life* (New York: Philosophical Library, 1951), D. H. K. Lee, *Climate and Economic Development in the Tropics* (New York: Harper, 1957), and such standard references as K. J. K. Buettner, *Biometerology* (Pergamon, 1962) and part 4 of S. W. Tromp's *Medical Biometerology* (Elsevier, 1963).

CHAPTER 5

Soils and Their Management

In previous chapters we have considered the rock types of Africa, the land forms they comprise, and the climates to which they are subjected. These factors are all relevant to the formation of soil and are responsible for some of the characteristic features of the soils found in Africa.

SOME CHARACTERISTICS OF AFRICAN SOILS

Many workers have been preoccupied with the importance of temperature and moisture on soil formation, and earlier work on the importance of mineralogic and microscopic examination of soils has tended to be overlooked. In 1950, however, the late Cecil F. Charter, then director of the Gold Coast Survey, demonstrated anew the supreme importance of the character of the mineral particles examined under the microscope. His work has shown the danger of arguing from one continent to another and has demonstrated the significance of the study of geomorphology — the evolution of land forms. It is, of course, universally known that when soils are subjected to mechanical analysis the mineral particles of which they consist can be graded according to

size into stones, coarse sand, fine sand, silt, and clay. An international classification has been drawn up which defines the size of particles as follows:

Diameter greater
   than 2 mm: stones
Diameter between
   0.2 and 2 mm: coarse sand
Diameter between
   0.02 and 0.2 mm: fine sand
Diameter between
   0.002 and 0.02 mm: silt
Diameter less than
   0.002 mm: clay

A "sandy" soil, for example, includes more than 60 percent of coarse and fine sand but less than 10 percent of clay. Loamy soils and loams contain a smaller percentage of coarse and fine sand but more of clay, and so on.

But what is the origin of these mineral particles? It is, of course, in general the underlying rocks, whether solid or "drift" deposits. Over vast areas of Europe and North America the underlying rocks are of sedimentary origin — superficial deposits laid down or redeposited by wind, river water, ice and melt water from ice, sea water, or older, solid deposits of sandstone, shale, and clay. When examined under the microscope, the tiny mineral fragments, especially of the all-important, stable mineral quartz, are found to be more or less rounded (partly rounded if deposited under water, more fully rounded and polished if windborne). By comparison, we have seen that a very large part of the African continent has been land for many millions of years. The old Miocene peneplanation surface has been subjected to atmospheric weathering for 15 million to 30 million years. The mineral particles of African soils are thus very frequently derived directly from the underlying solid rocks; the particles have *not* been transported. The underlying crystalline complex is commonly of varied metamorphic rocks seamed by quartz veins (Figure 5.1). The quartz veins, and the quartz of the various metamorphic rocks, have been shattered into tiny "sand" grains, but the grains are *sharply angular* and of different sizes. It was the Scottish road engineer, John Loudon McAdam (1756–1836), who realized that angular rock fragments of different sizes could be compacted into a solid, durable road surface by simple pressure or rolling. This is the principle of the macadam road. The rock fragments of an African soil thus present the ideal conditions for the formation of a "macadam" surface. It would seem that even the pounding by the raindrops in a tropical

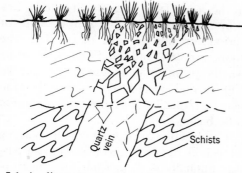

5.1 A diagram showing the formation of a sedentary soil from subsoil.

downpour may sometimes be sufficient to consolidate the surface. Although the bare foot of the humble cultivator may tread with impunity on the soil, a caterpillar tractor has the same effect as a road roller and consolidates the surface into a hard macadam layer. Immediately the majority of mechanical cultivators are ruled out. There are other consequential results of this soil structure. It was found in the East African experiments that disc plows lasted only a very short time. The angular quartz grains (harder than any steel) embedded in a clay matrix seem to have acted just like diamond dust in a circular iron wheel; they rasped the steel discs of a plow in an incredibly short time. There is no sound alternative yet, in many parts of Africa, to the hand cultivator with his hoe, quite apart from the costs associated with mechanized cultivation and other aspects, which are considered in Chapter 7.

Any student of elementary chemistry knows that a chemical reaction is normally hastened by the application of heat. That is why the test tube is heated in the Bunsen burner, why a hot solution of acid does its work more quickly than cold. Furthermore, a lump of sugar or salt dissolves more quickly in hot water than in cold. Although it is now recognized that some very interesting chemical reactions take place under cold conditions, it is still true to say that the majority of chemical reactions that can be observed in soils in midlatitudes are hastened in the tropics. With air and surface soil temperatures approximating 80°F (27°C), it would seem that downward leaching (the solution by percolating rainwater of substances in the surface layers and their removal to lower layers) takes place with greater rapidity than in midlatitudes, though this is not agreed upon by all workers. In the dry season, where a dry season occurs, evaporation is rapid, and with it the deposition of salts in the soil. According to local conditions, a "hardpan" primarily of ferruginous oxides may be formed either at the surface or at a varying distance below it. Perhaps of even greater significance is the rapid oxidation of organic compounds when exposed to the atmosphere. In mid-latitudes the turning of surface layers of the soil permits air to reach organic matter and encourages the work of aerobic (air-loving) bacteria which convert decaying organic matter into valuable humus and organic food directly available to plants. Plowing in the tropics, on the other hand, may expose organic matter (such as fibrous roots) which combines with the oxygen of the atmosphere so rapidly that it forms the gas carbon dioxide, which disappears into the air.

It was proved by actual experiments in Ceylon long ago that frequent plowing can literally plow all the goodness out of a tropical soil. It becomes increasingly doubtful whether plowing is the right treatment for the soils of vast areas of tropical Africa. The luxuriant growth of an equatorial rainforest suggests a soil of great fertility, and the fallen leaves suggest a ready source of organic matter. But when the forest is cleared and the atmosphere reaches the soil directly, it is rapidly reduced to complete sterility. The relationship of air temperature to humus content has been demonstrated in Java, where at an elevation of 3000 feet (914 m) and an average annual temperature of 68°F (20°C) the humus content of surface soil was 14 percent. It dropped to 5 percent at lower levels and a temperature of 76°F (24°C). In tropical lowland soils it is often below 2 percent. The beneficial action of frost, which, because water expands when it freezes, breaks up clods of clay soil and prepares a natural seed bed in the colder parts of midlatitudes, is absent in the tropics. Instead, the mechanical action of heavy downpours of rain may further consolidate an already heavy soil.

Although the incidence of soil erosion has cast doubts on the virtues and the value of huge plowed areas in middle latitudes, it is still true to say that there the well-managed farm in the fall is likely to exhibit a succession of neatly plowed fields, with the air reaching the soil. It will be a farm kept clean, and the land will be free of weeds. In tropical Africa it is scarcely too much to say that such a farm would be all wrong. The exposure of the soil to the atmosphere would result in rapid deterioration in nutrient status; it would be inviting soil erosion. When working in West Africa the worst example of soil erosion the authors of this book actually witnessed was on a government experimental farm which had been clean-plowed and was then unfortunately subjected to a fall of rain, 2.5 inches (63 mm) in one night. Every furrow was an incipient if not an actual gulley.

By the standards of cultivation common in both America and Europe the African's farm is very dirty; his land is full of weeds. But the golden rule in tropical Africa is to keep the soil covered with vegetation; the problem is to introduce a "cover crop" which will both keep the soil covered and add to its nutrient status. Various leguminous crops (with bacteria in the root nodules which convert atmospheric nitrogen to nitrogenous plant food) have been introduced for this purpose, and the African cultivator has been encouraged to hoe them into the soil. Because this hoeing is done by hand, the already heavy labor of cultivation is thereby doubled, and the hoeing-in of green crops has not proved popular with African cultivators. The custom has long been to clear a tract of land by burning it, cultivate it by hoeing in the ashes, and abandon it after a few years. The tract cleared is too small for serious erosion to take place. The tree roots are left and bind the soil, while weeds spring up unhindered to protect the soil. In regions of heavy rainfall the land may be ridged by hoes into a succession of little basins.

The practice of clearing land by burning as well as the practice of burning off pasture annually is almost universal in tropical Africa. Is this process injurious to the soil? No one needs to be reminded of

5.A Basin cultivation in southern Nigeria. This is a most effective means of preventing soil erosion. (Copyright L. Dudley Stamp.)

the effect of burning clay — it becomes a brick. It is well known too that peat bogs and soils very rich in organic matter may, in middle latitudes, actually catch fire and burn for long periods. Thus burning off the vegetation in tropical Africa may both bake the surface soil to a bricklike form and fire the organic matter in the soil. As a matter of fact this does not happen unless the fire is very fierce; the secret is to burn off early in the dry season before the vegetation is too dry. In that case the soil benefits from the dressing of ash. Some experiments seem to show that the results of burning off a cover crop are as good as hoeing it in (with an immense saving of labor), but other recent work throws doubt on this conclusion. Until mechanized cultivation becomes the rule, burning will doubtless continue because it is simple and saves labor.

The part played by organisms and micro-organisms in tropical soils is obviously very different from temperate soils. The microbiology of submerged riceland soils must obviously be very different from that of normally drained soils. Another interesting case of conditions

peculiar to the tropics is afforded by those lands where termites (commonly known as white ants) are abundant. Their termitaria, reaching many feet in height and believed in some cases to be centuries old, are familiar sights over much of drier tropical Africa. In a land suffering from leaching and with soils and subsoils almost free of lime, the material of the termitaria has been found so rich in calcium carbonate that it can supply fertilizer for a considerable patch of surrounding land. There are parts of the tropics where these afford the only fertile patches. Yet there does not seem to be any accumulation of phosphates, as might be expected, from termite excreta. Termites break down organic matter such as twigs and leaves falling on the surface, but it is not clear that they help to build up humus; they may merely aid rapid oxidation. The effect of termites in aerating and working over the soil makes up in part for the general absence of earthworms.

A well-known feature of the humid tropics is the extraordinary depth to which rock weathering may take place. This is accentuated in the many parts of

5.B A bush-fire in Uganda. Fire is perhaps the most important single ecological factor in the tropical savannas. (Photo: J. Allan Cash.)

Africa where there is no definite water table. Another complicating factor is found in those regions which have a long dry season. The stunted tree or scrub vegetation secures its continued existence by the development of extremely long roots, so that moisture retained at great depths can be used. Incidentally, the clearing of such scrub may be extremely difficult; a bulldozer is almost useless.

The effect of higher temperatures in increasing the rate of leaching has been mentioned, but the water to dissolve the minerals is also necessary. Here R. M. Scott demonstrated for East Africa the extent to which the availability of chemical plant nutrients is affected by the amount of rainfall and the consequent amount of vegetation.[1] In areas of low rainfall, mature well-drained soils had their clays fully saturated with bases (calcium, magnesium, sodium, and potassium), but as rainfall increased the percentage saturation fell to about 15 percent in areas with a mean annual rainfall of about 30 inches (760 mm). In areas of greater rainfall, more luxuriant plant growth enables the root system to bring

5.C A termitarium or "ant-hill" near Accra, Ghana. (Copyright L. Dudley Stamp.)

[1] R. M. Scott, "Exchangeable Bases of Mature, Well Drained Soils in relation to Rainfall in East Africa," *J. Soil Sci.,* **13** (1962) pp. 1–9.

the nutrients back to the surface and the percentage saturation rises again to a maximum of 55 percent at about 45 inches (1140 mm) rainfall. At still higher rainfalls, however, the downward leaching resumes its dominance and in areas with 75 inches (1900 mm) of rainfall, the saturation is found to be below 10 percent.

THE MAIN SOIL GROUPS

Modern pedologists quite rightly study soils as soils. The description of the soil profile, the determination of the soil series, chemical, mechanical, and biotic analyses, and the genesis of the soil are all studied without, necessarily, reference to the natural vegetation which the soil supports or its use, actual or potential, by man. The emergence of pedology as a distinct branch of knowledge has resulted in a certain loss, a divorce of the study of soil from cognate studies. Yet, looking back to the early days of soil science, we see that it was Dokuchaev, viewing the problem over the wide homogeneous plains of Russia, who showed that each major climatic type produced its own peculiar soil or range of soils. His pioneer studies were followed by the well-known work of his pupil Glinka. By contrast, in a country of relatively homogeneous climate but great variety of terrain and underlying rocks, it was the British who considered soils in relation to geological formation. A great advance was marked by the work of F. E. Clements and his collaborators, and few scientists today would doubt the validity of his general thesis that the living plant,

or assemblages of plants, forms an index of the sum total of environmental conditions, notably climate and soil. It seems clear, therefore, that there ought to be a close relationship between climate, soil, and vegetation. There ought, therefore, to be a distribution of great soil belts over Africa similar to that known in North America or Eurasia. Yet Marbut in his pioneer essay of 1922–1923 could say: "No book, paper, paragraph, or sentence dealing with this matter as a whole has been encountered, nor has any reference to the possibility or the probability of the existence of a series of soil belts covering the continent been found."[2] The foundation which he then proceeded to lay and his tentative map have proved very valuable. Milne and his co-workers in East Africa found it possible to develop a classification of soils applicable to their field studies based essentially on Marbut's scheme.

The tragically early death of Geoffrey Milne[3] deprived soil science of a great pioneer. He introduced the catena or catenary concept, which he mapped by vertical stripes of varying width ("pajama stripes") to indicate dominance of each constituent type (Figure 5.2). He wrote:

[2] H. L. Shantz and C. F. Marbut, *The Vegetation and Soils of Africa* (New York: American Geographical Society, 1923) p. 131.

[3] "A Provisional Soil Map of East Africa (Kenya, Uganda, Tanganyika, and Zanzibar) with Explanatory Memoir," *Amani Memoirs* (East African Agricultural Research Station, 1936). See *Geog. Rev.,* XXVI, (1936) pp. 522–523. See also *Transactions of the Third International Congress Soil Science,* I (1935) pp. 345–347.

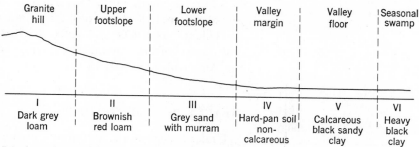

5.2 A typical soil catena in East Africa. (After G. Milne.)

Throughout districts characterized by an undulating or hummocky topography, certain sequences of changing soil profiles are found repeated. An example, met with over a large part of the dissected peneplain of Uganda . . . , consists of the sequence of soils between the crest of a low hill and the floor of the adjacent swamp, the profile changing from point to point of this traverse in accordance with conditions of drainage and past history of the land surface . . . a sequence of this kind is termed a catena or catenary complex . . . which can be made specific by prefixing a locality name.

It is clear that this principle is of very wide application.

In succeeding years a great deal of detailed work was done, but (quite apart from the complexity of the subject matter), differences in approach, terminology, and systems of classification made it impossible to obtain a coherent overall picture. That this is now available is due to the labors over ten years (1954–1964) of Dr. J. L. D'Hoore and his associates, who have published a map at a scale of 1 to 5 million, together with an explanatory monograph (See Table 5.1).

The classification used is necessarily a compromise based on the systems in use in Africa around 1960. Earlier syntheses had tended to assume that similar climates would give rise to similar soils—the "zonal approach" developed particularly in Russia. This was especially important when extrapolation was needed for areas where no other data were available. By comparison, the 1965 map gives a much greater importance to parent material. The terminology avoids the use of such terms as laterite, chernozem, and chestnut soils, which in Africa have tended to become misleading. The new pedological language of the Soil Conservation Service of the United States Department of Agriculture is not used but it is frequently possible to make a translation except, unfortunately, for the major group of Tropical Iron-rich soils.

A greatly simplified version of the 1965 map is provided in Figure 5.3 and the proportion of Africa covered by the various soil types is also given. Since the climate was not taken into account in delimiting the soil categories, the broad similarity in the pattern of distribution of climatic factors, especially of rainfall, and that of the major soil groupings is all the more striking.

Table 5.1 Proportion of Africa Occupied by the Principal Soil Types of Africa.[a]

Soil Type		Percentage
Raw mineral soils		28
Weakly developed soils		19
Brown soils		9.3
Iron-rich tropical soils		33
Vertisols		3.3
Pseudopodsolic		0.4
Mediterranean		
Brown and red	0.3	1.0
Calcimorphic	0.7	
Alluvium		1.8
Halomorphic		1.3
Hydormorphic		2.4
		100.0

[a] After J. L. D'Hoore.

RAW MINERAL SOILS

The first feature of note is the enormous area which is virtually devoid of soil, amounting to 28 percent of the continent. This is reputed to be double the proportion of that of a continent as notoriously desertic as Australia. D'Hoore classifies this cover as "raw mineral soils." However it is not defined as a soil in the U.S.D.A. system, but is regarded as a *non-soil*. It includes bare rock, ferruginous and calcareous crusts, and desert detritus. The deserts of the Sahara, the Namib, and the Afar consist largely of this cover.

WEAKLY DEVELOPED SOILS

Under less extreme conditions, shallow soils with little profile development occur,

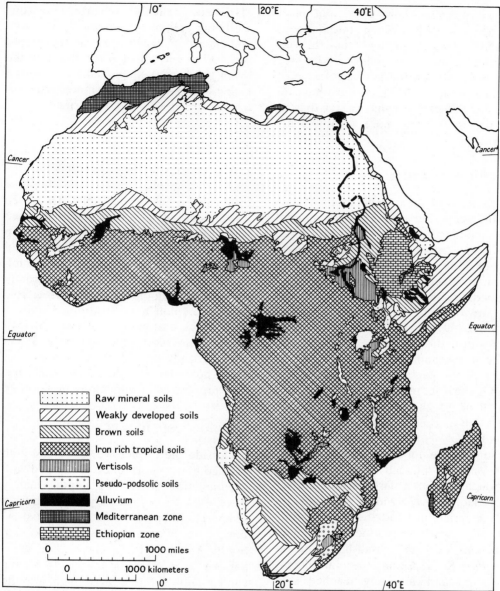

5.3 The soils of Africa. (After D'Hoore.)

Legend:
- Raw mineral soils
- Weakly developed soils
- Brown soils
- Iron rich tropical soils
- Vertisols
- Pseudo-podsolic soils
- Alluvium
- Mediterranean zone
- Ethiopian zone

0   1000 miles

0   1000 kilometers

also over wide areas. They include extremely stony soils or lithosols with solid rock within a foot (30 cm) of the surface. However, the deeper subdesert soils (7 percent of Africa) can be rich in nutrients although lacking in humus and liable to contain excessive soluble salts. If irrigation is possible, careful management can bring about reasonable yields.

BROWN SOILS

These are described by D'Hoore as brown and reddish-brown soils of arid and semi-arid regions. They are mostly found between the desert areas and the equatorial region under hot and dry climates where the annual rainfall rarely exceeds 20 inches (500 mm). The natural vegetation is typically short grass and bush ("steppe" in the French terminology) used for extensive grazing although, with irrigation, cotton and millet are grown. The same soils on the northern fringe of the Sahara, in the Mediterranean coastal area, are richer in organic matter than in the tropics and are more favorable for agriculture.

IRON-RICH TROPICAL SOILS

This is the most extensive group of soils in Africa covering a third of the continent and including most of the soils found within the tropics under normal conditions of drainage and with over 25 inches (500 mm) mean annual rainfall. They are grouped together in Table 5.1 because they are often found in association and interdigitated; however, they may be divided into three broad categories influenced by humidity but also by the nature of the parent material, relief, and age. On the drier margin with mean annual rainfall of 20–24 inches (500–1200 mm) and a well-marked dry season are the *Ferruginous Tropical Soils* or *Fersiallitic Soils*. These are the most typical "savanna" soils or the "plateau soils" of Milne. Although not particularly fertile and easily eroded, they are widely cultivated for shifting agriculture and are used for commercial groundnut production in West Africa. In the high rainfall areas are the *Ferrallitic Soils*. Among these are deeply weathered and intensely leached soils usually beneath a forest cover where the fertility and nutrients are contained in the vegetation and the superficial layer of humus. Once the clearing has taken place this fertility is quickly used up and the basic fertility of the soil is very low. In general the most fertile category of this group is that of the *Ferrisols*. This often seems related to an intermediate annual rainfall[4] and to being a younger or less senile soil, such as may develop in areas

of moderate relief where surface horizons are being continually removed—at a rate not exceeding weathering of the parent rock. Thus the soil is often found in the lower levels of the highland areas. At the higher levels an equally or more fertile *eutrophic brown* soil may be formed.

VERTISOLS

A less extensive tropical soil is the vertisol, a dark or black clayey soil, often in a form which swells into a sticky mass when wet and shrinks to a hard deeply cracked soil when dry. It is found in areas with a rather marked dry season and an annual rainfall of less than 40 inches (1000 mm). A basic source rock and flat topography assists its development and an intractable form is common in poorly drained hollows (the "black cotton soil" of East Africa). Vertisols are most important in the Sudan but are locally significant over wide areas. Their potential fertility can be high, but they present great difficulties in working.

PSEUDOPODSOLIC SOILS

Outside the tropics we find a soil with marked horizons, leached above and with accumulation layers at depth, mainly developed on sedimentary rock under a temperate, subhumid climate. Its most extensive occurrence is in the High Veld of South Africa and Lesotho and in comparable areas of the Maghreb. In Kenya similar soil is found at a high altitude where the climate may be regarded as temperate. In South Africa pseudopodsolic soils are used for large-scale grain farming and for grazing.

MEDITERRANEAN SOILS

North West Africa, the Maghreb area, has a varied topography with a wide range of rock types and climates differing over relatively small distances. There has also been a long period of use or misuse of these soils by man. The resulting pattern

[4] Scott, *loc. cit.*

of soils is therefore most complex. Those most characteristic of the region include distinctive *Red and Brown Mediterranean Soils* and calcareous soils including *Rendzinas*.

ALLUVIUM

Patches of alluvial soils are naturally widespread and often form the most productive soils within a locality. In the Nile Valley they form the major national resource, but elsewhere seasonally flooded or waterlogged alluvial plains wait for the major schemes of irrigation and water control necessary to develop them. Alluvial and *hydromorphic* soils are often associated and the latter often present great problems of reclamation. They include the swamp soils.

HALOMORPHIC SOILS

Rock type, topography, and a high water table under intense evaporation gives rise to salt and alkali-rich soils in limited areas of Africa, supporting especially adapted vegetation and presenting great difficulty in utilization other than for seasonal nomadic herding.

FERRUGINOUS CRUSTS

The typical soil of the more humid tropics is rich in iron, and a widespread associated feature is a ferruginous crust. This may range from a heavily iron-enriched layer (such as gives rise to the *murram* so useful for road making in East Africa) to a thick capping of a heavy, obviously metallic, rock or ore. The precise significance of these is still subject to debate but their distribution does not accord well with any one particular climate or set of conditions found today and it is commonly supposed that some at least were formed when the climate was different — perhaps more humid. The great extent of such crusts or *cuirasses* is shown by Figure 5.4. Comparable but cal-

careous crusts are found in Algeria and Morocco. Other classifications have used the term *laterite* for ferruginous crusts and the tropical iron-rich soils have also been described as *"lateritic."*

SOILS OF ETHIOPIA

Because of the great range in altitude and associated climatic conditions in Ethiopia, the distribution of soil types cannot be shown in Figure 5.3. The plateau surface and highlands of moderate relief carry iron-rich tropical soils of the Ferrisol variety but Vertisols are also common. Steep slopes and erosion, both natural and man-assisted, give rise however to shallower and younger soils.

MANAGEMENT OF THE SOIL

Over most of tropical Africa the traditional methods of land use did little to modify the soil. The widespread rationale of the system of "shifting cultivation," still common, is better explained by the use of the description "bush fallowing." Varying in its details from region to region, in its essentials it consists of clearing a relatively small patch of vegetation and using it for some years to grow crops until the fertility begins to decline. The initial fertility may be increased by the ashes of the burnt vegetation and (as in the *Chitemene* or "ash garden" of Zambia) the succession of crops is carefully arranged so that the most demanding crops are planted first and more tolerant crops planted in the following season. The plot is then abandoned to natural regeneration which takes place all the more rapidly because tree stumps have not been removed. After a period of years which varies with the soil, the vegetation, and the climate, natural fertility is restored to the point where clearing for another cycle of cultivation is justified. W. Allen has proposed[5] a "land use factor" to express

[5] *The African Husbandman* (Edinburgh: Oliver and Boyd, 1965).

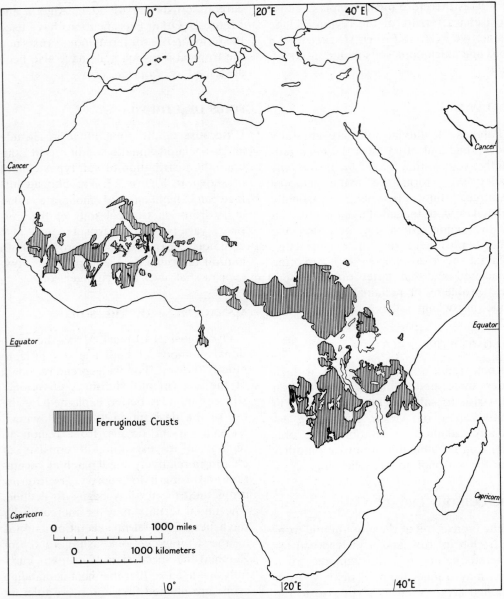

5.4 Ferruginous crusts in Africa. (After D'Hoore.)

the proportion of cultivated to recuperating land. Where alternative crop and fallow periods of equal duration are all that is required, the land use factor may be said to be 2, because the area need only be divided into two plots or "gardens," one cultivated and one resting. In the dry woodland of Zambia, however, a maximum of three years of cultivation will require a complete cycle of regeneration lasting thirty years giving a factor of 11 (one plot in use, ten in fallow). In such ecological zones only a low population density could be maintained by subsistence farming.

Unfortunately, this pressure on the land is now widespread throughout Africa. In part this is due to the rapidly increasing population densities described in Chapter 7 and is a case of *demographically in-*

5.D An aerial view of ash gardens or "chitemene" clearings of shifting agriculture in the woodland or *miombo* of Zambia. (Copyright: W. T. W. Morgan.)

duced land shortage. On the whole, however, Africa is not overpopulated and much of the increasing complaints of "land hunger" which disturb political leaders and excite agricultural consultants is due to other factors. When agriculture

was for subsistence, there was little point in extending the area of cultivation beyond what would provide for the family. With the entry of an exchange economy surplus harvests became of value, and it became worthwhile to cultivate more than one could consume. This is the case of *trade-induced land shortage*. But the amount of land which could be cultivated by one family with a digging stick or hoe was strictly limited. The introduction of the plough, however, enabled a much larger area to be cultivated. This gave rise to *technologically induced land shortage*. The effect of these last two factors is to reduce the carrying capacity of the land, in terms of employment. A given acreage will now support a smaller number of people, although at a higher standard of living. The extent to which this operates will also be influenced by changes in the yield per acre. There is nothing unusual in all this: the same pro-

5.E Cultivation by hoe, Jos Plateau, Nigeria. Using such a tool, the amount of land which can be cultivated per person will obviously be small. (Photo: Eric Kay.)

cesses were at work during the agricultural improvements in Europe which released labor from the land to work in mines and factories in the cities to make the goods and provide the services for the material advancement of all.

A buildup of pressure similar to that on cultivated land can be seen in pastoral land as well. Two technological improvements have frequently resulted in overstocking: one is the prophylactic injection, such as the one against rinderpest, which has led to a great increase in the number of Masai cattle; the other is the bore hole. Lack of water brought about the periodic resting of grazing lands away from the natural sources of water during the dry season. Where these have been provided with bore holes, grazing can be continued through the period when such sources of water dry up, leading to an increased and unceasing pressure upon the pasture. In this case it is generally hoped that a more commercial rather than a subsistence and status-value approach would lead to voluntary reduction in herds to enable better and more marketable stock to be raised. Unfortunately traditional practices have often been too entrenched to allow such

trade-induced management to be practiced.

The most immediately apparent result of overcultivation or overgrazing is soil erosion, and much effort has been expended by Agricultural Departments in Africa, as in parts of North America, to control erosion by such methods as terracing, contour ploughing, and rotational grazing through paddocking.

The mention of soil erosion introduces a subject of the utmost importance to all Africa. It is sometimes forgotten that erosion is a natural geological process; there is submarine erosion and, as soon as a tract of the earth's surface is raised up above the level of the sea, it is attacked by all the many forces of atmospheric weathering and subaerial erosion. High mountains are shattered by frost, bare rocks are split by the heating of the sun's rays, gulleys are cut in hillsides, the wind blows loose particles as surely as rain separates them from their parent source. The sum total effect is gradually to reduce all land surfaces to peneplains—almost planes or plains—and many examples of subaerial peneplanation can be found in the geological past. Since the greater part of Africa is

5.F Geological erosion in the Udi Plateau of Nigeria. Although hastened by bush clearing and overgrazing, this is natural land erosion—more than just soil erosion—and cannot be wholly prevented. (Copyright: L. Dudley Stamp.)

5.G An attempt to stop the gullying shown in the last picture. Banks were thrown across the gully, grass and quick-growing trees were planted, but the work was not successful. It was all swept away by flood waters after heavy rain. (Copyright: L. Dudley Stamp.)

a plateau high above sea level, these forces of nature are powerful and active. There are some plateau masses: the flat-topped hills of the Karoo and perhaps the sandy Udi plateau of Nigeria where rapid erosion of the hillsides is inevitable. Wherever, however, slopes are relatively gentle, nature herself slows down the process by providing a mantle of soil, itself protected by a mantle of vegetation in the form of forest, woodland, scrub, or grass. Over vast areas, the surface is kept stable long enough for a complete soil profile to develop, for a soil of good depth to form. There is little loss of soil from a forest, little from grassland.

Soil erosion may be looked upon as a disease which is a malignant form of a natural phenomenon. It has rightly been described as a disease of civilization, but one so serious that it threatens the very existence of mankind. A soil which has

taken hundreds of years to form may be lost in a single night. Although P. A. Yeomans working in Australia has shown that conversely, given the right conditions, both soil and a soil biota may develop very rapidly,[6] experience from many parts of the world has shown that soil erosion may have effects outlasting the civilization which gave rise to it.

The muddy waters of rivers in spate are ample evidence of soil erosion. But this transport of river mud is a natural phenomenon and not necessarily harmful. If caught and spread over the flat flood plain, it may build up fertile land at the expense of hill country of little value from whence it came. That this has been known of the Nile for centuries is evident from Shakespeare's words:

. . . The higher Nilus swells,
The more it promises: as it ebbs, the seedsman
Upon the slime and ooze scatters his grain
And shortly comes to harvest.

The drainage and economic use of alluvial plains and deltas are thus important aspects of development for Africa. The material removed by soil erosion may sometimes be "trapped" only a short distance away and valuable new land gained. Such methods, effectively followed in the Punjab, need to be adopted in Africa. Wind erosion and the "march of the deserts" present more difficult problems.

Remedial measures to check existing erosion are very necessary but a more comprehensive and fundamental approach to the management of the soil resources of Africa is evolving. If the people of Africa are to enjoy the prosperity which could be theirs they must make the soil of the continent yield much more than hitherto. This means transforming the soil from the natural state with the use of fertilizers, cultivating machinery, weed killers, carefully calculated rotations, irrigation and drainage schemes, and all the

---

[6] P. A. Yeomans, *The Challenge of Landscape* (London: Faber and Faber, 1958).

5.H Degraded land near Dakar in West Africa, exhausted by overcultivation with millets and peanuts. (Copyright R. J. Harrison Church.)

devices of modern agricultural science. Under the prevalent conditions of leaching, the use of fertilizers requires care if they are not to be wasted but many soils respond dramatically to applications of nitrogen, phosphates, and sulphur, and fertilizer factories are being established. The position has been succinctly expressed by Professor Sir Joseph Hutchinson who has himself been responsible for major improvements in yields, particularly of cotton:

Hitherto the maintenance of fertility has been ensured by allowing the reestablishment of natural vegetation at intervals determined by the nature of the soil and the effect of short periods of cultivation. Man has inserted a period of cropping into the biological system dominated by a wild flora and fauna. The condition of success has been that its insertion was not of such long duration or of such frequent repetition as to jeopardise the dominance of the natural vegetation. That condition we can no longer observe and man must now undertake, as he long ago undertook in temperate regions, responsibility for the complete management of the soil he cultivates. He must, in fact, undertake the domestication of the soil as

he domesticated plants and animal. . . . If we are prepared to face the complete change in soil management that is involved in the departure from dependence on natural vegetation for regeneration we may reasonably aspire to improvements in productivity of something of the order of magnitude that has been achieved in temperate regions and this we must do, since the population increases, achieved and in prospect, are such that reliance on natural regeneration is no longer possible. The choice lies between the establishment of a regenerative and improving cycle of fertility in fully managed soils and the progressive degradation of Africa's soil resources in the attempt to feed a population too great for the recuperative forces of natural vegetation.[7]

[7] From the introduction to *The Soils Resources of Tropical Africa,* A symposium of the African Studies Association of the limited Kingdom, edited by R. P. Moss (London: Cambridge University Press. 1968), pp. 2–3.

Further Reading

The basic document is undoubtedly the *Soils Map of Africa* and the explanatory monograph by J. L. D'Hoore published from Lagos by the Commission for Technical Co-operation in Africa in 1964. Most valuable papers on the characteristics of African soils and their use as a resource are contained in the report of a symposium of the African Studies Association of the United Kingdom, edited by R. P. Moss and published as *The Soil Resources of Tropical Africa* (Cambridge: Cambridge University Press, 1968). This includes a correlation by D'Hoore between the classification used and the leading American, Russian, French, and Belgian (Congo) systems. The characteristics and world distribution of ferruginous crusts and the use of the term laterite is dicussed in *Laterite and Laterite Soils* by A. Prescott and R. L. Pembleton (Farnham: Commonwealth Agricultural Bureaux, 1952).

The effects of traditional land practices are described in detail in *The Soil Under Shifting Cultivation* by P. H. Nye and D. J. Greenland (Farnham: Commonwealth Agricultural Bureaux, 1960) written from the University of Ghana. A classic anthropological account of shifting agriculture as practiced by one tribe in Zambia was given by P. de Schlippe in *Shifting Cultivation in Africa: the Zande System of Agriculture* (London: Routledge, 1956) but a broader view of its operation and significance for schemes of agricultural improvement is contained in the important work by W. Allan, *The African Husbandsman* (Edinburgh: Oliver and Boyd, 1965).

CHAPTER 6

Forest, Grassland, and Desert: Wildlife in Africa

It is a safe assertion that at least 80 percent of all Africans derive their sustenance directly from the land and its products. There are still those groups, now few and rare, so close to nature that they fall into the category of "gatherers," gathering wild fruits and roots and maintaining life on what nature provides and they can find. There are others, more numerous, who depend upon the spoils of the chase, coupled with a little vegetable food raised in small clearings. There are still larger groups of cattlemen and herders who rely on the natural grasslands for pasture. Finally those peoples, so often the hereditary rivals of the last, who have come to rely on food raised in their small clearings in the bush usually practice a form of land rotation, or shifting cultivation, and raise a series of crops dictated by the natural factors of climate, soil, and vegetation cover.

It follows logically that to all Africa the existing vegetation is of paramount importance. One is tempted to say the natural vegetation, for so it appears, but there is little doubt that the bulk of the vegetation which seems "natural" has been profoundly modified by man's long-continued activity. It is not uncommon to find evidence of former settlements in the heart of what seem to be primeval rainforests; it is still disputed to what extent the savanna or the bush veld of Africa is "natural," how much the result of periodic firing by the human inhabitants and grazing by their animals. This is the same problem as that of the campos of Brazil.

But whether it is truly "natural" or only "seminatural," the study of the existing vegetation of Africa assumes a very great importance. The trees, shrubs, herbs, and grasses are plant indicators affording an index of the total effect of the environment and so pointing the way to potential or agricultural use of the land. The taxonomic botanist and the systematist are interested in collecting and describing species, and some magnificent books have been published on the flora of different parts of Africa. An outstanding example of such is the *Flora Capensis*. This, as its title implies, deals with the flora of the Cape Province of South Africa. Recent multivolume floras exist or are being published in parts for West Tropical Africa, Tropical East Africa, North Africa, and for the *Flora Zambesiaca.* It has been argued by some that even those floras covering large areas are "local" in the sense that they do not give a continent-wide picture of the distribution of what may be widespread species described under other names elsewhere.

A remarkably complete map of the vegetation of Africa was published as early as 1923 in the pioneer work by H. L. Shantz at that time of the United States Department of Agriculture and C. F. Marbut, then of the Bureau of Soils of the same Department: *The Vegetation and Soils of Africa,* published by the American Geographical Society. The first part, on the vegetation, is by Shantz. It is based on the study of over 500 references, which are listed, followed by an account of a special journey of the entire length of the continent. The provisional map of the continent which had been prepared was revised in the light of the first-hand experience gained. We may regard Shantz's book as summarizing all important work which had been done prior to 1920. Since that time there have been some important studies, notably by I. B. Pole Evans and R. S. Adamson in South Africa; by Trapnell and Clothier in Zambia, by Gillman in Tanzania, and by Aubreville and Keay in West Africa.[1] Thirty years after his pioneer journeys and only shortly before his death, Shantz revisited the localities he had previously studied. He took pho-

tographs from the exact spots he had chosen before and published the two series side by side. The general result was to show much less change than had been expected.

Homer L. Shantz was also a keen observer of African agricultural practices and African uses of soil and vegetation. Like many scientists who later worked in Africa, he recognized the adaptability and skill of African farmers in using the environment under difficult conditions, as well as the possibility and need for improvements. Shantz's views on African agriculture were published in a notable series of long articles which, for the time, summarized the state of knowledge on the subject and formed a companion piece to his classic work on vegetation.[2]

Botanists working in Africa and on African plants have founded an organization with the pleasingly imperative title of "AETFAT" (*l'Association pour l'Etude Taxonomique de la Flore d'Afrique Tropicale*). A great number of localized and regional vegetation surveys have been combined by an editorial committee of the Association (A. Aubreville *et al.*) to produce a *Vegetation Map of Africa South of the Tropic of Cancer* at a scale of 1: 10 million with explanatory notes by R. W. J. Keay (*Oxford University Press,* 1959). This is the basis of Figure 6.1.

Although Africa did not directly suffer the glaciation which the Great Ice Age brought to North America, Europe, and Asia, the climate of the continent must have undergone wide fluctuations. It is one of the great scientific problems for the future to trace the effects of these climatic pulsations on the African vegetation and fauna. The ice ages in Europe seem to have been paralleled in Africa by relatively wet and dry periods — "pluvial" and "interpluvial" periods marked by fluc-

[1] The principal relevant works of these authors are: I. B. Pole Evans, "A Vegetation Map of South Africa," *S. Afr. Bot. Surv. Mem.,* XV (1936); R. S. Adamson, *The Vegetation of South Africa* (1938); C. G. Trapnell et al., *Vegetation-Soil Map of Northern Rhodesia* (1950); C. Gillman, "A vegetation-types map of Tanganyika Territory," *Geog. Rev.* XXXIX (1949) pp. 7–37; A. Aubreville, *Climats, Forests et Desertification de l'Afrique Tropicale* (1949) (and other works); R. W. J. Keay, *An Outline of Nigerian Vegetation* 2nd Ed. (1955).

[2] "Agricultural Regions of Africa," *Economic Geography,* XVI (1940) pp. 1–47; 122–161; 341–389; XVII (1941) pp. 217–249, 353–379; XVIII (1942) pp. 229–246, 343–362; XIX (1943) pp. 77–109, 217–269.

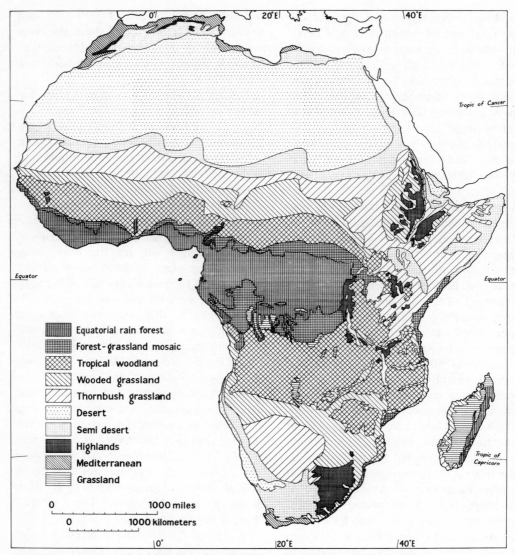

6.1 The vegetation of Africa (largely after l'Association pour l'Etude Tax-onomique de la Flore d'Afrique Tropicale).

tuating lake levels as well as alternating advance and retreat of ice on such mountains as Mt. Kenya. The dominant African vegetation must have waxed and waned between evergreen rainforest over huge areas and grassland or desert scrub. The present vegetation shows relics of former vegetation.

Although grouping into classes is necessary for descriptive purposes, it should not obscure the essential unity and continuity of the vegetation of tropical Africa.

In fact even the three-fold grouping into forest, grassland, and desert is artificial; they are best regarded as stages in a tropical vegetation continuum. Provided there is sufficient moisture, the climax vegetation in tropical Africa is high evergreen forest. This is naturally found along the equator wherever rainfall is high [60 inches (1500 mm), or over], where the dry season or seasons, if present at all, are very short, and where temperature range is small. But it also extends into the wettest parts of the bordering tropical regions, notably near the coast of much of West Africa as far as Sierra Leone, where the dry season, though marked, is not long enough to counteract availability of underground moisture reached by plant root systems, and the temperature is not high enough nor the air dry enough in the dry season to induce excessive transpiration. Similarly, forests of comparable type may line river banks, where abundant moisture is available from the alluvial soils throughout the year and evaporation from water and soil surfaces keeps the air humid.

On the margins of equatorial lands where a dry season becomes marked and the overall rainfall less, growth becomes seasonal. During the dry season leaves are shed as a protection against excessive transpiration and in general there is less of a struggle upwards to reach light and air. So the equatorial forest passes into what in India would be called "monsoon forest," which is deciduous, lower, and more open. With decreasing rainfall and an increasing length of dry season, the trees become smaller and more widely spaced and have adopted various protective devices. Some of these devices are designed to lower water loss by transpiration, seen in reduced leaf surface, umbrella-shaped form of the crown, and ability to wilt; others are designed to store water by development of fleshy stems and leaves, or make a permanent underground water supply available by very long roots. Still other devices are designed to avoid destruction by discouraging browsing animals; hence the numerous forms of spines and hooks.

With still lower rainfall, such thorn woodland passes through thorn thicket into thorn scrub, widely spaced thorny bushes on the desert margin. There are some species of tree which can exist through a wide range of environmental conditions and may be found from the margins of the rainforest almost to the desert. A very good example is *Acacia*

nilotica which forms well-grown trees 50 to 75 feet (15 or 23 m) high in the wetter situations, but appears as stunted, spiny bushes only a few feet high in its most arid habitats.

There would thus seem to be no place at all for grassland in this scheme, and it has been argued that extensive stands of pure grassland are exceptional and occur in a state of nature only where unusual environmental conditions, usually of soil or drainage, are found. Undoubtedly, in the more open woodland and scrub, grass and herbs form an important element in the ground vegetation which springs into life with the coming of the rains, but it is becoming increasingly certain that much, if not most, of Africa's grasslands are primarily the results of man's interference. Fires are difficult to start in the rainforests, but elsewhere they start and spread very easily in the dry season. Some may be started by lightning but the majority are the result of deliberate firing of dried grass or undergrowth. They have the effect of burning off the dry grass (but not harming the roots), nourishing the surface with ash, and so stimulating growth when the rains come. On the other hand, they destroy tree seedlings and even young trees and so favor the extension of grass at the expense of trees. In this they reinforce the action of grazing animals, both wild and domesticated, which eat off the grass and herbs without harm (unless to excess, because of overstocking) but destroy tree seedlings.

Thus, parallel to the sequence of woodland vegetation from rainforest to desert scrub is another of grassland with varying proportions of trees which have managed to survive. Another complication results from the very widespread practice of shifting cultivation, or bush fallowing. When a cleared patch is cultivated for a few years and then abandoned or left to recover, it is colonized in the first instance by a temporary assemblage of plants, replaced in due course by another; but it is often a long period of years before these "seral communities" are finally replaced by the "climatic climax vegetation." Some seres or seral communities become so firmly established that they show signs of permanence; a good example is afforded by thickets of bamboo.

A further complication in tropical Africa results from elevation. Parts of East Africa are sufficiently high and sufficiently wet for temperate rainforest to replace tropical vegetation, and mountain grasses or alpine meadows occupy considerable tracts.

All that has been said above applies to tropical Africa. In extratropical North Africa, north of the great desert barrier, are found those types of vegetation common to countries around the Mediterranean basin. Where rainfall permits, on well-watered hill slopes oak–conifer forest is the climax. Far larger areas are covered by the Mediterranean brush or scrub, resembling the chaparral of California, which in turn passes into desert scrub. On the high-level basins among the Atlas Mountains there are stretches of what may be called steppe.

Extratropical South Africa differs in that it is not cut off completely by a desert barrier from tropical Africa, and there is a merging of Mediterranean and tropical types of vegetation. The best-watered parts of Natal and the Cape, with the rainfall well distributed throughout the year, are clothed with a subtropical or temperate rainforest, but the natural vegetation covering those parts of the Cape with a winter rainfall is again a Mediterranean scrub, also merging with decreasing moisture into desert scrub. On the plateau of South Africa, over much of the Orange Free State and southern Transvaal, is the tall-grass–short-grass "prairie" of the High Veld.

Quite clearly, the AETFAT colored map, and still more the simplified version shown in Figure 6.1, involves much generalization. In making generalizations, both in the field and in the drawing office, it is difficult to avoid a subjective judg-

ment. It has been pointed out that the impressions which are gained of much African vegetation depend very largely on the time of year at which the traveler sees the country. The grassland with scattered trees, after the grass has been burnt off and where the majority of the trees are leafless, may appear but little removed from a semidesert waste. If, however, it is seen after the coming of the early rains, with tall, lush grass and herbs, perhaps high enough to hide a man, and trees in fall leaf, it appears comparable with an open forest having a very rich undergrowth.

Again, an important advance was made by Gillman in his recognition of complexes and catenas.[3] He correctly determined that distinct vegetation types, often widely different, occur nearly everywhere in close conjunction or juxtaposition, and the cartographical representation of such complexes is difficult. In his vegetation map of Tanganyika on the scale of 1:2,000,000, he used background color for the dominant vegetation, with dots indicating the relative frequency of associations of minor importance. Further refinement is possible by close or wide spacing of the dots. Much more important, however, is the recognition of a catenary complex. As described in the last chapter, the soil scientist, following particularly the work of G. Milne in East Africa, recognizes that the same sequence of soil types may be repeated over and over again throughout a large area. For example, where a plateau is intersected by broad valleys there will be certain types of soil associated with the valley floor, other types with the valley slopes, and still other types with the plateau surfaces or interfleuves. This sequence of soils is matched by a sequence of vegetation. Bearing this repetition in mind, both Milne for soils and Gillman for vegetation have used a system of coloring by vertical stripes (which quickly became known as

[3] Clement Gillman, "A Vegetation Types Map of Tanganyika Territory," *Geog. Rev.,* XXXIX (1949) pp. 7–37.

pajama striping) to indicate those areas dominated by catenary complexes.

Bearing these refinements in mind, we may now consider the broad classes of vegetation, which it should be noted are based on *physiognomic* rather than *floristic* criteria. Here yet another source of confusion arises because of the different names which have been given to the same vegetation types. Gillman and others have objected to the use of such terms as "savanna," "'steppe," and "veld" on the grounds that "legitimate doubt may arise as to whether such importations from the languages of lands harbouring their prototypes are correctly used out of their appropriate setting." Similarly Gillman objected to the use of African vernacular words and claims that it is possible to use simple English descriptive names. Here however he immediately encountered a difficulty because he succeeded in drawing a distinction between forest and woodland, whereas these two words are often used in English interchangeably. The names adopted for the AETFAT map are, with a few exceptions, those recommended by a meeting of specialists in phytogeography held at Yangambi in 1956.[4] A special effort was made at this international meeting to coordinate French and English terms but without complete success. Thus British workers on East Africa tend to use a nomenclature proposed by Dr. P. J. Greenway which is more suited to the vegetation types found in that region.

---

[4] Scientific Council for Africa South of the Sahara, Publication No. 22, *Phytogeography* (London and Lagos 1956).

Forest

EQUATORIAL RAINFOREST

Shantz, Richards, and others (see Selected Bibliography) use the term "tropical rainforest," and this well-known type of vegetation has also been known by the descriptive title, "evergreen rainforest." It is the dominant type of forest in those areas having more than 60 or 80 inches (1500 or 2000 mm) of rainfall annually and a consistently high temperature throughout the year. As a rule there is little variation in the mean temperature between one month and another, the mean annual range rarely exceeding 5 or 6°F, and averaging about 80°F (27°C). Night temperatures rarely drop below 70°F (21°C) or certainly 65°F (18°C); the day temperatures rarely rise above 90°F (33°C) or, still more rarely, above 95°F (35°C). This is the constantly hot, humid climate found on either side of the equator. As soon as there is a marked dry season, forest type tends to change.

A typical equatorial forest consists of large trees, approximately 125 feet (38 m) high, with a relatively dense and interlocking canopy. The equatorial forests of the Amazon are often described as gloomy in the extreme, with little or no undergrowth. This is not typical of Africa, since there is often an understory of small trees, and the undergrowth is usually dense enough to prevent a distant view. Certainly in the more open parts there is a thick growth of herbs on the forest floor. Woody climbers, or lianes, are usually abundant, and many of the trees are supported by flanking (plank) buttresses. The thick undergrowth and the woody climbers make these forests extremely difficult to penetrate except along defined paths.

As a rule, numerous species of trees are present, and it is rare that one finds a single dominant or even a number of codominants. Although some of the trees yield excellent and much-valued timber,

6.A Timber working in the rainforest of Equatorial Guinea. (Copyright: R. J. Harrison Church.)

usually hardwood of the mahogany type, and though softwood timbers do occur, the difficulty of extricating examples of the trees desired is so great that there has been no commercial exploitation over very large areas of this type of forest. It may be regarded as one of the great untouched reservoirs of timber in the world. One of the requirements is to develop markets for the less familiar kinds of timber.

The equatorial type of forest is not as extensive in Africa as was once supposed. It is broadly restricted to parts only of the Congo Basin and adjoining Equatorial Africa and to relatively small areas lying in the wetter parts of West Africa. It was long supposed that the African equatorial forests could be described as true primeval forests unaffected by man. It has been found, however, that under certain conditions revegetation is very rapid when the original forest is destroyed, and what appears today is in fact only second growth.

Where these forests occur bordering the great river courses, the underlying soil is alluvial and may be described as a rich, deep loam of natural fertility. The myth, however, that all equatorial forest soils are naturally of high fertility has long since been exploded. When the forests are cleared, there are often sandy or "lateritic" areas which need dressings of ash and organic matter before they will produce crops, and in the high-rainfall areas there are immediate dangers both of physical soil erosion and of the leaching of plant food by exposure to atmosphere.

These equatorial forests in Africa, because of their relatively open character, have an abundant animal and bird life, especially rich along the water courses where hippopotami and crocodiles are found. The nomadic pygmies of the heart of the Congo forests afford examples of groups of human beings still largely dominated by their physical environment, and just as animals and birds seek light and air by living in the treetops away from swampy conditions or ground likely to flood, so these peoples have in certain cases built their homes high up in the trees. But these are generally temporary dwellings for people who are essentially nomadic. Elsewhere the inhabitants have destroyed portions of the forest, particularly along the great waterways or where a short, relatively dry season makes burning possible.

Among the principal plants which are of economic value, the most important is the Guinea oil palm. It furnishes the oil prized for food and for a variety of other uses, including the making of soap. More inviting is the palm wine made from its sap. Beginning as a nutritious and innocuous beverage, a few days of fermentation converts it into a powerful brew. This has been the subject of a masterpiece of African imaginative fiction: *The Palm-wine Drinkard* by Amos Tutuola (London: Faber and Faber, 1952). Rubber is obtained from certain of the native trees and lianes, and is still exploited in some of the remoter areas. The importance of the forests for the ivory obtained from the enormous elephant herds belongs to an earlier stage. At the time when slave trading was widespread, it can be said that equatorial Africa yielded two main products to the outside world: ivory and black ivory.

Settlements in the equatorial forests are usually small clearings where a variety of crops can be, and are, grown: food plants such as yams, sweet potatoes, rice, manioc, and sugar cane; fruits such as bananas, mango, and guava; tobacco and beans; and of course the oil palm. Over vast areas of the equatorial forests little development has yet taken place under modern conditions, more, it may be said, because of scarcity of labor than because of climatic difficulties.

Comparable forests can develop where moisture is derived from groundwater rather than from rainfall. These include the long ribbons of forest which follow river valleys through drier areas (the riverine or "gallery" forests) and swamp forests.

FOREST–GRASSLAND MOSAIC

Bordering on the Equatorial Rainforest are areas where grassland is broken by patches of forest or *vice versa*. The trees are of the same species as the neighboring continuous forest and are not confined merely to river valleys. The grasses are usually tall and broad leaved and include the "elephant grass" (*Pennisetum purpureum*), looking like sugar cane and up to 10 or 15 feet (3 or 4.6 m) high. This is often referred to as "derived savanna" because some of it at least has been cleared by human action, especially with fire. The grasses are mostly too coarse to be good grazing but there are areas of dense peasant cultivation, as in Uganda. Elsewhere, however, are thinly settled, tsetse-fly-infested, regions.

Relatively isolated belts of this vegetation are found in the area of the dry cli-

6.B A coarse type of tropical grassland, Nigeria. There is little value in the grass as fodder. (Copyright: L. Dudley Stamp.)

matic anomaly of the Ghana coast and on the coast of east and southeast Africa. The forests of the last two are isolated from the main block of rainforest and have a distinctive flora including forest forms of the more typically "savanna" families.

TROPICAL WOODLAND

This is one of the most extensive vegetation types of Africa, indeed of the tropical world. The distinction between this category and that of wooded grassland can be argued on the grounds of proportion of tree cover and on floristic composition, but essentially there is a continuous although open cover of trees with grass and herbs beneath, rather than grassland dotted with trees. It is particularly well developed south of the equator in south-central Africa, occupying vast areas of Tanzania, Katanga, Angola, Zambia, Malawi, Moçambique, and Rhodesia. It may be described by its dominant genera as the *Brachystegia – Isoberlinia – Julbernardia*

6.C Tropical woodland or *miombo* in southern Tanzania. (Copyright: W. T. W. Morgan.)

Woodland but it is more convenient to use the indigenous term *miombo*. Over vast areas, conditions tend to a monotonous norm: infertile leached iron-rich sandy soils over extensive peneplains and a severe dry season of six or seven months with 40–50 inches (1000–1250 mm) of rainfall received in the summer. The trees, 25–50 feet (7.6–15 m) high, are sufficiently dense, together with the level surface, to limit visibility to one or two hundred yards. Conditions are hard, even for wild animals, which are much rarer than on the more grassy plains, and human cultivation must follow an extensive system of shifting cultivation (*chitemene*). The most flourishing and intrusive creature is the tsetse fly. The utilization of the *miombo* is one of the most intractable and widespread problems of African development. A certain beauty is not lacking in the red tints of the leaves during the dry season, faintly reminiscent of the fall in North America and the seasonal flush of greenery is like a concentrated spring—many trees actually flower *before* the onset of the rains.

The zone with comparable climate in West Africa has also a similar vegetation although differing in composition, especially in the absence of *Brachystegia*. It has been much more influenced by cultivation and burning although it has not been particularly attractive to settlement. In the terminology common to West Africa this is the northern Guinea Savanna, the southern extension of which lies within the forest–grassland mosaic.

WOODED GRASSLAND

Moving into the drier areas with a longer dry season, the trees become more widely spaced and the grass more dominant. The trees stand in the grassland in a proportion that in some places resembles that favored by the English landscape gardeners of the eighteenth century, so that it may be described as "parkland." The trees include many broad-leaved types, particularly species of *Combretum* and *Terminalia,* with winged and often brightly colored seeds. Although *Acacia* thorn trees may be common, they are of different species from those which dominate the drier zones, while the baobab (*Adonsonia digitata*) is particularly common. In West Africa, this is the Sudan Savanna which has been settled for centuries and heavily modified by burning and clearing for cultivation. Groundnuts (peanuts) are the most important commer-

6.D A large baobab tree (*Adonsonia digitata*) near Livingstone, Zambia. (Copyright: L. Dudley Stamp.)

cial crop, and the more open vegetation is less favorable to the tsetse fly, so that grazing is important.

This type is less extensive south of the equator where it forms the "low veld" of Rhodesia and South Africa including the *mopaniveld* (*Colophospermum mopanae*) of the Zambezi and Limpopo valleys.

THORNBUSH GRASSLAND

This is a type which is particularly variable in appearance. The grass is thin and usually less than 3 feet (1 m) high and too sparse for fire to spread easily. The trees are mostly thorny, of *Acacia* and *Commiphora* species. Their density may vary from a wide scatter to close stands and their form from rather spindly, often umbrella- or obconical-shaped trees to compact bushes. These can form thickets of regional extent, almost impenetrable except along game trails.

In West Africa this is the Sahel Savanna, although the current French terminology would prefer the use of the description "steppe." This is generally of a rather open form, as is the equivalent veg-

etation in the Kalahari (often incorrectly styled a desert). It is also common in East Africa and the Horn where it is often more dense, to the frustration of the tourist who cannot see the wildlife among the thorn bushes of the game parks. It is probable that the density of bushes is in part at least a response to human activity: where livestock, including camels, are grazed and fires are deliberately started, it may be more open. Dense "bush" may be encouraged by lack of grazing, which may

6.E Thorn bushland (*Acacia-Commiphora spp.*) in Kenya. Hanging from the tree are nests of "weaver birds."

result from lack of water, infestation with tsetse fly, or locally from intertribal raiding.

SEMIDESERT

On the margins of the desert, the thornbush grassland takes on an attenuated form with much bare soil, rock, and stony pavement between scattered bushes and sparse grass and herbs which, however, become much more conspicuous following rain. Although the *Acacia* and *Commiphora* spp. remain numerous, some curious plants can survive under these conditions, including the desert rose (*Adenium* spp.), the *Hyphaene* palm in the dry watercourses, and the evergreen "toothbrush tree" (*Salvadora persica*). Small succulents are common. Beyond the tropics this type is represented by the Karoo vegetation of South Africa and the equivalent types of North Africa.

DESERT

The term "desert" has a range of meanings, and in the absolute sense of "absence of living things" would refer to quite small areas. The area shown in Figure 6.1, however, is described as virtually devoid of vegetation except for widely scattered solitary plants. Outside of the great transcontinental belt of the Sahara, it is restricted to the Namib of South West Africa and the Danakil of Ethiopia.

MEDITERRANEAN TYPES

Beyond the tropics, in the areas of winter rainfall and summer drought of North and South Africa, is a distinctive vegetation type composed of evergreen shrubs which are usually small and wiry. Trees are rare and there is little grass. It is a "sclerophyllous" vegetation, adapted to the summer drought and is found in other parts of the world with comparable climates. Known in French-speaking North Africa as *maquis,* it is similar to the *chapparal* of California.

GRASSLAND

Only two types of vegetation of restricted extent are sufficiently lacking in

6.F Stony semidesert, after good rains, in northern Kenya. Dried stalks of seasonal grasses and small thorn trees (*Acacia reficiens*). (Copyright: W. T. W. Morgan.)

6.G Floating islands of papyrus on Lake Kioga, Uganda. The "island" in the foreground is about four hundred yards across. (Copyright: W. T. W. Morgan.)

tree or bush growth to justify the term grassland. One of these is a grass "steppe" found on certain plateaus of Kalahari Sand in regions otherwise dominated by *miombo* woodland. The other comprises much of the interior of Madagascar, where it is likely that it is at least in part derived by clearing for cultivation from original forest.

HIGHLAND VEGETATION

There are many localities, important although not always extensive, where the vegetation has been profoundly affected by altitude. The most striking are the equatorial high mountains of East Africa, Ethiopia, and Cameroun where endemic "alpine" plants are found. These include giant forms of common European flowers (*Sennecio* and *Lobelia*), the distinctive form and features of which are closely paralleled on other equatorial high mountains in South America and Indonesia, but completely different genera are involved. Below the alpine zone are montane grasslands and forests, including the "cedars" (*Juniperus* spp.) and the typical *Podocarpus* trees and mountain bamboo (*Arudinaria*). Most of the tropical highlands are now densely inhabited up to heights of at least 8000 feet (2400 m).

At a lower altitude is the grassveld of South Africa, from about 3600 feet (1100 m) but rising to over 10,000 feet (3000 m). Both here and in the tropical highlands, *Themeda triandra* indicates valuable grazing. This compact block of sub-

6.H Highland vegetation in the Ruwenzori mountains, Uganda, showing giant forms of *Sennecio*. (Copyright: J. Allan Cash.)

tropical or temperate grassland has been of great economic and historic significance.

WILDLIFE IN AFRICA

Tropical Africa can probably claim to be richer in wildlife than any other major region on earth. The diversity of animal—and vegetable—life in the tropics, as measured by the number of species, is much greater than in the temperate zones, and in Africa there is a full range of environments to accomodate them. Not only is there a graduation from continual rain to continual drought, but plateaus and mountains offer temperatures modified even to the point of maintaining tundra-like conditions in the "Afro-alpine zone." Each ecological niche provides different opportunities to be exploited by the creatures most adapted to it, and this leads to

specialization, both anatomical and geographical. The exquisitely apt build of a giraffe for browsing in tall thorn trees is paralleled by many more humble but no less remarkable examples ranging from the swift, slender, and beautiful cheetah of the open plains to the slow, powerful, and grotesque anteaters. Again the pervasive influence of rainfall can be seen so that, for example, the various species of gazelle and antelope can be placed according to their typical habitats along the continuum from rainforest to desert. In East Africa such a sequence might include: Bongo, Bush Buck, Impala, Grant's Gazelle, Gerenuk, Oryx.

Thus each habitat has a characteristic assemblage of wildlife, and the more varied the environments within a region, the greater the range of wildlife is likely to be. The transitional zone between two environmental zones (the "ecotone") is likely to be particularly rich and even to contain a greater quantity of animals than elsewhere.

Such wildlife, especially of the larger forms, appears to have been more widespread over the world in the past and it is its survival in some parts of Africa which is so notable. Certainly, to travelers from temperate lands the appearance of the rhinoceros, elephant, hippopotamus, and crocodile recalls reconstructions of Pleistocene or even earlier creatures rather than contemporary fauna. The extinction of so much wildlife on other continents has been attributed variously either to climatic change or to human action, and specifically to what has been termed "prehistoric overkill." The low density of population over so much of Africa, combined perhaps with relatively inefficient hunting

techniques, has given the big game a better opportunity for survival than where competition with *Homo sapiens* was more acute. Some of the greatest concentrations of wildlife are to be found in parts of East Africa where infestation with tsetse fly has kept man out. Also in East Africa, however, is the special case of the Masai lands where the culture of this tribe, occupying extensive areas, is such that the wildlife has been left virtually untouched. This attitude is in striking contrast with that of the early European travelers and settlers who appear to have been motivated by a compulsive urge to slaughter. Fortunately Europeans and their weapons arrived late in East Africa, but in North, West, and South Africa the extermination of big game has proceeded much further.

The future of the remaining wildlife is

6.1 Elephants in high grass of the Murchison Falls National Park, Uganda. Their food intake is enormous and competition for land with a growing human population has led to their withdrawal to National Parks and tsetse-infested areas. (Photo: J. Allan Cash.)

now under greater and more fundamental threat than before. The rapid increase in population of the African countries results in growing pressure on the land available. An eland eats as much as a cow and can carry disease to infect the regularly dipped domestic cattle. The arable farmer is similarly in direct competition and sees no reason to tolerate his fences being broken and his crops being eaten when modern rifles can quickly remove the cause of such costly damage. There is a case for preserving at least some of the wildlife, however, based on scientific and economic, as well as emotional, grounds. Such wildlife represents a stock of biological material—a genetic pool—from which mankind may well wish to breed in the future. Also, an economic return is almost immediately and widely recorded by its attraction for tourists. As the world becomes more urbanized and its landscapes tamed, the remaining areas, uncontaminated by man and his works, are becoming increasingly appreciated and air transport and rising standards of living enable the desire to view such regions to be gratified. Already receipts from tourism are more important than any more material export from such countries as Kenya, and although tropical beaches are also an attraction, the wildlife provides specific reasons for visiting one country rather than another. The returns per acre from the more popular and accessible National Parks are comparable to those from extensive ranching. Less well known, but with more revolutionary implications for land use, is the ranching of wildlife. Game animals flourish in areas where cattle can be introduced only after expensive anti-tsetse measures have been undertaken. It has been frequently pointed out that the biomass per acre in a state of nature is higher than if the same area is grazed by cattle. This is because the variety of species present ensures that all of the vegetation is grazed or browsed instead of only the grasses (and only some of those) which are all that are utilized by domestic cattle. The rate of growth of some of the gazelles has also been shown to be particularly rapid, and they contain a higher proportion of meat than cattle. Thus the individual animals are particularly efficient converters of plant matter into meat, and the complex of wild herbivores make the maximum use of the entire plant cover. The problems are of harvesting, processing, and transporting the meat and developing a market for it.

Even if such methods of extracting a financial return from wildlife areas prove to be less profitable than ranching or some alternative form of land use, in the final analysis many would change the argument from an economic calculation to a value

6.J Zebra in the Nairobi National Park, Kenya. The circle of tourist vehicles are surrounding a pride of lions. (Photo: Kenya Tourist Office.)

judgment: we want wildlife to be preserved and are willing to pay for this to happen. This emotion is particularly well developed among the prosperous peoples of the world and it is they who can easily afford to pay the costs involved. The potential income foregone, however, is lost by those who belong to the poorer nations of the world. There would thus seem to be a good case for a transfer payment on an international basis to make up the deficiency (whereby the net losses on wildlife farming, as well as wildlife sanctuaries, would be covered by those most able to afford to do so).

It has been increasingly necessary to delimit areas in which wildlife will be protected, and Africa has numerous (some famous) National Parks and other wildlife reserves.

Further Reading

The basic document for this topic is obviously the *Vegetation Map of Africa South of the Tropic of Cancer* with the brief explanatory notes by R. W. J. Keay (Oxford University Press, 1959). This has a very useful bibliography up to that date. Covering the whole of the continent and complete with map and bibliography is J. M. Rattray's *The Grass Cover of Africa*, FAO Agricultural Studies No. 49 (Rome: Food and Agriculture Organization, 1960). The work of Shantz and Marbut (1923) (see Chapter 5) is now only of academic interest but a fascinating set of pictures is contained in H. L. Shantz and B. L. Turner, *Vegetational Changes in Africa* (University of Arizona College of Agriculture Report No. 169, 1958). The site of 241 photographs of vegetation taken in 1919, 1920, and 1924 were revisited and rephotographed, 78 such pairs being published.

The literature on wildlife is extensive but of variable quality and follows many different approaches. Two very readable introductions to the subject, referring to specific regions, are: B. & M. Grizmek, *Serengeti Shall Not Die* (London: Hamish Hamilton, 1960) and Frazer Darling, *Wildlife in an African Territory* (London: Oxford University Press, 1960). The International Union for the Conservation of Nature focuses concern, especially at a scientific level, on the problem of survival, and many useful papers from a conference held at Arusha, Tanzania, are collected in *Conservation of Nature and Natural Resources in Modern African States* (1963). A very readable and beautifully illustrated introduction to the zoo-geography of Africa is *The Zoology of Tropical Africa* by J. L. Cloudsley-Thompson of Khartoum (New York: Norton, 1969). The possible reconciliation of economics and conservation is presented by Raymon F. Dasman in *African Game Ranching* (New York: Macmillan, 1964). Important articles appear in the *East African Wildlife Journal* and the *Journal of Wildlife Management*, which also publishes longer contributions in its series of *Wildlife Monographs*.

CHAPTER 7

Population and Peoples

THE POPULATION OF THE CONTINENT

The total population of the African continent has been estimated at 345 million (1969) and its distribution is shown in Figure 7.1. Immediately apparent is the lack of population over such great arid stretches as the Sahara, the Namib, Kalahari, and the Horn of Africa. Although rainfall is the most pervasive factor influencing the distribution of population, in the better-watered areas many other factors are at work. Two of the most important are soil fertility and disease, but natural factors are often insufficient to explain the population groupings. Many concentrations of dense settlement have historical origins in the attraction of powerful indigenous kingdoms such as those of Yorubaland and the Fulani/Hausa emirates in Nigeria or Buganda in Uganda. Conversely, the areas which suffered from the warfare conducted by such states or by more general intertribal conflict remain to this day relatively underpopulated. Similarly, slave raiding has left its mark, whereas the introduction of cash crops and the provision of roads and railways have brought about local concentrations of immigrant populations.

The overall population density of the continent is about 28.5 persons per square mile (11 p.km²), compared with about 65 per square mile 25 p.km²) for the land surface of the world as a whole, excluding Antarctica. Looked at in another way, every inhabitant of the African continent has a share of land of all types of about 22 acres (9 ha). The corresponding figure for the people of the continental United States is about 12 acres (5 ha). If we eliminate one-third of Africa as being desert or mountain incapable of supporting a permanent settled population, the share of potentially habitable land is still over 14 acres (5.7 ha) per head. By comparison with densely peopled Europe, the African continent appears almost uninhabited. The people of Great Britain have a little over one acre (0.4 ha) of land of all types per head of population [or taking England and Wales alone, about 0.75 acre (0.3 ha)]. In France the figure is about 2.7 acres (1.1 ha) per head; in Italy, with its large mountainous areas, only 1.4 acres (0.6 ha).

It would be wrong, however, to visualize Africa as a continent of vast open spaces and no people. In the first place there are great contrasts. In the Nile valley, which forms the cultivable heart of Egypt, population density averages about 1200 persons per square mile (463 p.km²); each person, therefore, is supported by the produce of about half an acre (0.2 ha) of land, and a surplus of some agricultural produce is available for export! Nor is there any doubt that, given the existing forms of cultivation, there is overpopulation in parts of Nigeria, where the density exceeds 300 persons per square mile (116

p.km²). Elsewhere there are both dry deserts and "forest deserts" virtually devoid of people. Broadly speaking, if one judges by densities in any other part of the world, much of Africa is underpopulated.

What population could the continent support? Calculations of potential population are likely to lead us into dangerous paths whether we are considering Australia, the United States, Canada, or Africa. Stamp has dealt with this question

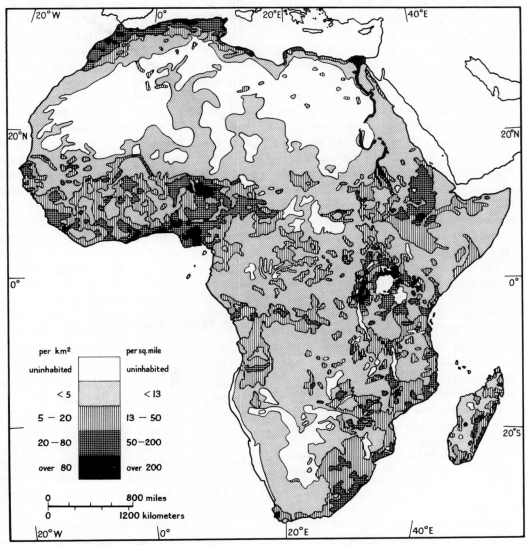

per km²	per sq. mile
uninhabited	uninhabited
< 5	< 13
5 – 20	13 – 50
20 – 80	50 – 200
over 80	over 200

0   800 miles
0   1200 kilometers

7.1 The density of population (rural only) around 1960. (After Else Schmidt and Paul Mattingley, 1966.)

at some length elsewhere.[1] It may be demonstrated that in the climatically favored lands of northwest Europe, using present systems of cultivation, one acre of cultivated land will support one person at a northwest European standard of living—measured in calories, 2500–3000 per day. Reasons are given in that work for believing that the most "underdeveloped" countries of the world are those lands in midlatitudes which practice large-scale mechanized farming rather than intensive mixed farming. Far too little is yet known of the possible output of tropical lands. It is certain that a rice economy in favored conditions will support over one person per acre; Egyptian experience suggests two, albeit at a low standard.

We have already seen how tropical Africa is hampered by vagaries of climate, by inadequate control of water, by soils difficult to handle, by numerous and serious plagues of man, beast, and plant. Western science has not by any means reached the point when those difficulties can be overcome, and at the moment much of Africa is supporting a maximum population, given the existing form of cultivation and land management and the present incidence of pests and diseases.

Thus, it is common to find local concentrations showing all the signs of overpopulation and land shortage. The problems of such areas are made more acute by the rapid rate of increase of the population. The average annual rate of increase in Africa is estimated at 2.4 percent compared with a world average of 1.9 percent. For the U.S.A. the rate of growth is 1.3 percent and for Europe only 0.9 percent. This is reflected in the large proportion of children which increases the pressure on the already inadequate facilities for education.

The significance of the densities quoted lies in the fact that for the most part the population is rural and derives its livelihood directly from the land. Commerce and industry are still less developed than in other parts of the world and consequently the extent of urbanization is also relatively small. Using United Nations data because of its comparability, although it includes quite small settlements, it can be said that the industrialized and prosperous nations tend to have at least a half and often over 70 percent of their population in cities and of these the majority are in large metropolitan centers. In Africa, by contrast, only the more prosperous countries have 20–30 percent of their population in towns of any sort, and for many countries the figure is less than 10 percent. Only in South Africa is the level of urbanization as high as 46 percent (1960). It is clear that if Africa is to advance economically and socially, a great increase in the number and size of her towns must take place; how to prevent this leading to slums and urban sprawl is just another of the problems facing her leaders in the future.

THE PEOPLES OF AFRICA

The striking differences between the various peoples found in Africa is an elementary fact which requires examination for its causes and its significance. The situation is a complex one and its interpretation is made more difficult by confusion over the basic classification. This is especially true where the distinction is not maintained between classifications based on race, on language, and on culture or society.

Race in this context means the presence of inherited characteristics, among which are some of the most obvious superficial differences of anatomy, skin color, hair form, etc. The traditional methods

---

[1] *Land for Tomorrow,* Pattern Foundation Lectures, University of Indiana, (American Geographical Society, 1952); rewritten and revised as *Our Developing World* (London: Faber and Faber 3rd Ed., 1968). By using a Standard Nutrition Unit (SNU) of 1 million calories of farm production per annum (a good average standard to support one person) it can be shown how much land is needed under given types of diet and methods of production to support one person. The world average is just over 1 acre (0.4 ha).

of anthropometry—deriving statistical means from measurements of such features—have been somewhat discredited with the realization that some of these are acquired characteristics, due to environmental influences or to diet rather than to inheritance. To this extent they represent *phenotypes* rather than *genotypes*. Studies of blood groups and genetic material are more hopeful but again it has been shown that some of these may be influenced by exposure to disease, perhaps operating over a few generations. The most widely studied instance is the distribution of sickle-shaped red blood cells in populations which have been subjected to malaria over some generations.[2]

[2] Another interesting distribution is a deficiency in the red blood cell enzyme, Glucose-6-phosphate Dehydrogenase, which also tends to correspond with that of subtertian malaria. Persons with this blood defect are liable to be ill after eating broad beans. Pythagoras, whose philosophical teaching included the sinfulness of eating beans, may have had such a reaction. He was certainly born in a malarial area.

A great volume of fascinating detailed work is now under way on human taxonomy and adaptability, in Africa as elsewhere, but a coherent picture has yet to emerge. It must be stressed, therefore, that the map of races (Figure 7.2) is provisional one. Movement of peoples, as well as intermixing, has complicated the scene.

LANGUAGE IN AFRICA

As in other parts of the world, in Africa the spread and consequent present distribution of languages tend to obscure race relationships. The map of languages given here (Figure 7.3) is simplified from one prepared by Joseph H. Greenberg and published originally in the *Southwestern Journal of Anthropology*, 1949–1950. Greenberg distinguishes sixteen families of languages, but some of these are spoken only by very small and restricted groups. Broadly, the whole of Negro-Bantu Africa is shown as speaking languages of one family (the "Niger-Congo")

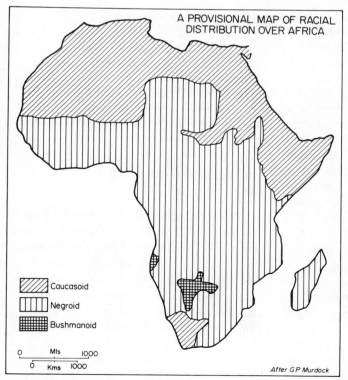

7.2 Racial types. (After Murdock.)

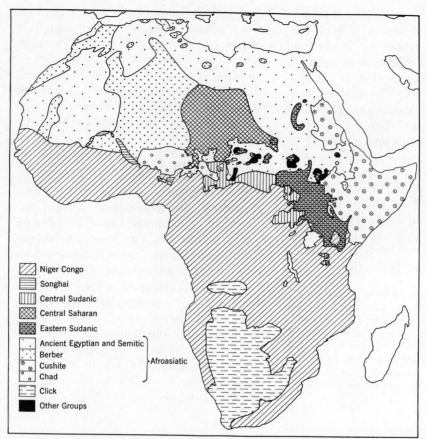

7.3 The languages of Africa. This map has been simplified from that of Greenberg and the classification used is subject to some disagreement.

and almost the whole of Bantu Africa, the "central branch" of this group. The term Bantu is widely used for the large family of languages extending from South Africa as far north as Cameroun and Uganda. Greenberg's map shows a large enclave in southern Africa as the click family, so called because there are click sounds incorporated in the languages. The Bushmen and Hottentots speak such languages, and there are clicks in the Bantu tongue of the Matabele. In reading Greenberg's map, we must remember that the more numerous Mashona and Bechuana of the Kalahari speak Bantu (Niger-Congo) languages.

Over the whole of North Africa are the Afro-Asian languages. The other smaller families of languages are those of the cul-tural borderlands, especially in East Africa where much mixture has taken place leading to specialized linguistic developments.

TRADITIONAL CULTURE AND LAND USE

The influence of the environment upon societies is a controversial topic but some relationship can generally be discerned and the multiplicity of tribes in tropical Africa provides many examples. The lands occupied by a tribe are often coextensive with a distinctive ecological unit, and intertribal boundaries commonly coincide with a change of environmental conditions—of rainfall, soil, or vegetation. Thus the Kikuyu tribe may be most expli-

7.A Baholo performing a hunter's dance with a mask representing an antelopes head. These people are Bantu from the Angola–Congo border. As in other parts of the world, there is a great need to record for posterity the amazing variety of traditional dance and music of which this is an example, as well as other cultural features.

citly defined by its language, but in some ways it may be more usefully described as those people who cultivate the rainy, forested, eastern slopes of the Aberdare range in Kenya.

Some of the environmental influences over land use have been described in previous chapters and one of the most limiting, the presence of disease, will be considered subsequently. These establish within each ecological zone a different and limited range of opportunities to wrest a livelihood from the soil, and thus the traditional ways of life of their inhabitants follow a similar zonation (Figure 7.4).

Along the Mediterranean borders we find an agriculture established from very early times, with cattle, the plow, cereals, and Mediterranean fruits (especially barley, wheat, olives, figs, and grapes). Southward, towards the desert margins, nomadic pastoralism based on sheep replaces cultivation; in the deserts cultiva-

tion is limited to oases, and human life depends on date palms and camels.

South of the deserts, in the semi-arid open lands of the Sudan, the people are again pastoralists depending for their livelihood on cattle, goats, sheep and, in some areas, camels. Southward, with increasing rainfall and a modest rainy season, there is again some cultivation, precarious, and dependent mainly on sorghum and millet. Cultivation is traditionally by the hoe; use of the plow is still rare.

The area of intermediate rainfall of the savanna between the steppes of the desert margins, which are too dry, and the forests of the equatorial margins, which are too wet, is favorable to cultivation. Large villages are the rule; there have been in the past empires of considerable size. Dependence for food is on millet and corn (maize), latterly on peanuts on the uplands and rice along the rivers. Tobacco is grown, sometimes cotton; kola nuts are

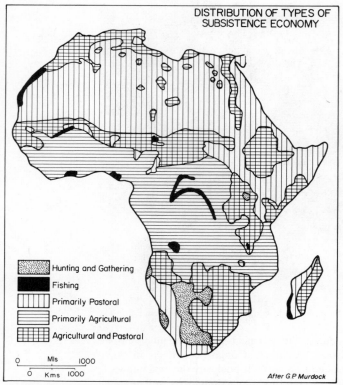

DISTRIBUTION OF TYPES OF SUBSISTENCE ECONOMY

Hunting and Gathering
Fishing
Primarily Pastoral
Primarily Agricultural
Agricultural and Pastoral

Mls   1000
Kms   1000

After G.P Murdock

7.4 Types of subsistence economy. (After Murdock.)

gathered. Often cattle are bred, sometimes sheep and horses, and among the cultivators or mixed farming communities are tribes that are almost exclusively pastoral. Unfortunately, in regions where the rainfall is more reliable and where mixed farming should reach its maximum intensity, we encounter the "fly belts" where the tsetse fly virtually eliminates domestic animals.

In the rainforest areas lack of grass and the presence of insect-borne diseases again limit the keeping of livestock, and root and tree crops become particularly important. These include yams, cassava, sweet potatoes, bananas, oil palm, cocoa, and robusta coffee. Exploitation of the rainforest has been particularly uneven, densely settled areas with large villages in Ashanti or Ivory Coast contrasting with areas of sparse population based on patches of shifting cultivation as in parts of Congo and Gabon.

At first sight Africa appears to be peculiarly poor in indigenous food plants. Of those widely cultivated, sorghum (Guinea corn or giant millet) and perhaps some strains of rice are native. Despite its wide use, corn (maize) was introduced from America, and so were tobacco, peanuts, yams, and manioc. Actually it was the Portuguese who, to feed their slaves before and during shipment, introduced into West Africa the many new food plants which have now become staple items of diet: cassava (manioc), sweet potatoes, yams, corn, peanuts, coconuts, and bananas coming from America, and oranges straight from Portugal.

The barley and wheat of the north were introduced from the Middle East and Europe at an early date, as was the date palm from Arabia. Coffee seems to be native to southern Ethiopia as the kola nut is to West Africa, but most other fruits have been introduced. Cloves were introduced by the Arabs into Zanzibar because there they could use slaves for picking the buds.

A close look at crops being grown for family or local consumption, however, reveals a wide range of indigenous plants, including legumes, cucurbits, root crops, and green vegetables. Most of these have not benefited from the intensive development which has been given elsewhere to the introduced plants, and scientific improvement could probably increase their yields greatly. Certainly they may be expected to be more suited to African ecologies than introduced crops. A major research and development program on sorghum is now under way, but there are many other lesser-known crops, any one of which might contain great potential.

7.B Girls of the Turkana, pastoral nomads in an arid area of Kenya. Traditionally their clothing is made of skins, the beads from ostrich shell and the lip plug from ivory but modern substitutes are now common. (Photo: J. Allan Cash.)

7.C Morning tea in a Moroccan village. The men are typical Berbers. The charcoal bellows, brass tray, teapot and glasses are practically the same throughout northern Africa. The tea is often flavored with mint and is made very sweet. (Copyright: Geographical Publications Ltd.)

The ass may be native to East Africa, and the camel to Egypt, but cattle and horses have been introduced, as well as European strains of sheep. West Africa gave us the guinea fowl.

Among the host of wild plants and large herbivores discussed in Chapter 6, it may be that new domestication is possible which did not occur in the African Neolithic. An obvious candidate for domestication is the eland, and there are many roots and berries which are at present collected but which could be cultivated and perhaps improved.

TRADITIONAL SOCIETY AND LAND USE

Traditional systems of land holding and management in Africa were evolved in relation to the needs of a subsistence economy and a given technology. The introduction of cash crops and trade, of new techniques and new aspirations, finds these traditional systems inadequate. Systems of shifting agriculture cannot support growing populations beyond a

very moderate density and hinder the introduction of permanent improvements and perennial crops. Fragmentation into numerous and excessively small plots is common and rights over land are generally communal rather than individual—a right of cultivation rather than ownership. This again makes difficult the building up of a modern large farm with capital invested in fencing, buildings, water supply, improvements in the soil, and long standing tree crops. Without clear title to the land, it cannot be used as security to raise the loans with which to make these improvements. Within traditional societies it is usually necessary to hold a plot of land to be a full member of the community, to be able to marry, to be buried, and to have any status. This leads to land being held by bad as well as good farmers, by those who have little interest in its development or who have employment elsewhere, as well as by those desirous and capable of making farming a commercial success. Thus agricultural development frequently requires drastic changes in the traditional system of land tenure as well as more technical innovations.

A communal system is similarly inevitable among traditional pastoral peoples, to allow access to water and seasonal changes in grazing and to accomodate the fluctuating fortunes of individual herds. This makes virtually impossible any effective management of the grass by paddocking and rotational grazing. Disease control is difficult, and the more progressive individual finds it hard to isolate and upgrade his own stock. Traditional social obligations to provide stock for bride price or other purposes may make it impossible for him to replace his numerous scrub cattle by smaller numbers of more productive stock.

TRADITIONAL SOCIETY AND POLITICAL STRUCTURE

It has been pointed out in Chapter 2 that the national boundaries in Africa were largely determined by negotiation between European powers during the nineteenth century and that they frequently bisect tribal areas. With the removal of the metropolitan power, these boundary problems add to the difficulties of the new nations learning to live with each other (compare Figures 2.13 and 2.15). It is within the states, however, that tribal conflicts cause most difficulty. The sense of belonging to a tribe is still likely to be far stronger than that of nationality. The tribe is linked by a common language and fellow tribesmen behave in keeping with tribal traditions. A tribesman will most likely marry from the same tribe and his inheritance will be a plot of tribal land. By contrast, the new nation is full of people to whom he can only speak in a foreign tongue, perhaps that of the former colonial power. Their behavior is strange to him and he does not feel at home in other parts of the country as he does within the tribe. Yet these strangers from other dis-

7.D The paramount chief of the Ashanti (Ghana) in 1951. The Golden Stool, symbol of the nation, is displayed. (Official photograph.)

7.E Unchanging household chores in a Fulani village, Nigeria, using subsistence crops and simple utensils of gourds, skillful basket work, pestle. (Photo: J. Allan Cash.)

tricts are making laws and decisions that affect his way of life and his prosperity and that of his people back home. Regional self-interest is a powerful political emotion in any country, as any member of the U.S. Senate is aware, but linked with tribal sentiment, it takes on a new intensity. It is therefore not surprising that a number of African states have been in danger of falling apart into tribal units; this has been so common that to quote examples would be invidious. A major task of many national leaders has been to lessen tribal jealousies. Federation tended to be favored by the departing British as a device to diminish tribal apprehensions; however, it also tended to perpetuate tribal and regional awareness. The growth of towns is helpful because it increases intertribal contact and lessens the social control of the tribe. Marriage outside the tribe is more likely in towns, replacing intertribal tensions by more personal ones, less damaging to the stability of the state.

CHRISTIAN MISSIONS

The factors leading to a transformation of the traditional societies of Africa are many and varied. Perhaps the most powerful and pervasive influence has been the spread of the exchange economy into previously self-contained communities. Among the more specific agents deliberately working for change in tropical Africa have been the missions.

The early navigator-explorers from Europe were followed shortly by missionary priests, but from then on the growth of the slave trade obviously rendered untenable any permanent stationing of missionaries drawn from the same peoples as the slavers. Nevertheless, as inland Africa became more familiar, all the great Christian churches sent missionaries and were vociferous in their condemnation of the evils they found. Livingstone's base was the mission in Bechuanaland. His reports and the reports of other missionaries roused public opinion in America and Europe against slavery to such a degree that governments, however, unwilling, had to take action, sometimes to the extent of expending millions of dollars with little prospect of return.

Missions have always realized that to reach the people their workers must know the local language. In the study of African languages missionaries have been pioneers. Since they came to convert the "heathen" and to teach them what they believed to be right and true, missionaries as a whole may have lacked the interest (which is basic to anthropologists) in the study of indigenous cultures for their own sake. Certain tenets of dogma and ritual may have been stressed in ways inappropriate to African circumstances; Western ideas of behavior may have been pressed with little realization of the effect. For ex-

ample, it is often said that by their insistence on a common Western attitude towards nudity (that it is of itself an evil), missionaries are responsible for the spread of an undesirable attitude towards sex. Certainly in education, curricula and methods of teaching have often been transplanted bodily from the home country. In the British areas African children were often taught the irrelevant details of English history and geography. The boy or girl educated in the mission school learns, it is said by some critics, to despise his fellows and to seek only to copy his teachers, with the disastrous result that he becomes an outcast from his own people rather than a leader. Yet Africa has emerged into an international community which has been in considerable measure framed for good or ill according to Western ideas. In familiarizing Africans with the background of this culture the missions have performed a useful function.

Some statistics of leading Christian denominations are published annually, but certain matters are not revealed by figures. One is the growth of indigenous African churches, in some, although not all, of which aspects of old pagan beliefs and customs may have been absorbed in forms of Christianity. Such local churches now number in the thousands throughout tropical Africa. Somewhat different is the Dutch Reformed Church of the Afrikaans-speaking South African, sometimes described as the strongest national church in the world. Of ancient origin is the Coptic Church of Ethiopia, to be considered later (see Chapter 15).

Christian teaching has always included the education of the young and the care of the sick. Almost everywhere in Africa the missionaries, supported by voluntary contributions from home and sometimes tolerated rather than helped, occasionally even obstructed, by administrators on the spot, were pioneers in establishing schools and hospitals. Often, when the

7.F A missionary church in southern Sudan. (Photo: J. Allan Cash.)

missions had successfully built up the framework of education and of medical services, governments stepped in and took over both management and credit.

ISLAM

Over much of Africa however, the religion which has had the most pervasive and lasting influence has been Islam. During the Middle Ages, the Christian churches of northern Africa were overwhelmed by Islam and that of Ethiopia survived only by constant struggle. As- sociated with the spread of Islam is a language and literature (Arabic), a style of art and building, distinctive systems of land tenure and of agricultural methods. This has given to northern and northeastern Africa a cultural homogeneity which is lacking for any large area south of the Sahara. In many parts of Africa Christianity is an important influence but where Islam is dominant it may be said to have formed a world in its image. This gives edge to what appears to be increasing competition between Moslem and Christian missionaries in some areas.

Further Reading

The First African Population Conference held at Ibadan in 1966 concerned itself only with the half of the population of the continent which lives within the tropics and primarily with that of the English-speaking areas. Nevertheless, the collected papers edited by John C. Caldwell and Chukuku Okonjo, *The Population of Tropical Africa* (London: Longman, 1968) provides valuable representative studies. More concerned with the distribution of the population are the *Essays on African Population* edited by K. M. Barbour and R. M. Prothero (New York: Praeger, 1961). National data is available from the *United Nations Demographic Yearbook*.

A conventional but outdated division of the peoples of Africa is set out by C. G. Seligman, *The Races of Africa* (London: Oxford University Press, 3rd Ed., 1957). A more recent and comprehensive survey, with useful bibliographies and a large and detailed map of the tribes of the entire continent is G. P. Murdock's *Africa, its peoples and their culture history* (New York: McGraw-Hill, 1959). For any one region or any one tribe, the first step is to see if it is included in one of the many volumes of the *Ethnographic Survey of Africa* published by the International African Institute under the general editorship of Daryll Forde. These volumes are concise summaries of the literature on individual tribes.

CHAPTER 8

The Plagues of Africa: Pests and Diseases

The evil reputation which Africa, especially tropical Africa, so long held as an unhealthy continent was linked essentially with climate. It was the "unhealthy climate" which caused West Africa to be known as the "white man's grave," and different parts of the continent are still referred to as unhealthy or contrasted with such areas as the healthy Kenya highlands. That climate has a direct effect upon the healthy, normal functioning of people is, of course, undeniable, but not to the extent, or anything like the extent, formerly believed. The dangers of life in most parts of tropical Africa are not due directly to climate but to the many diseases which flourish under the climatic or other physical conditions prevalent in the continent. Diseases to which man and animals are subject are numerous and severe, often fatal, and although their causes are now generally known, their elimination is another matter. It has been said with good reason that the tsetse fly, carrier of the germs of sleeping sickness in people and nagana in domestic animals, is still the real ruler of much of Africa. In the tsetse-fly belts both animal husbandry and mixed farming are impossible, so that agri-

cultural progress is virtually eliminated. Though the locust does no direct harm to man, a countryside devastated by locusts is a countryside of starvation. Pests and diseases thus constitute a very important factor in African development, past, present, and future.

MOSQUITOES

We are accustomed to summer plagues of mosquitoes in many parts of the world, and many a fishing or hunting vacation in the far north has been ruined by the unwelcome attention of mosquitoes. Annoying and even painful, mosquito bites are not in themselves serious, but when the mosquitoes are carriers of disease it is another matter. Malaria, the most widespread of all diseases in tropical Africa, and yellow fever, one of the most dreaded, are both carried by mosquitoes. Directly or indirectly, malaria is the chief threat to health and life in most parts of tropical Africa. It can be fatal, but its indirect effects (undermining health and so rendering its victims more susceptible to other infections) are even more important. It is a debilitating disease, and therefore the greatest contributor to inefficiency in the whole range of human activities. It is probable that over large areas of tropical Africa all children who survive to adolescence have been infected with malaria and have developed an immunity. Although apparently healthy, they have probably lost both stamina and efficiency. In such populations adults may develop an acute attack of fever which runs its course and after a few days terminates naturally just as in temperate latitudes a cold disappears after it has run its course. To the stranger, especially the European, coming into these malarial areas the diseases strike with devastating effect.

Malaria is caused by a minute animal parasite transferred by mosquitoes of the genus *Anopheles* from man to man. The female parasite is fertilized in the stomach of the mosquito. The resulting offspring pass into the saliva of the mosquito; when it bites a man they are transferred to his blood, and fever develops after a period of a few days. There are four types of malarial parasite of the genus *Plasmodium* which cause fevers of somewhat different types. The commonest is subtertian. Several species of *Anopheles* are known to be carriers, but it is *Anopheles gambiae,* widely distributed in Africa, which is the chief villain. It was formerly restricted to Africa but was accidentally introduced into Brazil. Incidentally, this is one of the great dangers of the speed of modern air travel—the accidental transportation of noxious pests—and explains the elaborate precautions now insisted upon by the health authorities of many countries. Blackwater fever, a consequence of malarial infection, has also been a most serious disease.

With the discovery by Ronald (later Sir Ronald) Ross in 1898 of the way in which mosquitoes transmitted malaria, it was realized that the disease could be controlled by eliminating its vector. Unfortunately *Anopheles gambiae* breeds very easily and does not bother greatly about the character of the water where it deposits its eggs; small rain pools, stagnant water left in riverbeds in the dry season, even marshes with up to 66 percent of seawater will all serve. Not unexpectedly, the incidence of malaria is greatest at the end of the rains and while there is still stagnant water not dried up. A thin film of oil over the stagnant waters prevents the larvae from breathing and so eliminates the mosquito. Careful and thorough spraying with insecticides can also be used. By such methods restricted areas, notably some islands, have been rendered malaria free but such control over the entire continent is still far in the future.

Long before the involvement of the mosquito was understood, malaria had been treated with quinine—a cure taught to Jesuit missionaries by South American Indians in the seventeenth century (or possibly earlier). The introduction of modern prophylactic drugs (e.g., paludrine, chloroquine, aralen, camoquin, and daraprim) has transformed the situation. If taken regularly, they provide a very high degree of personal immunity but, in addition, if an entire population is treated, it is possible to break the chain of infection and eliminate the disease throughout an area.

The American Geographical Society has devoted Plate 3 of its great *Atlas of Diseases, Geog. Rev.,* XLI (1951) pp. 638–639 to the chief species of malaria vectors. It shows the distribution in Africa of the chief species of *Anopheles* widely distributed in the world and also of other species important in Africa (Figure 8.1).

Yellow fever is a terrible infectious disease caused by an ultramicroscopic virus transmitted from man to man principally by the mosquito *Aëdes aegypti*. An attack of yellow fever confers immunity, that is, if a victim recovers from his first attack he is safe for life. It seems certain that immunity is earned by many Africans in early life by mild attacks, but if the disease strikes severely it is fatal in 90 percent of the cases. The unfortunate

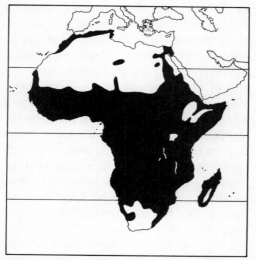

8.1 Malarial mosquitoes in Africa. Species of mosquito carrying malaria exist in all parts of Africa shown in solid black on this map. (Figures 8.1, 8.2, 8.4 to 8.6 and 8.10 are derived from the American Geographical Society Atlas of Distribution of Diseases.)

victim starts vomiting and goes on vomiting until the strain causes death by heart failure. There is little that the attendant can do but watch the patient die this horrible death. Every now and then there are epidemics, and, although the numbers involved are in ordinary years small, there is a constant fear of a serious outbreak. Fortunately there is a safe and effective inoculation against yellow fever, and for all travelers to and from tropical Africa it is an essential requirement so that it is now almost impossible for a traveler from abroad to contract it. Most African countries report annually that there have been no fatal cases. The mosquito *Aëdes aegypti* is very widely distributed (Figure 8.2), far more widely than the disease, and it breeds freely in anything which will hold water, especially, it would seem, in villages and towns. Old automobile tires are

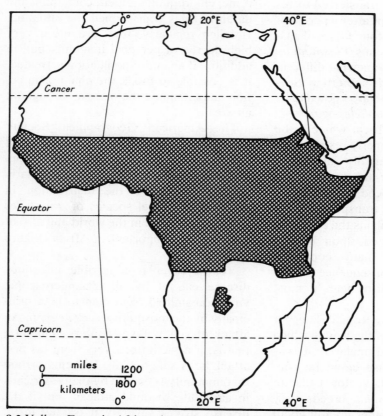

8.2 Yellow Fever in Africa: the endemic area as outlined by the World Health Organization, January 10, 1952.

particularly favored. The provision of piped water supplies and efficient drainage would make towns safe provided other water surfaces were controlled. In parts of West Africa efforts have been made to make illegal the growing of certain palms which hold stagnant water, but unfortunately even the banana holds water between its great leaves and the stem. The same mosquito in Africa is responsible for transmitting dengue, or "break bone," fever. Though rarely fatal, this fever throws the victims out of action for two or three weeks. New arrivals are particularly liable; they have high temperatures and a skin eruption while the pain in joints and muscles is acute. They feel as if every bone in their bodies were literally breaking. Dengue and associated fevers carried by *Aëdes aegypti* are widespread in Asia but yellow fever is thus far absent. This is probably due to the lack of yellow fever in the ports of East Africa, but air travel presents a grave threat of accidental infection.

There are other diseases transmitted by mosquitoes. The condition known as elephantiasis, the enormous swelling of the legs and sometimes of other parts of the body, is caused by a minute worm transmitted by mosquitoes. Since the 1940's, treatment with Hetrazan and certain arsenic compounds have achieved favorable results.

TSETSE FLIES

The name tsetse fly is given to the twenty-odd species of African blood-sucking flies of the genus *Glossina*. They are somewhat larger than houseflies and can be recognized by their prominent proboscis projecting horizontally in front of the head and by their habit of resting with the wings lying one upon the other. They are found in "fly belts," especially on the margins of bush or forest near rivers or lakes, and are particularly active and troublesome during the hotter parts of the day. Certain species carry the single-celled

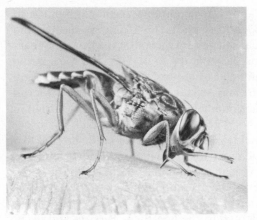

8.A A tsetse fly (*Glossina morsitans*) sucking blood from a finger. (Photo: Barnaby's Picture Library.)

organisms known as trypanosomes, which are the cause of fatal diseases in both man and animals. When the tsetse fly sucks blood from an infected subject it draws up some of these organisms, which undergo a developmental phase within the fly and are then passed into the blood of the man or animal on which the fly may next feed. The fly *Glossina palpalis* transmits *Trypanosoma gambiense,* causing sleeping sickness in man to the west of the western Rift Valley, while *G. tachinoides* carries the same trypanosome north of latitude 8° North. *Glossina morsitans,* and the similar *G. swynnertoni* and *G. pallidipes,* transmit *T. rhodesiense,* causing the Rhodesian form of sleeping sickness in man in the east and south of the continent. The Rhodesian form is a severe and often fatal disease that runs its course rapidly, whereas the less virulent Gambian type usually persists longer. These and other tsetse flies are also the main carriers of those trypanosomes which cause *nagana* disease among domestic animals, but this is also transmitted mechanically by the *Tabanid* biting flies which have an even wider distribution. It is possible that monkeys can act as "carriers" of sleeping sickness, and many wild antelopes, though unaffected themselves, are carriers of the diseases of cattle. Sleeping sickness spread from West Africa, where the population has acquired a certain immunity, to Uganda and East Africa generally, and caused severe mortality in the early years of the century. Not only are the insects difficult to control — clearing of vegetation around villages and elimination of scrub are important — but the pupae lie buried in shady ground difficult to attack by insecticides. The toll taken of cattle has led to a demand for the wholesale destruction of African wild animals, believed to be carriers. The accompanying map, for the material of which the authors are greatly indebted to the late P. A. Buxton and H. S. Leeson, shows the distribution of tsetse flies (*Glossina*) in general and, within that, the areas (shown in black on Figure 8.3) where sleeping sickness in man occurs. The huge size of the area is obvious.

In the early years of this century,

sleeping sickness produced an immense epidemic in Uganda, where it appears to have killed between 200,000 and 300,000 people within a very few years, amounting to two-thirds of the population in some areas.[1] The resulting depopulation of the most affected areas has left some localities uninhabited down to the present day. Similarly, the concentration of population over large parts of Tanzania into areas within which the fly could be eradicated has left much of the *miombo* woodland empty of inhabitants. Elsewhere in Africa it was a killing disease, especially when associated with insufficient food and consequent poor physique. The French in

[1] B. W. Langlands, *Sleeping Sickness in Uganda 1900–1920,* Occ. Papers No. 1. (Dept. of Geography, Makerere University College, 1967).

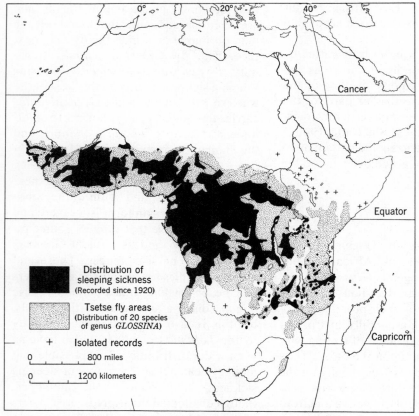

8.3 Sleeping sickness and tsetse-fly areas. (Compiled from information supplied by the late P. A. Buxton and H. S. Leeson.)

West Africa found that the annual mortality of patients treated by the best skill then available varied from 5 to 15 percent. Owing to advances in the production of drugs, the disease has now ceased to be a menace and no longer makes a large contribution to deaths in tropical Africa, although a certain number of people still die of it, coming for treatment too late, or living beyond the range of medical services. Several drugs, not chemically related, have contributed to this remarkable victory. A point in their favor is that the patient does not have to be admitted to a hospital; he can be treated in his village by an itinerant team. The most recent drugs are not used in treatment of the sick, but for the protection (prophylaxis) of those who are exposed to the risk of sleeping sickness. With these drugs, all individuals, as far as possible, are given an injection which protects them completely for a large number of months, so that the chain of infection between man and fly is effectively broken.

Cattle, horses, and dogs bitten by a *Glossina* sp. carrying the "fly disease," or nagana, usually die. At first no effect is seen, but a few days after the animal has been bitten the eyes and nose begin to run, a swelling appears under the jaw and the muscles become flaccid. The animal begins to stagger and may go mad before it dies. It is found on dissection that the cellular tissues under the skin have become injected with air. The result of this fatal effect is twofold. In the first place, there are severe losses on the margins of the fly belts in cattle country, as in East Africa. In the second place, it is virtually impossible to introduce these domestic animals into the fly belts, and consequently mixed farming is not a practicable method of improving the management of the land and increasing crop yields. The lack of meat and milk adds to dietary and health problems. It is also impossible to introduce the ox-drawn plough. Control by bush clearing and inoculation are both possible but much of the land which could be made available to livestock by such methods is insufficiently productive to repay the cost involved. Before the arrival of the railway and automobile, it was usually the presence of nagana and the consequent inability to use animal transport, that required human porterage and the foot safari.

HOOKWORMS

It is probable that hookworm disease, or ankylostomiasis, occurs among a very high proportion of Africans, but, because very severe cases are few and it is rarely fatal, it has been much neglected. The tiny worms, when adult, live in the human intestines attached to the gut wall, from which they suck blood. Thus the victim suffers a continuous loss of blood. Extreme cases result in marked anemia, and there are many who believe that hookworm disease in milder but pernicious cases is responsible for much mental and bodily lethargy. The eggs of the worms leave the human body in the feces; the larvae develop on the ground and then enter through the skin of feet and ankles of persons walking unshod on contaminated soil. People wearing shoes are rarely infected so that the local manufacture of cheap shoes and sandals plays a valuable part in preventive medicine. Similarly, proper sanitation eliminates contaminated soil.

WATER-BORNE DISEASE ORGANISMS

Throughout tropical lands diseases of the intestines and stomach, ranging from mildly upset digestions to killing diseases, are much more common than in temperate lands. Climate is only indirectly responsible by favoring the rapid decomposition of foodstuffs and lowering man's resistance. Infection may be conveyed by dust, by the hands' coming in contact with infected material (hence the imperative need of washing before meals), by house flies, but above all by contaminated water, especially that which has been infected by human excreta. Danger may come from water even if one does not drink it; it may simply be used for washing cooking utensils or on vegetables to be eaten uncooked. For this reason salads, so popular in temperate lands, are particularly dangerous in the tropics. Fruit with a firm skin (for example, bananas or oranges) is safe, but bruised or damaged fruit are best avoided. Both salads and fruit may be washed with a mild, tasteless disinfectant such as "permanganate of potash." Milk is also very liable to contamination and should always be boiled.

The two forms of dysentery, the one caused by an amoeba living in water and the other by a bacillus, are very common. Various forms of diarrhea are even more frequent.

The unpleasant disease known as bil-

harziasis, or schistosomiasis, of which one form is characterized by discharge of blood and mucus from the rectum and the other form affects the bladder, is common throughout Africa (Figure 8.4). It is caused by drinking water contaminated by the fluke parasite *Schistosoma* or *Bilharzia*. The intermediate host is a water snail, such as *Planorbis* or *Isidora* (much enjoyed by ducks) and the obvious control is by elimination of these hosts. Fortunately, if water contaminated by *Bilharzia* is kept for two days, it becomes innocuous for domestic purposes. The disease can be cured with relative ease, but is a killing malady because of the disorganization of the internal organs. The snails flourish in bathing pools near villages and are able to live in water fouled by urine or excrement. Unfortunately, the disease has spread in Africa with irriga-

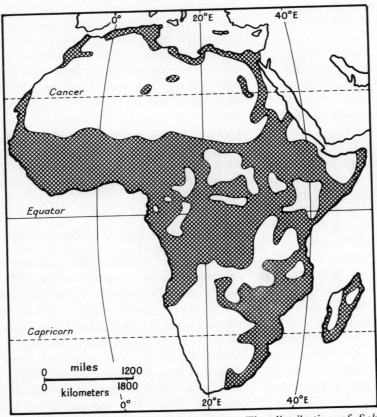

8.4 Bilharzia (Schistosomiasis) in Africa. The distribution of *Schistosoma haematobium* or *S. mansoni*.

tion works. Once again the control of the disease is dependent upon general improvement of sanitary conditions, and in this case calls for close collaboration between the irrigation engineers and the doctors.

Fortunately, diseases of the typhoid–paratyphoid group seem to be rare in Africa, and so is cholera, but with the increasing ease of transport, there is a risk of importing such diseases from other continents, from India, or from pilgrims returning from Mecca.

The Guinea threadworm (*Dranunculus medinensis*), though only a millimeter in diameter, lives under the human skin and may reach a yard or more in length. It causes ulceration and much incapacitation. The embryo lives in a minute freshwater crustacean, and once again infected drinking water is the source of infection.

LICE, TICKS, AND FLEAS

Unpleasant as the unwelcome attention of these parasites of man and animals may be, it is the diseases they carry which are far more important. Relapsing fever is caused by a blood parasite (*Spirochaeta spp.*) carried by a louse or a tick. Although diagnosis is easy by a microscopic examination of the blood, the fever has symptoms closely resembling those of malaria and may not be suspected in time to prevent a severe epidemic. If diagnosed in time it is readily curable, and the disease can be controlled by delousing the population; but epidemics of unparalleled intensity have occured in the past. In 1921–1922 an outbreak in French Sudan and Niger killed at least 10,000 persons; in 1926 one district in Darfur (Sudan) lost 10,000 out of a total population of 20,000.

Another louse-borne disease is typhus, but this — by way of contrast — is a scourge of colder lands and rare in tropical Africa. It has affected Morocco and Algeria with some severity, as it did in 1942.

It is well known that murine plague is transmitted from rats to man by rat fleas.

The domestic house rat, *Rattus rattus*, is the chief host, and fortunately is restricted in Africa to main ports, though a mouse, *Mastomys natalensis*, is known to be a host in certain areas. In World War I plague due to rats was a serious menace in Dakar, and in 1920, 15,000 human cases were reported from French West Africa. Because of an energetic campaign waged against the rats, cases of plague and resultant deaths dropped steadily; in 1938 only four cases were reported in French West Africa and for the first time no deaths. Normally, about 60 percent of cases are fatal. The other epidemiological form of plague, sylvatic plague, is confined to southern Africa (Figure 8.5). In that case the permanent hosts are certain wild rodents, mainly of the genera *Tatera* and *Desmodillus*.

OTHER HUMAN DISEASES

Africa does not escape the worldwide killing diseases of other continents. Tuberculosis is one of the most frequent causes of death in tropical Africa, despite the spectacular fall in mortality rates elsewhere in the world with the use of modern drugs. Pneumonia is especially dangerous to ill-nourished and scantily clad children liable to sudden changes of climate (as when the harmattan suddenly begins to blow); smallpox is likely to spread by movements of laborers and to assume serious proportions; gonorrhea is very widespread; syphilis has become the commonest cause of admission to the hospital in many districts of Africa. Polio affects Africa as it does other continents, especially in transient labor camps, and so do influenza and trachoma. It would seem that Africans are particularly susceptible to epidemic diseases when away from their homes or when vitality is lowered by heavy manual work coming on top of indifferent feeding. Thus mortality on railway construction work has frequently been very heavy.

A disease particularly prevalent in trop-

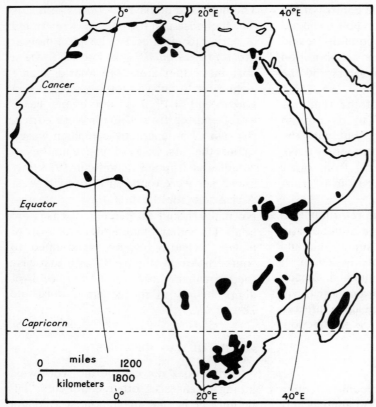

8.5 Plague in Africa. The distribution of human cases of plague, 1900–1952.

ical Africa (affecting children especially) is yaws, caused by *Spirochaeta pertenuis,* closely allied to *S. pallida,* which causes syphilis; it is not, however, a syphilitic disease. The germ enters the body through cuts, abrasions, or sores. It causes skin eruptions and ulcers all over the body, which themselves may lead to other infections. We may here blame the climate to some extent, for in the tropics cuts and wounds do not heal as easily as in cooler lands and are likely to become the seat of other infections.

Leprosy, caused by *Bacillus leprae,* is another contagious disease widespread, though irregularly so, in Africa (Figure 8.6). Although the disease is now readily curable in early stages, lepers have so long been regarded as social outcasts that the difficulty is to persuade those who have the disease to come for treatment.

LOCUSTS

So far we have been considering briefly the plagues which affect man directly; Africa has many others which attack his food supply — his crops and his animals. Many are pests and diseases of wide, if not worldwide, occurrence such as rinderpest and foot-and-mouth disease among cattle; some are ancient and well known, others seem to be new — like the swollen shoot disease of cocoa. We have already indicated that at present the tsetse fly makes improvement of agriculture over huge areas of Africa impossible. Similarly the wide prevalence of poultry disease has made poultry farming impossible over large areas. We cannot deal with the geographical distribution and possible causes of all these many pests and diseases, but for several reasons particular interest attaches to the study of the locust. Locusts are among the oldest enemies of mankind. The locusts brought by the east wind were the seventh of the plagues which Moses caused to harass Egypt in his effort to secure the release of his people from bondage. Throughout the Old Testament the destructiveness of the locust is proverbial. In Egypt, "Very grievous were they: for they covered the face of the whole earth, so that the land was darkened; and they did eat herb of the land, and all the fruit of the trees: and there remained not any green thing in the trees, or in the herbs of the field, through all the land of Egypt."[2] Yet it was not until about 1930, when a great locust plague seemed to be threatening Africa and western Asia, that several governments, including the Brit-

ish, French, Egyptian, and South African, realized the need for investigating not only the best means of killing locusts but also the reasons for their periodic swarmings. Later, in 1945, a permanent Anti-Locust Research Center was established.

Tropical Africa is subject to plagues of three different locusts: desert locust (*Schistocerca gregaria*), African migratory locust (*Locusta migratoria migratoroides*), and red locust (*Nomadacris septemfasciata*). Each has its own "invasion area," though they partly overlap (compare Figures 8.7, 8.8, and 8.9). It has been found that the normal cycle of locust life in each breeding area is closely correlated with the climatic cycle, especially rainfall, whereas migrations of swarms between breeding periods are largely connected with wind systems. Unfortunately

[2] Exodus, X, v. 14–15.

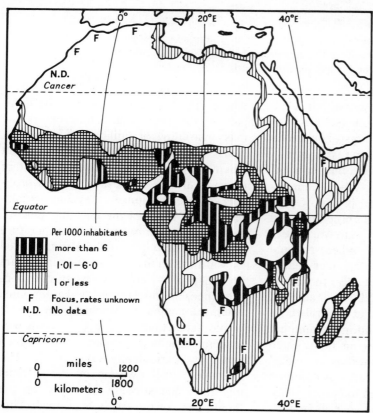

8.6 Leprosy in Africa, 1952.

8.B A plague of locusts in Morocco. As part of the international campaign assisted by the Food and Agriculture Organization of the United Nations, they are here being fought with the help of poison. (Courtesy of F.A.O.)

the convergence of airflows, which is the prime cause of rainy seasons (see Chapter 4), provides both the moist conditions favorable for breeding and the means whereby the locusts become concentrated into that very area. Where climatological data are adequate, it is now possible to forecast locust breeding and movement of swarms and so to warn areas of the impending danger. Where thermal convection currents develop over heated ground they provide a lift to locust swarms just as they do to birds or aircraft, and the swarms may fly at several thousand feet from the ground, maintaining a speed of about 11 miles an hour. Such swarms may travel hundreds of miles. Thus, during a plague year, it is common for desert locusts to breed in North Africa during the first half of the year and for the flying swarms then to be carried by major air currents to areas south of the Sahara

where they breed again during the latter part of the year. Quite different is the mass marching of millions of young locusts, or "hoppers." They march actively when warmed by the sun and maintain direction by the sun's rays (though probably actuated by hunger, they may actually march for this reason into the desert), resting by night when the temperature falls. Their activity is definitely stimulated by warmth. Each species of locust occurs in two phases: solitary, when the consequences are not serious, and gregarious, when the danger of swarming appears. It would seem that there exist certain permanent breeding grounds from which swarming periodically takes place. For example, small swarms of the African migratory locust were observed on the flood plains of the River Niger near Timbuktu in 1926–1927 over an area of some 50 by 120 miles. In 1928 the swarms in-

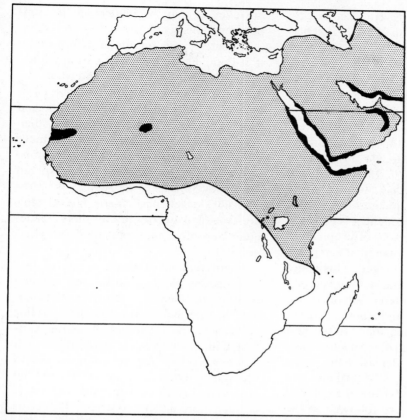

8.7 The maximum invasion area of the Desert Locust (stippled). Known and suspected outbreak areas are shown in black. (After Uvarov.)

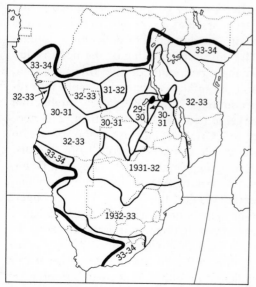

8.8 The annual spread of the Red Locust, 1927–1934. Black areas show the swarms of 1927–1929. (After Uvarov.)

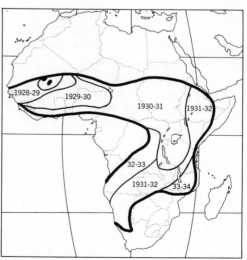

8.9 The annual spread of the Migratory Locust, 1926–1934. Black areas show the swarms of 1926–1927. (After Uvarov.)

vaded Senegal and Sierra Leone; by 1929–1930 the whole of West Africa had been invaded; by 1930 the plague had reached Khartoum; and by 1932 swarms which had, of course, bred on the way reached Rhodesia and Angola. From the small initial center some 4 million to 5 million square miles had been affected, and the plague lasted 14 years. Similarly, small swarms of red locust observed in what is now Zambia in 1927–1929 had become 6300 recorded swarms over 3,000,000 square miles by 1935. Although modern insecticides render the protection of a given area of crops comparatively easy, a well-planned campaign is needed to control a plague. This is not impossible, however, and in the recession of a plague which affected much of Africa, Arabia, Pakistan, and India between 1950 and 1960, it is claimed that for the first time in history control measures had played a major part in defeating the desert locust. Large swarms in Mauritania and Senegal were sprayed from the air and those that escaped were followed to the Souss valley in Morocco where they were eliminated. Similar action by the Pakistan Plant Protection Department north of the Rann of Kutch was followed up by the Plant Protection Department of India when the remnants moved south. Although the benefits are great, the costs are high and control requires continual vigilance and prompt action on an international scale. The danger is that when the immediate threat is absent, less money is made available and international cooperation withers away.

DEFICIENCY DISEASES

Among the many diseases and plagues of Africa are some which are the result of deficiencies, especially of diet, rather than the action of any direct agent. Periods of shortage between harvests are not uncommon among rural communities with a subsistence economy and at such times resistance to disease is lowered. Even when the volume of food is sufficient,

however, it may be inadequate in composition. This tends to be so where there is a great reliance on one crop, especially if it contains little except carbohydrate, such as bananas or cassava, and where the presence of nagana means the absence of livestock and consequently of milk and meat. The use of white maize rather than yellow and its substitution for the more nutritious sorghum or the millets is unfortunate. The most serious and widespread deficiency disease in Africa is kwashiorkor, which particularly affects children weaned on to starchy diets, inadequate in protein and vegetable foods (Figure 8.10).

There remains a whole range of diseases among plants, animals, and man due to some deficiency, often difficult to detect, in the land or the soil itself. Major deficiencies in the soil, such as low content of lime, phosphates, and nitrogen, can be detected by chemical analysis, and to the trained eye may be apparent from the growth and form of plants themselves. It is much more difficult to detect absence or excess of "trace elements," the full significance of which is not yet fully known.

A deficiency disease of worldwide occurrence is goiter, not so much a disease in itself as a symptom of ill health due to an unbalanced diet deficient in iodine. The unsightly swelling of the neck is due to malfunctioning of the thyroid gland, and the influence extends widely into reproduction, growth rate, intellectual development, and deaf-mutism. The people of Africa, living close to the soil are on the whole remarkably free from this disease, except in the Nile Valley and Delta, patches in the Abyssinian plateau, on high country near the source of the Niger, Northern Nigeria, around the Ebola River in northern Congo, and in the Katanga. In each case the incidence would appear to be due to the constant use of river water deficient in iodine. In a small but interesting area of the Langkloof Mountains near Knysna in South Africa local waters and soil are normal in respect to iodine content but very rich in available lime, though

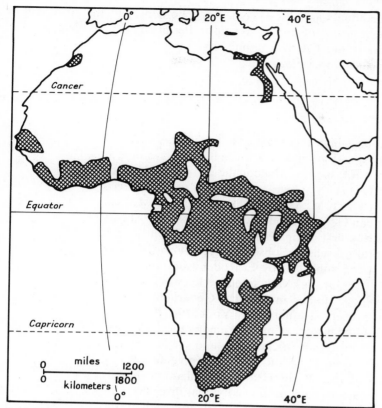

8.10 Diseases of protein deficiencies (kwashiorkor, nutritional edema) in Africa.

low in phosphorus. This lime–phosphorus imbalance seems to lead to increased demand for iodine and may explain the popular association of goiter with limestone areas elsewhere in the world.[3]

There were parts of Kenya where the mysterious disease "nakuruitis" swept away the settlers' cattle and sheep until it was traced to deficiencies of trace elements in the soil. With a dressing of cobalt the same land now carries excellent livestock.

THE CONTROL OF PESTS AND DISEASES

It is important for us to be aware of the multitude of serious pests and diseases which affect Africa today. They hinder

economic development and rob the people of health and of the expectation of life which the inhabitants of more fortunate lands have. Other lands were not always so fortunate, however, and in the history of Europe it is only relatively recently that malaria, leprosy, smallpox, cholera, and plague have ceased to be threats. These and a host of less spectacular infections and ailments have been eliminated by public health measures, inoculation, clinical treatments, and all the benefits of an increasingly higher standard of living and better diet, clothing, and housing. There is every reason to expect a comparable improvement in other parts of the world by the application of techniques already in operation or which may confidently be anticipated. The visitor to Africa is able to take precautions which make it extremely unlikely that any of the diseases mentioned here will affect him and an increas-

[3] World Goitre Survey, *Iodine Facts* (London, April, 1946).

ing proportion of the inhabitants are able to do the same. The deployment of preventitive medicine across tropical Africa is a massive and an expensive operation, but it can be done and the costs will be repaid in the prosperity and happiness of millions.

Further Reading

Much of the material on which this chapter is based was supplied from unpublished sources, and grateful acknowledgments are due to Professor P. A. Buxton, Professor G. Macdonald, Dr. C. J. Hackett, Mr. H. S. M. Hoare, Dr. H. S. Gear, and Dr. D. W. S. Davis.

Under the direction of Dr. J. M. May, the Department of Medical Geography of the American Geographical Society published 17 sheets of an *Atlas of Diseases,* the first comprehensive attempt to deal with the geography of the world's diseases. Subsequently, a *World Atlas of Epidemic Diseases* has been published by E. Rodenwaldt and A. L. Jusatz (Hamburg, 1961). Dr. Jacques May amplified his work with his *Studies in Disease Ecology,* studies in Medical Geography No. 2, American Geographical Society (Hafner: New York, 1961).

A fascinating account of the history of malaria among the early travelers in Africa is given by Professor Michael Gelfand's inaugural lecture *Rivers of Death in Africa* (London: Oxford University Press, 1964). The publications of the World Health Organization include useful summaries of the current position for individual diseases. One which exemplifies the relevance of a geographical approach is the report of the Seminar on the Ecology, Biology, Control, and Eradication of *Aedes aegypti* in *Bulletin, W.H.O.,* Vol. 34, No. 4 (1967) pp. 519–702. This is even more apparent in the report on Trypanosomiasis in *Bulletin* Vol. 28, Nos. 5 and 6 (1963) especially the article on the distribution of the vectors of African pathogenic trypanosomes by J. Ford (pp. 653–670).

CHAPTER 9

Transportation in Africa[1]

Animal power was one of the first of man's labor-saving devices. In common with other Mediterranean lands, the ass was in common use as a beast of burden in North Africa from very early times. In Roman times, horses were used to pull vehicles, and there was an ancient system of hard-surfaced roads in northwestern Africa. These roads deteriorated under the Vandals, Byzantines, Arabs, and Turks, who used only pack animals on trails—horses, donkeys, mules, and camels. In Egypt, donkeys, oxen, buffaloes, camels, and some horses have been used as work or riding animals for centuries. It is only necessary to mention in passing the obvious association of the camel, the "ship of the desert," with the desert regions, nor is there need to stress the well-known but nevertheless striking adaptations of the animal for desert life: the broad spreading foot, the arrangement of the stomachs, the safety reservoir of food in the hump, the tongue and mouth able to laugh at thorns, the nostrils closing at will against sand and dust. That the camel is fully conscious of its successful adaptation to environment, so vastly better than that of clumsy-footed man, is

clear from its supremely haughty bearing and supercilious expression.

In much of tropical Africa, by contrast, traditional society made little use of animals as beasts of burden. The presence of the tsetse fly is only a partial explanation because it is not universally present; and even if horses could not survive, cattle were widespread in east and southeastern Africa and yet bullocks were not used. (Although oxen are used as pack and riding animals in Mali and the Ahagger.) The donkey is a pack animal among some nomadic peoples, such as the Masai, today but it may well be a late introduction. The use of the camel has been mentioned and where conditions are suitable (disease permitting and grazing available) horses are used, as in the drier savannas of West Africa and in the highlands of Ethiopia and Lesotho. Probably more relevant to an explanation was the lack of trade and therefore of need for transport among societies based upon a subsistence economy. We may almost say in con-

[1] This chapter has benefited greatly from contributions and detailed advice made by Professor Benjamin E. Thomas, who is gratefully acknowledged.

9.A A typical path through farmland in Ghana, near Sekondi. Originating as footpaths, they can be negotiated by bicycles—with or without power assistance. (Copyright: L. Dudley Stamp.)

sequence that the wheel remained if not unknown at least unused until the advent of Europeans. Wheeled vehicles need roads, the construction and maintenance of which requires much effort and such administrative techniques as taxes or forced labor which were not common in the indigenous political systems of most of tropical Africa. In tropical Africa human porterage (where watercourses were not available for dugout canoes) was practically universal. So the routes from village to village, to the tribal meeting place, to the shrines in the forest were worn by human feet, traveling single file. There were no wheels, no wheeled vehicles, no cart tracks with the two deep wheel ruts so universal in India or Indochina. In the forests or closer type of savanna country the tracks made by human feet were narrow. In the early years of the present century it was suddenly realized that the ideal form of transport for these tracks already existed in the form of the bicycle. It was cheap, easy to ride and maintain, and millions were imported. The motorbike is equally well suited to footpaths but rising standards of sophistication as well as prosperity have encouraged the direct

jump from bicycle to secondhand automobile.

In the open savanna and the grassveld or steppe of southern Africa, where no tsetse fly hindered their use, the Dutch introduced at an early stage the lumbering ox wagon—the covered wagon of the Great Trek. With its standard "span" of sixteen oxen it was, until recently, still to be seen in parts of South Africa and Rhodesia. R. U. Sayce has claimed that the development of South Africa as a whole is intimately connected with the ox and he has stressed the many thousands of ox wagons which were in use, notably in the period 1880–1890.[2]

After World War I it became clear that the modern automobile could go, at least in the dry season, over much of unforested Africa with but little in the way of formal roads. It would be too much to say that the drier parts of Africa have now a network of roads, but, except in the rains, most parts can be reached by automobile. The qualification "except in the rains"

[2] R. U. Sayce, "The Transport Ox and Ox-Wagon in Natal," in *Studies in Regional Consciousness and Environment* (New York, 1930).

may exclude a period of 6, or even 8 months in parts of tropical Africa. Human porterage is usable, although with difficulty, throughout the year. The same is true of the bicycle, but for economic year-round movement of passengers and goods overland, either railroads or all-weather roads are essential.

RAILROADS AND THE OPENING UP OF AFRICA

Railroad construction began early in Egypt, Algeria, and South Africa. The first rail line on the African continent was started in 1852, by the famous railway engineer Robert Stephenson, to connect Alexandria to Cairo. Other lines in Egypt were built to serve the Nile delta and valley and, later, to connect them with the Suez canal. The French military built a line from Algiers to Blida in 1858. Under civilian control, the network was gradually expanded. By 1871, it served the area between Algiers and Oran and, after the French protectorate over Tunisia was established in 1881, the railways of the two territories were joined. By 1884, one could travel by rail from western Algeria to eastern Tunisia over a system that served all the major centers of both countries.

In South Africa the building of the line from Cape Town began in 1859. It was completed to Wellington in 1863, but it did not reach the Kimberley diamond mines until 1885, Johannesburg on the Rand until 1892, or Bulawayo until 1897. It may indeed be said that the "railway era" for tropical Africa began shortly after the partition of the continent and that strategic factors were stronger than economic ones in determining which lines were built. There was no coordination: gauges were chosen at the whim of the companies or of the governments who backed them. Most railways in tropical Africa were begun after 1890, and railway construction went on spasmodically and rather slowly until World War I. As the territories of the European powers became demarcated and widely accepted, so economic considerations (especially the exploitation of valuable mineral deposits)

9.B An ox wagon of the old type on the High Veld, with a full span of 16 oxen. Such ox wagons played a large part in the development of South Africa but it is doubtful whether a full span ox wagon still exists today. (Courtesy South African Railways.)

replaced strategic ones as the main factors determining routes. Many short lengths of line, especially in the Congo, were constructed to join navigable stretches of waterway either by circumventing rapids and falls or by linking one waterway with another.

In many areas of tropical Africa it was the railroad which arrived first, before the road, and it was not uncommon for a route to be traversable only by rail and not by road (e.g., from Tabora to Kigoma on Lake Tanganyika, across the Malagarassi swamp). With the increasing importance of the truck, the bus, and the automobile, a change of emphasis occurred which is well illustrated by the famous Victoria Falls Bridge over the Zambezi. It was designed and built as a railway bridge and completed in 1904–1905, but by the 1920's the adventurous, with or without permission would drive a model-T Ford (invaluable because of its high clearance) over the bumpy wooden surface. Later it was definitely converted to a rail and road bridge.

Some examples of early "strategic" railways may be quoted as interesting. The line from Lourenço Marques in Portuguese East Africa to Pretoria in the Transvaal, built by the Netherlands Railway Company, was completed in 1895. The Transvaal was an independent republic, but the line from Pretoria to Durban in the British colony of Natal was opened the next year. In 1891 the Imperial German government took over the administration of German East Africa from the German East Africa Company, and the Tanga railway was begun in the same year, though it did not reach far inland for many years. In 1892 the old Imperial British East Africa Company surveyed a railway route from Mombasa to Lake Victoria; construction was undertaken by and at the expense of the British government in 1896.

Farther north the French, under a concession from Ethiopia, started construction in 1897 on the railway from their port of Jibuti to Addis Ababa, the capital of Ethiopia—to this day the only railway link between Ethiopia and the outside world. It is perhaps indicative of the changing relative significance of road and rail that the Italians during their occupation of Ethiopia (1936–1941) built many motor roads but no railways and that at the end of World War II the Addis Ababa railway was not sufficiently important for through running to be resumed for some years.

Most of the railways in tropical Africa were begun after the Berlin Conference of 1884–1885. St. Louis was linked with Dakar in 1885; the line to link the Senegal River at Kayes with the Niger, though actually begun in 1881, did not reach Koulikoro on the Niger until 1904, and it was 1923 before there was through running from Dakar to the Niger.

Stanley is credited with saying that "without railways the Congo is not worth a penny." He knew well the great navigable stretches of the mighty river and its tributaries and realized how those navigable stretches must be linked up by railroads circumventing the rapids and falls (Figure 9.1). Because the force of his argument was appreciated, the line from Matadi to Kinshasa was opened in 1898, uniting the estuary with Stanley Pool and thus conquering the obstacle of the Livingstone Rapids. The short stretch of line from Kisangani to Ponthierville around the Stanley Falls in the heart of the basin was opened in 1909.

The expense and inefficiency of human porterage in the Africa of the past and the transformation wrought by the railroads is described in the contemporary *Handbook of Commercial Geography* by G. G. Chisholm, first published in 1889: A man carrying 100 pounds on his head might travel 15 or even 20 miles a day; two men driving a railway engine could haul, for example, 1,000,000 pounds 1000 miles in a day. Is it little wonder that goods valuable enough to stand the costs of human porterage were few in number—gold, diamonds, and ivory, to mention the tradi-

9.C The railhead at Nakuru in the Kenya Rift Valley in 1900. (Photo: East African Railways.)

9.D Nakuru sixty years after the railway arrived at the open grassland of the previous picture. (Photo: Camera Press Ltd.)

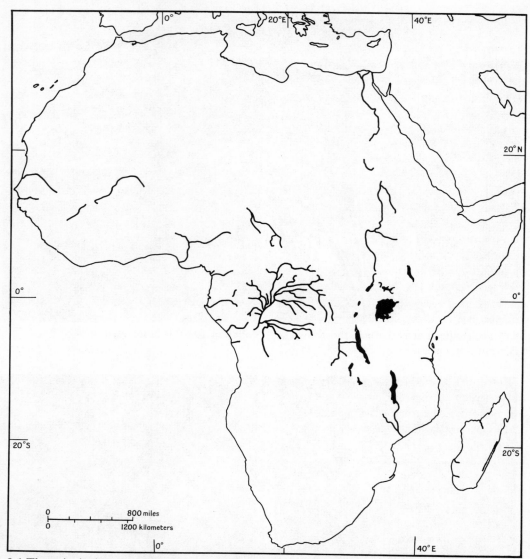

9.1 The principal navigable waterways of Africa. This map shows in dramatic fashion how the navigable stretches of waterway are isolated by falls and rapids or other obstructions so that no river affords penetration deep into the continent.

tional African ones — and the commercial opening up of Africa awaited the railroad? This is still largely true for such heavy commodities as minerals, though the truck and automobile have added greater flexibility and extended the range reached from a railroad. Sarraut[3] records that

[3] A. Sarraut *La mise en valeur des colonies françaises*. Paris: Payot, 1923.

during World War I the French needed to transport 4200 tons of cereals in the Ivory Coast. It took 125,000 porters 2,500,000 working days, with an incalculable loss in cultivation as a result!

THE CAPE TO CAIRO RAILWAY

Most of the continents have had their great railway romances. The destinies of

California and of British Columbia were both in the balance before the forging of the railway links which bound them to the East, and the concept of the railroad as a unifying as well as a civilizing influence was uppermost in the minds of the great empire builders before the automobile and air age. The idea of a through railroad from Cape Town to Cairo is associated especially with the name of Cecil John Rhodes—scholar, financier, statesman, dreamer, philanthropist. Born in England in 1853, he was never a strong lad, and at 16 he went to Natal to join his brother on a plantation to lead an open-air life. Within a few months the brothers joined in the diamond rush to New Rush, afterwards named Kimberley, and by subsequent financial organization of South African gold and diamond mining companies Cecil Rhodes was able to build up a vast personal fortune with which he set out to turn his dreams into reality.

By long tradition the territories of the old British Empire, now the Commonwealth, had been colored red on political maps, and it has been said that it was

Rhodes' ambition to "paint the whole of Africa red." He saw Africa on the road to progress and prosperity under the British flag. First he desired the union of South Africa and so, in 1881, he entered the Cape parliament. He was largely responsible for extending control over Bechuanaland in 1884–1885. He became prime minister of the Cape in 1890. At the same time he was chairman and virtual dictator of the chartered British South Africa Company (founded 1888), which, after the manner of the famous old chartered companies such as Hudson's Bay and East India, acquired, developed, and ruled the vast heart of Africa which became known as Rhodesia, now the Republics of Rhodesia and Zambia. In his other sphere of interest he endowed the Rhodes Scholarships to permit students from the United States and the British Commonwealth to study at Oxford University. He saw many of his hopes dashed by the Boer War in 1899–1902. He died on March 26, 1902, two months before the war came to an end.

The two maps (Figure 9.2) reproduced

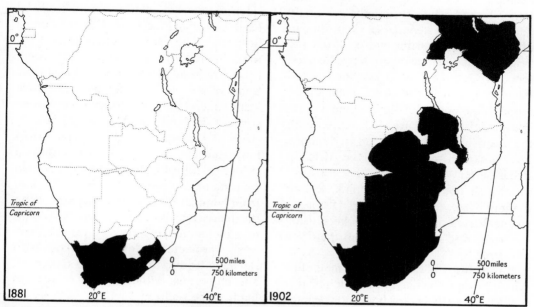

9.2 British territory in Africa in 1881 and in 1902. The plan for a "Cape to Cairo" railroad was a component in the British expansion in Africa during the nineteenth century.

here show the British sphere in southern Africa in the year 1881, when Rhodes entered parliament, and at the close of 1902, the year in which he died.

What of the Cape to Cairo railway? By 1885 it had reached Kimberley; five years later the territory in which Kimberley is situated (Griqualand West) had become part of Cape Colony. In 1885 a British protectorate was established over Bechuanaland, and during 1896–1897 the railway was constructed right through Bechuanaland to reach Rhodesia. Rhodes had obtained a mineral concession from the chief Lobengula covering the whole of Zambesia (Zambia and Rhodesia) in 1888, which was thus proclaimed a British sphere of influence the same year. Lobengula's kraal was on the site of the modern Bulawayo.

In 1905 the Victoria Falls Bridge was opened, and Zambia (then Northern Rhodesia) was linked directly with Cape Town. Construction continued across the territory to the mining area of Katanga on the border of the Congo and so to Kukama on the navigable Congo system, reached in 1918. By this time the automobile had come to supply the really flexible link, and steamer services filled in other gaps. Before the end of 1902, the year in which Rhodes died, only the existence of German East Africa interrupted the red on the map from the Cape of Good Hope to the border of Egypt, then a nominal vassal of the Turkish Empire. With the grant by the old League of Nations Mandate of former German East Africa to Britain after World War I, that territory became, if not red, at least pink. Before the outbreak of World War II tourist agents were issuing through tickets, using rail, road, and water links from the Cape to Cairo.

It is an irony of history that a major link which extends the line of rail much further on its way north, is now being constructed in a spirit of revulsion against the government of Rhodesia and much of what Cecil Rhodes stood for. This is the TanZam railway from Kapiri Mposhi in Zambia (formerly Northern Rhodesia) to Dar es Salaam. A change of gauge is involved, but this connects with the East African system which reaches into northwestern Uganda at Arua. With the Sudan Railways now as far south as Wau, another gap is narrowing, albeit to some 375 miles (600 km).

RAILROADS TODAY

New railroads are still being built in Africa and they are being constructed largely to serve the same purposes as those that already exist. Africa is part of the "developing world" and there is much to do before the transport infrastructure will be adequate for the expanded economy and greatly increased standard of living to which end so much effort is being expended.

The clearest case for a new railroad is one to serve a new mine. The exploitation of a mineral deposit necessarily involves calculations of the estimated life of the line, the labor and capital required, and the transport which will be needed (considering over how many years it could be used and what size freight charges could be borne). This enables firm commitments to be entered into upon which the feasibility of a railroad can reasonably be gauged. Some of the earliest lines built in Africa were mineral lines and today they include some of the largest and most rapidly constructed. Examples are the 419 miles (674 km) from the iron ore of Fort Gouraud (F'derik) to Port Etienne (Nouadhibou) in Mauritania or the 170 miles (274 km) from Nimba to Buchanan in Liberia. With the increasing pace of mineral exploitation, including the entry of Japanese interests, projected developments, with railways leading from them to the coast, are numerous, although some are less likely to be realized than others.

Harder to estimate are the likely returns on railroads built to aid general development, i.e., to improve the accessibility of regions of potential agricultural surplus. Building a railroad into an area of peasant farming permits the marketing of cash crops but does not inevitably lead to their production, or to the quantity and quality required. The whole process of agricultural improvement has still to take place. This involves research into crops suitable for the locality, consideration of the pests found there, the introduction of new cultivation techniques and fertilizers, a marketing system, and the diversion of effort from subsistence farming. Even when such commercially orientated activity has been stimulated, it is not uncommon for the most profitable part of the new traffic to be taken by road.

An instructive combination of the initial stimulus offered by a mineral deposit and the unsatisfactory agricultural response to a new railroad is offered by the western extension of the East African Railways from Kampala to Kasese (Uganda). The government had long wished for such a line to open up an area which was making little contribution to the national expansion. This was finally made possible by the decision to work the copper deposits on the eastern flank of Ruwenzori. The anticipated development of agriculture along the line of the rail however was very slow in arriving and when it did it was largely served by trucking into Kampala.[4] Nevertheless, the present prosperity of Kampala and the areas to the east could hardly have been realized without the construction of the Uganda Railway over forty years ago. Certainly there remains a case for extending railroads into densely settled agricultural areas or to areas of known high potential, provided that they require the long haul to a port or other internal markets for which rail is competitive with road haulage. The railroad to Kano in northern Nigeria made possible the great output of groundnuts and cotton,

so important to the economy of the country, and it is hoped that similar effects may follow from the 400 miles (644 km) of line to Maduguri.

We have stressed the part played by strategic considerations in the construction and alignment of African railroads from their beginning. They enabled the colonial powers to administer territory and convince their rivals that they were in effective occupation of the area claimed. Political considerations still loom very large in plans for future railroads. One of the major problems of the independent states which have succeeded the colonies is to create a sense of national unity and identity out of a portion of Africa which had a boundary flung around it as a result of the "partition." The precise extent to which such political judgments are involved is hard to tell. Thus, in the Cameroun, the short extension from Mbanga in the French-speaking province to Kumba, the main town of the English-speaking province, was an obvious political necessity. The completion of the Trans-Cameroun railway from Yaoundé to Ngaoundere, on the other hand, while providing access to the potential of Adamaoua Plateau, would also form an axis around which this curiously shaped and unintegrated country could be consolidated. The political motivation for the railroad connecting Zambia and Tanzania has been mentioned, and a similar connection, also to be built with Chinese assistance, was to have been made between Mali and Guinea (before a change of Government). The negative influence of politics can be seen in the closure for three years of the railroad linking Kayes with Dakar because of disagreement between Mali and Senegal.

Despite this new construction it remains true that the predominant alignment of African railways is as isolated units extending inland from a port. This reflects the historical fact of the entry of the rail-builders from overseas but, more fundamentally, it reflects economic ac-

---

[4] A. M. O'Connor, *Railways and development in Uganda* (Nairobi: Oxford University Press, 1965) pp. 51–87.

tualities. The different regions of Africa have less to offer each other in the way of trade then they have to offer the rest of the world, particularly the industrial nations, and it is from such countries that manufactured items, including the capital goods required for development, are imported. The only relatively dense railroad networks exist in South Africa and in the Maghreb, part of a more commercial and industrial economy. In 1900, Algeria had the densest and most mature network of railways in Africa but since 1920 many minor lines have been removed. The competition of the truck, bus, and airplane has been effective here as elsewhere in the world and some African countries now have less railway mileage than formerly. The two principal lines of the East African system, inland from Mombasa and from Dar es Salaam, are now connected and the TanZam railroad will extend this further. There is no sign however of any desire (or, indeed of any need) to link up the railroad systems of, for example, Ivory Coast, Ghana, Togo, Dahomey, and Nigeria (Figure 9.3).

ROADS IN AFRICA

Speaking in general terms, the importance of the surfaced all-weather road did not come to be appreciated until the growth in use of the automobile, and particularly the truck and motor bus, after World War I. Prior to that time reliance was placed essentially on the railroad for the "opening up" of territories. There is an interesting example of the road pioneer who was before his time in the story of the "Stevenson Road" planned by James Stevenson, a Glasgow business man and one of the founders of the African Lakes Corporation in 1878. It was designed to link Lake Nyasa (at Karonga) with the southern end of Lake Tanganyika near Abercorn and so to make river–road communication possible from the mouth of the Zambezi to the north of Lake Tanganyika.

At the same time another Glaswegian, William Mackinnon, was attempting to build roads from Dar es Salaam to Lake Tanganyika and from Mombasa to Lake Victoria. William McGowan, a young engineer who went to survey and assist in the construction of the Stevenson road, has left an interesting diary kept from his arrival at Quelimane in 1884.[5] The road was never finished. The railway from Beira via Blantyre to Lake Nyasa superseded the proposed use of the Zambezi, whereas Lake Tanganyika was reached at Kigoma direct by rail (begun in 1905) from Dar es Salaam in 1914.

Before considering the impact of roads and their provision in Africa, however, we should ask, what is meant by a road? In remote areas what is referred to as a road may be merely the route followed by an occasional landrover—which raises the question: how often must a landrover follow the same tracks through the bush before a track becomes a "road"? Such simple earth roads or tracks are acceptable for infrequent use (provided the rains are not too severe) preferably by a four-wheel-drive vehicle or at least by one with a high clearance; however, the running costs of vehicles on such tracks are high. The tracks are frequently unusable because of rain, and they cannot take much traffic, but since they involve very little or no construction or maintenance they form a relatively dense network in many of the drier savanna areas.

Of greater economic significance are the gravel roads which in most countries form the largest mileage of official "road." Throughout much of the tropical areas these are surfaced with laterite (known as "murram" in East Africa) which fortunately is widespread and forms a very convenient road material. With drainage ditches and simple roadworks and bridges, this is the standard "all-weather road," which implies that the road is

[5] *Scot. Geog. Mag.*, LIX (1943) pp. 31–36.

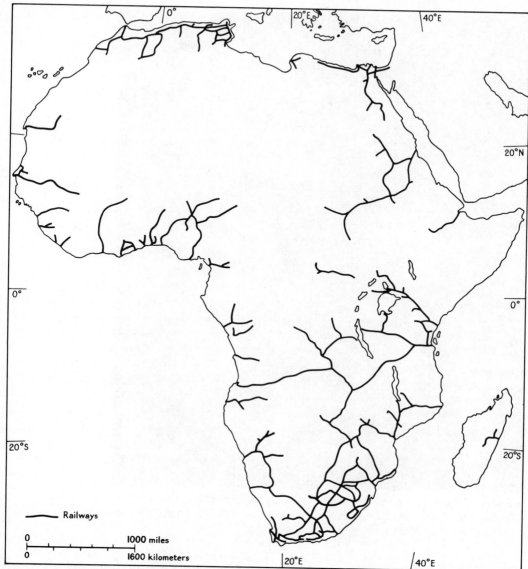

9.3 The railway network of Africa.

unlikely to be impassable on more than a few days in a year. Construction costs are low but, with an increasing volume of traffic maintenance costs rise rapidly; at a rate of about three-hundred vehicles a day it is generally considered more economic to lay a bitumen surface. It is these gravel roads which under pneumatic tires and spring suspension systems develop the notorious corrugations at right angles across the roads ("washboard roads") but,

if they are well maintained, the running costs of vehicles on laterite is reputed to be only slightly higher than on bitumen. With the general increase in traffic and the need to provide a more reliable surface, the mileage of hard-surface (bitumen or concrete) road is increasing rapidly. Much research has gone into reducing the costs of their construction by such techniques as "soil stabilization." The temptation is not always resisted, however, of permit-

9.E Muddy conditions on a Nigerian road. Many of the roads of Africa are still without a hard surface and are liable to become impassable during the rainy season. (Photo: J. Allan Cash.)

ting economical, light-construction roads to be used by heavy vehicles which soon break up the surface. A bitumen road which has broken up is more expensive to repair than one of laterite.

Whichever standard is used, roads are an essential investment for development. It has been estimated in Borneo that every mile of road into a previously uninhabited region opened up 250 acres of cultivable land. More typically, however, roads are improved or extended into areas already producing crops or livestock to lower the costs of exporting or reaching internal markets. Government investment can be

much smaller if farms are large or if there are big estates and plantations. Many of the roads will be on the farms or "estate roads," and plantations may have the resources and find it worthwhile to construct roads beyond their borders to link up with a main highway. In areas of peasant production, all the roads become a public charge.

Roads are, of course, essential for more than agriculture. In addition to the obvious needs of domestic industry, a number of projects are now classed as "tourist highways" to serve what in some countries is the fastest growing sector of the economy. These include the roads to and between the game parks of East Africa. In rapidly urbanizing centers, adequate roads can help to keep down the cost of food in the towns and lessen social distress and potential political unrest—and even keep labor costs competitive. As with the railways, noneconomic considerations are also involved, especially to assist the unification of the nation and to increase the accessibility of the capital from all regions. Regrettably, military strategic requirements remain.

The advantage of investing in roads rather than railways is that governments can provide merely the highway, leaving private enterprise to invest in trucks and buses. Operating a one-vehicle road haulage business is a particularly suitable way of acquiring management and entrepreneurial skills in a developing country. Although the government does not get back direct returns on its investment, this lack of receipts is attractive to national planning authorities because it is more difficult to prove that investment in a road has not been justified, than it is to prove it of a railroad. (Although the World Bank has established criteria, they are less blatant than a deficit on the railroad's annual account.)

AIR TRANSPORT

The pattern of air transport grew up during the colonial period with a strong emphasis on routes to and from the metropolitan country and with little connection between French- and English-speaking countries or between East and West Africa. Although the majority of the traffic is still to and from Europe, direct flights to America, on the one hand, and to India and the East on the other, are now well established. The network of routes within Africa is thus becoming more dense but the difference between the smaller and the more important airports is becoming greater. Those which were principally "staging points" have declined relatively (Benina, Wadi Halfa, Kano). Portugal still maintains "cabotage" routes with its overseas territories. (Cabotage routes are internal to a country—or empire—reserved to national operators, and not open to international competition or

9.F Dry rivers which suddenly flow during the rains are another road hazard, seen here in Turkana, Kenya. The landrover and similar vehicles have greatly improved communications in developing areas. (Photo: J. Allan Cash.)

9.G A steamer on the river Congo, typical of many African river services. (Courtesy United Nations.)

regulation.) Among the passenger traffic the growing importance of tourism should be noted. The European holiday maker is extending his range from the northern side of the Mediterranean to the southern, the African side. The next step is across the Sahara into the tropical world, where a beginning has been made in East Africa. The growth of this traffic is likely to be associated with an increase in holiday-taking during the European winter. The ever-increasing freight traffic includes the trade in fresh vegetables and fruit to the big cities of Europe, particularly of produce from the Kenya highlands being flown from Nairobi to London and Frankfurt, but also from the Ivory Coast to Paris.

PORTS AND SHIPPING

Ports are especially important in Africa because it is through them that the long isolation of the continent south of the Sahara was broken down, and much of the current economic development depends upon a healthy and growing overseas trade. It was estimated that in 1965 only 6 percent of the international trade of the African states was across land frontiers. Most of the markets for African goods are in the industrialized nations and it is from them that the flow of capital goods for development schemes derive. Expanding economies also give rise to rapidly increasing demands for oil imports. This concern with international, long-distance trade partly explains the lack of any voluminous coastal traffic. On the east coast, the dhow and schooner traffic, trading directly to the Persian Gulf and India, is dying out and trade is being concentrated on the principal ports. The concentration along this coast is being achieved by trucks rather than by a coasting trade.

The myth that the whole of Africa is deficient in good natural harbors is still sometimes propounded. This myth is probably derived from the fact that some of the first European contacts (and a long period of subsequent trade) took place along those parts of the West African coast which happen to have a smooth coastline, pounded by surf. This is the stretch between Ivory Coast and Nigeria and for this area the generalization is true, but it is of questionable significance. Some of the most active ports of tropical Africa including Abidjan, Takoradi, Tema, and Lagos are now located in this area. These rely heavily on artificial constructions replacing earlier surfports. Other parts of West Africa, such as the deeply indented coast between Senegal and Sierra Leone, are well supplied with harbor sites, and the same is true of the Maghreb and much of South Africa. The eastern side of Africa has many excellent sites, typically derived from drowned inlets protected by raised coral reefs.

In the development of these ports and their relationship with their hinterlands political considerations have frequently been important. The divorce between the port of Bathurst in Gambia and its "natural" hinterland in much of Senegal is very apparent, as is the curious route of the railroad from Fort Gouraud (F'derik) to Port Etienne (Nouadhibou), in Mauritania. Some English writers of the colonial period noted that the fine British port of Freetown was cut off from serving a vast "natural hinterland" because of French

control of the interior. Meanwhile, French authors observed that the upper Niger valley, under French control, was cut off from a direct "natural outlet" at the bay of Freetown by British control of Sierra Leone and, as a consequence, it was necessary for the French to build a railway inland from the less satisfactory port of Conakry and then curve it eastward behind Sierra Leone to reach the Niger River. Similarly the development of the port of Assab in Ethiopia in addition to that of Djibouti, and the close spacing of Lomé, Cotonou, and Lagos is related to political boundaries. The landlocked states present their own problems of which those of Zambia (discussed elsewhere) exemplify the political, strategic, and commercial considerations involved.

A political event with far-reaching effects was the prolonged closing of the Suez canal following 1967. This transformed the Red Sea from one of the world's great ocean highways to a backwater and the shipping services to Red Sea and East African ports were curtailed. Following the closure, a "Cape deviation surcharge" was added to freight charges to Europe amounting to 50 percent for

9.H Unloading an automobile onto two surfboats. This illustrates the difficulties which were faced in handling modern cargoes along much of the West African coast before the construction of artificial harbors. (Copyright: L. Dudley Stamp.)

9.I Unloading surfboats on the beach at Accra, Ghana, before the completion of Tema harbor in 1961. (Courtesy B.O.A.C.)

Port Sudan and 15 percent for Mombasa and Dar es Salaam. Cape Town regained its role as a major port of call and with the increasing size of ships, especially bulk carriers of oil and ores, the commercial significance of the Suez Canal was lessened.

Commonly the ports themselves are of great political moment. Because they were once sites of entry for alien powers which established the boundaries of the modern state, they are often capital cities. This is so common that the exceptions point to special circumstances—the great antiquity of the Egyptian state (Cairo) or a location in the frontier zone of the Kenya Highlands (Nairobi). In South Africa, there are two capitals—one at the first point of entry (Cape Town) and the other the point of furthest penetration (Pretoria).

For the developing nations of Africa, ports are also particularly attractive sites for the location of new industries. An early stage in commercial evolution is the importation of machinery in parts, and the

9.J The harbor at Dar es Salaam, Tanzania. This is typical of numerous harbor sites of the east coast of Africa, formed from a lagoon behind a raised coral platform. (Photo: East African Railways and Harbours.)

point of entry is a very suitable place for an assembly plant. Similarly, the so-called import substitution industries generally need to import much of their raw material. If the home market is inadequate to support the new industry at an economic scale, by locating at a port, it may be possible to export sufficiently to build up production to an economic scale.

TRANSPORT AND TOURISM

The development of tourism, and the prosperity it can bring, is obviously related to the provision of transport. The modern period of tourism in Africa apparently began when the luxurious Mena House was built at Giza in Egypt so that Empress Eugenie of France, and other visitors, would have a suitable place to stay in 1869 when they came for the opening of the Suez Canal and a visit to the Sphinx and Pyramids. Other famous hotels became established in Cairo and there were regular tours from Europe to Cairo, Giza, and Luxor. By 1940 there were organized tours to several other parts of Africa as well but especially to the cities, mountains, and beaches of Morocco and Algeria, to the big game and national parks of East Africa, to South Africa, and to the spectacular Victoria Falls on the Zambezi river.

In tropical Africa, the first hotels and rest houses were built at seaports, to serve European administrators and visitors, and were added to inland centers when railways and roads reached them. Africans traditionally stayed with kinsmen or friends when they visited towns, but with the rise of commercial agriculture and urbanization many became customers for hotels and restaurants. The rise of airlines after World War II, and the growth of African cities preceding and following independence, led to a great increase in air travel, and a need for improved airports and hotels. This was also encouraged by the arrival of diplomatic corps and international civil servants in the new capitals. Many independent African countries, with new airways and hotels, began advertising for tourists. Instead of using steamships and railways, the new flow of tourists, with moderate means, came mostly by air and used buses or private cars for local transport. Traffic on the international airlines, originally mostly of European administrators, teachers, and technicians, changed with the times and came to include African diplomats, university students, and businessmen, as well as vistors on business or pleasure from other continents.

TRANSPORT AND DEVELOPMENT

We have spelled out the part played by the different forms of transport in the development of Africa. That investment in transport is essential if economic growth is to be achieved has been widely recognized in the development plans of many African countries. Between one-third and two-thirds of the government investment is commonly allocated to transport and, on a world scale, some 40 percent of the loans from the World Bank to the developing countries have been concerned with transport improvements.

Further Reading

Most studies on transportation in Africa deal with a part of the continent and often with only one of the forms of transport. These are listed in the bibliography.

PART **II**

The Countries and Regions of Africa

CHAPTER 10

Egypt and the Nile:

The United Arab Republic

Nearly every country in the world has its own individuality, but of Egypt it may be said that here is a country in many ways unique. Because it is unique, it is not in any sense typical of Africa. In population, Egypt is much larger than its neighbors (Libya to Iraq, and including Saudi Arabia), and it is inevitably the center of political gravity in the Near East. It has a strategic location between Europe and monsoon Asia on the one hand and between Asia and Africa on the other, and it is not solely dependent upon the functioning of the Suez Canal. Added to its remarkable environmental setting and its ancient history, such features mean that we find the United Arab Republic a country very distinct from the remainder of the continent of Africa.

THE UNITED ARAB REPUBLIC

Although the total area of the Republic of Egypt is recorded as being 386,198 square miles (1.0 million km²), the settled and cultivated areas comprising the Nile valley, the Nile delta, and the inhabited desert oases cover only about 13,500 square miles (35,000 km²)—less than a third the area of Pennsylvania. In its physical setting the whole of Egypt is part of the enormous desert belt stretching from the Atlantic shores across the whole of the North African continent and, interrupted only by the Red Sea, into Arabia and Iran. It is in fact one long oasis, 700 miles (1,100 km) from north to south, but only 10 to 15 miles (16 to 24 km) wide, except where it is enlarged towards its seaward end into the delta (Figure 10.1). If Egypt of the Nile is thus to be described as an oasis, it is a unique oasis where two factors, the annual flooding of the Nile and the alluvial soils which have been deposited by that river, combine to render the oasis not only unmatched in natural fertility but, as long as the traditional "basin cultivation" was practiced, having that fertility annually renewed.

Whether Herodotus, when he wrote of Egypt some 3000 years ago, was already quoting some previous authority, or

10.A The Nile valley in Upper Egypt at Thebes, Luxor. The air view shows clearly the rocky wall of the Nile valley and the desert which lies beyond. It is clearly impossible to extend the irrigated land shown in the foreground. At the foot of the cliffs is the temple of Queen Hatshepsut (Deir el Bahari) c. 1500 B.C. (Copyright Aerofilms Library.)

whether his *bon mot* was indeed original, it is to Herodotus that we commonly give credit for a statement which has perhaps been repeated more times than any other in geographical literature: that "Egypt is the gift of the Nile" (see Figure 10.2). However banal the statement may be, it remains eternally true. Thanks to the Nile, what would otherwise be a complete desert is a fertile and prosperous country with a history of human settlement unrivaled anywhere in the world.

Apart from a small and irregular amount along the Mediterranean fringe of the delta, Egypt receives practically no rain during the whole of the year.

The country as a whole falls quite simply into a number of physical divisions. The Nile itself runs between parallel lines of cliffs, in some places only 220 yards (200 m) wide, but normally a few miles apart. From the edge of the bounding cliff on the east, the Arabian Desert rises towards the shores of the Red Sea, culminating in a mountain range with peaks reaching between 4000 and 7000 feet (1200 and 2100 m). The drop to the Red Sea is sudden, and northwards, where the Red Sea narrows into the Gulf of Suez, the

rugged relief is continued in the peninsula of Sinai. By contrast, to the west of the Nile valley, the Libyan hills subside gently into the broad flat plain of the great Libyan Desert. In places the surface of this plain sinks in shallow, broad depressions in which are found a series of scattered oases. The Libyan Desert as a whole becomes lower in its general elevation from south to the north, and it is in the north that, locally over a considerable area, its surface lies below sea level before rising slightly into the Libyan Plateau, which itself overlooks the Mediterranean Sea in a low scarp. One depression in this western desert, lying near the Nile itself, is the famous oasis of El Faiyum, lying below sea level and in such a position that flood waters from the Nile can be directed into it. It is thus extensively cultivated and able to support a large population. Below Cairo the Nile divides into its distributaries which pass through the delta on their way to the Mediterranean. As previously noted, the shape of the Nile Delta is the capital Greek letter Δ (delta), and it may even be claimed that the word "delta" is one of the oldest geographical terms in existence.

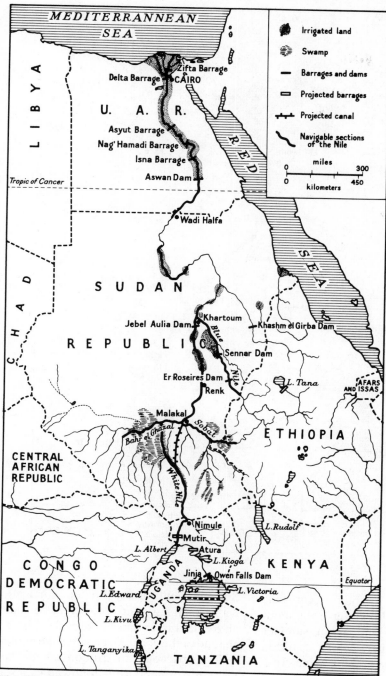

10.1 The Nile Basin.

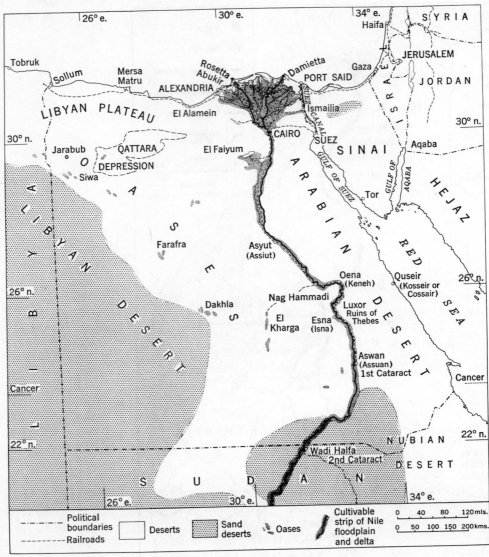

10.2 A general map of Egypt.

Climatically, the Egyptian year falls into two parts—a mild winter from about November to April and a hot summer from May to October, which is often ushered in by that scorching wind from the south known as the *khamsin*. As understood in midlatitudes, there is no spring and no fall. The virtual absence of the cyclonic disturbances which are so usual in midlatitudes results in a monotony of climatic conditions during most of the year; sudden variations in temperature are rare, except occasionally in winter.

Since agriculture depends upon irrigation water, man has control to a very considerable extent over times of harvest. There is the end of the cool season when the midlatitude crops come to fruition (*chetoi* harvest) in April and May, followed by a second (*nili*) harvest when subtropical crops are ready for gathering, in July and August. Despite the fact that Egypt is 700 miles (1100 km) from north to south, stretching over some 8 or 9 degrees of latitude, there is little difference in the main crops which can be grown throughout the country. We shall consider later in this chapter the regime of the River Nile in detail with its spectacular seasonal flood, coming between July and December — a natural phenomenon long unexplained, but recognized for 5000 years as the basis upon which cultivation and settlement depend.

HISTORICAL OUTLINE

Such in brief is the physical background of the country whose history recorded in substantial monuments from the past is longer and less interrupted than that of any other land. Although some writers distinguish Upper, Middle, and Lower Egypt, the time-honored division is Upper Egypt (broadly speaking, the Nile valley above Cairo) and Lower Egypt (the delta below Cairo).

It was Menes, the founder of the First Dynasty, who united Upper and Lower Egypt, and from that time to the present day, between six and seven thousand years, Egypt has remained a unit and under a single government, except for very brief periods. Although this unity may be explained by saying that Egypt is an oasis naturally isolated by sea and desert, it remains a remarkable fact. It is true that where irrigation has to be planned and executed in terms of the country as a whole, unified control is essential. It may also be said that once the foreign invader has braved the sea and the desert and reached the fertile oasis his task of conquest is easy, and no natural barrier remains to prevent his hold over the whole.

The oasis land which is thus Egypt has had another and most interesting effect upon its people. Though there are some slight differences between the people of the delta with somewhat lighter skins and the people of Upper Egypt, there is an essential unity among Egyptians in both their physical and mental characteristics. If one can judge from the representations of their ancestors in the days of the Pharoahs they have remained physically the same for thousands of years.

Through all these thousands of years of their history the Egyptian people have enjoyed, or perhaps one may say have suffered from, an essentially autocratic and highly centralized government. In Dynastic Egypt the Pharoahs were absolute rulers with a few carefully selected and autocratically appointed ministers. Their rule was absolute throughout the country. There was no tradition of local autonomy, no hereditary feudal aristocracy so general in other lands. It may be said that Egypt has known bureaucracy from its earliest days. The rank and file of the Egyptian people, the peasants (or *fellaheen,* of today) have thus always been subject to a strict, sometimes harsh and oppressive, government. The effect of this has been clearly assessed by Charles Issawi in his interesting book, *Egypt: An Economic and Social Analysis.* He suggests that " . . . the result has been greatly to weaken individualistic feeling and completely to uproot the spirit of municipal enterprise. Several millennia of centralized autocracy have accustomed the Egyptians to look to the government for the initiation of any business whatsoever. At the same time the rapacity of the governors has led to a proven distrust of the government, the effects of which are still unfortunately too visible. In addition to political oppression Egypt has always suffered from intense economic exploitation." He goes on to instance the enormous amount of human labor which must have gone into the erection of the pyramids and how at intervals even the long-suffering Egyptians attempted to unite in popular revolts.

The autocratic centralized government of Egypt has always, it may be said, been superimposed, and throughout practically the whole of their history the Egyptian people have been liable to foreign domination. In dynastic Egypt there was the invasion and the control of the country by the Hyksos or Shepherd Kings (1700 B.C.)

10.B The great temple at Abu Simbel on the Nile in Upper Egypt. The picture shows the work in progress in 1964 to raise the entire facade to the top of the cliff above the waters of Lake Nasser, impounded by the High Dam at Aswan. (Photo: Barnaby's Picture Library.)

from the heart of Arabia and also by Nubians from the south (c. 700 B.C.). Even if the Pharoahs of ancient Egypt are regarded as assimilating themselves with the people of the country which they ruled, and in that sense are regarded as Egyptians, they often chose foreign advisers to carry out their designs. The favorite Old Testament story of Joseph is a most interesting example. Because it was reported that Joseph, languishing in prison, was an able interpreter of dreams, the Pharaoh of the day had him brought forth, and because his interpretations of Pharaoh's dreams appeared authentic and carried conviction he was immediately made second only to Pharaoh himself in control of the whole country.

Complete outside control of Egypt definitely came into existence with the Persian conquest in 525 B.C. The Persians, in turn, were ousted in 332 B.C. by the Macedonians under Alexander the Great, and in 30 B.C. the Romans took the place of the Macedonians. The varied interpretations which have been given to the story of Cleopatra, from Shakespeare to George Bernard Shaw, may serve to illustrate the relationship between Roman governors and Egyptian leaders. As the Roman Empire faded and Byzantium took its place, Egypt was left open to conquest by the Arabs, and to its lasting incorporation in the Moslem world. The Arabs acquired the country in A.D. 642 and controlled Egypt for two centuries, always from outside the country, from Medina, from Damascus, and from Baghdad. In A.D. 868 the first Turkish dynasty was established. Almost exactly a century later the Moslem Fatimite king—this time from the west—overran the country, but it was a Kurdish successor to the Fatimites who saved Egypt from the Crusaders. Although the country was conquered again by the Ottoman Turks in 1516, Egyptian rulers preserved their identity and acknowledged in a somewhat perfunctory way the nominal authority of the sultan of Turkey.

When Napoleon I turned his attention to Egypt and the French expedition of 1798 reached the country, Egypt was a poor, isolated, and neglected backwater of the Ottoman Empire. Its once prosperous trade, centered on the ancient port of Alexandria, had been ruined by the diversion of world trade routes from the Mediterranean to the Atlantic after the discovery and development of the Americas. Although the conquest of Egypt by Napoleon Bonaparte was itself ephemeral, it was the beginning of a new era in Egyptian development. It marked the return of Egypt into the sphere of European commerce and laid the foundation for the future role of Egypt in the life of the world around the Mediterranean Sea.

Napoleon was less interested in the internal development of Egypt and the restoration of the age-old agriculture of the country than he was in the possibilities of developing Egypt on a colonial model, its destiny being to supply such tropical products as cotton and cane sugar which could not be produced in the homelands of France herself, but which were of enormous importance in the Napoleonic French World Empire. The seeds were sown, and when, a few years later, the dynasty under Mohammed Ali (an Albanian) became established, Egypt herself went ahead, and more and more the economic prosperity of the country became linked with the expansion of cotton cultivation, the development of the delta, and commerce with Europe. Although Egypt remained nominally a part of the Ottoman Empire, the influence of the Sultan at Constantinople became less and less. Mohammed Ali himself, following the autocratic procedure of his innumerable predecessors, attempted to create an industrialized, closed, and state-controlled economy, and to expand Egypt so as to include part of the remains of the Ottoman Empire. But in the meantime European powers had come to have other interests in Egypt, and Mohammed Ali's plan was defeated by those European powers in 1841. This is another key date in Egyptian history.

It was Napoleon Bonaparte who, if he did not originate, brought to the fore the concept of a canal through the isthmus of Suez to link the Mediterranean Sea with the Red Sea and thus to provide a seaway from Europe to India and the Far East. As British interests in India expanded and were consolidated it was naturally they who would appear to have had the main interest in such a project. Actually British personnel of the great East India Company passing to and from Britain and India were taken by ship to Egypt, to the old port of Alexandria. They traveled by river boat up the Nile to a point above Cairo, where they transferred to desert caravans for the land passage across to the shores of the Red Sea, there to embark on the second sea stage of the journey to their Indian destinations. The ships of the old Peninsular and Oriental Steam Navigation Company (P. and O.) provided the means, and when any such route, however tedious and inconvenient, has become established, vested interests are unwilling to see such a radical change as would result from the construction of a canal and a through route. We deal below with the story of the Suez Canal, but, although the British even more than the French had become concerned with the destiny of the project, so essential to the development of easy communication from the home country to India and the Far East, the British government officially opposed the scheme!

In 1870 came the defeat of France by the Prussians, only one year after the opening of the Suez Canal. Britain, under the circumstances, felt that it was necessary to have control if not over Egypt herself at least over Egypt as part of the vital sea route to the east. The opportunity came in 1882 when the Egyptian ruler asked for Britain's help in quelling a nationalist revolt marked by antiforeign riots in Cairo and Alexandria.

From 1882 to 1914, although remaining nominally a vassal of the Turkish Empire, Egypt became in effect a British protectorate. British troops were stationed in the country to maintain order and in particular to guard the Suez Canal. With the outbreak of World War I in 1914, Turkey allied herself with Germany and thus became ranged on the side of Britain's enemies. Consequently on December 18, 1914, Egypt was declared a British protectorate. This was a wartime expedient, and the protectorate came to an end on February 28, 1922, when the sultan of Egypt became hereditary ruler and was proclaimed king on the fifteenth of March. From that date Egypt has been an independent state, and steadily the evidences of independence became more and more marked. Extraterritorial privileges enjoyed by European powers were abolished in 1937. Later, after the conclusion of World War II, when Egypt so nearly became a victim of German invasion,

British troops were withdrawn from Egypt. They left the quarters which they had so long occupied in Cairo, although a small number remained for guard duties along the Suez Canal.

Thus with the proclamation of the late King Fuad I as king in 1922, the dynasty established by Mohammed Ali became the recognized ruling house of Egypt. In 1952 a military group, focusing widespread discontent, forced the abdication of Fuad's successor King Farouk. Although for a year his infant son was nominally accepted as king, in 1953 a republic was proclaimed, and in due course the military leader, General Nasser, became president. By the time of his death in 1970, Gamel Abdel Nasser had become not only the dominant figure in Egypt but had also achieved a wider reputation as a supranational Arab leader.

In 1958 Egypt, Syria, and Yemen joined the United Arab Republic but Syria broke away again in 1961 and the federation with Yemen was ended. Subsequently a union with Libya and Sudan has been proposed.

THE POPULATION PROBLEM OF EGYPT

Few populations are as homogeneous throughout as the people of Egypt. This is to be expected from an existence over a long period within the Nile valley, separated by desert from other populations but within which communication was easy. The fundamental element is constituted by the *fellaheen,* or peasants. Moderately tall, slightly built, with long limbs and broad shoulders, and a pronounced nose, they are very strongly contrasted with their Negro neighbors to the south. The two distinctive physical types are clearly delineated in bas relief on the walls of the ancient monuments. Although there has undoubtedly been some mixture between the Arabs of the north and the Negroes of the south, this seems to have exercised but little influence on physical type, and still less on manners and customs. The habitation of the poorer *fellaheen* is still built as it was in the time of the Pharaohs of dried mud over a framework, a house often without any opening save the door, and the sole furniture of which is a chest for clothes, a low table, and a few cushions and mats. There is an advantage in the absence of other openings, for the smoke which accumulates within acts as a deterrent to the eternal plague of mosquitoes.

The *fellaheen* were converted to Islam, and consequently Egypt is a keystone in the great Moslem world. Next in importance is that element of the population represented by the Coptic Christians, descendants of those ancient Egyptians who adopted Christianity in the fourth century, and whose head is the Coptic Patriarch of Alexandria. They are grouped especially in Middle Egypt, around Asyut, which is sometimes called the Coptic Capital, and in the Faiyum. Unlike the *fellaheen,* who are almost exclusively farmers and who remain essentially dwellers in the country, the Copts have tended to drift into towns and become artisans, traders, merchants, and money lenders. Until recent times they often lived in walled and guarded enclosures, as in Cairo. Together with Greek Orthodox Christians they number well over a million.

These are the two essential elements in the indigenous population of Egypt as far south as Aswan. South of Aswan lies Nubia; the people of the valley are Nubians with some Negro affinities. There are besides half a million mixed Bedouin Arabs in the deserts of Lower Egypt, and pure Bedouins in the Nubian Desert.

The population of Egyptian towns is much more mixed. By the side of indigenous Egyptians there may be found Arabs, Nubians, Turks, Greeks, Syrians, Armenians, and especially that mixture of races so typical of the ports and bazaars of the eastern Mediterranean, commonly called Levantine. It is in the towns that the European communities are found. Historically the French, English, Belgian, and Italians have been most numerous.

In common with other countries of the Mediterranean the population of Egypt has shown a remarkable rise in the last century and a half. The French mission of Napoleon Bonaparte estimated the number in the whole country rather under $2\frac{1}{2}$ million people. In 1821 Mohammed Ali found a little over this figure—2,536,000. (Incidentally, Egypt is the only African country for which adequate and accurate population statistics exist over a considerable period.) In 1846 the population had reached nearly $4\frac{1}{2}$ million, in 1882 nearly 7 million; by 1927 this had doubled to $14\frac{1}{4}$ million. Since then the population has doubled again and by 1970 it had reached an estimated total of 33 million. This gives an average density for the "settled" area (excluding the deserts) of some 2400 per square mile (926 per km^2)—about a quarter of an acre per head (0.1 ha). This is more than can be supported and large imports of wheat and wheat flour are necessary. This rapid growth of population, currently of the order of 2.5 percent per year, means that strenuous efforts to increase the national product have had little success in raising the average standard of living. Yet the rate of population growth has declined slightly and there is increasing support for a policy of population limitation.

By contrast with tropical Africa, but more typical of North Africa and the Near East, a large proportion of the population live in towns, amounting to 38 percent at the census of 1960. Most of this is contained in Cairo and Alexandria. Together with its suburbs, the built-up area of Cairo has an estimated population of $5\frac{1}{2}$ million, by far the largest single city in Africa, and greater Alexandria numbers well over 2 million. Other towns are much smaller (e.g., Suez: 245,000 in 1960) but they are numerous as befits a highly organized

10.C Modern Cairo, with hotels and Radio Cairo building along the Nile.
(Photo: Eric Kay.)

society and long established commercial economy.

IRRIGATION AND AGRICULTURE

This large and dense population is sustained, as it has been for thousands of years, by an agriculture based on irrigation by the waters of the Nile. In its course through Egypt the Nile runs smoothly and evenly, usually nearer the eastern side of its valley. The river level falls slightly from January to May and June, when it reaches its lowest level. In July the water rises rapidly and continues to do so through August and September, reaching its highest point in Lower Egypt in the month of October, when it is normally $7\frac{1}{2}$ meters or about 25 feet above its low level of May–June. The level of the river then falls rapidly through November and December, more gradually through the succeeding months.

As in so many eastern countries, water can be lifted from the river, and equally from wells, by the *shadoof*, which consists of a bucket, or bag of skin, suspended from the end of a long pole balanced by a counterweight. By the shadoof water is commonly and easily raised 7 to 10 feet or more, and a succession of lifts may raise

water considerably higher. Another method of lifting water a short distance is the Archimedean screw, and the more elaborate types of lift operated by cattle or donkeys are still widely used, including the *saqia* or Persian waterwheel, although small mechanical pumps are now common. The traditional form of irrigation in Egypt, however, is basin irrigation. The waters of the river at the time of flood are led off into carefully constructed inundation or flood canals, from which the water passes into a basin where the flat field or fields are enclosed by low earth banks. These basins vary in size and may be anything up to 100,000 acres. The Nile waters at flood carry a reddish-gray silt, which is naturally deposited and left behind in the basins. Unbeknown to the ancient Egyptians, the slime or ooze to which Shakespeare refers is derived from far-away Ethiopia. It represents the results of natural geological as well as soil erosion from distant areas, and, since much of the silt is derived from areas of basic volcanic rocks, it is naturally rich in mineral salts.

The peasant sows his seed broadcast in the damp mud which is left when the waters are led off from one basin into the next. There follows for the cultivator a period of comparative rest until the harvest is ready. The grain which has been sown at the beginning of November is ripe by early February. Other plants, sown a little later or with a longer vegetative period, may not be ready until April or May. This is the natural winter harvest, known as the *chetoi*.

It happens naturally that the borders of the valley are too high to be covered by the river floods which inundate the basins. Water must be lifted to these higher fields by a shadoof, or a succession of shadoofs, or by other means. The water that is thus distributed is free from sediment, and it becomes necessary to fertilize the fields with such material brought to the spot as dung and organic debris from the villages. There is more work for the farmer, and he sows his seeds later; the harvest, in this case known as the *nili*, is also later.

The traditional crops of Upper Egypt, sufficient for feeding—and clothing—of a dense population, are cereals (wheat, barley, rice and maize, i.e. American corn) cotton, vegetables (beans, peas, lentils, onions), and especially lucerne or bersim for cattle. Grapes, date palms, and olives are perennial plants likewise made possible by irrigation.

It will be seen that such a system of basin irrigation is dependent upon the height of the flood, which fortunately in the case of the Nile is remarkably constant, and also on a system of cooperation between landowners, which will permit the development of a system of basins.

It was Mohammed Ali in the early part of the nineteenth century, following doubtless upon the lead given by the members of the French Commission, who saw the possibilities of a system of permanent irrigation by canals. The French were not interested so much in extending the existing production of traditional Egyptian crops as they were interested in securing from Egypt those products of warm climates which Europe needed, notably cane sugar and cotton. The concept of Mohammed Ali was that every peasant should have enough land to support himself and his family, which he calculated to be between a hectare and a hectare and a half, or $2\frac{1}{2}$ to 4 acres. Two factors made the materialization of such a partition of the land impossible. In the first place the Islamic law ordains that property shall be divided between all the heirs, and hence the subdivision of land. On the other hand, large-scale perennial irrigation is only possible under some unified system either of land ownership or land control. The question is so important that careful statistics have long been kept of land ownership.

As recently as 1948, 95 percent of Egyptian landowners were small holders with less than 5 acres of land but holding all together less than 35 percent of the cultivated land surface. By contrast, there were about 2000 landowners holding over 50 acres but totaling one-third of the whole. The Agricultural Reform Decree of September 1952 limited agricultural ownership to 200 feddans (207.6 acres) and by the end of 1959 about 350,000 acres had been distributed among 111,000 farmers.

The modern system of canal irrigation may be regarded as having begun with the construction of the delta barrage, at the head of the delta below Cairo, from 1861 onwards (replaced in 1942 by the great Mohammed Ali barrage). The barrage of Zifta was added to this system in 1901, and the year 1902 marked the completion in Upper Egypt of the great Asyut dam, followed in 1909 by the barrage at Esna (Isna) and still later, in 1930, by the dam at Nag Hammadi 150 miles above Asyut. The Nem barrage is used for a diversion dam as distinct from one for storage.

Although these various dams both increased the area of cultivable land during flood water and assured more abundant harvest, what was needed to provide water during the long dry period when the level was low was a reservoir along the southern border of Egypt. It was for this purpose that the great dam at Aswan was constructed. Completed in 1903 at an original cost of $15,000,000, it was successively enlarged in 1907, 1912, and 1933.

The ever-growing population, however, outgrew these improvements and massive imports of food became normal. To meet these needs and provide power for industrialization, the "High Dam" has been built a short way upstream. This has created a massive reservoir extending 310 miles (500 km) to the south and averaging 14 miles (22 km) in width. In so doing it has required the displacement of some 70,000 people both in Egypt and Sudan and involved the movement of the Sudanese town of Wadi Halfa. Many ancient monuments of the Nile valley have been totally submerged although the most famous of all, the giant statues of the rock temple of Abu Simbel have been raised, at great cost, above the waters. The stored water will enable another 1.3 million acres (525,000 ha) to be irrigated for the first time. Some of these will be marginal to existing irrigation along the lower valley and especially in the delta. It is planned also to irrigate a string of oases lying west and parallel to the Nile, known as the "New Valley." In addition, it will be possible to convert 700,000 acres (280,000 ha) from seasonal to perennial irrigation, giving two or more crops in the year. The total effect should be to increase agricultural output by 25 percent.

The planned output of hydroelectricity is immense—about 2 million kilowatts when fully operational. Some of this will be used for water pumps on the irrigated lands, while transmission lines already carry power to Cairo, 450 miles (725 km) away. Transmission losses are considerable and Aswan has obviously become an attractive industrial location for some branches of industry.

AGRICULTURAL PRODUCTS

In addition to providing most of the food for Egypt's millions, the intensively worked irrigated fields are also the source of the principal export, cotton. For many years, cotton accounted for between 60 and 70 percent of exports, but new categories of exports, especially rice and petroleum, are reducing this preponderance.

Two main types of cotton are grown, the long staple and the medium staple. For a long time the famous long-staple cotton with a silky luster ($1\frac{1}{2}$ inches staple) known as *sakellarides*, usually contracted to *sakel*, was recognized as being second in quality only to the famous Sea Island cotton of the West Indies. From 1935 onwards a new and heavier-yielding variety perfected at the experimental station at Giza, opposite Cairo, and consequently known as *Giza 7*, surpassed *sakel* both in acreage and yield. Other long-staple cottons have been produced, and the possibilities are by no means exhausted. The shorter-staple cotton, *cashmuni*, though of good quality, is not up to the standard of *sakel*. It is grown to some extent in Upper Egypt. A remarkable feature of cotton production in Egypt is the very high yield per acre. The average of between 400 and 500 pounds of ginned cotton per acre is still well above the average American figure, despite recent improvements, and more than five times that of the yield common in India.

Though spinning and weaving mills have been developed, mostly in Lower Egypt, the bulk of the crop is exported from Alexandria as raw cotton, particularly to the U.S.S.R., China, Japan, India, and the cotton-consuming industrial countries of Europe such as Czechoslovakia, Poland, and Germany. Formerly the largest customer was the United Kingdom.

It was the American Civil War which, by cutting off supplies to Europe, especially to Britain, was mainly responsible for the rapid development of the Egyptian cotton cultivation and export. Although the high quality of Egyptian cotton gives it a favored place on world markets, so great a reliance on an export liable to competition from synthetics is unfortunate.

Another major export is rice, of

growing popularity because of its high yields. It is particularly grown in the delta where it has the advantage of tolerating slightly saline soils. Smaller exports are made of onions and potatoes but the increased output of cane sugar has been absorbed by the home market.

The basic importance of the cereals for home consumption has been mentioned but, especially near the cities of Cairo and Alexandria, there is a marked specialization in the intensive production of vegetables. It is conceivable that these could be used for another export line aimed at the European market.

Over much of the cultivated area, however, the most extensive single crop is lucerne or *bersim,* grown to feed livestock and especially the bullocks and domestic buffaloes necessary for ploughing, transport, and raising water. (The field buffalo should not be confused with the wild and fierce Cape Buffalo of East and South Africa—a very different creature.) If these processes could be mechanized, a large area in total would be released to contribute more directly to domestic food production or to export crops.

THE EGYPTIAN ECONOMY

Although agriculture remains the largest single contributor to the national income and to exports, industry is rapidly gaining in importance, as is also the exploitation of minerals. By 1966–1967, 22 percent of the Gross Domestic Production was derived from mining and manufacturing. Of most immediate significance has been the discovery and exploitation of new oil fields. The loss of production from the Sinai fields following the June War of 1967 was quickly made up from fields on the western side of the Gulf of Suez, and from beneath its waters. Subsequently large fields were discovered west of the Nile, some of which are probably a continuation of those of Libya. This has converted Egypt from an importer to an exporter of oil. Other mineral deposits contributing to exports are manganese

and phosphates. There are hopes of greatly increasing the production of phosphates, both for export and for fertilizers for domestic agriculture, based on deposits at Wadi Jadid.

The completion of the Aswan Dam, which became fully operative in 1970, provided power for some major industrial projects. The largest of these is the Helwan steel complex, also being expanded with Soviet aid, to a capacity of 1.5 million tons. This will make Egypt the biggest steel producer in Africa outside of South Africa. It will use about one-tenth of the electrical output of the Dam. Other major producers are the superphosphate factory and a ferrosilicon plant. Most industrial employment, however, is in agricultural processing and smaller scale manufacturing of consumer goods. About 40 percent of all industrial jobs are to be found in Cairo.

Tourism has a unique resource base in the great quantity of spectacular and widely renowned ruins of antiquity and it has been a major source of foreign receipts since early in the nineteenth century. Cairo itself has more medieval structures, mosques, etc. than any other Arab city and has all the facilities, shops, museums, opera house, appropriate to one of the great cities of the world. Another source of invisible exports are the profits from the Suez Canal but these were interrupted by the war of 1967 and the conflicts following it. It was this military confrontation, however, which moved certain oil-rich states of the Arab world (Libya, Saudi Arabia, and Kuwait) to make grants-in-aid to Egypt.

THE SUEZ CANAL

So long as the world's commerce was focused on the countries around the Mediterranean Sea between Europe on the north, Asia on the east, and Africa on the south, the existence of the isthmus of Suez was mainly of importance as providing part of the land route between Egypt and its Asian neighbors, or from

10.D Traditional craft, *feluccas,* on the Nile at Aswan. Such transport along the Nile has unified Egypt over the millenia. (Photo: J. Allan Cash.)

10.E Iron ore barges at Esna on the Nile, carrying iron ore from Aswan to the steel works at Helwan. River transport on the Nile still has a part to play in modern Egypt. (Photo: Eric Kay.)

farther afield between the extremes of the Arab domains of the Middle Ages and the Turkish Empire which succeeded it. With the extension of European interest in India and the Far East, the isthmus became a barrier, interrupting the natural line of sea communications from the Atlantic seaboard and the Mediterranean to the Red Sea and the Indian Ocean. A glance at a physical map shows that the Gulf of Suez and equally the Gulf of Aqaba (Akaba) on the other side of the Sinai Peninsula are continuations of the system of rift valleys so marked throughout eastern Africa. From the head of the Gulf of Suez to the Mediterranean seacoast is less than 70 miles in a straight line. The land between is flat, at most only a few feet above sea level, and in part occupied by shallow salt lakes, known as the Bitter Lakes. It is not always realized that the Suez Canal as we know it today was not the first waterway to unite the Mediterranean with the Red Sea. The earlier idea, of course, was to link the heart of Egypt with the Red Sea at a time when the largest ships then in use were shallow built, using the lower branches of the Nile. Consequently a canal was constructed—a fresh-water canal, known as the Canal of the Pharaohs—leaving the Nile in the neighborhood of Heliopolis, following a course due east to the neighborhood of the modern Ismailia, whence it passed southwards to the Gulf of Suez near the present site of the town of Suez. In the days of the later Roman Empire, it fell into disuse, but was resuscitated in the days of the Arab domination, since the Arabs always had the great idea of trading between the Mediterranean and the East. The Ottoman Turks, seeking always to preserve the isolation of the Moslem world and to interrupt any means of communication between Christians and Moslems, abandoned the canal. With the discovery of the Cape route to India the former canal seems to have been completely forgotten.

When France, at the beginning of the sixteenth century, took the initiative for eastern development and exploration, and when Richelieu founded the *Compagnie Générale du Commerce,* the idea of a canal came under consideration. The idea remained, however, one of a route from Alexandria, using the Nile, and thence from the neighborhood of Cairo to the Red Sea. It was the struggle between the French and the British in the time of Napoleon Bonaparte which gave birth to the idea of a direct canal from the Mediterranean to the Red Sea in order to enable the French to wage war against England in Indian waters. Mohammed Ali, as in so many other things, took up the idea left him by Napoleon Bonaparte, and it is recorded that he referred to making "a Strait of Bosphorus in the Desert of Suez." (Figure 10.3.)

After the idea had been discussed for some 50 years it was the Frenchman, Ferdinand de Lesseps, who brought the plan to realization, securing the approval of Napoleon III and the support both of the Turkish sultan and of the Egyptian ruler, Mohammed Said, successor to Mohammed Ali. Britain under Prime Minister Palmerston opposed the whole scheme. But the *Compagnie Internationale Maritime de Suez* was formed, with a capital of 200 million francs.

The Canal was constructed rapidly from 1860–1869, and on November 18, 1869, a flotilla of 68 ships carrying the Empress Eugenie of France, the Emperor Francis Joseph of Austria, the Khedive of Egypt, and many other dignitaries passed through the Canal and inaugurated it, after it had received both a Christian and Moslem blessing. It is interesting that the British themselves played no part, other than one of opposition, in a project afterwards of greater importance to them than to any other country. The original shareholders in the Suez Canal Company included the Khedive of Egypt. Knowing that the Khedive was particularly hard up for funds and anxious to dispose of his holding, the British Premier Disraeli (afterwards Lord Beaconsfield) in 1875 made an instantaneous and personal deci-

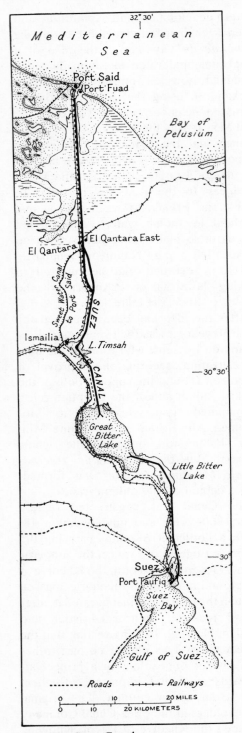

10.3 The Suez Canal.

sion to acquire the Turkish holding on behalf of the British government. He borrowed $20,000,000 in the name of the Cabinet and presented the British Parliament with what was virtually a *fait accompli*. Had it not been for this bold stroke of an individual, the opportunity would doubtless have been lost by which the British government held 295,026 shares out of a total issued of 652,932 and had three representatives on the governing board of 32. The concession granted to the Suez Canal Company was for 99 years from the date of inauguration; hence it was due to expire on November 17, 1968. However, on July 26, 1956 President Nasser proclaimed the nationalization of the Suez Canal Company. It was clear that Egypt, by excluding Israel, would no longer observe the convention of 1888, whereby the canal was open equally to vessels of all nations. Britain and France landed troops to protect their interests, but this show of force was not fully endorsed by the British people or by Britain's allies, and the troops were withdrawn. In 1958 Egypt agreed to pay £28 million in compensation to the shareholders of the Suez Canal Company, spread over a period of years. In 1959 the World Bank granted a loan of U.S. $56.5 million for the general improvement of the Canal. This aimed at widening and deepening the canal to allow the passage of ships of 55,000 tons and speeding their passage by lining the banks and constructing some lengths of twin canal. Further plans were announced in 1966 to allow ships of up to 100,000 tons to pass through. With the occupation of Sinai by Israel in June 1967, however, the canal was closed, trapping some ships in transit, and in the absence of dredging, silting began.

The effect of the closure of the Suez Canal was not so great as had been expected. It had long ceased to be a key link in the communications of the British Empire, particularly between Britain and India. More important had become the flow of oil from the Persian Gulf to

Europe. However, the increasing size of tankers was causing anxiety, hence the need for improvements. Subsequent to the closing of the Canal, supertankers were introduced, and it is inconceivable that they would be able to use any foreseeably enlarged canal except in ballast. Ore carriers are developing towards comparable dimensions. The decline of empire, the increasing size of bulk-carrying ships and the switch of passenger traffic from ships to aircraft have lessened the world reliance upon the Suez Canal. Its closure affected some naval dispositions and increased shipping charges especially from Europe to the Red Sea and East African ports, but the excitements of 1956 were not repeated in 1967.

THE REGIONS OF EGYPT

For a consideration of the country as a whole, we may regard Egypt as divided into: the Western Deserts (Libyan Desert); the Eastern Deserts (Arabian and Nubian Deserts); the Nile valley, or Upper Egypt; the Nile delta, or Lower Egypt; the Faiyum. The two great desert tracts represent 97 percent of the surface of the country but have less than 2 percent of the population.

The Western Deserts (Libyan Desert). The plateaus which make up the greater part of the surface of the country consist, in the extreme southwest, of the ancient metamorphic rocks and granites of the great African Massif. These are covered, as we proceed northward, by gently inclined sheets of sediment, giving rise, as a result of weathering, to great flat-topped, table-like hills or mesas. The sedimentary rocks dip gently northward, but at a slightly higher angle than the surface of the country, so that geologically the beds become younger and younger as one goes towards the Mediterranean. North of the southern outcrops of ancient rocks are found the wide stretches of Nubian sandstone, then northward wide expanses of limestone. This explains the essential

structure of the Libyan Desert to the west of the Nile valley. In the south the surface is covered with superficial deposits of sand. It is one of the least habitable parts of the whole Sahara, avoided by nomads and caravans alike, no oasis relieving its arid surface, no settlement of significance existing.

The northern portion of the Libyan Desert formed by the lower plateau surfaces of limestone is relatively more habitable. A long line of oases, shown in Figure 10.2, occupies the depressions over a distance of 600 miles (966 km). There are numerous salt lakes, but in places wells reach fresh water. Where this is the case the oases can support populations which run into the thousands. The oasis of Dakhla, for example, has at least 15,000 people and a permanent capital town with as many as four mosques. Development schemes based on drilling for water from deep aquifers have had some success but

10.F Water from a bore hole in the Western or "Libyan" Desert. (Photo: Monitor.)

the natural reservoirs are not being re-plenished as freely as some had hoped, and the water levels have been falling. More ambitious is the "New Valley" project which visualizes the diversion of Nile waters from Lake Nasser, behind the Aswan High Dam, into the oases of Kharga and Dakhla. Between the actual oases several nomadic tribes contrive to find sufficient pasture for their camels and provide means of transport for the oasis inhabitants. It is one of the great features of life in the Islamic world that the pilgrimage to Mecca demands movement, and even these remote oases supply their quota of pilgrims for the sacred journey. Catering for pilgrims is one of the great occupations throughout Islam. Thus these oases of the northern Libyan Desert are linked by a regular and frequented route, leading particularly to the capital.

Into this harsh environment has moved a new population dependent upon neither oases nor camels. The sedimentary rocks were found to contain oil and the first two fields to be exploited—at Alamein and Umbaraka—were sufficiently productive to allow exports to begin.

The Eastern Deserts (Arabian and Nubian Deserts). To the east of the Nile, to which the Sinai Peninsula is naturally attached, the desert tract between the Nile and the sea is relatively narrow, but its surface is much more varied than to the west, and the country has in places considerable natural resources. The mountain belt, partly of volcanic origin, which borders the shore of the Red Sea is continued along both sides of the trough or rift valley of the narrow Gulf of Suez, and so into the southern part of the Sinai Peninsula. As any voyager by ship down the Gulf of Suez is able to recognize, the arid shore is far from hospitable. Actual access to the shore is rendered dangerous by coral reefs, so that there is no port between Suez, the southern end of the Suez Canal, and the little harbor of Quseir or Cossair. Here and there in little basins amid the rugged sandstone or basalt mountains are

agricultural villages; and along the south there is an inhabited trench, the depression of Keneh, lying between the volcanic belt and the true Arabian Desert.

In the Peninsula of Sinai the desert plateau fades northeastwards into the Negev or Israeli desert, inhabited by a few nomadic pastoralists. In the southwestern parts of the peninsula, along the shores of the Gulf of Suez and the Red Sea, there are little cultivated basins among the rocky mountains and numerous fishing villages. The Peninsula of Sinai is indeed a land of transition. The east looks to and fades into Asian lands, the west looks towards and is dependent upon Egypt proper.

The eastern deserts of Egypt and the Peninsula of Sinai are not without economic significance. There are precious stones, also the famous turquoise, some deposits of phosphate rock and nitrate, and the small but significant oil fields which have long been worked along the western shores of the Gulf of Suez. To this must be added the larger oilfields discovered from 1949 onwards at Sudar, Asl, and elsewhere in the peninsula and the more recently exploited offshore Morgan field, beneath the bed of the Gulf itself. There are salt deposits, too, and from the mountains of the Arabian Desert Egypt obtained and still obtains some of those magnificent building stones (porphyry, granite, and sandstone) used in Egypt's famous monuments dating from the time of the Pharaohs, though the most famous of all is the pink granite of Aswan.

The Nile Valley or Upper Egypt. This valley is the *Khem* (signifying "dark") of the Egyptians, a name which points the contrast with the white shimmering desert stretches on either side. The Nile is navigable throughout Egypt as far south as the town of Aswan at the First Cataract. The navigable Nile is paralleled also to Aswan by the main railway. Here are both the old Aswan Dam and the new High Dam above which the vast reservoir of Lake Nasser carries a regular service to the town of Wadi Halfa, just inside the Sudan Republic. Wadi Halfa is the northern terminus of the Sudan Railways running to Khartoum and Port Sudan. Above Aswan begins the ancient land of Nubia.

Upper Egypt consists of a succession of irrigated basins marked off from one another by those points where the two clifflike walls of the river valley approach close to one another. Those who distinguish a Middle Egypt regard Upper Egypt as stretching as far northwards as the Thebes Basin. This basin, the ancient site of Thebes, was perhaps the richest of all the basins of the Nile valley in ancient times, and it was around it that the Middle Empire developed. The incredible richness in ruins of temples and palaces of this part of the Nile valley, at Thebes, at Karnak, and at Luxor in particular, is lasting evidence of ancient glories. At the present day the ancient system of basin irrigation has been almost completely replaced by perennial irrigation from the Aswan dam. This area has become the principal region of cultivation of the sugar cane and the site of the principal sugar factories, a part of the new prosperity of modern Egypt.

On the whole the valley widens northwards and is lined by a succession of towns and large villages, among which one may regard Asyut as the chief of this very rich region of Middle Egypt.

The Nile valley stretches as far as Cairo (Figure 10.4). Curiously enough, Cairo has been the capital of Egypt only since 1863, unless one regards Cairo as merely the resiting of ancient Memphis after the Moslem conquest. The fact that Cairo has become the heart of Egypt is due to the economic development of the delta in the past century and a half. From the point of view of modern Egypt, Cairo is perhaps

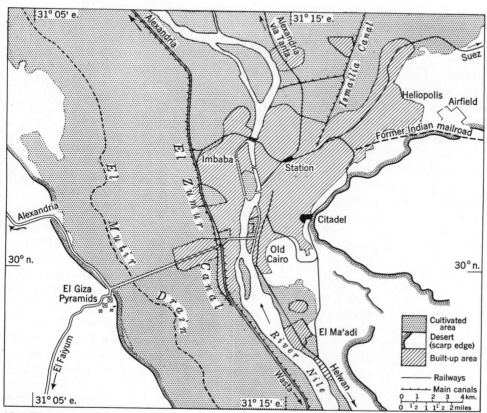

10.4 The site of Cairo.

the most rationally situated capital in the world. Its predecessor, Memphis, was on the western or left bank of the Nile, nestling under the low limestone cliff on which were built the great pyramids and the Sphinx. In contrast, Cairo originated on the right or eastern bank of the river, on or below a projection of the desert plateau. There the Arab conqueror of Egypt, 'Amr, built a mosque on the site of the former Roman citadel. To the Arab town was added later the Turkish town, the citadel built by Saladin and, in due course, the Levantine town built by Mohammed Ali and his son. For centuries, Cairo has been a major cultural center of Islam and today it contains numerous universities and publishing houses besides, for example, the headquarters of the Arab League. The modern cosmopolitan city of Cairo has extended from the foot of the hills, across the alluvial plain, to the Nile itself, and its suburbs have crossed over the river to the western side and now stretch all along the road from Cairo to the pyramids, displacing the cultivation of the Nile alluvium.

The Nile Delta or Lower Egypt. The area of the delta is double that of the Nile valley or Upper Egypt. If, therefore, the whole could be placed under cultivation it would play a dominant part in the Egyptian economy. Whereas Upper Egypt, the Nile valley, has a history of cultivation going back for thousands of years, the final conquest of the delta is the result of the comparatively modern activity of man, armed with the knowledge and the tools of science. For a long time the outer delta of the Nile was simply an immense area of sand, traversed by the seven branches of the river, two of them reasonably navigable, interrupted by long lagoons, or land periodically flooded or impregnated by salt. Ancient Egypt used only the inner delta lands. The outer delta in fact remained a desert barrier between Upper Egypt and those centers of commercial activity, the ports of Alexandria, Abukir, Rosetta, and Damietta. The branches of the river were the commercial routes which linked the Mediterranean ports with Egypt proper. Today modern perennial irrigation and the drainage of marshes and lagoons have made the delta the principal economic region of Egypt, with cotton as the chief cash crop and rice becoming more important. The population has become widely distributed and dense, but it is the land and not the sea which matters. Much of the delta coast itself is still deserted and cut off by lagoons from the cultivated lands.

Alexandria, founded by Alexander the Great in 332 B.C., was a naval base against the Persians as well as an outlet for Egyptian commerce, and it remained for over 2000 years the largest city in Egypt. Like most ports associated with the world's great deltas it lies not on the delta but to one side (in this case the western side) where it is free from silting up, which would have resulted in the past from deposits of Nile alluvium. Thanks to the Island of Faros, the port enjoys shelter from Mediterranean storms and suffered an eclipse in fortune only when the Atlantic sea routes replaced the Mediterranean. Although it might be thought that the opening of the Suez Canal would have taken trade and traffic exclusively to Port Said, Alexandria more than shared in the great redevelopment of Mediterranean commerce.

The Faiyum. Properly speaking, the Faiyum is a depression in the Libyan Desert, comparable with those previously mentioned, in which are found the oases. The only difference—but it is an essential one—rests in the fact that it is situated below sea level, and by a connecting channel with the Nile valley receives the vitalizing waters from the main river. Although this connecting channel is doubtless natural, it has been carefully remade and controlled by the hand of man. It is a large basin, over 500 square miles (1,300 km^2). Already in 1882 it had more than 200,000 inhabitants; by 1927 the total had reached over half a million, and in 1960, some 840,000. The capital,

Medinet el Faiyum, is a town of considerable size, surrounded by numerous villages in which the inhabitants live by the exportation of fruits, baskets made from local reeds, and pottery made from local clay. In addition to the ordinary crops cultivated throughout Egypt, the oasis of the Faiyum specializes in fruits such as oranges, lemons, grenadines, figs, apricots, nectarines, olives, and the traditional grape. As a result of this fruit cultivation, the area has a delightfully wooded appearance, quite different from that of the open Nile valley.

THE RIVER NILE

So far we have considered only the course of the River Nile as it passes through Egypt. From time immemorial, because the life of Egypt depended upon the annual flooding of the Nile, the behavior of its waters was carefully studied. The Nile in Egypt affords us the earliest known examples of river gauging, by the famous Nilometer at Cairo. The annual flooding was accepted perforce as the gift of the gods. It was not indeed until the nineteenth century was far advanced that this water regime came to be understood and the source of the Nile itself discovered (Figure 10.5). With a total length of 4060 miles (6530 km), the Nile is one of the world's greatest rivers. It ranks second in length only to the Missouri–Mississippi [4500 miles (7240 km)], unless the Amazon can be found to be slightly longer than the 4000 miles (6440 km) commonly claimed. The basin of the Nile falls naturally into some seven major divisions (Figure 10.6).

The Lake Plateau. The Nile has several sources rather than one, but the farthest headstream may be regarded as the Kagera, which rises in the highland of Burundi over 4000 miles (6460 km) from the Mediterranean, and flows into Lake Victoria. Lake Victoria is a huge though shallow lake. There is little variation in its level. Though it lies in the equatorial region of well-distributed rainfall, there is a great loss of water by evaporation. The Nile flows out of Lake Victoria at Jinja over the Ripon Falls (now submerged), followed at a short distance by the Owen Falls, site of a large dam and power station. The dam has made the Lake immeasurably the largest storage reservoir in the world. Below the Owen Falls, the river, known as the Victoria Nile, traverses Lake Kioga and then flows over the magnificent Murchison Falls before entering the northern end of Lake Albert.

The waters which drain into Lake Albert form another source of Nile water. Unlike Lake Victoria, Lake Albert is a deep, narrow lake, with precipitous, mountainous sides. At its lower end it receives the Victoria Nile before the united waters pass on northwards as the Albert Nile. A dam to increase the storage capacity of Lake Albert would maintain an enormous reservoir of water to serve the whole basin.

The Basin of the Bahr el Jebel. This is a huge, almost level expanse of land lying some 1200–1500 feet (366–457 m) above sea level through the center of which flows the mainstream, here called the Bahr el Jebel (literally, Mountain River). The extreme flatness of the basin results in enormous areas becoming inundated during and after the rainy season, promoting the growth of vast quantities of swamp vegetation, including tall grass and giant reeds, known as *sudd*. Since 1957 there has been a rapid spread of the South American water hyacinth (*Eichornia crassipes*). Constant effort is needed to maintain the navigable channel. Much more serious is the huge loss of water by evaporation from this great basin, with the result that the White Nile leaves the basin unenriched by the rainfall over this huge area, and possibly with a smaller volume of water than that which passed into it 500 miles (805 km) farther south. Part of the scheme, therefore, for the regulation of the Nile is the cutting of a straightened channel through this basin and its maintenance as an open waterway. This would also reduce evaporation.

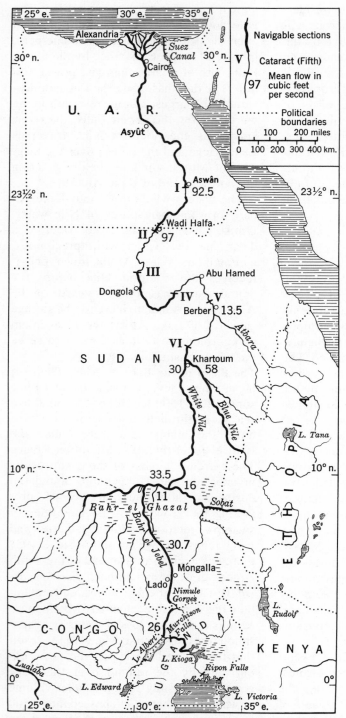

10.5 The regime of the Nile, showing flow at selected points. (35.3 cu. ft. = 1 cu. metre. 1 cu. ft. per second = 102 cu. m. per hour.)

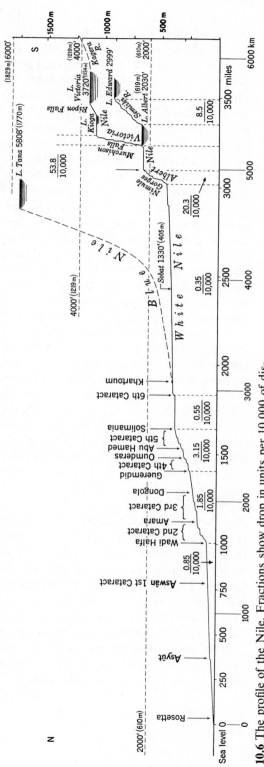

10.6 The profile of the Nile. Fractions show drop in units per 10,000 of distance.

Actually, numerous streams, especially from the southwest (from the Sudan–Congo border), drain into this basin. One, the Bahr el Ghazal, joins the Nile at Lake No. Other streams drain from the Ethiopian mountains to the southeast, collecting together as the Sobat which joins the White Nile a short distance above Malakal. The Sobat is a more important source of water than the left-bank tributaries and makes good the loss of water through evaporation in the marshes.

The White Nile Valley from Malakal to Khartoum. Here the White Nile passes through the increasingly arid region of the central Sudan. Throughout the whole of this stretch it receives no tributary of importance.

The Blue Nile Basin. The Blue Nile drains from the lofty mountains of Ethiopia north-northwestwards, to join the White Nile at Khartoum. Whereas the White Nile at Khartoum is a river of almost constant volume, it is the Blue Nile which, receiving the monsoon rains from Ethiopia, contributes that volume of water in the high-water season which is later responsible for the Nile floods in Egypt. The Blue Nile has in the heart of the Ethiopian mountains a natural reservoir in Lake Tana. Quite obviously the agreement of the Ethiopian government is an essential part of a comprehensive regulation of Nile waters, yet there is little reason why Ethiopians should have any interest in what happens after the Nile leaves their territory. On the Blue Nile at Sennar has been constructed the magnificent dam which has made possible the irrigation of the Gezira (see "Sudan," Chapter 14 and Figure 4.F).

The Desert Cataract Course. Below Khartoum the united Nile flows at first northwards until it reaches the Sixth and highest Cataract and, after receiving the important but seasonal Atbara, commences the succession of descents to its lower levels over the Fifth, Fourth, Third, Second, and First Cataracts, each of which marks the outcrop of resistant grantic rocks of the ancient African complex. This desert course of the Nile serves mainly to transport the life-giving water from Khartoum to the Egyptian border. The land on either side, for reasons which will be discussed at length in Chapter 14, is unsuitable for extensive irrigation, and so the water reaches the Egyptian border. Lake Nasser, formed behind the Aswan high dam, is reached before the border, where the site of Wadi Halfa has been flooded and the town and the railway terminus moved to higher ground.

The Nile in Upper Egypt. Since this course of the Nile has already been described, no further comment is necessary, except to emphasize the utter dependence of Egypt on the waters received from Ethiopia even more than on the waters received from the southern Sudan and the plateau of East Africa. During the low-water season 80 percent of the water is derived from the White Nile, but during the flood season only 14 percent, leaving 70 percent at that season to come from the Blue Nile, 16 percent from the Atbara.

The Delta Course. The map given above (Figure 10.1) illustrates the existing and projected control points for the Nile waters. It reinforces the discussion in Chapter 3 which suggested that the essential division of Africa for purposes of development must be on a basis of river basins. Unity of purpose within the whole Nile basin among all the peoples concerned is obviously a *sine qua non* for future African development and peace.

Further Reading

An invaluable comprehensive account of the geography of the U.A.R. is Raye R. Platt and M. B. Hefny, *Egypt: A Compendium*

(New York: American Geographical Society, 1958). To follow the changing economic structure, one may begin with *Egypt in Revolution* by C. Issawi (London: Oxford University Press, 1963) and *The Egyptian Agrarian Reform, 1952–1962* by G. S. Saab (London: Oxford University Press, 1967). To change the daily life of the toiler in the field, however, is a major and prolonged task and its continuing character is well described in *The Egyptian Peasant* by Henry Halib Ayrout (Boston: Beacon Press, 1963).

The Nile river and its basin has, understandably, been the subject of massive studies by Egyptian officials. These are best consulted in the sequence of volumes on the Nile Basin beginning with Vol. I, *General Description of the Basin, Meteorology, Topography of the White Nile Basin* by H. E. Hurst and P. Phillips (1931) and including Vol. X, *The Major Nile Projects* by H. E. Hurst, R. P. Black, and Y. M. Simaika (1966). A popular account by H. E. Hurst is *The Nile: A General Account of the River and the Utilization of its Waters* (London: Constable, 1957, 2nd Ed.).

CHAPTER 11

Mediterranean Africa or the Maghreb[1]

In many respects the three countries, Morocco, Algeria, and Tunisia, which together make up northwest Africa, may be regarded as an island cut off from the rest of the world. To the northwest is the Atlantic Ocean, to the north and northeast the Mediterranean Sea, to the south the great wastes of the Sahara (Figure 11.1). But from the earliest times the Mediterranean Sea has exercised a unifying influence on the countries which border it. It has permitted travel from one shore to another of peoples, of their religions and cultures, at times of their conquering armies. Northwest Africa was long called on the older maps "the Barbary States" from the name "Barbers" or "Berbers" then commonly used for the inhabitants. Northwest Africa of today bears the impress of several distinct cultures resulting from its geographical position.

The basic substratum of the population, the Berbers, reached the area overland along the North African desert coastal routes. However, the great city of antiquity, Carthage, was established by sea power and when Rome overcame Carthage, the Romans in their turn left their impress upon the Berber people

(Figure 11.2). Following the Romans were the invasion and control by the Vandals and the Byzantines, who sometimes intermarried with the local people, but had less permanent impact on the culture of the region than the Romans who preceeded them or the Arabs who followed. By the land route came the Moors, or Arab conquerors, bringing with them Islam. Across the eight miles of the Straits of Gibraltar, from one Pillar of Hercules to the other, they could see the lands of Spain which lay beyond and so they swept on, extending their conquests and their influence over most of the Iberian Peninsula. Thus for some centuries a part of Europe was a colonial dependency of a politically and culturally superior power based in Africa. In due course, when the great Arab domains gave place to the Ottoman Empire, northwest Africa became nominally part of the Turkish realm except that Morocco maintained a greater independence. Too remote to be under direct control of Constantinople, as the

[1] This chapter has benefited greatly by advice and contributions suggested by Professor Benjamin E. Thomas, who is gratefully acknowledged.

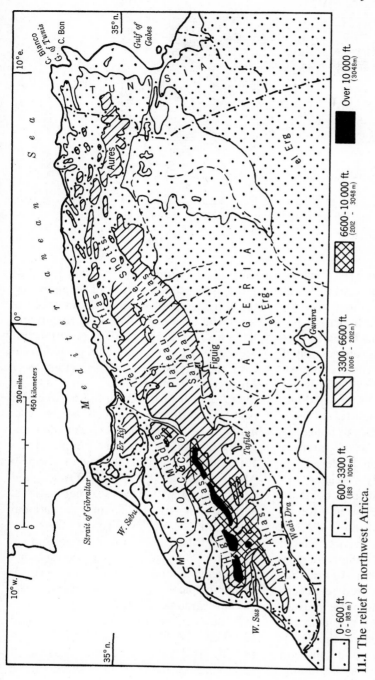

11.1 The relief of northwest Africa.

0 - 600 ft.
(0 - 183 m)

600 - 3300 ft.
(183 - 1006 m)

3300 - 6600 ft.
(1006 - 2012 m)

6600 - 10 000 ft.
(2012 - 3048 m)

Over 10 000 ft.
(3048 m)

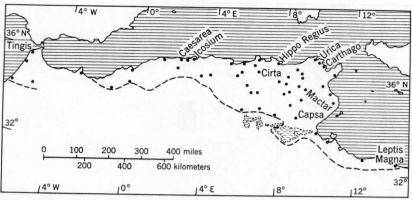

11.2 Roman Africa. The dots show the principal towns and the broken line the limits of control.

Turkish power waned the area became divided among a number of local rulers of Turkish or other origin, leading to a decline in law and order. Both British and American naval expeditions failed to produce decisive results in the suppression of the Barbary pirates. The French conquest of the territory now known as Algeria started in 1830 but was neither rapid nor consistent. The French themselves were at first not agreed on whether to hold only the ports, or occupy the whole interior. Also, the famous Algerian leader, Emir Abd-el-Kader, with only meager resources, kept the conquest from being an easy one. He harried the French forces from 1841 to 1847. But by 1851, all northern Algeria was in French hands. The year 1951 thus marked the centenary of the real French hold over Algeria, but in the early part of that hundred years economic progress was slow. The railway from Algiers to Oran was begun in the year 1860, and from that event the development of agricultural and mineral resources may be regarded as beginning. At first slowly, later more rapidly, the development of these resources continued to expand. French influence extended southwards over the great desert area now forming Southern Algeria.

In 1881 the Bey of Tunis, until then under nominal Turkish control, was forced to recognize a French protectorate

over his territory. But it was not until 1912, after a long period of dispute, that the appearance of German claims and the territorial interests of France, Spain, and Britain resulted in the partition of Morocco. France obtained a protectorate over the largest part of the sultanate of Morocco. Spain aquired a protectorate over Spanish Morocco in the north and a part of southern Morocco which was added to Spanish Sahara. Under the leadership of Abd-el-Krim, the people of the Rif resisted Spanish control in Spanish Morocco until 1926. Britain, France, and Spain, along with several other nations, worked out, by 1923, an international status for the city of Tangier. Germany approved the partition of Morocco in return for a voice in the commercial arrangements and an addition of territory to her tropical colony of Kamerun from French Equatorial Africa.

France called the area it controlled "French North Africa" and intentionally provided a certain amount of unity through the railway system (Figure 11.3). Short, north–south railway were at first extended from Algerian ports to iron mines and farming areas in the interior and linked by an east–west line. Later, the east–west Algerian line was joined to the railways of Tunisia and French Morocco when France aquired protectorates over them. *La ligne imperiale*, running from

Casablanca and Rabat through Fez, Oran, and Algiers to Tunis, connected the major cities of the three territories. It was important to the French for political and military purposes, as well as for passenger services, but it had little through freight because the products of the three countries were similar. Shorter rail lines, some in standard, and some in narrow, gauge connected the imperial line with all major productive areas of the interior and with all ports of importance, and played a large part in economic development.

After World War II developments were rapid. On March 20, 1956, France recognized the full independence of Tunisia. In 1957 the monarchy was abolished and Tunisia became a republic. The relatively smooth transition to an independent Tunisia owes much to President Habib Bourguiba who has also worked with some success towards the modernization of the country. His relatively moderate approach to Arab politics and affairs generally is also distinctive.

In Morocco the monarchy was central to the struggle for independence. Because of his insistence on governmental reforms for French Morocco, Mohammed V was deposed as sultan of Morocco by the French administration in 1953 and exiled to Corsica and then to Madagascar. Under the pressure of Moroccan demands and increasing disorders, France was forced to restore him to Morocco in 1955 and he led the country to independence in 1956. His title was changed from sultan to king in 1957. Upon his death in 1961, his eldest son, the crown prince, ascended the throne as King Hassan II. Following the termination of the French protectorate in 1956, independent Morocco gained control of Spanish Morocco in the north and the territory in the south (Southern Morocco) which had been added to Spanish Sahara. The international status of Tangier was abolished and it too was rejoined to Morocco. Spain had aquired the towns of Melilla and Ceuta on the Mediterranean coast in 1470 and 1580, respectively, and the enclave of Ifni on the Atlantic coast in 1860. These places were therefore a part of Spain long before the partition of Morocco in 1912 and were not part of the Spanish protectorate. Spain relinquished Ifni to Morocco in 1969 but retained control of Ceuta, Melilla, and her other tiny enclaves on the Mediterranean. Spanish territory also includes the Canary Islands, which have an

11.A The main entrance to the walled city of Fez. (Copyright: L. Dudley Stamp.)

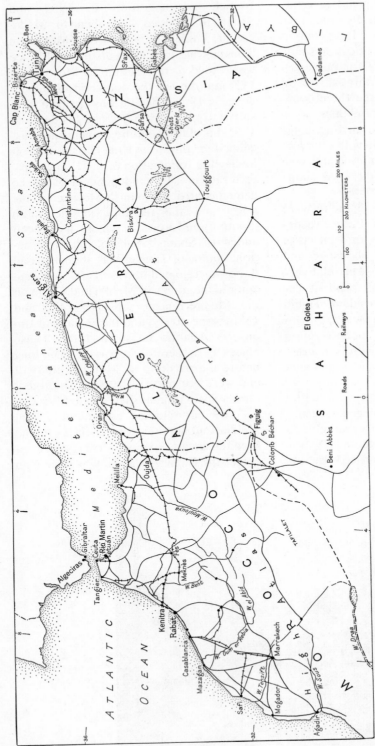

11.3 Northwest Africa: main roads, railways, and towns.

11.B The Karaoiune mosque, Fez. The ancient cities of the Maghreb were centers of Islamic culture. (Photo: Monitor.)

overwhelmingly Spanish population and are considered to be integral parts of Spain, and the lightly populated Spanish Sahara, formerly known as Rio de Oro.

When de Gaulle was recalled to power in France in 1958 and the constitution of the Fifth Republic was adopted in 1960, the "French Republic" was constituted so as to include (a) Metropolitan Departments, (b) Algerian Departments (Algeria), (c) Saharan Departments (Sahara), (d) Overseas Departments, and (e) Overseas Territories. Thus the distinction was maintained between the old Northern Algeria and the vast area of the Sahara previously called Southern Algeria. Northern Algeria had become the home of a million Frenchmen—many second and third generation—or about 10 percent of the total population, estimated at just

under 10 million on January 1, 1960. The principle of self-determination would mean handling over control to the Moslem majority, but this was accepted by a general referendum throughout France. A joint Council was set up in 1962 after agreement had been reached with the Moslems who had been waging a war of independence, but French extremists with their cry "Algerie française" and an underground army inaugurated a reign of terror and destruction. However, de Gaulle persisted with his policy of self-determination. A referendum in Algeria was, as expected, overwhelmingly in favor of independence. An independent republic was accordingly declared on July 4, 1962. It is estimated that by late 1963 fewer than 100,000 Frenchmen remained in the country.

THE PHYSICAL BACKGROUND

The Arabs called their great country of Arabia the Isle of the Arabs. Recognizing that the desert isolates as much as the sea, they gave the name *Djezira-el-Maghrib,* or the Western Isle, to that area of northwest Africa isolated by sea, ocean, and the great desert. Maghreb is indeed a convenient name and a better one than the Barbary States. The term is sometimes extended to include Libya. The island, if we regard it as such, is structurally a part of Europe. The great folded mountain ranges which form such conspicuous features in the European lands bordering the Mediterranean Sea, the Alps, the Apennines of Italy, the Sierra Nevada of southern Spain, are continued in North Africa, where they form not one continuous mountain range but a succession of mountain ranges separated by lofty plateaus or at times by narrower mountain basins. Collectively this is the Atlas system, the alignments of which run, broadly speaking, from west-southwest to north-northeast, that is, roughly parallel to the sea coast, and are cut across by the political divisions of Maghreb. Perhaps the simplest way to regard the structure of the whole area is as a lofty plateau wider in the west, narrowing towards the east, with a corrugated surface, and flanked by great ramparts to the north overlooking the Mediterranean, and to the south overlooking the Saharan wastes. Thus a traveler, journeying from the north, from the Mediterranean shore southwards, will pass through a succession of mountain ranges and intervening plateaus from the relatively well-watered Mediterranean coastal slopes, across mountain ranges often capped with snow, to basins which become increasingly arid, until at last the real desert is reached. Such a traverse made by a geographer is described in Griffith Taylor's article entitled "Sea to Sahara: Settlement Zones in Eastern Algeria."[2]

[2] Geog. Rev., XXIX (1939) pp. 177–195.

The arrangement of the mountain ranges affords a natural division for the whole area. Starting in the west, in Morocco, the central and highest range is the Great or High Atlas, with a core of crystalline rocks, reaching in its highest points some 12,000 feet (3,700 m). South of the High Atlas lies the triangular depression known as the Sous, being broadly the valley and plain of the small river of that name. The Anti-Atlas range to the south is considerably lower and of less extent. To the north of the High Atlas is the parallel range of the Middle Atlas, and between the High and Middle Atlas lies the Moulouya depression. Both the Great and the Middle Atlas are separated from the Atlantic Ocean by a broad plateau roughly 1000 feet (300 m) in elevation, dropping gradually to the coast. This largely cultivated plateau watered by snow-fed streams from the high mountains is a well-settled agricultural region, familiar to many travelers because it is traversed by the main road from the great port of Casablanca to Marrakesh, an old capital of Morocco, which lies almost in the shadow of the High Atlas.

To the north the plateau passes into the plains, likewise well settled and cultivated, with the magnificent old walled cities of Rabat, Meknes, and Fez, until a new mountain rampart is reached in the curved range of the Rif Mountains (otherwise Er Rif). This range was obviously formerly continuous with the Sierra Nevada of Spain before the cutting of the Strait of Gibralter.

Eastward into Algeria the High Atlas of Morocco fades out, and instead two parallel mountain ranges, the Tell Atlas, continue the line of the Rif in the north; and the Saharan Atlas continues the line of the Anti-Atlas in the south. Between them they enclose a broad plateau generally known as the Plateau of the Shotts. A "shott" (in French, "chot") is a shallow lake, frequently salt and frequently only semipermanent. Along part of the Algerian coast the Tell Atlas drops steeply to the Mediterranean, the northward slope often being known as the Tell. A separate coastal range is sometimes developed, as near Oran, separated by a deep valley from the Tell Atlas itself.

Still farther east, in Tunisia, the two main ranges of Algeria approach close to one another, thus almost eliminating the Plateau of the Shotts. The mountains reach the eastern shores of Tunisia in high cliffs, Cape Blanc marking the termination of the Tell Atlas and Cape Bon that of the Saharan Atlas. Between these two promontories is the Gulf of Tunis, which afforded such an attractive, protected site to the builders of Carthage as well as to its successor, the modern town of Tunis.

Climatically the whole of the Atlas lands experience a Mediterranean climate of winter rainfall associated with cyclonic disturbances and a summer when Saharan conditions spread over the whole, and a hot, sunny, rainless period results. Almost everywhere, more than 80 percent of the total precipitation comes in the winter half of the year. With such varied relief local variations in climate are very marked and often very sharp. The Moroccan coast is washed by the cold Canaries current flowing southwards, and the cool air from over it lowers the summer temperatures, resulting in considerable fog (as on the Californian coast) but only a moderate rainfall. The Moroccan coastal plain and plateaus are indeed dry and depend largely on irrigation water, but the lofty mountains attract a high-relief precipitation of 60 inches (150 mm) and more (Figure 11.4).

The Western coastlands of Algeria form a sort of rain-shadow area, the bulk of the rainfall having been precipitated on the Rif Mountains, but farther east the Tell Atlas is well watered and contrasts strongly with the dry enclosed plateau, with some 10–15 inches (250–375 mm) of rain. Despite nearness of the ocean in terms of miles, the Plateau of the Shotts with an elevation of 2000–3000 feet (600–900 m) is so cut off from maritime influences as to experience great extremes of temperature. Rapid changes in natural vegetation as well as of agricultural development reflect these climatic contrasts.

On the best-watered regions, as on the slopes of the High Atlas, the Middle Atlas, and the Rif, and in eastern Algeria, there are forests of cork oak, holm oak, and conifers (the Aleppo pine, cedar, and juniper) together with stretches of grassland. Much of the former forest cover, however, has been destroyed by the collecting of firewood and overgrazing by goats and sheep through many centuries. This has led to soil erosion and an arid appearance of the mountainsides which is not justified by the actual rainfall. In the drier areas, or where the soil is poor, the forests give place to that characteristically Mediterranean bush vegetation commonly called *maquis,* closely comparable to the Californian *chaparral.* It has stunted oaks together with numerous evergreen bushes and flowering shrubs, among which the heaths (*Erica*) are conspicuous. The *maquis* often forms very dense thickets. On such areas as the plateau of western Morocco and other dry areas, the *maquis* becomes impoverished, the shrubs are scattered, there are coarse wiry grasses, but small palms appear. With a still smaller rainfall we find a very stunted Mediterranean vegetation which is sometimes described as *steppe* or *dry steppe.* It is here that the wiry, tufted, drought-resisting grasses of the alfa or esparto types occur. The esparto is of some economic importance as a source of paper-making material.

South of the Anti-Atlas and the Saharan Atlas the whole merges into true desert, often with considerable stretches of erg, or sand. A conspicuous feature is a line of mountain-foot oases, most of which are now reached by modern means of transportation and form the outposts of civilization from which the trans-Saharan journeys may be attempted.

Throughout the whole area abundant and assured sunshine favors the ripening

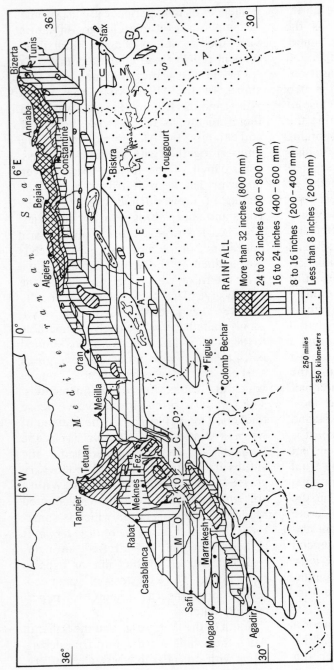

11.4 Northwest Africa: annual rainfall.

RAINFALL

More than 32 inches (800 mm)
24 to 32 inches (600 – 800 mm)
16 to 24 inches (400 – 600 mm)
8 to 16 inches (200 – 400 mm)
Less than 8 inches (200 mm)

of cereal crops and fruits wherever adequate water is available. Wheat and barley are the principal cereals; and among fruits the grape, with very extensive production of wine (especially in Algeria), and the olive are most important, with date palms in the oases. On the semi-arid pastures and maquis, sheep and goats are numerous, especially the Merino and other wool-producing sheep. Though the irrigation works of North Africa are small rather than large and spectacular (there are no large rivers), irrigation has been practiced from at least Roman times onwards. The French in the last century did much to extend the cultivable area by their careful, systematic control of available water supplies. (Figure 11.5.)

Reference has already been made to the population of the Maghreb. A large proportion of the population is a mixture of Arab and Berber stocks, usually known as Moors. The more purely Arab population has come to be associated with the desert margins and the more arid areas, whereas the Berbers are the cultivators of the more moist highlands. The Berbers, even more perhaps than the Moors, are European both in paleness of skin and cast of countenance, and it is not surprising that with the mixture of blood in Spain they should closely resemble Spaniards, or indeed the southern Italians. This alone marks off Maghreb from the rest of Africa, and yet the American or North European tourist to Morocco or Algeria is able to find in the flowing white robes commonly worn, in the characteristic architecture, in the prevalence of mosques, in the inevitable bazaars, with their mingling of camels, mules, and donkeys, an oriental flavor as distinctive as anything which he is likely to find in the Far or Middle East.

MOROCCO (MAGHREB–EL–AKSA, THAT IS, THE FARTHEST WEST)

Morocco is a kingdom over which the king, formerly sultan, exercises supreme civil authority as well as, in his capacity as Commander of the Faithful, the supreme religious authority. The present dynasty has been in existence for some three centuries; prior to that, Morocco, from the time when Islam was introduced at the end of the seventh century and more especially from the time of the great Arab influx of the eleventh century, had a colorful history, with the rise and fall of various Arab and Berber dynasties. Many rulers of the past have left their mark in the great cities. Fez was founded early in the ninth century (808), Marrakesh in 1062, and a number of other walled towns have remained well preserved to the present day. Perhaps one of the most colorful of them all, because of its situation on the seaboard, is the capital Rabat. It is here that the king normally resides, though occasionally also at Fez, Marrakesh, and Tangier.

From 1912 to 1956, the Empire of Morocco was divided into three unequal zones as described above. The French zone, by far the largest, had an area of approximately 200,000 square miles (500,000 km²), and in it the effective authority was exercised by the French as the protecting power, represented by a resident-general, with headquarters at Rabat.

The Spanish Zone, the Rif, was an area of about 8000 square miles (20,000 km²). The sultan's powers were here delegated to a caliph, whom the sultan chose from two candidates presented by the Spanish government. The Spanish high commissioner resided at Tetuan. The Rif Mountains include some wild and inaccessible country where tribesmen were brought under effective control only in 1927.

A third zone was the International Zone at Tangier, only some 225 square miles (583 km²) in area, around the well-situated and well-equipped port of Tangier, the natural gateway from Europe into Morocco.

The former Spanish Zone, which may be called now the Northern Zone, with a population somewhat over a million, is an

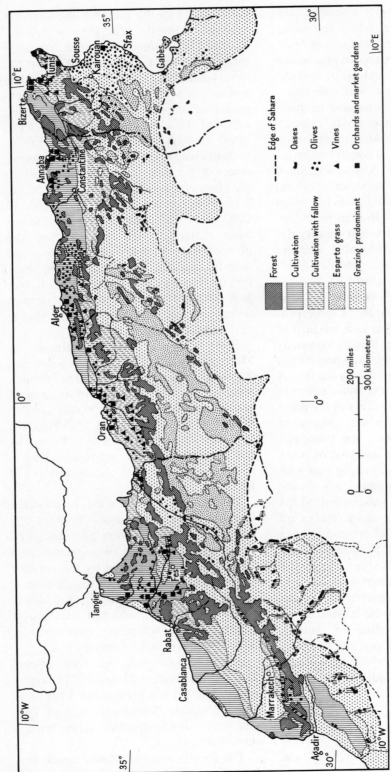

11.5 Northwest Africa: land use. (After Despois and Raynal.)

11.C A portion of the bazaar in Fez. Commercial life has been long established in the many urban centers of North Africa. (Photo: Monitor.)

11.D Place jemaa-el-Fua in Marrakesh. The heart of an ancient city still full of vitality. (Photo: Barnaby's Picture Library.)

area of very limited natural resources. In the western coastal part, especially around Larache, there are small areas of arable cultivation, but the area is not self-supporting and imports foodstuffs. The pastoral highland districts yield wool, hides, and skins, mainly from sheep and goats, but such forestry resources and mineral resources as exist have been little developed except for the recent production of iron ore.

The two principal Spanish possessions are the small ports and resorts of Ceuta (one of the "Pillars of Hercules") and Melilla. Iron ore from the interior is exported through Melilla but in decreasing quantities. The portion of southern Morocco formerly incorporated in Spanish Sahara has been returned. With the loss of its international status, Tangier is no longer so attractive as a location for certain types of business enterprises and residents, although a free port has subsequently been established. It still retains, however, many foreign residents.

The remainder of Morocco was formerly under French protection and still has a large French minority although it has decreased from a maximum of about 350,000 just before independence. Its character has also changed, comprising fewer farmers or settlers and more Frenchmen sent under technical assistance and as teachers. An estimate at the end of 1968 gave the foreign population of all Morocco as 190,000, including 92,000 French. Morocco also had a long-established minority of Jews, the largest in the Maghreb, amounting to about 225,000. These numbers have also greatly diminished following the establishment of Israel and following each outbreak of anti-Jewish felling. Both minorities are principally urban, being especially concentrated in Casablanca.

The bulk of the population is itself divided between the speakers of Arabic and Berber. Berbers are more numerous in Morocco than elsewhere in the Maghreb, comprising some 35 percent of the total.

Their homeland is in the mountains where, in the past, the rule of the sultan was much weaker – the dissident zone of *Bled el Siba* compared with the *Bled el Makhzen,* in the lowlands.

Morocco has the largest population (over 14 million) and also the fastest growing one, in northwest Africa. With the rate of increase a frightening 3.2 percent a year, modest increases in the national product have had little effect on the standard of living so that, despite an unfavorable social climate, official plans for birth control have been introduced as an integral part of the development plan.

Some fine forests of cedar and pine survive on the high mountains but they are sadly reduced from their former considerable extent. Oak forest woodland is more widespread, including the cork oak, which yields some export. Conservation measures have been introduced both to maintain a supply of timber and local fuel and to protect the watersheds from soil erosion. Plantations of eucalyptus and wattle by contrast are mostly in the lowlands, especially of the Rharb, behind Rabat. The dry plains beyond the mountains support natural growth of alfa or esparto grass which is cut for paper making.

The French presence introduced improved agricultural practices on the farms of both settlers and progressive Moroccans so that an area of about $3\frac{1}{2}$ million acres (1.4 million ha) cultivated in the "modern sector" is sharply contrasted with the up to $8\frac{1}{2}$ million acres (3.4 million ha) in the "traditional sector" (Figure 11.5). Traditional peasant farming is based largely on the cultivation of barley and of hard wheat using a simple plough but also using some form of irrigation (usually not involving any storage) over some $1\frac{1}{2}$ million acres (600,000 ha). Olives are also a peasant crop for home or local consumption, a part of which is essentially a subsistence economy. The total French farmland amounted to about $1\frac{1}{2}$ million acres (600,000 ha) at its maximum extent. It is being taken over more carefully than

11.E Moroccan women weeding the wheat fields. They work in gangs of thirty or forty. Later in the year they will work at harvesting beans, peas, and other crops. (Copyright: Geographical Publications Ltd.)

in some other countries with less disturbance to the manning of what are sometimes complex commercial enterprises. This large-scale commercial and export-oriented agriculture is located especially on the coastal lowlands, and around Fez and Meknes and the valley of the Sus. Where wheat is grown, it is of the soft variety. The important crops in value, if not in acreage however, are the vine, citrus fruits, and vegetables. The vine had been grown for its fresh and dried fruit but the French settlers brought improved varieties for the production of wine. The future of the large wine exports is uncertain here as elsewhere in the Maghreb in the face of market difficulties in Europe and the restricted local outlets in an Islamic country. Citrus fruit and vegetables are also produced for the European market for which Morocco can grow spring vegetables a month or so ahead of local producers. A large proportion of these are irrigated and plans exist to extend the area to over 700,000 acres (300,000 ha).

The pastoral way of life has been much less affected by modernization, partly through lack of interest by French settlers. With a climate of strongly differentiated seasons and a topography of marked relief, transhumance between winter grazing on the lowlands and movement into higher and more moist pasture in the winter is common. Goats are more numerous than sheep on the mountains while camels are more widespread than merely in the desert margins, being common in the vicinity of Casablanca.

Off the Atlantic coast of Morocco the cool waters are very valuable fishing grounds. Fishing vessels from France, Portugal, Spain, and even distant Britain fish in Moroccan waters, but the coastal fishing industry is largely in the hands of Moroccans, who have adopted European methods for sardines, anchovy, and tunny fishing. Fishing vessels from Casablanca, Mohammedia, and Mehdia supply fresh fish to the local markets but over half of the total catch is landed at Safi and Agadir, the main centers for canning sardines.

Morocco has relatively few metallic minerals, apart from some manganese, but very extensive deposits of phosphatic chalk. Where the proportion of phosphate reaches a certain percentage, the deposits form resources of immense actual and potential value. The workings are in pockets scattered over the "phosphate plateau" in the middle west of the country in two main concentrations, around Khouribga and around Youssoufia where recent developments have expanded into the Ben Guerir area. Mining is both underground and by opencast methods, with exports handled by Casablanca and Safi, respectively. The ore must be treated on the spot to improve the quality before transport, and the fertilizer industry (both for foreign and domestic consumption) is growing rapidly. In a world hungry for fertilizers it is difficult to overemphasize the importance of Moroccan deposits. Between one-half and one-third of the total exports of the country are represented by phosphates going almost entirely to those countries of Europe where intensive agriculture is practiced, such as Denmark and Holland, or where poor soils benefit enormously by phosphatic dressing, as in Spain, Italy, and France.

Small deposits are worked of cobalt, lead, and zinc, and anthracite (from the Jerrada mine, near Oujda). In striking contrast to Algeria, only two small oil fields have been located but exploration continues, most hopefully offshore in the southwest, near Agadir.

The old Moroccan railways of narrow-gauge lines which the French constructed for military purposes mainly between the years 1911 and 1915 have almost all been replaced by standard-gauge lines, but it is the growth of the road network in this relatively dry country where road construction is easy that has been the outstanding development of recent years. Although Tangier is reached by excellent roads as well as by railway, this has not succeeded in diverting the bulk of the traffic from Casablanca and Rabat.

The ancient walled cities of Marrakesh, Fez and Meknes are regional centers with populations in excess of 200,000. The capital of Rabat is of a similar size but the commercial heart of the country is at Casablanca, a cosmopolitan city of well over a million people. It is the major port of the country, accounting for two-thirds of total cargoes, and has naturally attracted most industry.

Its present boundaries are unsatisfactory to the kingdom of Morocco which harkens back to a period when Sherifian control or influence extended much further to the south and east. The arid and thinly populated regions concerned have become immensely more desirable since the discovery of oil in what is now Algerian territory and of further phosphate deposits in Spanish Sahara.

ALGERIA

The vast territory long designated as Algeria on maps of Africa, and shown as covering more than 950,000 square miles (2,466,833 km²), divides clearly into the vast stretch of Southern Algeria (until 1962 known as the Sahara departments) and the settled country of the north or Algeria proper. The line of oases along the Saharan foot of the Atlas ranges is broadly the dividing line between the two. Algeria proper, some 114,000 square miles (295,000 km²) contains only 12 percent of the total area but 94 percent of the population.

In contrast to Morocco, Algeria was a French possession. The thirteen *departments* into which Algeria was divided in 1959 were organized into *arrondissements* and *communes,* with administration on French lines, the inhabitants electing representatives for all local and national assemblies and French citizens electing senators and deputies to Parliament in Paris.

In the century and more of French occupation Algeria became a field for French settlement and colonization. More than one million Europeans, mainly French, resided in Algeria, and these immigrants from Europe and their descendants constituted between 10 and 15 percent of the total population. Although of

French citizenship, many of these were of Spanish, Italian, or other origins and this, together with the large proportion of the European community which had been born in Algeria, led to a reluctance to face leaving the country and going to France. In effect, of course, many decided they had no option. From 1871 to 1962 the numerous Jews were also regarded as French citizens. Reference has already been made to the exodus of more than four-fifths of the French settlers in 1962 as a consequence of the grant of independence.

The amount of land favorable to agriculture is distinctly limited but intensive efforts by French settlers supported by favorable entry to the French market led to a large export trade of agricultural products. Thus the "modern sector" of farming developed as a component of a larger economy which made the break with France particularly disruptive. This has been especially true for viticulture which supplied the largest agricultural exports and was the principal support of settlers' farming. But these exports of wine amounted to a third of the production of France itself and whereas some

overproduction could be tolerated for political reasons, the tendency to a wine surplus within the EEC countries has led to a great reduction in French purchases of Algerian wine. Sales to eastern Europe have only been made at much reduced prices. Similarly the outlets for fruit, vegetables, and tobacco have become more competitive. In contrast to Morocco, much farmland was abandoned by settlers or was quickly requisitioned and taken over by "workers' committees" in a process known as "*autogestion.*" An attempt to remedy the managerial inefficiency of these committees was made by the military government which appointed advisors to each. The contrast with the traditional peasant farming remains, but reference is now made to the "socialist sector."

The principal concentration of the "socialist sector" of farming, as of the colonial settlement which it has succeeded, is the western Tell, between Algiers and Oran (Figure 11.5). Here the modern farming flourished on the plains and plateaus between the hill ranges and confined between them and the coast. Much of the latter needed reclaiming from

11.F Terracing on steep slopes near Algiers. The terraces are planted with vines, various fruits, and vegetables. (Copyright: G. M. Hickman.)

11.G A vineyard in Algeria. While a part of France, Algeria flourished on the export of wine but since independence it has been necessary to cut down the acreage of vineyards and to attempt to safeguard the market by improving the quality of the wine produced. (Photo: Ministry of Information, Algeria.)

marshland while, conversely, production elsewhere required irrigation works. In the absence of major perennial rivers, these consist of numerous small- or medium-scale schemes. This commercial agriculture required and supported a well-developed intrastructure of roads, railways, local town centers, and ports; the decline in wine shipments particularly depressed Oran. Population is therefore concentrated on the lowlands rather than on the hills from whence, however, come seasonal laborers. In contrast, the eastern Tell contains fewer well-watered plains and the dense population is in the rainier hills where Berber peasants continue a traditional and largely subsistence agriculture based on wheat, olives, figs, and sheep. This is inadequate to support the dense and rapidly increasing population and many men travel to the towns, to the larger farms of the western Tell or to France to work and send remittances home. The settlers, less numerous than in the west, settled on the drier and less fer-

tile high plains of Constantine growing soft wheat, some by dry farming methods, and on the few small coastal plains behind Annaba (Bône) and Skikda (Philippeville).

The dry lands of the plateau of the shotts yield cuttings of esparto grass for paper making but are essentially grazing country, extending across the Saharan Atlas to the margins of the great desert itself. Irrigation has a role here (and a greater potential) in providing fodder for the hardest, driest parts of the year, and oases supply dates, some of which are exported.

The recent exploitation of oil and gas in the south has diverted attention from the useful mineral deposits being worked elsewhere. The most important is the opencast iron-ore mine at Ouenza, near the Tunisian border. The ore is taken to Annaba where an iron and steel industry is being built up, or is exported to eastern Europe. Lead, zinc, and copper come from a number of small mines (the largest is the lead–zinc mine at El-Abed on the

Moroccan border) from which the ore is processed, when political stresses permit, by the Zellidja washing plant in Morocco. A small coal field is worked at Bechar, also near the Moroccan frontier and unfortunately remote, especially from Annaba. New phosphate deposits are being developed to the south of those nearly exhausted near Tebessa, at Djebel Onk, to supply a fertilizer factory also at Annaba.

The value of such mineral products, however, is dwarfed by that of oil and gas. It was fortunate for Algeria that the economic disaster of the precipitate departure of the French settlers was offset by the oil boom. The FLN began open warfare against the French administration in 1954 while the first well was successful at Hassi Messaoud in 1956, and Algeria has become the second largest producer of oil in Africa (after Libya). Hassi Messaoud is some 350 miles (560 km) from the coast and more discoveries have been made still further south (see Figure 12.3). Pipelines reach the coast at Arzew and Bejaia in Algeria and La Skhirra in Tunisia with a fourth under construction to Skikda. Gas is also piped to Arzew from the vast deposits at Hassi R'Mel. Proximity to European markets is an advantage, particularly following the closure of the Suez Canal, but exploitation has been affected, and probably limited, by government suspicions of and restrictions upon foreign enterprises. Nevertheless, oil comprises over seventy percent of Algeria's exports and twenty percent of the country's gross domestic product. Refineries have been built at Algiers and Arzew and oil and gas provides a power and raw material base for the policy of industrialization.

In contrast to Morocco, the main emphasis of development planning in Algeria is on industrialization rather than on improving the agricultural sector. Although ideological considerations undoubtedly are involved, this also reflects the poorer prospects for agriculture in Algeria, including less opportunities for irrigation, and the greater mineral and power base. Industrialization will necessarily be most marked in the existing coastal towns. These are largely modern creations with the traditional quarters less prominent than in Morocco, reflecting the population for which they were built; before independence over half the inhabitants of Algiers, Oran, Bône (Annaba), Philippeville (Skikda), and Sidi bel Abbès were European rather than local Algerians, and Constantine had little less.

TUNISIA

Tunisia is the smallest of the Maghreb states both in area and population and is the least well endowed with natural resources. Since independence, four-fifths of the French settlers and almost the entire Jewish population have left. Former French farms have been taken over by "cooperatives" which are in fact more like state-managed farms but opposition to their system has led to a relaxation of state control.

The line of the Tell and the Saharan Atlas approach one another in the north of the country where the most favored, best watered, agricultural lands lie north of the rain watershed, the "Dorsale." French colonization was concentrated here, around Tunis and Bizerta and on the peninsula of Cap Bon, producing wine, citrus fruit, vegetables, and wheat. The Medjerda Valley also attracted settlers to land which in many places needed draining. This is now the scene of a major river-valley development scheme based on irrigation and flood control by three dams and requiring strict regulation by a controlling authority. The major agricultural export however is olive oil and this derives from much drier areas along the coast of central Tunisia. There is a long tradition of olive growing in the hinterland of Sousse, and French enterprise extended this to yet drier areas behind Sfax, establishing very large plantations of widely spaced trees. The still more arid

11.H A portion of the extensive olive groves in the vicinity of Sfax, Tunisia. (Photo: Paul Popper.)

regions of the south contribute dates, those from the oases of Djerid being of particularly excellent export quality. Esparto grass is reaped from the dry steppes of the interior plateaus.

Phosphates and iron ore were the only significant mineral products until oil was discovered. For some years following the discovery of oil in Algeria and then in Libya it appeared as if there might not be any deposits in the relatively small area of possible geological formations in the far south of Tunisia. The discovery of the Al Borma and Douled fields, however, has provided Tunisia with a much needed addition to its resources for export and for domestic consumption. Oil from both Tunisia and part of the Algerian fields is piped to the port of La Skhirra on the Gulf of Gabes. A refinery had already been constructed at Bizerte, based on its strategic situation for importing crude and exporting refined oil.

A certain individuality and sophistication is generally attributed to Tunisia and it is tempting to consider how much may be due to distinguished historical predecessors. Tunis is near the Phoenician capital of Carthage, for so long a rival to Rome itself and subsequent Arab capitals at Kairouan and Mahdiya ruled over

"Ifriqiya." The population is more uniform in that there are fewer Berber speakers than in Morocco or Algiers and the city of Tunis has a greater than usual primacy — 16 percent of the population of the country live in the capital and the next largest city is less than one tenth its size.

THE ECONOMIC DEVELOPMENT OF NORTHWEST AFRICA

The foregoing descriptions will have made it clear that Morocco, Algeria, and Tunisia, though situated in Africa, form a region so apart from the remainder of the continent that they might almost have been excluded from a book dealing with Africa, the tropical continent.

They provide an instructive contrast however, not only in terms of climate and structure, but also in the different response to the experience of colonization, shared with most of the rest of the continent. In the Maghreb, the incursion was into less of a "power vacuum" than elsewhere. It was indeed the lack of control over the exercise of force by pirates and brigands which provided one reason for European intervention and the pacification of the Rif was not completed until 1927, while that of the Sahara area of

Southern Algeria was only achieved in 1934. The glamorous reputation of the Foreign Legion survives from this era. In contrast with many tropical African colonies, France met a culture with a long and written history, a major world religion, organized states and a less inferior technology. This offered a greater natural resistance to a cultural and economic takeover, but it was also subjected to greater pressures. The number of French and other European settlers (nearly two million) was greater than anywhere else on the continent except in South Africa and the problems and human tragedies of decolonization were therefore more intense. Over a million are believed to have died in Algeria in what was virtually a civil war, and for a period a three-sided one, spilling over into France itself.

Such a colonization by settlers rather than merely by administrative officials results in a much greater and more pervasive creation of infrastructure. This is seen in the number and equipment of ports, the length of railways and roads, and the numerous irrigation schemes. With private investment in addition to that of governments, modernization was spread among thousands of individual farm buildings and small commercial enterprises. New towns or quarters were added to old cities which provide a well-developed urban network. These are part of a widespread market-orientated economic system.

This economic orientation was and continues to be towards Europe. Politically, by contrast, the Maghreb states themselves became part of the Middle East, the Arab world of related language, religion, and culture. The trade among the Arab countries, however, is insignificant and in foreign trade, especially of oil, they are competitive rather than having common interests. With the common use of French as the language of commerce, the declining significance of religious differences, and the termination of the provocation of colonization, relationships with Europe should improve. The Maghreb has interests in a special relationship with the E.E.C. (the "Common Market") and it has much to offer in exchange, including conveniently placed oil. Tourists from Europe find more than the climate to attract them: charming and ancient cities from Marrakesh to Tunis and Kairouan and the scenery of mountains, seacoast, and desert. Complementary resources and material self-interest seem likely in the future to confirm the relevance to the Maghreb of a fundamental geographical factor — its position on the southern shore of the Mediterranean Sea.

Further Reading

On this topic there is a large literature (in French) much of which is cited in the great standard works by Jean Despois and René Raynal. A primarily systematic approach is given by Jean Depois: *L'Afrique du Nord* (Paris: Presses Universitaires de France, 1964, 3rd Ed.) while a thorough regional treatment is in Jean Despois and René Raynal: *Geographie de l'Afrique du Nord-Ouest* (Paris: Payot, 1967). Very useful too is Professor Despois' chapter, in English, on "Development of land use in Northern Africa" in *A History of Land Use in Arid Regions,* edited by L. Dudley Stamp (UNESCO, 1961).

Among more specific works in English should be especially mentioned *Northern Morocco: a Cultural Geography* by Marvin K. Mikesell (1961) and Benjamin E. Thomas's *Trade Routes of Algeria and the Sahara* (1957). Both are University of California Publications in Geography.

CHAPTER 12

The Sahara and the Saharan States

The world's greatest desert, the Sahara, stretches right across the north of the African continent from the shores of the Atlantic Ocean to the shores of the Red Sea (Figure 12.1). The long, narrow Red Sea serves only to interrupt the desert stretch, to be continued on its Asian side across Arabia and into Iran. Three thousand miles from east to west across Africa, the Sahara is nowhere less than a 1000 miles wide; in round figures, the desert occupies more than 3 million square miles (7.8 million km²), or between a quarter and a third of the whole continent. Not by any means the whole of this vast area is "true" desert. There are very large areas of "tame" desert or poor scrub and steppeland where at least some vegetation can exist, and the margins fade into steppeland supporting sparse nomadic pastoral populations.

Such an obvious geographical unit has no separate political existence. The southwest quadrant is occupied by the group of states which have arisen from the former French West Africa, the northwest forms the territory of Spanish Sahara along the coast, Mauritania, and the vast southern extension of Algeria inland. Portions of Morocco and Tunisia also extend into the desert. The northeast quadrant lies in Egypt and Libya; the southeast section lies in the Republic of the Sudan, and, surprisingly enough, in the Chad Republic, part of former French Equatorial Africa. Though the boundaries between these political units are but lines through the desert wastes, they are clearly defined by treaty and in some cases demarcated. The geographical unity of the whole is such that a general account seems justified.

Every traveler by one of the desert caravan routes is familiar with the spectacle of bleached bones showing through the sand, grim reminders of some unfortunate camel or ass which perished by the way, in a country where nature is hard on the weak and unprepared. In somewhat the same way, on a gigantic scale, there appear at intervals through the desert plains of sand and gravel, rocky mountain ridges which are the bare ribs of once huge mountain chains formed early in the earth's history. Some of these mountain remnants are still mighty masses in their own right, especially the Tibesti and Ahaggar mountains, rising to heights of 10,000 feet (3,000 m) in the very heart of the Sahara. By the trend of the folds in the

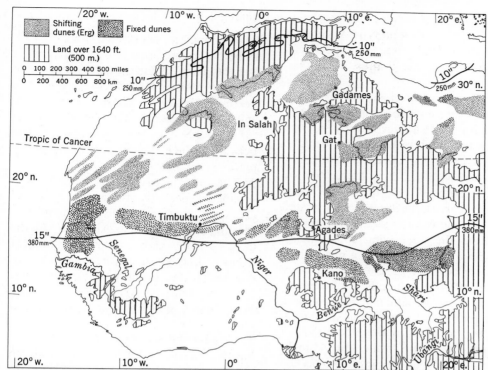

12.1 The Sahara. The Sahara may be regarded as lying between the annual rainfall line of 10 inches (250 mm) in the north and 15 inches (375 mm) in the south; the true desert within somewhat narrower limits. (Map in part after A. Bernard.)

rocks and the ridges to which they give rise, geologists distinguish the remnants of several distinct periods of earth movement, at least two of which are well marked. Much of the higher ground is actually volcanic material, and many of the peaks are extinct volcanoes.

The old, fanciful idea that these mountain masses were once islands and that the sands of the Sahara were of marine origin and its salt lakes remnants of a once extensive ocean, is entirely without foundation. The features of the Sahara as they appear today are the results of atmospheric weathering. Nowhere in the world are there better opportunities for the study of the phenomena of arid lands. Although the desert is broadly the area with an average of less than 8 inches (200 mm) of rain a year, with decreasing average fall there is increasing irregularity. The regime along the Mediter-

ranean border is naturally that of the neighboring lands, with the rare rains coming in the winter, whereas along the Sudan border the season of possible rain coincides with that of the neighboring tropical lands during the hot season. In the heart of the Sahara the mountain masses exercise a distinct influence of their own, and many storms of great violence have been observed, for example, at Tamanrasset in the Ahaggar massif. Short, sharp storms may occur two or three times a year, or it may be that several years will pass without one. When such storms do happen, the mechanical action of the rain on the unprotected ground is at a maximum, and the normally dry watercourses are filled with turbulent muddy water.

Some of the watercourses derive from a former period of greater rainfall. There is abundant evidence that in the past rainfall was sufficient over much of the Sahara to support a light savanna-type vegetation and the associated animals included elephants, rhinoceroses, giraffes, and hippopotami.

With its normally cloudless skies and the consequent intense radiation, most of the Sahara is characterized by a great range of temperature from day to night. The range even of shade temperature may be over 60°F (33°C); it is double that on surfaces exposed to the sun. Consequently, bare rocks are intensely heated by the sun and expand so that they crack away from the underlying cooler mass, often with a loud report like a pistol shot. Where rocks such as granite are composed of different minerals, each mineral may have its own coefficient of expansion, and the rock may be broken in small fragments by no other action than that of insolation—exposure to the sun. At night the temperature of the ground may be 15°F (8°C) or more less than that of the air and so may record as much as 20°F of frost (11°C). The "skinning" of rock surfaces which results is clearly seen in the case of granite.

At least along the northern part of the Sahara the thermometer commonly falls below freezing in the winter, and every year ice forms at places like Touggourt or Biskra, much more frequently than along the Mediterranean itself farther north. In the summer the Sahara can lay claim to have recorded the highest known shade temperatures on the earth's surface. Azizia in Tripolitania recorded 58°C or 136.4°F in September 1922. (This is an unofficial record by the National Geographic Society. It was exactly equaled in 1933 at San Luis Potosi, in Mexico). There are other records at least as high as 133°F (56°C). These extremes of temperature are associated with a clear atmosphere and dry air; relative humidity may drop below 10 percent.

Returning to the rocky deserts which form a large part of the Sahara, we may distinguish:

1. The ancient crystalline rocks which form the Precambrian base of much of the Sahara. They include granites and metamorphic rocks, often intensely folded in north–south trends. These are most conspicuous in the great dome of Ahagger, in the central Sahara, the highest and wildest peaks of which however, are formed by more recent volcanoes.

2. The old Paleozoic sedimentary rocks grouped especially around the updomed areas of the crystalline basement and forming uplands such as Air. They are the basis of the high mountain block of Tibesti, although the greatest altitudes are reached by the superimposed volcanoes. In many areas they have been subject to Hercynian folding on a north–south alignment.

3. Continental sediments formed in huge basins and laid down by wind or in shallow fresh or saline water. These are mostly sandstones and can form extensive plains or plateaus. They are comparable in date with the upper Karoo of South Africa and, since they were preceded and followed by marine transgressions with limestone deposits, they are also known as the "continental intercalaire."

4. Marine sediments, especially of Cretaceous and Tertiary age, which are found far into the interior. They include the extensive limestone plateaus of the northern hamadas (e.g., Hamada el Homra) and are of great economic significance as potential resevoirs of oil.

It would seem that quite late in its geological history, probably at the same time as the formation of the rift valleys of East Africa, the Saharan area was rent by great faults. Some blocks of country were elevated, others depressed. Through the cracks great sheets of lava were poured out or volcanoes piled up to great heights. As a result of the differential uplift of the blocks, clifflike scarps are of frequent occurrence.

The wind plays a more important part in sculpturing the desert surface than in more vegetated areas. Apart from strong constant winds such as the harmattan, violent whirling storms produce the dreaded sandstorms. Particles of rock, already detached by insolation, are constantly rolled against one another, gradually rounded, reduced in size, and smoothed until, when desert sand is examined under the microscope, even the smallest grains are rounded and polished. But before this happens angular fragments are hurled against rock faces, undercutting them and sculpturing them into fantastic shapes. Some hard rocks appear polished by this action, but nature has here its own protection. The sun, bringing to the surface of the rocks, by capillary action, any moisture contained in the surface layer, causes the water to evaporate, and a thin hard skin of iron and manganese salts is formed which protects the rock surface. This desert *patina* or crust is often black in color, giving an appropriate although incorrect impression that fire has passed over the rocks. The process is not fully understood, and it is probable that some of the moisture comes from dew.

The action of wind erosion in deserts is most noticeable because it creates unusual forms but it is clear that the main work of erosion and deposition in arid zones is achieved by the action of water, as in other climates. This is particularly effected by sheet flood and gully erosion following the occasional torrential storms over areas of bare, weathered rock.

Rock and gravel surfaces occupy the largest part of the Sahara. Sand dunes, which have so fired the public imagination, do not in fact occupy more than about a fifth and that includes rolling sand plain as well as dunes.

In detail, the character of the desert is the result of a combination of several factors. There are, first, the character of the underlying rocks; second, the force of torrential water erosion produced by the rapid runoff after the occasional severe storms; and, third, the conflicting character of desert weathering consequent upon a rapid alternation of heat and cold, which results both in the formation of the protective hard crust or desert patina and also in the shattering of the rocks.

Broadly speaking, there are three main types of surface and resulting scenery. The *Erg* desert is the desert of shifting sand dunes, the distribution of which is shown in Figure 12.1. A distinction is made there between those areas where sand movement is still active and what may be called "fossil" sand dunes, where movement appears to have ceased.

Then there is the *Reg* desert, a firm-surfaced naked plain, where the surface is strewn with an accumulation of gravel and small stones left behind by the sorting action of the wind which has carried off the finer, lighter sand to be deposited elsewhere to form *erg*. The result can be a uniform and level "desert pavement."

Third, there is the *Hamada,* or rocky, desert, where bare rocks outcrop, most commonly the exposed surface of limestone plateaus.

From the point of view of caravan movement preference is for the finer types of reg, or gravel plains.

In contrast to some of the deserts of Asia there are no great stretches in the Sahara of fine alluvium, and even if water were available there is less land suitable for irrigation than we find, for example, in Iraq, or in Western Pakistan in the Indus basin.

A scanty vegetation is to be found over most parts of the Sahara except the erg. Naturally in the north it is a very stunted and attenuated representation of the vegetation of neighboring Mediterranean lands, whereas in the south it is the tropical grassland with scattered spiny shrubs, which fades gradually into the true desert. Both the coarse wiry grasses growing in tufts and the spiny bushes, and more especially the succulent plants, af-

12.A The *reg* type of desert in the Sahara. (Courtesy of the Department de la France d'Outre-Mer.)

ford some rough pasture for camels, and few areas are completely despised by the desert nomads.

Oases occur wherever water is sufficiently near the surface for vegetation to be able to reach it, and often desert plants have amazingly long roots. It would be wrong to think of the typical oasis as a well surrounded by a clump of palms. Although the date palm is the character-istic tree of oases large and small, the oasis often has a margin of coarse shrubs and grass, and the larger ones have con-siderable tracts of land which can be cul-tivated by permanent settlers. Water is not always reached in depth from wells, but by striking horizontal channels into the surrounding country at a higher level and there reaching the water table so that the water flows into the oasis in the hollow

12.B The edge of the sand sea or *erg* surrounding the oasis of Brak in the Fezzan province of Libya. (Photo: Esso.)

12.C The spring at the center of the oasis of Brak, Libya. The view is characteristic of many small North African Saharan villages with mud-faced inward-facing houses beneath a forest of date palms. (Photo: Esso.)

by gravity. These horizontal channels are found especially in Algeria, and are known as *foggara* (Figure 12.2). They are similar to the *karez* of Baluchistan. Various types of oases may be distinguished by their physiographic origins. Thus there are: the riverine type (e.g., Wadi Saoura), oases formed on piedmonts or alluvial fans (e.g., El Kantara), in sand basins (e.g., the Souf), and the artesian springs found in parts of Egypt and Algeria.

Most maps of the Sahara indicate the extensive watercourses which may, on rare occasions, be occupied by surface water. Many of them do mark the lines of underground streams, and from the air it is often possible to distinguish whole underground river systems by the sparse but nevertheless distinct lines of vegetation, plants with roots long enough to reach the water below. At intervals the vegetation becomes richer, and an oasis develops wherever the water table is near enough to the surface. The linear arrangement of oases is thus explained. Taking southern Algeria as an example, it would seem that water from the Atlas ranges drains as underground rivers southeastwards, water from the Ahaggar massif by a system of radial drainage. The underground water can of course be reached by wells and is

12.2 Section through a *foggara*. The foggara, shown by a heavy line, taps the underground water table at X, and the water flows by gravity to the grove of date palms.

usually cold, fresh, and pure in contrast to the occasional scanty surface supplies impregnated with magnesium sulphate (Epsom salts) and other salts. There has been some discussion whether, as in deserts elsewhere, the water tapped by modern French wells is "fossil" water and therefore exhaustible, or is fresh water renewed from rainfall or snow on distant mountains and therefore inexhaustible. Whichever is true, continuous heavy pumping, as has occurred in western Egypt, is beginning to reduce the level of the water table. The use of the water in irrigation has made possible a doubling of the size of the palmeries in several oases.

On the whole the numerous peoples of the Sahara belong to Eurasian groups rather than African. The core of the Sahara, with its focus in the massif of Ahaggar, is occupied by Berbers, of whom the principal people are the Tuareg. The Tuareg are the "People of the Veil," so called because the men (but not the women) wear veils. The Tuaregs stretch right through the country of Air almost to the Nigerian border, and they are essentially nomadic camel men. Over the whole of the western desert and the northern area the people are of Arab stock, and are often called, very vaguely, Moors.

In contrast to the Tuaregs, who are no more than nominal Moslems, the Moors know and observe the Moslem religion, its history, and Islamic law. They fall into three occupational groups: the camel nomads, the seminomadic cattle raisers of the northern Sudan stretch, and the cultivators of the oases. Their habitation is essentially the tent; their connection with the peoples of northern lands is suggested by the appellation *Beidan,* or white, in contrast to the appellation *Sudan,* or black.

As long as the French had possession both of the north and south they had an interest in routeways across the Sahara. These north–south trade routes were in contrast to those east–west movements, which were in some ways of more fundamental historical and cultural significance, such as the one situated to the south of the desert region through the grasslands of the Sudan, a route followed by Moslem pilgrims from the Islamized parts of West Africa through the Republic of the Sudan on their way to Mecca.

In the years between the wars the

12.D Traditional transport in the Libyan desert using camels and donkeys and accompanied by a dog. Firewood and water bags are conspicuous loads. Notice the horizontal sedimentary strata in the lower depths of which, oil is found. (Photo: J. Allan Cash.)

French built motor roads equipped with rest houses, refueling stations, and a system of telegraphic communication to prevent the possible loss of tourist cars. One of these main desert highways (*piste automobile*) linked Colomb Bechar, at that time the railhead of the Algerian railway system, with Gao on the Niger River, and connected from there with Timbuktu and other points in West Africa. Another route, the Hoggar route, ran southwards from Algiers, through the remarkable center of Tamanrasset and Agades, to Zinder and so to Kano in northern Nigeria, thus linking with the Nigerian railway system. It is notable that the first route follows along the course long proposed by the French for the trans-Saharan railway. This railway was constructed southwards from the Algerian system to Colomb Bechar, within desert territory but separated by 1400 miles (2250 km) from the proposed terminus of Gao on the Niger in French Sudan (now Mali), whence an extension to Niamey lower down the Niger was also planned, while a branch line was intended to reach Timbuktu and the great irrigation area of the Niger inland delta.

The second, or Hoggar, route passes through Tamanrasset and skirts the Ahaggar massif (a remarkable region in the heart of the Sahara) actually in the former administrative area of Southern Algeria. In general the region is an immense plateau averaging more than 3000 feet (900 m) high; more exactly a succession of platforms separated by abrupt edges and consisting of ancient schists penetrated by basic rocks. These are remnants of Precambrian (Algonkian) mountain chains. Local peaks are formed of old volcanic necks and reach their highest point in Tahat (9550 feet, 2918 m). This island mountain mass in the midst of the Sahara is also a climatic island with violent thunderstorms which from time to time fill the deep watercourses before the streams lose themselves in the surrounding desert. Bernard has described Atakor, as the highest part of the Ahaggar is called, as a formless mass, without harmony, without line; a skeleton robbed of its flesh yet transformed by its colors into country of wild beauty. Black basalt plateaus rest on a foundation of rose-colored granites; the volcanic peaks take on a lilac tint at sunset. The scene is so different from those to which we are accustomed that it appears entirely unreal. On the flanks of the mass lies the remarkable settlement of Tamanrasset, a town with poplar-lined avenues, electric light, and a modern hotel where passing travelers mingle with the various local officials. Because of the interest of this route, it is the one most used by tourists. The more westerly route through Tanezrouft is comparatively level and fast but passes through a particularly barren and relatively less interesting area.

With oil developments deep in the Sahara and the powerful attraction of the remote and unusual to ever increasing numbers of tourists, interest in trans-Saharan routes is growing rapidly. They now cross international boundaries and their maintenance requires appropriate cooperation.

ECONOMIC DEVELOPMENTS IN THE SAHARA

Although the Sahara was carved up by France, Spain, Italy, and Britain in the latter part of the nineteenth century, and French "pacification" of the 1,500,000 square miles (3.9 million km²) of French territory went on almost until the outbreak of World War II, little change took place in the life of the desert. Neither nomadism nor the concept of the unity of Islam were compatible with fixed political boundaries—they were just lines on a map. The whole position has been changed by the rising tide of nationalism and the suddenly enhanced importance of boundaries consequent upon discoveries of oil, gas, metallic ores, and underground water (Figure 12.3). There are reasons for the late geological exploration of the Sahara; first, the difficulty of working in waterless deserts many miles from a base; second, the mantle of sand and superficial deposits masking so much of the underlying geology. Modern equipment, notably air conditioning; specialized transport, including helicopters; and new techniques, notably aerial photography and geophysical prospecting, have led to numerous and often spectacular discoveries. It must be remembered that even now only the very rich deposits are economically exploitable. The major mines of iron ore and phosphate represent concentrations of wealth in sharp contrast to their surroundings, producing an income which transforms the expectations of the states concerned, and of their citizens. Other occurrences including copper and rarer metals are known but in areas such as the Hoggar, at present too remote for economic exploration. The greatest and most rapidly developed of all the mineral resources has, of course, been oil, and gas.

The country which has benefited most from an alignment of boundaries inspired largely by French colonial convenience has been Algeria where the vast oil and gas fields have been discovered in what was little more than a military appendage. The dissatisfaction of Morocco with this situation has been mentioned, and the boundary between Algeria and Tunisia is also subject to dispute. Libya has fared well but an adjustment of the boundary with Chad made by the French causes some resentment. The discovery of very large deposits of phosphates in Spanish Sahara has made Spain less willing to consider the competing claims of Algeria, Morocco, and Mauritania to the territory.

SAHARAN STATES

The general pattern is that the Sahara is divided between countries whose centers of population and of administration are outside, beyond the Sahara's northern or southern limits. In three cases, however, so great a proportion of the area lies within the great desert that we should consider them here.

Libya. Most of the population of Libya and of the land used for settled agriculture, as distinct from nomadic pastoralism, is contained in a narrow discontinuous strip within twenty miles of the

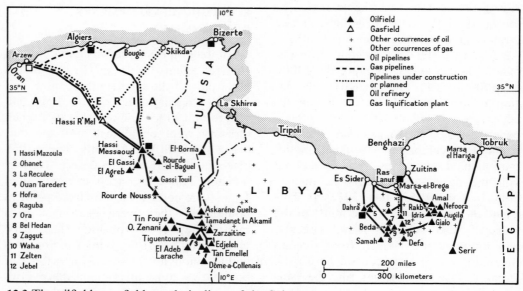

12.3 The oilfields, gasfields, and pipelines of the Sahara.

12.E Floods in winter at Benghazi. Occasional winter storms can bring devastating floods to the Mediterranean coastal regions of Libya and Tunisia. (Photo: J. Allan Cash.)

coast. So overwhelming a proportion of the land area, however, lies within the Sahara that Libya must be regarded as a Saharan state and it is from the otherwise largely barren tracts that the great oil wealth is derived. Along the borders of the Mediterranean Sea are those parts which enjoy a sufficient rainfall or can command sufficient water to make habitation possible. In the extreme south is the land of Fezzan, where isolated oases of considerable size are cut off by great stretches of desert. The Mediterranean coastal fringes fall into two main parts — Cyrenaica and Tripolitania. Cyrenaica includes Benghazi, Tobruk, and the town of Al Bayda (Beida) built as a legislative capital following independence. The western parts of the Mediterranean coastlands, likewise capable of settlement and some development, form Tripolitania, centering around the attractive town of Tripoli (Figure 12.4). Tripolitania came under Turkish domination in the sixteenth century, and, although the Arab population retained or later secured some measure of independence, the country in 1835 was proclaimed a Turkish vilayet or province. In 1911, when a quarrel had broken out between Italy and Turkey, the Italians occupied Tripoli, established an army there, and shortly afterwards the Italian chamber passed a measure which decreed the annexation of the country,

later confirmed by treaty. Though there had been earlier Italian settlements, this marks the beginning of a period of rapid development of Libya as an Italian colony.

By 1938 there were 90,000 Italian settlers in Libia Italiana, that is, in Tripolitania and Cyrenaica. The land hunger at home, the extreme pressure of population on the resources of the home country, had long resulted in a constant stream of emigrants from Italy to the New World, and in large numbers of Italian laborers seeking work in France and elsewhere. But Italy still claimed it needed territory for settlement. In her colonies in Africa, all of them in desert tracts — Somaliland, Eritrea, and Libya — it cannot be said that Italy spared money or materials in her efforts to develop her new territories for settlement. The Italians were great road builders, and they gave Libya some excellent roads through areas capable of settlement. The buildings in the towns and the farms, if not on a palatial scale, were ambitious. There was a touch of grandiloquence in some of the monuments which were erected rather in advance of successful colonization and development. The Italian language remains widely spoken while the number of Italian nationals has varied with political and economic vicissitudes, and was estimated at 29,000 in 1962.

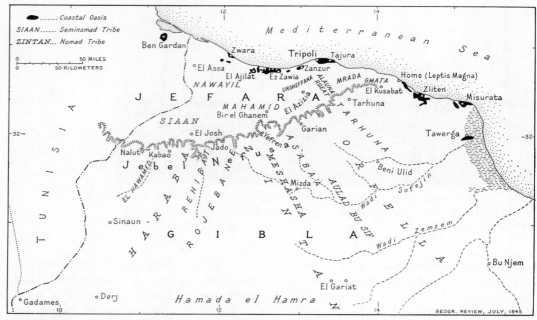

12.4 Tripolitania, showing the main regional divisions and population groups. (From Jean Despois, *Geog. Rev.*, 1945. Courtesy of the *Geographical Review,* American Geographical Society.)

The whole of Libya has an area of approximately two-thirds of a million square miles (1.8 million km²), and the boundaries were fixed after agreement with Egypt in such a way that Italy secured the oasis of Jaghbub (or Giarabub) in 1926, in exchange for which Egypt's claim to a rectification in the frontier at Salum on the Mediterranean Sea was accepted. This vast territory, according to the census of 1964, had 1,564,369 people, Arabs and Berbers as well as a considerable Egyptian population. After campaigns of fluctuating fortunes, the Italians, with their German allies, were expelled in 1942 and in 1951 Libya became an independent kingdom under the Amir of Cyrenaica. King Idris was the spirited leader of the Sanusi and held office under the Italians before going into exile under Mussolini. This consisted of a federation of the three provinces of Tripolitania, Cyrenaica, and the Fezzan until 1963 when a unitary government was established. In 1969, a military coup established a republic.

An interesting account of Tripolitania, in English, has been given by Jean Despois,[1] together with several instructive maps (Figures 12.4, 12.5, and 12.6). The rainfall map shows at once the small area of the country which enjoys more than 8 inches (200 mm) of rain on an average, and how very tiny the area is just around Tripoli itself which receives the not particularly large total of 14 inches (350 mm).

Strung out along the seacoast between lagoons and the sands of the dunes are oases with numerous palms, dotted with villages. Their existence is possible because of the thousands of wells from which water is constantly being obtained. Immediately behind are the plains of the Jefara, sandy steppes with stunted vegetation and occasional muddy depressions into which water seeps at times. Deeper aquifers are now being tapped by bore holes with mechanical pumps. Increased pumping has resulted in a lowering of the

[1] "Types of Native Life in Tripolitania," *Geog. Rev.,* XXXV (1945) pp. 352–367.

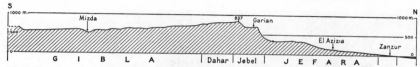

12.5 Section across Tripolitania from south to north. (From Jean Despois, *Geog. Rev.*, 1945. Courtesy of the *Geographical Review*, American Geographical Society.)

water table and some infiltration of sea water. The Jefara is bounded on the south by the bare rock cliff known as the Jebel, or the mountain. Its steep edge, which we may look upon as the beginning of the inevitable African plateau, is serrated by dry watercourses. In places the Jebel is 2500 feet (760 m) in height but falls eastwards.

On the heights of the mountain, altitude has resulted in an increased precipitation, and some dry farming is possible in a land with stunted Mediterranean plants; but otherwise from this area—known as Dahar or "the back"—the country fades quickly into the desert itself. Tripolitania forms the larger of the two population concentrations and contains the largest town and port for general cargo (other than oil). Tripoli is the commercial capital, and also the location of most of the government administration.

Cyrenaica has points of comparison. There is a main coastal plateau and the southern zone or depression of the Kufra. On the coast, Benghazi has about 10 inches (250 mm) of rain a year. The Ital-

ian population was concentrated in the agricultural zones of the oases at the foot of the hills along the coast. Once again the area capable of settlement and development is extremely limited. Along the coast, sometimes called the Marmarican coast, are one or more systems of terraces ending seawards in cliffs, diminishing in general from west to east. There is thus less of a coastal plain than the Jefara of Tripolitania but the rainfall on the plateau is greater, in some places exceeding 20 inches (500 mm) a year. The resulting vegetation is more plentiful (e.g., Jabal el Akhdar or Green Mountain) with some remnants of natural woodland and several valleys were the site of Italian colonial settlements. A few miles from the coast is a water parting, south of which are the flat, bare surfaces of the highlands region tilted slightly southwards and consisting of a limestone *hamada*. This gives southwards to a depression in part below sea level, in which are found the Siwa oasis (in Egypt) and the oases of Jaghbub and Jalo. Finally, to the south, is the great Libyan erg with long lines of sandhills. The

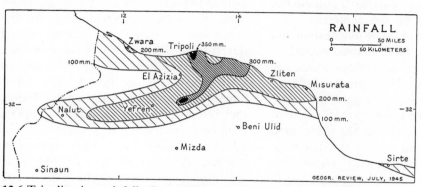

12.6 Tripolitania—rainfall. (From Jean Despois, *Geog. Rev.*, 1945. Courtesy of the *Geographical Review*, American Geographical Society.)

12.F The extensive ruins of Cyrene, the ancient Greek capital of Cyrenaica. This is a reminder that for centuries "Africa" was essentially the southern shore of the Mediterranean seas and part of one world with the northern coastlands. (Copyright: Aerofilms Library.)

Jaghbub oasis is described as occupying a rock-girt basin some 350 square miles (900 km²) in area in which there are three large intercommunicating irregular basins, each in turn subdivided into small *hatiya*. A hatiya has a flat bottom with a salty alluvial soil, covered with halophytic vegetation and sometimes with a salt lake. There are occasional springs which give potable but bitter water, and all the numerous wells have a high proportion of magnesium and calcium salts. A few hundred people at most live in the *zawiya* enclosure focusing on a small mosque; there are palm groves and some small vegetable gardens.

Cyrenaica is the lesser of the two population concentrations and has the second largest town and port of Benghazi. Whereas the population in Tripolitania includes Berbers as well as Arabs and is generally more cosmopolitan, Cyrenaica is the homeland of the Sanusi Arabs, with only some small minorities.

Oases similar to Jaghbub are widely spaced within the desert of the interior. Those of the Fezzan in the southwestern part of the country were given Federal status under the former constitution with a capital at Sebha. They have contributed little to exports in the past, providing only some generally indifferent dates for the home market. Oil developments in the desert have given them a strategic service role, disturbed their isolated and enclosed economics, and disrupted their labor supply. In the large Kufra oasis, drilling techniques have been diverted to tapping the vast reservoir of groundwater of which the oasis is a surface expression. Successful crops have been raised but the question of the source of the water is still unsolved: is it a renewing resource or a deposit of fossil water which may be "mined" but which will then be exhausted? (Figure 12.7.)

With the discovery and exploitation of oil, the otherwise barren wastes of the desert have become the focus of economic activity and the prime source of the nation's wealth. The transformation of the national income has been prodigious. In 1952, a United Nations report was able to comment that "Libya is an excellent example of universal poverty in an extreme form." Although oil exploration got under way in 1955, exports on a large scale did not begin until 1962; but by 1969, Libyan production had overtaken that of Saudi Arabia. The gross domestic product per head jumped from $40 a year in 1952 to $893 in 1967: from one of the lowest to one of the highest in Africa.

The rapid rise in production has been greatly helped by the closure of the Suez canal and the proximity to the European market. Other factors have included favorable conditions offered by the government with prospecting rights being withdrawn if not quickly taken up, and the low sulphur content of the oil. The conditions offered by the kingdom compared favorably with those in Algeria but the revolutionary government is less accommodating.

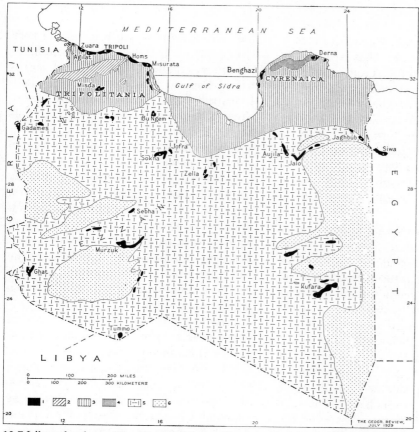

12.7 Libya: land use. The boundaries are those that existed when Libya was an Italian colony. (1) Cultivated land and oases; (2) dry farming with olives, figs, and barley; (3) steppe and scrub used for pasture (4) dense scrub; (5) rocky desert (*hamada*) and pebbly desert (serir); (6) sandy desert. (From S. Dainelli, *Geog. Rev.*, 1929. Courtesy of the American Geographical Society.)

12.G Drilling in the Zelten oil field, Libya. The oil lies in limestone at a depth of 6000 feet. (Photo: Esso.)

The location of the oil and gas fields is shown in Figure 12.3. They are mostly south or southwest of the Gulf of Sirte but prospects and recent discoveries fill the gap westward towards the Algerian fields. A network of pipelines link the wells to simple tanker loading terminals, mostly on the Gulf and not at any major port. Local consumption is relatively small but there are refineries at Marsa el Brega and at Tripoli, and plans exist for petrochemical industries.

The best use for the oil revenue poses problems for a country where the other natural resources are such as to offer only poor prospects for returns on investment. Agriculture still occupies about a third of the labor force but it only contributes 4 percent of the gross domestic product. Investment in this sphere could lead to permanent improvement with a long term continuing benefit to a large number of people. Projects under way, or obviously desirable, include boreholes and dams, afforestation, rehabilitation of the extensive soil-eroded areas, and stabilization of sand dunes. The use of fertilizers has been encouraged and agricultural prices have been artificially supported. Prosperity has increased demand for food so that Libya has become a substantial importer rather than exporter as it had been in the past. Crops include barley, wheat, groundnuts, tomatoes (canned), olives, and citrus fruits. Esparto grass is also harvested. Industrialization is proceeding more slowly, hindered by lack of raw materials and by the size of the market.

Spanish Sahara. Spanish Sahara has an area of some 103,000 square miles (266,000 km²) but a population of only 30,000–50,000 nomads together with some 10,000 Spanish civilians and another 15,000 troops. The phosphate deposits, estimated at 1,700 million tons, are reputed to be among the richest in the world. A 60-mile (97 km) long conveyor belt connects the deposit at Bu-Craa to a jetty at Villa Cisneros.

Mauritania. Although at one time a part of French West Africa, Mauritania is essentially a Saharan state. Over most of its territory rainfall averages less than 8 inches (200 mm) a year, and at its capital, although on the coast, water has to be supplied by a large desalination plant. About 85 percent of the population is Moslem, either Arab or Berber, and the official designation of the country is "Republique Islamique de Mauritanie." During the eleventh century it became the center of the Almoravid Empire which founded Marrakesh, overthrew Ghana, and extended into Spain as far as Cordoba and Granada. With an area of 419,260 square miles (1,085,805 km²) it contains only an estimated 1.2 million population and large areas are virtually empty.

Apart from a few oases, cultivation is limited to the valley of the Senegal River on the southern border in the Chemama district where crops include maize, millet, sorghum, rice, tobacco, and vegetables. Here are the greatest rural densities and a Negro minority of about 150,000. Dates are derived from the interior oases (Atar,

Tidjika, and Kiffa) but the main support of the population is pastoralism, and livestock is driven southwards for export. Gum arabic is still obtained from the *Acacia* spp. thorn trees. Even so, there is little population of any sort in the very arid regions north of about 18° latitude. The cold offshore waters are rich in fish and, like Morocco, Mauretania has extended its territorial limits to twelve miles. This has enabled the government to extract some licensing fees, etc., from the numerous foreign fishing vessels, particularly from Japan (fishing for the highly

12.H A new mosque and office building in Tripoli, Libya. Oil discoveries have brought wealth and a building boom to the cities of Libya. (Photo: Esso.)

prized Devil Fish), Spain, and France. The center of the fishing industry is Port Etienne with its own fleet and processing plants.

Such economic activity is small and has little effect on exports compared with mining. Very large deposits of rich iron ore (65 percent Fe content) have been discovered in the vicinity of Fort Gouraud in the barren north where three mines have been established. (Kediat Idjil, Rouessa, and F'Derik). This is exported 420 miles (675 km) to Port Etienne on a railroad which takes a circuitous route and tunnels through an escarpment to avoid traversing Spanish Sahara. After several false starts, the copper resources at Akjoujt are now being worked, with the output taken by road to Nouakchott. Minerals probably account for over 90 percent of exports — and much of government revenue. The volume of other exports however is probably undervalued because of unrecorded movement over the Senegal border. Much of the trade of the south goes through Rosso or Kaedi using the Senegal ports of Dakar or St. Louis.

Further Reading

The principal reference on the Sahara is undoubtedly *Le Sahara Français* by Robert Capot-Rey (Paris: Presses Universitaires de France, 1953) which includes a bibliography of over 800 items. A convenient summary of the geology is provided by *Le Sahara: Geologie — Resources Minerales, Mise en Valeur.* (Paris: Payot, 1957). Theodore Monod and Charles Tonpet have made a remarkably concise account of "Land Use in the Sahara — Sahel Region" in *A History of Land Use in Arid Regions,* edited by L. Dudley Stamp (UNESCO, 1961, pp. 239–253). Good reading based on sound scholarship and experience is offered by *The Golden Trade of the Moors* by E. W. Bovill (London: Oxford University Press, 1958) and *Tribes of the Sahara* by Lloyd Cabot Briggs (Cambridge: Harvard University Press, 1960).

A recent full-scale account of Libya does not exist although *The New Libya* by Salem Ali Hajjaji (Tripoli: Government Press, 1967) is a locally produced, useful description. The International Bank for Reconstruction and Development published their *Economic Development of Libya* in 1960 (Baltimore: Johns Hopkins Press). Detailed studies, mostly in Tripolitania, are given in *Field Studies in Libya* (University of Durham Department of Geography, Research papers series No. 4, 1960), edited by S. G. Willimott and J. I. Clarke.

CHAPTER 13

West Africa

West Africa forms a well-marked division of the continent, whether it is defined geographically or politically. Geographically it may be defined as stretching from the westernmost point of the continent, Cape Verde near Dakar, for some 1750 miles (2800 km) eastward to the Cameroun mountains. There in the east the natural limit is a line of volcanic mountains and uplands trending along fault lines from northeast to southwest, including the mighty volcanic peak of Cameroun Mountain itself [13,352 feet (4070 m)] and extending out to sea to embrace Fernado Póo, Principe, São Tomé, and Annobón. The southern limit of West Africa is undeniably defined for all purposes by the Atlantic Ocean, or that large section of it commonly called the Gulf of Guinea. Speaking generally, the coast trends east and west and, roughly parallel to the coast, there exists in West Africa a succession of vegetation zones. Forest and swamp of the coast give place inland to savanna and scrub, until some 600 or 700 miles (1000 km) from the coast cultivable West Africa fades into the Sahara desert. This is the geographical limit, and where the rainfall drops to 15 inches

(380 mm) or less the desert may be said to begin. This great block of country, offering a variety of environmental conditions to its human inhabitants but broadly all permanently inhabited or capable of supporting a settled population, has an area of about a million square miles (2.6 million km²).

Politically West Africa comprises the series of republics which have replaced the vast lands of French West Africa (Afrique occidentale française) with the four enclaves of former British colonial territory (the Gambia, Sierra Leone, Ghana, and Nigeria), Portuguese Guinea, and Liberia. On the eastern limit the islands of São Tomé and Principe are Portuguese while the former Spanish-held islands of Fernando Póo and Annobón are now united with the mainland territory of Rio Muni to form the Republic of Equatorial Guinea. The boundaries of States succeeding former French West Africa do not, however, recognize the existence of the Sahara, and several stretch across the barren wastes, there to adjoin the southern boundaries of North African territories (especially Southern Algeria). If, therefore, one uses the boundaries of

13.A Air view of typical mangrove forests in the Niger Delta. The larger growth along the margins of the delta stream is characteristic. (Copyright: Aircraft Operating Company of Africa.)

former French West Africa to define "West Africa," one includes another million square miles (2.6 million km²) of desert to the north of what is geographically West Africa.

Geographical West Africa consists of a succession of strips running east and west. This is clear at once from Figures 13.3–13.6. The lowland coastal strip gives place to a rolling plateau; the normally wet coast gives place to parallel bands merging into one another, but becoming steadily drier inland until the desert is reached. Equatorial rainforest is succeeded by deciduous forest, savanna, scrub, and then desert, each with its own characteristic products.

HISTORICAL BACKGROUND

Whoever may have been the original human inhabitants of West Africa, perhaps people of pygmy stock, the West African Negroes came early on the scene and penetrated to the coasts, taking their system of shifting cultivation in forest clearings wherever they went. From the Maghreb, Egypt, and the Sudan successive waves of adventurers came, helped greatly from Arab times onwards by the possession of camels. Especially noteworthy were the cattle-keeping Fulani who, like the other cattle keepers, rarely penetrated the tsetse-infested forest belts. The nomads mixed freely with the Negro peoples, often adopting their language and sometimes their customs, but it was the nomads who brought Islam to West Africa. The marked distinction between the agricultural, pagan, pure Negro, coastal peoples and the inland pastoral-agricultural Moslem mixed peoples is thus very old and very fundamental. For knowledge of West Africa in the Middle

Ages we owe much to a Moor, Leo Africanus, who was born at Granada in Spain in 1494 or 1495, but was brought up in Fez (Morocco) and subsequently traveled extensively and left written accounts of the great Negro empires of his day.

The first great empire was the Ghana Empire (Figure 13.1) which reached its zenith about A.D. 1000. Its capital was at Ghana, now in the desert some 250 miles (400 km) west of Timbuktu. This empire was succeeded by the Mali Empire (from its thirteenth-century capital Mali on the left bank of the Niger above the modern Segou) but more commonly named from its ruling race the Mandingo Empire. The Keita family, to this day providing small chiefs in the Bamako area, can be traced back to the seventh century, and in the fourteenth century ruled over the greatest Negro empire the world has ever known and one of the world's great empires. In 1660 the last Mandingo emperor was forced to abandon Mali, the site of which is now a waste of scrub.

The Gao or Songhai Empire lay to the east of the Mandingo Empire, with its capital at Gao on the Niger. It came to an end in 1591 by conquest from across the desert by a Moorish army largely composed of European mercenaries and equipped with cannon. The Songhai and Mandingo Empires gave place to many small kingdoms, some ephemeral, some like the Mossi Empires or the Fulani Kingdoms of remarkable and lasting stability (Figure 13.2).

The story of these Negro empires is important for at least two reasons.[1] In the first place they demonstrate the governing abilities of the African. Pride in their former glories led to the adoption of the name Ghana for an entirely different area (the Gold Coast) when it became independent and the similar resuscitation of the name Mali. In the second place they were based on a mixed economy in areas which today have become semidesert. Does this prove the desiccation of Africa?

The foregoing descriptions make it

---

[1] The Ghana Empire is believed by some to be the origin of the word Guinea (as a corruption), later applied to the whole west coast. The British gold coin, the "guinea," took its name from the fact that it was minted from gold from the Guinea coast. The guinea, comprising 21 shillings (£ 1.05) is still used in Britain by some traders and professions as a unit of price, though no coins or notes have been issued for a very long time.

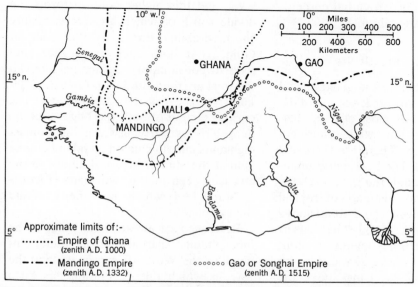

13.1 Ancient empires of West Africa. (The Mandingo empire is also known as Mali.)

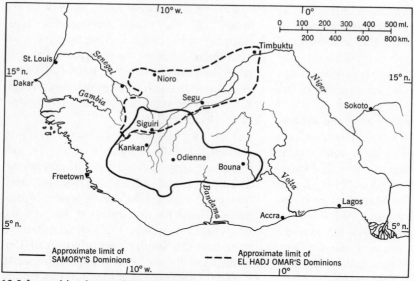

13.2 Later kingdoms of West Africa.

clear that the natural geographical divisions of West Africa run east and west. In sharp contrast the majority of modern political divisions run north and south. Each major political division thus tends to be a transect of the whole. Political boundaries cut right across environmental zones and in fact take no notice of human distributions. Frequently a single tribe, such as the Ewe, discussed later, is divided by a boundary created during the European partition of Africa but perpetuated by modern national units.

THE PHYSICAL BACKGROUND

Using West Africa in the geographical sense, we see that this great section of the continent partakes of most of those features common to the whole continent south of the Sahara. There are the usual huge plateaus with level or gently undulating surfaces, though the general elevation is here less than most parts of tropical Africa: 500–1000 feet (150–300 m) above sea level (Figure 13.3). The desert country of the north lies mainly at about 1500 feet (450 m) above sea level, with occasional hill masses rising above the general level. South of this lies the shallow

depression or basin, an ancient sea and later lake bed, through the heart of which the River Niger makes its great northward bend via Timbuktu. Westward a low divide separates the basin of the middle Niger from the basin of the Senegal; to the east a somewhat similar divide separates the Niger from the basin of Lake Chad. Southward of the central Niger basin the land rises again to rolling country 1000–1500 feet (300–450 m) above sea level, and this higher country forms the divide south of which are rivers, mainly short, draining direct to the Gulf of Guinea. At both ends this higher land rises to considerably greater heights. To the west are the Futa Jallon-Guinea Highlands; to the east the Jos Plateau. The curious course of both the Niger and the Sengal rivers deriving from the Guinea highlands and flowing on an inland course behind the shorter rivers draining to the coast, is seen in the two maps (Figures 13.3 and 13.4) which show the relief and the drainage.

Reference has already been made to the inhospitable, harborless character of much of the West African coast, and the way in which this reputation has been somewhat misleadingly applied to the rest

13.B The western edge of the northern Nigerian plateau. (Copyright: Aerofilms Library.)

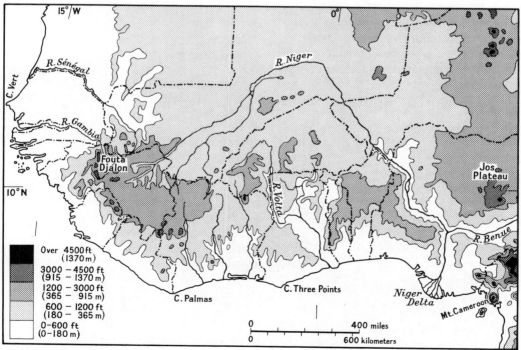

13.3 Relief map of West Africa.

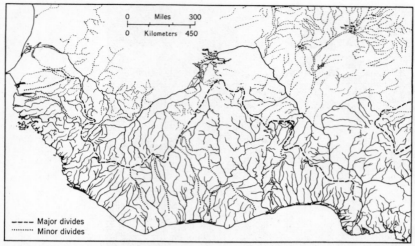

13.4 Drainage of West Africa.

of the continent. Where the desert reaches the sea, north of St. Louis and Cape Verde, longshore drifting has caused long curving sandy beaches offering no shelter (except at Port Etienne), with dangerous offshore shoals and heavy surf. Cliffs are rare on much of the African coasts, so that those of Cape Verde, behind which Dakar seems to hide, call for comment. Southward, however, the coast is largely one of mud flats with mangrove forests intersected by innumerable channels; a number of estuaries, though with variable channels and impeded by sandbanks, offer shelter and access to the interior. Most important of these are the mouths of the Gambia, Casamance, Cacheu, and Rokel rivers—respectively in Gambia, Senegal, Portuguese Guinea, and Sierra Leone. Beyond, and until the numerous creeks of the Niger delta area (the "oil rivers") are reached, the coast again is smooth and surf-pounded. The economic and political necessity for ports to serve the well-populated hinterland, however, has led to a row of ports established despite difficulties of site.

GEOLOGY

In common with the greater part of the continent, West Africa consists essen-

13.C Fishermen of the Fanti tribe launching their boats at Lumley, Sierra Leone. These Ghanaian migrant fishermen work up and down the West African coast. (Photo: Eric Kay.)

tially of an ancient crystalline complex, widely exposed, with various groups of overlying sediments in certain regions. The basement complex includes great masses of granite-gneisses, ranging from true granites to orthogneisses and para-gneisses, and highly folded metamorphic rocks which show trend lines broadly termed Huronian, from north to south. Sediments, usually gently folded and only slightly if at all metamorphosed but believed to be Precambrian, rest on these and are sometimes important because of the inclusion of gold-bearing conglomerates (as in Ghana). There are also groups of Paleozoic sediments, likewise gently folded but into northeast to southwest folds. Later sediments include Mesozoic and Tertiary. The sediments of the lower group, known to the French as *Continental Intercalaire* and broadly contemporary with the Nubian sandstones of Egypt and Libya, were probably laid down in an inland basin over a very long period of time from the Permian to the Lower Cretaceous. Later a shallow sea invaded the interior or occupied gulfs extending from the eastern part of the present Gulf of Guinea. At a later stage there were the huge inland Quaternary basins, such as those of the Middle Niger and Chad, in which were deposited various lacustrine, fresh-water, and terrestrial deposits. Volcanic rocks of various ages add the final major feature to the long geological story.

Although substantial mineral deposits are known to lie in former French West Africa, many localities are remote, and not all the ores are high grade or worth exploiting. The impressive output up to World War I was essentially from British West Africa. Though the gold-bearing "bankets" of Ghana are not known in neighboring territory, there are some alluvial and eluvial deposits, especially in the Republic of Guinea. Alluvial diamonds, probably derived from some ultrabasic rocks but not yet traced to their source, are widespread and industrially important in Ghana, the Ivory Coast, Sierra Leone, and Guinea. The local exploitation of highly ferruginous laterite as iron ore has

long been widespread, and such ores are now of commercial importance near Conakry in Guinea. Hematite iron ores of international significance worked in Sierra Leone are now worked elsewhere, as in Liberia and northern Mauritania. Bauxite is widely distributed, and some is of high grade and now being exploited in the Los Islands off Conakry and in Ghana. Though the working of manganese ore up to 1950 was restricted to Ghana, (then the Gold Coast), there are known deposits in the Ivory Coast and Niger. Mineral-bearing sands with ilmenite, zircon, rutile, and titanium ores occur along the Senegal, Sierra Leone, and Ivory Coasts. There are phosphates which rank with the lower grades of Morocco now being exploited near Thiés in Senegal and in Togo, and deposits occur elsewhere. Unfortunately limestones suitable for making cement or agricultural lime are relatively rare. Rock salt and saline earths by contrast are common and worked in Mauritania, Senegal, Mali, and Niger.

NATURAL REGIONS AND POLITICAL DIVISIONS IN WEST AFRICA

The relief features shown in Figure 13.3, which afford a series of strips roughly parallel to the coasts, are reinforced by the character of the natural vegetation—itself dependent upon climate—shown in Figures 13.5 and 13.6 The general arrangement of vegetation belts is agreed, but several different detailed schemes have been proposed. It is indicative of the isolation in which each national group worked in Africa before World War II that even the scientists and technical officers such as foresters and agriculturists in the French and British spheres rarely met, scarcely ever collaborated. Inland, the evergreen rainforests extend as a broad belt except where they are interrupted by the Ghana dry belt. Floristically, French workers have distinguished a Casamancian forest area in the west related to the rainforest but more

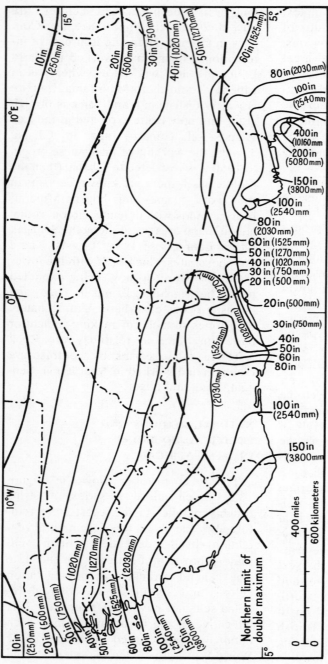

13.5 Mean annual rainfall over West Africa.

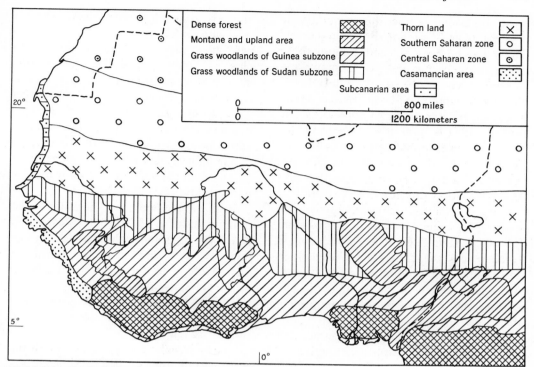

13.6 Natural vegetation of West Africa. The classification and terminology used here is that which has been commonly used in West Africa but may be compared with that used for the entire continent in Chapter 6.

bushy and deciduous. Its characteristics may partly be derived. Beyond are the savannas which in West Africa are aligned in zones essentially in response to increasing aridity and for which a widely used terminology exists. Precise definition and the floristic components are more arguable as in the use of the word "savanna" for some vegetation types where others would prefer "steppe" (see Chapter 6). Closest to the rainforest is the Guinea Zone, divided into distinctive southern and northern sections. In the south is a lush growth of tall, broad-leaved grasses with trees often of the same or related species as those of the forest, and including the shea butter tree (*Butyrospermum parkii*). Some at least of this vegetation is probably derived from clearing of the forest itself. In the northern section, trees are more important and the forest has more of the character of a deciduous woodland—losing its leaves in the dry

season. This is similar to the great block of "miombo" woodland south of the equator, and similarly is much infested with the tsetse fly. The Sudan Zone is next with more widely spread trees standing in seasonally revivifying grasses, characteristic trees being of the *Combretum* and *Terminalia* genera and the more luxuriant *Acacias*. Most conspicuous is the fleshy-trunked baobab (*Adonsonia digitata*). Here the tsetse fly is less common and more easily eradicated, cattle are kept in great numbers and agricultural populations flourish, with an export of peanuts and cotton. In the direction of increasing aridity, grass becomes thinner and the *Acacias* more bushy and dominant and we enter the Sahel Zone, a pastoral rather than agricultural domain. As the Sahara is approached, the thorn bushes become more widely spread and the general vegetation cover thinner until the desert is entered. On the higher plateaus, relief rain or mist and cooler temperatures modify the vegetation and montane forests and grasslands may be distinguished. Among these approximately parallel zones many observers have described an "empty belt", an almost unpopulated zone between population concentrations to the north and south, and it is tempting to try to fit this around a vegetational category. The closest fit is with the tsetse-infested Guinea Savanna, and this is similar to the very low population densities of the southern "miombo." The correlation is poor, however, and it is clear that a number of other influences have been at work including in some places the coincidence of geologically unfavorable conditions for groundwater and elsewhere the heritage of slave raiding and warfare between peoples of the forest and the savanna.

The important point is, of course, that each of these zones forms a distinctive environment to which the human response has been very different. The shifting cultivation of the formerly pagan or animistic Negroes of the coastal zones contrasts utterly with the life of the Moslem Fulani cattlemen or the sedentary Hausa of the northern zones. Yet political divisions cut right across all these natural zones. The new states therefore tend to contain peoples of different cultures and regional interests forming a built-in source of political tension. In economic terms, however, these contrasting natural regions have much to offer each other in their differing agricultural products and the recognition of the mutual advantage of such north–south trade offers a hope for some increasing stability (Figure 13.7).

Until the emergence of the independent African states in 1958–1960, West Africa could be regarded politically as French territory occupying the whole vast interior and reaching to the coast in four main areas: (1) Senegal, (2) French Guinea, (3) the Ivory Coast, and (4) Dahomey with Togoland, separated by enclaves not under French control.

The first enclave was the narrow British territory of the Gambia; Senegal and French Guinea were separated by the enclave of Portuguese Guinea; French Guinea from the Ivory Coast by the broad enclave of British Sierra Leone and Liberia; the Ivory Coast from Dahomey by

13.D A "pagan" village and lands, northern Nigeria. Such irregular but compact fields are typical of areas of hoe cultivation. (Copyright: Aerofilms Library.)

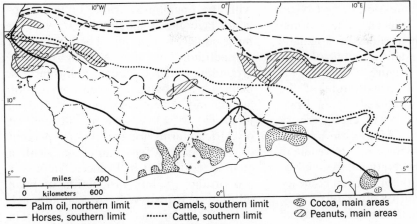

Palm oil, northern limit — — — Camels, southern limit Cocoa, main areas
— — Horses, southern limit ······ Cattle, southern limit Peanuts, main areas

13.7 Some agricultural distributions in West Africa.

the British Gold Coast and the trusteeship territories of Togoland.

The French approached West Africa both by sea and by land, and French West Africa administratively met Southern Algeria in the heart of the Sahara. The British and Portuguese approached West Africa from the sea, and Liberia, too, was established by coastal settlements. From the coasts there was gradual penetration inland, but the four British enclaves of the Gambia, Sierra Leone, Gold Coast, and Nigeria, like Portuguese Guinea and Liberia, were based essentially on coastal settlements. The same was true of the former German Togoland and Kamerun (Cameroun). The fact that French West Africa formed a continuous tract encouraged unification of the territories, whereas the British areas, cut off from one another, each developed along individual lines. Differences in colonial rule have left differences in political and administrative inheritance but most immediate of course is language. Because of the number of vernacular languages in use, French or English have been retained, and we can conveniently refer to Francophone and Anglophone Africa.

FRANCOPHONE WEST AFRICA

The reorganization of the former French Empire into the French Union (Union Française), completed after World War II, had certain important effects in West Africa. The seven former "colonies" of Senegal (Senegal), Mauritania (Mauritanie), French Sudan (Soudan Français), French Guinea (Guinée), the Ivory Coast (Côte d'Ivoire), Dahomey (Dahomey), Upper Volta (Haute-Volta, revived in 1947), and the Niger Territory (Niger) all became "territories" within the Federation of French West Africa with its capital at Dakar. The trusteeship territory of Togoland remained outside the Federation. As already explained briefly in Chapter 2, the recall to power of General de Gaulle in 1958 and the framing of a constitution for the Fifth Republic had speedy and far-reaching effects for French West Africa. The eight territories listed above were offered a choice between complete independence or autonomy within the French Community (La Communauté). French Guinea voted for independence and became the Republic of Guinea (République de Guinée, with French as the official language) on October 2, 1958. The other seven voted to remain in the French Community, but before the end of 1960 each had become a republic with the titles, respectively, of Senegal (République du Sénégal), Mauritania (République Islamique de Mauritanie), Mali (République du Mali, formerly French Sudan), Ivory Coast (République de Cote d'Ivoire), Dahomey (République du Dahomey), Upper Volta

(République de Haute-Volta), and Niger (République du Niger). The former French trusteeship territory of Togoland became the independent Republic of Togo on April 27, 1960 (Figure 13.8).

Under the earlier constitution of the French Union, crystallized at the Brazzaville Conference of 1944, each territory elected its deputies (African or French) whose duty and privilege was to reside in Paris and sit in the National Assembly, there to legislate both for French home affairs and for African or other territories. The African deputy thus began to play an important part in the government of France itself. The Africans settled down to European ways of life in Paris; conversely, French settlers established themselves as private traders, shopkeepers, and craftsmen in considerable numbers in tropical Africa. They took with them French ways of life and gave a remarkable atmosphere of metropolitan vitality and racial cooperation to the towns of French West Africa where they settled. By 1950 there were 30,000 Europeans, mainly French, in the unique city of Dakar (12 percent of the population) and 10,000 in the Ivory Coast capital of Abidjan. After 1945 new building and modernization took place in Dakar on a scale unparalleled elsewhere in tropical Africa, and the changes in Abidjan, especially

with the opening to traffic of the deep-water lagoon port in July 1950, were almost equally staggering. There was keen competition for the African farmers' groundnuts, coffee, cocoa, palm kernels, palm oil, and bananas; keen competition among middlemen and exporters. The big jump was in coffee growing—80 percent on African farms and less than 20 percent on European-owned plantations, with a guaranteed market in France. There was proportionately less production of palm oil than in British West Africa, although some was being made into soap locally in Senegal and the Ivory Coast. The same postwar period was marked by such industrial growths as oil-seed crushing of peanuts on a large scale in Senegal, cement and lime making, brewing, boot and shoe making. These industries were run both by Africans and by French.

The development of iron ore and bauxite mining in French Guinea was by large-scale private enterprise, but the social services and public works were financed by the Metropolitan Government, through the organization known as F.I.D.E.S., comparable with the Colonial Development and Welfare Acts of Britain.

The French system in Africa was designed to make the African a good citizen of Greater France, to bring him into part-

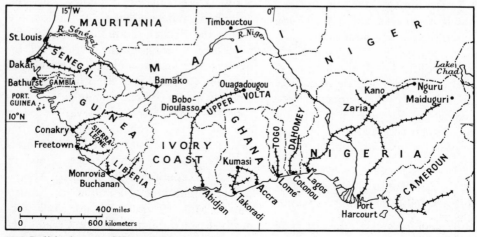

13.8 Political map of West Africa.

nership even to the extent of governing France. There was no place in the scheme for the conservation of any indigenous African social structure. The coming of independence found a considerable number of French-speaking Africans with experience in matters of government and organization, with a tradition of interracial cooperation, and so the transition was made with remarkable smoothness.

ANGLOPHONE WEST AFRICA

The trends in British West Africa after World War II offered some remarkable contrasts to French West Africa. The introduction of universal franchise leading to democratic self-government would seem the quickest way of completing the disappearance of the British Empire, which indeed it was. Whereas the French until 1958 held up the ideal of citizenship of Greater France (just as the Romans did 2000 years ago, by the lure of the magic words, *civis romanus sum*), the British held to the ideal of a Commonwealth of Free Nations.

Progress was rapid. Before 1939, broadly speaking, the administrations of the British colonies were largely bureaucratic and almost entirely white. The governors were appointed by the Colonial Office in London, and ultimately policy was the responsibility of the British Parliament acting through the Secretary of State for the colonies. Not unfairly the British colonies were described not as countries but as collections of tribes in a steel framework of British administration.

During World War II Africans entered in large numbers the higher circles of administration, notably in financial committees, but also in an advisory capacity.

In the postwar period the rapidity of African cultural and political development was recognized by the successive establishment in each colony of entirely new constitutions based essentially on democratic principles as understood in Anglo-Saxon countries. The form varied slightly from one area to another, but the principles were the same: a large legislative council, elected directly by universal adult (or adult male in Northern Nigeria) suffrage or through electoral "colleges"; African ministers in charge of departments and forming a cabinet in complete control of the countries' affairs, except for the governor's right of veto — the governor appointed as before. The changes were accompanied by the development of a party system, the rapid Africanization of the civil service and the development of local government. The old distinctions between "colony" and "protectorate" largely disappeared.

General satisfaction with the new constitutions was tempered by one consideration. Africans had no direct representation in London, where the Colonial Office appointed governors and where Parliament determined major policy. In contrast to the situation in French West Africa, each British territory was treated as a separate case. In the Gold Coast the 1951 elections under universal adult suffrage for the House of Assembly put into power Kwame Nkrumah, leader of the Convention People's Party, who at the time was in prison for seditious activities. He was immediately released and took office as Leader of Government Business.

The Gold Coast was thus operating a system of democratic elections and a party system, so that the country was deemed to be ripe for independence with the goodwill of both main parties of the British Parliament. The General Assembly of the United Nations agreed in December 1956 that the new country should absorb the trusteeship territory of British Togoland; it chose the title Ghana from the ancient African empire of that name (though not in the same area; see Figure 13.1); and the British Parliament passed the Ghana Independence Act. The State of Ghana thus came into existence on March 6, 1957, choosing dominion status within the Commonwealth. On July 1, 1960, it was declared a republic within the Commonwealth with Dr. Kwame Nkrumah as president.

The story of Nigeria is not dissimilar. It became a federation under a governor general on October 1, 1954; six years later to the day the Federation was declared a sovereign independent state within the Commonwealth.

The question of the trusteeship territory of the British Cameroons on Nigeria's eastern borders — in two separated portions — was left open, to be decided by the vote of the people. The small northern area was added to the Northern Region of Nigeria; the southern portion elected to join the Cameroun Republic, the former French trusteeship territory.

Sierra Leone presented the problem of the viability of a much smaller state, but independence was achieved on April 27, 1961. Even little Gambia became an independent state on February 18, 1965.

Although political divisions between French and British territories cut indiscriminately across tribal areas, there is little if any tendency either for realignment of boundaries of the newly independent states or for mass migration one way or another. There continue to be seasonal movements of labor, such as the "strange farmers" in the Gambia and a general movement of men from Mali, Upper Volta, and Niger into the richer coastal states. Unfortunately such minorities, even though they are of Africans among Africans excite distrust and dislike when political or tribal passions are excited.

The British developed, notably in Nigeria, a system of government-controlled marketing boards for the chief export crops. In Nigeria such boards were established for cocoa, peanuts, and palm oil products. The boards fix the price to be paid to the producer, who therefore knows in advance what he will receive. It is held that this is conducive to an even spread of wealth, to a balanced cropping and to fair prices in times of depression. There is no lure of a sudden high price to tempt the cultivator to neglect to grow food. The marketing boards use the "profits" they make on world markets for the benefit of the industry; it is in fact a form of taxation. The upsurge in coffee production in the Ivory Coast and cocoa in Ghana suggests that producers appreciate the benefits, though there are those who argue that the minimization of the profit motive lowers the incentive of the progressive individual. Somewhat later the

13.E Sitting beneath cocoa trees, the farmers are splitting open the pods to extract the beans. (Photo: United Africa Company.)

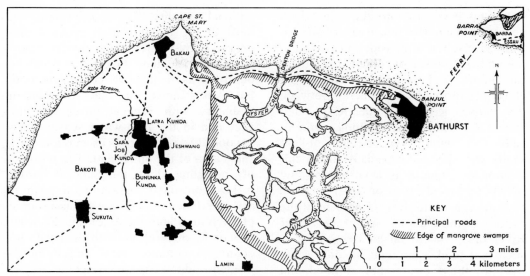

13.9 The site of Bathurst at the mouth of the Gambia River.

French introduced a system of guaranteed markets (in France) and prices.

THE GAMBIA

The Gambia River as a natural routeway into the West African hinterland early attracted the attention of British traders. The "Company of Adventurers of London Trading into Africa," which received its charter from King James I in 1618, later in the century (1664) built Fort James on an island some 17 miles (27 km) from the mouth of the river. In the wars with France in the eighteenth century the Fort changed hands several times and was finally destroyed. The Treaty of Paris in 1814 recognized British sovereignty over the banks of the Gambia River, although there was no longer a British post in the area. After the abolition of slave trading by the British Parliament in 1807, the British navy had used Gorée (a small island off the site of Dakar) as a base against slave carriers in the Gambia. The restoration of that islet to France by the Treaty of 1814 led Britain to select the site where Bathurst now stands (Figure 13.9). In 1816 the chief of neighboring Kombo ceded an island—little more than a low, uninhabited sand bank—on the

south bank of the river, where the mouth is only 2 miles (3.2 km) wide. Renamed St. Mary's Island, a military post was established in 1819 following a traders' settlement in 1816. Linked with the mainland by a line of sand banks, bordered on the south by a large area of mangrove swamp, well sheltered from Atlantic storms, it was an excellent defensive site for the original purpose but a poor one for the location of a capital from which to develop an extensive colony. Because the island is liable to flooding, especially in the low ground between two original higher parts, the drainage problem (until the mid-fifties there were insanitary open sewers) has never been fully solved. An adequate water supply remained an additional problem until 1951. As usual with African rivers, there was a bar at the entrance to the intricate channel, now dredged to 26 feet at high water. Although Bathurst harbor is sheltered, it had only shallow-water wharves, and vessels of more than 2000 tons had to load and offload by lighter until a deep-water wharf was provided in 1952.

Most of the country consists of a long narrow strip on either side of the river, at most only 20 miles (32 km) in total width, though extending more than 200 miles

(320 km) eastward into the interior. A century and a half of effective British control has resulted in considerable differentiation from the surrounding French territory in which the Gambia forms an enclave. The former local distinction between the Upper River, Middle River, and Lower River has a justification geographically. The *Upper River* is a region of light sandy soils devoted especially to the cultivation of peanuts as a cash crop and millets (especially *coos* or *kous*) for food. Peanuts constitute over 95 percent of the exports of the Gambia, and in the Upper River the pressure on land resources is such that food is brought in; only small tracts by the river are liable to flood, and these too usually have sandy peanut soils. The *Middle River* has tracts of alluvium liable to river floods along the Gambia (known as *banto faros*) flanked by sandstone terraces yielding sandy soils. The flood lands have been reclaimed by building "bunds" or banks of mud and reeds, and the fields so formed are cultivated year after year for rice by the women. The men work the higher ground by the usual African system of bush fallowing, with an emphasis on peanuts. In the *Lower River* there is the same distinction into the low-lying areas liable to flood and the uplands. Here, however, the flooding is by brackish water; there are extensive mangrove swamps, and the utilization of the banto faros depends upon the breeding of a rice which can withstand brackish water. Much development effort has gone into the preparation of rice fields on a relatively large scale on the Lower River, assisted by technical advice from Taiwan.

Detailed land-use surveys, with published colored maps on the scale of 1:10,000, showed a remarkable shift in cultivation between 1947 and 1957. As the reclaimed mangrove swamp lands become more fully used, there is a tendency to abandon the higher land.

Gambia has an estimated population of about 350,000, and it may be regarded as an illustration of the relevance of scale to national viability. There are roads, but most of the movement of produce and people is by river, though the ferry services are inadequate. Georgetown may be described as the head of ocean navigation, but river steamers can reach the eastern boundary with Senegal throughout the year and in the high-water season even beyond. The river serves as an outlet for a small area of the hinterland. The problem of smuggling along the Senegal border makes controlled marketing of peanuts and rice difficult to enforce and is a source of friction. Plans exist for much closer economic integration with Senegal, including a common tariff and a much-needed bridge across the river.

PORTUGUESE GUINEA

The Portuguese were early among the European explorers of the coasts of West Africa and claim to have discovered what is now Portuguese Guinea as early as 1446. Sovereignty was claimed by the kings of Portugal from 1462 onwards. In 1669 a station was established on the Corubal, and by 1690 Bissau, or Bissao, was a flourishing slave port. The territory was separated from the governorship of the Cape Verde Islands only in 1879, and in 1886 a long series of disputes with France was ended by a boundary settlement. By this settlement Portuguese Guinea is entirely surrounded, except on the seaward side, by former French territory—Senegal to the north, Guinea to the south.

Although the area is 13,948 square miles (36,125 km²) and the total population over half a million, Portuguese Guinea remains one of the least developed parts of West Africa. The coastline is here extremely intricate. The coastal plain devolves into a succession of low peninsulas and innumerable islands between which lie a maze of channels. The deep estuaries of the Cacheu, Mansôa, Geba (with its tributary the Corubal), and Cacine afford access to considerable distances inland. Though less than in Sierra Leone, the rainfall is high, and mangrove swamps give place inland to dense forest and then savanna. Rice is the principal crop of the coast being grown by peasants in fields laboriously created from mangrove swamps; bananas and oil palms are grown on the slightly drier lands, giving place to peanuts in the interior. There are few cattle, but some sheep and goats of low quality.

The Portuguese are a mere handful, mainly officials. This is apart from considerable armed forces. Such trade as there is (with export of peanuts, rice, wax, palm oil, and hides) is mainly in the hands of Lebanese or French, with the chief port at the capital, Bissau. This port is on a fertile island and can be reached even at low tide by vessels drawing 36 feet through the Geba Canal; it has deep-water wharves. Both Cacheu and Bolama can be reached by comparatively large vessels. The main disadvantages of the coastal strip are the poor drainage and the bad health reputation. There are very few Portuguese plantations, and production and export is largely from peasant farmers. Geologically the area is part of a larger geological basin and exploration for oil continues.

Most of the people of the interior are Mandingos or Fulani, nominally Moslem, who are both agriculturists and pastoralists, while the rice-growers of the coast are the Balante.

SIERRA LEONE

The West African coast from Portuguese Guinea to Cape Palmas in southern Liberia trends almost directly from northwest to southeast and thus at right angles to the rain-bearing airstreams of the wet season. In the typical wet month of July, Sierra Leone and Liberia, its neighbor, receive the full force, and nearly everywhere the rainfall in that one month exceeds 15 inches (380 mm). Both countries belong, therefore, to the wet forested regions of West Africa, with evergreen forests of equatorial type forming the natural vegetation cover over the greater part of the whole. On the coastal belt of Sierra Leone some 150 inches (3800 mm) of rain falls in the rainy season from May to October. Rightly or wrongly this excessive rainfall was long regarded as particularly unhealthy for white people, and it was Sierra Leone in particular which gained the name of the "white man's grave." In the interior the rainfall decreases, and orchard bush or savanna is reached.

Like Portuguese and Republican Guinea, Sierra Leone has a much-broken coastline and a series of rivers draining direct from the interior highlands to the coast, with estuaries sometimes affording good natural harbors. By far the best of these is the mouth of the Rokel, with Freetown nestling under its protecting headland called The Peak, perhaps the finest natural harbor of the whole coast.

Although the inland boundary of Sierra Leone does not correspond strictly with the water parting, in general rivers rise either within its territory or only just over the border. A short distance farther inland, over the mountains which continue the Futa Jallon southeastward, the water drains northeastward into the headstreams of the Niger. In contrast to the Gambia or Nigeria, no great river gives access to the far interior.

The history of Sierra Leone has been briefly recounted in Chapter 2. Although the British in early days took an active part in the African slave trade, they have every reason to be proud of their pioneer work for its abolition. Settlement was begun in Sierra Leone in 1787 with 400 runaway African slaves who were waifs in London, and for those rescued from slave-ships. Though the first settlement failed, it was followed by others, and Free Town (later Freetown) was refounded in 1794. Behind Freetown is a mountainous peninsula some 25 miles (40 km) long; it was the roaring of the winds in the mountains which gave rise to the Portuguese name meaning "Lion Mountain." The history of Sierra Leone repeats many features common to the West African coast. For a long time British interests were restricted to the coast. It was not until 1896, more than a hundred years after the foundation of Freetown, that a British protectorate was proclaimed over the hinterland of 27,669 square miles (71,663 km²) in contrast to the "Colony" on the peninsula extending to only 256 square miles (663 km²). Sierra Leone had a Legislative Council as early as 1863, but not until 1924 was there direct representation of the protectorate. In 1958 a democratically elected House of Representatives came into existence; on April 27, 1961, Sierra Leone became independent and was later elected a member of the U.N. It remains a member of the Commonwealth.

Sierra Leone falls naturally into a number of tracts roughly parallel to the coast.

The coastal belt is one of swamps. They are built up to a large extent by eroded soil from the uplands. They develop into mangrove-covered swamps or *Raphia* swamps covered to a few inches by high spring tides and heavily flooded by fresh water during the rains. Back from the coast they may be flooded only by fresh water. More than half a million acres of reclaimable swamp exist; only 10 percent are at present cultivated. Indeed, a large proportion of the rice, which is the staple food grain of Sierra Leone, is upland rice grown in the interior. Much of the land actually used is along the lower reaches of the Great and Little Scarcies rivers. These potential ricelands could undoubtedly relieve the pressure on the existing food-producing lands and provide a surplus for export, but the necessary land reclamation is difficult and expensive.

Behind the coastal belt is one of undulating ground where shifting cultivation has caused the destruction of much of the original high forest. Here forest products include palm oil and palm kernels, providing the largest agricultural contribution

to the country's exports. Coffee and cocoa are also exported. Although the solid rocks of Sierra Leone away from the coastal plain are mainly granite and gneisses, there is usually a thick covering of laterite which hinders the discovery of minerals. Some of the lateritic deposits are sufficiently rich in iron to have provided the basis of an African smelting and blacksmith industry, but the iron-ore deposits which have been worked for export since 1933 are hematites near Marampa, to which place a 52-mile (84 km) railway was completed from Pepel 15 miles (24 km) upstream from Freetown and on the northern side of the estuary. Access to the port has been deepened and production increased with new markets being found in Japan in addition to the traditional export to Europe.

Bauxite and rutile are also mined but the principal mineral wealth of the country is in diamonds which normally account for over a half of the value of exports. They are derived from the alluvium of the Sewa and Moa river systems and are worked both by large private companies and on a small scale by individuals. The widespread occurrence of the diamonds gave rise in the past to fears of illicit mining and dealing.

Inland the country rises as a much-dissected plateau towards Futa Jallon highland. In the east are forest reserves in high forest country. Elsewhere are clearings growing cassava, yams, and upland and swamp rice. In the north is sparsely populated orchard bush country supporting 25 persons or less per square mile (10 p.km²) in contrast to Sierra Leone's average of about 85 (or 33 p.km²). This is a high figure for tropical Africa.

The focus of the whole country remains Freetown. The government railway to the interior at Pendembu, with a branch to Banya, was built at the very narrow gauge of 2 feet, six inches (76 cm) and with the increase in road haulage, it is being phased out. That to Marampa has a more sensible gauge of 3 feet, six inches (107 cm) but it is purely a mineral line. Unfortunately, maintenance costs on roads are high, and in view of the very heavy rainfall, bridges need to be numerous and able to withstand swollen streams. In the years following the end of World War II many ferries were replaced by bridges built with the help of the Economic Cooperation Administration (E.C.A.).

Freetown is a much-used port of call and is also served by the airport at Lungi on the opposite side of the estuary. Fourah Bay College at Freetown is proud of the fact that it is the oldest university college in Africa south of the Sahara, founded in 1827 and affiliated with the University of Durham until 1967. It is now a constituent member of the University of Sierra Leone together with the Njala University College. These two colleges reflect a distinction between the creole society of Freetown and that of the mainland.

LIBERIA

The story of the establishment of Liberia ("Free land") is well known and has been briefly outlined in Chapter 2. The high hopes which the American Colonization Society entertained in 1821 when they selected the present site of Monrovia as the new African home for freed American Negro slaves were not to be realized quickly. In the first place the American Negroes had lived in contact with Western civilization; they were just as alien to the untamed African jungle as a white settler might be. Although after the establishment of the first settlement others sprang up along the coast, they were under the aegis of the American Society, usually with white governors, and relied on American aid for their continued existence. Apart from the "independent African State of Maryland" which had been established at Cape Palmas in 1833, there were by 1847 only about 3000 Americo-Liberians. In that year the Society suggested that the settlers headed by an octoroon from Virginia, Joseph Jenkins

Roberts, should devise a constitution on American lines. This was done, and the constitution of the Republic has remained closely modeled on that of the United States. The Liberian flag even follows the parent model, horizontal stripes of five white and six red with a blue field on the upper corner next to the flagstaff. On that blue field there remains the original one single star. Independence was declared in 1847, and Roberts held office as first president until 1856. Maryland was absorbed the following year.

But Liberia stagnated. There were doubtless some Americo-Liberians, who, having been slaves themselves, were inclined to look upon the new country as constituting their turn and to regard the existing inhabitants as creatures of a lower order, if not to be slaves at least to be ruled over as menials. On the whole, however, it is probably true to say that Liberia wished to develop on national lines and to cooperate with the native-born Liberian tribes, but that the latter had no desire for cooperation. And so, after a hundred years, the Liberian government exercised authority over a narrow strip of coast and was ignored 20 miles (32 km) inland. In 1925 it was estimated that there were only 25,000 Americo-Liberians, more than half of whom lived in the capital, while the hinterland remained the least-known region in all tropical Africa and one where government control was nominal or nonexistent. This was despite the vigorous forward policy initiated by President Barclay in 1904 of offering concessions to American and European interests and of permitting their advisers and technicians full access to the country. The turning point was really 1925 when a large land grant for rubber planting was made to the Firestone Company. This was followed by something of a "boom" when a number of estates were laid out and big houses were built of timber imported from America.

With a coastline of about 350 miles (560 km) Liberia has a total area of 43,000 square miles (111,000 km²), roughly the same as the State of Pennsylvania (Figure 13.10). A census taken in 1962 gave a population of 1,016,000, lower than previous estimates. This gives a rather low density now estimated at about 25 per square mile (10 p.km²), and some of the forests are virtually uninhabited. Apart from the Americo-Liberians some 60,000 of the coast Negroes have been in sufficiently close contact with Western influences not to be tribally identifiable. Of the six main groups inhabiting the rest of the country the Mandingos are Moslems, but the Gissi, Gola, Kpwesi, Kru, and Graboes may be called pagans, except where they have been influenced by Christian missions. The Kru of the coast—indeed the southeastern coast is

called the Kru coast—are great seamen and are employed on ships trading to West Africa. All the coastal peoples like the water and make great use of it. They build their villages near the high-water mark and make extensive use of dugout canoes in the tidal estuaries. Some of these traditional canoes (the Accra type) are fitted with sails and are thoroughly seaworthy. Only those who can handle a boat with skill would dare the work of handling cargoes by surfboat. Except at Monrovia, Buchanan, and one of the river mouths which can be entered by small steamers, coastwise shipping depends on these surfboats just as elsewhere at the minor ports on the West African coast. Some of the coastal people have penetrated into the

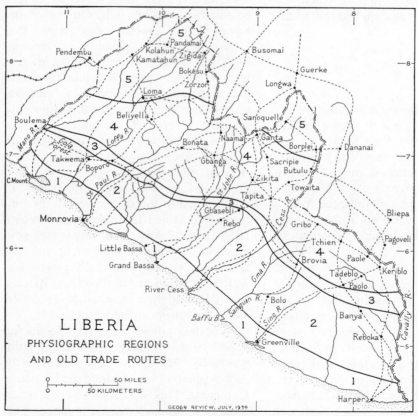

13.10 Liberia, showing the old trails and the broad physiographic divisions: (1) coastal plain (2) rolling hills (3) hills rising steeply to 600 feet (180 m) or more (4) dissected plateau, average elevation 900 feet (275 m); (5) mountainous country. (From G. W. Harley, *Geog. Rev.,* 1939. Courtesy of the *Geographical Review,* American Geographical Society.)

interior by river and settled on the banks, but, broadly speaking, behind the coastal belt live people whose only contact with the sea is to come at certain seasons to fish and take back home the smoked fish. Some such tribes, the De for example, have actually reserved narrow corridors to the sea.

Many writers have referred to what they describe as Liberia's "colonial system." By this was meant the old contention among Americo-Liberians that a very sharp line existed between them and the aborigines whose function should be to pay hut taxes and to contribute foodstuffs and cheap labor to the national economy. The aborigines regarded the Americo-Liberians as intruders of foreign origin, often in council referred to them as "Americans," and regarded the future of the country as being one of self-determination in which the Americo-Liberians would be excluded. However, two factors have here intervened. In 1944 President W.V.S. Tubman initiated a policy designed to secure equality of citizenship throughout the country. In the second place the ties between Liberia and the United States have become increasingly close, increasing the pace of change throughout the country. During World War II an American force was established in Liberia (later withdrawn), a large and efficient airport was constructed and maintained at Roberts Field, the construction of a commercial deep-water port at Monrovia by the United States Navy was begun, a health mission was maintained, and a road was undertaken from Monrovia into French Guinea. On their part, the Liberians granted a concession to an American company to work rich iron ore at Bomi Hill about 40 miles north of Monrovia, and a mineral line was built to bring out the ore. On January 1, 1944, the Liberian dollar was raised to parity with the United States dollar, and Liberia is in the Dollar Area in contrast to the rest of West Africa which is in the Franc or Sterling Area.

Liberia can readily be divided, as shown in Figure 13.10 into five belts parallel to the coast. The first (1 on Figure 13.10) is the coastal plain with rivers and lagoons navigable for small boats where clearings in the forest yield a few palm products and citrus fruits can be grown. Behind this is a belt (2) of rolling hills, 100–300 feet above sea level, adapted to rubber plantations where the forest can be cleared. The narrow belt marked 3 on Figure 13.10 is the main rise to the African plateau—hills rising steeply to 600 feet (180 m) or more. Beyond this lies a dissected plateau (4) at an average elevation of 900 feet (275 m) which has a low density of population but has much commercial forest and is the home of the kola tree. The interior (5) is mountainous country with elevations up to 3000 feet (900 m) in the northwest, 4000 feet (1200 m) in the center, and even reaching, in Mt. Nimba on the frontier, 5800 feet (1768 m). Like the remainder of Liberia this country too is forested.

At the mission station at Ganta (see Figure 13.10) Harley[2] has described the climate with care. The year begins with the dry month of January, with the harmattan blowing. This wind continues till about mid-February; it then reduces the temperature by promoting evaporation of residual moisture. Some rains then arrive, but it is not until about mid-March that the ground has been sufficiently softened for a heavy fall to be followed by a flight of termites. This is taken as a sign for bush cutting and the planting of cassava on the uplands, rice in the swamps. The harvest of rice (of which at least thirty-five varieties are known) begins in July, main crop in August, late varieties in December. In July and August the harvest is helped by a decrease in rain, the "little dries." October and November have heavy dews and are best for growing vegetables, cotton, and tobacco.

[2] G. W. Harley, "Roads and Trails in Liberia," *Geog. Rev.,* XXIX (1939), 447–460.

Rice may be called the staple food of Liberia. Not enough is produced, however, for the town population of the coast, and there is a large import of rice, as well as of other less basic foodstuffs. This reflects the way in which the striking economic advance of recent years has been the result of large scale enterprise in rubber planting and iron-ore mining and associated investments. Agriculture has remained little affected and still largely subsistence oriented.

Although there is some production and export of palm kernels, coffee, and cocoa, the principal cash crop remains rubber. The industry is dominated by the giant Firestone estates, but production is shared with other plantations and by a large number (over 10,000) of small producers who market latex or coagulum to be further processed by the companies. For many years, rubber accounted for ninety percent or more of exports but its relative importance has declined with the rise of iron-ore mining.

Iron ore is of widespread occurrence in the crystalline rocks of the interior although they had not been immediately detected beneath deep laterite soils and heavy forest. Exports began in 1951 and iron ore now accounts for two-thirds of the total. Three mines export through Monrovia while the largest, which is removing much of the summit of Mt. Nimba on the Guinea border, is connected by rail with the artificial port, also specially constructed, at Buchanan. A fifth mine is under development. Other minerals are known but not worked and although diamonds are exported, an unknown proportion are believed to be derived from Sierra Leone.

These large mining and plantation ventures have required massive investment in infrastructure, particularly in the ports of Monrovia and Buchanan, the construction of railroads [e.g., from Nimba to Buchanan, 170 miles, (274 km)] and of roads. The companies as well as the government provide schools and hospitals. Government revenues have increased greatly by its holdings in the equity of the mining companies but their mechanized operations do not provide as much employment as the plantations.

The pace of development has been particularly dramatic in the transformation of the capital city of Monrovia. In the early 1950's it was a small town of some 30,000 inhabitants characterized by old and rather dilapidated buildings and with most streets unpaved and unlit. Twenty years later, the population had jumped to 100,000, streets were paved and lit and there were many air-conditioned buildings and a central boulevard. Dirt roads to Robertsfield and the Firestone plantations had been replaced by modern paved highways.

A source of government revenue which has given rise to some international controversy has been the registration of shipping under the Liberian "flag of convenience." Liberia now has the largest merchant marine in the world, consisting largely of tankers belonging to companies with international interests, the ships of which would never expect to see their country of registration. Restrictive regulations both by government and trade unions make American owners anxious to register their vessels under what has been described as a "flag of necessity."

GHANA

Despite the absence of good natural harbors and the dangerous surf which pounds everlastingly along the sandy shores, the stretch known as the Gold Coast exhibited a combination of geographical factors which rendered it particularly attractive in the eyes of the early European explorers and traders. It is here, east of Cape Three Points, that a climatic anomaly brings drier conditions, the causes of which are still under dispute. The different direction of the coast, so that rain-bearing southwesterly winds are parallel, has been suggested, also upwelling cool waters offshore are a factor. In contrast to the totals (exceeding 120 inches) of the Sierra Leone and Liberian coasts, the seasonal fall drops to less than 60 inches (1500 mm), over a long stretch to less than 40 inches (1000 mm)—at Accra to less than 30 (760 mm)—and at Lomé on the eastern border it is only 31 (787 mm). Instead of a coastline of mangrove swamp backed by lofty evergreen forests, the savanna zone reaches the coast. To the coast came Africans with gold dust; along the coast were occasional headlands offering defensible sites for forts or fortified trading posts.

The Portuguese were the first to establish permanent stations, starting in Elmina in 1481. In the seventeenth century the Dutch ousted the Portuguese but had to share with the British. Denmark and Brandenburg (now part of Germany) were there too. The abolition of slave trading in 1807 caused the British to reduce their forts from twelve to four, and even those would have been given up had they not served a useful purpose, by the irony of fate, as bases for the British navy *against* slaving. An early attempt at government taking a hand in trading was unsuccessful, but a handful of merchant traders refused to leave the coast. George Maclean, their leader, was probably the first man to adopt indirect rule, encouraging the chiefs to apply their own laws to the orderly control of their territories, provided they were "in harmony with civilized ideas of justice."

When the British government realized the determination of those interested in the Gold Coast to remain, they reluctantly appointed a governor, and in 1850 a charter established a separate government from that of Sierra Leone, of which the Gold Coast had been nominally a dependency. Even then the object of the British government was ultimately to withdraw. But there was no turning back. The great legend of Queen Victoria as the mighty mother protector was growing. In 1844 the Fanti tribes had voluntarily made a bond renouncing human sacrifice and agreeing that all cases of murder and robbery should be tried by British officers according to British law. So in 1865 a Report to the British House of Commons advised against any extension of sovereignty but stated: ". . . it is not possible to withdraw the British government wholly or immediately from the West African coast." But the little British territory could not remain static. The Fanti tribes threatened the remaining Dutch ports, and in 1871 the Dutch asked the British to take them over—at the price of the few stores they contained. So the British took on a war, the Ashanti war of 1873. By this time the French had been active. Their main objective had been to consolidate their interest in the Ivory Coast and its hinterland and to prevent the British in Sierra Leone from linking up with the Gold Coast. Germany secured the long narrow strip running inland of Togoland adjoining the Gold Coast on the east simply by hoisting the German flag at Baguida, Lomé, and Porto-Segouro in 1884, and notifying Britain that a protectorate had been established.

Thus the British colony of the Gold Coast (capital Accra) was defined by the actions of France and Germany. It was not until 1901 that Britain finally settled a protectorate over Ashanti (capital Kumasi), the Northern Territories having been delimited in 1897. Part of Togoland was placed under British mandate after World War I and under trusteeship in 1946. The Gold Coast in that same year became the first African dependency to secure a legislature with a majority of elected members (18 against 12), Ashanti and the Northern Territories being specifically represented. The subsequent story leading to independence in 1957, and the adoption of the historically inspiring but geographically misleading name of Ghana, has already been told.

The rapid recent political growth is closely bound up with economic development, which in turn is closely bound up with cocoa. It was an African worker returning from Fernando Póo in 1879 who brought half a dozen cocoa beans and planted them on his farm. There were later importations, and in 1891 there was the first recorded export of 80 pounds. The cultivation of cocoa spread rapidly through the Gold Coast Colony, and in 1898 was introduced into Ashanti, where it spread with equal rapidity throughout all parts of the country having suitable physical conditions. Within a fews decades the Gold Coast as a whole was producing between 200,000 and 300,000 tons, two-thirds of the world's total output. It is not commonly realized that cocoa is grown entirely on African farms by Africans. It is not a plantation crop as is commonly believed. The European's part has been in buying the crop and also in helping with research, control of pests and diseases, provision of best seed and fertilizers, and, where needed, government supervision. The cocoa is bought by the great international cocoa firms through the Marketing Board. Yet the swollen shoot disease, which assumed alarming proportions in the nineteen-forties, threatened the whole industry and with it the economy of the country. Happily science found the answer.

Cocoa has made Ghana rich, but it has brought problems. As a source of wealth the government encouraged planting, but in Ashanti the Confederacy Council (then the supreme African authority) wisely showed itself afraid of a single-crop economy. Every third chocolate, from every candy box in the world, comes from Ghana. In fancy we may visualize running from the chocolate boxes everywhere in the world a constant river of money that seeps and percolates into the humblest homes of the country, and brings a standard of living amongst the highest in tropical Africa — cars, bicycles, radios, clothes, and homes. It is easy for a government to see in cocoa a crop readily salable and the country's most efficient dollar earner. Although dependence on cocoa

has declined, it normally accounts for over a half of the value of exports; Ghana is therefore still at risk when disease appears or when the world price declines.

The success of cocoa production brought increased population, especially to Ashanti, by immigration from the Northern Region (formerly Northern Territories) and from the neighboring Francophone states. The population of Ashanti jumped from 406,000 in 1921 to 578,000 in 1931, 824,000 in 1948, and 1.1 million in 1960. Urbanization is also most marked; Kumasi jumped from 35,800 in 1931 to 78,500 in 1948 and to 190,400 in 1960. Mining centers trebled. The towns have to be fed by food imported from other areas; even many of the cocoa villages no longer have enough land to grow their own food. The pressure on the land has involved destruction of much forest. Runoff of rainwater is increased, soil erosion encouraged, protection from the drying harmful harmattan lost.[3]

The total area of modern Ghana is 92,100 square miles (238,537 km²), with a 1948 census population of 4,111,680, which by 1968 had more than doubled to an estimated 8.4 million. The whole is roughly rectangular, having a coastline of 270 miles (430 km) and an extent from north to south of 300 miles (480 km).

In its relief Ghana repeats the usual West Coast features. There is a coastal plain, though in the center this gives place to higher ground with cliffs. Behind lies an undulating upland rising gradually to the wedge-shaped Ashanti plateau with its exposures of ancient crystalline rocks. From the crest of this upland short streams drain southward straight to the coast, but northward from the crest, the land falls again to the broad valley plain of the Volta and its tributaries. Two-thirds of the whole country lies in the basin of the Volta, the main stream of which, the

[3] These and other problems are discussed by R. W. Steel, "Some Geographical Problems of Land Use in British West Africa," *Trans. Institute of British Geographers* (1948), No. 14 (1949).

13.F Within the artificial harbour basin of Takoradi, Ghana, logs await shipment. (Photo: Jack Barker by courtesy of the United Africa Company.)

Black Volta, rises far to the northwest in the Republic of Haute-Volta (Upper Volta) to which it gives its name.

Although not ranking with the Niger or the Congo, the Volta is one of Africa's major rivers. In its lower reaches it has cut a gorge which was noted as a potential power site as long ago as 1915, and a complex Volta River Project began to be considered during the 1950s. With World Bank and other contributors construction of the dam at Akasombo began in 1961 and the first electricity was generated in September 1965. The final installed capacity (after allowing for a generator on standby reserve) will be 640 megawatts. This compares with the previous annual consumption for the entire country of 120 megawatts. Part of this great output is used by an aluminium smelting plant at Tema using imported raw material and exporting ingots and billets. Schemes to utilize large local deposits have not materialized. Electricity is also to be exported to nearby Togo and Dahomey. The resulting lake Volta has flooded a significant pro-

13.G The Akasombo Dam on the Volta River, Ghana. (Photo: The United Africa Company.)

portion of the country (3.5 percent) but fortunately the area concerned was not very productive, a part of the "middle belt," but some 80,000 people had to be resettled before the 250-mile-long lake drowned their lands. The lake offers opportunities for fishing and for communication by boat with the northern regions.

Both the relief and the climate prevent Ghana from exhibiting the simple zonation of environmental conditions parallel to the coast seen in other parts of West Africa. It does, however, fall into a number of well-marked climatic-vegetation regions, each with characteristic human response. In the extreme southwest, west of Cape Three Points, is a coastal plain enjoying almost equatorial rainfall and temperatures where swamp rice can be grown. Its focal point is Axim.

Inland in the southwest is undulating country covered naturally with evergreen forest. This yields cabinet woods of the mahogany, ebony, and teak types exported from Takoradi. This country and its extension eastward form the oil-palm belt. The production of kernels and oil has, however, greatly diminished because of the greater attraction of cocoa cultivation.

Over the plateau of crystalline rocks which makes up a large part of the west, the rainfall is sufficiently heavy and well distributed through the year for the natural vegetation to be that of a dense equatorial forest. Here are the words of a Fanti whose home was at Sekondi:[4] "I have walked mile after mile through narrow meandering paths bounded on either side by great forest lands, primeval forests in whose depths are the farms and cocoa plantations of the African farmers and cocoa planters . . . . only here and there could I see streaks of sunlight penetrating through the branches and the leaves to lighten our paths . . . . in these forests the most prominent tree is the silk-cotton,

which rises like a column to a height of over 100 feet and measures 8 to 10 feet in diameter. . . . The forest is the home of wild animals . . . . the elephant has been almost exterminated by ivory hunters . . . . the forest growth is gradually being cleared in order that the land may be reclaimed for agricultural purposes and also for the building of new townships."

This word picture conveys the essential idea that the great cocoa region is still one of untidy African farms (averaging only about 3 acres, 1.2 ha, in extent), largely hidden by forest — untidy but thus escaping the evils of soil erosion. But here conservation of appropriate areas of forest is vital to maintain an essential resource, maintain even flow of water, and afford a protection against the drying harmattan. The preservation of the native fauna is another worldwide problem.

The areas of densest production of cocoa are around Kumasi. The development of cocoa production has depended largely on a growing network of roads and a considerable mileage of railways. It is the presence of mineral deposits, however, which necessitated the construction of railways. Northward the cocoa-equatorial forest area gives place to forest where leaf fall in the hot season is marked; this is the region of kola nuts. Northward the forest merges gradually into savanna.

Gold is often second in value to cocoa among exports. Gold-bearing conglomerates are widely distributed, and the gold is both panned from streams — as it has been since long before the Gold Coast earned its name — and mined. The chief workings lie along the Takoradi–Kumasi line and its branch to Prestea. Diamonds with stones of industrial quality were first found in quantity in 1919 in the Birrim Valley, reached by the Central Region Railway. The industry here has some advantage over an industry depending on stones of gem quality; the industrial demand is steadier. Large deposits of manganese ore have been found and are worked opencast

[4] Joseph S. Annan, "The Gold Coast Colony," *Scot. Geog. Mag.,* LIX (1943) pp. 55–59.

at Nsuta near Tarkwa junction. Ghana ranks as a leading world exporter of this metal vital in the steel industry. Bauxite is worked at Awaso, having there been reached by a branch line; the opening up of other deposits is possible following the completion of hydroelectric power works.

Brong-Ahafo, the Northern and Upper Regions, are savanna, relatively sparsely populated but with some production of shea nuts, from which shea butter is produced. The main export is of labor to work in the cocoa farms and the towns of the south.

For a long time the chief outlet of the Gold Coast was Accra, an open roadstead where all goods had to be taken to and from the shore by surfboats while the ocean-going vessels rode at anchor in the heavy swell. Despite the consummate skill with which these surfboats were handled (a grand piano was seen to be successfully lowered onto two surfboats lashed together) delay, damage, and expensive handling were inevitable. The western railway reached the coast at Sekondi, which was also an open roadstead, until the construction and completion in 1928 of a fine harbor at Takoradi a few miles away led to the abandonment of Sekondi. Takoradi is a deep-water harbor protected by long breakwaters built of local gneiss. It has commodious wharves, so that most trade from western Ghana goes to the port, mostly such bulky raw materials as cocoa, manganese ore, gold, bauxite, and timber. In 1961 the roadstead port of Accra, and of the minor ports like Axim, Cape Coast, Saltpond, and Winneba, were replaced by the opening of a second deep-water port at Tema. This is designed to serve the general traffic of the Accra area, the aluminum smelters and other industries associated with the Volta River development, and connects by a bridge across the Volta with the old Togoland. At the same time Accra is being transformed into a modern city, already with a population of over half a million.

Kumasi has grown to be a focal point of Ghanaian communications, of railways and roads. Two roads from Kumasi reach the northern borders of the country, one in the west, the other through the heart of the Northern Region and continuing to Ouagadougou in Upper Volta.

The economic and political advancement of Ghana is matched by a lead in education. The University College of the Gold Coast has become the University of Ghana, with a fine modern campus at Legon, near Accra. Kumasi has a University of Science and Technology while the University College of Cape Coast specializes in teacher training.

NIGERIA (FEDERATION OF NIGERIA)

Nigeria is the largest and most populous of the Commonwealth countries in Africa. Its area, approximately 356,669 square miles (923,773 km^2), makes the country comparable in size to Texas and Arizona together, or six times the area of New England. The population of about 61 million (U.N. estimate of 1968) is distributed in such a way that locally Nigeria faces serious problems of overpopulation, at least with the existing system of cultivation. Pressure on the land has in turn led in the south to such a shortening of the period of rest in the system of shifting cultivation as to induce serious soil erosion, in the north to such overstocking as also to encourage soil erosion.

Historical Development. Nigeria, although roughly the basin of the lower Niger, had little claim to be considered as a unit until its emergence as one of the new independent African states. It resulted from the almost fortuitous association of diverse territories under one British administration after Northern and Southern Nigeria were joined together in 1914. At independence, Nigeria was given a federal structure with Northern, Eastern, and Western Regions to a considerable extent autonomous and with a federal capital at Lagos. This reflected the contrast between the Moslem Hausa and Fulani of the northern savannas with the Christian or pagan peoples of the southern forest lands, and, within the south the strongly marked cultural differences between the Yoruba peoples, with their local kings or "Obas" and the mobile and commercially oriented Ibos. The distrust bred by these differences led to the tragic attempt at the formation of a breakaway Republic of Biafra, 1967–1969. The Federation now consists of twelve states.

Under the name of the Oil Rivers (from the association with palm oil) the channels of the Niger delta had been known for 300 years to European traders before H. L. Lander in 1830 proved their connection with the Niger. Wilberforce, who headed the antislavery movement in Britain, was succeeded in the eighteen-thirties by J. F. Buxton, who argued that naval or military force would never crush the slave trade but that profit from legitimate trade must be offered to the African chiefs in lieu of what they might lose by the suppression of the slave trade. A Niger expedition was organized in 1841–1842 to establish trading posts, but disease proved fatal to nearly all concerned. Later attempts to establish permanent trading stations likewise failed.

Farther west, Lagos had long been a headquarters of the slave trade. The British enthroned there in 1851 an antislaving king, but he did not prove strong enough for the task. It was his son who, in 1861, ceded Lagos to Britain, and so Lagos became an antislaving base. In the meantime British trading interests established firmer holds in the Niger delta and were consolidated into the United Africa Company in 1879. When West Africa was debated at the Berlin Conference of 1884–1885, British interests in the Niger coastlands were established and, by the agreement of 1886 delimited, from French Dahomey on the west to German Kamerun on the east.

British trading interests received a charter from the crown and became the Royal Niger Company in 1886, with extensive powers. Lagos remained a British colony and protectorate. The Royal Niger Company established stations on the Niger and Benue until its advance brought the British into contact with the powerful Moslem emirates of the north, especially of Kano and Sokoto. Because there were differences to be settled with France, in 1889 the company's charter and governing powers were withdrawn and its sphere of operations reorganized into the

13.H A general view of Ibadan from Mapo Hill. Ibadan is the largest truly indigenous city of tropical Africa. (Photo: Shell.)

Protectorates of Northern and Southern Nigeria. In the succeeding years, Lugard, as High Commissioner of the Protectorate of Northern Nigeria, slowly and steadily forced the emirs to abandon slavery and accept Western ideas of law and order.

In Southern Nigeria there were pagan kingdoms where a rule of fear yielded slowly to the system of indirect rule under Britain. In 1906 Lagos was combined with Southern Nigeria, and in 1914 they were united with Northern Nigeria to form the Colony and Protectorate of Nigeria with Lagos as the seat of government. There followed a period of steady development in which the building of railways played an important part, later the building of roads. The enormous importance of modern transport in African development has been repeatedly emphasized in this book. Nigeria affords many examples. The prosperity of the southern coastlands has long depended largely upon palm oil, and the oil-palm belt can be reached to a large extent by navigable channels of the delta. But the production of tin ore from the Jos Plateau, which permitted Nigerian output at one time to reach a fifth or a quarter of the world's total (now about six percent), would not have been possible without the provision of rail access. The same is true of the coal deposits at Enugu.

The autocratic pagan kingdoms of Southern Nigeria with their colorful and picturesquely styled chiefs felt the full force of the political movements which reached their peak in the years following World War II. Large numbers of West Africans served in the armed forces in many theaters of war (including Burma) and came back critical of much in their homeland. Serious rioting took place in several places such as Abeokuta and Benin. The ruler of the former, the Alake of Abeokuta, went into exile, to return amid scenes of triumphal splendor some two years later. Again Western concepts of democracy came into conflict with the traditional African tribal organization.

In general terms throughout this book considerable emphasis has been placed on the sameness of conditions throughout tropical Africa. Although there are important differences between the major regions—such as West Africa and East Africa—and divergencies which increase under the varied European influences, naturally some parts stand out from others in social, economic, or political development. It is in this regard that Nigeria, despite the diversity of its parts, is outstanding. Nowhere have the Moslem emirates retained their distinctive character so well as in the north of Nigeria; nowhere have the erstwhile pagan, now largely Christian, Negro kingdoms retained the individuality and the pageantry that they have among the Yoruba of the south. A description of the ancient city of Benin as recently as 1951 referred to the pageantry whereby a new local chief in traditional garb of starched white linen skirt, coral necklet, anklets, and wristlets, supported by a young man on whose shoulders he rested his arms, preceded by sword bearer and followed by a band, received confirmation of his office from the Oba or king of Benin. The sprawling palace of the king, partly of mud and partly of sheet iron or brick, was still lit only by an occasional hurricane lamp, yet the Oba spoke English perfectly and made frequent visits to England. His son was educated at Cambridge University. Benin is the city which has produced some remarkable carving and brass work over several centuries.

The Physical Background. These human contrasts between north and south in Nigeria merely reflect the climatic conditions, which have resulted in a series of climatic–vegetation–agricultural zones roughly parallel to the coast. Before, however, the railroads, and later motor roads, came to link north and south, the Niger and its great navigable tributary, the Benue, played their part. Broadly, the coastal swamps of the Niger delta and the lagoonal coastline give place inland to

13.I and J Old and new methods of tin working in Nigeria. In the upper picture the earth is being dug by hand and the heavy baskets are being carried away by women. In the lower picture the same type of ground is being worked by hydraulic sluicing with a minimum of labor. Such technological improvements lead to economic efficiency but render worse the chronic problem of unemployment in developing countries. (Copyright: R. J. Harrison Church.)

high plains in the Yoruba country and to the Udi Plateau reaching 1000 feet (300 m) above sea level. In the lower Niger–Benue basin Cretaceous and Tertiary sediments obscure the ancient crystalline rocks, and the coal seams in the Cretaceous sandstones of Enugu are economically significant. It is north of the Niger–Benue that the Jos Plateau of crystallines

averages 4000 feet (1200 m) and has tin ores of great importance. Northward the plateau descends by steps to the Chad basin. The eastern margins of the country are marked by a great line of disturbance, with volcanic rocks culminating in the huge pile of Cameroun Mountain, since 1961 included in the Cameroun Republic.

Climatically, the almost equatorial belt

of the south enjoys in places over 100 inches (2500 mm) of rain (Figure 13.11), with a double maximum (April–July and September–October) and a very equable temperature ranging throughout the year only a few degrees on either side of 80°F (27°C). Northward the amount of rain decreases, the length of the dry season increases (reaching as much as 9 months), there is a single rainfall maximum but the total fall varies greatly from year to year, and the daily and annual ranges of temperature increase. In the coastal belt some very heavy rainfalls are recorded. 150 inches (3800 mm) over much of the delta and up to 400 inches (1000 mm) over the border on Cameroun Mountain. Storms of hurricane force tend to occur at the beginning and the end of the rains.

Mangrove forests cover large areas of the delta and coastlands, the trees ranging from 5 to 60 feet (1.5 to 18 m) in height (Figure 13.12). Inland is the equatorial rainforest with its great buttressed lofty trees, some of which yield timber of mahogany type. This is the oil-palm belt, and it is the Guinea oil palm, wild or cultivated, which is still a major export. The rainforest is a belt of poor sandy soils, badly leached in the east, and affords ample proof that the luxuriant forest growth is no criterion of soil fertility. How much of the forest is "primeval" is an interesting problem. Traces of human settlement under the largest trees when felled have demonstrated that much is in fact second growth. Some African plantations of Hevea rubber have been established in Benin and Calabar. The succeeding "monsoon" or deciduous forest belt yields mahogany and bamboo but is more significant as the home of the kola nut. The great heart of Nigeria is savanna land with *Acacia, Terminalia,* and baobab, and this gives place northward to thorn forest and scrub.

Agriculture. Agricultural belts follow those of natural vegetation (Figure 13.13). Generally subsistence farming is giving place to farming where subsistence crops are combined with one or more cash crops. In the coastal and wet belts common crops in the temporary forest clearings (often with basin cultivation, described on p. 86), include yams, cassava, maize, sugar cane, plantains, bananas, and oil palm. Cocoa cultivation is very important in the west, but it is difficult to dry the beans before they become moldy.

In the intermediate forest areas cultivation is similar, with kola nuts as a cash crop. Over the savanna or plateau areas the agricultural Hausas practicing permanent or shifting cultivation cultivate millet or guinea corn (sorghum), groundnuts (usually known as peanuts in America), cassava, tobacco, and cotton, together with shea nuts. On the irrigated lands around Sokoto rice is grown and sugar cane is also grown under irrigation. The Hausas share the land with the pastoral

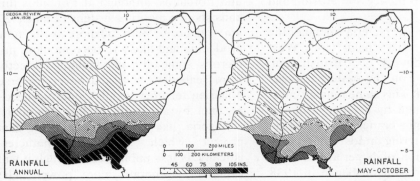

13.11 Rainfall map of Nigeria. (From L. Dudley Stamp, *Geog. Rev.,* 1938. Courtesy of the *Geographical Review,* American Geographical Society.)

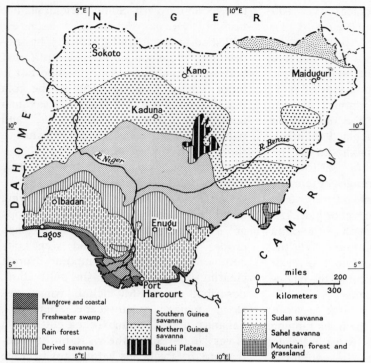

13.12 Vegetation zones of Nigeria. Compare this map with that of rainfall, Figure 13.11. (After R. W. J. Keay, 1953.)

Fulani, with their 10 million cattle and many sheep and goats. Local varieties of cotton have long been cultivated, but improved types, with staples up to one inch, as well as American long-stapled cottons, have become general along the Lagos–Kano railway line. Zaria is a leading center. But the great cash crop of the north is the peanut. The introduction of light steel plows to replace the traditional hoe was found to induce soil erosion and was abandoned.

The minerals of Nigeria include the only worked coal fields of West Africa—the discovery of a British geologist—at Enugu, on the eastern railway to Port Harcourt. This same railway, after crossing the Benue by a great bridge at Makurdi, gives off a branch which taps the tin ore fields centering on Jos. The leading mineral production of Nigeria, however, is oil. Exploration for oil began in 1938 but the first exports were not made until 1958 since when it has reached the posi-

tion of leading export commodity with a rapidly increasing output. The geological setting seemed favorable for oil in the delta of the Niger river and it was at Oloibiri, to the west of Port Harcourt, that the first field was discovered. Productive areas have since been found across the Niger in the Middle West State and eastward in Calabar (South Eastern State) (Figure 13.14). Exporting ports are Bonny and Forcados, although at Forcados this consists of a mooring system 17 miles (27 km) offshore. With offshore wells now producing and likely to become more numerous, some oil may be pumped directly from seabed to ship and never traverse Nigerian territory at all. Domestic needs are met by a refinery at Port Harcourt.

Nigeria, like Ghana, has a major dam project which, however, characteristically, is less publicized although it will eventually generate more power. The Niger does not have a gorge section but between Yela and Jebba its course is con-

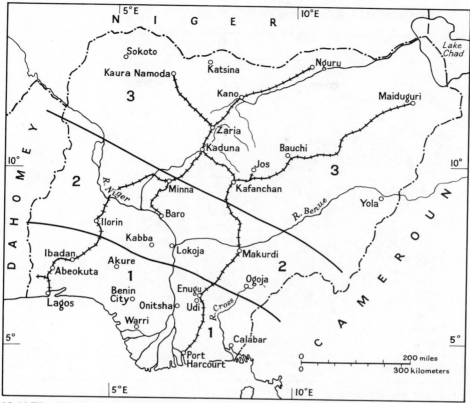

13.13 The three broad agricultural zones of Nigeria. (1) Southern belt of yams, cassava, maize, oil palms and cocoa; (2) middle belt of orchard bush; (3) northern belt of open savanna merging into scrub, with cultivation of guinea corn, millet, peanuts, and cotton; cattle and goats.

13.K Traditional looms at Keffi, Nigeria, weaving narrow strips of cloth which are then sewn together. (Photo: Eric Kay.)

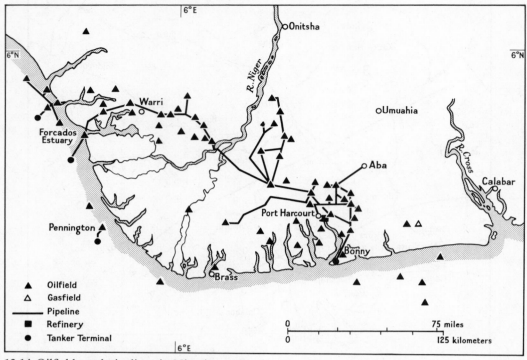

13.14 Oilfields and pipelines in Nigeria.

fined and it is interrupted by a number of rapids. Suitably solid foundations were found at Kainji although the dam had to be $2\frac{3}{4}$ miles (4.2 km) long and another of a similar length was necessary to control a low watershed. The dam has a maximum height of 215 feet (65 m) and will be able to supply generators to a capacity of 960 megawatts. Again, such a great increase in available electricity cannot be absorbed immediately. There is no major project requiring electricity comparable to the aluminium plant at Tema but power lines have been constructed to go through Ibadan to Lagos in the south and to Kaduna in the north. Locks at the dam, together with a canal to bypass the Awuru rapids downstream, and improved control of water flow downstream, makes navigation possible for most of the year as far as the border with the Niger Republic. This should greatly lower the cost of transport for groundnuts, cotton, livestock, and other products to the south and for export. Improved flood control should permit

more agriculture on the flood plains downstream and fishing in the lake will be an economic resource. The reservoir covers an area of 480 square miles (1240 km²) and 50,000 people were displaced. Fortunately the area covered is of poor Guinea-type savanna of low productivity. Further dams are planned for Jebba, also on the Niger which would have a capacity of 500 megawatts and at the Shiroro Gorge on the major tributary of the Kaduna River, with a capacity of 480 megawatts.

Towns and communications. The Niger is navigable by flat-bottomed steamers all the year round from the sea to near the Kaduna confluence (460 miles, 740 km), and in the high-water season (July to October) through the Kainji dam (which has greatly improved navigation) to the Niger border. The Benue is seasonally navigable for 470 miles (760 km) above its confluence with the Niger to Garua on the Cameroun side of the frontier. The Cross River is of great local value in reaching the palm-oil belt and has an oil-exporting port at Calabar. Behind the coastal sand bars navigable waterways connect the Lagos lagoon with the Niger delta.

Lagos, the federal capital, is partly situated on an island in a lagoon reached over a dredged bar from the ocean (Figure 13.15). Although Lagos has deep-water wharves, most of the trade is handled at the well-equipped railway wharves of Apapa on the mainland. Thence the main line runs inland through the large, sprawling old Yoruba capital Ibadan, one of the largest cities (800,000 estimated in 1970) of tropical Africa, and now the seat of a great university. The line reaches and crosses the Niger at Jebba; beyond, the administrative industrial center of Kaduna (chosen as a healthy site) has largely replaced the old town of Zaria. It is at Kaduna that the eastern line to Port Harcourt (now Nigeria's second port) on the Bonny River joins the main line. Reference has been made elsewhere to the way in which in Nigeria railway and mineral development went hand in hand. Later motor roads have played an increasingly important part, and air transport is important both internally and internationally. A particularly fascinating example of a major center surviving and adapting itself to change is afforded by Kano, which accordingly merits special study.

Kano. The walled cities which are the capitals of the Moslem kingdoms or emirates of Northern Nigeria and neighboring states are among the most fascinating features of West Africa. An excellent example is offered by Kano, though many others might be chosen—Sokoto or Katsina, for instance. Kano is fundamentally as it was when studied and described by Dr. Derwent Whittlesey,[5] except that there has been a great expansion of the modern township outside the walled city and the whole area is undergoing the mod-

[5] "Kano: A Sudanese Metropolis," *Geog. Rev.,* XXVII (1937) pp. 177–199.

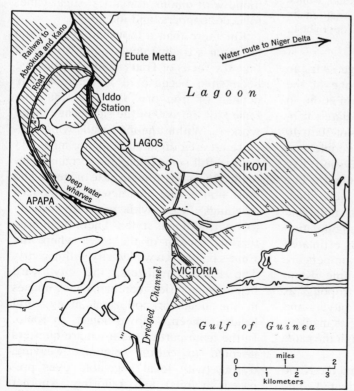

13.15 The site of Lagos.

13.L A merchant's town house in Kano. Notice the flat roof and elaborate and traditionally nonrepresentational decoration. (Copyright L. Dudley Stamp.)

ernization typical of all large African centers. It is the center of one of the major pockets of dense population in West Africa. In the area immediately tributary to the city within a radius of 30 to 40 miles live more than a million people, and within the administrative division live more than double that number. The *umland* or tributary area is well tilled: there are hamlets every half mile and about forty walled towns. The population of the urban area of Kano was estimated at 300,000 in 1968 but these numbers are greatly increased at harvest time. Kano well deserves the title of "metropolis" as there is a constant stream of buyers and sellers into and out of the city; as many as 25,000 may pass inward through the gates in the wall during the day.

In contrast to most of Africa, the Kano *umland* is continuously cultivated. The soils, derived from underlying granite, are light and easily worked and benefit greatly from manuring. The Hausa cultivators pay the nomadic Fulani who own all the cattle in the neighborhood to pasture their herds on the stubble fields during the dry season and thus to benefit the land by animal and human manure and "treading." The soil is enriched also by the manure of the sheep, goats, and pack animals—especially asses and mules— which are kept by the farmers. The light land of the Kano area has also benefited greatly from the increased cultivation of peanuts, which, though they require other manures, add nitrogenous material made from atmospheric nitrogen to the soil. The field crops raised in the rainy half of the year are chiefly Guinea corn (*Sorghum vulgare*), spiked millet (*Pennisetum spicatum*), and peanuts, with smaller proportions of cotton, manioc, sweet potatoes, and sesame. Where water can be obtained throughout the year from well or stream (by *shadoof*), gardens are found with onions, tomatoes, sugar cane, tobacco, peppers, and indigo.

For more than a thousand years Kano has been a trading center, and for a long time the focus of Hausaland. It may have been sited because of a locally usable deposit of iron ore; the city was long famed for the skill of the smiths and metal workers. Within the mud walls which enclose an area of some 9 square miles (23 km²) is still some open land, originally intended to supply food in case of siege. The mud houses are characteristic; modern dwellings faced with concrete usually follow traditional styles. There is an aristocratic section of the town where the Emir's palace is a walled city within a city. The Emir's ministers, the city ward headmen, and rich merchants have houses in the neighborhood, and many rural headmen keep a "town house" in Kano. In the main part of the town are quarters devoted to cotton spinning, weaving, dyeing (with local vegetable dyes prepared in pits) and tailoring. Another leading industry is tanning of leather (goats, cattle, sheep, camels, and asses all supply hides and skins, with goats easily leading), some tanning materials being derived from the seeds of a local Acacia. Kano has a main market, well stocked, and many smaller ones, including one which, before the British entry in 1903, was the slave market.

Outside the city walls is the township established by the British, with government buildings, a European residential quarter, and two African towns where many of the immigrants into the area reside. Such immigrant settlements beyond the town walls are common in the north and are generally named "Sabon Gari." Though no longer the railhead, Kano has a large transshipping trade from camel caravans to the railway. The large trade in peanuts, cotton, and skins is outward; the inward trade includes kola nuts from the south as well as a large range of imported goods.

Kano has become a great international and local airport as well as a focus of an increasing number of all-weather roads. The old city has been equipped with electricity, it has a good water supply, and some improvement has been made in sanitation. Its walls have tended to disintegrate; its old narrow gates have been widened to admit automobiles and the now widely used buses. Nevertheless, Kano retains much of its medieval charm.

Kano has been chosen as an example of a walled capital of an ancient Hausa state. There are others equally worthy of detailed study; a good example is Katsina. **Nigerian problems.** Nigeria is the largest state in West Africa in terms of population and productive area. Its problems are therefore on a greater scale and it has been the scene of the fiercest and most determined effort to break up the national unit left by the colonial powers. The demise of parliamentary government and the

13.M Fulani nobility riding through Kano at the feast of Id-el-Fitr at the end of Ramadan. The gorgeously apparalled rider of royal blood (indicated by the turban) is acknowledging the greeting of the man on the left. (Photo: Barnaby.)

13.N Looking across the roofs of the ancient city of Kano in northern Nigeria. The hill in the distance is within the city walls and is capped with a thick layer of ironstone. (Photo: J. Allan Cash.)

13.O Herdsmen bringing Fulani cattle into Lagos. There is an extensive internal trade in the products of the differing ecological zones of northern and southern Nigeria. (Photo: Jack Barker, courtesy of the United Africa Company.)

failure of carefully designed safeguards against communal distrust in Nigeria has probably caused more distress to British well-wishers than the troubles of any other former colonial territory. Fortunately the national assets of the country, its well-developed infrastructure and the standards of education and initiative are such that Nigeria has the opportunity of a prosperous future.

FRANCOPHONE WEST AFRICA

Historical background. French interest in West Africa really began in 1483 when Louis XI sent an expedition to Cape Verde in search of a remedy for the leprosy from which he died before the expedition returned. Although French vessels anchored off the site of Saint-Louis in 1558, the first French company (the Norman Company) to receive a charter to trade with Senegal and the Gambia was founded in 1624, a few years after the British had established themselves on the Gambia. Within the next few years three French companies were granted rights by Richelieu extending from Cape Verde to the mouth of the

Congo. In 1635 the first Christian mission was established; in 1658–1659 Gorée and Saint-Louis were founded. Although the French companies were established for purposes of trade, they soon became interested in territorial accessions, and the Compagnie du Sénégal (the successor of the Norman Company) undertook to provide 2000 slaves annually to the French possessions in America.

In 1698 the Frenchman André Brue built a fortified post on the Senegal 400 miles (640 km) from the coast, the first attempt by a European to establish a permanent station away from the coast. The century which followed was one of constant strife between British and French; the Treaty of Paris in 1814 marked the end of the struggle. At that time France was the only European power with any claims to possessions inland. France kept her possessions as they were in 1792 – Arguin, Portendik, Saint-Louis, Gorée and its dependencies, Cape Verde, Rufisque, Portudal, and Joal. The British retained only trading rights.

Although the Revolutionary Convention of 1794 abolished the status of slavery in the dominion of France, slavery

13.P In Kano, Nigeria, pyramids of groundnuts (peanuts) in bags await transshipment by rail to the ports, while camels carry salt into the Sahara. (Photo: Jack Barker, courtesy of the United Africa Company.)

was not finally abolished throughout the Empire until 1848. But the concept of French citizenship grew gradually, and the French tried to reorganize the economy of Senegal on the basis of agriculture. The turning point was the beginning of the export of peanuts in 1840, and French development was concentrated in Senegal, based on Saint-Louis.

In 1845 the French possessions were divided into two governments: Senegal based on Saint-Louis and Rivierès du Sud based on Gorée. In 1847 the French created a corps of African cavalry (Spahis); in 1848 the first Senegalese *Tirailleurs* were enlisted from freed slaves. The French military tradition was thus introduced very early into Africa.

A little later the French clashed with El Hadj Omar who had set up a Moslem state over a large area to the southwest of Timbuktu. French development at this time owes much to General Faidherbe, who was appointed governor of Senegal in 1854. He established schools, banks, and a survey organization, and he was the real founder of Dakar, where a military port was set up in 1857 and the first jetty built in 1863.

French interests in West Africa were well established at the time of the Berlin Conference in 1885. The same year France recognized German claims to Togoland, and boundary agreements with Portugal, Britain, Liberia, and Spain followed gradually. Until the German occupation Togoland, with a seaboard of about 30 miles (48 km) and a depth of 300 (480 km), had not existed as a unit, and its status as a German colony from 1885 to 1914 was typical of the entirely artificial units created by European powers in Africa. On the outbreak of World War I Togoland fell to British and French forces in the first month. Later the division of land between Britain and France was accepted by the League of Nations and the United Nations.

Senegal was thus the earliest area of French penetration into West Africa.

France's rights in French Guinea were recognized by Britain in 1882, and Conakry was occupied in 1887. In the Ivory Coast the French had a factory at Grand Bassam at an early stage — lasting until 1707 — and treaties with local chiefs were revived in 1842. The French were later concerned to maintain an access from the coast to the Upper Niger basin. In Dahomey they obtained rights to establish a trading post as early as 1669 at Ouidah, but it was not till 1851 that a treaty of friendship was concluded with the king of Dahomey. Porto Novo accepted the protection of France in 1863.

Consolidation of French West Africa came with the establishment of a central government in 1895, when the governor of Senegal became governor-general with his capital at St. Louis. The capital was moved to Dakar in 1904, and Dakar, described below, continued to grow in political and economic importance. The emergence of the independant African states in 1960 reduced Dakar in status to the capital of Senegal, but it continues to serve in several ways as a focal point of French-speaking West Africa.

The Peoples of Former French West Africa. The people fall into the two main groups: the Islamized peoples of the north and the Negroes of the south. But northern religions, organizations, and languages have invaded the south, and Negro blood has penetrated far into the north. The lands are not neatly parceled out into tribal areas, but broadly the peoples of the north are Moslems of Arab, Berber, and Fulani stock, the Negroes of the south are Christians or Animists. The Negro villages usually comprise "clans," each of families descended from a common stock; there was no intermarriage between members of the same clan under French administration.

Each territory was divided into *"cercles"* under a *"commandant du cercle,"* who was often virtual ruler of his province. He appointed the village chief (after consultation with the village elders) and the canton chief, supervising a group of villages.

SENEGAL (RÉPUBLIQUE DU SENEGAL)

Historically Senegal was the bridgehead for French penetration into West Africa. Here the French established St. Louis on a remarkable island site (obviously for defensive purposes) near the mouth of the Senegal River, an important highway into the interior. Dakar has replaced and now completely overshadows St. Louis as the capital of the Federation (and subsequently of Senegal) and chief port, and the railway inland from Dakar to Kayes on the Senegal (and then to Bamako on the navigable Upper Niger) supplanted the old Senegal River highway. The town has spread from its congested sandbank island to the main sandspit (the "Langue de Barbarie") facing the Atlantic Ocean. A long road bridge spans the Senegal River to the railhead at Sor, whence a line runs to Dakar. St. Louis, like Bathurst in the Gambia (and to some extent Lagos), is a good example of a town site well suited to its original function as a European trading outpost but not permitting expansion to meet modern conditions. With the independence of Mauritania to the north, it has also lost traffic to Nouakchott and its population has declined.

Senegal lies partly in the Sudan savanna, and partly in the "Sahelian Zone" of French writers, where the dominant vegetation is a sparse grass brush with spiny bushes. Much lies within the basin of that important navigable highway, the Senegal River. Floods permit the cultivation of millet and guinea corn in the river valleys, and along the coast between St. Louis and Dakar there is a line of oases behind the coastal sand dunes. Elsewhere settlement and cultivation are restricted to the more fertile pockets where water is available; it is the peanut which has made the fortune of Senegal. Commercially cultivation is important only where the crop

land can be reached by river, rail, or road. At the head of the estuary of the Saloum is the rapidly growing port and town of Kaolack, linked by a branch line with the Dakar–Niger railway. The river Gambia, navigable through the British strip to the border, also taps peanut country. The story is always the same — the dependence of economic development on modern transport.

The southern part of Senegal, the Casamance, between Gambia and Portuguese territory, has a higher rainfall and thicker vegetation. Unfortunately it is also more troubled by tsetse fly and heavily lateritic soils. It is relatively isolated from the rest of the country and rather less developed.

Dakar.[6] Dakar is unique among the settlements of tropical Africa, and as such merits special attention. When it replaced St. Louis as the capital of French West Africa and seat of the governor-general, it became, despite its situation near the sea level well within the tropics (it is less than 15 degrees from the equator), a European city. This is true both because the European residential center with its tall apartment houses, its shops, cafes, and hotels (run by Europeans) is unlike anything else in tropical Africa and because large numbers of French and other Europeans settled there, to all appearance permanently. There were schools for their children, bathing beaches, and yachting facilities for their outdoor recreation, cinemas and dance halls for indoor. The congested site on the peninsula, cut off by the African town, led to a closely knit city, but the suburbs, now mixed African and European, have spread beyond the airport to the Atlantic beaches (Figure 13.16). The vast increase in sea and air traffic has concentrated much business in Dakar. With a magnificent natural harbor protected by

[6] Derwent Whittlesey, "Dakar and Other Cape Verde Settlements," *Geog. Rev.,* XXXI (1941) pp. 609–638. "Dakar Revisisted," *Geog. Rev.,* XXXVIII (1948) pp. 626–632; A. Seck, "Dakar," *Les Cahiers d'Outre-Mer* (1961) pp. 372–392.

13.Q Modern housing in Dakar. A major problem in rapidly growing African cities is to provide decent housing at low cost. Here a blown-up balloon forms a "frame" over which the cement is poured. The result is a beehive-shaped home not unlike a traditional African pattern. (Copyright: R. J. Harrison Church.)

Cape Manuel and extensively improved, the site is unmatched in West Africa, and the isolated rocky site supports Dakar's claim to be considered an "African Gibraltar." Within present-day West Africa, however, Dakar is placed at the geographical margin, and a position where ships from Europe or America would make Dakar their first and last point of call along the coast, is now of less importance with direct air flights. Nor does Senegal provide the productive base for a preeminent city, while both of these factors favor Abidjan in Ivory Coast.

The Cape Verde Peninsula, behind which Dakar is sheltered, owes its origin to sheets of recent volcanic lava, partly covered with sand dunes. West Africa affords many examples of the importance of such geological "accidents"; Freetown is another.

It has been argued that, although Dakar is well within the tropics, the local climatic conditions link it with midlatitude rather than lowland tropical conditions. It is from Dakar or Cape Verde northward that the cool Canaries current with upwelling cold bottom waters tempers the air temperatures, and there are pleasant sea breezes, especially from November to

February. The January average is 73°F (23°C), with a mean of daily minima and maxima from 64°F to 82°F (18°C to 28°C). There is no doubt that immediately to the *south* of Dakar the humidity becomes higher throughout the year, and the tempering effect of breezes off the sea is less where the Canaries current does not exist.

In the sheltered bay of Dakar is the tiny island of Gorée, so important in the history of French expansion in Africa but no longer of any significance.

MAURITANIA (RÉPUBLIQUE ISLAMIQUE DE MAURITANIE)

Mauritania was part of French West Africa under the governor-general at Dakar but it is essentially a Saharan state and is described in the previous chapter. A considerable trade, partly unrecorded, takes place across the Senegal river with Senegal and with Mali.

MALI (RÉPUBLIQUE DU MALI)

For a short time the territory of the French Sudan (Soudan Français) on achieving independence became known as

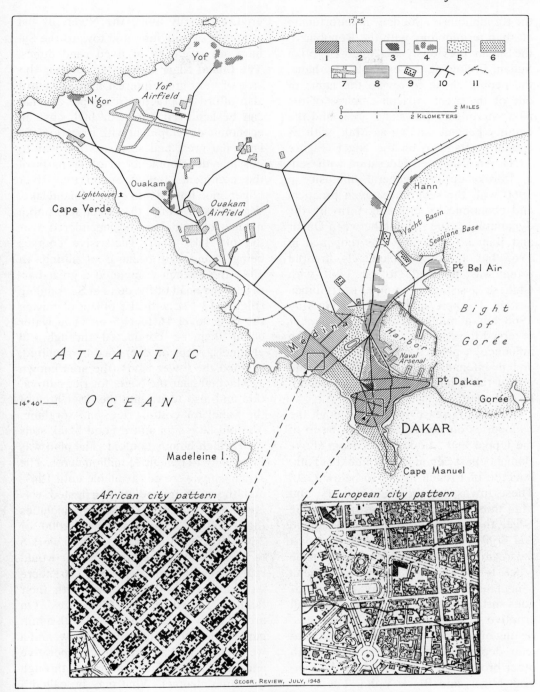

13.16 Dakar, Gorée, and Cap Vert (Cape Verde) in 1946–1947. (1) European
city; (2) African city; (3) African market; (4) African village; (5) sanitary zone;
(6) military reservation; (7) airfield; (8) factory district; (9) tank farm; (10) main
roads; (11) railroad. (From Derwent Whittlesey, *Geog. Rev.,* 1948. Courtesy
of the American Geographical Society.) Dakar has expanded greatly since this
map was prepared but it demonstrates clearly the site of the town and the
typically separated components of a colonial town of the time.

the République du Soudan, an unfortunate clash in terminology with the Republic of the Sudan, previously the Anglo-Egyptian Sudan. Following the example of Ghana, the people chose to revive the name of one of the great African empires of the past, in roughly the same area, and the country became known as Mali, with its capital at Bamako on the Niger (Figure 13.1). An attempted federation with Senegal broke up amid general animosity in 1960 with the severance given practical and economically crippling form by the dynamiting of the rail link between Dakar and Bamako. The line was reopened in 1963 but a more ideologically favored route was planned, to be built with Chinese assistance, to link the Guinea system. The agreement was signed in May 1968 but a military *coup* in November reversed the decision. This illustrates the influence of politics on the establishment and maintenance of communication and one of the complications of being a landlocked state.

Mali comprises essentially, though the boundaries do not coincide, the basin of the Upper and Middle Niger from above Bamako, past Ségou and Timbuktu (Tombouctou of French maps) to below Gao. These towns are the main centers, and Mali thus includes the great bend of the Niger, the heartlands of the old Mandingo and Songhai Empires. For the most part the region is one of uniform and feeble relief. In the east and south the Archean peneplain is dominant, and its monotonous surface is varied only rarely by small eruptive masses. Horizontal sandstones, resting on the peneplain, form a large plateau depressed in the center and with other broad valleys occupied by the Senegal, Niger, and Black Volta. The sandstone plateau has a marked edge 1000–1500 feet (300–450m) in height — even reaching 3000 (900 m) in the Hombori mountains — forming a great semicircle. Erosion has left flat-topped mesas such as the Manding plateau near Bamako. The sandstones are often cov-

ered, especially along the Niger, by flat stretches of alluvium, and toward the Sahara are stretches of fixed sand dunes. **The Inland Niger Delta.**[7] Not only is this area of very great interest in itself, but it also affords a practical example of what can be achieved, albeit at high cost, in economic development with irrigation of a large flat area, and so points the way to possible developments in other parts of the continent. Below Ségou the River Niger once flowed into a large inland lake. When this dried up, the Niger split into a number of branches and meandered over the old lake floor, successive courses being abandoned because of silting. In 1941 the French completed a great barrage at the head of the delta at Sansanding (Figure 13.17), with the object of raising the river level 16 feet (5 m). The water could then be conducted through old channels, recut or deepened as required, to flood the lower lands (the area known as Macina) near the Niger for rice cultivation and also to irrigate the drier area of the Sahel for cotton, rice, and sorghum. The old lake silts afford good black soils with a high humus content. The plan was eventually to benefit $2\frac{1}{4}$ million acres. The sluice gates were not available until 1947, and the area immediately irrigated was about 50,000 acres. The scheme includes the eventual settlement of 200,000 or 250,000 African colonists, each to work 8 to 13 acres. With their families this would represent a million people. By 1961 there were about 27,000 colonists with their families settled on 100,000 acres. On arrival each settler is provided with a hut, garden, three head of cattle, a plow, and a well. They market through a cooperative and purchase further equipment through the same channel. What may be called a pilot scheme on a smaller scale (about 5500 colonists and families) was carried out higher up the Niger at Sotuba near

[7] R. J. Harrison-Church, "Irrigation in the Inland Delta of the French Sudan," *Geog. Jour.*, CXVII (1951) pp. 218–220.

13.R Large scale mechanized cultivation on the Inland Niger Delta. This may be contrasted with the fields of the "pagan" settlements in Nigeria. (Courtesy: Office du Niger.)

Bamako. Unfortunately cotton production has not been very successful and the principal crop is now rice. The scheme was very ambitious, requiring much capital and careful direction and the date of its final completion is problematical.

UPPER VOLTA
(RÉPUBLIQUE DE HAUTE-VOLTA)

In 1919 the colony of Upper Volta was carved out of the old colony of Upper Senegal and Niger, but later, in 1932, the colony was suppressed, its territory being divided between the Ivory Coast, Sudan, and Niger. Then, in 1947, the separate division was reestablished as a territory, with an area of about 106,000 square miles (274,000 km²) and a population of about 5 million. It became a member of the French Community in 1958 and an independent republic in 1960.

This country lies in the same latitude as the populous parts of Northern Nigeria. The French made great efforts to counteract the disadvantages of its inland situation. There are numerous but not very good roads which focus on the two chief centers of Bobo-Dioulasso and Ouagadougou (sometimes anglicized as Waga-

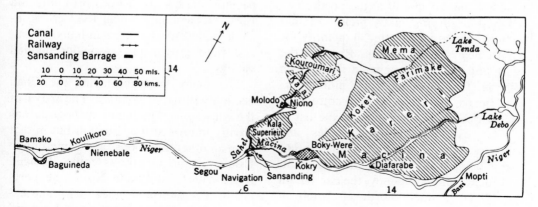

13.17 The Inland Niger Delta.

dugu), the capital. Both are served by air. The railway from the greatly improved port of Abidjan to Bobo-Dioulasso was extended to Ouagadougou in 1954.

Most of the country is a flat, poor savannaland with numerous cattle, sheep, goats, horses, and donkeys. Shea butter is produced, and cultivated crops include corn, sorghum, millet, rice, beans, peanuts, and cassava. Exports include cattle and peanuts, but trade is small; most agriculture is primarily for subsistence and there is a large movement of labor to work in the cash crop zones and the mines of Ivory Coast and Ghana.

NIGER (RÉPUBLIQUE DU NIGER)

The vast Republic of the Niger, with over 3 million people, lies mainly to the north of the Federation of Nigeria and stretches roughly from the Niger in the west to Lake Chad in the east. The north is desert; the southern strip has sufficient vegetation to support large numbers of cattle, sheep, and goats with smaller numbers of asses, camels, and horses. The main difficulty of the country is scarcity of surface water. Indeed only four areas have sufficient water to permit settlement: the western districts watered by the Niger and its tributaries; the parts of the southern zone where the water table can be reached by wells and the water is potable; the area near Lake Chad; and the wadis of the Air massif in the north.

Dried or drying lakes yield salt and sodium sulphate (the latter in quantity for export near the Komadugu River in the east), and there is a demand for both in Nigeria. The Hausa cultivate millet, peanuts, beans, and cassava, with cotton and locally rice near the rivers. To the list of modest exports (livestock, hides and skins, peanuts, cotton) a welcome addition is being made of uranium from Arlit.

A focal point is Niamey, the capital, on the Niger. Zinder, north of Kano in Nigeria and linked with it by road, is another center, from which the trans-

Saharan Hoggar road passes northward through Air and the towns of Agades and Tamanrasset (see p. 217). The boundary with Nigeria divides an area of ecological and cultural coherence and there is a large trade across it of cattle for more southern markets.

The vast open savannas of Niger abound in game and form a favorite area for big game hunters — for lions, elephants, buffaloes, and various antelope.

CHAD (RÉPUBLIQUE DU TCHAD)

Although Chad was a part of French Equatorial Africa, in its situation and physical and human geography, it has much in common with these states of the "sudan zone," Niger, Upper Volta, and Mali. In the south is a belt of higher rainfall, savanna largely of woodland type, and relatively dense populations of settled cultivators, either pagan or Christian missionized. Stretching northward into the Sahara are the vast expanses of sahel savanna or semidesert with rainfall negligible in places and occupied by nomadic pastoral tribes of Muslim religion and culture. Both are essentially Negro people, however.

Cattle are driven into neighboring countries for sale and dried and smoked fish from Lake Chad is similarly a local export. The principal export, however, is cotton from the southern savanna, especially south and west of Fort Lamy and Fort Archambault. Local food crops include millet, sorghum, groundnuts, wheat, and rice, grown in seasonally flooded valleys.

The major problem facing the Chad economy is that of isolation. The arrival of the railway at Maiduguri in Nigeria has greatly improved the situation but in that as in all other directions (via Cameroun to Doula or the circuitous route, Bangui, Brazzaville, and Pointe Noire), seaports are over a thousand miles away and export and import requires transshipment.

Numbering only an estimated 3½ million, the population of Chad exceeds that of its former associates, Gabon, Congo (Brazzaville), and the Central African Republic put together. The vastness of the northern arid lands reduces the overall density to about 8 per square mile (3 p.km²) but most of the population in fact forms part of the relatively densely settled east–west zone of the Sudan Savanna.

IVORY COAST (RÉPUBLIQUE DE COTE D'IVOIRE)

The capital of this republic of 124,500 square miles (322,463 km²) is the thriving town of Abidjan on the northern side of a large lagoon (Figure 13.18). As an example of French enterprise in Africa, Abidjan rivals Dakar both in interest and in importance. It has a richer hinterland both within the Ivory Coast and extending into Upper Volta and even Niger. The whole orientation of the area was changed with the completion of the ship canal through the obstructing sandbar and the opening

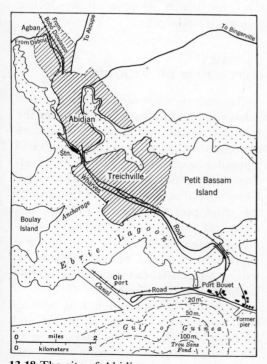

13.18 The site of Abidjan.

to traffic of the deep-water wharves in July 1950. Prior to that time Grand-Bassam at the mouth of the Comoé River and where the lagoon is connected with the sea served as an inadequate roadstead port. Later a port was established at Port-Bouet (Petit-Bassam), where deep water (*Trou sans fond*—the "deep without bottom") approaches the coast, but the situation was obviously open and exposed. From the wharf at Port-Bouet a rail link was thrown across the lagoon to Abidjan. In the meantime the former administrative center of Bingerville had been gradually abandoned in favor of Abidjan. With the completion of the canal from the lagoon to the *Trou sans fond*, Grand-Bassam, Port-Bouet, and Bingerville have all become ghost towns. From Abidjan the railway is the great highway to the interior. In the 716 miles (1152 km) to Ouagadougou it cuts through roughly the same zones as exist in Ghana to the east, except that the coastal zone has the heavy rainfall of the Axim area of Ghana and is naturally covered with an equatorial type of forest which it traverses at the narrowest point.

The prosperity of the Ivory Coast is derived from the southern portion of the country, the belt of rainforest and the moist, partly derived, savanna adjacent. This has been achieved by a "mixed" economy with foreign (largely French) plantations permitted together with the dominant peasant-type farms. In this the policy of President Felix Houphouet-Boigny has been in sharp contrast to that of President Sekou Touré of Guinea. Coffee is the major export and Ivory Coast is the largest producer in Africa, mostly of *robusta* or *liberica* types. Access to the French market was valuable in building up exports and, although the degree of preference has been reduced, the EEC is still the principal market. Coffee is widely grown in the forest belt whereas bananas for export and pineapple (for canning and for juice) are more restricted with a highly organized trade

13.S The Vridi Canal at Abidjan. This canal connects the lagoon with the open sea (notice the breakers) and has permitted Abidjan to develop as a modern ocean port.

through Abidjan and Sassandra. Cocoa is also exported although not in such quantities as neighboring Ghana. The forest is being so rapidly cut for timber that fears are expressed for the maintenance of future supplies, but some loss of stock is an inevitable corollary of clearing land for agricultural advancement. From the northern savannas come peanuts, cotton (being encouraged for a local textile industry), and livestock, but perhaps more important is a supply of temporary or permanent migrant labor for the south. Bouaké is the focus of transport and trade in the north and is the second city.

The exports of the country are thus reasonably diversified among a number of agricultural products and timber but minerals have so far been unimportant except for a small production of alluvial diamonds and manganese. Prospecting is active, with most hope for iron ore.

The massive investment in creating the port of Abidjan enabled the economy of Ivory Coast to make a big leap forward. Much of the development has been concentrated in the eastern portion of the forest belt, in the vicinity of Abidjan and

the railway to it. A new port being constructed at San Pedro may similarly serve and stimulate the southwestern portion of the country. Between lies the Bandama river on which a major hydroelectric scheme is under way.

DAHOMEY
(RÉPUBLIQUE DU DAHOMEY)

Dahomey lies between the Republic of Togo (former German Togoland) on the west and Nigeria on the east. With an area of 43,000 square miles (122,000 km²) and a population of some 2½ million, its coastline is only about 70 miles (110 km) long. From the old port of Grand-Popo through the chief port Cotonou, a railway runs along the coast to the capital, Porto-Novo, a few miles away, and thence a short distance inland. The main line inland leaves this coastal railroad and serves the southern half of the country.

Naturally the vegetation and agricultural zones link with those of Nigeria and of Togo and Ghana. The forest zone of the south furnishes palm oil and kernels—the chief products of the country – but coffee and cotton have been successfully introduced farther north as commercial crops. Palm oil for export is mostly derived from African-owned plantations established with slaves who could not be sold abroad following the abolition of slavetrading. Rainfall is too moderate to allow cocoa to be important. The economy has been described as "catastrophic," due at least in part to political factors of extreme sectionalism, numerous changes of government and an excessively large civil service derived from Dahomeian officials employed by the French in other colonies and subsequently repatriated. The local market is small and natural resources modest. The most realistic hope is for mineral discoveries, most likely being offshore oil. The completion of a new harbor at Cotonou in 1965 was a necessary precondition for economic development.

GUINEA (RÉPUBLIQUE DE GUINÉE)

In the referendum of September 28, 1958, Guinea voted for complete severance from France and was proclaimed an independent republic four days later under the control of President Sékou Touré. The Republic of Guinea stretches from the coast between Portuguese Guinea and Sierra Leone inland to the headwaters basin of the Niger. The capital and chief port, Conakry, sheltered by the Iles de Los which were ceded by Britain to France in 1904, is itself on an island linked by a bridge with the mainland. Thence a railway runs through the territory to Kouroussa on the Niger, below which point the great river is navigable. The coast is part of the drowned section seen also in Portuguese Guinea and Sierra Leone so that Conakry is free from the sandbars which are the curse of so many African ports.

Guinea, in its 95,000 square miles (245,857 km²), comprises several very different regions. The coastal plain, 30 to 50 miles (50–80 km) wide, is a very wet region inhabited by the Susu (Soussou). Rainfall is of monsoonal intensity, with Conakry receiving an average of 169 inches (4300 mm) a year. Cultivated plants include the oil palm, and there are banana plantations. Inland are rolling plateaus which form a foothill zone to the Fouta Djallon. These are inhabited by the cattle-rearing Fulani, living in villages of round huts surrounded by fruit trees. Crossing the Fouta Djallon, a considerable stretch of which lies more than 3000 feet (900 m) above sea level, the land slopes toward the north, draining to the Senegal, or northeast, to the Niger. This part of Guinea is linked naturally with neighboring parts of Mali – the savanna country with peanuts and sesame. An important center and terminus of the rail from Conakry is Kankan. Finally, in the southeast is the forested Guinea Highlands, much dissected and extremely difficult of access, lying behind Sierra Leone and Liberia, which together cut it off from the sea. It is now, however, penetrated by roads from Kankan as well as being linked by road with the Liberian port of Monrovia.

Agricultural exports from French Guinea were mostly integrated into the French market and included coffee, bananas, citrus, pineapples, and peanuts, often grown on plantations behind Conakry or on the Fouta Djallon plateau. These have declined in relative and often in absolute importance and exports are now largely made up of bauxite and alumina, and iron ore, together with a contribution from small scale gold and diamond mining. Iron ore is shipped from Conakry from opencast workings conveniently sited only five miles along the peninsula. Unfortunately they have an unwelcome chrome content but further iron ore exports are likely by an extension of the workings on Mt. Nimba from the Liberian to the Guinea side of the mountain, with Liberian agreement, and transport along the existing railroad to the port of Buchanan. Guinea is particularly rich in bauxite which is already quarried on the Los Islands, offshore from Conakry. On the mainland, bauxite is mined at Fria, 90 miles (150 km) from Conakry where it is reduced to alumina with local hydroelectric power before being shipped to Cameroun to be processed into aluminium. A large World Bank loan has enabled an even larger mining operation to be begun at Boké, in the north of the country, including the construction of an 85-mile (137 km) railroad and a new port at Kamsar. Eventually it might also be possible to process this ore into alumina if power plants were constructed on the Konkouré river.

With a population of over 3½ million and a wide range of natural resources, Guinea has the prerequisites for a prosperous and a powerful state. Eccentric economic policies and rather quarrelsome foreign relations may have played a part in the failure to achieve any greater success so far.

TOGO (RÉPUBLIQUE TOGOLAISE)

Togoland surrendered unconditionally to British and French forces in August 1914, shortly after the outbreak of World War I. It was ruled under mandate from the League of Nations (approved 1922) until December 14, 1946, when the United Nations agreed on the terms of the trusteeship. Of the total area of 33,700 square miles of the former German territory, the French were given control of 21,600 square miles (56,000 km²), including the whole of the coast. Under the mandate and trusteeship systems Togoland could not become an integral part of French West Africa, and so when, in the 1958–1960 period, the French territories became republics within the French Community, Togo became an independent republic on its own.

Togo illustrates the way in which African peoples remain divided by political frontiers. The Ewe people, for example, have occupied the same area continuously since the sixteenth century. But half of them found themselves in French Togoland, about two-fifths in British Togoland, and the remainder in southern Ghana. Somewhat similarly placed are the Dagomba, who lived partly in British Togoland, partly in the northern part of Ghana. Yet so far have modern political concepts replaced old tribal ties that when the indepent republic of Togo was formed, the former British Togoland had already in 1956 elected to join Ghana, and the division remains.

Togo is entirely an artificial unit, even more so than its neighbors. Its people resemble those of neighboring lands, Ghana and Dahomey. Its geographical divisions are those of its neighbors. There is a lagoon coast, somewhat arid as in Ghana, succeeded inland by a terrace some 200 to 300 feet (60–90 m) above sea level, which gives place to a marshy but fertile depression (with oil palms, bananas, maize, and cocoa). Northward is the zone favorable to cotton, before the country of the Fulani and the Hausa is reached. There are railways totaling 270 miles (440 km) running inland from Lomé, where a modern port was finally completed in 1968.

Small exports of cocoa, coffee, cotton, peanuts, and cassava (to neighboring Ghana) have been supplemented by phosphates from near the coast but other mineral deposits are not at present deemed adequate to work. Favorable indications off Dahomey have encouraged a search for oil offshore of Togo. Yet Togo has many economic and political disadvantages including its small size, awkward shape, ethnic disunity, and lack of any major resources. However, cooperation with Dahomey and Ghana could assist and the deep-water port (with a "free port" zone proclaimed) is a step forward.

Further Reading

Most conveniently, West Africa is covered by two major works. *West Africa, A Study of the Environment and of Man's Use of it* by R. J. Harrison Church (London: Longman, 6th Ed., 1968, and frequently revised) achieves a completeness and a wealth of detail within a reasonable compass. It is particularly well balanced between a systematic and a regional approach and between English- and French-speaking countries. A more extended systematic and topical analysis is offered by W. B. Morgan and J. C. Pugh in *West Africa* (London: Methuen, 1969). Both are rich in bibliographical references.

For this large and populous region, divided among many states, there is an extensive and thorough literature in greater detail. This is indicated in the Selected Bibliography at the end of this book.

CHAPTER 14

The Sudan

The word Sudan is used in several different senses. Literally it is the plural of the Arabic word *suda,* meaning black; hence the Sudan is properly the land of the blacks. It has long been and is still frequently applied to the whole belt of country stretching approximately from the Atlantic Ocean in the west to the Ethiopian Mountains in the east, with the great Sahara Desert on the north and the hot, wet forest belt of the West African coastlands and Equatorial Africa on the south. In this sense it is essentially the belt of grassland, usually with scattered trees, constituting what is more frequently called the savanna country. In the west are the Republics of Mali, Niger, and Chad, which are considered in Chapter 13.

A very important part of the belt lies in the east. In this chapter we are concerned both with the eastern Sudan as a geographical unit and with the political division of Africa known as the Republic of the Sudan (Jamhuryates-Sudan). This area was formerly known as the Anglo-Egyptian Sudan and it was under the joint control of Egypt and Britain as a condominium from 1898 effectively to 1951, and nominally to 1955, becoming independent on January 1, 1956. The Sudan is the largest country on the continent of Africa with an area of nearly a million square miles or $2\frac{1}{2}$ million square kilometres [967,500 square miles (2,506,000 square km^2)]. Its total population however is only about 15 million.

THE GEOGRAPHICAL LIMITS OF THE REPUBLIC OF THE SUDAN

The Sudanese Republic stretches from the heart of the great desert in the north, where the boundary with Egypt is for the most part a straight line drawn across wastes of sand, to the borders of equatorial forest lands in the south. In broad terms it coincides roughly with the basin of the Central and Upper Nile, but excluding the sources of both the White and the Blue Niles. Thus the Sudan as a whole, like Egypt, draws its life blood, the water of the great rivers, from territories beyond its control. The waters of the White Nile come from the plateau lands of Uganda, Kenya, Tanzania, and even to a small extent from the Republic of Zaire. The source of the waters of the still more important Blue Nile (which below Khartoum supplies three-fifths of the total volume of Nile water) is in the mountains of Ethiopia.

It might be theoretically possible to divert the whole of the Nile waters reaching the Sudan for purposes of irrigating lands in that country, in which case Egypt might virtually cease to exist. In Chapter 3 of this book, emphasis was placed upon the natural division of Africa into river basins and how existing political boundaries cut across the natural water partings or watersheds, with little regard for the ever more obvious fact that the future prosperity and development of the African continent must be based upon unified control of the waters in each of the great river basins. A call for the unity of the Nile basin is a recurring theme in Egyptian history, one expression of which

was in October 1951 when the Egyptians abrogated the treaties with Britain and declared Farouk king of Egypt and the Sudan.

THE REGIONS AND PEOPLES OF THE SUDAN

In broad general terms the Sudan consists of a succession of belts of country stretching from east to west, that is, from the margins of neighboring countries, Chad and the Central African Republic, in the west to the Red Sea or the borders of Ethiopia on the east (Figure 14.1). Following a course from south to north, and therefore cutting across these zones at right angles, is the White Nile, entering Sudanese territory from Uganda as the Bahr el Jebel in the extreme south. It will be convenient to consider these belts of

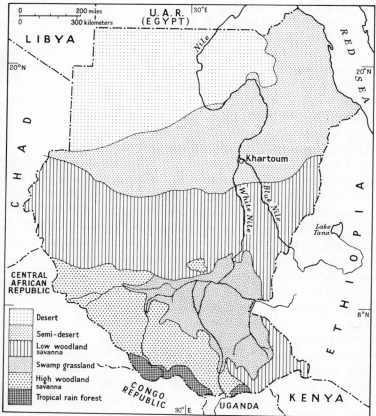

14.1 Vegetation of the Sudan. (After J. H. G. Lebon.)

country from the north, that is from the Egyptian border, to the south.

The Desert Belt. The frontier between Egypt and the Sudan crosses the Nile some distance below the Second Cataract, which itself is just above the Sudanese town and railhead of Wadi Halfa (which has been resited following the creation of "Lake Nasser"). To the west lie the great sandy stretches of the Libyan Desert, to the east the almost equally arid wastes of the Nubian Desert, extending to the rugged Red Sea hills and the shores of the Red Sea.

Through this desert belt the united Nile passes in its course, making a huge S-shaped bend. The Libyan Desert, to the west, is uninhabited, but to the east, near the Nile, there are a few desert nomads, Berbers, who give place towards the Red Sea to the Beja. They possess camels, mainly, and some sheep and goats, which become more numerous in the south. Both desert feed and water are scarce; when the rains fail, animals die, and the Beja suffer great hardships.

The Nile valley which passes through this desert belt may be described as an attenuated version of the Nile valley in Egypt below Wadi Halfa. The Egyptian cultivators, the *fellaheen,* are not found south of the Egyptian border. Their place is taken by Nubians, who in Egypt were found side by side with the Egyptian cultivators between the Egyptian border and Aswan, but who have now been evacuated from their villages before flooding by the High Dam project. In the Sudan they have established a chain of little agricultural villages on both banks of the Nile as far south as Korti. Upstream from Korti these little villages are occupied by sedentary Arabic-speaking tribes.

Cultivation has for centuries been carried out by using the Persian wheel, or *saqia,* to raise water from the river, also by the *shadoof,* the Archimedean screw, and, although to a relatively small extent, basin irrigation from the Nile floods. In the last thirty years these traditional methods of irrigation have been largely displaced by diesel-engined pumps. Small towns, such as Dongola, Karima, Abu Hamed, Berber, and Shendi are markets. Because there are few oases in the desert belt outside those associated with the Nile, little cultivation exists away from the river.

The stretch of the Nile between Khartoum and Wadi Halfa, being interrupted by cataracts, is not used for through navigation; however, the sections between the cataracts are still used by sailing craft (*feluccas*), and there is a river steamer service between Karima and Dongola. The railroad from Wadi Halfa to Khartoum leaves the valley itself and cuts straight across the Nubian Desert between Wadi Halfa and Abu Hamed. The landscape is so empty and featureless that the railroad stops are given numbers instead of names. At Atbara is the junction from which another main line cuts across the desert and the Red Sea hills to the important port of Port Sudan on the Red Sea. It is natural that Atbara should have become a "railway town" with extensive locomotive and carriage repair shops. It is at Atbara that the river of the same name draining from the northern hills of Ethiopia joins the Nile.

The Semidesert or Steppe Belt. To the south the desert belt gives place gradually to one where vegetation, though sparse, becomes slightly more abundant. The number of people increases, and life becomes richer and more varied. North of El Obeid, reached by rail from Sennar and Khartoum, are numerous nomadic Arab tribes. They have camels and flocks of sheep and goats. They follow the movement of the sun southward during the dry season, and then return toward the north during the rains between June and October. Herding is much helped by shallow ponds or "*hafirs,*" some now being excavated by machinery. Between the Blue Nile and the Atbara are tribes who own very large flocks of sheep.

It will be seen that in this semidesert

belt there is no permanent agriculture, so that the well-cultivated Gezira, that famous triangular area between the White and Blue Niles before their union, depends for its prosperity entirely on the great irrigation scheme described below.

The Savanna Belt. South of latitude 15° summer rainfall increases, vegetation becomes more rich, one passes into the grassland with trees, or savanna, and agriculture becomes general.

The Nile seems to have provided a line of communication through this country in such a way that northern and southern influences have intermingled. So it is by no means uncommon to see side by side the little square hut of hard mud, so characteristic of the Nile valley through its desert stretches, and the round hut with conical roof made of straw or grass and typical of the people of the savanna lands of so much of tropical Africa.

In the typical savanna country the people combine cultivation of sorghum millet, peanuts, and sesamum. In the dry months they collect gum arabic. Most of the world's supply comes from the Sudan and it forms a major export. The acacia trees or bushes are cut with small incisions, from which "tears" of gum are later collected. There are also transhumant cattle-owning tribes (Baggara), who move toward the Bahr-el-Arab and Sobat in the dry season; these people market live cattle and hides. To translate the words of Professor Maurette, "Nothing is more mixed than the population of these steppes and of these savannas, vast spaces without natural limits between the desert of the north and the forest or marshes of the south. There was the southern limit of the advance of Arab tribes and of the Nubians. The first Nilotics appear with the people known as the Shilluk. But above all, from Darfur to the region of the Blue Nile the Sudanese tribes are numerous."

Local favorable conditions give rise to concentrations of population and agriculture. Thus higher rainfall and water supplies from drainage channels deriving from Jebel Marra [10,073 feet, (3071 m)] support a mixed population of cultivators and nomads in western Darfur, centered on El Fasher. The leading regional center of the western savannas is El Obeid, well placed to serve the sandy Qoz plains, the Nuba mountains and the range lands shading into the desert to the north. A plentiful supply of groundwater is its greatest asset.

These open savannas have for very long periods been a line or belt of communication from east to west. As the people on the fringes of Negro Africa became converted to the Moslem religion, there followed the necessity of the pilgrimage to Mecca. Pilgrims who pass along the routeways do not always return, but sometimes remain to settle and form colonies among the indigenous peoples. In later times disturbed conditions in the Sudan led to much movement along this belt, and in still more recent times the movement of laborers, perhaps remaining to become settlers, has been equally marked. The study of migration, past and present, along this belt is one of fascinating interest, if of extreme complexity.

The Southern Clay Plain. The southern part of the Sudan is a huge shallow basin situated essentially on the great African plateau surface of crystalline rocks, through which meanders sluggishly the upper White Nile, or Bahr el Jebel, after it leaves the Uganda border. As already described, it is joined by the Bahr el Ghazal and the numerous tributaries which flow down from the watershed which lies between the Congo basin and the Nile basin. In the heart of the basin is a marshy area known as El Sudd, from which the great masses of floating vegetation find their way into the river courses and into the Nile itself.

In addition to permanent swamps there are much larger areas which are inundated every rainy season but dry out between December and May.

In the Sudd Region there are immense

14.A Shilluk tribesmen with dried fish in the southern Sudan. In the savannas of southern Sudan, nomadic pastoralism is often combined with fishing in the rivers and swamps of the upper White Nile and its tributaries. (Photo: Barnaby.)

numbers of fish in the shallow pools which attract vast flocks of fishing birds. The people of the region spear or trap the fish in the early months of the year when many have been cut off in natural ponds by the fall of the flood waters. They are dried and can then be used throughout the year. But mainly the population, known as the Nilotics or Nilotes, are cattle-keeping. They seek areas above the flood waters between June and October. As the floods recede they seek moist pastures near the rivers, called *toiches*.

The margins of the basin, including much of that province of Sudan known as Equatoria, are remote regions where the Negroid peoples practice their shifting cultivation on the old soils of a plateau 2000–3000 feet (600–900 m) above sea level. This is a vast area, and the population is sparse. There is considerable truth in the assertion that the Sudan from the point of view of its human geography consists of two utterly different and contrasting parts: the Islamized north and the part-Christian, part-pagan south.

The remoteness of Equatoria led to a development scheme among the Zande people based upon supplying a manufactured product to a local market, rather than the more usual aim to export a raw material. The Zande traditionally practice shifting agriculture and it was their system which was described by P. de Schlippe in his classic account: *Shifting Cultivation in Africa* (1955). They were persuaded to settle on planned holdings, growing cotton which is manufactured into cloth by a factory at Nzaria, which has since been joined by other small industries. Distance here provides a degree of local protection, in the form of transport costs, against competition from imports.

THE HISTORY OF THE SUDAN

Such in brief outline is the geographical background of the Sudan. Because of past British interests in the Sudan a brief historical account given by a Frenchman may provide an objective view of one having no reason to side with any particular group. The following is an approximate translation of the account given by Fernand Maurette in the *Geographie Universelle,* published in 1938, the year after the death of the author:

From the nineteenth century B.C. Egyptian Pharaohs had an interest in "Nubia." An inscription of 1879 B.C. found 40 miles south of Wadi Halfa forbids "Negroes" to pass farther down the Nile. From this time onward all the masters of the moment in the east tried, whether from the north or from the east, from the Mediterranean or the Red Sea, to lay their hands on the country which was the source of precious materials—ivory, ostrich feathers, gums, and, above all, slaves. In the time of the Emperor Julian the Roman power advanced as far as Ethiopia. The Coptic form of Christianity established itself at Soba, near Khartoum, and at (Old) Dongola, the foundation of which dates from this time. In A.D. 641 the Arab government of Egypt invaded Nubia, took (Old) Dongola, and demanded from the Nubian chiefs an annual tribute of slaves; the treaty was observed for the next 500 years. In 1169 the Turkish sultan, Saladin, famous champion of Islam, founded in Egypt a dynasty whose raids into the Sudan were numerous. Then there were Arab sultans from the Yemen who, coming by the Red Sea and landing at Suakin, advanced as far as the Nile and to Darfur, which they Islamized, thus cutting off for a long time the Christians of the north from those of Ethiopia. Islamized and Arabic-speaking tribes also came from the northwest. After them and concurrently in the sixteenth century, the Islamized Negroes living between the Blue and White Niles, the Fung, founded a vast empire, with Sennar as its capital, which stretched from Ethiopia to Dongola. They systematically exterminated Christianity from all the low country lying below the Ethiopian massif. The Ottoman Turks themselves advanced from the other direction as far as Dongola. From the sixteenth century up to the time of Mohammed Ali the Kingdoms of Darfur and Sennar and the Turkish power divided the country among them; but they were concerned mainly with that lucrative trade, the supply of slaves to the Lower Nile or to the Red Sea.

In 1822 Mohammed Ali established an Egyptian government in northern Sudan. His son, Ismail Pasha, obtained from the Turkish Sultan the right to establish himself at Suakin and Massawa. The whole of the eastern Sudan was in the hands of the ruler of Egypt. The temporary unification resulted in a sort of nationalism and an increase of trade (in slaves, ivory, ostrich feathers, and gum), but this was the time

14.B Pyramids on the site of the ancient city of Meroe, center of an important kingdom between 550 B.C. and 300 B.C. (Photo: J. Allan Cash.)

14.C The remains of an early Christian church at Senna South, near Wadi Halfa, on the Nile. (Photo: Barnaby.)

when the antislavery campaign reached its peak in Europe. Ismail, who needed Europe's support, was forced to accept a policy of reform. From 1869 to 1880 three European governors were named by him to the Sudan (Equatoria Province): Samuel Baker, then Gordon, then Emin Pasha (see Chapter 2). They suppressed the slave trade between Khartoum and Uganda. Economically, however, there was nothing to replace the profit, immoral and illicit but lucrative, and this spelt ruination for the country.

The revolt of the Mahdi, which began in 1881 and which was an explosion of Moslem fanaticism, undoubtedly gained strength by exploiting the discontent of the impoverished Sudanese chiefs. In four years, from 1881 to 1885, Mahdism conquered the whole Sudan. General Gordon, who had returned as governor-general, was killed at Khartoum in 1885. The British, in partial control of Egypt since 1882, kept only the Red Sea ports. For eleven years, until 1896, the country remained in the hands of the Dervishes or Mahdists. The commerce in slaves began

again, although it was hindered by the Anglo-Egyptian occupation of the ports. This occupation was, besides, the base for a pincer movement for encircling the Dervishes. From 1885 the Berlin Conference had declared war by the whole of Europe on the slave trade.

In Uganda in 1893 a British company had given place to a government protectorate. In 1891 an Anglo-Italian treaty fixed the frontiers of Eritrea. Against the Dervishes, thus cornered, an expedition under the command of Kitchener was sent in 1896 (from Egypt). It finished in 1898 with the complete conquest of the Sudan by Anglo-Egyptian forces.

So it was that the Anglo-Egyptian Sudan, as its name implied, came under the governments jointly of Egypt and Britain. The treaty of 1898 laid down that the flags of the two countries should fly side by side; that the governor-general of the Sudan should be named by the Khedive, like the governor of Egypt, on the recommendation of the British government.

This arrangement was, says Maurette, ". . . a sort of mandate, without the letter, and which lacked only the control of the League of Nations." The British government guaranteed also to the Egyptian government the defense of the southern frontier of Egypt and guaranteed to Egypt such volume of waters of the Nile as was necessary to the country. It was this question of the Nile water which was partly the basis of the Anglo-Egyptian Treaty of 1898 and the subsequent development of irrigation in the Sudan.

A treaty between Britain and Ethiopia in 1902 guaranteed the interests of Great Britain and Egypt as far as the waters of the Blue Nile were concerned, and the tripartite agreement among Britain, France, and Italy in 1906 extended a similar arrangement. A new agreement with Ethiopia in 1933 went into technical details in that it dealt with the construction of a dam at the exit from Lake Tana in Ethiopia, thus covering one of the points of a great plan for the control of the waters of the Nile which had been prepared after a long enquiry by the great British hydrologist, Sir William Garstin. The Garstin plan had five essential parts.

The first part of the plan was to preserve part of the waters of the White Nile for the period of drought following the flooding of the Blue Nile, and for this purpose a dam was to be constructed at Jebel Aulia, some 29 miles (47 km) above Khartoum. In the second place, in order to secure this regular volume of water, a large canal was to be constructed through the Sudd Region. In the third place a dam at the exit from Lake Tana was to be constructed to maintain reserve water for the flooding of the Blue Nile and to regulate its contribution for perennial irrigation. These three parts of the plan concerned not only the Sudan but Egypt also, and the third required the agreement of Ethiopia.

The parts of the plan which concerned only the Sudan were the first to be carried out. Outside the Nile proper was the irrigation of the deltaic plains of Gash (below Kassala) and of the Baraka around Tokar near the Red Sea. From 1929 the canals constructed resulted in the perennial irrigation and cultivation of about 45,000 acres (18,000 ha) at Gash and 55,000 acres (22,000 ha) at the Baraka. The much larger scheme was the construction of a gigantic dam at Sennar across the Blue Nile for the purpose of irrigating part of the Plain of Gezira between the two Niles. The dam was finished in 1925 and the canal works by 1929, but continual expansion and development have taken place since.

ECONOMIC DEVELOPMENT OF THE SUDAN

The economic development and present economy of the Sudan rest upon two bases. The first is the production of traditional commodities, the second is the production of cotton, which is based essentially on the modern irrigation works.

The traditional production of the country is designed primarily for human consumption and consists mainly of cereals — wheat and barley in the valley of the Nile, sorghum and millet (*dura* and *dakha*) in the remainder of the Sudan. The harvest has always been adequate for the population except locally after drought. A feature of the drier northern Sudan has long been the storage of grain in specially constructed elliptical silos in the ground known as *matmuras*. Farther south grain is stored in simple storehouses or "elevators" above ground. There are also the products of the herds of cattle, sheep, and goats.

The Sudan is the world's chief source of gum arabic of which there are two kinds, obtained from two different species of small acacia tree. With low rainfall these trees may degenerate to mere bushes. The better gum is obtained from *Acacia senegal*, the inferior but more abundant from *Acacia seyal*. The greatest source of material is in the heart of the country in the Province of Kordofan, but production is also active in Darfur, Blue Nile, and Kassala Provinces.

There are inexhaustible supplies of papyrus which might be collected in the Sudd Region, and with a world shortage of paper materials this is a possibility still to be explored.

Other agricultural products include sesamum and peanuts, both of which are exported; some of the sorghum also goes to Egypt for cattle and poultry feed. In the northern desert regions dates are produced, and melon seeds are important and are exported. By far the most important crop cultivated for export is cotton. Some American cotton is grown as a rain crop, notably in the Nuba Hills region of Kordofan, and also in Equatoria and the Upper Nile Provinces. This is a development which took place almost entirely after World War I.

The great development, however, is that of the Egyptian varieties — sakel and types which have succeeded or replaced it — on permanently irrigated land. There are three major areas of production. The oldest are the inland deltas of the Gash and Baraka streams already mentioned, streams which descend from the mountains of northern Ethiopia and disappear in fan-shaped silt plains. But the great area is that of Gezira, irrigated by the Sennar Dam and its canal systems, and where the area under cotton has steadily increased to reach over 200,000 acres (80,000 ha) in the years following World War II and nearly half a million acres (200,000 ha) by 1962, thanks especially to the Manaqil extension (1958–1962). Much of the Egyptian type of cotton is also grown on state and privately owned pump schemes drawing water from the Blue and White Niles.

The development of the Gezira irrigation area is a fascinating story. It is the supreme example in Africa of a successful cooperative scheme between a European management and African cultivators settled in an orderly way on the reclaimed land. Until it was nationalized in 1950, the Gezira scheme was run on a unique system of triple partnership — between the government, the two concession companies, and the Sudanese tenant cultivators. It was in fact the largest peasant agricultural cooperative in the British Commonwealth and probably in the world, covering close to a million acres along the banks of the Blue Nile. The land is now the main cotton-producing area of the Sudan. It is irrigated by free flow from the Sennar Dam. Before the construction of this dam the Gezira, a name which applied to the *doab* between the White and Blue Niles, was a flat clay plain with a precarious rainfall on which cultivators grew an uncertain crop of *dura* (sorghum). They lived in scattered villages, usually on the higher ground, and embanked small fields in an endeavor to conserve moisture. When the irrigation scheme was decided upon, the land was surveyed and the owners' titles registered. The government then rented the land from the owners or purchased that required for permanent works, about a quarter of the whole.

The railway reached Sennar in 1910;

14.D The Roseires Dam across the Blue Nile, during the course of construction and while the river is low (April, 1965). The water stored by the dam has doubled the supplies available for irrigation. (Photo: United Nations.)

14.E Ploughing on the Gezira prior to irrigation. (Photo: J. Allan Cash)

the great Sennar Dam, built by the government but delayed by World War I, was completed in 1925. Two companies, Sudan Plantations Syndicate Limited and Kassala Cotton Company Limited, were given concessions (which expired in 1950) to carry out subsidiary works and generally to manage the land and market the crops. The third partner, the Sudanese cultivators, grew their crops under guidance as well as providing labor and sharing in profits of the whole scheme. Although cotton is the cash crop, the crops are carefully rotated to provide sorghum (*dura*) for food and a leguminous fodder, *lubia* (*Dolichos lablab*), for working bulls and other livestock. These food crops occupy together considerably more land than the cotton. Of all profits on the sale of cotton 40 percent goes to the tenant cultivators, the remainder being shared by the government and the companies. From a few acres in 1912 the area under cotton approached an average of a quarter of a million acres in 1940–1950. Of the tenants about 20 percent are also the owners of the land; 60 percent are local peoples. Other tenants come from countries to the west, especially Moslem pilgrims to or from Mecca who have stopped to obtain work and funds and sometimes to settle.

The history of the Sudan Plantations Syndicate Limited is interesting. In 1904 the American philanthropist Leigh Hunt obtained an option over about 11,000 acres (4000 ha) along the Nile at Zeidab, but his plan to settle American Negroes there proved a failure. An English company took over his option, and it was this company which made a new agreement with the government in 1907, changed its title slightly, and took over the management of the Gezira lands. It was an example of successful private enterprise cooperating with and approved by the government, but with a minimum of government interference.

With the nationalization of the scheme and under an independent Sudan, progress has continued. The urban focus is Wad Medani, now a considerable town of 60,000 and capital of the Blue Nile Province. The controlling authority is the Sudan Gezira Board.

TRANSPORTATION AND COMMUNICATIONS IN THE SUDAN

It may be said that the million square miles (2.5 million km²) of the Sudan fall naturally into two zones. The first zone can be reached by modern means of communications, the second zone is a vast hinterland within which life remains unchanged and resources relatively undeveloped, primarily because of difficulties of access. The transportation routes, excluding airways, are shown in Figure 14.2.

It will be noticed that the 3000 miles (5000 km) of railroad of the common African 3 feet, 6 inches (1.07 m) gauge make the important irrigated tracts, including the Gezira together with Khartoum and the Nile valley settlements, accessible to the modern port of Port Sudan, which has replaced the old Arab port of Suakin, a few miles to the south on the Red Sea coast.

Over 2400 miles (4000 km) of river steamer routes exist, and apart from communication by air these provide the only

permanent link between the northern and southern parts of the country. Stern-wheel steamers of shallow draft are principally employed. The cataracts of the Nile result in three separated stretches of navigable river. There is first the connection from the Sudanese railhead at Wadi Halfa, down the reservoir behind the High Dam to Shellal in Egypt, where connection is made with the Egyptian railway system. Between the Third and Fourth Cataracts there is a short stretch where the Nile settlements are connected by river services and linked with the terminus of a branch railway at Karima. By far the most important navigation is that above Khartoum, from which steamers ply up the White Nile

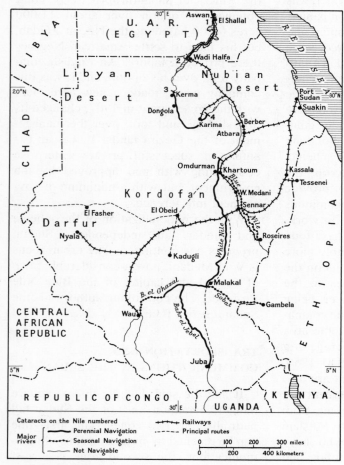

14.2 Transport in the Sudan.

14.F A general view of Port Sudan, a modern structure and town.

to Juba, whence road motor services operate to the Uganda frontier and into Uganda as well as into the Congo.

The steamer routes up the Sobat into Ethiopia and up the Bahr el Ghazal are used in the high-water season only and there is some seasonal traffic on the Blue Nile.

As in so many other parts of Africa, road transport has increased enormously in importance. In the Sudan tracks suitable for use except after rain are comparatively easily prepared in the steppe and savanna belts. But the Sudd remains an impenetrable barrier which must be skirted by road transport. The road from Khartoum to Juba is open only from December to March, when the early showers in the south turn the clay plain into a quagmire. When the heavier rains come in June, water covers the road; the grass is fired or cut in December. There are, however, all-weather roads in Equatoria and Bahr el Ghazal Provinces beyond the clay plains.

Khartoum, the capital, has of course become the focus of the Sudan. It is a modern town with broad streets laid out according to a design by the British general Kitchener. From about April to December the heat is often intense for long periods, broken only by rainstorms with torrential and damaging downpours, frequently following sandstorms, in August and September. From January onward days are hot and sunny but nights are cold enough for Europeans to appreciate a warm coat, even if heating of houses is rare. Khartoum is the center of higher education, with the University of Khartoum, which has evolved from a collection of colleges to independent status; there is also a branch of Cairo University. Khartoum is expanding as an industrial town, especially in Khartoum North, across the Blue Nile and reached by a road and rail bridge, and there is light industry in Khartoum itself.

Facing Khartoum, on the other side of the White Nile, is Omdurman, also reached by a fine road bridge, which is one of the largest market towns in Africa. It became the capital and a center of caravan traffic during the Mahdist period (1885–1896); it is now a center for truck traffic. Omdurman has over 170,000 inhabitants, and it also is changing rapidly, with much modern building replacing some of more traditional construction. With growing population, the "three cities" area around the junction of the White and the Blue Nile is becoming more integrated.

The steady growth in importance of Port Sudan since its completion as a modern port in 1926 is reflected in the fact that it handles over 80 percent of the foreign trade of the Sudan. To the casual visitor its coral gardens, seen through glass-bottomed boats, are perhaps the finest in the world to be visited so easily.

14.G A street scene in Port Sudan with a load of firewood brought in on a camel. (Copyright: L. Dudley Stamp.)

Further Reading

From former staff of the Department of Geography of the University of Khartoum have come two essential texts. Most comprehensive is *The Republic of the Sudan, A Regional Geography* by K. M. Barbour (London: University of London Press, 1961). A massive task of compilation and interpretation is represented by *Land Use in Sudan* (Bude, England: Geographical Publications Ltd., 1965, World Land Use Survey, Monograph No. 4) by J. H. G. Lebon. An older work now becoming a classic is *Agriculture in the Sudan* edited by J. D. Tothill (London: Oxford University Press, 1948). The heart of the modern economy is described in *Gezira: A Story of Development in the Sudan* (London: Faber and Faber, 1959) by A. Gaitskell.

CHAPTER 15

Ethiopia and the Horn of Africa

A glance at the physical map of the African continent reveals the presence of a great knot of mountainous country stretching from the shores of the Red Sea to the northern borders of the East African plateau in the neighborhood of Lake Rudolf. This great knot of mountains forms a continuous barrier cutting off both the Nile basin of the Sudan and the Sahara Desert from the part of the African continent which projects eastward for some hundreds of miles into the Indian Ocean, and which is occupied by the country of the Somalis.

Referring back to the rainfall map of Africa on p. 67, we see at once that the mountain knot enjoys a heavy precipitation, whereas the whole of Somalia to the east is a continuation of the desert lands stretching across Arabia on the other side of the Gulf of Aden and the Red Sea. The mountain knot coincides in general extent with the ancient Empire of Ethiopia. This is another part of Africa to which the much-used adjective "unique" can be applied.

THE ETHIOPIAN EMPIRE

The whole of Ethiopia is nearly 400,000 square miles (1 million km^2) and, although no census has ever been taken, the population is estimated to be more than 23 million. The Empire of Ethiopia is a sovereign independent state, which has grown out of a combination of a number of kingdoms which used to recognize the king, or Negus, of Ethiopia as their King of Kings. The smaller kingdoms, such as Tigre, Gojjam, Gondar, and Shoa, have become mere provinces, as have other parts which previously enjoyed at least some autonomy. Haile Selassie I, who was born in 1891, was crowned king in 1928, proclaimed and crowned emperor in 1930.

The long history and fluctuating fortunes of Ethiopia include an experience of colonialism from Italy, brief in Ethiopia proper, more prolonged in Eritrea.

Overpopulated Italy's colony in North Africa, Libya, her colony along the Red Sea in Eritrea, and the large area of Italian

291

15.A The Tississat Falls on the Blue Nile or Abbai where it leaves Lake Tana. (Photo: J. Allan Cash.)

15.B Searching for ibex on the cliffs of the Simein mountains in northern Ethiopia. There is international concern for the survival of the ibex. (Photo: J. Allan Cash.)

Somaliland were all mostly desert. But the establishment of Italy in both Eritrea and Somalia not unnaturally brought Ethiopia into the sphere of Italian interests. At a time when the Negus of Ethiopia was consolidating his hold over the surrounding peoples from bases in Amhara, Tigre, and Shoa in the period of 1880–1900, the Italians were consolidating their position on the Red Sea coast, and the French were already in possession of Jibuti (Djibouti), which they had annexed in 1884. An Italian force, invading from the Red Sea coast, was annihilated by the Ethiopians at Aduwa in 1896. Undoubtedly this resounding defeat rankled in the minds of Italians for many years. Although the three European powers concerned, Britain, France, and Italy, reached an agreement with Ethiopia in 1906 confirming the independence of the Ethiopian ruler and acknowledging his right over the terri-

tories he had conquered in consolidating the Empire, the Italians accepted this settlement with the memory of the past defeats still in mind.

In 1936 Benito Mussolini, the Italian dictator, felt himself sufficiently strong and independent of adverse European opinion to invade Ethiopia and to annex it to the Italian Empire. The emperor fled to Britain and there lived in exile until, with the outbreak of World War II, British Imperial troops drove the Italians from Ethiopia and gave the country back to the control of Haile Selassie, who reentered his capital Addis Ababa in 1941.

It should first be made clear that Ethiopia is not a simple kingdom but an empire with many different communities, often physically distinct, and distinguished by language and religion; many of the communities have long histories of separate existence. At the heart of Ethi-

15.C The cathedral church in Addis Ababa. The Coptic church is at the historic, cultural, and political heart of the Ethiopian empire. (Photo: J. Allan Cash.)

opia are the Amhara who inhabit the plateau of the central Ethiopian highlands. They were converted to Christianity in the early days of the Christian era and, until recently, maintained close contact with the Egyptian Coptic Christians. In fact, the Abuna, or Metropolitan Archbishop of Ethiopia, had always been an Egyptian Copt appointed and consecrated by the Coptic Patriarch of Alexandria. The church is very strong in the country, having numerous clergy and holding large possessions of land. It was a natural consequence of recent events that Ethiopia should seek a greater degree of independence in this as in other directions. In January 1951, an Ethiopian became archbishop of the country, and in 1959 the Ethiopian Church became autocephalous with a Patriarch second only to that of Alexandria.

To the north of the area which forms the homeland of the Amhara are the Tigreans, closely akin, and also Coptic Christians. The most numerous people of Ethiopia are, however, the Gallas, constituting about half the entire population. They are a pastoral people some of whom

are Christian, some Moslem, some pagan. The Empire also includes Nilotic tribes in the southwest, Falashas of Jewish origin north of Lake Tana, and numerous tribes either of Somalis or allied to the Somalis in the plateau country of the southeast of the Empire. Various Negro peoples live in the southwest, bordering the Sudan. As in East Africa, an Arab and Indian commercial element is found in the towns.

The importance of appreciating the racial complex within the Ethiopian Empire is great because of the widespread belief in America and Europe that Ethiopia is the supreme example of an African country where the people have determined their own destiny (see the map of languages, Figure 15.1).

Between Ethiopia proper, which nowhere reaches the seaboard, and the southern coasts of the Red Sea lies Eritrea, which was part of the pre-1939 Italian African Empire. The people of Eritrea, who number more than 1 million, consist of Coptic Christians living on the plateau areas and Moslems, with few exceptions, on the lowlands of the western province and the Red Sea littoral. Italians

15.D A traditional form of Coptic church in rural Ethiopia, at Zeguie. (Photo: Camera Press.)

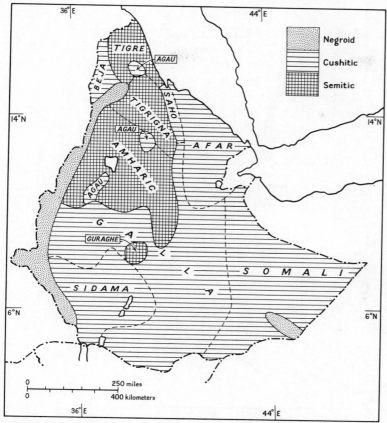

15.1 Languages of Ethiopia. The historic nucleus of Ethiopia is the area occupied by the Amharic speaking Coptic Christians. (After the Atlas of Ethiopia.)

settled at Assab in 1869, and Eritrea became Italy's first colony in 1889. When the time came to decide the future of the country, from which the Italians were driven by British Commonwealth forces in 1941, there was clearly opportunity for a difference of opinion as to whether Ethiopia should be allowed to extend its empire over the whole of this country, on the grounds of uniting together all the Coptic Christians, despite the alien character of the coastal Moslem population. By virtue of the decision made by the United Nations it was agreed that Eritrea should be federated with Ethiopia (that is, should enjoy partial autonomy) by 1952. It was, however, fully integrated into Ethiopia in 1962.

With regard to its physical setting, if

Ethiopia is examined in some greater detail, it will be seen that the western half includes most of the lofty mountain area, where large tracts are more than 10,000 feet (3000 m) above sea level (Figure 15.2). This extensive mountainous western half is bounded by a great fault scarp overlooking the rift valley previously described. The rift valley in fact forms a great trench southeast of the capital, Addis Ababa, occupied by a succession of lakes, but northward it broadens out into the lowlands abutting Eritrea and the Red Sea; a considerable area is below sea level. To the east of the rift valley trench in the south of the country there are other lofty mountains, but the country passes thence into a plateau, eventually fading into the lower elevation of the Somaliland

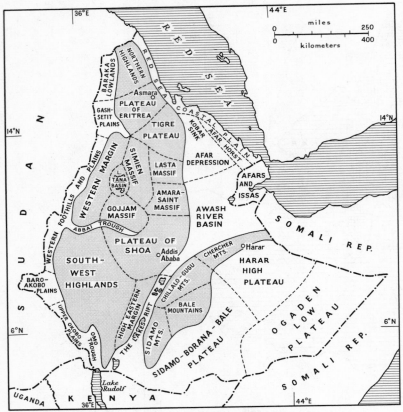

15.2 Physical regions of Ethiopia. (After J. C. Last.)

desert plains. The highly mountainous character of western Ethiopia is a direct result of an immense number of volcanic lava flows poured out in old fissure eruptions one above the other. They give rise to huge plateau areas, often more than 10,000 feet (3000 m) above sea level and with some points reaching over 13,000 feet (4000 m). This mountain massif enjoys a heavy rainfall, coming at the time of the Indian monsoon. The rainy season in the mountains is thus the rainy season of India, June to October. Average annual rainfalls are over 40 inches (1000 mm) over most of the plateau rising to 80 inches (2000 mm) in the southwest where rain is received during most of the year (Figure 15.3). This mountainous heart of Ethiopia is a land of abundant rainfall, of swiftly running mountain streams carving their way through deep and tortuous gorges up to 5000 feet (1500 m) deep,

many of them eventually finding their way to the Blue Nile or to other Nile tributaries, the Sobat in the south, the Atbara in the north. The western rift valley edge is the main water parting of the country. Eastward the water drains toward the Somali desert.

In the well-watered mountain land cattle, sheep, and goats are numerous. The horses of the country are small and hardy, donkeys sturdy and well adapted as baggage animals; mules are also available as pack animals. The immense range of environmental conditions has meant that Ethiopia is just as able to produce cotton and coffee as sugar cane and cereals like millet, wheat, and barley.

From the point of view of agricultural production the Ethiopian highlands may in fact be divided into three zones. The lowest, called *Kolla*, comprises the lower slopes of the plateau itself and the deeper valleys up to 5000 or 6000 feet (1500 or 1800 m). Where rainfall is adequate it is forested with a vegetation of tropical character, for here frost is unknown. Here may be found rubber vines, ebony trees, and bananas with coffee, which grows wild in abundance in the higher parts. There could be an enormous output of coffee of the Mocha type of Arabia from this zone. The banana is mostly the "false banana" or ensete (*Ensete edule*) of which the content of the fleshy stem is eaten, rather than the fruit. In the zone of heavy rainfall in the south and southwest of the Highlands, this is the basis of the diet. In the drier highlands near Harar, a major crop is chat (*Catha edulis*) the leaves of which are chewed as a narcotic drug. Maize, sorghum, and millets are grown and cattle are important in the drier areas.

Above the Kolla is the *Woina Dega*, or wine highlands, extending up to 7000 or 8000 feet (2500 m), a healthy tract with numerous trees, where such Mediterranean fruits as the orange, fig, and apricot as well as the vine will flourish, where cereals can be grown, and cattle and sheep are reared in large numbers. This is the most typical agricultural landscape of the highlands, growing teff, barley, and wheat on ploughed fields over large areas where the original vegetation has now been completely removed. Teff is a cereal, *Eragrostis teff* which grows rather like a field of good thick hay and its flour is used to make a type of bread, *indira,* and also a beer.

Above the *Woina Dega* rises the *Dega* proper. The degas provide pastures of open grassland with bushes, but there such cereals as wheat and barley can be cultivated, and there is abundance of pas-

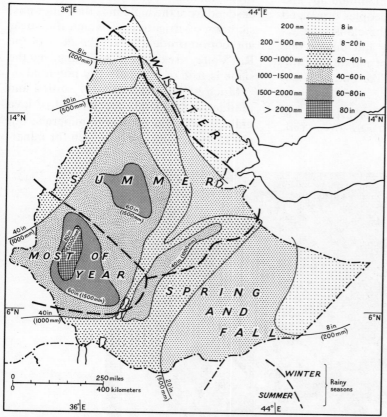

15.3 Mean annual rainfall and seasonality in Ethiopia. (After the Atlas of Ethiopia, 1962.)

ture for cattle and sheep. The very highest levels, above 10,500 feet (3500 m) and known as *Wirch,* represent Alpine pastures with distinctive elements in the flora related to that on the high mountains of East Africa.

In the arid regions gum arabic and gum tragacanth are collected, and also those aromatic substances so prized by the people of former days, frankincense and myrrh. Beeswax too is obtained, from the honeycombs of wild bees, and an excellent drink is made from the honey.

Ethiopia has been described as the Switzerland of Africa, a description more apt of the mountainous western half of the country than the unkind designation of its arid northeastern plains in Danakil as the "hell-hole of creation."[1] Mountain Ethiopia shares some of its features with other mountain lands—its great scenic beauty, its invigorating mountain air, and its sturdy, independent peoples organized on a feudal clan basis, the clans long accustomed to fight, raid, and pillage one another. A description of mountain Ethiopia today reads not unlike one of High-

[1] L. M. Nesbitt, *Hell-Hole of Creation: The Exploration of Abyssinian Danakil* (New York, 1935).

land Scotland a few centuries ago. One day it may well become a Mecca for tourists, a jewel in the great deserts protected by forbidding escarpments. It contains monuments at Axum dating from "the Queen of Sheba," richly decorated Coptic churches, and fascinating towns such as the walled city of Harar. Ethiopia boasts an ancient civilization, of which all members of its society are proudly aware.

Around the great mountain heart of Ethiopia proper are wastes of rock and sand where existence in an environment of heat and drought is possible only when wells are known whose life-giving waters enable the desert nomads to keep their camels, donkeys, and mules or their herds of wiry goats, lop-eared sheep, and big-horned gaunt cattle alive. Wild and domestic animals alike live precariously on the scrub vegetation under the eyes of the ever-watchful vultures. Where rivers descend from the highlands they offer possibilities of irrigation of which the sugar and cotton production on the floor of the Rift Valley are only the beginning, and the same is true of hydroelectric potential.

Much of the most densely settled and productive highlands are formed of lava unlikely to yield economic minerals, but elsewhere the intensive search for miner-

15.E One of the churches at Lalibela carved out of the rock, the horizontal lavas and tuffs which can be seen forming the extensive plateaus ("*ambas*") beyond, bounded by deep valleys. (Photo: Camera Press.)

15.F The largest of the ancient obelisks at Aksum. Aksum derived from the Sabean culture of southern Arabia and was the origin of a Christian state in the Ethiopian highlands. Notice the representation of a building with doors, windows, and beam-ends. (Photo: Camera Press.)

als has only recently begun. The discovery of oil on the Red Sea littoral of Egypt has encouraged exploration which has located gas offshore from the Eritrean coast.

The principal route into the Ethiopian Highlands is through the port of Djibouti in the French Territory of the Afars and the Issas, from which a meter gauge railway was constructed to Addis Ababa over the years 1897 to 1926. This serves irrigation developments on the Rift Valley floor and it is proposed to extend it southwards. The Italians built a railway across the arid escarpments from their point of entry at Massawa to their colonial capital in Asmara and on to Agordat. The third port of Assab is not served by railroad and cargo is transported by trucks across the desert lowlands and up the great wall of the highland edge at Dessye. Its use, however, avoids dependency upon a foreign port. In the five years that the Italians occupied Ethiopia, they characteristically carried out some remarkable work in road building with hairpin bends reminiscent of the Alps in Europe. The Imperial Highway Authority has an important role in improving communication between the parts of the Empire formerly difficult of access and in facilitating the marketing of export crops in an economy largely aimed at very local markets. Particularly difficult is the task of linking the sections of lava plateaus or "*ambas*" separated by very deeply cut river gorges. A strategic road is also being built to improve communication with Kenya.

By far the largest town of Ethiopia is the capital city of Addis Ababa, with over 600,000 people. It stands in the highland zone at 8000 feet (2,400 m), so that the three hottest months (before the rain breaks as in India) are March, April, and May, but they average only a little above 60°F (16°C). On winter nights temperatures drop to 40°F (4°C) and even below, but the average is 58°F (14.4°C) for the coldest month. These figures of small range compare closely with the figures for Nairobi. In contrast to the old walled cities, Addis Ababa is modern. It was deliberately selected as a site for the capital by the Negus Menelik II as recently as the end of the nineteenth century and has benefitted greatly from the introduction of Australian eucalyptus—supplying large quantities of firewood from the surrounding hills. It is conveniently centrally situated and is near the border of Amhara and Galla country. Reflecting favorably on the reputation of Ethiopia is the selection of its capital for the headquarters of the Economic Commission for Africa of the United Nations and of the Organization for African Unity.

Harar, the ancient walled city and center of the coffee district, is the traditional starting point for caravans to the coast. It is a Moslem stronghold and the former commercial capital, with a large Arab and Indian population. The old city is on a plateau; a new city has grown up at Dire Dawa on the railway on its way through the Rift Valley below. This modern commercial and industrial town has something of a French atmosphere.

Eritrea consists of two regions. The first is the narrow coastal plain, backed in the north by the wall-like fault scarp of the Ethiopian highlands and in the south by the uplands of Danakil. The second region, the highlands, drains westward to the Nile plain. The population is partly nomadic, engaged in the occupations of animal rearing and the collection of gums and resins. The Italians sought to develop irrigation agriculture, especially for cotton and food grains in the coastal plain. In the highlands agriculture is possible only in the more favorably watered parts and little of the Italian farming remains.

Most of the trade passes through Massawa. A railway runs from Massawa to Asmara, the administrative center, and thence to Agordat. From the latter there are roads southward and to the Sudan frontier. Asmara is a progressive modern town with an international airport and is situated near the plateau edge overlooking the Red Sea plains.

AFARS AND ISSAS
(TERRITOIRE FRANÇAIS DES
AFARS ET DES ISSAS)

This small French territory has little economic importance apart from the port of Djibouti, which replaced the original French port of Obock, acquired in 1867,

when Djibouti was chosen as the terminus for the railway to Addis Ababa. The Afar are a Danakil, Galla people and the Issas are a Somali clan. The number of Somali has greatly increased by immigration to seek work in the town and port, whereas the Afar tend to keep to their traditional herding. Demands for unification with Somalia led to a referendum and a 60 percent vote to remain as an overseas territory of France. Dispute was caused over the voting rights of some of the Somali and Ethiopia threatened action if Djibouti, its principal outlet, was taken over by Somalia. Its strategic position as a port of call obviously depends on whether the Suez canal is in operation, as does that of its rival, Aden.

SOMALI REPUBLIC

Somalia became an independent republic on July 1, 1960 when the British Somaliland Protectorate and the Italian trusteeship territory of Somalia merged. The area is about 245,000 square miles (638,000 km²) and the population, almost entirely of Somalis, is estimated at over 2.6 million. It occupies the prominent "Horn" of Africa. The aridity is derived from the same combination of winter Arabian high pressure and divergence of the summer winds towards the great Indian monsoon which is responsible for the anomalous dry conditions over equatorial East Africa. Only in the southern part of the country and on the escarpment of the northern region does annual rainfall exceed 20 inches (500 mm). It is generally much less and falls in two seasons, as in eastern Kenya. Aridity confines land use over most of the country to nomadic pastoralism depending heavily on camels but also on goats, sheep, and cattle. The herds must follow the grazing into regions outside the national boundary, especially in the "Haud" of Ethiopia and these movements are regulated by treaty. These boundaries also divide the permanent grazing areas of other Somali and this has led to conflict with Kenya, Ethiopia, and the French Territory of Afars and Issas. The Somali claim is that their nation has been partitioned between five states (represented by the five-pointed star on the flag) of which only two have so far been regained. The recognition of ethnic unity as constituting a right to sovereignty, however, would tear apart the painfully established order of Africa, and the O.A.U. agreement of 1964 regards the inherited colonial frontiers as inviolable.

The former protectorate of British Somaliland, dating from 1882, consists of a narrow coastal plain only about a dozen miles wide, backed by a steep fault scarp. The highlands rise abruptly to a height between 4000 and 7000 feet (1200m—2100m), and then the surface of the plateau slopes gradually southward. The whole country is extremely arid, the population almost entirely nomadic, with a dependence upon sheep and goats and a few cattle. Some gums and resins of different kinds are collected from the bushes of the semidesert, and there is a small production of salt. The administrative center and now the third town of the country (pop. 50,000) was Hargeisa and the principal port Berbera. Berbera has long acted as an outlet for products of the Harar and the Somali plateau.

Italy's first concession dated from 1889, largely extended in 1901, and later by treaty with local chiefs. The Italians, who invaded British Somaliland on the outbreak of World War II in 1940, were driven out the following year, and the British also took Italian Somalia. After nine years of British administration Italy was allowed to resume control, on a trusteeship, on April 1, 1950, with the express objective of preparing the country for independence after ten years. In 1960, Italy completed her trusteeship and Britain withdrew from British Somaliland, enabling the two territories to join and form the independent Somali Republic.

The former trusteeship territory consists essentially of a plateau 2000 to 3000 feet (600 to 900 m) above sea level, sloping gradually eastward and presenting a series of steep scarp faces toward the coastal plain and the Indian Ocean. Much is close to absolute desert, but from the capital of Mogadiscio (est. pop. 250,000), formerly part of the domains of the sultan of Zanzibar, a fair road runs inland to a cultivated belt along the Webi or River Scebeli. The Juba River is navigable and at its mouth is Chisimaio (Kismayu). Rainfall increases in a southward direction and between these rivers is the Benadir coast of the Swahilis. Here some cul-

15.G Old buildings of the sea front at Mogadishu. (Photo: Nigel Watt, Camera Press.)

tivation is possible relying either on the rain or on irrigation. Bananas are the leading crop, exported from Chisimaio (Kismayu) and the old Arab port of Merca. The bananas are of only moderate quality and high labor costs for handling and loading them prevent the Somali product from competing on the open market, so that this important export is dependent upon a duty-free Italian market. Rain-grown agriculture between the Scebeli and the Giuba (Juba) rivers has sorghum and maize as major crops with sesame and groundnuts as secondary ones. Irrigated crops near the rivers include bananas, sugar cane, citrus fruits, cotton, and vegetables. Projects are under way to increase agricultural production to serve local needs and to permit modest exports, especially of cotton and citrus fruit, in addition to bananas.

A uranium deposit may prove useful, and suitable geological conditions exist for oil, especially in the region adjacent to, as well as in the area in dispute with, Kenya.

Further Reading

No recent comprehensive studies have been published of either Ethiopia or Somalia and data and maps are, partly for security reasons, insufficient. A school text by Geoffrey C. Last, *A Geography of Ethiopia for Senior Secondary Schools* (Addis Ababa, 1963) gives a general overview and a helpful short bibliography is appended to his "Introductory Notes on the Geography of Ethiopia" (*Ethiopia Observer,* VI, No. 2, 1962). Also see E. W. Luther, *Ethiopia Today,* 1958, and F. J. Simoons, *Northwest Ethiopia; Peoples and Economy* (Madison: University of Wisconsin Press, 1960).

For the former Italian portion of Somalia see the report on *The Economy of the Trust Territory of Somaliland* made to the International Bank for Reconstruction and Development, 1957. The former British section was reviewed in *A General Survey of the Somaliland Protectorate* 1944–1950, (Hargeisa: Govt. Printer, 1951). The historical background to the division of the Somali nation is given by I. M. Lewis in "The Somali conquest of the Horn of Africa," *Journal of African History,* 1 (1960) pp. 213–30.

CHAPTER 16

Equatorial Africa

Equatorial Africa coincides in general with the great basin of the Congo River, together with a region between the Congo mouth and the Cameroun Mountain drained directly to the Atlantic Ocean. Politically it thus includes both Zaire, formerly the Congo Democratic Republic, once Belgian, with its capital at Kinshasa (formerly Leopoldville), and the Congo Republic, which was formerly French and has its capital across the Congo River at Brazzaville. The states of Gabon and the Central African Republic were also within French Equatorial Africa and so was Chad, but that country has more in common with West Africa (Chapter 13). Cameroun includes the former French trusteeship territory and the southern portion of the British one — the northern section joined Nigeria. Equatorial Guinea unites the former Spanish territories of Fernando Póo and Rio Muni.

Through the heart of the great area runs the line of the equator, but equatorial Africa in the sense generally understood does not stretch right across the continent, since to the east lie the high plateaus occupied by Tanzania, Kenya, and Uganda, with a very markedly contrasted character. The Congo Basin is essentially an enormously broad flat basin in the great African plateau. Although there are considerable differences from one part to another over such a huge area, there are many features common to the whole drainage area of 1,600,000 square miles (4,144,000 km²).

The heart of the area enjoys an equatorial climate with no dry season, and this extends to the coast of southern Cameroun. The so-called rainfall equator lies about 3° North of the true equator, and along this line rainfall is well distributed throughout the year; the total reaches 60–80 inches (1500–2000 mm). The range of temperature between day and night does not commonly exceed 10 or 15°F (6 or 8°C), and the difference between the mean of the hottest and coldest months is not more than 3–5°F (2–3°C). This is the region of the hot wet forests so closely associated with true equatorial regions.

To the north one passes into a subequatorial region of northern type, with rainfall maxima in June and September, and an appreciable dry period in December and January. Southward from the rainfall equator the southern type appears, with rainfall maxima in March and November, and a distinct or relative drought in June, July, August, and September.

Where the southern margins of the basin are reached in the Katanga, the daily temperature range has become considerable [15–20°F (8–10°C)], and the annual as much as 15°F (8°C). The rainfall regime has become that of the southern tropical areas, with a rainy season from November to April.

There are fascinating local differences. Where the heights of the Cameroun mountains are reached there is a rapid rise in rainfall so that stations on a slope of the mountain itself show an average fall of 400 inches (10,000 mm) a year. Circumstances closely associated with the upwelling of cold water and offshore winds bring the arid coastal belt of South West Africa and Angola almost to equatorial latitudes in the neighborhood of the Congo mouth, where the rainfall is only 30 inches (750 mm) per year.

Equatorial forests of the evergreen type naturally occupy the heart of the basin, but give place as the land rises to a high savanna type of forest where trees lose their leaves in the dry season, though evergreen forests stretch as long tongues up the river valleys. Drier types of forest succeed towards the margins of the basin and pass naturally into the African savannas.

Along the coasts there are extensive mangrove swamps, especially north of Cape Lopez. It should be noted that the true equatorial forest is of much more limited extent than was supposed in the early days of the African explorers, who rather naturally penetrated by rivers and were unaware of the relatively open character of the ground between the main streams. How far the large areas of savanna are natural and how far they owe their existence to the long-continued system of rotation or "shifting" cultivation practiced by the widespread though not very numerous inhabitants is an open

question. What strikes one in flying over the more populated parts of the Congo basin is the amount of forest which has been destroyed and the numerous areas either under cultivation or recently deserted. It is doubtful how much of the high forest is original; even in the depths of the forest evidences of former human settlements are frequent. Unfortunately when the land is cleared of forest the soil is very rapidly leached by the heavy rainfall and recovery takes a long time.

In the early days of European penetration equatorial Africa was chiefly of interest as a source of slaves. Later under white influence the tapping of forest trees and the collection of palm oil from the wild oil palms attained large proportions, and so too did the trade in ivory, one of the few commodities whose value enabled it to stand the high cost of transport by human porters from the heart of the forest to the rivers, or the coast. Overtapping and ruthless destruction of the rubber-bearing trees killed that trade. It became more profitable to grow oil palms in less remote plantations. Some of the more accessible parts of equatorial Africa have come to make an appreciable contribution to world commerce, with plantation rubber, plantation palm oil, cocoa, and coffee. Though valuable timbers, mostly heavy wood of the mahogany type, have been worked, the great variety of trees in the equatorial forests makes the working of any one type difficult.

Three main ethnic groups are to be found in equatorial Africa. There are the pygmy tribes, who still live a seminomadic existence in certain parts of the equatorial belt. They keep to themselves, though they are in friendly relationship especially by trade with their Bantu neighbors. Some of the tribes have achieved an exotic allure in school textbooks in the English language from their sensible habit of building shelters among the branches of trees, away from the danger of floods and certain wild animals. Some of them do still depend to a considerable extent on animals which they can kill for food, or on fruits and roots which they gather, but the majority practice some form of agriculture.

In the north of the region are people of mixed racial origins, forming a distinctive group of agriculturists. Over the remainder of equatorial Africa the people are Bantu. They live for the most part in straggling villages, often of great size. For some centuries before European penetration these Bantu peoples had established and organized extensive empires. Indeed, the Congo derives its name from the Congo Empire, which covered much of this area in the fifteenth century when the first Portuguese discoveries were made.

It was Stanley who said that the Congo, without railroads, is not worth a penny. To an extent unusual in Africa, however, communication has been possible by river transport; railroads were first constructed to supplement steamer services and they still perform this function.

Flowing as it does through the heart of equatorial Africa, the great Congo is a more constant stream than the Nile or the Zambezi (Figure 16.1). The tributaries from the south, such as the Kasai, have two periods of low water and two of high in the year, but the tributaries from the north such as the Ubangi have a single maximum. Consequently the regime on the main river varies from place to place; at Stanley Pool the river is at its lowest in July and August. The emphasis, however, should be on the relative constancy of the flow. Below Stanley Falls the river is unimpeded by rapids for a thousand miles to Stanley Pool. The central navigable channel is never less than 10 feet (3 m) deep, though the river with its shallows and islands is often 8–10 miles (13–16 km) wide. It should be realized that the Congo, with its enormous basin and huge volume, is probably the largest undeveloped source of hydroelectric power in the whole world. One must remember too that the river in about 220 miles (350 km), descends nearly 900 feet (275 m) in a series of thirty-two rapids, known collectively as the Livingstone Falls, from Kin-

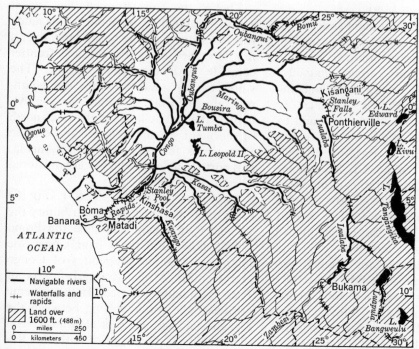

16.1 The Congo Basin.

shasa to Matadi. What a dream for a water engineer!

ZAIRE (FORMERLY THE CONGO DEMOCRATIC REPUBLIC)

Zaire Republic or Congo (Kinshasa) covers an area of 895,000 square miles (2,345,000 km²). This is nearly eighty times the size of Belgium, of which it was formerly a colony.

The Congo Free State was set up in 1885 by the Association of the Congo, which was dominated by Leopold II, king of the Belgians, and for more than 30 years it was virtually the personal property of the king. It was only in 1907 that it was annexed by Belgium. The boundaries were defined by declarations dating from 1885 and by successive treaties with the powers interested in neighboring lands. An interesting adjustment took place as late as 1927 when Portugal exchanged 3 square kilometers—a little over a square mile—near Matadi in the Congo estuary for 3500 square kilometers (1350 square miles) in the extreme southwest.

Although the eventual independence of the Belgian Congo had been envisaged, it had fewer Africans in political and administrative positions (town councils, army and police officers, etc.) than in comparable British or French colonies. It would have been difficult for Belgium to maintain a colonial status for the region when adjoining territories of French Equatorial Africa had already become independent, but the declaration of independence on June 30, 1960 can now be seen to have been premature. The period between the decision for independence and its implementation was only six months. Independence for Kenya was agreed at the same time but a carefully phased handover occupied four years. The departure of many (although not all) Belgian administrators, teachers, and doctors on the day of independence left no effective organization behind, and

neither of the two rival African leaders, Kassavubu and Lumumba, succeeded in establishing his authority. Personal, tribal, and regional rivalries flared up; the rich Katanga province broke away, and Lumumba called upon both the United Nations and the U.S.S.R. for intervention and help. The Secretary General of the United Nations sent out a military force of 20,000 (mainly African and Asian troops) but was himself tragically killed in an air disaster while visiting the area; Lumumba was murdered by tribesmen. There were mutinies, massacres by rival groups, massacres of European missionaries, the use of mercenaries, and a precarious semblance of law and order in a few centers maintained by United Nations troops. The only recompense is that a few politicians elsewhere may have learned and remembered for some time at least, the fragility of an ordered society. Those who had heard of him may have recalled the description by Hobbes of the absence of government when the life of man (and perhaps more of woman) is "solitary, poore, nasty, brutish, and short."

Though the Zaire Republic lies almost entirely within the Congo basin, it is much less extensive than the basin. Only over a few stretches does the political frontier coincide with the water parting. The whole vast area has but a tiny though immensely important coastline on the Atlantic—the deltaic lands of the river north of the main stream, hemmed in between Portuguese territory to south (Angola) and north (Cabinda, which is administered as part of Angola).

For some 1500 miles (2400 km) the main river, and then its great tributary the Ubangi (Oubangui), and then the Bomu (which flows into the Ubangi) form the boundary with the Republics of Congo and Central Africa (formerly parts of French Equatorial Africa). In the extreme northeast the water parting between the Congo basin and the Bahr el Ghazal basin of the Nile is the frontier with the Republic of the Sudan, and in the extreme south the water parting with the Zambezi is in part the frontier with Zambia. In the east Zaire stretches to Lake Tanganyika.

In general terms the Congo basin is a shallow depression on the surface of the great African plateau; most of the heart of the republic is less than 1600 feet (500 m) above sea level. The geological structure is essentially simple (Figure 16.2). The basin is geologically very ancient. Recent alluvium borders the main river and stretches around Lake Leopold II; older alluvium—once the bed of a great lake—occupies the lower core of the basin. These give place on the higher ground to vast stretches of soft sandstone known as the Loubilache (Lubilash) Beds. Older than these are the famous Koundeloungou (Kundelungu) Beds, more localized in distribution. These are the oldest sedimentary rocks found resting on the ancient crystalline massif. They are probably Permian-Triassic in age and have been folded, not very severely, by the movements responsible for the folded mountains of the Cape in the extreme southwest of Africa. These beds include limestone, shales, and sandstones, but the adjective "famous" refers particularly to the basement beds with great boulders scratched by ice. It would seem that at this period the whole of the heart of Africa was covered by great ice sheets, and it is held by many geologists that either the North or the South Pole of the earth was then over the heart of Africa.

Apart from the actual or potential value of the younger rocks in providing the material for agricultural soils, economic interest centers on the ancient crystalline rocks and mineralized ancient sediments. In the Katanga district in the extreme

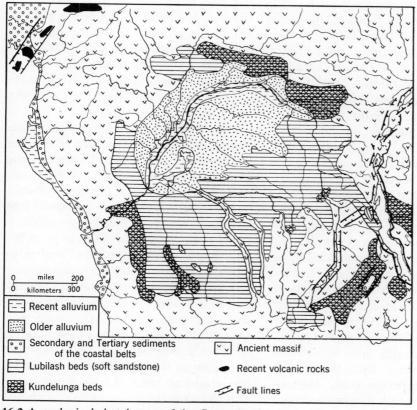

16.2 A geological sketch map of the Congo Basin.

south on the Congo–Zambezi divide is one of the richest mineral-bearing tracts in the world.

The population of Zaire is estimated to be almost 20 million (1969–1970), an average density of only 22 per square mile (9 p.km²). There are some pygmies in the forests and Nilotics in the northeast, but the bulk of the Africans are Bantu with some Sudanese. On the basis of the 1941 census, Pierre Gourou prepared a detailed population-density map, published in color as one of the sheets of the *Atlas general du Congo* by the *Institut Colonial Belge* on the scale of 1:5,000,000. His commentary is still very relevant to the distribution of the rural peasants with their largely subsistence economy in relation to the features of the natural environment. He used the 1047 administrative divisions known as *circonscriptions indigenes,* and apart from groups of forest pygmies who may have escaped enumeration the map may be accepted as an accurate representation of the facts. It showed some very remarkable contrasts in population density. Some 10 percent of the whole Congo could be described as a "forest desert" with fewer than 0.3 person per square kilometer—less than 1 person per square mile—and three-quarters of the whole Congo had less than 12 to 13 persons per square mile. Gourou found an east–west belt roughly 5° South of the equator, including Kikwit and Luluabourg, of relatively dense population, and a less pronounced one north of the equator. Surprisingly, Kinshasa (then Leopoldville) was an "island" of population in a sparsely inhabited area. Local factors which influence the number and variety of insect carriers of disease are responsible, Gourou believed, for local population growth, and he instances the good health record of Coquilhatville (now Mbandaka) right on the equator with the poorer record of Elizabethville (now Lubumbashi), nearly 12° South. Gourou ascribed the freedom of Coquilhatville from

malaria to the character of local waters which, draining from laterized surfaces, have a high content of aluminium hydroxide in solution. He believed that the well-populated belt south of the equator coincides with a belt where the forest, though of equatorial type, is sufficiently dry in some years to be burnt but where the fires do not become so intense as to damage the soil. Nevertheless he admits that the distribution of population as a whole is not explicable only in terms of the influence of natural factors. The effects of tribal warfare and of slave raiding in the past are among other complicating factors. Gourou's map affords an interesting example of a factual survey used as a starting point for an analysis of the influence of geographical factors.

The capital of Zaire (then the Congo) was changed in 1927 from Boma to Léopoldville (Kinshasa). Boma and Banana are now of little importance, but Kinshasa has become a great modern city with a population of about 1.5 million. The same is true of Matadi, the chief ocean port, with its extension known as Fuca Fuca and the associated oil port of Ango Ango, from which a pipeline takes fuel to Kinshasa for Congo river steamers (see Figure 16.3).

The modern history of Zaire falls into several marked stages. In 1877 when Stanley arrived from the east and solved the problem of the Congo itself, the whole territory had long been in the hands of scattered tribes, sometimes grouped into ephemeral and ill-defined Negro empires. It had been a reservoir of slaves going latterly eastward by Arab slave traders to the Indian Ocean, previously to the west and so eventually to America. Stanley found, in Europe, one man able to understand the importance of his discoveries: Leopold II of Belgium. He thought out a comprehensive scheme of transport development to open up the whole basin: first a portage railroad from Kinshasa to Matadi on the estuary, second a combined rail–river route to the Katanga, which he

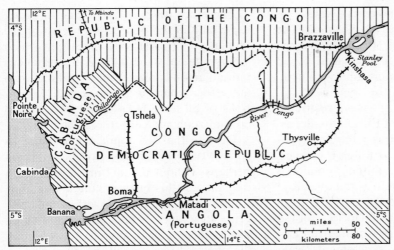

16.3 Countries at the Congo mouth. Congo D. R. was renamed Zaire in 1971.

secured, and third a direct rail to the Atlantic. All of these were eventually constructed. It was Leopold who had established in 1876 at the Brussels meeting of the International Geographical Union a Commission for the Exploration of Central Africa. After several expeditions Leopold established the *Association internationale du Congo*. This Association, under the active presidency of Leopold, rapidly followed political and economic rather than scientific aims, and, despite French and Portuguese objections, was "recognized" by the United States and Germany in 1884. Leopold granted numerous concessions to companies and, although the slave trade had ceased, there followed a period of exploitation in the companies' efforts to obtain, in particular, ivory and wild rubber. Gradually stories of harsh treatment of Africans came out, but many stories were found to be exaggerated for political reasons.

In 1900 four-fifths by value of all the exports from Leopold's domain were represented by wild rubber from vines such as *Funtumia elastica*. But Leopold, being a farsighted as well as an ambitious man, had secured control over a part of the plateau to the extreme southeast of the Congo basin known as the Katanga. This he secured in 1892 at a time when local

chiefs were considering asking Britain for protection. The mining period may be said to date from 1906, when the Katanga copper deposits began to be exploited, though there was but a small output until after 1911. Africa, had, of course, shared with other continents the stories of fabulous wealth in minerals, but although copper, tin, iron, and even gold were brought out of the interior, the stories of the trackless forest and its perils had prevented anything approaching a "gold rush." The discovery of substantial copper deposits in the Katanga may be credited to the Belgian geologist Jules Cornet, who explored the area in 1890 to 1892.[1]

Vast concessions were granted by Leopold to land and mining companies, notably to the *Compagnie du Katanga* (1891) and its later subsidiary the *Comité spécial du Katanga,* and these had to be recognized when the territory became a Belgian colony in 1908. From that time the Katanga became the focus of European activity in the Congo with much of the mining activity in the hands of the great combine formed in 1906 (involving

[1] The late Sir Dudley Stamp studied geology under Cornet at Mons in 1919 and recalled him working in the field in striped trousers and a tail coat, and carrying a black umbrella.

Belgian and British interests), known as the *Union Miniére du Haut Katanga*. The assets of this company were nationalized in 1967 but it has been replaced by an equally large state organization with managers, many of whom are Belgian.

At first production was restricted mainly to the vicinity of Elizabethville, especially from the famous mine known as the Star of the Congo (Etoile du Congo), but later the center shifted a hundred miles north-northwest to Kambove. Rail access was first provided in 1910 from Zambia, but the completion in 1931 of the Benguela railway across Angola from Lobito Bay provided a convenient "side door" much nearer Europe. Less convenient but all-Congo routes using river and rail were opened in 1911 via Stanleyville and in 1928 via Port Franqui and the Katanga Railway. Three developments of great importance took place. One was the establishment of smelting works at Lubumbashi (Elizabethville) and Likasi (Jadotville) so that nearly all the export is in the form of crude copper. Then, from 1925 onward, came the increasing use of coal from two fields within Zaire instead of from Wankie in Rhodesia. The third was the growing development of hydroelectric power first from the Cornet Falls on the upper Lufira River. In consequence of all these developments the southern Katanga has become a major area of white settlement in tropical Africa, and the industries are dependent on immigrant African labor drawn from many parts of Zaire as well as from Angola, Portuguese East Africa, and even farther afield. The mineral resources of Katanga are far from exhausted and Japanese interests are active in the area.

Apart from the great copper deposits the Katanga also yields tin and zinc, as well as the greatest output of cobalt of any region in the world, and for some time, almost all the world's output of radium. Many of the early developments in the use of atomic energy used uranium ores from Shinkolobwe.

There are other mining areas in Zaire, especially in the Kilo-Moto region of the highlands northwest of Lake Albert which yields alluvial diamonds. Zaire produces more diamonds measured by volume than any other country in the world. Indications of oil have been found in the small coastal zone adjacent to Cabinda.

Despite the developments in Zaire as an entity the Katanga forms a region perhaps without parallel in the world. In the heart of this busy mining area stands Lubumbashi, the capital, with its magnificent skyscraper blocks of offices which would be a credit to any city anywhere in the world. The layout of the modern towns is on comparable lines. Much has been written of the importance of access in Africa, and the story of the opening up of the Katanga is well known. Focusing on the mineral-rich area of the Katanga and adjacent Zambia are a number of competing routes leading to Matadi and Lobito on the Atlantic and Beira, Lourenço Marques, and Dar es Salaam on the Indian Ocean (Figure 16.4). The least convenient is the route through Zaire territory which involves transshipment onto a river steamer but it is hoped that an all-rail, all-Zaire route will be constructed. These routes are described further in Chapter 18.

The development of the Katanga had placed it in a very different position from the other provinces of Zaire. It was certainly not surprising that, in the midst of chaos elsewhere, the Katanga should have sought to break away and establish its independence. It will be clear from the account of its mineral resources given above that the Katanga has the resources to stand alone, but without the revenue from this one vital province Zaire as a whole would have been precariously placed.

Given conditions within which investment and orderly trade is possible, Zaire offers great opportunities for economic development with a great extent of well-watered and potentially arable land in

16.A Potential water power in the Katanga. The waters of the southern Kalulo River plunges over a wall of horizontal schists over 260 feet (80 m) high. Zaire has one of the greatest reserves of hydroelectric power in the world.

proportion to the population and large known and prospective mineral resources. It also contains a hydroelectric site with one of the largest potential capacities in the world. The vast and relatively even flow of the Congo River cuts through the Crystal mountains on its way from the Congo basin to the sea. The Inga scheme could realize an installed capacity of 26,280 megawatts. Unfortunately the principal market within Zaire would be in the distant Katanga but there would still be a great surplus. A small component of this scheme will be working in 1972.

RWANDA AND BURUNDI

At the end of World War I Belgium, as one of the Allies, received under mandate from the League of Nations the territory of Ruanda-Urundi, a tract of some 20,900 square miles lying east of the main western rift valley, that is, east of Lake Kivu and the northern end of Lake Tanganyika.

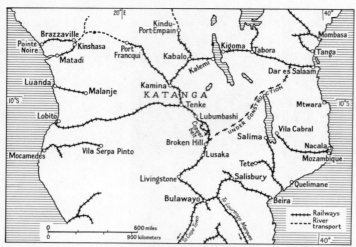

16.4 Transport routes serving the Katanga (Zaire) and Copperbelt (Zambia).

Formerly part of German East Africa, it belongs geographically to East Africa but formed administratively an integral part of the Belgian Congo after 1925 — adjoining the progressive province of Kivu, although it was made a trusteeship territory of the United Nations. Refusing independence as a united country, they became separate sovereign states with the names Rwanda and Burundi in 1962 and the limited common functions were ended by 1964. Both were traditional kingdoms but there has been much bloodshed between the agricultural *Hutu* majority and the pastoral *Tutsi* former aristocracy and both are now Republics. There are large numbers of refugees in Uganda and Tanzania, but refugees from Zaire are also found in Burundi.

Rwanda and Burundi occupy the eastern portion of the high land formed by the structural dome across which the western Rift Valley has cut, together with associated volcanism, some still active. Thus most of the area lies at over 5000 feet (1500 m) rising towards the Rift Valley to a crest over 10,000 feet (3000 m) and the Mfumbiro Range of perfectly shaped but extinct volcanoes rising to 14,786 feet (4507 m) at Mt. Karisimbi. These lie on the northern border of Ruanda which has the more attractive

scenery, including Lake Kivu as well as a lake-studded national park.

Climatically there are five regions. First there are two long narrow belts running north and south parallel to Lake Tanganyika. This is in the tropical lowland of the rift, with about 35 inches (900 mm) of rain. Here is situated Bujumbura, on the shores of Lake Tanganyika, capital of Burundi and a lake port, exporting through Kigoma and Dar es Salaam. High-forested mountains with heavy rainfall (and a double maximum) follow to the east and form the Congo–Nile watershed. The Central Plateau with about 50 inches (1250 mm) occupies most of the heart of the two countries, and here, in the north, is Kigali, capital of the Republic of Rwanda. Farther east is the warm, dry eastern depression. Finally the volcanic district of the northwest forms a distinct area of Rwanda.

The land is intensively cultivated using the hoe on small fields and terraces to support an overall density of population in excess of 300 persons per square mile (120 p.km²) and locally much higher. Agriculture is necessarily mostly food production for subsistence, including maize, millet, sorghum, beans, and cassava, the cultivation of which was encouraged by the Belgians as a famine reserve. The British did the same in their adjacent East African territories. Exports have to face a long haul to the coast but *arabica* coffee is widely grown as a peasant cash crop. On a much smaller scale are exports of cotton, pyrethum, and tea. Cassiterite (tin ore) is mined in Rwanda. Cattle were formerly under the control only of the Tutsi, but are now more widely owned. They are of the large-horned variety valued more for their prestige and beauty than as a source of meat and milk.

Rwanda and Burundi offer a remarkable comparison with Zaire, with which they were formerly associated. With an area only 2.3 percent that of Zaire, yet they support a population 40 percent as large (about 6.4 million compared with 16 million). Although containing good soils and a favorable climate, the broken relief makes mechanization of agriculture difficult and isolation hinders trade. By comparison, Zaire harbors vast potential resources for agriculture and mining and a low density of population so that a resumption of the labor migration begun under the Belgians should be of mutual benefit.

FORMER FRENCH EQUATORIAL AFRICA

Afrique Equatoriale Française (or A.E.F.) was perhaps the least homogeneous of all the political divisions of Africa, stretching as it did from the Tibesti Mountains in the middle of the Sahara to the Congo River and Atlantic margins, actually as much as 5° *south* of the equator. French settlements on the Gabun or Gabon River date from 1839, and Libreville on the Atlantic coast was founded in 1848, as its name implies, for liberated slaves. From these settlements as bases the sphere of French influence was steadily expanded and limits defined

16.B Intensively cultivated hillsides in central Rwanda. (Courtesy of United Nations.)

by a series of treaties. The boundary between French Equatorial Africa and the Anglo-Egyptian Sudan was not fixed until February 1924, and the later organization into the four territories of Gabon, Middle Congo, Ubangi-Shari, and Chad dated only from 1946. In 1960 they became the four independent republics of Gabon, Congo, Central Africa, and Chad.

GABON (RÉPUBLIQUE GABONAISE)

Gabon is the French Sierra Leone. The capitals of Libreville and Freetown were both founded for resettled slaves and both have an extent of highly indented coastline. The population, however, is small, and large areas of its heavily forested interior are virtually uninhabited. The total population is less than half a million, giving an average density of about 5 per square mile (2 p.km²). For a long time exports consisted mostly of timber, especially such attractive furniture wood as *okoumé*. Some cocoa and coffee is also exported but minerals are becoming more important. Gabon is a major supplier of manganese, exporting via Point Noire in the Congo (Brazzaville). Since 1956 oil has been produced at the coast near Port Gentil, where a refinery has been built, and production is more than adequate for the home market. Several large reserves of iron ore have been formed and production is beginning at Belinga from which a new railroad leads to a new port at Owendo, near Libreville. This small country is one of the most prosperous in tropical Africa. It is well endowed with minerals, hydroelectric power sites, forests, and potential agricultural or plantation land. Lack of population could limit output in the immediate future.

CONGO (RÉPUBLIQUE DU CONGO)

Congo (Brazzaville) was the former colony of Middle Congo and its capital was the capital of French Equatorial Africa. The town is therefore rather larger and more well developed than otherwise might have been the case, and the country has more industries serving the local market than its former colleagues — and more civil servants. Brazzaville is strategically situated on the north shore of Stanley Pool on the Congo, receiving river traffic from upstream, including from the Central African Republic and transshipping it by rail to the Atlantic port of Point Noire. Congo is less fortunate than Gabon but its exports have similarly been dominated by timber, now running at about 50 percent of the total. There is a small export of palm oil and sugar but most agricultural production is for subsistence or the local market. Diamonds are the second export item with small amounts of lead and gold. A small petroleum output is obtained from near the coast. Production is increasing from a large potash deposit at Holle St. Paul, only 25 miles (40 km) from Point Noire. The total population is less than a million and the density similar to that of Gabon at 5 per square mile (2 p.km²).

CENTRAL AFRICAN REPUBLIC (RÉPUBLIQUE CENTRAFRICAINE)

The Central African Republic (formerly Ubangi-Shari) extends from the north bank of the Ubangi, a major tributary of the River Congo across the broad watershed into the Chad basin. Lying between 4°North and 10°North, it receives a tropical rather than an equatorial rainfall regime with a marked dry season and a savanna rather than a forest vegetation. Cotton is the leading cash crop of the savannas and the major export, followed by coffee. Peanuts are growing in importance but yielding little for export. The forested areas of the south are near the Ubangi and other rivers suitable for transport, and despite the long haul, timber is exported. The only considerable mineral production is of diamonds although uranium is worked. A position in the middle of the continent hinders trade with the outside world most of which involves transshipment between the Pointe Noire to Brazzaville railway and river steamers. A direct route through Cameroun would be of great benefit although the natural resources and the size of the population [1.5 million at 5 per square mile (2 p.km²)] which would be served make the project of dubious profitability. Its relationship with its neighbors also pulls in several directions providing as it does a route into Chad, a refuge for Sudanese, and a hinterland competed for by Congo (Brazzaville), Cameroun, and Zaire (Kinshasa).

CAMEROUN (RÉPUBLIQUE FEDERALE DU CAMEROUN)

As briefly noted in Chapter 2, the Germans secured a hold on the Cameroun coast in 1884. British traders and missionaries had already established settlements in the country near the present Victoria and Debundja within sight of the great Cameroun Mountain, but Britain had declined the request of the Duala chiefs to extend a protectorate over their lands.

The Germans were quick to appreciate the value of the highland zone, and in 1901 moved their administrative headquarters from Douala to Buea (now the capital of West Cameroun) on the southeastern slopes of the mountains. On the healthy heights above the equatorial rainforest they looked to establish European settlements. In particular they set to work to study scientifically the problems of tropical agriculture and established a fine botanic garden at Victoria. Their buildings were constructed with double roofs for insulation and they were built to last. At first the wealth of the country came from palm oil and rubber gathered from the forest, but then they introduced plantation agriculture, notably of bananas, which were sent in large quantities from Victoria to Hamburg before World War I. The Germans pushed their territorial claims inland to Lake Chad, passing thus

(like neighboring Nigeria) out of the forest through the savanna zone to the Saharan margins. They adopted over the people of the grasslands a form of indirect rule, recognizing the integrity of tribal groups.

In 1911 the French were forced to cede to Germany 100,000 square miles (260,000 km²), giving German Kamerun direct access to the Ubangi and to the Congo, thus cutting the French equatorial empire in half. Almost as bad was the inclusion of a strip of land reaching the Atlantic only a few miles north of Libreville. This was the price of Germany's noninterference with French plans in Morocco.

Early in World War I British and French forces took the Camerouns; the French reincorporated the territory they had been forced to yield three years earlier and the remainder was divided — 166,000 square miles (430,000 km²) going to France and 30,000 (78,000 km²) to Britain, including Victoria and Buea. This was recognized by the League of Nations under the mandate system, and later trusteeships under the United Nations. Britain divided her territory into northern and southern parts. In 1961 the north voted to join Nigeria and the south to join the former French territory which had become independent in 1960, forming a federal republic.

To a considerable extent the French built on the economic foundations laid by the Germans. The port of Douala was progressively improved (formerly ocean vessels anchored 25 miles away); a railway was constructed to Yaoundé, on the plateau, which is now the federal capital and the focus of an important road system. One road goes through to Fort Lamy, the capital of the Chad Republic, crossing the upper Benue at a point from which it is navigable through Nigeria. Though the European-owned plantations advanced but little, the plantations for coffee, oil palm, and cocoa which the Germans encouraged African chiefs to establish have now a considerable output.

Cameroun is relatively well served by domestic industry and has one large scale industry in the two aluminium plants at Edeah. These are based on local hydroelectric power and at present use bauxite and alumina imported from Guinea, although there are also bauxite deposits in Cameroun itself.

The unification of the two parts of Cameroun has obviously presented problems, with differences in language, trade relations, education, currency, etc.

EQUATORIAL GUINEA

Equatorial Guinea consists of the former Spanish territory of Fernando Póo and Rio Muni, including the distant island of Annobón and the offshore islands of Corisco, and Great and Little Elobey, which became independent in 1968.

Fernando Póo is unique in West Africa. The volcanic line of the Cameroun mountains extends southwestward. Fernando Póo is thus a collection of extinct volcanoes rising from ocean depths to heights of nearly 10,000 feet (3000 m) above sea level. The fine harbor of Santa Isabel is part of an old crater invaded by the sea; elsewhere on the island are volcanic peaks rising from the ash and lava plains and fascinating crater lakes. The heart is forested or grassed, with some Dutch and Swiss cattle on the grasslands. On the west, north, and east fringes of the island, up to about 2000 feet (600 m), are extensive plantations. Fine-quality cocoa is by far the most important crop and, with coffee, accounts for four-fifths of the cultivated area, the rest being occupied by African foodstuffs. Export crops are produced on plantations, many of which were owned by Spanish settlers and companies but their number has been reduced following disturbances in 1969. The population of Fernando Póo contains distinct communities, resulting from a complex history. The indigenous inhabitants, are the Bubis (almost 15,000) with some 5000 Fang from mainland Rio Muni and 4000 creole Fer-

nandinos. These are outnumbered however by a fluctuating population (40,000–70,000) of immigrant workers who come to work for the Spanish and Fernandino landowners. They are mostly Ibos from eastern Nigeria and it was from Fernando Póo that mercy flights to Biafra derived.

Santa Isabel is essentially a Spanish town set in the tropics (fully as European as Dakar or Abidjan) in which Africans happen to live. It houses a quarter of the people of the island; its fine Spanish-type houses and public buildings suggest both prosperity and a lively interest in the island's welfare by the former administration. There are excellent macadam roads, and there is even a pleasant hill station (Moka) with chalets, where conferences can be held, at 4500 feet (1400 m).

Tiny Annobón has some 1400 people and is heavily overpopulated; many seek work in fishing off Fernando Póo. Its inhabitants speak Portuguese.

The prosperity and sophistication of Fernando Póo contrasts with Rio Muni on the mainland. Although with an area 13 times as large, its population is only three times as great (still less than 200,000), without including the migrant laborers on Fernando Póo. It is a continuation of the forested plateau of Cameroun and Gabon inhabited by the same Bantu people, the Fang. The only significant export is timber, although exploration for oil continues along the coast. Spanish plantations have been abandoned.

SÃO TOMÉ AND PRINCIPE

These Portuguese islands lie between Annobón and Fernando Póo and form part of the same line of volcanic peaks. They constitute a province under a governor. With an area of 372 square miles (964 km²), they have over 60,000 people, including a thousand Europeans and three thousand of mixed blood. São Tomé in particular is prosperous and well developed, with roads and numerous well-equipped plantations. Exports include cocoa, coffee, copra, palm oil, and cinchona. Here with favorable physical conditions is proof that the Portuguese are not backward in fostering the economic development of their colonies. The soil is extremely fertile. Settlement and development on a permanent basis by the Portuguese date from 1493. The earlier prosperity was based on sugar. Labor shortage, as in Fernando Póo, led to the introduction of contract labor from Angola and elsewhere, now forming the bulk of the population.

There are interesting historical survivals in many parts of Africa. A good example was the tiny fortress of São João Batiste of Ajuda on the coast of Dahomey, claimed by Portugal and forming part of the province of São Tomé and Principe, until it was seized by Dahomey in August, 1961.

Further Reading

See the Selected Bibliography, p. 416.

CHAPTER 17

East Africa

THE PHYSICAL BACKGROUND

Each of the great regions into which the continent of Africa naturally falls has certain points of distinctive individuality. Over much of the continent the point of individuality is the river basin—the basin of the Nile and the basin of the Congo and to a lesser extent the basin of the Zambezi, for example. East Africa is different in that there the emphasis is on the unity suggested by a great continuous plateau on the surface of which, occupying a shallow depression, is that enormous stretch of shallow water, Lake Victoria, lying between two arms of one of the most remarkable features to be found on the earth's surface, the East African rift valley, marked in the west by a chain of long, narrow, deep lakes. To the east are coastal lowlands of varying widths (Figure 17.1).

The greater part of the East African plateau lies at an elevation of more than 4000 feet (1200 m) above sea level. Large sections in Kenya where the plateau is crossed by the equator are at an elevation of over 6000 feet (1800 m). An entire modification of climatic conditions results, in such a way that under the very

equator itself are lands which settlers claimed to be ideal for the settlement and development of white men nurtured in cool midlatitude lands. As elsewhere around the fringes of Africa the plateau descends to the coast by a series of steps, and as soon as lower land is reached physical conditions afforded by the terrain and the climate are utterly different. Hence the eastern half of Kenya with the port of Mombasa, or the islands of Zanzibar and Pemba off the coast offer marked contrasts to the regions high up on the plateau itself.

Structurally the East African plateau does not differ in any marked degree from the other parts of the African continent. There is the same complex of ancient metamorphic rocks of gneisses and schists, of ancient sandstones, and there are huge areas occupied by granite, all making up the plateau mass. As elsewhere in Africa, prolonged erosion has over large areas obscured the solid rocks by a varied mantle of decomposed rock and soils predominantly of a red color, a mantle sufficiently deep to hinder the discovery of those mineral riches sought by man and which occur scattered through the ancient complex. In consequence

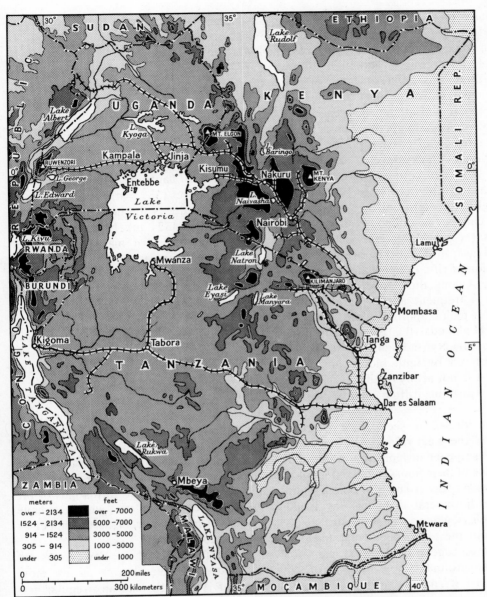

17.1 East Africa. The considerable elevation of most of East Africa is apparent. The Rift Valley faulting is shown in Figure 3-3.

there are important mineral deposits still in course of discovery, and doubtless others to be discovered, with prospecting encouraged by the example of the virtually single-handed discovery of some of the richest diamond-bearing ground in the world.

We have discussed elsewhere the development in Africa of peneplain surfaces, that is, of surfaces which are almost plains and which in terms of years are very ancient. At a time when great mountain-building movements in other parts of the world were folding the weaker rocks to form the great mountain chains, the western Cordillera of North America, the Andes system of South America, the Alpine and Himalayan chains of Europe and Asia, and even the Atlas of northwest Africa itself, the bulk of the African continent was a great rigid block, resistant to any further folding movements. Its very rigidity, however, resulted in the development of great cracks, and along these cracks there was differential movement. In particular it would seem that in East Africa, to compensate for the great movements of compression in other parts of the world, a region of crustal tension developed. Parallel cracks developed, and long narrow blocks of country were let down between them, giving rise to rift valleys. Although an eastern and a western Rift Valley can be described, both trending towards the single feature occupied by Lake Nyasa, in detail they are seen as a succession of rifts rather than continuous faulting. Among their general characteristics is a frequent alignment along the crest of a major uplifted dome as in the Kenya Highlands, the Rwanda-Burundi dome and the Nyasa Highlands. They are also bordered by fault blocks and their alignment is not always uniform, while in central Tanzania rifting almost disappears.

If one draws a section across the country of the great rifts to true scale the rift valleys appear insignificant in that the foundering of their floors to the extent of a few thousand feet is small in comparison with the horizontal distances involved. Nevertheless, when seen on the surface of the ground they are spectacular indeed. To reach the edge of the East African rift, to see the ground falling away at one's feet, and, if atmospheric conditions permit, to catch a glimpse of the mountain wall on the far side are experiences never to be forgotten.

It would be surprising indeed if such a fracturing of a large section of the earth's surface did not give rise to another of the earth's phenomena. It was associated with a great outburst of volcanic activity. Huge sheets of lava cover enormous areas in Kenya and extend southward into Tanzania and westward into Uganda, to be continued northward by still larger areas amid the mountains of Ethiopia. These stretches of lava have in many areas broken down to form some excellent soils. More conspicuous than the sheets of lava are the gigantic individual extinct volcanoes which tower to great heights above the plateau surface. Among the outstanding giants are Mount Kenya itself, almost on the equator, and rising to heights [17,058 feet, (5200 m)] which permit a fringe of glaciers round the peak. Southward within Tanzania, Kilimanjaro rises to 19,340 feet (5895 m). On the Kenya-Uganda border is the notable Mt. Elgon, 14,178 feet (4321 m). Near the western rift, on the western margins, the great mass once known as the Mountains of the Moon and now as Ruwenzori rises to 16,763 feet (5110 m) but is quite different in character, being a faulted block or horst.

Between the two great branches of the rift it would seem that the old plateau surface sagged, hence the reason for Lake Victoria, so different from the other lakes of East Africa. It is a shallow, island-fringed lake with gently shelving coastlands. Similar, though much smaller, is Lake Kyoga to the north, through which the waters from Lake Victoria drain on their way to make the White Nile. Thus the heart of the plateau forms part of the great Nile basin, that part which we have discussed in Chapter 11 as the upper or plateau course.

East Africa as a whole, however, is not dominated by river basins as are most parts of Africa. Instead an irregular network of streams join up to form rivers important locally, though ones whose names are little known outside the country, whose waters may yet be used for storage and irrigation works. Unfortunately in the driest areas, as in north and eastern Kenya, the volume of water available is small. Elsewhere it is the alternation of extensive flooding followed by seasonal drought that needs correcting, as in the Kilombero and Malagarassi valleys of Tanzania.

Professor Trewartha has drawn attention to the major climatic anomaly presented by East Africa.[1] Located in the same latitudes as the continuously rainy Congo and Amazon basins, the principal problem of land use in East Africa is seen to be inadequate rainfall (Figure 17.2). The minimum rainfall desirable for permanent cultivation in these latitudes is a reli-

[1] Glenn T. Trewartha, *Earth's Problem Climates* (Madison: University of Wisconsin Press, 1961).

able 30 inches (750 mm) a year — received in at least four years out of five. Some 55 percent of East Africa receives less than this. The basic cause of this anomaly has been described in Chapter 4 as due to the stable conditions in the airflow curving round to join the Indian monsoon, together with a dry air mass from Arabia during the other part of the year. The rapid passage of the Inter Tropical Convergence Zone brings a twin rainy season

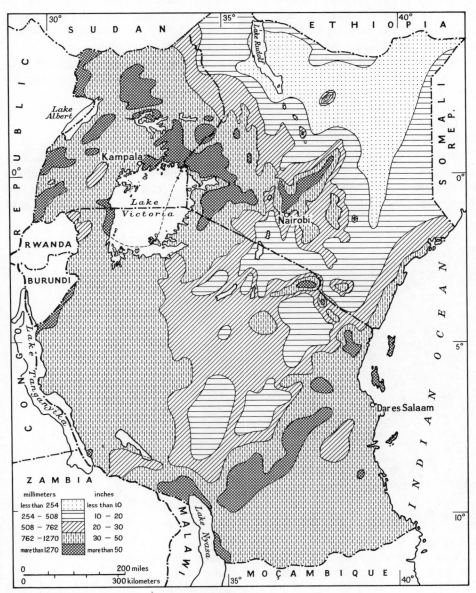

millimeters		inches
less than 254		less than 10
254 – 508		10 – 20
508 – 762		20 – 30
762 – 1270		30 – 50
more than 1270		more than 50

0 ———— 200 miles
0 ———— 300 kilometers

17.2 Mean annual rainfall over East Africa.

regime over much of the area: the "long" and the "short" rains. The aridity is most marked in the northeast bordering the Horn of Africa (see Chapter 15).

Rainfall along the coast is generally greater than inland although rarely beyond the range of 30–50 inches (750–1250 mm) a year. Westward, drier conditions prevail, averaging 10–30 inches (250–750 mm) a year, until totals increase with the approach of the highlands, or the atmospheric systems derived from the Congo Basin or of Lake Victoria. The influence of relief is very marked and can be highly localized. Mountains receive relief rainfall which may be in excess of 100 inches (2500 mm) on the windward aspect (generally east or southeast) with an abrupt rain shadow on the lee side. Highlands may therefore stand out as islands of higher rainfall carrying forests, cultivation, and dense settlement among a sea of arid, thinly populated thorn bush (Figure 17.3). The reduction of temperature with altitude is such that at

about 5000 feet (1500 m) the climate no longer comes into Köppen's tropical category. This is well indicated by the vertical zonation of vegetation types and also of the kinds of garden plants which may be grown. On the high mountains unique, often giant, forms have adapted themselves to a climate which has been well described as "summer every day and winter every night."

Such are the essential features of the climate of eastern Africa which distinguish it so clearly from that of humid equatorial Africa. They exercise a marked influence on the river regime, on the vegetation, on the life of the indigenous peoples, and on the possibilities of agricultural development.

HISTORICAL BACKGROUND

The pioneer journeys of exploration by David Livingstone quickly inspired others to follow him. The early missionaries and traders into east and central Africa found

17.A Intensive cultivation on steep slopes around Lake Bunyoni, Kigezi, Uganda. This mountainous area of southwestern Uganda is an extension of the Rwanda–Burundi dome and has attracted a dense population because of a high rainfall, freedom from tsetse fly and ease of defense in troubled times. (Photo: Eric Kay and N. R. Shave.)

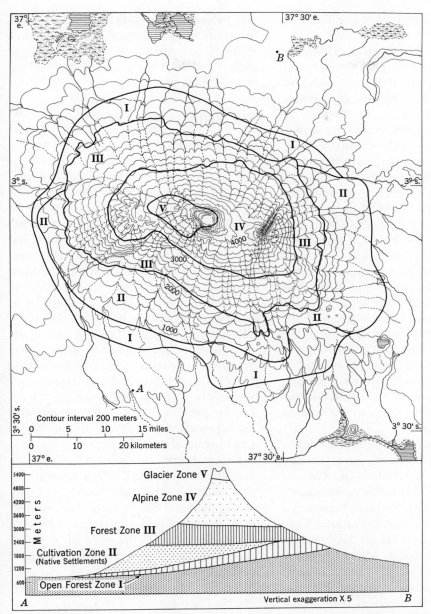

17.3 Vegetation zones around Kilimanjaro. (After Geog. Univ., Figure 28.)

the vast lands of East Africa sparsely populated by peoples menaced by famine and disease, the prey of intertribal warfare, and under the perpetual shadow of the slave trade. At that time the slavers were Arabs based primarily on the island of Zanzibar, whose sultan (himself of Arab descent) claimed a loose sovereignty over a great part of East Africa. Reference has already been made (Chapter 2)

to the efforts of the British consul to persuade the sultan to take strong action against the slave trade and to the way his authority was undermined when Karl Peters concluded treaties with local chiefs leading to the establishment of German East Africa. In 1886 the sultan's authority was limited to a coastal strip. The mainland was divided between German and British interests defined by treaty in 1890, in which year Zanzibar became a British protectorate.

The British East Africa Company began trading in 1887, but incurred such losses that by 1893 it had to withdraw from Uganda. The British government was persuaded by F. J. D. Lugard, afterwards Lord Lugard, not to break faith with the Africans with whom the company had made agreements but to take over responsibility. This led to a protectorate over Buganda in 1894 and East Africa (later Kenya) in 1895. It was in the latter year that the railway from Mombasa inland to Uganda was begun, a vital line of communication if Uganda was to be freed of the slave traffic and opened up economically. Labor was short and had to be brought from India, but the supply was hindered by plague. Disease killed off the transport animals as well as many of the workmen themselves, while the failure of the rains in 1898 led to famine over all of Kenya. The railway did not reach Kisumu on Lake Victoria until 1901, and Kisumu remained the port of entry to Uganda for the next 25 years.

Farther south, slave trading had a strong hold, but missions were successfully established at Blantyre in 1874 and Livingstonia in 1875, followed by trading companies. In 1891 Portugal recognized British rights to the country around Lake Nyasa, and to the west lay the country where the British South Africa Company had been accorded rights in 1889. In 1891 Lewanika, paramount chief of Barotseland, asked for and received British government protection. Arab slave traders who had been encroaching from north and west were defeated in a pitched battle by Sir Harry Johnson in 1894, and the last slave train, intercepted on its way to the coast in 1898, was set free at Fort Jameson. King Lewanika was a great ruler who foresaw the inevitability of change. He granted trading and mineral rights to the British South Africa Company and later land rights. The company in return extended railway and telegraph lines northward from South Africa. In 1924 the British government took over administration of the country, which had then come to be known as Northern Rhodesia, now Zambia. The further history of the territories is given later.

THE PEOPLES OF EAST AFRICA

Apart from a few pockets in remote areas occupied by the primitive pygmies, the vast majority of Africans in East and Central Africa are Bantu Negroes. For centuries they have been subjected to constant pressure from the north such that there is a zone of ethnic contact and mixing through Uganda, Kenya, and northern Tanzania. Early Hamitic (Cushitic) and Nilotic invasions gave rise to aristocratic class among the indigenous kingdoms around Lake Victoria. Later Hamitic movements brought the Galla and Somali into northeast Kenya with resulting conflicts of loyalties referred to in Chapter 15. Nilotic and Nilo-Hamitic (or Paranilotic) invasions brought well-known pastoral tribes south largely following grazing country, with the Masai reaching deep into Tanzania.

In the absence of a written language the various tribes of East Africa have gradually evolved forms of speech mutually unintelligible. This, in turn, has resulted, with improved communications following European entry, in the need for a *lingua franca* and the use of Swahili (Kiswahili) for this purpose. The choice between Swahili and English as the medium of government and education is a hard one.

For many centuries the Arabs had been active traders along the East African coast, and it was they who drove the Portuguese from their last stronghold at Mombasa toward the end of the seventeenth century. In 1832 the Iman of Muscat transferred his capital to Zanzibar, and in 1861 his son established Zanzibar as a separate sultanate, with wide claims in East Africa. A coastal urban civilization had existed along the coast for over a thousand years and presented a sharp contrast with conditions in the interior. It was derived from the Persian Gulf and Arabia and was in contact with the wider world including India and China.

European settlement was one of the objectives of the British South African Company in Rhodesia from the start, but in East Africa it came later as the attractiveness of the climate of the Kenya highlands was increasingly appreciated and the first true settlers took up land in 1902. The land which was granted to them was largely uninhabited except when, every few years, the warlike Masai drove their cattle into the pasture from which they had long before frightened away potentially permanent agriculturists. The agriculturists, however, owed some debt to the Masai whose presence kept the slave traders away from Kenya and northern Tanzania, in contrast to the situation further south.

It was the British who brought, for the building of the Mombasa-Uganda railway, large numbers of indentured laborers from India. Some 6000 elected to remain, and they have been joined by many who handle much of the import and export trade and retail distribution, as well as providing artisans, craftsmen, and clerical workers. It is this minority which is suffering most from policies of "Africanization."

World War I, 1914 to 1918, resulted in the voluntary mobilization of every British settler and the abandonment of most of the farms and the conquest of German East Africa. That territory, renamed Tanganyika, became a mandated territory entrusted to Britain, but the uncertainty of its political future did not encourage either settlement or economic investment. However, the discovery of gold and diamonds in Kenya and Tanganyika (Tanzania) and the development of the great copper zone in Northern Rhodesia (Zambia) gave new incentives; white settlements in the Kenya highlands grew, and Nairobi developed into a modern city. The arrival of independence is described below.

References are made below to the careful work of the late Clement Gillman who showed so clearly the remarkable contrasts in population distribution which are such a prominent feature of East Africa (Figure 17.4). There are fertile coastlands around Lake Victoria where 400 persons are crowded on each square mile (150 p.km^2); the islands of Zanzibar and Pemba support more than 250 per square mile (100 per km^2). On the other hand, vast areas in the heart of Tanzania are virtually uninhabited, yet they are far from being desert lands.

UGANDA

At the time of European intervention in East Africa, the kingdoms around Lake Victoria were the focus of commercial, political, and missionary interest. The greatest of these was Buganda and it was from the establishment of a protectorate over this kingdom in 1894 that British rule spread over the whole of Uganda. The Protectorate provided an interesting example of the policy of "indirect rule" with a ruler and a parliament ("Lukiko") for each of four kingdoms and the British Governor with his secretariat located in a small settlement on a peninsula in Lake Victoria, rather than in the principal city and railhead of Kampala which was the capital of the Kabaka of Buganda. Uganda became independent in 1962 and the special position of the four kingdoms was ended in 1967.

Although the total area of Uganda is only 80,000 square miles (200,000 km^2), if one excludes the tracts of inland water which lie within its boundaries, it has a population of nearly 8 million. This represents a very high density for Africa, of no less than 100 per square mile (nearly 40 p.km^2). On the slopes of Mount Elgon and on the shorelands of Lake Victoria the density exceeds 200 (75 p.km^2). The dam across the Nile at Owen Falls has attracted industry to Jinja, although the pull of the commercial center and principal market of Kampala makes it a major center of manufacturing, especially for smaller factories. The final installed

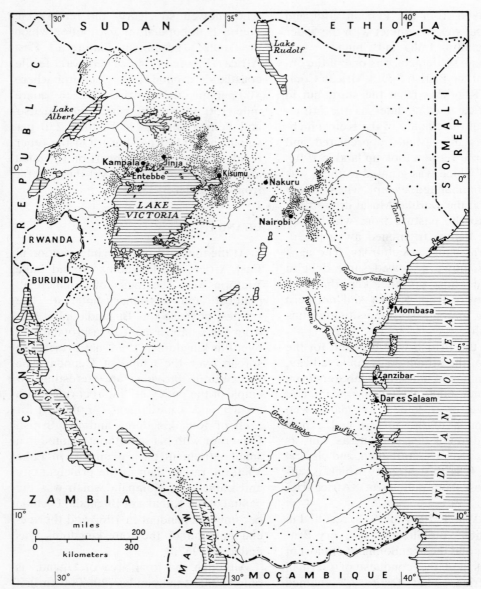

17.4 The distribution of population in East Africa. (After P. W. Porter and W. T. W. Morgan.) Each dot represents 5,000 people.

capacity of the dam was some 13 times that operating in Uganda at the time of its construction. Consumption was very slow in increasing to utilize this and a power line had to be constructed to Nairobi to increase sales. When planning for the production of electricity it is also necessary to plan for its consumption, industrial or domestic.

The eastern boundary of the country is

roughly the line of highlands which separates the Nile drainage from the Lake Rudolf basin. In the west Uganda includes part of the western rift valley, and here the Bunyoro Plateau overlooks from great scarps the deep trough occupied by Lake Albert. This plateau is an expression of a zone of uplift parallel and just east of the Rift Valley. The uplift lay across the previous east–west drainage, reversing the flow of some rivers and resulting in valleys where rivers flow in opposite directions.

As a result of its elevation the country has a modified equatorial climate. Thus Entebbe at 3900 feet (1190 m) has a characteristically small annual range of 70–73°F (21–23°C), and over most of the plateau the rainfall, averaging between 40 and 60 inches (1000 and 1500 mm), shows two maxima. The first is about April to May, and the second about October to December, but at Entebbe the intervening "dry" periods are dry in the relative sense only. Though there is considerable variability in annual fall of rain associated with variations in the strength of the air masses which converge on this part of Africa, there are not the periods of drought which are such a curse over much of Africa. And, although the rain — largely convectional — may fall during thunderstorms, sometimes with great violence, it does not do the damage that heavy falls may do on land left dry by months of drought, as happens farther south in Tanzania. In the northern and northeastern parts of

Uganda, rainfall is less and, being further from the equator, the two maxima are more closely spaced, leading to a distinctive dry season.

In southern Uganda the absence of marked seasonal rhythms makes cultivation possible throughout the year, but this type of climate did not attract European settlers as did that of Kenya. Uganda had been subject from time to time to very serious epidemics of sleeping sickness and other insect-borne diseases, though it enjoys a climate conducive to great agricultural development. On the whole the natural vegetation is that of moderately open forest or a dry savanna with abundance of trees. There are large stretches of papyrus swamp and swamp forest on the lower ground around the lakes resulting from the disruption of the drainage lines caused by warping of the land surface as described above. With decreasing rainfall toward the northeast, the savanna becomes poorer. Other local variations include stretches of grassy downland, and as elsewhere in Africa, the existing vegetation pattern is doubtless in major part

17.B The Owen Falls Dam and hydroelectric power station. This lies across a gorge where the River Nile leaves Lake Victoria, seen in the distance. The town and industrial center of Jinja lies beyond right. (Copyright: W. T. W. Morgan.)

due to human interference and cultivation.

In contrast, however, to the shifting cultivation so common in Africa, the Baganda in the populous areas have developed an intensive system of permanent garden cultivation. A large proportion of the Baganda are Christians, and the church is often a central feature of a group of homes. A modern home would probably have a corrugated iron roof, plastered walls, doors and windows, and a cement floor. The thatched kitchen is a separate building at the back, and the house is surrounded by a carefully swept yard with a shade tree or two and a few flowers. The surrounding garden consists of several parts. First there is the banana garden, tended by the wife, then plots with sweet potatoes, cassava, maize, and beans. Then there is the cotton patch, tended by the husband, who weeds the crop. The family does the harvesting about January, and the cultivator takes his

sacks of cotton tied to his bicycle to the ginnery.

Such is the life of the people within reach of modern roads, but throughout the country the large population naturally practices subsistence agriculture, with cereals, particularly millets, cassava, and bananas being the most important. The great cash crop, cultivated commonly by the Africans mainly in small plots from one-fourth of an acre upward, is thus cotton. The local varieties formerly grown for current use have been largely replaced since the introduction of American and Egyptian seed in 1903, so that most of the crop is now American Upland. Grown all over the country, the acreage reached 1,565,000 acres in 1959–1960, with an output averaging 65,000 tons, with a peak in 1958–1959 of 72,000. Acreage in 1969 was 1.25 million acres. The bulk of the crop is grown for export, and it is interesting that the local ginneries were until very

17.C A Baganda family and homestead near Kampala, Uganda. The prevalence of square houses with metal roofing reflects relatively prolonged commercial contacts overseas as the busuute dress reflects the fashions of early Christian missionaries. (Photo: Eric Kay and N. R. Shave.)

recently often owned by the immigrant Indians.

Agriculture in the humid south of the country is typified by the banana garden of Buganda. Crops grown for subsistence or local sale are bananas, maize, beans, and sweet potatoes. Many different varieties of banana are grown for cooking, fruit or beermaking, and the basic dish is of steamed bananas or "*matoke.*" The principal cash crop and leading export is robusta coffee. This has overtaken cotton which remains, however, very important and is more widely spread, extending into the areas of the moister savannas. These two crops usually account for 75 to 80 percent of total exports.

The western highland zone in the Toro and Ankole districts has attracted attention because of the possibilities of growing tea with good yields and both here and also on the slopes of Mt. Elgon, the better quality and higher priced *arabica* variety of coffee is grown. Tobacco is a crop especially of the high rainfall savanna of West Nile Province and sugar is grown, with the aid of irrigation, on two large plantations near Jinja.

Generally, however, the distinctive feature of the garden agriculture compared with Kenya has been that it became commercialized without the introduction of more than a few plantations or European settlers. British policy turned against such alienation in 1926, but equally important was the preexisting pattern of society and of land holding in the highly organized Buganda state which was able to adjust to the new commercial orientation and which had a land-owning middle class able to see the opportunities opened up by the arrival of the railway.

Livestock are the principal support of the drier areas of Karamoja, bordering on the arid north of Kenya and of Ankole, famed for its distinctive long-horned cattle — similar to those shown in paintings of ancient Egypt. Large areas are still unusable because of the tsetse fly which has in the past caused disastrous outbreaks of trypanosomiasis in cattle and humans. Some of these virtually uninhabited areas have been turned into game parks which in Uganda are especially noted for their numerous elephants.

The emphasis in Uganda has been upon agriculture rather than upon minerals, the exploitation of which has been hindered by the high cost of transportation to the coast. There has been a small output of tin ore, but the extension of the railway from Kampala has made possible the development of important copper deposits at Kilembe in the Ruwenzori massif. The ore is sent down to the railhead at Kasesi and thence to Jinja for smelting.

Uganda may be cited as an object lesson for other parts of Africa. It has natural advantages of soil and climate, but not without the disadvantages inherent in African conditions, such as infestation with tsetse fly. The relatively favorable natural environment is reflected in the number and the standard of living of its African population. Insofar as trade with the outside world is concerned, such advantages are of no use without modern means of transportation. Thus the modern development of Uganda began in fact with the completion of the railway through Kenya to Mombasa, though actually the first railway in Uganda ran from Jinja to Namasagali, bypassing some major rapids to link Lake Victoria with the head of navigation on the Victoria Nile. As elsewhere in Africa, development of roads has played and is playing an enormously important part in opening up the country. With the prosperity resulting from the export trade in coffee and cotton Uganda has now thousands of miles suitable for motor traffic throughout the year, and the truck and the station-wagon "taxi" are to be found everywhere transporting agricultural produce.

KENYA

Before becoming independent in 1963, Kenya had been a British protectorate since 1895. It was proclaimed a crown colony in 1920, when it took the title of Kenya Colony from the famous volcanic peak, almost exactly on the equator, which is its highest point. Along the coastlands are territories (at that time rented from the sultan of Zanzibar) which became the Kenya Protectorate. A treaty with Italy signed in 1924 ceded to Italy (Italian Somaliland) the whole of the Juba River and a neighboring tract of arid country, formerly in Kenya. In 1926 the area around Lake Rudolf in the northwest was transferred from Uganda Protectorate to Kenya.

The whole of Kenya now covers a land area of 219,790 square miles (569,180 km²) with a population of 8.6 million at the 1962 census. Ethnic divisions are particularly marked in Kenya with an African population approximately 65 percent Bantu, 16 percent Nilo-Hamitic, 14 percent Nilotic and 5 percent officially termed Hamitic. Significant minorities include about 40,000 Arabs largely resident on the coast, nearly 200,000 Asians (Indians and Pakistani), and Europeans whose numbers have fluctuated in recent years between 40,000 and 60,000. The distribution of the population is markedly uneven, reflecting the distribution of rainfall, and 80 percent of the population is concentrated onto 15 percent of well-watered land in the southwest of the country, consisting of the highlands and the Kenya portion of the Lake Victoria basin.

A simple physical division would recognize four major regions in Kenya. The coastal zone is distinguished by greater rainfall and lower altitudes than the plateau behind it. It has had a long history of trading port towns and successive Portuguese/Arab/Zanzibari control. Islam is predominant, and Swahili is widely spoken as a first language rather than merely as a *lingua franca*. Inland are the arid plains and plateau made up largely of peneplains or the sedimentary basin of the Tana embayment. Occupying three-quarters of Kenya, they support only

some 10 percent of the population who are largely nomadic pastoralists with herds of camels, goats, sheep, and hardy cattle which subsist on thorn bush and semidesert grasses and shrubs. Beyond are the highlands where the 5–20 inches (125–500 mm) of rain a year increases to 30 and up to 70 inches (750–1750 mm). The Kenya Highlands consist essentially of an upraised dome upon which lavas and volcanic cones have been superimposed and across which has been sliced the slightly sinuous north–south Rift Valley. A massive single volcano flanks the Highlands on either side — Mt. Kenya on the east and Mt. Elgon on the west. The eastern flanks of the highlands (on the lower slopes of the Aberdare Range and Mt. Kenya) is the home of the Kikuyu and closely related peoples, the largest tribe in the country. Between the Highlands and the Lake is another area of high and more reliable rainfall also densely populated and including two more tribes each numbering over a million: the Nilotic Luo and Bantu Luhya.

In the Highlands the area of greatest fertility and most reliably high rainfall had been occupied by cultivating peoples before the arrival of the Europeans. Large areas, however, were found to be used only for grazing by the Masai or were actually empty. These were not well suited for traditional African cultivation but to Europeans they appeared as good farming lands. Indigenous crops would not thrive at these altitudes, but introduced crops and livestock from Europe did well. Inadequate water supplies were met with bore holes and dams, and the cool climate with substantial houses, warmer clothing, and an appreciation of the climate based on comparison with that of Britain. To Lord Delamere and others, this was an inviting "White Man's Country." The first land in the "White Highlands" was taken up in 1902 and it eventually extended to 12,000 square miles within which only Europeans could own or manage farm land. Thus Kenya

17.D Large scale farming in the Kenya Highlands at Molo, over 8000 feet (240 m). This was a part of the "White Highlands." (Photo: East African Railways.)

had a true "settler" community which persisted long enough to enter into the second and third generation and gave a distinct character to the landscape and to Nairobi and the smaller towns of the "up country." This racial restriction of land holding was ended in 1962 and "decolonization" has proceeded apace. Since the majority of the exports at independence was derived from settlers' farms, there was a sensible attempt on the part of both the Kenya and the British government to avoid a precipitate flight from the land. Many of the large farms have been divided into small holdings but others have been maintained as large units.

Much farming is still for subsistence needs, but with little mineral wealth, Kenya relies heavily on certain export crops. Chief among these is high-grade *arabica* coffee, introduced on missionary and settlers' plantations but increasingly a peasant crop. This is typically grown at 5000–6000 feet (1500–1800 m) but at higher levels, and if rainfall is sufficiently reliable through most of the year, its posi-

tion is taken by tea. Another high altitude crop is pyrethrum, grown for insecticide. At lower altitudes, down to sea level and able to survive drier conditions of 25 inches (725 mm) of rain a year, are extensive estates of sisal. Fresh fruit and vegetables air freighted to Britain and elsewhere in Europe is a growing trade.

Although gold has been produced in western Kenya, the only substantial mineral production is soda ash dug out of alkaline Lake Magadi on the floor of the Rift Valley. A large and increasing income, however, is being obtained from tourism which is more important in Kenya than in either of the other East African countries. This is based on the attractions of wildlife in the game parks, tropical beaches, and highland scenery. A certain sophistication, especially noticeable in Nairobi, is also helpful.

The first capital of the East African Protectorate was Mombasa, an ancient Arab town with its Portuguese fort overlooking the old harbor still used by dhows from across the Indian Ocean (Figure

17.E Intensive peasant cultivation in the Kenya Highlands. This shows Kikuyu land after consolidation and terracing of steep slopes. (Photo: Kenya Information Services.)

17.F Nomadic pastoralists (Rendille) on the move in the arid north of Kenya. (Photo: J. Allan Cash.)

17.5). It is on the other side of the island, however, that the modern port has arisen on the harbor of Kilindini, the largest port of East Africa. Mombasa is the second town of Kenya and has a hinterland of the whole of Kenya, Uganda, and northern Tanzania. With the construction of the railway to Uganda, however, the capital was soon moved from the point of entry of the colonial power to the edge of the Highlands, where great future developments were obviously going to take place. This was Nairobi, a "forward capital."

Nairobi was selected as a site for a railway settlement at a point where the plains had been passed and the Highlands and the Rift Valley were yet to be crossed. It has become the largest city of Kenya and of East Africa, with a rapidly increasing population, estimated at nearly half a million in 1970. In the middle of the Highlands, and on the floor of the Rift Valley, is the third town, Nakuru. Kisumu, the terminus of the old main line to Lake Victoria, is the next largest center. Other towns originated as administrative centers or as small service centers in the commercial farming areas of the highlands.

Considering the extent of European settlement and the bitterness of the "mau mau" fighting by Kikuyu nationalists during 1952–1956, the eventual orderly transition of the colony to independence was remarkable. A number of favorable factors may be invoked, but a major consideration must have been the stature of the nationalist leader, President Jomo Kenyatta.

TANZANIA

Tanzania had its origins in the creation of German East Africa, out of lands which the sultan of Zanzibar claimed but was unable to hold and lying between the Portuguese and the British sphere of influence. After the war of 1914–1918, it was

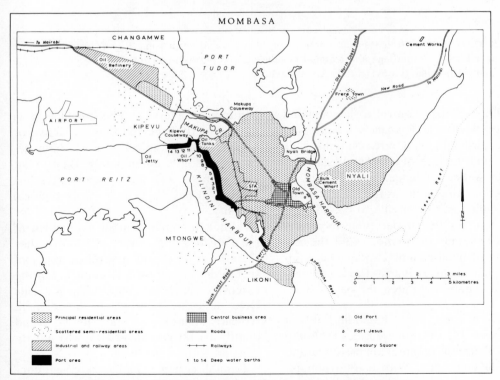

17.5 The site of Mombasa. The island is formed by two drowned river courses which provide excellent harbors.

17.G East Africa offers tourists a combination of two principal attractions: Big game in natural surroundings and tropical beaches. Here is the Nyali Beach Hotel near Mombasa. (Copyright: J. Allan Cash.)

left under British control as a mandated territory known as Tanganyika, converted to trusteeship by the United Nations. This status and the lack of internal dissensions due to settler influence, as in Kenya, or indigenous kingdoms, as in Uganda, made it possible for Tanganyika to be independent first, in 1961 under Julius Nyerere, the "Mwalimu" or teacher. After the federation of independent Zanzibar with independent Tanganyika in 1964, the new federal republic adopted the name 'Tanzania."

With a total area, excluding inland waters, of 342,000 square miles (886,000 km²), Tanzania is larger than Kenya and Uganda combined. With a total population approaching 12 million, its density of 35 per square mile (13 p.km²) is near the continental average. The population is more widely dispersed than in Kenya or Uganda and ethnically more homogeneous, being predominantly Bantu, but also without any particularly numerous tribe or tribes — a help towards political stability.

Although annual rainfall over much of the plateau is of the order of 30–50 inches (750–1250 m) a year, there is a long and severe dry season of 5–7 months. On the extensive peneplains, sandy, leached soils have developed on which this climate typically supports a deciduous woodland of little use for grazing and anyway mostly infested with tsetse fly.

Rainfall is higher along the coast, continuing the land use and the cultural world described for Kenya. Among the ruins of

17.H Nairobi: the sophisticated capital of Kenya, which was only a watering place for cattle until 1899. The pace of change has added several major buildings to the skyline since this photograph was taken. Note the originator of it all: the railway. (Photo: Kenya Information Services.)

ancient settlements, those of Kilwa Kisiwani stand out. Mangroves are extensive especially in the delta of the Rufiji and tree crops are important, including coconut, mangoes, cashew, and citrus. Maize, cassava, some rice, cotton, and sisal are grown. In the interior a wedge of marked aridity extends southwards from Kenya, supporting thorn bush (*Acacia* and *Commiphora* spp.) This is mostly occupied by pastoral Masai who have contributed to the survival of wildlife in their area by not hunting it and here are the major game parks of Tanzania including those of Serengeti, Manyara, and Ngorongoro.

The greater part of Tanzania however consists of the deciduous woodland over vast peneplains as mentioned above. This *miombo* vegetation is similar to that of the northern Guinea savanna of West Africa, a woodland with trees 25–40 feet

(8–12 m) high whose leaves die off during the dry season with colors reminiscent of the European autumn, although not the New England Fall. It falls into two main blocks, in the southeast and in the west (where it is known as the Central Plateau). Sleeping sickness was so serious here that in many areas the trusteeship government had to gather up the population into concentrations which could be isolated from the tsetse fly. Even the natural biological productivity—wildlife—is low and the yield of honey ranks as one of the major products.

South and west of Lake Victoria, intensive clearing has taken place and, with high rainfall, dense populations are supported. West of the Lake, the Bukoba district has an agricultural population which has grown coffee since before the Europeans arrived, in gardens mixed with

17.I The ancient Arab town of Lamu facing directly on to its sheltered harbor. The east coast of Africa has been a part of the world of maritime trade in the Indian Ocean for centuries and sailing *dhows* still trade with the Persian Gulf and India. (Photo: East African Railways.)

17.J The mosque is a symbol of the distinctive Swahili and Arab culture of the coastal regions of East Africa. This is at Shella, near Lamu. (Photo: East African Railways.)

bananas and maize. South of the Lake is the area known as Sukumaland after the name of the people, and centered on the Lake port of Mwanza is an extensive settled area with an economy based on cattle, sorghum, and maize, and on cotton as a major export crop.

Highland areas are widely scattered and each has a distinctive environment and system of land use. The largest are the Northern Highlands which extend from the coast near Tanga consisting of the block mountains of Usambara and Pare, the great volcanoes of Kilimanjaro and Meru and the Crater or Winter Highlands (including Ngorongoro) which are formed by Rift Valley faulting. All of these carry pockets of dense agricultural settlement and in the past attracted European settlement, although never on the scale of Kenya. Arabica coffee is the leading export crop. Attempts by Europeans to settle in the "Southern Highlands" centered on Iringa were much less successful partly because of isolation but also because of lower rainfall, although a limited zone supports tea plantations. The high rainfall areas had already been preempted by peasant farmers in the Nyasa highlands still further south, now growing pyrethrum, wattle, and wheat. Other, rather remote, highland areas include the Ufipa Highlands around Sumbawanga, and north of Kigoma.

Much of the foundation of our scientific knowledge of the geography of Tanzania was laid by Clement Gillman who, in a remarkable one-man effort, contributed successively articles on population, vegetation, and white settlement to the *Geographical Review*.[2] Most revealing was his population map, a remarkable achievement in detail for the period (Figure 17.6). Among factors which have influenced the irregular distribution of population are the historical effects of slave raiding by Arabs from Kilwa Kivinjie, Bagamoyo, and Sadani; the rampage of Bantu armies from the south, especially the Ngoni, and the putting down of revolts by the Germans, particularly in the southeast and around

[2] "A Population Map of Tanganyika Territory," *Geog. Rev.*, XXVI (1936) pp. 353–375; "A Vegetation Map of Tanganyika Territory," *Geog. Rev.*, XXXIX (1949) pp. 7–37; "White Colonization in East Africa," *Geog. Rev.*, XXXII (1942) pp. 585–597.

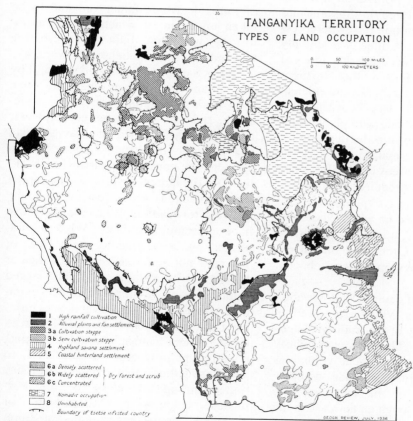

17.6 Types of land occupation in mainland Tanzania, as classified by Clement Gillman in 1936. The huge areas uninhabited or occupied by a widely scattered population were (and in considerable part remain) areas without permanent surface water, or infested by tsetse fly. (From C. Gillman, *Geog. Rev.*, 1936 and 1949. Courtesy of the *Geographical Review*, American Geographical Society.)

Sadani. Gillman particularly noted the effects of water supply and of tsetse infestation. He suggested that there was a critical density of population. If the land was sufficiently productive (which depended largely on rainfall and water supplies), the densities of settlement would be such that bush-clearing would eliminate the conditions suitable for breeding by the tsetse fly. At lower densities, the bush and undergrowth would not be kept down, the tsetse could establish itself, and disease, either of cattle or of humans, would require the evacuation of the area.

Agriculture provides subsistence and income for the great majority of the population. Exports are dominated by cotton, coffee, and sisal. The production of cotton is heavily concentrated in Sukumaland with smaller production elsewhere, especially at the coast. Coffee is essentially a highland crop, mostly from the slopes of Kilimanjoro and Meru in the Northern Highlands where a very large and efficient peasant cooperative has flourished for many years, side by side with plantations. Sisal was a German introduction and for many years was the mainstay of exports. It will thrive in dry areas but the low price of the bulky product requires cheap transport, and the extensive plantations are confined to the coast or within short distance of the railway, up to 200 miles (320 km) or so inland. Other agricultural exports include cashew nuts, tea, tobacco, and pyrethrum.

The discovery of diamonds at Mwadui, near Shinyanga, by Williamson added an export equal to any of the traditional agricultural products. This was particularly fortunate because the small goldmines which between them have made an important contribution in the past are now mostly closed (although an increase in the price of gold would open up some of them). Similarly the lead mine of Mpanda has closed. Considerable coal reserves have been located and proved in the interior but so far isolation has kept them unused. Oil exploration continues, especially offshore and on islands such as Mafia.

Lacking any single major concentration of population, transport has always presented a problem in Tanzania. The first railroad to be built was inland from Tanga to serve the Northern Highlands and eventually to reach Lake Victoria. The latter aim however was dropped after the Uganda Railway was completed. The Central Line was built as a strategic line across the center of the country from Dar es Salaam to Kigoma approximately following the caravan route from Bagamoyo to Ujiji, with a branch to Mwanza to tap the richer lands bordering Lake Victoria. Tanzania has had an unfortunate history of railroads which failed and had to be taken up again of which the most notorious was that built to serve the Groundnuts Scheme behind Mtwara.

Dar es Salaam was selected as a port by the sultan of Zanzibar when the open roadstead of Bagamoyo became inadequate. It is one of the better deepwater creeks which provided the East African coast with numerous harbor sites, although the entrance is narrow and awkward for the largest vessels. As the capital it has grown to be the largest, and a rapidly growing, town although it cannot be said to have any natural nodality. While its hinterland was restricted to those parts of Tanzania not better serviced by Tanga or Mombasa, its volume of traffic lagged behind that of Mombasa. The confrontation with Rhodesia however has been of great material benefit to Dar es Salaam. A route through Tanzania enables Zambia, notably the prosperous copper belt, to avoid using those politically embarrassing routes through Rhodesia or the Portuguese colonies of Moçambique or of Angola, or the uncertainties of Zaire. Temporary measures using road transport are being replaced by an oil pipeline and a railway, while the road is also being improved. Political factors also influence the amount of traffic received from eastern Zaire and Burundi down the railroad from Kigoma.

ZANZIBAR

From a littoral empire extending from Oman down the entire East African coast and with a sphere of influence extending into eastern Zaire, the dominion of the sultan of Zanzibar shrank to the two islands of Pemba and Zanzibar itself. Independence on December 24, 1963 was soon followed by revolution on January 12, 1964, which caused the slaughter of an unknown number of the dominant Arab community and which extinguished the rule, although not the life, of the last sultan. During the nineteenth century, the strategic situation of this offshore island had made it a center of trade including, for some time, a large slave trade. The prosperity and significance of Zanzibar declined under the successive blows of the ending of the slave trade, the freeing of the slaves who worked the plantations, the loss of the mainland to the colonial powers of Germany and Britain, and the rise of the ports of Dar es Salaam and Mombasa.

The island of Zanzibar is some 53 miles (85 km) long and with an area of 640 square miles (1660 km²) it is nearly twice as large as Pemba with 380 square miles (980 km²). They are composed of the same sedimentary and coral rocks found on the coast of the mainland with infertile limestone on the east restricting the main agricultural areas to the western half of each island. Rainfall is high, averaging 60–80 inches (1500–2000 mm) a year. The principal and distinctive export of cloves derives from deliberate importation by one of the sultans. Other crops include coconuts, mangoes, rice, and maize, and fishing is important. Zanzibar City is situated on the western side of the island facing a sheltered but reef-studded roadstead. Nearly half of the population of the island is concentrated in the city; this, and the dependence on cloves for export, indicate an economic malaise.

Although a part of Tanzania, Zanzibar has, in fact, little contact with the mainland and even information is scarce. The economic significance of the offshore location has gone but its strategic potential remains.

COOPERATION IN EAST AFRICA

Following the World War I, 1914–1918, Britain controlled all of what we have included in East Africa either as a colony, a protectorate, a protected state, or a mandate or trusteeship territory. Attempts at a closer political union were always frustrated, and even the British administration became fiercely defensive of the separation or "independence" of their charges. In particular there was always suspicion of the influence of the white settlers in Kenya. However a large measure of cooperation was in fact achieved. Partly as a result of the Congo Basin Treaties, there were no tariff barriers between the territories and there were no barriers across the roads between them. A pooling of administrative services was achieved in 1947 with the establishment of the East Africa High Commission handling such subjects as posts and telegraphs, much of the tax collections, and a host of research and scientific services. Perhaps most important was the creation of a unified East African Railways and Harbours Administration. Even such modest steps towards unification are incompatible with the full exercise of sovereignty, and following independence of the three countries, barriers to movement and trade have been erected. This has been accompanied by changes in name first to the East African Common Services Organization and then to the East African Community and the headquarters have been moved from Nairobi to Arusha. This loosening of the structure makes it easier for other countries to be included and membership may be widened to include Zambia, Ethiopia, Somalia, Rwanda, and Burundi.

THE EAST AFRICAN GROUNDNUT SCHEME

No example illustrates better the difficulties which beset any attempts to develop tropical Africa than Britain's ill-fated attempt to grow peanuts (groundnuts) on a large scale in East Africa.

Britain emerged from World War II with many acute shortages, not the least being margarine and cooking fats. It was Frank Samuel, Managing Director of the United Africa Company, itself a subsidiary of the vast Unilever concern, who visualized during a tour in 1946 the possibilities of the empty spaces of East Africa for growing peanuts, an annual crop and so one with a quick return. Britain's harassed Minister of Food seized on the idea and sent out a mission of three experts. John Wakefield, former Director of Agriculture of Tanganyika; David Martin, plantations manager of the United Africa Company; and John Rosa, banker. After nine weeks on the ground, the Wakefield Report[3] was written, soon to be accepted by the British government as a major contribution to the African population and development problem and the home food problem. This decision was reached after careful scrutiny of the report in which two strong voices, W. M. Crowther and Dunstan Skilbeck, were raised in favor of making haste slowly by pilot experiments, but the socialist government, through Minister of Food Strachey, decided on full speed ahead. The United Africa Company acted as managing agents until a gov-

ernment corporation, the Overseas Food Corporation, could be organized and take over, which it did in March–April 1948. In the meantime, secondhand, heavy bush-clearing machinery was collected, especially bulldozers from American army surplus in the Philippines. Massey-Harris had already agreed to supply Canadian tractors.

The scheme was to clear 3,210,000 acres (1,335,000 ha) by 1953 of scrub—the dreary, useless, closely matted tangle of vegetation through which only a rhinoceros could force a way with difficulty—in "units" or farms of 30,000 acres (12,000 ha) and to secure at the end of the five years an output of 600,000 tons of peanuts. The areas chosen were:

	Acres	Hectares
Tanganyika Central Province (Kongwa)	450,000	182,000
Western Province (Urambo)	300,000	121,000
Southern Province	1,650,000	667,000
Kenya	300,000	121,000
Northern Rhodesia (Zambia)	510,000	206,000

The Central and Western Provinces were reached via the Tanganyika Central Railway from Dar es Salaam; the Southern Province by a railroad to be constructed from the new deep-water port of Mtwara near Mikindani. Advance guards of European personnel arrived at Dar es Salaam early in 1947; the first "cut" in the bush was actually made on April 30, 1947. Alan Wood has well described the effect on local life under the title "From Tribe to Trade Union." The chiefs cooperated in many ways, notably in securing labor, but soon their authority faded away. In the haste to get labor, a large daily ration of food [totaling 3500 calories a day, basically corn (maize), beans, meat, sugar, and oil] was issued, supplemented by cash wages ranging from 15 shillings (2 dollars) a month upwards. Even that was too much! Prices soared, and local economies were completely upset. Although medical skill became available and was beneficial, the workers in crowded quarters missed their womenfolk and sought satisfaction elsewhere. The Dar es

---

[3] Alan Wood, *The Groundnut Affair* (London, The Bodley Head, 1950). *A Plan for the Mechanical Production of Groundnuts in East and Central Africa,* H.M.S.O., Cmd. 7030 (1947) (The Wakefield Report). *The Future of the Overseas Food Corporation,* H.M.S.O., Cmd. 8125 (1951).

17.K Land in southern Tanzania cleared in preparation for planting peanuts. This illustrates the large scale of operations in the "Groundnut Scheme" and raises the question whether such denuding of the soil surface is wise. (Copyright: Aircraft Operating Company of Africa.)

Salaam dockers organized the first trade union. There were ugly strikes. Those Africans who had served in the army seemed to have lost their mechanical skill, and, although others quickly picked up the handling of heavy machines and could maneuver them with the best, running repairs were another matter. Soon three-quarters of all the machines were out of action.

There are many reasons which may be given for the failure of a scheme, conceived in the grand manner, which might have been an African T.V.A. Too much bureaucratic control was one. In January 1951, there were 1283 Europeans on the corporation staff compared with 384 on Earthmoving and Construction Limited, the company actually doing the work. The organization did not work smoothly, but primarily failure was due to lack of knowledge of the conditions. The machinery failed in its task partly perhaps because it was "secondhand," but mainly because the immensely long roots of the brush provided a tougher proposition than bush

clearing in middle latitudes; the microstructure of the soil defeated the disc plows; the sandy soil was "packed" by the machinery and rendered unfit for peanuts; the vagaries of the rainfall were not sufficiently appreciated. Consequently the first crops are said to have been less than the seed put in the ground.

By September 1949 it was clear the objectives could not be reached, and a revised plan for a total of 600,000 acres (242,000 ha) by 1954 was introduced, concentrating on a rotation of crops rather than only peanuts. Then in January 1951 the British government was forced to abandon, in its original form, the whole project. Against an original total estimated cost of 23 million pounds, in January 1951 36 million were written off as lost, roughly 2 dollars for every man, woman, and child in Great Britain. Land already cleared was to be used for experimental purposes: four farms with about 10,000 acres (4,000 ha) under crops in Kongwa and 60,000 acres (24,000 ha) in Urambo with 13 farms. The Southern

Region seems to have proved that "fully mechanized land clearing is far too costly and could be reduced by substituting hand labor," and experience suggested that cropping with peanuts, corn (maize), and millet (sorghum) should be combined with cattle grazed on grasses.

The proposals for Kenya and Northern Rhodesia (Zambia) were early abandoned, but permanent works of lasting value include the southern port of Mtwara, although the railway planned for extension westward to Lake Nyasa did not get far and was torn up in 1962.

The groundnut scheme reinforces Julian Huxley's words that "the most important lesson of history for Africa is to go slowly." It is an expensive lesson but the day will come when with increased knowledge development will go ahead in these areas.

The Overseas Food Corporation as part of its work in East Africa set up a Scientific Department under the direction of Dr. A. H. Bunting as Chief Scientific Officer in charge of a staff of 30 or 40 scientists. His summary[4] of the work undertaken during the life of the department, 1947–1951, is a good example of the range of studies needed in tropical Africa. The soil scientists found top dressings of

[4] *Nature,* CLXVIII, No. 4280 (1951) pp. 804–806.

phosphate and nitrogen were required on all soils, but how to retain nitrogen (possibly by use of grass courses) remained unsolved. There was some evidence that a common weed played a major part in the mobilization of soil phosphate, and the retention of the weed was therefore vital. Unless there is an exact balance of nitrogen and potash, plants seem to develop abnormally; tobacco notably has a "tang" which renders it commercially of little value. It seemed that continuous cropping allowed no accumulation of moisture in the soil, whereas fallowing did. Thus, following the African's traditional system of bare fallowing, an increase of nearly 50 percent in peanut yield resulted. Among the plants it was found that successful American types of soybean were not adapted to the equatorial equal day and night temperatures throughout the year. Sorghum needed a horny peripheral layer at maturity of the grain as a protection against storage pests; sunflowers failed to pollinate because the bees or other pollinators were too few; destructive stem borers were not affected by insecticides successful elsewhere. The *Aphis,* which carries rosette disease of peanuts, needed to have its life cycle traced before it could be controlled. Thus the scientists indicated dozens of problems to be solved before success in development could be achieved.

Further Reading

The most comprehensive reference is the collection of authoritative chapters in *East Africa: Its Peoples and Resources* edited by W. T. W. Morgan (Nairobi: Oxford University Press, 1969) which is accompanied by seven specially drawn maps. Also covering the entire area is *An Economic Geography of East Africa* by Anthony M. O'Connor (New York: Praeger, 1966). For Uganda, *A Subsistence Crop Geography of Uganda,* a detailed study made by David N. McMaster while on the staff of Makerere University College, Kampala is most illuminating. It was published as Occasional Paper No. 2 of the World Land Use Survey (Bude, England: Geographical Publications Ltd., 1962). *Uganda,* by H. B. Thomas and Robert Scott (London: Oxford University Press, 1935) is now very old but it was a thorough piece of work and still has much of value. Professor Simeon H. Ominde of University

College, Nairobi, has written a book with wider relevance than its title in *Land and Population Movements in Kenya* (London: Heinemann, 1968). A detailed sample study of seven thousand square miles of varied country and of a major town is provided by the studies contained in *Nairobi, City and Region* edited by W. T. W. Morgan and published in Nairobi by Oxford University Press (1967). Now aging but still mines of information are *Tanganyika: A Review of its Resources and their Development* by J. F. R. Hill and J. P. Moffett (London: Crown Agents, 1955) and the second edition of the *Handbook of Tanganyika,* edited by J. P. Moffett (Dar es Salaam: Govt. Printer, 1958). For Zanzibar see "The Land Use of Zanzibar Island" by Margaret E. Caistor in *Four Island Studies* being Monograph No. 5 of the World Land Use Survey (Bude, England: Geographical Publications Ltd., 1968).

In honour of S. J. K. Baker, for many years Professor of Geography at Makerere College, Kampala, a distinguished offering of *Studies in East African Geography and Development* has been edited by Professor S. H. Ominde (London: Heinemann, 1971).

CHAPTER 18

South-Central Africa:
The Southern Savanna Lands

There are several reasons why separate considerations should be given to that belt of southern Africa stretching from the Atlantic shores of Portuguese Angola to the coast of the Indian Ocean in Mozambique, or Portuguese East Africa.[1] It is a belt of Africa which lies between the equatorial forests of the Congo and the lofty plateaus of East Africa on the north and the extratropical white man's land of South Africa to the south (Figure 18.1). In very general terms the area to be considered is the basin of the great Zambezi with the addition of various peripheral tracts. In terms of political units we shall consider the great territory of Angola on the west and the huge area of central Africa occupied by Zambia, Rhodesia, and Malawi and Mozambique.

Although so large an area must contain a variety of land forms and ecology, it is overwhelmingly characterized by extensive peneplains cut across a Precambrian shield at elevations of several thousand

feet. Soils are often ancient residual ones, the climate is dominated by a long dry season and the vegetation by deciduous woodland: the *miombo* (*Brachystegia-Isoberlinia-Julbernardia* spp.). There are also large areas of Kalahari sands.

This is not a favorable environment for either agriculture or pastoralism and, except where special factors are found, the density of rural settlement is low. The exceptions include higher areas of better farming land in Rhodesia and Angola, which have attracted white settlement. Economic developments, especially mining, although to a lesser extent including pockets of introduced commercial farming, have made these countries dependent upon one another, to some extent unwillingly. This is particularly true of transport to and from the interior, but also of hydroelectric and coal supplies, local food production, and migrant labor. Such economic interdependence already exists but the future economic development of the area would greatly benefit from an increase in cooperation and joint use of major projects.

---

[1] The correct spelling is Moçambique, but it is usually anglicized as Mozambique.

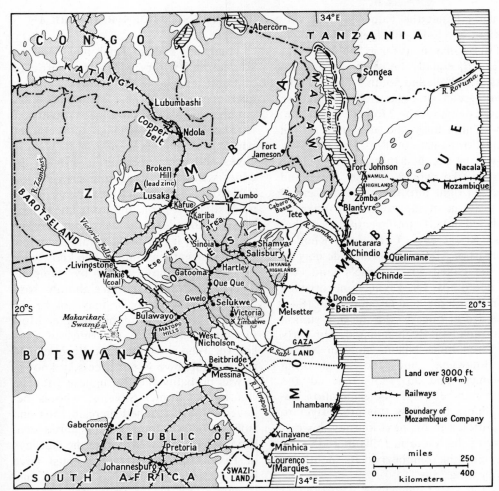

18.1 South-central Africa and the Zambezi basin. For Gaberones read Gaberone and for Namula read Namuli.

This makes the political disarray of the area an economic as well as a human disaster. These countries also share a common experience of settlement by whites to approximately the same degree. Thus white settlers form a larger portion of the population than in West or East Africa, but they are much less numerous than in the Republic of South Africa.

HISTORICAL GEOGRAPHY

The story of the exploration and subsequent organization of this part of Africa has been briefly considered in Chapter 2. The Portuguese established settlements at an early date on both the Atlantic and the Indian Ocean shores. The discovery of Angola was claimed by the Portuguese Diogo Cão in 1482, and points on the coast have been occupied continuously by the Portuguese since 1505, with the exception of the years 1641–1648, when the Portuguese were temporarily ousted by the Dutch. Comparatively little, however, was done to develop the vast area. The great drain of population from Portugal to Brazil in the sixteenth, seventeenth, and eighteenth centuries drew Portuguese attention away from Africa. As a result the boundaries of the Portuguese sphere in Angola remained loosely defined, and along the south the long-disputed frontier was not finally settled until 1926, when it was agreed that the Cunene River with the Rua Cana Falls, 406 feet (124 m) high, were to be shared, as far as the water was concerned, equally between the governments of Angola and South Africa. On the Indian Ocean side the great Portuguese trading company, the Mozambique Company, administered the area long settled by the Portuguese until as late as 1942.

It will be recalled that the Portuguese claim to the whole of the hinterland stretching right into the heart of Central Africa and an attempt to exclude other nationals led directly to the activities of that British Rockefeller, Cecil John Rhodes. The heart of Africa in this latitude may almost be called Livingstone's land. We have noted how Dr. Livingstone, arriving in Africa as a medical missionary in 1841, proceeded at once to the mission station at Kuruman in Bechuanaland. He early discovered Lake Ngami, now in Northern Botswana, and the neighboring Okovango, and in 1850 reached the Upper Zambezi. His determination despite illness to follow this great river to its mouth led to his next journey, his discovery of the Victoria Falls in 1855, and his tracing the Zambezi to its mouth by the following May.

Thus it was Livingstone who brought the knowledge of this heart of Africa directly to the English-speaking peoples. It was Rhodes who brought the territories into the British sphere of commercial and political influence. Rhodes worked with amazing speed. In 1887 the Portuguese attempted to close the Zambezi basin; in 1888 Rhodes secured from the king of the Matabele exclusive rights to work minerals. Matabeleland is the core of Rhodesia. In 1889 the British South Africa Company, formed by Rhodes for the purpose of exercising these rights, set to work, and by 1891 the limits of Portuguese and British spheres of influence had been settled. Nyasaland (now Malawi) became a British protectorate, and the huge territories, subsequently Northern and Southern Rhodesia (now Zambia and Rhodesia) were handed over to Rhodes's company.

THE BRITISH IN CENTRAL AFRICA

There are ancient ruins and mines in Rhodesian territory which have intrigued and still intrigue anthropologists and archeologists. The earliest inhabitants of the country, who may have been Bushmen, left behind rock carvings and colored paintings of hunting scenes on the walls of caves and rocks. Scattered through the country there are large numbers of workings from which former inhabitants gained gold, silver, copper, and iron. Though extensive, the deposits were not worked below water level, and it would seem that the workers at that time had no knowledge of how to remove water by pumping. There are several hundred elaborate stone buildings which may or may not be the work of the same mining people. Most famous of these are the ruins of Zimbabwe. Who was the first European to reach Zimbabwe is not precisely known. It was probably the Portuguese Franciscan monk, Franci Silveira, who is believed to have reached there in 1561 and suffered martyrdom. In the three centuries which followed, before the journeys of Livingstone, the country must have been visited from time to time by missionaries and traders, but otherwise remained forgotten. Although gold was discovered in the area in 1865, the discovery did not give rise to any immediate movement, so that it was the concession granted by King Lobengula to Rhodes and his associates which really started the development of the area.

It is interesting that when the territory was proclaimed a British sphere of influence on July 20, 1888, it was known as Zambezia, thus emphasizing the association of what are now Zambia and Rhodesia with the Zambezi River. The pioneer column of settlers, consisting of 187 Europeans and 150 Africans, left Cecil Rhodes's farm near Kimberley on May 6, 1890. They were joined by police and guides, reached the site of the present town of Salisbury on September 12, 1890, and commenced the building of a fort. The

British protectorate over Bechuanaland (Botswana) was declared on May 9, 1891, thus protecting the route to the new settlements.

South African farmers soon evinced an interest in the new lands, and there was never any prohibition to Boer farmers. They were dissuaded from occupying part of the country by force but were invited to take up farms, which some of them later did. The arrival of the settlers and various restrictions necessary for the preservation of peace led to some resentment by the Matabele. In 1893 they attacked a post of the British South Africa Company, and war followed. It was brought to an end by the occupation of Lobengula's kraal near the present site of Bulawayo, which was founded on its present position in the following year, 1894.

In 1895 Northern and Southern Zambezia officially became Northern and Southern Rhodesia. The subsequent history of Rhodesia includes the revolt of the Mashonas, but is closely bound up with the improvement of means of access by the coming of the railway. That from Kimberley reached Bulawayo in 1897, that from the Portuguese port of Beira reached Salisbury in 1899. The Zambezi gorge was bridged below the falls in 1904, and one enters upon the modern phase.

The question whether Southern Rhodesia, which then had a European population between 30,000 and 40,000, should join the Union of South Africa or have a resident governor was decided by referendum in 1923. The result was for a resident governor, and on October 21, 1923, Southern Rhodesia became a self-governing colony of the British Commonwealth. Gradually the new state acquired mineral and other rights from the old South Africa Company, and Southern Rhodesia developed along modern lines.

Referring briefly to the history of Zambia (Northern Rhodesia), we see that it was not until 1911 that the separate territories of Barotseland, or Northwestern Rhodesia and Northeastern Rhodesia joined, and it was not until 1924 that a first governor was appointed in Northern

18.A The rail and road bridge over the Zambezi gorge below the Victoria Falls. This bridge, completed as a rail bridge in 1903 was for long the only bridge across the Zambezi linking what are now Zambia and Rodesia. (official Photograph: J. Rau.)

Rhodesia, taking over the administration of the country from the South Africa Company. Thus the development of Northern Rhodesia came later than that of Southern.

Though geographically Malawi falls within the Zambezi basin, being drained by the Shire—that important tributary of the Zambezi—its history has been somewhat different. Modern roads now make it possible to travel between Zambia and Malawi, but the natural outlet of the country was along the general line of the Shire River to the Zambezi at Chindio, and from these down the navigable stream to the port of Chinde near its mouth. Not until the bridging of the Zambezi in 1935 did Malawi become part of the commercial hinterland of the port of Beira. Formerly known as the British Central Africa Protectorate, the area was renamed Nyasaland in 1907, having been transferred to the control of the British Colonial Office in 1904.

The three British territories in the heart of Africa clearly had certain common interests. An advisory and consultative body to deal with nonpolitical subjects, such as communication, health, education, and statistics, known as the Central African Council, was in due course set up. The question of the closer association of Northern and Southern Rhodesia and Nyasaland came to the fore in 1951, when active consideration was given to the possibility of forming a British Central Africa with dominion status, or its equivalent. By this time the three territories had developed along rather different lines. By virtue of its southern situation, the elevation of the great central tract of the country above 3000 feet (900 m), and its well-distributed and adequate rainfall, Southern Rhodesia had become a land of white settlers predominantly of British origin, though relying to a large extent on African labor. Its chief towns, Bulawayo, Gwelo, and Salisbury, are European in concept and execution. European agricultural production had taken on a dominant note,

despite the existence of the important coal field at Wankie, and despite the development of the iron-ore deposits for the works at Que Que.

The larger territory of Northern Rhodesia, with savanna or bush cover, nearer the equator, generally lower in elevation, had not been recognized to the same extent as a white settlers' country. But its richness in minerals, not only in the part of the country which lies along the Congo-Katanga border and is part of the great Copperbelt of central Africa, but also in the mineral deposits still being explored and developed in other parts of the territory, had given Northern Rhodesia an importance in world economy of a different character from that of Southern Rhodesia. In some respects Northern Rhodesia had overtaken in importance its older settled neighbor to the south.

Nyasaland, the most densely peopled of the three, had but a handful of white settlers, and there was a widespread migration of workers especially to South Africa, and the Copperbelt.

Could these three territories, with their different gackgrounds, have formed a satisfactory union? The Federation of the Rhodesias and Nyasaland was set up in 1953, and the first federal parliament met at Salisbury in 1954. The influence in the Federation of white-governed Southern Rhodesia however, was too strong to satisfy the emerging African leaders of Northern Rhodesia (Zambia) and Nyasaland (Malawi). In 1963, Nyasaland withdrew and the Federation was terminated.

There was no difficulty over independence for Nyasaland, which became Malawi on July 6, 1964, or for Northern Rhodesia, which became Zambia on October 24 of the same year. Southern Rhodesia however had for a long time been a self-governing colony with less control by Britain, and it emerged from the Federation with enhanced powers. The government however represented a small, largely European electorate (in a country with an overwhelming African majority) to which the British government was unwilling to grant independence. A unilateral declaration of independence ("UDI") was therefore made which was followed by the imposition of international sanctions. Economic patterns, and relationships between countries in this region are therefore more than usually influenced by political considerations, and this should be borne in mind below.

RHODESIA

Rhodesia consists of a broad belt of high plateau more than 4000 feet (1200 m) above sea level running from southwest to northeast. The northern side drains to the Zambezi, the southern to the Limpopo. The plateau is generally of rolling relief, and the 3000-foot (900 m) contour may be taken as separating the healthy high veld from the low veld, where malaria is one of the disadvantages associated with climatic conditions. The natural vegetation is a savanna grassland, passing into open forests, and in the Zambezi lowlands to denser forests where Rhodesian teak and Rhodesian mahogany are obtained.

Along the eastern border between Umtali and Melsetter the elevation increases and the country is more dissected so as to become mountainous in character. This is a well-watered area, and the average rainfall between 20 and 35 inches (500 and 900 mm) over the bulk of the plateau renders it excellent agricultural country. It is in the south and west that irrigation becomes necessary as a precaution against drought. Soil erosion is a problem, especially owing to the heavy character of rainstorms.

On the European farms which occupy the upland belt, corn (maize) is the main crop, and cattle rearing is of great importance (Figure 18.2). Rinderpest, which seems to have broken out first in 1895, has played great havoc, but strenuous efforts have succeeded so well in curbing the disease that there are huge ranches for beef cattle, and near the main railway through Bulawayo, Gwelo, and Salisbury dairying is firmly established, with creameries at each of the large towns. With the development of cold-storage facilities there is a growing export in chilled beef, while pig and poultry rearing flourish, dependent largely on the corn crop, with associated bacon factories. The Witwatersrand and the mining districts of the Katanga offer markets which are not very far distant.

There is a general correlation between the more infertile soils and lower rainfall in Matabeleland with cattle ranching. Where better soils and more reliable rainfall permit, arable cultivation on the European farms becomes dominant. Tobacco, introduced as a commercial crop in 1910, has become of paramount importance on areas of light sandy soil overlying granite. Citrus fruits grow well, and there is an export of oranges as far as Europe. Other crops include cotton, peanuts, sunflowers for seeds, beans, fiber plants, and vegetables for local use. Irrigation is becoming increasingly common. In the African belts subsistence agriculture is the general rule, with corn occupying four-fifths of the cultivated land.

The fact that the lower lands draining to the Zambezi remain seriously infested with tsetse fly deters development there, whereas the Sabi and Limpopo valley are being actively opened up with large ranches and irrigation schemes.

Turning to minerals, we see that the coalfield at Wankie with its output of 4 million tons a year is insufficient to meet all demands. Some goes north to the Copperbelt, much is consumed by the railways and the towns of Rhodesia, and coke is made and supplied to the iron and steel works at Que Que, which began production in 1948 using local ores. Gold, worked from time immemorial in small scattered mines, remains an important mineral product, but the small scattered copper mines do not compare in significance with those of Zambia. However, Rhodesia is a major world supplier of

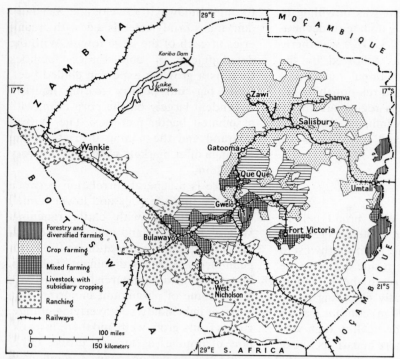

18.2 European agriculture in Rhodesia. Notice the correlation with the higher altitudes and with the railway. (After R. Anderson and N. Edmundson.)

18.B The Wankie Colliery in Rhodesia. Such a scene is unusual in Africa outside the Republic of South Africa. To avoid using this coal, Zambia has developed its own deposits on the other side of the Zambezi valley. (Official photograph.)

chrome, high-quality asbestos and lithium. Although the coalfield remains a valuable resource, it is the supply of electricity from Kariba (beginning in December, 1959, see p. 359) which has provided a secure power basis for subsequent expansion in mining and manufacturing.

The railways in both Zambia and Rhodesia were constructed in part to permit the development of minerals. In order to avoid expensive bridging over streams they followed where possible main watersheds. They do not thus necessarily tap the richest agricultural districts; but the development of roads, marked in Rhodesia as elsewhere in Africa, has to a considerable extent obviated the necessity for further railway construction.

Rhodesia has attracted well over 200,000 white settlers. They are settlers in the sense that they make their permanent homes in the country but only a very small proportion are settled on the land. A large number are town dwellers. Roughly one-third of the population of both Salisbury and Bulawayo is white, and the larger towns have more than half the total white population of the country. When World War II ended there were about 75,000 Europeans. A large influx began, rising from 7000 in 1946 to 17,000 in 1948 and over 18,000 in 1956, dropping in later years. But the immigrants were of a different character from those of prewar years. It is recorded that in 1948, 28 percent of all new arrivals went to manufacturing industries in the towns, only 7 percent to the farms, leaving a large proportion for administrative, distributional, and other occupations not directly productive; this general trend has been continued. At first sight it might appear that this urban growth is undesirable in a country where so much remains to be done in the open lands. Actually it enables a balanced urban-rural economy to be developed; there is not the pressure of the white farmer to encroach on African farmlands that there was in Kenya. Much European-owned farmland could be handed over to African occupation with little damage to European employment. In Rhodesia are the basic requirements of modern industry: coal, iron, metals, water power, and a good climate. Secondary industries like the Gatooma textile mills and the machine-tool industry of Salisbury illustrate the current trend.

About half of the African population lives in the reserves. The remainder is employed directly or indirectly by Europeans.

Rhodesia entered the iron and steel business in a substantial way when the Rhodesian Iron and Steel Commission established a plant located at Que Que near good deposits of iron ore and supplies of limestone and in direct main rail communication with the coking coals of Wankie [500 miles (800 km)] and supplied with electric power from Umniati. The plant consisted of a blast furnace, an open hearth furnace, and Bessemer converters, with a capacity of 33,000 tons of finished steel. Since 1950 developments have been favored by iron-ore deposits nearby at Buhera, coal deposits near Beit Bridge, and the availability of Kariba power. The political situation has led to a slowing down of the economy and to a lack of data which has become secret information in an economic war against much of the world. Of long term relevance, however, is the prospecting and development work that has been proceeding in the sphere of minerals, particularly involving nickel, copper and magnesite.

ZAMBIA

The economic heart of Zambia is an undistinguished piece of plateau just south of the border with the Katanga Province of Zaire. Here in a zone about 70 miles long by 30 miles wide (110 by 50 km) is the Copperbelt which for years has been the third or fourth world producer of that essential metal (Figure 18.3). Cobalt is also produced. Copper accounts for over 90

18.C Mufulira mine in the Copperbelt of Zambia. The vast plateau of low-fertility deciduous woodland was found to contain pockets of rich copper ore, leading to the construction of large mines and company-built towns and other facilities, such as the stadium seen here. The woodland provided fuel for the early stages of mining and the towns and mines stand as islands amid an encircling expanse of secondary-growth *miombo*. (Photo: RST)

percent of Zambia's exports and the industry for over 50 percent of government receipts. The belt of mines and associated prosperous little towns is centered on the town of Ndola. Some 120 miles (193 km) to the south is the older settlement of Broken Hill with its large output of lead and zinc, which was one of the reasons for the early extension of the railway line northward from Livingstone.

The principal concentration of commercial agriculture is a belt within reach of the railroad between Kalomo and Lusaka, the capital. With better than average soils, the railroad allows the export of tobacco (formerly via the Salisbury auction of the much larger Rhodesian crop) and access to the market of the Copperbelt for dairy products, vegetables, meat, and other foodstuffs. Such farming was introduced

by a relatively small number of white settlers.

There are two other interesting pockets of white settlements, both far removed from the railway. One is at Mgala (formerly Abercorn) in the highlands south of Tanzania, where there are government plantations, and here the outlet is via the lake and the Central Tanzanian railway, to Dar es Salaam. The second is around Chipata (formerly Fort Jameson) on the Malawi border where tobacco planting has become important. This area is linked by motor road to Blantyre in Malawi and from there by rail to the port of Beira.

The extreme south of the country, in the Zambezi valley west of Livingstone, is an area yielding hardwoods—Rhodesian teak and Rhodesian mahogany. In this area Livingstone, which until 1935 was

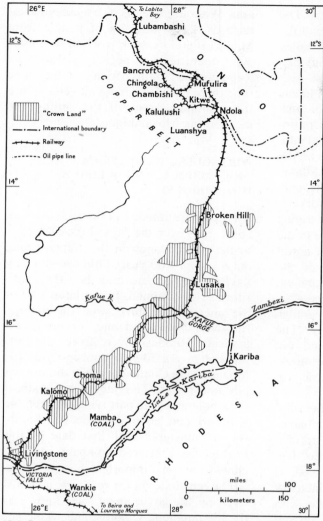

18.3 Central Zambia. The economic core area of Zambia lies in the Copperbelt and along the line of the rail. Most of the large scale farming is on former "Crown Land." For Lubambashi read Lubumbashi.

the administrative capital of Northern Rhodesia has sawmilling establishments. The location of towns in Africa was subject to some trial and error. It was agreed that the original site of Livingstone was proving itself to be unhealthy, with the result that shortly after it ceased to be the capital the whole town was bodily moved to higher and supposedly healthier ground some miles away. The capital was shifted to Lusaka, farther north along the railroad. Recent urban growth has put modern Lusaka, Ndola, and Kitwe (a major copper mining town) among African cities with over 100,000 population.

MALAWI

The long narrow strip of Malawi lies mostly along the western shores of Lake Malawi and on either side of the Shire Valley which drains it southward to the Zambezi. The lake, known as Lake Nyasa in Tanzania, fills two adjoining sections of Rift Valley trough and although its surface is 1550 feet (472 m) above sea level, it is some 2500 feet (760 m) deep. The Shire Valley is also down faulted and the land on either side of both lake and valley rises into up-faulted highlands and plateaus reaching to 7000 and 8000 feet (20000 and 24000 m) in the Nyika Plateau of the north. The principal areas of agriculture and rural settlement are discontinuous. The small areas of European plantations were established in the south, on the Shire Plateau and the flanks of Mlanje Mountain, east of the Shire trough. Although this led to an influx of workers, the principal areas of African farming were on the other side of the Shire in the Ncheu and Lilongwe area of Central Province. At the opposite end of the country, at the north end of Lake Malawi, is a densely settled area with fertile alluvial or volcanic soils with very high rainfalls, in the Karonga locality. The Shire Valley was little populated but modern developments include cotton estates with irrigation and hydroelectric production.

Much of Malawi has better, higher rainfall conditions than most of Zambia or Rhodesia and exports are made up of a range of crops, especially tobacco, tea, groundnuts, and cotton. Lake Malawi supports a prosperous fishing industry which even achieves some trade with neighboring countries. There are no significant mineral workings. The main port for the country is Beira in Mozambique, reached by railway from the south of the country (including the main commercial center of Blantyre–Limbe) by the Sena Bridge over the lower Zambezi. A new outlet has been constructed to another Mozambique port, Nacala. Urban growth is proceding and the construction of government and commercial buildings and related housing has filled in much of the area between the twin towns of Blantyre and Limbe, which together contain a population of over 100,000.

The total population of Malawi is over 4 million which is greater than that of Zambia which has more than six times the

area. Without minerals or considerable industries, large numbers of people from Malawi therefore seek work in neighboring countries, especially Rhodesia, Zambia, and South Africa. At the same time there has also been a movement into the plantation areas of the south from neighboring Mozambique.

PORTUGUESE EAST AFRICA (MOCAMBIQUE, ANGLICIZED AS MOZAMBIQUE)

Portuguese interest in the East African coast dates from the days of the early Portuguese ascendancy in the Indian trade, but for some 300 years little was done by the Portuguese to develop the African territories they claimed. In the latter part of the nineteenth century, when the boundaries with Nyasaland and the newly established Rhodesia were fixed, the Portuguese gave a 50-year concession to the Mozambique Company which did not expire until 1941. Thus about one-sixth of the whole area, the part lying between the Zambezi and about latitude 22° South, was administered until that date by this Portuguese chartered company, and included the very important port of Beira.

The remainder of the territory, administered by the government, was known as the Mozambique Colony. The whole has now passed under unified state control, but the major part of the development of the country in the present century has been the result of foreign investment, notably in the two great ports and in the railway communications, including the great Zambezi Bridge, linking Beira with Malawi.

A large part of Portuguese East Africa south of the Zambezi lies less than 500 feet above sea level and consequently is covered by vegetation of the low veld which extends also into the eastern Transvaal. Portuguese territory extends far inland up the Lower Zambezi to the small frontier post of Zumbo. Zumbo is well below the great Kariba Gorge and there is a navigable stretch below Zumbo through a somewhat narrow gorge to the Cabora-Barsa Falls. Here the river descends by a series of cataracts over a distance of some 50 miles (80 km) to the coastal lowland, where there is a broad navigable channel from Tete, past the junction with the Shire, to the delta. Along the lower Limpopo is good irrigated farmland.

North of the Zambezi, hilly country projects much closer to the coast. Here Portuguese territory occupies the whole width between Lake Malawi (Nyasa) and the Indian Ocean and, overlooking Lake Malawi, includes the Namuli Highlands, rising in places to over 6000 feet (1800 m) and giving Portuguese East Africa a range of climatic conditions not yet fully exploited.

Most of Portuguese East Africa is occupied by younger sedimentary rocks fringing the crystalline plateau. Mineral wealth as far as metallic minerals are concerned is thus restricted to the interior zone of crystalline rocks with which communications at present are limited. Iron-ore prospects exist along the railroad inland from Nacala.

The territory has compensation in the occurrence of some useful coal deposits in the Zambezi valley near Tete and finds of natural gas have intensified the search for oil.

Climatically the coastlands of Portuguese East Africa offer some interesting points. There is the southward-flowing ocean current of warm water derived from equatorial latitudes, known as the Mozambique Current. As a result the waters in the port of Mozambique are several degrees warmer than those of Mombasa 800 miles (1300 km) nearer the equator. Though the regime of rainfall is that of a normal trade wind type, with a rainy season (December to May) and a dry season, the coastal lands suffer from constant high humidity as well as a small temperature range, not more than 10°F (6°C) in the year. The latter part of the hot season is not infrequently characterized by destructive cyclonic storms (see Chapter 4). As was seen further north in East Africa the rainfall decreases inland from the coast, followed by an increase as higher ground is reached and orographical rainfall results.

Broadly speaking, African subsistence agriculture is the rule throughout the country, with the exception of the regions more immediately around the major ports where food is grown for consumption in the towns and there is a small development of commercial agriculture. Thus sugar cane, supplying raw sugar to Portugal, is cultivated behind Lourenço Marques in the Incomati valley, behind Inhambane, and in the Limpopo valley, as well as in the Zambezi valley around the great bridge at Sena and in the hinterland of Quelimane. Among other comparatively recent developments which point the way to future progress are cotton growing and fruit growing (bananas, pineapples, and citrus fruits, especially in the Lourenço Marques district). The uplands and the drier areas have parts suitable for sisal, peanuts, and other oil seeds. Exports consist of a wide range of agricultural products, mostly with Portugal as the largest customer. They include cotton, cashew nuts, sugar, copra, tea, and sisal as well as timber. The ubiquitous corn (maize) is the mainstay of African diet. Livestock is unimportant, owing to the low-lying nature of much of the territory and the prevalence of disease.

It is clear that just as the development of Portuguese East Africa to date has depended upon the happy collaboration of the interested powers, in this case Britain and Portugal, so does the position of the country make development in isolation unthinkable. The international implications are well seen in the story of the port of Beira. It is an example of a port whose hinterland is distant and not immediate. More than 80 percent of its total trade, exports and imports, come from or go to Rhodesia, Zambia, Malawi, and the far-off Katanga region of the Congo. The

Rhodesian railways operate the line between Beira and the Rhodesian frontier at Umtali; similarly the great main line northward crossing the Zambezi by the bridge at Sena has been constructed with British capital and is operated by British interests. Somewhat similar is the position of Lourenço Marques, only 55 miles by railway from the Transvaal frontier, which handles nine-tenths of the trade of Portuguese East Africa as well as a large volume of trade with the industrial area of the Rand. British capitalists have spent many millions of dollars on the improvement of the port, and the expansion of the port has enormously stimulated the development of the surrounding agricultural lands, which have unusually rich soils and a climate favoring bananas and sugar. It is the principal industrial center of Mozambique, with access to markets in South Africa, Rhodesia, and Zambia, as well as in the most developed southern sections of the country. Industries include oil refining, chemicals, fertilizers, and small-scale steel.

By comparison, the purely Portuguese East African ports, though situated where there are rich agricultural hinterlands, like Mozambique, Quelimane, and Inhambane, remain small and undeveloped. The changing fortunes consequent upon development of modern communications are well illustrated in the case of the port of Chinde, just north of the Zambezi mouth, and the river port of Chindio, both of which have been eclipsed by Beira since the construction of the railway bridge.

Climatically Mozambique is not so attractive to European settlers (although vacationers from South Africa and Rhodesia enjoy the beaches) and the land is not so thinly populated as Angola. There are only about 100,000 Europeans resident but there have been a number of plans to settle Portuguese farmers on the land. These have generally involved smaller farms than in Angola, and sometimes irrigated. Some plans have also been multiracial.

ANGOLA

Angola, otherwise known as Portuguese West Africa, is the largest of the Portuguese colonies and stretches from the Cunene River in the south to the Congo estuary in the north. Along the coastline north of the Congo mouth is a small enclave lying between Zaire and Congo, known as Cabinda, which is administered as a detached portion of Angola (see Figure 16.3).

The total area of Angola is a little short of half a million square miles (1,247,000 km²), but the population is little more than 5 million, so that the average density is low. Its capital, the multiracial city of Luanda, has an estimated 250,000 inhabitants, which makes it the third largest Portuguese city. Its full name is São Paulo de Luanda (or Loanda) and it was founded in 1575 and was for a long time the slave port for the African–Brazilian slave route. The slave trade was officially abolished in 1836.

Angola occupies a transitional position between the Congo basin to the northeast, the plateau of southern Africa to the southeast, and the coastal semideserts of the southwest. The east–west axis, along which runs the Benguela railway, is the Bié or Benguela plateau, averaging over 5000 feet (1500 m) and rising in places to more than 7000 feet (2100 m) above sea level. Along the 1000 miles (1600 km) of Atlantic coastline is a belt of lowland of varying width which is dry [20 inches (500 mm) rainfall in the north, less than 10 inches (250 mm) in the south] but surprisingly cool owing to the influence of the cool Benguela current. The average temperature for the year at Moçâmedes is only 69°F (21°C). Inland the country rises, often by a series of terraces, to the plateau. Over most of the interior the rainfall is between 40 and 60 inches (1000 and 1500 mm), with a long rainy season in the north and a shorter one in the south. On the higher parts frosts are common in the dry season. Practically the whole of

Angola is covered by savanna, mostly a woodland, with a little forest along the river valleys of the north which just reaches the Zaire oil-palm country.

African subsistence agriculture depends largely on corn (maize), cassava, beans, and tobacco, with upland rice, peanuts, and even wheat on the higher parts of the plateau. Commercial agriculture depends upon transport facilities. The export of coffee (about 45 percent of total exports), mainly from Luanda to America, is largely responsible for the rapid growth of that city. The north produces palm oil, sugar cane, and cocoa (Cabinda). Cotton is a natural crop of the savannas, and sisal is produced in certain drier areas. Cattle are reared extensively on the upland savannas, and there is some farming of Karakul sheep in the dry southwest. There is a considerable amount of coastal fishing. Both salted fish and salt itself are sent inland.

The Zaire Kasai diamond fields extend into Angola, and diamonds are the second export. Major iron-ore fields exist in the Cassinga area in the south of the country and increasing quantities are being exported through Moçamedes; other minerals, including copper, are known to exist, and oil was discovered just south of Luanda in 1955. More oil has been found further north, the largest sources being both on and offshore in Cabinda. Oil refineries have been built at Luanda and Lobito Bay.

Angola possesses large areas of thinly populated high plateau country attractive to European settlement, and there are about 300,000 Europeans in the country. Luanda in particular is a modern Europeanized city comparable in many respects with Nairobi and Salisbury. It is the center for a major concentration of Portuguese farm settlements and of commercial agriculture in both European and African hands. This is based on a hinterland which receives a high rainfall and is served by the northern railway. Again, however, most of the Europeans are in fact in the towns rather than in the rural areas. Undoubtedly, Angola is a land of great potential for agriculture, mining, and hydroelectric power. Much, however, will depend on political developments.

Angola has a growing mileage of metalled highways, and much of the existing economic development has taken place along the four railways inland from the coast. The Luanda railway from the capital, which is also a good port, serves coffee- and cotton-producing lands. From Porto Amboin, unfortunately with few facilities, a short line serves a rich agricultural hinterland. From the growing port of Lobito (replacing Benguela) the railway was completed right across Angola to the Zaire border in 1928 and reached the Katanga in 1931. It serves the higher part of the plateau, including the city of Nova Lisboa. In the south the port of Moçâmedes (Mossâmedes) has another line on to the plateau which has been extended to the major iron-ore workings at Cassinga. Porto Alexandre has a better natural site but has no railway into the interior.

THE RAILROAD SYSTEM

The railroad system of South-central Africa has grown in response to the major focus of economic activity being located in the center of the continent, that is, the Copperbelt of Zambia, together with the mines of the adjacent province of Katanga in the Republic of Zaire (Figure 16.4). Commercial competition and the calculations of colonial governments provided a variety of routes serving this area, but these were subject to a sharp and instructive reappraisal following the independence of Zambia and Rhodesia.

Mining had attracted a railroad as far north as Broken Hill by 1906 whereas the Benguela Railway did not reach the Katanga border until 1928 when large scale copper mining was beginning. The direction in which the copper was ex-

18.D The port of Lobito Bay, Angola. This is a superb natural harbor formed behind the sandspit (*restinga*) to the left which is 3 miles (4.8 km) long and which encloses an area of some 2 square miles (5.2 km²) (Photo: Gulf Oil.)

ported was influenced by financial connections. The British South Africa Company owned mineral concession rights on the Copperbelt and also owned the railroad to Beira and the port itself. After the railway was nationalized in 1949, the government itself had an interest in the copper traffic travelling via Beira. By contrast, the Benguela Railway to Lobito Bay was owned by Tanganyika Concessions who had holdings in the *Union Minière* which controlled mining in the Katanga but not on the Copperbelt. Another factor was the traffic in coal from Wankie. It was in the interests of overall development of the three British territories that the Copperbelt should use the Rhodesia railway system rather than the "back door" through Katanga and Angola. With congestion at Beira, a new line to Lourenço Marques was opened in 1955.

In addition to these two principal competitive routes, it is possible to export through Zaire via Port Franqui, Kinshasa, and Matadi, or via Kigoma and Dar

es Salaam, but both involve transshipment.

With the declaration of independence by Rhodesia, Zambia found its major link with the outside world under the control of a country unfriendly and a potential enemy. The Benguela and other routes are inadequate and routes through colonial Angola and the Republic of South Africa are also not desired. The Zaire routes are unsatisfactory technically and in the recent past have been unreliable. A new route direct to Dar es Salaam is therefore being developed. An emergency service of trucks over dirt roads has been improved by constructing a hard surface road and by conveying oil by a pipeline. China has agreed to construct a railroad, the "Tan-Zam" line. This could assist economic development along the route including irrigation schemes for the Kilombero Valley and the possible exploitation of some coal deposits, both in Tanzania. At the same time, improvements are being made to the Benguela Railway which will increase its capacity and there are plans to construct a railroad to close the gap between Port Franqui and Kinshasa.

THE DEVELOPMENT OF THE ZAMBEZI BASIN

Unfortunately political divisions have distracted attention from the great advantages which would follow if the Zambezi basin could be planned as a whole.

In Chapter 3 the Zambezi was referred to as a typical African river. In the 1700 miles (2740 km) of its course it flows through three distinct regions. The first is its plateau course, lying partly in Angola, partly in Zambia, but receiving also intermittent streams from the great Okovango swamplands of northern Botswana. The second part of its course is the Middle Zambezi or Gwembe trough, essentially the part lying below Victoria Falls where the river passes through a succession of relatively narrow valleys over waterfalls and rapids. The key to its development

lies at the lower end of this course in the Kariba Gorge, where the Zambezi narrows to less than 100 yards as it cuts through a rocky barrier. Shortly below, it reaches its third course through the Mozambique plain.

Reference has been made elsewhere to the possibility of small irrigation works, using the upper headstreams of the Zambezi (Chapter 4) but the Kariba Gorge offered an ideal site for the construction of a large-scale dam. After rejecting alternative proposals for a dam on the Kafue River, work was started on the Kariba Dam in 1955, and the first stage completed in December, 1959, when a supply of power from the first machine of 100-megawatt capacity became available, the first step towards a final capacity of 900 megawatts. The Kariba Lake is 175 miles (280 km) long and has an average width of 12 miles (19 km). Fortunately the population which had to be moved was small, and fishing in the new lake is expected to provide a needed source of protein. As the waters rose many animals were trapped

18.E The Kariba Dam across the Zambezi from the south bank. Friction between Zambia and Rhodesia has been enhanced by the construction of the first power plant on the Rhodesian bank. (Photo: Monitor.)

on temporary islands, and their rescue gave rise to the much-publicized "Operation Noah." An unexpected difficulty arose when the very rapid growth of a waterweed threatened to clog the power station.

The Kariba Dam provides essential power for the growing needs of the mines of the Copperbelt and the mines, manufacturing, industry, and towns of Rhodesia. Rather than proceed with the planned installation of further generators on the Zambian side of the dam, Zambia has been able to raise funds to construct an independent hydroelectric plant on the Kafue River. Other smaller dams exist elsewhere within the basin but another major project is under way further down on the main stream. This is the Cabora Bassa scheme, above Tete. It is claimed that the dam will be the fourth largest in the world. Eventual capacity is planned for 2000 megawatts, some of which will be transmitted 865 miles (1400 km) to Irene near Pretoria, South Africa. Up to 3.5 million acres may be irrigated and the flow of the Zambezi will be further controlled to the advantage of navigation.

Separated from the Zambezi basin by only the lowest of divides is the Okovango system of inland drainage.

18.F The site of the Cabora-Bassa dam across the Zambezi in Mozambique. Opposition to a colonial system endangers the implementation of this major development scheme. (Photo: Portugese State Office.)

In a survey of the whole Zambezi basin and various projects (Figure 18.4) Professor J. H. Wellington[2] drew this conclusion about the northern Kalahari: "There seems to be no other place in Africa where so much agricultural development is possible at so little cost, and the success of the French in the swamps of the upper Niger shows what planning, engineering skill, and sound irrigational practice can accomplish in terrain of this character. One looks forward to the time when the trans-Kalahari railway will not only connect Southern Rhodesia with the west coast but will also serve a great food-producing area of two million acres [800,000 ha], now only the playground of crocodiles, hippos, and fish hawks." The project still remains in the future.

THE BANGWEULU SWAMPS

Although lying in the part of Zambia outside the Zambezi basin, these great swamps were investigated by Professor Debenham,[3] who drew attention to problems common to other parts of Africa.

In the first place, we have here another of the great inland deltas, a natural consequence of the plateau character of the surface of the heart of Africa. Here there have been periodic rises and falls in the level of water, and because of the accumulation of vegetation the swamp water is not level but has a gradient from northeast to southwest of some 3 inches in a mile. The swamps not only cover 3000 square miles (7800 km²), but also are the home of some thousands of people engaged in fishing and the growing of cassava.

Should such an area, if possible, be

[2] "Zambezi-Okovango Development Project," *Geog. Rev.,* XXXIX (1949) pp. 552–567; *Geog. Rev.,* XXXVII (1947) pp. 351–368. Also see I. Langdale-Brown and R. J. Spooner, *"Land Use Prospects in Northern Bechuanaland* (Tolworth, England: Directorate of Overseas Surveys, 1963).

[3] *Geog. Rev.,* XXXVII (1947) pp. 351–368.

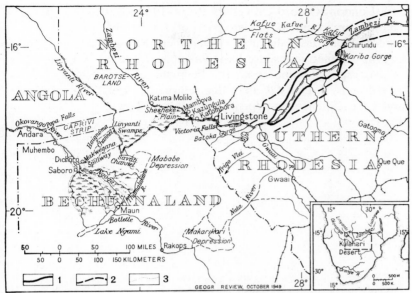

18.4 The Zambezi-Okovango relationships and the Kariba and Kafue gorges. (1) the Kariba resevoir; (2) faults bounding the middle Zambezi; (3) border of present and former swamps of the Okovango delta. (From F. Debenham, *Geog. Rev.*, 1949, Courtesy of the American Geographical Society.)

drained with the idea of adding to Africa's productive capacity and vast area of fertile alluvial soil, or would this simply destroy the important fishing industry and upset the African cultivators' careful adjustment to existing conditions? That adjustment can be only partial. Changes in water level are at once evident in drowned villages and gardens, and the now submerged Lunga Bank was once densely populated. Surely there could be no clearer proof that Africa still holds many problems for which we have no ready solution.

Further Reading

Professor J. H. Wellington's *Southern Africa* (Cambridge: Cambridge University Press, 1955, 2 vols.) extends as far as the "southern continental divide" between the Congo and the Zambezi and thus includes Mozambique, Malawi, Rhodesia, most of Zambia, and the south of Angola. A useful wide-ranging compilation with bibliographies is the *Handbook to the Federation of Rhodesia and Nyasaland,* edited by W. V. Brelsford (Salisbury: Government Printer, 1960). More recent one-country studies have been George Kay's *A Social Geography of Zambia* and *Rhodesia: A Human Geography* (London: University of London Press, 1967 and 1970) and *Malawi* by J. G. Pike and G. T. Rimmington (London: Oxford University Press, 1965). But for land use and the natural environment, the two parts of *An Agricultural Survey of Southern Rhodesia* (Salisbury: Government Printer, n.d., 1960?), including the detailed maps, are most valuable. Little is written in English of geographical value about the Portuguese territories but *Portuguese Africa* by J. Duffy (Cambridge: Harvard, 1959) may be consulted and C. F. Spence on *Mocambique* (Cape Town: Howard Timmins, 1963).

CHAPTER 19

South Africa

Mastery of the Cape of Good Hope meant the control of the commerce between Europe and India. That was the reason for the early Portuguese interest in the Cape; that was the reason that the Dutch East India Company sent Jan van Riebeeck in 1652 to establish a settlement on the shores of Table Bay under the shadow of Table Mountain; that was the reason that the British dispossessed the Dutch temporarily in 1795 and permanently in 1806. It is van Riebeeck's ship which was for a long time pictured on the penny stamps of the Union of South Africa, and the Afrikaans-speaking South Africans regard this as their "Mayflower." Little remained of former Portuguese interests, and it was not the intention of the Dutch to establish a colony —simply a rewatering and revictualing halt on the way to India. But, as we have already indicated in Chapter 2, when the settlement became firmly established, expansion was inevitable. The hinterland was occupied by Hottentots, who, their tribal organization broken down and decimated by plague, became the white man's servants while nominally remaining free. From the first the

settlement and later the colony depended upon these Hottentot servants and on imported Malay and African slaves. Unlike the Hottentots, the Bushmen farther in the hinterland were less capable of serving the white man and sought only to preserve their isolation by bows and poisoned arrows. They became almost extinct.

By 1795 the Dutch colony had expanded to some 15,000 free "burghers" who had retired from the company and remained in South Africa, together with a few pioneer settlers on the one hand and the servants of the Dutch East India Company on the other. The whole colony resented the harsh restrictions imposed by the company, and they were ripe for revolt when in August 1795 the Dutch capitulated to the British, whose occupation of the Cape was a strategic move against the French. Actually the British held the Cape from 1795 to 1803 in the name of the Prince of Orange, then a refugee from the French, living in England. Although the British removed all restrictions on trading, things did not go smoothly for long. The flow of European goods was cut off; the Dutch Settlers, although willing to work hard for themselves, had the tradition that to work for others was for blacks and slaves. The British objected to the harsh Boer attitude toward the Africans, though it differed but little from the attitude of white people in European North America at the time. It has already been indicated how eventually the Great Trek started in 1836. The establishment of the Orange Free State and the Transvaal Republic followed. By way of contrast, Natal was proclaimed British in 1843 and made a province of the Cape Colony the next year. With the recognition of the independence of the Transvaal in 1852 and of the Orange Free State in 1854, the four provinces of the future Union of South Africa—two British (Cape of Good Hope and Natal) and two Boer—were broadly defined.

In 1877 the impoverished Transvaal was suffering attack by several African tribes. The British stepped in and annexed the country, but the old problem remained. The Boers needed military assistance but hated interference by the British government; the British felt the need to protect whites against blacks but regarded the Boer treatment of Africans as the root of the trouble. The result was the First Boer War (1880–1881), with a British defeat and the Transvaal again independent.

Then came the discovery of the richest goldfield in the world, the Rand Goldfields. The Boers had no capital to work the deposits; British capital and Western industrialization poured into the country. The patriarchal Boers, headed by President Paul Kruger, hated these "outlanders" (*uitlanders*); they tried to tap their wealth by taxation while denying them rights of citizenship. The coup d'etat, known as the Jameson Raid, failed, and the British found themselves involved in the costly Boer War of 1899–1902 against a skillful foe, thoroughly used to the terrain. The British were several times besieged, notably at Ladysmith and Mafeking. The relief of the latter on May 17, 1900, resulted in such wild rejoicing by crowds in London that the word "maf-

19.A The statue to Paul Kruger, the Afrikaner leader, in Church Square, Pretoria. (South Africa Official Photo.)

ficking" was long used to denote extravagant crowd behavior.

By the Treaty of Vereeniging (1902) the Boers surrendered. Fortunately great men on the British side like Lord Milner were matched by great men among the Boers — General Botha and General Smuts. The Boers were granted British citizenship and given 15 million dollars with which to restock their farms, and other measures were immediately put in hand to restore the devastated areas. Within three years the Transvaal and Orange Free State were granted responsible government; a little later, after two years of discussion, the four colonies joined to form the Union of South Africa with dominion status (1910). In the World Wars of 1914–1918 and 1939–1945 South Africans, Boer and British alike, fought side by side with Britain.

Before considering subsequent events it will be well to examine the population problem.

THE POPULATION OF SOUTH AFRICA

In order to maintain the domestic life of the settlement the Dutch East India Company, especially between 1685 and 1688, sent out numbers of orphan girls as well as about 150 Huguenot refugees. There was little to tie either the Dutch orphans or the French refugees to their mother countries, and the growth of illiteracy is not surprising. With little contact or fresh immigration from Holland after 1688, they even abandoned their own language of Holland for a limited patois, the *Taal*—the origin of Afrikaans, which includes many African words. For twenty years after the British occupation in 1795 the colony remained essentially Dutch, but the British supplied troops as protection against Hottentot and Bantu inroads. It was largely to secure a new frontier that 4000 selected (out of 90,000 who applied) British immigrants were settled on the west side of the Fish River in 1820 (the Albany settlement). By that time the European population mainly of Dutch descent, numbered 42,000. The Albany settlers founded Port Elizabeth and Grahamstown and drifted into Cape Town. The more influential worked for freedom of speech and forced not only a more liberal government policy but a substitution of English institutions for Dutch. With the abolition of slavery and the Great Trek, the stage was set for the Cape to become predominantly English speaking.

The other English-speaking stronghold was Natal. The original settlers of 1824 whose presence deterred the Boer trekkers formed a small group, so that Natal was annexed to Cape Colony in 1844, placed under a separate government

19.B A statue to Cecil Rhodes, the British leader in South Africa. The contrasting attitudes represented by Kruger and Rhodes have had an enduring impact on the political geography of southern Africa. (South African Official Photograph.)

in 1845, but in 1856 was established as a separate colony. Zululand was added to Natal in 1897 and some districts of Transvaal transferred in 1903.

The need for labor led to importation of slaves from other parts of Africa and Malaya and later of indentured labor from India and elsewhere. The immigrant labor has remained to constitute a race problem — in which East Indians in South Africa may be compared with Negroes in the United States.

To the United States and Canada the Indian problem has become essentially a moral one — responsibility for the remnants of erstwhile fine people. To the United States the Negro problem is one of integrating a minority. Here South Africa is in a very different and vastly more difficult position. The whites are in a minority of about 1 to 4; there is a bottomless reservoir of Negro Africans in the whole continent to the north. A democracy of equal citizenship for white and black and equal voting rights would immediately give the Negro African control of South Africa and of white South Africans who have been governed by themselves or their own kind for over 300 years; hence the present dilemma.

The policy of the government in power since 1948 has been that of *apartheid* involving the segregation of Africans into specific areas, in sharp contrast to what we have seen happening in most of the rest of Africa. The whole policy of racial discrimination is opposed to world trends and to the policy of other members of the Commonwealth. In that regard, coupled with South Africa's refusal to admit United Nations authority over Southwest Africa, the Union of South Africa had become an embarrassment to Britain and the Commonwealth. On October 5, 1960, a referendum was held among the 1,800,426 white voters for or against the Union's becoming a republic on May 31, 1961. The voting was 52 percent in favor, the voting in the Cape being almost equal, that in Natal overwhelmingly against. A republic was declared, and almost immediately South Africa left the Commonwealth.

Table 19.1 illustrates the very rapid population growth after the establishment of the Union of South Africa.

Increase of Europeans (white) over 42 years, 1904–1946, was 2.6 percent per annum, but in 9 years, 1951–1960, was 1.6 percent per annum. Increase of non-Europeans over 42 years, 1904–1946, was 2.9 percent per annum, but in 9 years, 1951–1960, was under 1.0 percent. The distribution of these two population groups is shown in Figures 19.1 and 19.2. The diminishing proportion of whites to nonwhites is demonstrated by a comparison of Figures 19.3 and 19.4.

Officially the Republic of South Africa, or Republiek van Suid-Afrika, is bilingual; government servants are required to know both Afrikaans and English. At the census

Table 19.1. South Africa: Area and Populations of the Four Provinces

Year	Area in square miles	Europeans	Non-Europeans	Total	Density
1904	472,550	1,116,806	4,059,018	5,175,824	11
1911		1,276,242	4,697,152	5,973,394	13
1921		1,519,488	5,409,092	6,928,580	15
1936		2,003,857	7,586,041	9,589,898	20
1946	472,494	2,335,460	8,923,398	11,258,858	24
1951	472,359	2,641,689	10,029,763	12,671,452	27
1960		3,067,638	12,773,490	15,841,128	33
1970 (prelim.)		3,779,000	17,503,000	21,282,000	45

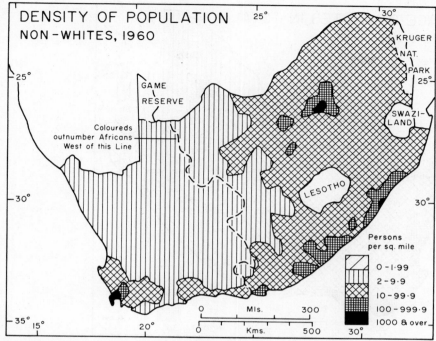

19.1 The density of the nonwhite population over South Africa, 1960.
Figures 19.1 to 19.5 inclusive are redrawn from T. J. D. Fair and N. Manfred Shaffer, 'Population Patterns and Policies in South Africa 1951-1960,' *Economic Geography* vol. 40 (1964) pp. 261-274, by kind permission.

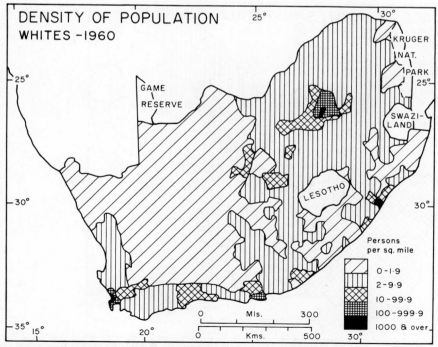

19.2 The density of the white population over South Africa, 1960.

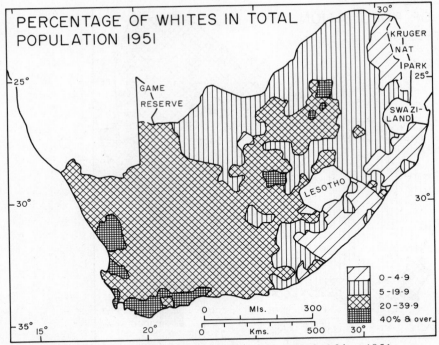

19.3 Percentage of whites in the total population of South Africa, 1951.

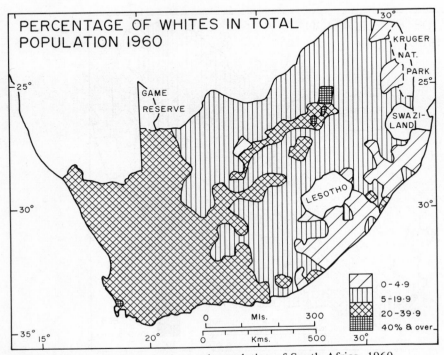

19.4 Percentage of whites in the total population of South Africa, 1960.

of 1960, Afrikaans was the home language of 1.79 million whites, English that of 1.15 million. Thus Boer descendants definitely outnumber the English speaking. This is predominantly the case in the Orange Free State and in rural Transvaal, but not in the other two provinces or in the urbanized Witwatersrand. Of the non-Europeans the majority are Bantu, but 3 percent (624,000 in 1970) are Asian and over 10 percent (nearly 2 million) are "other races", including the numerous "Cape Coloured" discussed later.

The Republic (formerly the Union) of South Africa never has been a black man's country in the sense that its development has almost entirely been determined by white settlement and enterprise, but the essential labor has been provided either by those of nonwhite races brought in for the purpose or who have been recruited from the African areas of the north and east. The question now is: can a vast territory controlled by only less than 4 million whites, so opposed to world trends, for long survive? The first years of the Republic included a further development of *apartheid* but also a strengthening of the national economy.

THE AFRICANS

In the Republic of South Africa the Africans are described officially as "natives" and their affairs are in the hands of the Department of Native Affairs. Practically all the Africans in the Republic are Bantu; the majority belong to the two major groups, the Nguni and the Sotho. Originally they were all tribally organized and lived in kraals or small villages. Whether or not the dwellers in an individual kraal were actually related, the kraal was regarded as a family unit, and there was no marriage permitted between dwellers in the same kraal. The kraals were controlled according to tribal law by a headman, who was usually a member of the traditional Bantu aristocracy, and nominally all allocation of tribal land was carried out autocratically by the chief. In actual fact, though grazing was common, cultivated fields tended to remain in the hands of the same families for many decades. Under the old organization the men provided food by hunting and took care of the stock, whereas the gathering of fruits and roots and the cultivation of fields were women's work.

Broadly speaking, the Africans in South Africa can now be divided into three classes. There are the tribal natives, living in the reserves, where to a varied extent the old tribal organization is still maintained. There are the "squatters" on the farms belonging to the white Africans, who in many cases continue to recognize more or less directly their tribal obligations. And, third, there are the town dwellers, who do not recognize any such obligation. In addition to these three groups are the African workers recruited for work in the mines, especially the gold mines of Witwatersrand. They come mainly from Mozambique, Lesotho, Botswana, Swaziland, and from various parts of tropical Africa. The recruitment of these workers in the mines is carried out systematically by the Native Recruiting Corporation Limited for the three former High Commission territories, and under various agreements and regulations where other countries are concerned. For example, in Mozambique there is a convention between the South African government and Portugal dating from 1928 and revised at intervals since then whereby a maximum number is permitted (it was fixed at 100,000 in 1940) and whereby conditions of work such as a period of acclimatization of 28 days of service are laid down. On leaving the mines the workers are not allowed to remain in the Republic.

The steady breakdown of tribal organization among the Bantu may be attributed to several causes. There is a poll tax, early fixed at 20 shillings ($2.60) for every adult male, and there is also a local hut tax, then 10 shillings ($1.30) per hut, imposed on the occupier of every dwelling in a native location. These taxes must be paid in cash, and thus there is an immediate incentive for the earning of money. It is still the rule for young men to pay in kind or cash to the parents of their brides, and the increasing tendency is to pay in cash rather than in cattle. Thus the desire on the part of the young men to obtain the necessary cash is probably the strongest inducement for them to leave their kraals and to obtain work in the mines, on farms, or as laborers in the towns. There is a constant demand for domestic servants in all the larger towns, and the number of Bantu female servants has been increasing rapidly. It is urged by some that missionary enterprise is also largely responsible for the process of detribalization. Approximately half the total native population in the Republic is recorded as belonging to various Christian denominations. With missionary enterprise has come the spread of education, and as we have pointed out elsewhere modern ideas of democracy are in conflict with autocratic tribal organization.

The squatters on the farms provide the greater part of such farm labor as is available. Arrangements differ in different parts of the country. A common arrangement in the Free State is for the head of a family to contract to serve the farmer throughout the year in return for which he receives a small cash remuneration plus the right to graze an agreed number of stock and to cultivate an agreed area of ground free of charge. In the Transvaal the agreement is to work for the farmer without wages for 90 days, with complete liberty for the remainder of the year, either to hire himself out to the best bidder or to work land provided by the farmer.

It is illegal for the farmer to sell land to the African squatters. It is generally agreed that the system is unsatisfactory and the labor indifferent. Residential segregation of the three "racial" groups, white, colored, and native, with Asiatics included in the colored group has been given the force of law. Under the Group Areas Act passed in July 1950 persons of one group are not permitted to own or occupy property in the controlled area of another group, except under permit. This involves registration, together with details of race, of all persons resident in the Union; and under the Immorality Amendment Act, also passed in July 1950, sex relations were entirely prohibited between Europeans and non-Europeans, that is, both colored and native groups. Previously the prohibition had applied only to marriages between Europeans and natives.

This segregation is enforced both on a small scale, within towns, and also on a much larger scale aiming at the establishment of self-administrating "Bantustans," based upon the African "reserves" (Figure 19.5). It is proposed to encourage industry to locate near these so that labor will be available without living in white areas.

It will be seen that the trend in legislation is diametrically opposed to the general trend in other parts of the African continent. It is based essentially on the concept that South Africa is and should remain a white man's country. The initial step was really taken as long ago as 1913 with the passing of the Natives' Land Act, in which native reservations were demarcated. This at the time was as much for the protection of the Africans as anyone, and they have since obtained some increases in their land.

THE "CAPE COLOURED"

The community known as the "Cape Coloured" is a critical element in the complex population structure of the Republic. It owes its origin to three centuries of miscegenation between the immigrant Europeans—especially of Portuguese, Dutch, and British stock—with the original Bantu, Hottentot, and other African peoples and also with slaves of West African, Malayan, East Indian, and other ori-

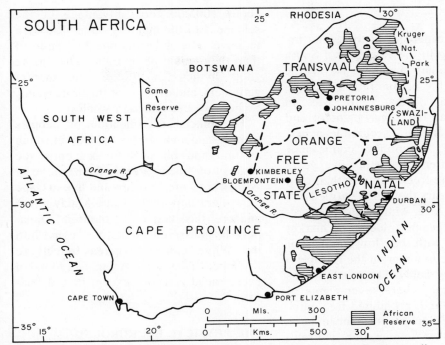

19.5 African reserves in South Africa. These are the bases of the "Bantustans" created by the policy of "apartheid."

gins. It is reported on contemporary evidence that in the early years of European settlement in the Cape three-quarters of the children born to slave mothers had European fathers. Officially the term covers the relatively pure-blooded non-Negro peoples, such as the Bushmen, Hottentots, and Griquas, about 25 percent of a total of about 2.0 million. The remaining three-quarters are the mixed peoples properly speaking, whose cultural affinities are with the mass of Europeans. Nearly 90 percent live in the Cape Province, where they are concentrated in the western parts, constituting there over half the total population. Except for the small English-speaking groups in Natal, the majority of Cape Coloured speak Afrikaans. Large numbers are employed on Afrikaans farms, especially in the more intensively farmed districts. In the towns they provide unskilled labor, domestic servants, and industrial workers. Only a small "upper class," tending to remain aloof from the majority, includes teachers,

skilled workers, and professional men. The worst elements drift to the underworlds of the larger towns, especially Cape Town. Nearly all the Cape Coloured are nominally Christians but adhere to English denominations even more than to the Dutch Reformed church. Among the Coloured the birth rate is 50 percent above that of the Europeans, but poverty, bad housing, and malnutrition have resulted in high mortality. On the whole the position of these people has steadily deteriorated. Employers prefer Europeans wherever possible, and the tendency under the racial discrimination policy of the Nationalist government which came into power in 1948 was to squeeze them out of the slightly advantageous position which they had held over the African.[1]

[1] An excellent study of these people by K. M. Buchanan and N. Hurwitz appears in the *Geog. Rev.*, XL, July 1950, pp. 397–414 ('The "Coloured" Community in the Union of South Africa').

THE ASIANS

Ninety-seven percent of the Asian immigrants[2] living in the Republic of South Africa speak Indian languages, so that the designation in the census return "Asian" may be read "Indian." It was in 1859–1860 that the sugar planters and other colonists in Natal secured legal permission to bring "indentured" coolie labor from India. After completing five years the Indians were free to choose their own job; after ten years they were entitled to a free return passage. Many came, few returned. They became traders and market gardeners, and with their low standard of living were able to undercut the European settlers in many fields. The reaction was inevitable. Natal, where seven-eights of the total are found, prohibited free entry in 1896; the Union government in 1913 prohibited further immigration entirely. By that time the numbers had come to exceed numbers of Europeans in Natal, but with cessation of Indian immigration numbers of Europeans drew slightly ahead after about 1925. At the census of 1970 there were 620,000 Asians in South Africa.

The Indians came from many parts of India; Muslim Gujaratis from Bombay and Tamil-speaking Indians professing Hinduism from the Madras coasts are most numerous, but there are many Hindu speakers from North India and Telegus from the south. Muslims constitute nearly a fifth of the total.

Among the Indians men heavily outnumber women (a legacy from the old days), but the birth ratio is high and the total is rapidly increasing. In 1927 inducements in the form of a free passage and a bonus were offered to Indians to return to India, and in the following twenty years

about 100,000 took advantage of the scheme. But the majority have little wish to leave. The are economically better off than they would be in India. They make good livings as traders, as market gardeners, and in some of the professions. Some have become very wealthy.

The official classification of peoples from Asia demonstrates the way in which cultural and physical factors enter the concept of "race." People from southeast Asia, if they are Muslims and live in Cape Town, are part of the Cape Malay group and are classified as "Coloured." Japanese business representatives come into the "White" category whereas Indians are "Asiatic." Thus some Asians are found in every racial category except that of "natives."

THE PHYSICAL BACKGROUND

What are the essential characteristics of the land into which Briton and Boer penetrated, and which is today the Republic of South Africa?

In common with other parts of the African continent there is in the south a great central plateau separated from the shores of the Indian and Atlantic oceans by a varied width of lower country.

In southern Africa the plateau reaches remarkably high elevations, especially over the eastern half. Nearly all this eastern half has an elevation of more than 4000 feet (1200 m), and considerable stretches exceed 6000 feet (1800 m) above sea level. The eastern and southeastern edge of the plateau forms a remarkable feature known as the Drakensberg or the Quathlamba Mountains, and the gigantic rocky wall viewed from the east is one of the world's spectacular features. It is particularly striking on the eastern borders of Lesotho where it is formed of thick layers of horizontal lavas. Although the edge of the plateau is somewhat less marked along the south, where it receives various names, it is nevertheless a distinctive feature. In the dry country of

[2] K. M. Buchanan and N. Hurwitz, "The Asiatic Immigrant Community in the Union of South Africa," *Geog. Rev.*, XXXIX, July 1949, pp. 440–449. In South Africa the word Asiatic is retained; the modern trend elsewhere is to substitute Asian.

the west the edge is less distinct and the elevation reached, though almost everywhere over 3000 feet (900 m), is less, and only a few points reach the level of 6000 feet (1800 m). The plateau itself is over large stretches almost flat. At other times it is rolling, and sometimes low, flat-topped hills rise from its surface. The latter feature is associated particularly with the presence of the almost horizontal sheets of sandstone associated with igneous rocks, belonging to the Karoo[3] beds (see above, Chapter 3). A marked change of scenery is associated with a change from the Karoo beds to the underlying ancient rocks.

In southern Africa the surface of the plateau sinks greatly towards the center, and over the heart of the dry land of Bot-

swana the average elevation drops below 3000 feet (900 m). In the Republic of South Africa the greater part of the plateau lies in the basin of the Orange River, together with its main tributary, the Vaal. Only the northern half of the Transvaal comes within the drainage of the Limpopo.

Climatically the elevation of the plateau lowers the general temperature 10 to 20°F (6–12°C) throughout the year, and the frost danger is of considerable importance (Figure 19.6). Since the plateau is a region of summer rain and falls in the winter are infrequent, snow is rare except on the mountains of the edge.

The plateau lies in the so-called trade wind belt. The rain-bearing air masses of summer are from the Indian Ocean, and the heaviest fall is consequently in the east; but only on the higher eastern parts of the plateau does the average exceed 30 inches (760 mm) a year. It is possible to

---

[3] Linguists now agree that the spelling "Karoo" is to be preferred to the older "Karroo." Previously, "Karoo" was the Afrikaans spelling; "Karroo" was commonly used in English works.

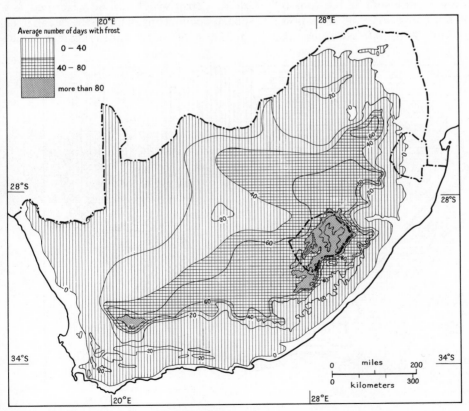

19.6 Incidence of frost over South Africa.

consider the high plateau as divided into eastern and western halves by the isohyet of 15 inches (380 mm) a year (Figure 19.7). With less than this amount cultivation except by irrigation becomes impossible. Even where the fall is between 15 and 20 inches (380 and 500 mm) a year crop production is precarious, and perhaps it is better to say that normal arable farming is limited to those eastern regions of the plateau which have more than 20 inches (500 mm) a year. Furthermore, the rain tends to fall in sudden storms, and the quantity from year to year is subject to serious variation. The sudden falls are conductive to serious soil erosion and the rapid formation of deep *dongas,* or gulleys. Soil erosion remains an intractable problem in the dry margins of the cultivated plateau, together with the degeneration of pasture. In addition to direct soil erosion, the rain falling suddenly on the hard parched surface of the land does not readily soak in but runs off instead of enriching the soil. It follows that most of the South African rivers, the

tributaries of the Orange, are liable to sudden floods, whereas for a large proportion of the year the watercourses are mainly dry.

The country between the high plateau and the sea is not in southern Africa a coastal plain. In the east throughout Natal under the great scarp of the Drakensberg Mountains there is a belt of very varied hilly land, and visitors to Pietermaritzburg who pass through the Valley of a Thousand Hills will recognize in that name the essentially broken-up nature of this tract. Here the underlying rocks are the same Karoo Beds that underlie neighboring parts of the plateau. But they are here gently folded, and the process of subaerial weathering has cut through the horizontal or gently inclined layers to carve out a varied relief which, became it is still actively in the course of being sculptured, geologists would describe as a "young relief." Only along the coasts of Natal is there a strip which can be described as a coastal plain, fringed along the ocean itself by lines of sand dunes against which

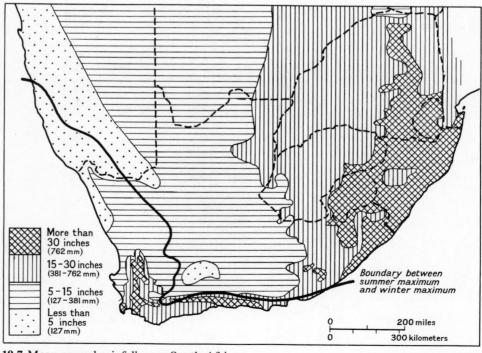

19.7 Mean annual rainfall over South Africa.

pound the everlasting breakers from the Indian Ocean.

In the south, that is, in Cape Province, the land between the plateau edge and the sea is much more varied. Here, in contrast with the whole of the heart of Africa but in common with the northwest of the continent, the rocks have been considerably folded, and one gets the familiar features of folded mountain ranges. Though these ranges differ in the details of direction, elevation, and degree of dissection, on the whole they tend to be parallel to the edge of the plateau. Between them are broad or narrow valleys, sometimes wide enough to form extensive plains. And it may be said, therefore, that the descent from the plateau to the sea is by a series of gigantic steps, each separated from the next by a range of mountains. In the most typical development the lowest step is a narrrow coastal plain, or coastal plateau, then a range of mountains (the Langeberg and Outeniquas) followed by the second step, a dry plateau known as the Little Karoo. The Great Black Mountains (Groote Zwarte Bergen) are followed by the third step, the plateau of the Great Karoo. The Great Karoo itself is overshadowed by the scarp here known as the Nuweveld, which forms the edge of the plateau.

This southern tract is the one where the summer rains of the type associated with the trade wind belt alternate with the winter rains from the westerlies and so receive a rainfall well distributed throughout the year. The rainfall is largely relief rainfall, with the consequent sharp differences between an exposed hill ridge and a sheltered valley. But there are numerous small rivers, rising among these favored mountains of the Cape Province. They naturally tend to flow as far as possible along the valleys, but at intervals they cut through the intervening mountain ridges by great gaps known in South Africa as *poorts*. Several of the rivers are naturally of considerable importance in providing water for irrigation of the flat valley plains.

Best known of South African mountains are those which lie in the southwest. Table Mountain, under which nestles the town and port of Cape Town, is in fact a prototype of flat-topped mountains found throughout Africa wherever beds of resistant rock are approximately horizontal. Nearby, overlooking Gordon's Bay, are those more varied mountain forms associated with irregularly folded rocks. This southwest region, of course, is the region of winter rain, South Africa's belt of Mediterranean climate, with the consequent reproduction of so many physical features reminiscent of southern California or southern Portugal.

Farther north and in Southwest Africa the land between the plateau edge and the sea is the desert stretch known as the Namib, of varied but not very distinctive relief. Throughout the vast stretch from 30° South to the border of Angola at 17° South only one permanent stream, the Orange River, reaches the coast.

GOLD

For many decades South Africa has led the countries of the world as a producer of gold. Generally it may be said that the African continent is responsible for about three-fifths of the world's output, and of this total some 80 percent comes from South Africa. In recent years, South Africa has supplied nearly three-quarters of the world output, excluding the U.S.S.R. Through recent discoveries an important part is now played by goldfields in the Orange Free State. From 1887 to 1949, inclusive, nearly all the gold came from the single goldfield of the Witwatersrand, with a total yield approaching 500 million ounces. This field alone in 1948 was furnishing 97 percent of South Africa's output, nearly 48 percent of the estimated world output, and its value represented two-fifths of all the commercial exports of the whole continent of Africa, excluding Egypt. Although serious production only began in 1951, by 1959, the new Orange Free State goldfields were producing a quarter of the total output and by 1966 the figure had risen to 36 percent. New fields had also been opened up in the Far West Rand, at Klerksdorp and in the "far east" Rand at Evander.

The Witwatersrand Goldfield has been described from the geographical point of view by Peter Scott[4] (Figures 19.8 to 19.11). He points out that the field, commonly known as the Rand, extends for 50 miles (80 m) from Randfontein eastward to Springs and for 20 miles (32 km) southward from Springs to Heidelberg. Structurally it comprises the areas where gold-bearing conglomerates called "reefs", of Precambrian age, either outcrop at the surface or dip steeply southward under a cover of younger rocks. Twelve-thousand feet (3700 m) is regarded as the possible limit to economic mining. At a depth of 9000 feet (2700 m) in the Crown mines the rock temperature is 109°F (43°C), and in order to protect the miners from phthisis and silicosis the air has to be kept saturated with moisture; deeper mining is possible only if dry methods with dry air can be adopted.

Structurally the Witwatersrand field may be divided into four main regions: the Central Rand, the Far East Rand, the West Rand, and the Far West Rand. As shown in Figures 19.8 and 19.10 these areas are separated by structural features.

The gold was discovered in 1884, the field was proclaimed in 1886, and production became important in the following year; by 1888 the whole length of the outcrop of the Central Rand was being mined by numerous companies. Gradu-

ally, as surface working gave place to mines and the mines had to go ever deeper, the work passed into the hands of large units. The Central Rand dominated production until 1897, and it was during this period that the cyanide process made possible the recovery of gold from pyritic ores which had previously been regarded as valueless. The process was introduced in 1890 and generally adopted from 1892 onward.

There followed the great development of the West Rand from 1898 to 1911 and then the Far East Rand (1912–1923), which became dominant in the years 1924–1938 when the Far West Rand, previously insignificant, began to be important. The years since 1951 have been marked not only by further expansion east and west but also by the rise of the new fields in the Orange Free State to the south. In the Rand itself a production peak of over 14 million ounces was reached in 1941. By 1966 production in the older area of the Rand had declined to 5.3 million ounces (17.4 percent) compared with a total production by South Africa of 25.1 million ounces (31.2 million ounces in 1968). In 1898 for every ton of reef which was milled, 9.78 pennyweights (0.489 ounce) of gold was obtained. By 1948 this had fallen to 4.01 pennyweights (0.2005 ounce), but vast additional areas had been proved. With great effort the world price of gold has been kept stationary. Technological improvements have kept costs down but mines are having to be made deeper and the future of gold mining in South Africa is in doubt over the long term. Some mines have been

---

[4] *Geog. Rev.,* XLI, October 1951, pp. 561–589.

Four maps (Figures 19.8 to 19.11) of the Witwatersrand Goldfield. In 1948 map (Figure 19.11) the large circles represent companies producing between 500,000 and 1,000,000 ounces a year, the smaller circles 100,000 to 500,000 and under 100,000. (From Peter Scott, *Geog. Rev.,* 1951. Courtesy of *Geographical Review,* American Geographical Society.)

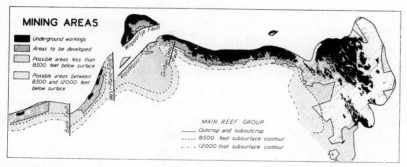

Fig. 19-8

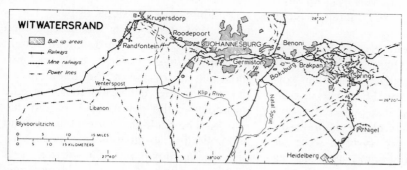

Fig. 19-9

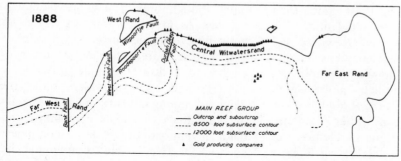

Fig. 19-10

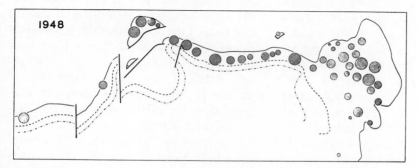

Fig. 19-11

able to stay in production only because of receipts from the extraction of uranium as a by-product.

It should be noted that the development of the goldfield was made possible by the nearby existence of coal, first in the neighborhood of the Far East Rand itself, latterly from the Witbank field where the seams are almost undisturbed, the coal of excellent quality, and the reserves very great. An electric power supply, vital to deep mining operations, was built up after 1907 on the basis of unlimited coal resources.

The great problem of the Rand has always been labor. There was an early attempt to use demobilized European soldiers as unskilled labor. There was also an attempt to recruit Africans in Central and East Africa. In 1904 Chinese laborers, on a three-year indenture system, were introduced, and at one time as many as 53,000 Chinese were employed in the mines; but repatriation was decided upon and was completed in 1910. Since then Africans have been recruited under the regular systems mentioned elsewhere, and increased technical efficiency has steadily lowered the average number of employees per 1000 tons of ore milled — now under 6.

The development of the Rand has given rise, naturally, to many other problems. One of the most serious is adequacy of water supply, which may prove to be a limiting factor in the future. Supplying water to the cities of the Witwatersrand is made more difficult by their situation on a watershed. The spread of the gigantic conurbation based on Johannesburg has been rendered difficult by the huge areas occupied by mining dumps of white crushed quartzose conglomerate. Naturally, apart from the important iron and steel industries, the development has given rise to a wide range of industries designed to supply local needs.

DIAMONDS

Gold is far from being the only mineral of importance in South Africa. Until the discovery in 1908 of diamonds in Southwest Africa and later discoveries in Tanzania and elsewhere, South Africa was almost the only source of diamonds in the world. A pebble from the banks of the Orange River was identified as a diamond in 1867; but the most famous diamond field is at Kimberley in Cape Province, where diamonds were first found in 1871. They were found in a decomposed rock known as *yellow ground* outcropping at the surface in oval or circular patches corresponding to depressions, or pans. It was found that underneath the decomposed yellow rock was a hard igneous rock, known as *blue ground,* and the momentous discovery of the diamond industry was the realization that this blue ground was the parent rock of the diamonds. The geologist knows blue ground as kimberlite, an igneous rock occupying pipes going down into the earth's crust which probably represent old volcanic necks. There are large numbers of these pipes though only a few are diamond-bearing. At first they were excavated in great pits from the surface to depths of 400 feet or more. Then it became necessary to follow the blue ground by underground mines, which took the diamond-mining industry out of the hands of individuals or small companies and made it a monopoly of large combines, such as De Beers, able to command the necessary capital, human skill, and technical equipment. In due course the great diamond combines were able to control and restrict the output in order to maintain prices. Their principal mines were near Kimberley, at Jagersfontein, Koffiefontein and finally, the largest single mine of all, the Premier diamond mine near Pretoria, from which the world's largest diamond, the Cullinan, was obtained in 1905. In the years 1925–1927 when discoveries of rich diamond-bearing alluvial deposits were made elsewhere, especially in Southwest Africa, diamond mining was temporarily shut down to counteract the output of alluvial stones. Alluvial diamonds in great quantity now derive from

19.C Probably the most famous hole in the world: the old Kimberly Diamond Mine. Much of it is below the water line. (Copyright: Aircraft Operating Company of Africa.)

many other areas of Africa including Zaire, Congo (Brazzaville), Ghana, Sierra Leone, and Angola.

OTHER MINERALS

If gold and diamond mines were the foundation on which the prosperity of South Africa was built, other minerals are playing a major and increasingly important part. This is fortunate because the future of the traditional minerals must necessarily be uncertain. The Precambrian shield forming most of the northern part of the plateau is highly mineralized, and especially is that true of the northern Transvaal.

The extraction of uranium as a by-product from the gold mines has already been mentioned. South Africa also ranks among the largest producers in the world of platinum, chrome, asbestos, manganese, antimony, and corundum. Also important are copper, iron ore, and fluorspar, followed by a wide range of minerals produced in smaller quantities.

The development of South African gold

mining, including the treatment of very large quantities of rock, was greatly assisted, as has been mentioned, by the availability of coal from the Karoo measures, fortunately mostly in the Witbank field near to the Witwatersrand. The coal is of good quality, in shallow mines, and cheaply mined. South Africa has one of the highest outputs of coal per head of population of any country in the world—more than the United States or the U.S.S.R.—and is a major exporter. This is in great contrast to the rest of Africa.

The wealth in coal is a consolation for the lack of any oil fields, for which an intensive search continues. Indications have been obtained in drilling offshore of the southeast coast. As a precaution against any attempted sanctions, a strategic reserve of oil is being built up in disused mines.

THE IRON AND STEEL INDUSTRY

The development of the South Africa iron and steel industry affords a very interesting example of progress towards economic self-sufficiency which marks the growth of so many of the "newer" countries of the world. The start dates only from 1910 to 1916, when three plants using scrap were established in the Witwatersrand, mainly to supply some of the needs of the gold-mining industry, and another also using scrap was located on the Vaal River at Vereeniging and received government support. The curtailment of overseas supplies during World War I (1914–1918) helped the industry, but it was hurt by the postwar depression. Nevertheless, the Union Steel Corporation (USCO) of Vereeniging established a blast furnace at Newcastle in Natal in 1926 and an additional steel works on the Klip River at Vereeniging in the same year. The South African Iron and Steel Corporation (ISCOR) was established at Pretoria in 1934 to use the local medium-grade quartzitic bedded ore deposits, and by 1949 it was producing three-quarters of South Africa's output of about 650,000 tons of steel. The discovery of rich hematite deposits at Thabazimbi, 156 miles from Pretoria by a railway which was pushed there in 1934, soon made that the chief source of ore. Though only some of the seams are suitable for making metallurgic coke, the Witbank coal workings are only 70 miles (113 km) from the ISCOR works. But Vereeniging has proved to have an even better location; it is actually on a coal field, other suitable coal from northern Natal is near, water supply is good, and the location is central for South Africa's railway system. In 1944 a site at Vanderbijl Park, 10 miles (16 km) west of the old works and on the bare veld, was chosen. Five years later this South African Gary had blast furnaces and steel and engineering works and was a fast-growing town of 20,000 people. Despite expanding demand South Africa by 1950 was on the verge of being completely independent of imports of iron and steel, and has remained so since. A new plant was opened at Witbank in 1968 and

the industry may be moving towards building up exports. The old steel works on the goldfield have expanded into a considerable industry but have been completely overshadowed by Pretoria and Vereeniging.

THE REGIONAL DIVISIONS OF SOUTH AFRICA

As Wellington very rightly says, "Two facts stand out in any consideration of land development in South Africa. The physical environment is inexorable, and the geographical advantages can be realized to the full only when the country realizes its true economic relationships with the rest of the world. Of the inexorable physical circumstances rainfall is of foremost importance."[5]

On the basis of rainfall Wellington recognizes three main divisions. The eastern division is where the rainfall is adequate and land may be utilized in the production of crops requiring a summer fall. The southwestern is where crop production is also possible because of sufficient rainfall, either coming this time in the winter or distributed throughout the year, or where there are perennial streams which permit continuous irrigation. The third, which he calls the middle area, perhaps more appropriately the western, is where rainfall of less than 15 or 20 inches (380 or 500 mm) a year is insufficient for crop production.

The three main divisions and subdivisions proposed and named by Wellington are indicated on Figure 19.12. We may consider each in turn.

The Cape Region. This is essentially the area of winter rainfall where the rainfall is sufficient for crop production. It is an area of mountain ridges and intervening valleys or plains. This is the birthplace of European agriculture in South Africa, and it is the region which bears the closest comparison to other parts of the world en-

[5] *Geog. Rev.*, XXII (1932) pp. 205–224.

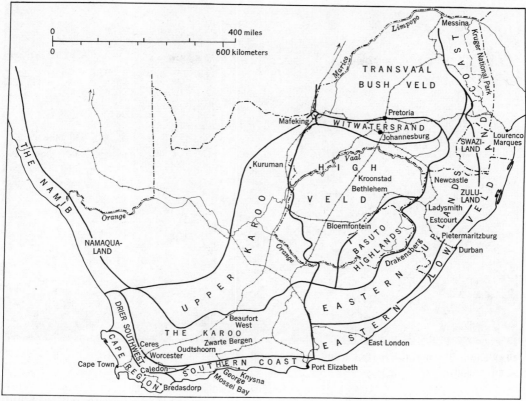

19.12 The regions of South Africa.

joying a Mediterranean climate, but notably to southern California.

The farmlands are used mainly for wheat production, with about half the land under crops and the other half lying fallow. But there is a natural infertility of the soils, and the yields are lower than in other countries relying chiefly on wheat production. In certain areas there is a specialized development of viticulture, and the holdings are naturally smaller. On the scanty natural pasture of shrubby Mediterranean type, sheep farming is a profitable secondary industry, and the animals graze also on the stubble and fallow lands. There is little cattle farming; the summer is too dry.

The production of wheat has tended to rely to a considerable extent on the protection afforded by duty on imported wheat. This is not a region, however, which need necessarily rely primarily on agricultural production. Its climate has the attractive features of sunny southern California. Quite apart from the early start enjoyed by Cape Town and the facilities which it has for easy communication by rail and lately by road with the whole of the subcontinent, this Cape region is one which naturally attracts those who have worked elsewhere and saved sufficiently to retire into a part of the country climatically most attractive. The Atlantic coast near Cape Town itself now has a succession of resorts with hotels and holiday apartments; the sheltered nature of False Bay attracts bathers and pleasure boatmen.

Incidentally, the botanists include a large tract of southwest Africa in the region of the "Cape flora," the richest in the whole of Africa and one characterized by a great wealth of flowering plants, especially those of shrubby habit. Typical

19.D Table Bay and the harbor from Table Mountain, Cape Town. (Photo: J. Allan Cash.)

and most loved is the "sugar bush" (*Protea* sp.).

The Drier Southwestern Region. This region differs from the preceding one in that the rainfall is almost everywhere too small for agriculture. It includes many of the folded mountain ranges, but interest centers on certain of the valleys which lie between them. These include the valley of the Olifants River in the north, the Breede River and its tributaries in the south, as well as the famous Ceres valley and the Hex River valley. Both the Olifants and the Breede are perennial streams, and therefore water can be used for irrigation during the dry summer season. This is the main area of production of grapes, but it also includes some of the best deciduous fruit orchards of the country, notably plums and apples. Some tobacco, especially of Turkish types, is grown and there are winter crops of oats and barley. This fruit-producing region has the advantage that the seasons are the reverse of those of the northern hemisphere and con-

sequently there is a large export of South African fruits to British and other European markets at a time when local supplies are nonexistent.

The expansion of quick freezing has opened up new possibilities in the marketing of fresh fruits. Much progress has been made in the technique of wine production. In particular South Africa has succeeded in producing excellent wines of the sherry type, able to compete on their own merits with the long-favored products of Spain. Light table wines, though they cannot be matched directly with German hocks or with French wines, have been proving their popularity, especially in Canada and Britain. Though originally introduced by the early Dutch settlers, both viticulture and fruit farming owe much of their development and success to the influence of the French Huguenots who, after the revocation of the Edict of Nantes in 1685, settled in this part of South Africa.

In contrast to other Mediterranean climatic regions, neither climate nor soil seems suitable to olives.

The Southern Coastal Region. This is the region where there is a gradual merging of the winter type of rainfall into the area of summer rain. Heavy mists are frequent on the southern slopes of the boundary ranges known collectively as the Lange-bergen, and the more even distribution of rainfall results not only in perennial streams but in soils with a character different from those of other parts of southern Africa.

Where the soils are derived from the Table Mountain sandstone they tend to be poor and leached, but where they are formed from shales and the rainfall is moderate or low, soil acidity tends to disappear and the land is particularly productive. Unfortunately the area concerned is strictly limited in extent. Among field crops oats and potatoes are important, wheat relatively less so. The well-distributed rainfall results in a comparatively luxuriant grass growth in wetter regions. There is obviously great variation from place to place according to local conditions, with the result that land values, types of farming, and intensity of production also show marked variation. Some of the best land is on the alluvial soils by Gamtoos River between Port Elizabeth and Humansdorp. Irrigated land commands a high price.

George is a fruit-growing center with special interest in apples; Knysna, with a heavier rainfall, lies in a forested area where afforestation has assumed importance on the neighboring hill slopes. Mossel Bay is a port lying in a sheltered bay commanding two passes into the interior, so that it is an outlet for the Karoo country behind. But in this respect it does not rival Port Elizabeth on Algoa Bay, which is the natural outlet of a large and productive hinterland, including not only the eastern part of Cape Province but also much of the Orange Free State which lies behind, and has also been provided with a good harbor.

The Karoo. Both the Great Karoo and the Little Karoo are treeless plains hemmed in by mountains and lying below the main scarp of the great African plateau. They both suffer from a small rainfall—everywhere less than 15 inches (380 mm) and in the west less than 10 inches (250 mm)—and a rainfall which is very irregular in its incidence during the year as well as from year to year. On the whole the flora is that of the Mediterranean Cape region, with an admixture of those plants characteristic of the dry Upper Karoo on the surface of the plateau itself. Usually drab and monotonous, with the gray-leafed shrubs separated by tracts of bare soil, after a shower of rain the shrubs and the succulent plants burst into flower. The streams are nearly all intermittent in flow, with the exception of a few which derive from the Swartberge range. Here it is possible, at the foot of the great escarpment and near the higher mountain ranges of the region, to use the water for the cultivation of crops of wheat or lucerne, together with tobacco and grapes. Where major conservation dams have been constructed on the Dwyka, Olifants, and Sundays Rivers, lucerne and citrus fruits are intensively cultivated. The Sundays River valley is a leading area.

Outside such specialized irrigation settlements, the Karoo is essentially a pastoral area, supporting considerable numbers of Merino sheep and Angora goats from which mohair is obtained. The bushes typical of the Karoo vegetation appear to have a high nutritive value as well as medicinal properties which keep the animals in good condition, though the carrying capacity of the land is low. Farms are 4000–10,000 acres (1600–4000 ha) in area; their value where they cannot be irrigated is less than a dollar an acre.

The Dry Regions of the Plateau. To the north of the Great Karoo and beyond the great escarpment are the dry regions of the plateau. In general, aridity increases toward the west and north, and a dry pastoral region where cattle can find a fair pasturage fades into the Kalahari Bush Veld and Kalahari semidesert.

The southern part of the region immediately north of the great escarpment is often known in South Africa as the Upper Karoo or the Karoid Plateau. This vast flat or very gently undulating treeless plain is broken by flat-topped hills, sure indication of the existence of horizontal beds of Karoo sandstone and Karoo dolerite. Everywhere the soil is shallow and rocky, and the vegetation consists of small scattered bushes capable only of supporting a few sheep and goats. The small population depends upon underground water which may be reached by wind-driven pumps.

Not only is the rainfall low, but it is extremely irregular, and it is not unusual for two or three years to pass without appreciable rainfall. Such small towns as Carnarvon and Victoria West are centers of the pastoral industry, but the farmers require anywhere from 4000 to 20,000 acres (1600 to 8000 ha) in order to maintain a flock of reasonable size. The Persian fat-tailed sheep seems to be the best adapted to the area where the Karoo shrubs occur. The industry which has brought at least a tolerable prosperity to this region is the Karakul fur industry. Karakul is the name given to the fur obtained from newly born lambs of this fat-tailed sheep. Northward in Namaqualand the bushman grass and other coarse grasses provide winter pasturage for a few thousand cattle. In the bush veld to the north of the Orange River cattle may find a fair pasturage in the summer, which here becomes the nominal rainy season.

Although little water reaches the Atlantic Ocean, the Orange River itself is a perennial stream, and along its banks are terraces large enough to be worth irrigating. As shown in Figure 19.6, winter frosts occur over most of the area, but summers are long enough and hot enough for cotton growing to be possible on the alluvial soils of these terraces.

The Namib. Although the greater part of the Namib Desert lies in Southwest Africa, it stretches into the Cape Province and is in fact the coastal strip where are to be found the most extreme of the desert conditions known in South Africa. The irregular rainfall even on an average does not exceed 5 inches (127 mm) a year.

The High Veld. The regions so far considered lie within the Cape Province of the Republic of South Africa. Although the surface of the high plateau as a whole may be called and often is called the High Veld, this term can be properly restricted to the eastern part of the plateau surface, covering the larger part of the Orange Free State together with the neighboring parts of the Cape Province and stretching northward into the southern Transvaal. Geologically, the surface is of almost horizontal beds of the Karoo system, sandstone predominating in the south and east with some dolerites and lavas in the northwest. The whole is a great expanse of rolling grassland, treeless except where shade trees have been planted around some of the farms and near villages or towns. It is in this area that the rainfall, more than 15 inches (380 mm), tends to average between 20 and 30 inches (500 and 760 mm) a year, and is of greater reliability than in the drier parts. The even surface has moderately fertile, loamy soils, but the elevation, usually between 4000 and 6000 feet (1200 and 1800 m), results in a great range of temperature, as well as a frost period extending certainly for more than 100 days in the year. Although there is much land in pasture, this is essentially a region of South Africa characterized by extensive arable cultivation. Although some wheat is grown in places as a winter and early summer crop, corn (maize) is the mainstay of the region. This is the so-called "maize triangle," where this is outstandingly the most important crop. With the development of mixed farming, however, the term has become something of a misnomer.

Although the dry climate results in a dry and compact grain, yields are low. Commonly the yield is little over four bags, or 800 pounds, an acre, which can

19.E Large scale farming on the high veld near Heilbron in the Orange Free State. (Photo: South African Information Services.)

be doubled or even trebled by the use of fertilizers, but is only about one-third of yields which have now become common in the corn belt of the United States.

Corn is the staple food grain of the Africans, and a considerable proportion is used as human food. It might be thought that a better use of the corn would be for the development of cattle, pig, and sheep farming. It is true that silage has been made regularly for Hereford and Friesian cattle on the better farms in the Standerton area, but this is far from general. The High Veld is indeed a great sheep area, but with Merino rather than mutton sheep. It would seem that the natural grasses of the High Veld are far from being as nutritious as they should be. It is believed that this is due to a lack of phosphorus, and that the comparatively poor quality of South African beef and mutton is in large measure due to this deficiency. It has been shown that a ration of bone meal or calcium phosphate can double the milk yield and more than double the market value of cattle or sheep intended for slaughter. In the meantime this has long been a corn-exporting region. The High Veld is dotted all over with its attractive little farms, each often sheltered by a plantation of pines or gum trees, or the Australian wattle, the bark of which

has a value in tanning leather. Many farms too have their apple orchards, and a windmill pumping water is an almost inevitable adjunct to the whole.

Edward Ackerman has expressed the view that even the relatively favored "maize triangle" is a problem area. More than three-quarters of the cultivated land of South Africa is inside the triangle, which has long been a one-crop region, though changing to mixed farming. Crop failures recur because of uncertain rainfall, with heavy summer thundershowers (when much-needed moisture is lost in runoff), high evaporation, and destructive hailstorms. The possibilities of crop failure do not encourage permanent investment in farm buildings, implements, or fertilizers. Plentiful early rains encourage shallow root systems, a liability for the plant if dry months follow.

Since 1951 the economic position has materially changed with the development of the new goldfields.

The Rand. Although this is not an agricultural land-use region in the same sense as those already described, the Rand, or correctly the Witwatersrand, is so distinctive that it merits separate consideration. It lies where the ancient rocks of the great complex crop out from beneath the Karoo beds which hide them farther south. It lies in fact between the High Veld properly speaking and the region of the northern Transvaal known generally as the Transvaal Bush Veld. As already described, it is the greatest gold-producing region of the world. The ore, extracted from depths of up to 9000 feet (2750 m), must be crushed by powerful machinery before the gold can be extracted by chemical means.

This implies large-scale organization with adequate capital. An essential factor in the development of the region has been the supplies of cheap coal from the great field which extends from the eastern end of the Rand over the edge of the plateau into Natal. The focal point of the Rand is the great modern city of Johannesburg (Figure 19.9), with a population of 1.4 million. East and west of Johannesburg are such industrial towns as Springs, Germiston, Benoni, Krugersdorp, Brakpan, and Boksburg, which together form the nearest approach in Africa to a conurbation.

Johannesburg was founded in 1886, and its progress was rapid. At first the surrounding veld was scarred by the huge dumps of waste white sand left after the gold-bearing banket was crushed and the gold extracted. But Johannesburg itself has been beautified by plantations of trees, notably Australian gum trees, which not only add character to the region but also are economically important as supplying pitprops and mining timber.

Rather naturally subsidiary industries have developed in the Rand, including chemicals, engineering works, and the preparation of agricultural products for food.

The Transvaal Bush Veld. This complex and interesting region occupies the northern two-thirds of the Transvaal between the Witwatersrand and the Limpopo River. There is thus a full range from the temperate climatic conditions characteristic of the high plateau at 6000 feet (1800 m) to the tropical climate of the Limpopo valley at under 2000 feet (600 m).

The gently rolling surface of the High Veld of the south gives place to a more broken and diversified relief where the older rocks outcrop. It is possible to distinguish a whole succession of low hill ranges, separated by relatively flat areas,

19.F Part of the great city of Johannesburg with its skyscrapers looking across to the mine dumps of white quartz in the background. (Courtesy of B.O.A.C.)

19.G Daveyton Bantu township near Benoni. One of the vast low-cost housing estates on the Witwatersrand. (Photo: South African Information Service.)

in fact a number of distinct physiographic regions in each of which a distinctive agricultural economy is developed.

The name Bush Veld suggests that here the treeless, grassy, High Veld gives place to a vegetation so characteristic of tropical Africa as a whole, here one with scattered bushes rather than trees. As the altitude drops towards the north, average temperatures become higher and the frost decreases until along the Limpopo itself frost is completely absent, or at least rare. In comparison with other parts of the Republic of South Africa this is a region of recent development.

Apart from the first modern iron smelting works in all Africa being at Pretoria, where smelting began early in 1934, there have been many other recent developments in the northern Transvaal. The completion of the railway through to the Limpopo River, which is crossed by the famous Beit Bridge, made it possible to work copper deposits at Messina. It was the intention that this railway should link up directly with the Rhodesian system, but the connecting link in Rhodesia has been long delayed, though the Beit Bridge is used by through road traffic. Changed commercial relationships following the Rhodesian unilateral declaration of independence and the subsequent economic sanctions are leading to a reconsideration of such a link.

Where communications make settlement attractive in the northern Transvaal have come the development of spacious orchards, the cultivation of cotton, tobacco, and peanuts, and the possibility of extensive development of other tropical or semitropical crops.

The Basuto Highlands. Returning to the southeastern margin of the High Plateau, the High Veld in the Orange Free State gives place southeastward, before the crest is reached, to country where the horizontal

19.H Citrus farms in the Rustenburg area. The farmhouse is of traditional Afrikaans design. (Photo: South African Information Services.)

Karoo sandstones, capped by resistant basaltic beds, reach elevations of 6000 feet (1800 m) and over, but where the land has been deeply dissected to form a series of precipitous crags and deep narrow valleys. Most of the country of this type lies outside both the Free State and the Cape Province and for the most part within the limits of Lesotho which is separately considered below.

The Eastern Uplands. Wellington uses this name—perhaps not a very satisfactory one—for the broad stretch of foothill country below the great escarpment, lying mainly in Natal, and including the middle veld.

The great scarp of the Drakensberg needs to be seen to be appreciated. Its highest point (incidentally the highest point in South Africa) is Giant's Castle, reaching over 11,000 feet (3350 m). There are forests in some parts, but many slopes are covered with grass, so that this area has been called the Mountain Grass Veld or Sourveld.

Basaltic rocks of the plateau cap the great scarp, and below are the almost horizontal Karoo beds with their seams of coal. It is, therefore, in this belt that the Natal coalfield has been developed, the focal point being the town of Newcastle. There is an obvious advantage that the export of coal to the Port of Durban is es-

sentially downhill, and gravity does much of the work of haulage.

Towards the coast the mountain grassveld stretches into what is sometimes called the grassveld and thorn bush veld, where much more cultivation is possible and where there is a very extensive population of Africans.

The Sourveld (where the word "sour" indicates the occurrence of grasses lacking in food value) gives place to a grassveld where the rooi grass is much more nutritious and where others have been introduced to provide even better grazing. To some extent this has become a dairying and even a beef-producing region. It includes the old land of the Zulus, Zululand. The staple food grain over much of the tract is "Kaffir corn" (sorghum), but Indian corn, or maize, is very extensively cultivated.

South Africa is a major world supplier of wattle bark for tanning, and 70 percent of the acreage of plantations is in the intermediate belt of Natal between 2000 and 4500 feet (600 and 1400 m) above sea level.

The Eastern Low Veld and Coastal Region. This is the coastal strip itself, and broadly can be taken to include the land below the 2000–foot (600 m) contour. Here frost becomes rare and near the coast completely absent. Although rainfall averages well over 40 inches (1000 mm), there is both seasonal and local variation; but everywhere rainfall is adequate for agriculture. Temperature variations on either side of a 70°F (21°C) annual average are low when compared with the plateau. At Durban, for example, the range is from 64 to 76°F (18 to 24°C). Both temperature and rainfall conditions are naturally most reliable near the coast itself. Though there are good alluvial soils in the valleys, elsewhere the ancient rocks with their granite intrusions which here outcrop give rise to some sandy and poor tracts. The whole region carries a heavy population, whether in the European areas of Natal or in Zululand and other areas occupied mainly by Africans. The development of commercial crops has laid emphasis on tropical products. Sugar cane comes first, and with its development South Africa became self-supporting in sugar. Now, with a production of well over a million tons of sugar, there is a surplus for export. Cotton is of some importance. Tropical fruits, citrus fruits, bananas, pineapples, and pawpaws are widely cultivated and sent to the interior parts of the country. Market gardening, the production of vegetables for consumption in the towns, has also extended greatly, and it is here that one sees the conflict between European and Indian.

Climatic conditions, British settlers, the introduction of fodder grasses and the local urban demand have combined to encourage a flourishing dairying industry so that a section of Natal has become the foremost dairying belt of South Africa.

Northward from Natal, the coastal belt passes into Portuguese East Africa, and Swaziland, which is separately described, lies inland. The Low Veld along the eastern margin of the Transvaal remained until World War I but little developed, and it is here that the enormous nature reserve, the Kruger National Park, is to be found.

The administrative center of Natal is Pietermaritzburg, founded as early as 1839. In size it is eclipsed by Durban (the port of Natal). The harbor of Durban is a natural bay of very considerable size with a narrow entrance which was formerly obstructed by a sand bar. This has in large part been removed by constant dredging, and the largest vessels using the Indian Ocean are able to dock alongside the quays adequately protected from the stormy seas of the South Indian Ocean. Durban has naturally become the principal coal (and mineral ore) exporting center of the Republic. It is the third town in order of size, and the population is roughly one-third African, one-third Indian, and one-third European. It still has a whaling industry.

The sandy coasts in the neighborhood form attractive holiday resorts, and surf bathing under adequate safeguards is as popular in South Africa as anywhere in the world. Safeguards are required against both sharks and strong undertow. Resorts like Warner Beach, with their crowds of sun- and surf-bathing Europeans, add a final touch, if such were needed, to South African contrasts. Although geographically Natal and the coastal regions have here been treated as a whole, it might have been more logical to describe separately the European areas and the African reserves.

MINING VERSUS AGRICULTURE IN SOUTH AFRICA

It is often urged that the economy of the Republic of South Africa is insecurely based because of its marked dependence upon the production of one commodity, which is gold. If for some reason or other world demand for gold should cease, it is argued that the whole country would find itself in a very precarious position. Gold accounts for up to a third of total exports and output is still increasing, although slowly.

It has been said with considerable truth that a tremendous part of South Africa's effort is directed towards digging gold out of the deep mines in the Witwatersrand for it to be buried, not quite so deeply, in vaults at Fort Knox, Zurich, and elsewhere. How long is this process likely to continue? Deeper mines and the exhaustion of the richer seams inevitably increase costs. A great question mark hangs over receipts in the form of the world price for gold. Determined efforts to hold down the price for monetary reasons or even to "demonatize" gold completely or in part could drastically affect receipts and therefore profitability. On the other hand, such policies could fail.

Fortunately the dependence of the economy on gold has been diminishing with the increasing production of other minerals and the rise of domestic manufacturing. The importance to exports of such minerals as uranium, diamonds, copper, asbestos, manganese, iron ore, chrome, coal, and antimony has already been mentioned so that although there is a heavy dependence upon minerals, they are in fact a highly diversified group. Domestic manufacturing makes the economy more self-reliant although politics deprives South Africa of the potential and obvious markets for its manufactures in the rest of Africa. The only concentration of industry on any scale in Africa is in the Republic of South Africa (Fig. 19.13).

In the meantime agricultural development proceeds steadily and against considerable difficulties. To a large extent South African agriculture is primarily the concern of the Afrikaans-speaking population (with the exception of the tropical products in Natal) whereas mining has become rather more the concern of the English-speaking section. This is admittedly only a very broad half-truth. Those who look to the future development of South Africa as bound up with agricultural production, though pointing to such factors as good sunshine records, are

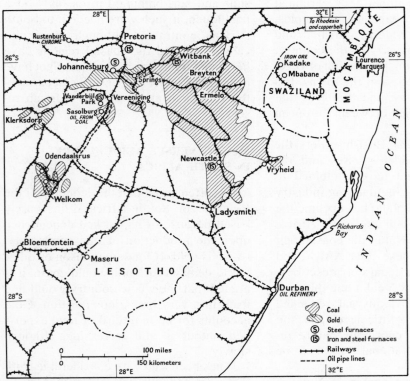

19.13 The South African industrial zone. Most coal mines are grouped in the Witbank, Newcastle-Ladysmith, Vryheid, and Breyton-Ermelo areas.

forced to recognize the numerous natural disadvantages – the inadequacy and irregularity of rainfall, the poverty of soils and liability to soil erosion, all of which combine to result in low and irregular yields. There is also the unsatisfactory labor position which many regard as being made worse rather than better by the restrictive racial legislation. If, however, South Africa is forced to rely more than in the past on agricultural production, this account should have made it clear that there are considerable possibilities, especially in parts of the country still largely underdeveloped. Thus the lines of future development in the Republic of South Africa would seem to rest especially with (1) the development of irrigation, (2) the control of soil erosion, (3) the introduction of fodder crops and nutritious grasses which have proved so successful in New Zealand, and the consequent development of more intensive mixed farming with high yields of crops, meat, milk, and other products. Long discussed, a vast project to regulate the Orange River has been started. This includes the construction of a tunnel $51\frac{1}{2}$ miles long to divert water into the Fish River and the eventual irrigation of an extra 700,000 acres.

Nothing has been said in the foregoing account of the important fisheries around the coasts of South Africa, which are described in detail in a paper by Peter Scott.[6] The author concluded: "Unlike other areas of the world's fisheries, South African coastal waters could be far more intensively fished than at present without depleting resources." He commended a longterm program of survey and research, since fishing had previously been restricted to certain areas only. The home consumption of fish in the country was only 7 pounds per head per annum. Existing taboos against the eating of fish held by many Bantu tribes are doubtless des-

tined to disappear. There is little doubt that the health of these people, who suffer seriously from protein deficiency, would be improved by the addition of fish to their diet. Since Scott wrote, the industry has expanded enormously, and South Africa is the largest producer of fish in the Southern Hemisphere. Together with Southwest Africa 7500 fishermen and a further 20,000 employed on shore handle over 2 million tons of fish annually – notably, pilchard, maasbanker, and mackerel. Much is converted to fishmeal and oil or is canned. Trawlers, especially from Cape Town, land the bulk of fish consumed locally. The three other ports concerned are Port Elizabeth, East London, and Mossel Bay. The bulk of the fish caught is known as "stock fish," otherwise Cape hake, which is a cold-water species, closely allied to the European hake. It is obtained by trawling in the cold waters off the southwest coast. The other principal fish is the Agulhas sole, representing 5 percent by weight, but 16 percent by value. Rock lobster or crayfish, of which the tails are exported frozen or canned, are much appreciated in many parts of the world. The abundant supplies of fish off South Africa have also attracted fishing by many other countries from such distant parts of the world as Japan and Russia among many others.

COMMUNICATIONS IN SOUTH AFRICA

South Africa is well served by an excellent railway system, despite the fact that the guage is only 3 feet, 6 inches (1.07 m). The first railway from Cape Town to Wellington was begun in 1859 since when some 14,000 miles (22,500 km) of railroad has been constructed in the Union. The railways and harbors are owned and controlled by the government, being administered by a special department. South Africa may be quoted as a good example of the excellent results which may be achieved with a narrow gauge and unified control.

---

[6] "The Otter Trawl Fisheries of South Africa," *Geog. Rev.*, XXXIX (1949) pp. 529–551.

At first the construction of lines from Cape Town was based partly on strategic considerations; then it was dictated by the discovery of the gold of the Rand and the diamonds at Kimberley, and later by the need to develop productive or potentially productive agricultural regions and to provide a comprehensive network to all habitable parts of the country. The later functions are clear from the special arrangements made by the railways for the handling of coal direct from the collieries to the wharves in the main harbors. The construction of a series of maize elevators in the corn-growing districts and at the ports was undertaken to secure ease and economy in handling one of the principal agricultural exports of the country. In comparison with the rest of Africa the Republic is fortunate in its adequate and accessible reserves of coal. This has not prevented the extensive use of electrification, and Natal was able to boast one of the earliest and longest stretches of electrified main line in the world.

The railway map now shows how the lines serve the four main ports of South Africa—Cape Town, Port Elizabeth, East London, and Durban—and also the eastern Transvaal with its natural outlet at the Portuguese port of Lourenço Marques. These lines leading to the main ports have now been joined up in such a way as to give a reasonable network, but it is still a tortuous journey, for example, from Cape Town to Port Elizabeth by rail. The concentration of development on the four main ports has meant that in many years the trade passing through the minor ports, such as Mossel Bay, Port Nolloth, Simonstown, and Knysna, is less than 1 percent of the whole.

By comparison with the countries of tropical Africa, the Republic stands out as being served with a network of railroads rather than isolated systems and by the much greater extent of roads with a tarred rather than a gravel surface. This reflects the nature of the economy which is more commercial, industrial, urbanized, and

wealthy. National income per head is estimated by the United Nations to average over three times the average for Africa (in 1963, $396 compared with $120).

SOUTHWEST AFRICA (SUIDWES AFRIKA OR NAMIBIA)

This vast territory, totaling nearly one-third of a million square miles (800,000 km²), occupies the drier side of the continent from the arid scrublands of the Botswana border to the absolute desert or Namib which parallels the Atlantic Ocean from the mouth of the Orange River northward to the lower course of the Cunene River, which forms the frontier with Angola. Throughout the whole of this stretch no permanent watercourse reaches the ocean. The southern tropic runs through the heart of the country in such a way that a larger area lies to the north within the tropics than south outside the tropics. Only locally, as near Windhoek, does the African plateau rise to suficient heights to cause marked amelioration of the hot dry climate. The white population in 1970 was only 90,000 out of a total of 749,000 (70,000 in 1960)although they dominate the economy. The average of all inhabitants over the whole territory is under two per square mile.

It is believed that this territory was inhabited at an early date by wandering Bushmen, who some six or seven centuries ago were replaced along the coastal regions by Hottentots. They were followed in due course by the Ovambos, and early in the eighteenth century by the Hereros. The last were checked in their southern movement by the Hottentots under a leader known generally as Jonker Afrikaner, who has since become a legendary figure. Living near the banks of the Orange River, he organized the Hottentots, equipped them with firearms, and became their leader and champion until his death in 1860, when the Hereros succeeded in forcing the Hottentots southward.

As early as 1486 Bartolomeu Dias landed at Angra Pequena, now known as Luderitz, and erected a cross to record his landing. Later travelers recorded that the Hereros in the area had great herds of cattle, and it was in 1792 that the Dutch took possession of the chief natural harbor of the coast, Walvis Bay.

In 1805 missionaries of German nationality, though in the service of the London Missionary Society, established missions in Namaqualand. It was an American shipmaster, Captain B. Morrell, who in 1828–1830 explored the coast, made journeys into the interior, and drew attention to the deposits of guano on the islands off the coast. This led to the exploitation of these guano islands in 1843–1845, and to their annexation by Britain between 1861 and 1867. In the following year, 1868, the great German leader, Bismarck, became interested in the area and asked whether the British government was prepared to safeguard the lives and properties of German missionaries. The British reply was noncommittal, though a few years later the Cape government sent a special commissioner who fixed limits for the territories of the two chief tribes, the Namaquas and Damaras.

A couple of years later, in 1878, Walvis Bay was annexed by Britain. In the 1880's, when Germans were active in so many parts of Africa, a German merchant, Luderitz by name, acquired land south of Walvis Bay and soon after purchased the harbor of Angra Pequena where, with the approval of Bismarck, the German flag was hoisted. This led naturally to the annexation by Germany of the whole territory north of the Orange River, excepting only Walvis Bay and the guano islands. The German government took over responsibility for the administration of the territory from the German company, the Deutsche Kolonial Gesellschaft. Jonker Afrikaner's old headquarters were made the seat of administration and renamed Windhoek.

The Germans were subsequently concerned with long and costly wars with the Hereros and Hottentots, but it was the discovery of diamonds on the Luderitz Bay coast in 1908 which showed the whole potential importance of this arid area.

When World War I broke out, the Germans advanced into Union territory but were quickly countered by Union forces under General Botha; on July 9, 1915, the German army surrendered. In 1919, at the end of World War I, the League of Nations granted a mandate to the Union of South Africa to administer the area, which became known as the Territory of Southwest Africa. Germans, including all officials, were repatriated. This was a Class 3 mandate, under which the territory was to be administered as an integral part of the territory of the Mandatory Power. The South African government has subsequently refused to recognize the competence of the United Nations over the territory and has incorporated it within the Republic. The United Nations has officially placed the mandate in the hands of its Council for Namibia. The security and apartheid systems of the Republic were extended to Southwest Africa in 1966, retrospective to 1950 and ten "ethnic homelands" are planned for the majority of the population. The largest of these is that for the Ovamba, a Bantu people numbering around 270,000 living in the north of the territory—and into Angola—who have been allocated 16,220 square miles (42,010 km²).

The country as a whole is essentially a stock-raising country, scarcity of water and poor rainfall rendering agriculture virtually impossible. Rainfall improves towards the north where a limited agriculture of uncertain harvests of sorghum is possible. The capital is at Windhoek on the central plateau where altitudes in excess of 5000 feet (1500 m) moderate the summer temperatures and provide better grazing. Between 3 and 4 million sheep and goats and more than 2 million cattle exist in the area, and considerable attention has been paid to the improvement of the quality of cattle and to the production of butter for home consumption and export. An important product is Karakul pelts, a valued fur in temperate lands. The area producing diamonds has been steadily expanded, and their recovery from alluvial sands and gravels takes place over a 300-mile (480 km) stretch of the coastline from the Orange River northward together with some offshore dredging. In the north of the country ores of vanadium (important), tin, lithium, lead, copper, and zinc are worked, the last three especially from the Tsumeb mine. Walvis Bay, the chief port, is linked by railway with the main South African system at De Aar Junction. Within the territory of Southwest Africa are over 1400 miles of railway of the South African 3 feet, 6 inches gauge. The railway administration also operates well-developed road-motor services, covering several thousand miles of road.

Despite aridity it is clear that Southwest Africa is far from being an unimportant area. There are some parts where subterranean water can be reached by wells, and this makes possible the extension of cattle rearing. Salt is obtained from some of the salt pans in the Kalahri, which occupies the northern and eastern parts of the country. Export figures are not collected separately from those of the Republic but commercial production is divided between those from livestock (live cattle to the Republic, fresh and canned meat, wool and karakul pelts), from mining (especially the Tsumeb complex ores) and from fishing (canned pilchards, fishmeal, fish oil, and rock lobsters). Considerable development should follow from the agreement with Portugal to utilize the Cunene River. A hydroelectric station is to be built at Ruacana and an irrigation scheme is to be supplied.

THE FORMER HIGH COMMISSION TERRITORIES OF SOUTH AFRICA

Within the area which may broadly be called South Africa are three territories which for various reasons remain distinct from the four countries which united in 1910 to form the Union of South Africa. They were placed under the direct protection of the British government in London which was represented by a High Commissioner who was also the United Kingdom Ambassador in South Africa.

LESOTHO

The story of this little mountain state reads more like a romantic historical novel than a story from real life. Its foundation dates from the troubled times of 1820 when the Bantu, including the Zulus, Matabele, and Korannas, were sweeping southward from central Africa, exterminating all those who stood in their path. A warrior named Moshesh welcomed refugees fleeing from the invaders and constituted himself their leader. The territory he chose was well suited for guerilla warfare; it stretches westward from the edge of the Drakensberg and is for the most part more than 6000 feet (1800 m) above sea level. Only the western border and the westward-draining valleys are at a lower elevation. Moshesh succeeded in building up what was almost unique in Africa: a nation as opposed to a tribe. In due course the Voortrekkers reached the country (1835–1837), and Moshesh took a hand in the troubled political relationships between the Boers and the Cape government. The latter was anxious to avoid trouble, and when action had to be taken in 1852 Moshesh was too good for the punitive force. The British abandoned the territory. The local Boers constituted it an independent Boer republic, but their attitude towards the Basutos was such that the chief appealed to Britain for help. So Britain intervened, and in 1869 Basutoland became a British Territory under the direct protection of the British government in London. When the Union of South Africa was formed by the South Africa Act of 1909, provision was made for the transfer of Basutoland to the

Union, but the inhabitants showed no wish to come under the Union. In 1966, Basutoland became independent under the title of the kingdom of Lesotho.

Lesotho has few assets. Its greatest advantage at one time was its mountainous relief which gave refuge against both Zulu and Boer but provides little arable land to support today's dense population. Cattle supplied to the Republic and wool and mohair exported overseas form the majority of exports, although the narrow strip of farmland along the western border yields a surplus of wheat as well as of peas and beans. An attempt is being made to establish deciduous fruit — cherries and pears. The only minerals of note are diamond deposits with a growing production. Although its position as an enclave of the Republic of South Africa has political disadvantages, Lesotho obtains some economic benefit from the remittances home of the Sotho who have gone to work, especially in the gold mines and collieries, of their rich neighbor. At the census of 1966, out of a *de jure* population of just under a million, over 100,000 were in the Republic and remittances from workers to Lesotho for the Year 1968/69 were estimated at nearly $3\frac{1}{2}$ million dollars. Lesotho also hopes to "sell" water from

19.I A man of Lesotho wearing a traditional hat and blanket and riding a horse — which is quite common because of the availability of healthy pasture. They are particularly useful in this mountainous land, the dissected sediments and lavas apparent in the distance. (Photo: R. Lamb, Camera Press.)

the Basutu highlands to the Republic where urbanization and the ever increasing demands of industry are in need of it. Following independence, the economy was sustained by and from Britain at the rate of about $12 million a year.

The capital, Maseru, is located in the less mountainous zone close to the border with the Republic of South Africa, and is connected to its railway system. At Roma is the growing University of Botswana, Lesotho, and Swaziland, serving those three countries and providing an African alternative to the racially segregated education of the Republic.

SWAZILAND

Swaziland[7] was settled in the early part of the nineteenth century by the Swazis, who had retreated northward in the face of Boer settlement only to find themselves menaced by the warlike Zulu raiders. It was at a time when British prestige was high; Mswazi, the Swazi chief, sent a deputation to Theophilus Shepstone seeking protection. Shepstone used his influence with Mpande, the Zulu chief, to such good effect that the Swazis and the Zulus have remained ever since on friendly terms. Mswazi died in 1868. Both he and his successor Mbandeni made numerous "concessions" to individual prospectors with the result that the country was overrun by undesirable characters, often in conflict. Again came an appeal to the British in 1887, but this time it was in vain. So the chief simply appointed the son of old Theophilus Shepstone as his resident adviser! There followed a short period of self-government by European residents with Swazi consent, then administration by the South African Republic, then by the Transvaal until 1907. Swaziland then entered a period of being administered by its own paramount chief with a resident British commissioner. In

[7] D. M. Doveton, *The Human Geography of Swaziland,* Institute of British Geographers, Publication 8, 1937.

1924 the Swazis objected strongly to the suggestion that their territory should be incorporated in the Union of South Africa, and in 1968 the country became independent. The country has an area of 6705 square miles (17,400 km²) and a population at the census of 1966 of 389,492.

By comparison with Lesotho, Swaziland has a lower density of population and much greater natural resources. The country extends from the high veld [4000 feet (1200 m)] in the west where it borders on the Transvaal down to the low veld of the Mozambique border. It is not entirely surrounded by the Republic and has direct and convenient access to the major port of Lourenço Marques in Mozambique. Sugar is grown under irrigation in the low veld and provides a major export. Other major cash crops include citrus fruit, also with supplementary irrigation, and cotton. Timber and wood pulp are exported from large plantations of pine and eucalyptus in the high veld. Ecological conditions provide a variety of agricultural possibilities but land use has also been powerfully affected by a division of the land between that in customary tenure and mostly used in subsistence farming, based especially

on maize or pasture, and that under individual, freehold title. The latter derives from concessions to Europeans, especially Afrikaners, made in the past and now the principal source of commercial production but also representing a political irritant.

Geological conditions are also varied and this is reflected in the mining industry. Most of the country consists of Archaen rocks of the African shield and this yields asbestos and iron ore. Asbestos has for long been a leading export from the Havelock mine in the west of the country, with a new working nearby. More important, however, has been the exploitation since 1964 of the haematite iron ore of Ngurenya, near the capital of Mbabane, for export to Japan. Not only is the value of the export greater, but it required the construction of the railway to Lourenço Marques. This is of general benefit to the economy but it also led to the opening up of the Mpaka coal mine to supply the railroad and to a subsequent small export trade. The coal is derived from rocks of Karoo age in the low veld.

Further plans for the economic advancement of Swaziland include the increased utilization of the Usutu river

19.J Some of the extensive plantations in Swaziland (Photo: Paul Popper.)

system for hydroelectric power and irrigation.

BOTSWANA

Botswana is as large as the whole of France and thus much more extensive than the other two territories.

Unlike Lesotho, which is entirely surrounded by Republic territory, and Swaziland, which is essentially an enclave of the eastern Transvaal, the third of the former British High Commission territories in southern Africa, Botswana, stretches away northward from the Cape Province and the Transvaal to occupy a huge area in the heart of the continent only separated from the Zambezi itself by a narrow tongue, known as the Caprivi Strip, which was ceded to Southwest Africa. To the northeast is Rhodesia and a point where the boundaries of Botswana, Rhodesia, Southwest Africa, and Zambia meet. The southern boundary is the Molopo River, a nonpermanent stream which drains or should drain to the Orange. The southern half of the country is essentially the Kalahari "Desert," without any surface streams; the northern half is in the basin of Lake Ngami and the Okovango swamp, from which the water overflows in favorable seasons to the Zambezi. We may, therefore, regard northern Botswana as lying in the Zambezi basin.

Few political divisions in Africa coincide either with natural features or frontiers between tribes, and Botswana is no exception. The southern part of the land of the Bechuanas lies in the Cape Province of the South African Republic. The country south of the Molopo was first declared a British crown colony under the title of British Bechuanaland, and a protectorate was established over the northern area by agreement with the leading chiefs. In 1895 the British area was incorporated in Cape Colony and today forms part of Cape Province. The protectorate was administered for a short time by the South Africa Company, but the chiefs protested and in 1896 the protectorate came under the direct administration of London. The Protectorate of Bechuanaland became the sovereign state of Botswana in 1966. In 1896–1897 the Bechuanaland Railway Company constructed the line linking South Africa with Rhodesia. It runs through the entire length of eastern Botswana and makes the country an essential link in African communications. The railroad runs through the zone of higher rainfall and of greatest population concentration, with the best grazing and some possibility of subsistence agriculture based on maize and sorghum. It was here that the new capital was built at Gaborone. The Protectorate had been administered from Mafeking, within the Republic and in deciding where to locate the capital, the choice was clearly limited to a site which was on the railway and near a perennial river which could be dammed for a water supply. Although placed on one edge of the country, the distribution of rainfall and therefore of population is such that a third of the population of Botswana lives within 90 miles (145 km) of Gaborone.

Eight different Bantu tribes, each with an elaborate tribal organization, inhabit Botswana together with a few nomadic Bushmen and some Damaras who fled from the Germans in Southwest Africa before the 1914–1918 war. Most of the usable country is in eight territories within which land is held under traditional systems.

Over that greater part of the protectorate which coincides with the Kalahari, misnamed a desert, the fine yellow Kalahari sand is an almost universal covering of the surface. The African population is mainly in the eastern half of the country, leaving 60,000 square miles (155,000 km²) in two large areas of State Lands. These have practically no population because there is no surface water but might be made suitable for large-scale ranching. The first need would be deep wells to provide watering points for cattle. There is need of fencing for control of grazing because overstocking for even a short time could begin a dust bowl and serious erosion. The natural grasses are said to be excellent in some places and at least edible in others, but droughts occur about one year in every three so that other fodder, best provided by hay in good years, must be available. All this clearly means large-scale operation; there is real danger of land damage in small-scale ranching or private ownership. Just as most of the country suffers from lack of water, so the northwest corner, the tsetse-fly-infested Okovango swamps, suffers from too much. There development is possible only with improved communications as well as control of water and the provision of incentives to the inhabitants—the Batswana.[8] The Okovango River rises in the Angola plateau where there is a good summer rainfall and after a course of some 800 miles (1300 km) enters the Ngami depression by the Popa Falls. There its waters spread out into a great swamp towards Lake

[8] The views expressed here are those of Frank Debenham; see *Geography*, XXXVI (1951) pp. 107–109. See also Chapter 18 p. 361.

Ngami, which lies at the southern end of this inland delta. Lake Ngami is being steadily invaded by thorn bush and is a mere fragment of the lake Livingstone saw. At times waters from the swamps and lake escape southeastward to the Makarikari depression (which has water only after floods), the lowest part of the northern Kalahari. At other times it seems that the waters of the Okovango escape into the Linyoti swamps and so into the Zambezi. Apparently the Zambezi is capturing the waters of the Okovango. Whatever may be the exact hydrological relationships, these swamplands are potential rich farmlands if the same methods can be applied as were used by the French in the Inland Niger delta.

Unfortunately the potentially mineral-bearing Precambrian platform is masked over most of Botswana by thick layers of Kalahari sands. In the northeast, however, it is exposed and here there have been promising prospects of copper, nickel, and other minerals, and rich diamondiferous pipes which are being exploited at Orapa.

Further Reading

The wealth of South Africa and the long tradition of its universities is reflected in its large scientific literature. The two standard texts are J. H. Wellington's *Southern Africa* (Cambridge, England: Cambridge University Press, 1955, 2 Vols.) and Monica Cole's *South Africa* (London: Methuen, 1961). Covering a large portion of Africa and serving as an illustration of some principles in geomorphology is *The Scenery of South Africa* (London, 1963) by Lester C. King. A lucid analysis in economic geography concentrating especially on southern Africa is *Development in Africa* (Johannesburg: Witwatersrand University Press, 1962) by L. P. Green and T. J. D. Fair. The long and fateful history of the Republic is set against the natural conditions and human dispositions in *An Historical Geography of South Africa* by N. C. Pollock and Swanzie Agnew (London: Longmans, 1963). An informed and humane discussion of the question of black and white is contained in "Southern Africa: bonds and barriers in a multi-racial region" by T. J. D. Fair in *A Geography of Africa* (London: Routledge and Kegan Paul, 1969), edited by R. Mansell Prothero. Much basic data is presented in the *Atlas of South Africa* (Pretoria: Government Printer, 1960), edited by A. M. and W. J. Talbot.

CHAPTER 20

African Seas and Islands

CONTINENTAL AND OCEANIC ISLANDS

Emphasis has already been placed upon the uninterrupted character of so much of the coast of Africa. The absence of deep bays and gulfs is a marked feature, and associated with this smoothness of so much of the African coastline is the absence of islands, which are to be found in such numbers bordering the coasts of other continents. Geographers commonly distinguish between continental islands and oceanic islands. Those belonging to the first group rise from the continental shelf at no great distance from the mainland. They are associated structurally with the neighboring parts of the mainland, and consequently the environmental conditions which they offer to human inhabitants differ but little from those of the neighboring shores. Oceanic islands, on the other hand, frequently rising from great ocean depths and cut off from the continental masses by stretches of water which are commonly both deep and wide, may bear no close relationship with the continental masses, and are not infrequently the summits of submarine volcanoes or the higher peaks of otherwise submerged mountain ranges.

Africa has but few continental islands or groups of islands and but few oceanic islands in the neighboring seas. But members of both groups have in Africa assumed a rather special significance.

CONTINENTAL ISLANDS

The coastlands of Africa have been described earlier in this book as inhospitable. Their inhospitality in the physical sense is particularly marked where large stretches of desert shore are fringed by sandy coastlands, against which pound the oceanic rollers in everlasting lines of surf. Through these breakers boats propelled by hand—for the larger modern vessels cannot approach within miles—make their way in constant danger of damage or destruction.

Other stretches of the coastline are backed by mangrove swamps, in turn giving place to thick forests affording constant cover to enemies. It is not surprising that those who sought to explore or establish trading relationships with the peoples of Africa, approaching the continent by sea, placed particular value on any natural inlet which might serve as a haven.

Later, when they sought to establish bases from which to carry on their trading, whether the nefarious slave trade or more legitimate efforts at commerce, it is obvious that they would choose easily defensible sites. Some such sites are afforded by rocky promontories, sheltering some bay to serve as a harbor, with land approaches which could be defended with relative ease. Considerations of this sort entered into the choice of sites for such settlements as Dakar in Senegal, or even Freetown in Sierra Leone. It is not surprising that maritime peoples approaching by sea, used to life on the sea and able to use their ships for escape purposes in case of need, favored especially the use of continental islands close to the coasts for their trading settlements. Examples are numerous around the coasts of Africa.

With the development in modern times of peaceful trading relationships these island sites have often proved inconvenient for establishing lines of communication with the interior, as with Gorée. In some cases the best has been made of a bad job. In other cases, new settlements have been chosen and developed. An interesting example of an island site is afforded by Bathurst, the capital of Gambia, built on an island at the entrance to the Gambia River and consequently developed with difficulties which have not yet been fully overcome in an attempt to improve communications with the interior. In Portuguese Africa and Nigeria are examples of settlements on islands, where the irregular swampy coast still remains undeveloped. Lagos is on an island in a sheltered lagoon, but what might have originally been a good choice has necessitated the construction of deep-water wharves and the commercial terminus of the railways into the heart of Nigeria on the opposite mainland at Apapa.

Elsewhere around the coasts of Africa are examples of larger islands which have served, and some which continue to serve to this day, as more extensive bases for European powers. Spain was for a long time in possession of Fernando Póo; Portugal remains in possession of the islands of São Tomé and Principe. The British occupancy of the Guano Islands off the southwest African coast (now Southwest Africa) had a different objective, the recovery of a substance of economic importance.

But the general story is repeated along the east coast of Africa, where islands are few but of considerable importance. The large and relatively fertile island of Zanzibar and its neighbor Pemba formed the base from which the sultans of Zanzibar exercised control over very large stretches of the mainland. Subsequently, in World War I, during the campaigns against German East Africa, British troops from India landed on and used the island of Mafia. The great Arab stronghold and port of the east coast, Mombasa, was built on an island, which again has presented certain difficulties in the development of the railway system through Kenya to Uganda.

Farther north a very interesting example of the changing importance of islands is offered by the tiny island of Perim in the midst of the narrow entrance to the Red Sea. Like so many islands of strategic importance, its significance was appreciated by Britain in the days of imperial expansion. Perim became a naval base, a signals station, a point for recoaling and refueling. But with their increasing size, warships and merchant ships were no longer able to use its limited facilities. Its functions were transferred to the port of Aden on the mainland coast of Arabia, another defensible position, but one with a harbor of magnificent size and depth.

There are other groups of islands farther removed from the coasts of Africa which may still be considered continental islands. In the northern Atlantic Ocean, lying off the northwest African coasts, are the Canaries. These partly volcanic islands with their rich soil, favorable climate, and moderate, well-distributed winter rainfall and abundant sunshine proved attractive to the Spaniards. The islands are administered as an integral part of Spain. The existence of natural harbors, or harbors improved without difficulty to meet the needs of modern vessels, has led to the use of Santa Cruz de Tenerife and Las Palmas as ports of call for ocean liners from Europe bound for South America or South Africa.

The important island of Madeira, farther off the continental shores of the northwest, long in the hands of Portugal, provides an alternative, again with a good harbor, at Funchal. Like the Canaries, Madeira is an island intensely productive and extremely attractive climatically and scenically. In the early days of exploration and of trading with merchant vessels equipped only with sails, the group of the Azores, much farther out into the Atlantic, afforded like and equally important facilities, immortalized in the lines, "At Flores in the Azores Sir Richard Grenville lay" and the story of the *Revenge*. But they are in the latitude of Portugal, not of Africa.

Nearer the coasts of desert Africa are the Cape Verde Islands, climatically much more arid and less favored for settlement, whose significance therefore has tended to wane with the passing of time. These are almost the only groups of islands in the Atlantic.

In the Indian Ocean special attention must of course be given to the great island of Madagascar. Excluding the island continent of Australia and the great island of Greenland, Madagascar can claim to be one of the largest islands in the world. Although it is structurally connected with continental Africa, it is a subcontinent which has had a long story of development of its own. Associated with Madagascar to the north are several groups of islands, but of no very great importance.

OCEANIC ISLANDS

In the midst of the Atlantic Ocean there are several truly oceanic islands, far re-

moved from land, notably Ascension, St. Helena, and the Tristan da Cunha group. It might be thought that mention of these has no place in a book on Africa, but, in the days when exploration of the African coastlands was still actively taking place, these oceanic islands had an immense significance as ports of call, as havens of refuge in time of storm or other need, and as stepping stones on far-flung ocean routes. They took on a new significance with the development of submarine electric telegraph cables, when some of them became cable stations. For a brief period it seemed that the development of transoceanic air transport would bring them once more into permanent prominence, but increases in the speed and range of aircraft soon enabled them to be bypassed.

In the wide expanses of the Southern Ocean there are other islands which again have strategic importance and a significance in the whaling industry.

In the Indian Ocean islands are far more numerous, but certain ones, notably Reunion, Mauritius, and the Seychelles, have played a part comparable with that of the oceanic islands of the Atlantic. Mauritius and Reunion are sufficiently large to have a permanent existence and life of their own.

No excuse need be offered, therefore, for a consideration of at least some of the features of these islands which lie in the oceans around the African continent.

THE AZORES

The three groups of islands making up the Azores have a total area of a little over 900 square miles (2300 km²) and a population of approximately 350,000. They lie well out in the Atlantic between latitudes 37° and 39°, which is in the extratropical high-pressure belt, but far enough north to receive an adequate rainfall from the winter cyclones of the westerly wind belt. They are volcanic, and the peaks of the old volcanoes reach considerable elevations, for example, 7610 feet (2320 m) in Pico, so that the islands attract a sufficient relief rainfall to prevent serious drought. The chief town and port of Ponta Delgada is on the largest island, São Miguel, on which are over half of the total population.

The islands produce, in adequate quantities for the people, foodstuffs such as cereals, fruits, wine, cattle products, and fish, and there is a small trade with Portugal, which lies almost due east. The scenery and climate are attractive to tourists, but the islands are somewhat off main ocean routeways.

MADEIRA (OR THE MADEIRAS)

This group consists of the one large island, Madeira itself, about 300 square miles (800 km²) in area, and four smaller ones.

Farther south than the Azores, the dry summer season is longer, the period of winter rainfall shorter. But again the volcanic rocks of Madeira rise to 6100 feet (1860 m), and a considerable relief rainfall results even at Funchal, on the southern coast, where the average is 30 inches (760 mm). The climate, with abundant sunshine even in the winter, and the scenery are both delightful, so that very large numbers of residents have been attracted to Madeira to live their years of retirement.

The once forested hillslopes, which might easily suffer from very serious soil erosion, have been carefully terraced. Attractive little houses, each with a terraced garden resplendent throughout the year with flowers, climb up the hillsides in the vicinity both of Funchal and of other settlements.

Careful cultivation yields abundant harvests of wheat and barley, but it is for its fruits—its pineapples and bananas, and particularly its grapes—that Madeira is famous. The Madeira wine, for so long a specialty of the island, is only one of the types which are made.

Though the local handcrafts, such as lace making and the making of cane chairs, are maintained to a large extent for the benefit of the numerous passing

20.A Terracing on the steep slopes of Madeira. (Copyright: Geographical Publications Lt.)

20.B The major industry of the Canary Islands has become tourism. La Canteras Beach at Las Palmas, Grand Canary. (Photo: Barnaby/Gerald Clyde.)

tourists, they form a lucrative sideline for the peasant population. Clearly also Madeira has a strategic significance in its position. The old treaties of friendship which have existed between Portugal and Britain for the past two centuries form the basis on which rather special commercial relationships have been established between Madeira and Britain, and it was in full accord with this tradition of friendship that Britain obtained temporary air bases in the Azores during World War II, when Portugal remained neutral.

THE CANARIES

The Canaries form a larger group of seven main islands, again of volcanic origin, with a total area of 2800 square miles (7250 km²) and a population of nearly a million. On the island of Tenerife the dormant snow-capped volcano, Pico de Teide, rises in a magnificent cone to a height of over 12,000 feet (3718 m). As a

result of these elevations rainfall may be considerable on higher ground, though near the coast on the eastern sides of the islands it may fall to 10 inches (250 mm) or less. In addition, the drying harmattan blows from the African mainland, which is nearer than in the case of Madeira.

Shrubby Mediterranean vegetation with numerous succulent plants is found on the hillslopes, though Mediterranean trees such as the holm oak (*Quercus ilex*) are found in the damper areas. Again careful cultivation, especially with irrigation, has made possible the cultivation of cereals and vegetables, notably onions for home use, together with olives, citrus fruits, and tobacco. A small and very sweet variety of banana, which is much liked in European markets, has been very specially developed.

Again there is an extensive tourist trade. Santa Cruz, on the island of Tenerife is rivaled as a tourist center and a port of call for steamers by Las Palmas, which is located on the northeastern coast of the island of Gran Canaria and has an excellent modern harbor developed on the eastern side of a tombolo.

The delightful smaller island of Palma is essentially the top of a single extinct volcano with a huge blown-out crater. Less frequently visited, it is an island of great beauty inhabited by a cheerful agricultural peasantry.

The Canaries form an integral part of Spain, just as the Madeiras are administered as an integral part of Portugal.

THE CAPE VERDE ISLANDS

Ten islands and a few islets form the Cape Verde Islands, a Portuguese colony, covering over 1500 square miles (4000 km²), and with a population of about 200,000. Being situated in latitude 15° to 17° due west of St. Louis in Senegal, they lie in the belt of the trade winds throughout the year and are extremely dry. The total rainfall, between 5 and 10 inches (125 and 250 mm), falls mainly in August, September, and October, in contrast to the Mediterranean rainfall of the Canaries or Madeira.

Sisal, a vegetable oil, purgeira, resembling castor oil, oranges, and a little coffee are among the agricultural products produced in excess of local requirements.

The capital of the islands is Praia, but the chief port, a former coaling station mainly used by vessels on the South American run, is São Vincente.

ASCENSION

Ascension is an isolated volcanic island in the South Atlantic less than 8° South of the equator, but no less than 700 miles (1100 km) from its neighbor to the southeast, St. Helena, and a still greater distance from the African coast.

It was occupied by the British in 1815, and its importance was as a haven or refuge in case of need by vessels of the British fleet. Consequently it was for a long time controlled by the British admiralty and organized as if it were a battleship, governed by a British naval officer. In 1922 it became a part of the colony of St. Helena.

Ascension takes its name from the fact that it was discovered by the Portuguese on Ascension Day in 1501. The several volcanic cones of which it is formed have rocks colored red and brown, but the central and highest one, rising to 2817 feet (859 m), owes its name, Green Mountain, and its covering of vegetation to the mists which frequently clothe the summit and a relief rainfall exceeding 30 inches (760 mm). This is in striking contrast to the arid and often bare lava surfaces occupying the lower levels of the island.

It became and still is a cable station, and the handful of people living there are all employees of the British Cable and Wireless Limited, now under government control.

In World War II it suddenly became again of immense strategic importance. An airstrip of the size suitable for the largest transport planes, together with the necessary buildings, was built by the American forces and became known as Wideawake Field. When the American forces left the island in 1947, transatlantic air transport had already become virtually independent of such stepping stones. Radio has made cable communication out of date so that this question almost automatically arises: is there a future for this little island of 34 square miles (88 km²), other than as a breeding ground for the sooty tern, which comes to Ascension three times in every two years to lay its eggs, or the sea turtles, which use the warm sands for the same purpose between January and May? It has a possible temporary function in the United States rocket testing through the South Atlantic.

ST. HELENA

St. Helena, though only slightly larger—47 square miles (122 km²)—than

Ascension and similarly an isolated volcano, with its peak rising to 2500 feet (823 m), is by comparison an important island. It too was discovered by the Portuguese, in 1502. It too is just a rocky top of a gigantic volcanic pile resting on the floor of the Atlantic Ocean, but St. Helena has been British for over 300 years, since 1571, and has a greater importance for several reasons. Its position in 16° South is right in the path of the southeast trade winds, so that the island was of utmost importance as a haven of refuge in the days of sailing ships. It was first occupied by the East India Company for the benefit of their ships rounding the Cape of Good Hope to India. Naturally the port and chief settlement, called Jamestown, is on the sheltered northwestern side of the island.

When vessels began to use coal it became a coaling station, especially for the ships of the British navy. It is 1200 miles (1900 km) from the nearest point, the Port of Moçâmedes, on the African mainland, and its very isolation led to its being used as a base for whalers. It is now, however, too far from the chief whaling grounds to serve this function.

The first time that the British captured Napoleon Bonaparte of France he was imprisoned on Elba, off the coast of Italy, and escaped. The second time, after his defeat at Waterloo in 1815, the British took no chances, and he lived a prisoner on St. Helena until his death in 1821. St. Helena is famous, therefore, as the place of exile of perhaps the most dangerous prisoner-of-war of all time. At a later stage St. Helena became a cable station, with the cable running from Cape Town on the one hand to Ascension and Europe on the other. The island still has a function in collecting messages from the feeble radios of small ships and passing them on. The pleasant climate is another factor which has led to a population approaching 5000 living happily on this island. They have as much meat as they need; they grow such excellent potatoes that some in the past have been exported. New Zealand flax has been introduced, and the industry started by the government mill in 1908 includes the preparation of rope, string, and lace for export.

Again, however, the question clearly arises: What is the future of such an island? Efforts to establish an airstrip during World War II revealed the absence of any suitable land.

St. Helena is a British crown colony, with a resident governor.

TRISTAN DA CUNHA

Even more remote and inaccessible than St. Helena is the group of islands which make up Tristan da Cunha, and which since 1938 has formed a dependency of St. Helena. Tristan da Cunha itself is another old volcano of which the highest point reaches 6760 feet (2060 m). The islands lie in 37° South, which is south of the southernmost point of Africa, and in the belt of the westerly winds, almost in the latitude of the "roaring forties." The handful of people, between 200 and 300, who lived there on the main island were descended mainly from shipwrecked sailors. Despite the cold, stormy climate and the extreme isolation, because Tristan da Cunha, unlike Ascension and St. Helena, is not near well-used oceanic routeways, they had a deep affection for their island and no desire to leave. They lived on a low plateau on the northwestern side of the island, growing potatoes and fruit, apples and peaches, and rearing cattle and geese. They had abundant fish in the surrounding seas.

During World War II the isolation of Tristan da Cunha was broken and the island became officially a British warship, under the name of H.M.S. Atlantic Isle, its function being primarily as a meteorological and radio station.

In 1961 the volcano, long believed extinct, showed ominous signs of activity and later erupted. The inhabitants were compelled to leave and were evacuated

20.C A volcano threatening the simple cottages of the inhabitants of Tristan da Cunha in 1961. (Photo: United Press International.)

via South Africa to Britain. After a scientific investigation of the position the majority returned early in 1963.

RÉUNION OR BOURBON

Turning now to the oceanic islands of the Indian Ocean, there are three volcanic islands, Réunion (French), Mauritius (British), and Rodriguez (British), forming a chain sometimes called the Mascarenhas, from the name of their Portuguese discoverer. Like the isolated islands of the Atlantic, they are volcanic. They lie in the trade wind belt, approximately in latitude 21° to 22° South, with a moderate to heavy rainfall derived from the Southeast Trades and augmented in the summer months by frequent tropical cyclones which are sometimes of a very violent nature. Only on the low-lying sheltered parts is there any real dry season,

but the oceanic position moderates the temperature which at sea level ranges only between monthly means of 68 and 69°F (20°C). Prior to their discovery by Europeans, the islands, densely covered with forest, were uninhabited. In the course of time forests have been almost entirely destroyed. Their place has been taken by plantations of sugar cane, the chief economic crop of the islands. The population has been derived mainly from settlers from France and Britain, settlers or imported laborers from India, together with a few Negroes, the descendants of slaves, or immigrants from Madagascar. A certain number of Chinese have also settled on the islands.

Réunion was occupied by France in the middle of the seventeenth century, and, except for a short period during the Napoleonic wars when it came into British hands, it has remained French. The

400,000 inhabitants are largely of French descent. With an area a little under 1000 square miles (2500 km²), it rises to over 10,000 feet (3000 m). The range of altitude makes possible the cultivation of a great variety of crops. The earlier ones of coffee, cloves, vanilla, and sugar have given place to a greater variety, including, tea, cinchona, cocoa, manioc (cassava) and rice. Wheat and temperate fruits and vegetables can be grown at higher levels. The principal economic crop is sugar cane, so that large quantities of sugar and rum are exported.

It is to be noted that much of this production is achieved on a tropical island with white labor, or labor of predominantly white descent.

The capital is St. Denis. The only harbor accessible to large vessels is Pointe-des-Galets, which is a partly artificial port.

MAURITIUS

Mauritius is situated some 500 miles (800 km) east of Madagascar and almost on the direct line between South Africa and Ceylon and India. It was certainly known to early Arab or Moorish sailors, and, though it was discovered by the Portuguese, the Dutch first settled on the island in 1598. They left, however, in 1710, and it was more than fifty years before the French arrived in 1767 and named the island Ile de France. The British occupied the island in 1810; it was formally acknowledged as British by the Treaty of Paris in 1814.

Like Réunion, it is a large island for an oceanic island, having an area of about 720 square miles (1800 km²). It is less elevated than Réunion, the highest point rising to 2711 feet (1827 m). In consequence there is a much larger proportion of cultivable low ground with rich volcanic soils, and very large numbers of emigrants have crowded into Mauritius from densely peopled India, so that the population approaches 800,000. Vegetables and farm crops are grown for home use. Salt is obtained by evaporating sea water in salt pans around the coast. Sandy areas of the coastlands are covered with coconuts and yield copra, but the mainstay of the island is its production of sugar. Mauritius is essentially a sugar island; its prosperity depends on the pro-

20.D The two landscapes most characteristic of Mauritius: steep mountains with sugar growing on the flatter land. (Photo: Camera Press.)

duction and the price of sugar. The porous volcanic soils, the marked seasonal rhythm, the low to moderate rainfall, are just those conditions, so well known in the West Indies, that are eminently suitable for the growth of sugar cane.

The principal town of Mauritius is Port Louis, situated on the northwestern side of the island and now linked to all parts by the motor roads which have replaced in function the former island railways. Port Louis is a little too hot and humid for Europeans, who favor the small hill sta-

tion of Curepipe, 1800 feet (550 m) above sea level, but only a dozen miles away. In contrast to Réunion, however, there are few pure Europeans in Mauritius. Apart from the Indians, the Mauritians are largely of mixed blood, together with Negroes and Chinese.

Despite the fertility of the island and the large sale of sugar to the British market, the density of population, which is rising rapidly, is such that there can be little hope for any major improvement in the standard of living. With over a thou-

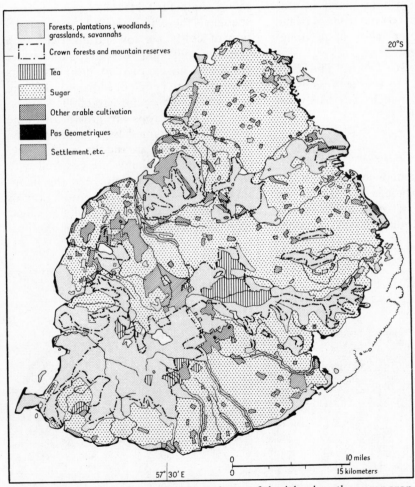

    Forests, plantations , woodlands, grasslands, savannahs

    Crown forests and mountain reserves

    Tea

    Sugar

    Other arable cultivation

    Pas Geometriques

    Settlement, etc.

20°S

57° 30' E

0   10 miles
0   15 kilometers

20.1 Land use in Mauritius. The dependence of the island on the sugar crop is graphically apparent. The *Pas Géometriques* are protective belts around the coast maintained under public ownership which may be leased to private individuals who are obliged not to damage the trees. (Map after J. E. Meade and others, *The Economic and Social Structure of Mauritius*. London: Methuen, 1961.)

20.E A house in the French colonial style on a sugar estate in Mauritius. It was built by the ancestors of the present owner during the first half of the 19th century. (Photo: Camera Press.)

sand persons per square mile (400 p.km²), dependent upon one export crop (sugar comprises over 95 percent of exports) and subject to devastating hurricanes (called cyclones in the Indian Ocean), Mauritius has much in common with those other problem islands in the Caribbean. The island became independent in 1968.

Rodriguez, lying 300 miles (480 km) northeast of Mauritius, is much smaller. Only 40 square miles in area (104 km²), it has only a few thousand inhabitants, who engage in fishing and the cultivation of food crops for their own sustenance.

MADAGASCAR
(MALAGASY REPUBLIC OR REPUBLIQUE MALGACHE)

The huge island of Madagascar covers an area of 229,233 square miles (594,180 km²). It is not far short of 1000 miles (1600 km) from the extreme northern to the extreme southern point, and in places its breadth reaches 360 miles (580 km). It supports a population of 6,800,000

(1967), yet it is true to say that this island remains almost an unknown land to English-speaking peoples. As a former French colony nearly 90 percent of the shipping visiting Madagascar is French; the air services which of recent years have linked it with Paris by three different routes are also French. There is a very extensive, voluminous, and well-informed literature on the geography and resources of Madagascar, but very little published in English.

Although it is only separated from the African continent by the Mozambique channel, some 250 miles wide (400 km), and although the basic crystalline complex which occupies the eastern two-thirds of the island does not differ greatly from the crystalline complex of the African continent, Madagascar has had a history entirely its own. Populated from the far side of the Indian Ocean as much as from the continent of Africa, isolated for a very long period previously so that both its fauna and flora have many distinctive characters, Madagascar can claim to be an island continent. In the island there are no large quadrupeds, but a number of distinctive species of lemurs. There are no poisonous snakes, and its flora is equally distinctive.

Outline of History. Although the peoples of Madagascar may have come at least in part from the African mainland, many highly distinctive cultural features derive from the fact that the island was settled by those who traveled across the Indian Ocean. This peopling began somewhere about the twentieth century B.C. and continued until recent times. The first inhabitants were probably Indonesians of Negro characteristics, whose descendants still constitute one of the important elements of the population. These were reinforced by large incursions of the Hovas, allied to the Malays racially and linguistically. In later times the island became well known to the Arabs, who came from the Persian

Gulf as well as from the east coast of Africa and who settled on the northwest and part of the eastern coastlands. Indians also came by sea and populated part of the southeast coast.

There are strong Negro elements, especially on the western side of the island. Some of these may have come as free settlers, or may have been mainly brought as slaves. The final Malayan migration to the island seems to have finished actually after the first appearance of European explorers. This was in fact the main invasion by the Hova, who may be said to constitute perhaps one-quarter of the population, and who have profoundly influenced the character of the other island peoples. They offer many points of contrast physically and in attitudes to the Negroes of Africa.

The influence of Arab culture in the north has tended to result in peoples who

20.F A village scene in Merina (Hova) country of Madagascar. The substantial brick houses have an un-African air. Rice is growing in the valley. (Photo: Richard Harrington, Camera Press.)

are industrious and frugal and who make both excellent cultivators and good merchants.

The island was definitely sighted by the Portuguese Diego Dias in 1500. At the time when the French were active in the Indian Ocean they had military posts on the east coast for part of the seventeenth century and most of the eighteenth century, but early in the nineteenth century they relinquished them all except the island of Ste. Marie. In 1811 Tamatave was occupied by British troops, and under the Treaty of Paris, 1814, the French settlements in Madagascar were recognized as coming under British control. The British, however, made no attempt to settle on the island and were content to leave it to the control of the Hovas, whose king — Radama I — established friendly relations with the British government; a British agent was sent to reside at his court. The London Missionary Society established the first Christian missions in 1820, but when Radama was succeeded in 1828 by one of his wives, she persecuted the local Christians to such an extent that most of them lost their lives. In 1836 all missionaries were compelled to leave the island, and for some years all Europeans were excluded from the country. Radama II, though he ruled for only two years (1861–1863) before being murdered, reopened the island to European trade. His wife, who succeeded him, effected treaties with British, French, and American governments.

Queen Ranavalona II, who ruled from 1868 to 1883, became a Christian, and during her reign Christianity became more widespread and much progress was made in education. But relations became strained with France because the Hova queen refused to recognize the French claim that certain tracts on the northwest coast had been transferred to them by local chiefs, and in 1883 Tamatave was bombarded and occupied by French marines. In the subsequent peace terms it was agreed that Madagascar's foreign relations should be directed by France, that a French governor should remain in the capital, and that Diego-Suarez should be ceded to France. In 1890 Britain recognized this French protectorate over Madagascar. After further disputes, a French expeditionary force in 1895 effected the conquest of the island; consequently, in 1896 the ruling Hova queen was exiled, and Madagascar became a French colony.

With the recall to power of General de Gaulle in 1958 and the institution of the Fifth Republic of France, Madagascar, in common with the other French colonies in Africa, was offered the chance to decide its own future. The vote was to remain a member of the French Community (1958) followed by the declaration of an independent republic on June 26, 1960 and admission to the United Nations later that year under the name of République Malagache (Malagasy Republic).

Structure and relief. The essential structural element in the island of Madagascar is a high plateau, part of the ancient continent of Gondwanaland, built up basically of crystalline rocks, with a whole range of granites and other igneous rocks which outcrop over vast stretches of the country. Here and there gold-bearing veins have decomposed to give rise to small placer deposits, and there are deposits of graphite which constitute one of the main mineral resources of the island. There are areas where precious stones occur, deposits of radioactive ores of nickel, copper, and lead. But over a very large part of the country the ancient rocks are hidden beneath a mantle of laterite or of lateritic decomposition products. The red soils which result are liable to extensive erosion and cause many of the streams draining to the coast to be red in color; hence the name sometimes given to the island is "Red Isle."

The crest of the plateau lies nearer the east than the west, and outcrops of volcanic rock give rise to high ground reaching to more than 6000 feet (2000 m).

Around the crystalline plateau, sedimentary rocks have been deposited which are especially important on the western third of the island, and become younger in age as traced towards the Mozambique Channel. Although it is tempting to regard Madagascar as structurally a mirror image to Mozambique, in fact the sedimentary strata are more closely related to those of the Tanzania coast, further north.

The eastern coast tends to be straight, free from indentations, and fringed with coral reefs. There are an onshore wind and a constant swell, and anchorages are very few and far between. From the crest of the plateau the land descends very sharply to the east coast, but to the west the drop is less, though there are some steep scarp faces overlooking the lower territory formed by the sedimentary rocks. Along the east coast is an almost continuous string of lagoons between the coral beaches and the steep rise inland. Linked by cuts this forms a valuable waterway.

Climate. Climatically the island lies within the Trade Wind Belt, so that southeasterly winds predominate. They bring a heavy rainfall to the eastern side of the island, comparatively little to the west (Figure 20.2). Thus four climatic divisions are distinguished:

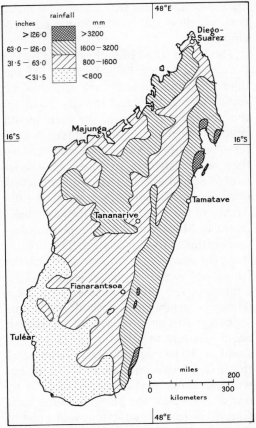

20.2 Rainfall of Madagascar. Note the range from the high rainfall of the east coast to the relative aridity of the south west.

1. The eastern slopes and the coast, much of which has a rainfall of over 100 inches (2500 mm) even at sea level with a rainy period from December to July, but where a considerable fall comes in every month.
2. The plateau, where altitude reduces the temperature from the 70 to 80°F (21–27°C) usual on the coast to a range of 55 to 67°F (13–19°C), typical of Antananarivo, 4600 feet (1400 m) above sea level.
3. The south and southwest, where the prevailing winds are descending from the plateau and become warm in the process. They deposit little or no rain, so that southward the southwest coasts are really to be described as arid and receive only some 15 inches (380 mm) of rain. For two-thirds of the year the rivers are dry.
4. The northwest, which resembles the southwest but has some northwesterly winds during the midsummer period, with a heavy rainfall in January and February and a dry season lasting from about May to November.

Vegetation. The vegetation corresponds closely with these climatic divisions (Figure 20.3). It may be hazarded that the original vegetation cover consisted of a continuous evergreen rainforest over the wetter areas of the east and north, giving place to a savanna or perhaps to steppe on the plateau and to semi-arid types in the driest regions. French workers in Madagascar believe, however, that the natural vegetation has been almost completely destroyed throughout the whole island by the process of burning by the inhabitants, so that over at least four-fifths of the whole surface a vegetation resulting from human interference has replaced that which is natural. Many species have been thereby extinguished, and the density of woodland or savanna is much less than it would otherwise be. The map of vegetation (Figure 20.3) shows the distinction which is drawn between the evergreen forests of the east and the deciduous vegetation of the west. The bamboo forests which are common at high altitudes are

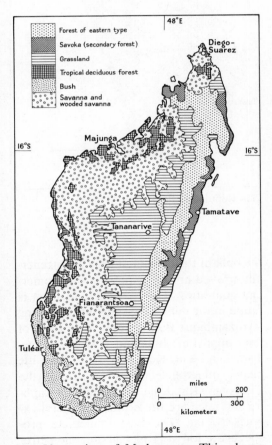

20.3 Vegetation of Madagascar. This shows the effect of rainfall (Figure 20.2) but also of human activity (compare with the population distribution, Figure 20.4). Much of the grassland as well as of the Savoka is believed to be secondary.

probably entirely secondary, and the laterite soils found when forests have been cleared are not very fertile, so that clearings are soon abandoned and allowed to degenerate into bush, locally called "*savoka.*" This is easily burnt, but often as a result there is bare soil with a hard barren crust, rendering the land virtually useless. Some attempt has been made to combat this damage by the preservation of natural forests and establishing new plantations. A small amount of timber, notably ebony, is produced, and products collected from the woodland include gum copal.

Agriculture. It will be clear that this island which seems to be favored climatically is not as agriculturally rich as might be expected. Little plantation agriculture has been developed. Rice is the principal food crop. Some upland rice is grown in forest clearings but sophisticated traditional irrigation is widespread, including on terraces reminiscent of the hillsides of Java. Cassava is second to rice as a food crop, especially in the wetter regions. Corn (maize) can be grown even in the dry parts during the rainy season, and is therefore of first class importance in the southwest. Sorghum, yams, and beans are other food crops, and sugar cane may be grown where irrigation is possible. The major export crops include coffee, rice, vanilla (of which Malagasy is the world's leading producer), sugar, sisal and cloves. The agricultural people of the east have few animals, but on the plateau cattle rearing is a mainstay of the local agricultural economy. The tsetse fly is absent. Fat-tailed sheep and goats are to be found in drier regions, and every Madagascan farm has a few pigs (another contrast with the mainland).

Human geography. The bulk of the African population lives in small villages, often surrounded by a stockade. Most of their cities owe part if not the whole of their development to European influence. Antananarivo, now more usually called Tananarive, is a mountain capital situated far from the sea or a river port. A jumble of villages linked by tortuous streets and ancient stairways can scarcely be reached from the more modern sections, and the rugged terrain presents sudden obstacles to building as well as to water supply and drainage. Before the French occupation of Madagascar it was the seat of government of the Merina (or Hova) people, an old trading and once a slave-trading center. The French established their rule there in 1895, and the population rapidly increased to make it the commercial and cultural as well as the political capital. It is situated on the edge of the Imerina plains, and in the capital and the surrounding highland plains live possibly one-third of all the people of the island[9] (Figure 20.4). It is connected by railway with Tamatave, the principal port, and a branch from this railway runs northward to Lake Alaotra. Whether the planned extensions of Madagascan railways will ever take place becomes increasingly doubtful, because of the rapid modern development of roads.

The exports of Madagascar are little per head compared with the small islands of the Indian Ocean such as Mauritius or Réunion which must "export to live." Compared with the exports typical of a country of mainland Africa, those of Madagascar are singularly varied. They are mostly agricultural and coffee, both *robusta* and *arabica,* makes up over a third of the value but sugar, rice, and vanilla all contribute between 5 and 10 percent, and there is a long list of significant cash crops including cloves (with a rapidly increasing output), raffia, sisal, essential oils, and tobacco; meat is also exported. The numerous livestock present an opportunity for development with upgrading, investment in packing plants, and building up of overseas markets.

Many mineral occurrences are known in the Precambrian massif which forms

[9] W. A. Hance (*Focus,* May 1958) has a striking map showing the concentration of population in a few parts of the island.

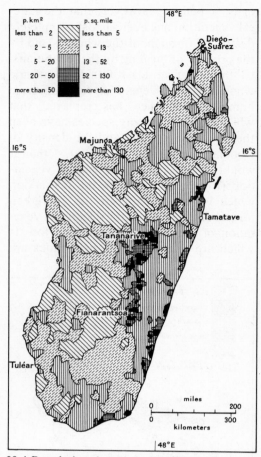

20.4 Population density in Madagascar.

the bulk of the island but they have generally proved not to be present in commercial quantities. This is similar to what is found in the mineralogically disappointing "Mozambique Belt" of the eastern side of the opposite mainland (Mozambique, Tanzania, and Kenya) rather than the heavy mineralized shield rocks of the Transvaal, Rhodesia, and Zambia. Graphite and mica are the principal mineral exports so far. The best immediate prospects are for working bauxite, and petroleum exploration continues in the sedimentary province of the west of the island, both onshore and offshore.

Although small deposits of coal have been located, power supplies are mostly of hydroelectricity. Heavy rainfall and the scarps in the east of the island offer many more sites for further power schemes.

Seen against its resource endowment, the economy of Madagascar appears to be surprisingly weakly developed. Some commentators have invoked the inhibiting effect of the religious "cult of the dead" which is so distinctive a part of the cultural life of the people. A relevant geographical factor, however, could well be a degree of isolation not to be expected from such an island situation. This is derived from the location of the capital in the middle of the interior plateau, in the center of the leading Merina community and with another Hova people, the Betsileo in Fianarantosa Province, also in the interior. The road and rail system have been too poorly developed to make much improvement. Extensions to the ports of Tamatave and Majunga and in the road system are helping.

THE COMORO ISLANDS

This group of islands lies midway between the northwest coast of Madagascar and the mainland of Africa and is administered by France as the *Territoire des Comores*. There are four main islands, with a total population at the 1966 census of 248,517. The chief two are Grand Comoro [720 square miles (1148 km²)] and Mayotte [140 square miles (374 km²)].

The climate is wet tropical. The natural forests have been largely cleared for agriculture, but some timber (exported as railroad ties) is obtained from those that remain. Sugar cane was formerly a leading crop, but it has suffered from more effective production elsewhere. The principal export crops are vanilla and essential oils. Cocoa, coconuts, sisal, and rice are also grown. Economic opportunities are limited and as a result there has been considerable emigration to Madagascar and the mainland.

Further Reading

The various islands discussed in this chapter are separately described in detail in the sources listed in the bibliography on p. 435.

Selected Bibliography[1]

1. AFRICAN HIGHLIGHTS

Bohannan, P. and G. Dalton. *Markets in Africa*. Evanston, Ill.: Northwestern University Press, 1962.

Brokensha, David (ed.). *Ecology and Economic Development in Tropical Africa*. Berkeley: Inst. Int. Studies, University of California, 1965.

Carter, Gwendolen M. (ed.). *National Unity and Regionalism in Eight African States*. Ithaca, N.Y.: Cornell University Press, 1966.

Collinson, Robert. *The SCOLMA Directory of Libraries and Special Collections in Africa*. London: Crosby Lockwood, 1967 (2nd Ed.).

de Blij, Harm de. *A Geography of Subsaharan Africa*. Chicago: Rand Mc-Nally, 1964.

Ewing, A. F. *Industry in Africa*. London: Oxford University Press, 1968.

Fordham, Paul. The Geography of African Affairs. Harmondsworth: Penguin, 1965.

Green, L. P. and T. J. D. Fair. *Development in Africa*. Johannesburg: Witwatersrand University Press, 1965.

Grove, A. T. *Africa South of the Sahara*. London: Oxford University Press, 1967.

Hailey, Lord. *An African Survey*. London: Oxford University Press, 1957 (revised).

Hamdam, G. "Capitals of the new Africa." *Econ. Geog.* **40** (1964) 239–53.

Hance, William A. *The Geography of Modern Africa*. New York: Columbia University Press, 1964.

Hance, William A. *African Economic Development*. New York: Praeger, 1967 (revised).

---

[1] References already given at the end of Chapters under "Further Reading" are not repeated here.

Hance, William A. *et al.* "Some Areas of Export Production in Tropical Africa." *Geog. Rev.* **51** (1961) 487–499.

Hodder, B. W. "Some Comments on the Origin of Traditional Markets in Africa South of the Sahara." *Trans. Inst. Brit. Geogrs.* **36** (1965) 97–105.

Hodder, B. W. and D. R. Harris (eds.). *Africa in Transition.* London: Methuen, 1967.

Jackson, E. F. (ed.). *Economic Development in Africa.* Papers presented to the Nyasaland Economic Symposium. Oxford: Blackwell, 1965.

Kimble, George H. T. *Tropical Africa.* Garden City, N.Y.: Doubleday, 1962 (Abridged Ed., 2 vols).

Mair, Lucy. *The New Africa.* London: C. A. Watts, 1967.

McEwan, Peter J. M. and Robert B. Sutcliffe (eds.). *The Study of Africa.* London: Methuen, 1965.

Pelletier, R. A. *Mineral Resources of South-Central Africa.* Cape Town: Oxford University Press, 1964.

Prothero, R. Mansell (ed.). *A Geography of Africa: Regional Essays on Fundamental Characteristics, Issues and Problems.* London: Routledge and Kegan Paul, 1969.

Robinson, E. A. G. (ed.). *Economic Development for Africa South of the Sahara.* London: Macmillan, 1964.

Robson, P. and D. A. Lury. *The Economics of Africa.* London: Allen & Unwin, 1969.

Rubin, Neville and W. N. Warren (eds.). *Dams in Africa: An Interdisciplinary Study of Man-Made Lakes in Africa.* London: Frank Cass, 1968.

Stamp, L. D. (ed.). *Natural Resources, Food and Population in Inter-tropical Africa.* Bude, U. K.: Geographical Publs. Ltd., 1955.

Steel, R. W. and C. A. Fisher. *Geographical Essays on British Tropical Lands.* London: Philip, 1965.

Steel, R. W. and R. Mansell Prothero. *Geographers and the Tropics: Liverpool Essays.* London: Longmans, 1964.

Sommer, John W. *Bibliography of African Geography, 1940–1964.* Hanover, N.H.: Department of Geography, Dartmouth College, 1965.

Thomas, M. F. and G. W. Whittington (eds.). *Environment and Land Use in Africa.* London: Methuen, 1969.

Wall, David. "Export Prospects for Africa South of the Sahara." *African Affairs* **68** (1969) 26–41.

Wolstenholme, G. E. W. and M. O'Connor (eds.). *Man and Africa.* London: 1965.

Periodicals:

African Affairs.
Journal of the Royal African Society. London.

2. UNROLLING THE MAP OF AFRICA

Barbour, K. M. "A Geographical Analysis of Boundaries in Intertropical Africa." *In* K. M. Barbour and R. M. Prothero *Essays on African Population.* 1961.

Clark, J. Desmond. *The Prehistory of Southern Africa.* Hardmondsworth: Penguin, 1959.

Cole, Sonia. *The Prehistory of East Africa*. London: Weidenfeld and Nicholson, 1964.

Dale, Edmund H. "Some Geographical Aspects of African Land-Locked States." *Ann. Ass. Amer. Geog.* **58** (1968) 485–505.

de Lusiggnan, Guy. *French-speaking Africa Since Independence*. New York: Praeger 1969.

Hallett, Robin. *The Penetration of Africa to 1815*. London: Routledge & Kegan Paul, 1965.

Hallett, Robin. *Africa to 1875. A Modern History*. Ann Arbor: University of Michigan Press, 1970.

Hallett, Robin. *Africa Since 1875. A Modern History*. Ann Arbor: University of Michigan Press.

Hodgson Robert D. and E. A. Stoneman. *The Changing Map of Africa*. Princeton, N.M.: van Nostrand, 1968 (2nd Ed.)..

Howell, C. and F. Bourlière (eds.). *African Ecology and Human Evolution*. London: Methuen, 1964.

McBurney, C. B. *The Stone Age of Northern Africa*. Harmondsworth: Penguin, 1960.

Neumark, S. Daniel. *Foreign Trade and Economic Development in Africa: A Historical Perspective*. Stanford: Ford Research Institute, Stanford University, 1964.

Touval, Saadia. "Africa's Frontiers: Reactions to a Colonial Legacy." *Internat. Affairs* **42** (1966) 641–654.

Touval, Saadia. "Treaties, Borders and the Partition of Africa." *J. African Hist.* **7** (1966) 279–293.

Zartman, I. W. "The Politics of Boundaries in North and West Africa." *J. Mod. African Studies* **3** (1965) 155–173.

Periodical:

African Historical Studies. The African Studies Center of Boston University.

3. THE BUILD OF AFRICA

De Kun, N. A. *The Mineral Resources of Africa*. Amsterdam, 1965.

Dixey, Frank, "The East African Rift System." *Colonial Geology and Mineral Resources Bulletin,* Supplement No. 1. London: H.M.S.O., 1956.

Haughton, S. M. *The Stratigraphic History of Africa South of the Sahara*. Edinburgh: Oliver and Boyd, 1963.

4. AFRICAN CLIMATES AND THE WATER PROBLEM

Bargman, D. J. (ed.). *Tropical Meteorology in Africa*. Nairobi: Munitalp Foundation, 1965.

Bennett, Merrill K. *An Agroclimate Mapping of Africa*. Ford Research Institute Studies, Vol. 3, 195–216 (1962).

Bunting, A. H. "Some Problems of Agricultural Climatology in Tropical Africa." *Geography* **56** (1961) 283–294.

Carter, D. B. "Moisture Regions of Africa." *The Johns Hopkins University Lab. of Climatology, Publications in Climatology,* **7** (1954).

Davies, J. A. and P. J. Robinson. "A Simple Energy Balance Approach to the Moisture Balance Climatology of Africa." *In* M. F. Thomas and G. W. Whittington. *Environment and Land Use in Africa.* London: Methuen, 1969.

Graham, Anne. "Man–Water Relationships in the East Central Sudan." *In* M. F. Thomas and G. W. Whittington. *Environment and Land Use in Africa.* London: Methuen, 1969.

Johnson, D. H. "Rain in East Africa." *Q. J. Roy. Met. Soc.* **88** (1962).

Kenworthy, J. M. "Rainfall and the Water Resources of East Africa." *In* R. W. Steel and R. M. Prothero (eds.). *Geographers and the Tropics.* London: 1964.

Ledger, D. C. "Some Hydrological Characteristics of West African Rivers." *Trans. and Papers, Inst. Brit. Geog.* **35** (1964) 73–90.

Ledger, D. C. "The Dry Season Flow Characteristics of West African Rivers." *In* M. F. Thomas and G. W. Whittington. *Environment and Land Use in Africa.* London: Methuen, 1969.

Pereira, H. C. *et al.* "Hydrological Effects of Changes in Land Use in some East African Catchment Areas." *E. Afr. Agric. For. J.* **27** (1962).

Rodier, J. *Bibliography of African Hydrology.* Paris: UNESCO, 1963.

Periodical:

Quarterly Journal of the Royal Meteorological Society.

5. SOILS AND THEIR MANAGEMENT

Biebuyck, D. (ed.). *African Agrarian Systems.* London: Oxford University Press, 1963.

Chambers, Robert. *Settlement Schemes in Tropical Africa.* London: Routledge and Kegan Paul, 1969.

Clayton, Eric. *Agrarian Development in Peasant Economies: Some Lessons from Kenya.* Oxford: Pergamon Press, 1964.

de Wilde, John C. *Experiences with Agricultural Development in Tropical Africa.* Vol. 1: *The Synthesis.* Vol. 2: *The Case Studies.* Baltimore: Johns Hopkins, 1967.

Makings, S. M. *Agricultural Problems of Developing Countries in Africa.* Lusaka: Oxford University Press, 1967.

Milne, G. *A Provisional Soil Map of East Africa.* London: Crown Agents, 1936.

Mohr, E. C. J. and F. A. van Baren. *Tropical Soils.* The Hague: Uitgeverij W. van Hoeve, 1954.

Moss, R. P. "Soils, Slopes and Land Use in a Part of South-Western Nigeria: Some Implications for the Planning of Agricultural Development in Intertropical Africa." *Trans. Inst. Brit. Geog.* **32** (1963) 143–168.

Murdock, George P. "Staple Subsistence Crops of Africa." *Geog. Rev.* **50** (1960) 523–540.

Phillips, J. *Agriculture and Ecology in Africa.* London: 1959.

Schokalskaya, S. J. *Die Boden Afrika.* Berlin, 1953.

Young, Anthony. "Mapping Africa's Natural Resources." *Geog. J.* **134** (1968) 236–241.

Periodicals:

Sols Africains—African Soils.
Journal of Soil Science.

6. FOREST, GRASSLAND, AND DESERT:
WILDLIFE IN AFRICA

Brooks, A. C. *A Study of Thomson's Gazelle (Gazella thomsonii Gunter) in Tanganyika.* London: H.M.S.O., 1961.

Davis, D. H. S. (ed.). *Ecological Studies in Southern Africa.* The Hague: 1964.

Hedberg, O. "Features of Afro-alpine Plant Ecology." *Acta Phytogeographica Sueiaca* **49,** Uppsala, 1964.

Hedberg, Inga and Olov Hedberg "Conservation of Vegetation in Africa South of the Sahara." *Acta Phytogeographica Sueiaca* **54,** Uppsala, 1968.

Michelmore, A. P. S. "Observations on Tropical African Grassland." *J. Ecology* **27** (1939) 282–312.

Moreau, R. E. *The Bird Faunas of Africa and its Islands.* New York: Academic Press, 1966.

Richards, P. W. *The Tropical Rain Forest.* Cambridge: Cambridge University Press, 1952.

Scientific Council for Africa South of the Sahara. Publ. No. 22. *Phytogeography.* Lagos/London: C.S.A., 1956.

Shantz, H. L. and C. F. Marbut. *The Vegetation and Soils of Africa.* New York: American Geographical Society, 1923.

Talbot, L. M. and M. H. Talbot. *The Wildebeeste in Western Masailand, East Africa.* Wildlife Monographs No. 12., September 1963.

Periodicals:

Journal of Animal Ecology.
Journal of Applied Ecology.
Journal of Ecology.
Journal of Mammology.

7. POPULATION AND PEOPLES

Brass, William *et al. The Demography of Tropical Africa.* Princeton: Princeton University Press, 1968

Bryan, M. A. *The Bantu Languages of Africa.* London: International African Institute, 1959.

Clarke, J. I. *Population Geography and the Developing Countries.* London: Pergamon Press, 1971, Chap. 3.

Deschler, Walter. "Cattle in Africa: Distribution, Types and Problems." *Geog. Rev.* **53** (1963) 52–58.

Edinburgh University. *African Urbanization: A Reading List of Selected Books, Articles and Reports.* London: International African Institute, 1965.

Gibbs, J. L. *Peoples of Africa.* New York: Holt, Rinehart & Winston, 1965.

Greenberg, J. H. *The Languages of Africa.* Bloomington, Ind.: Research Center in Anthropology, Folklore and Linguistics, 1963.

Guthrie, Malcolm. *Classification of the Bantu Languages of Africa.* London: International African Institute, 1948 (reprinted 1967).

Hunter, Guy. *The New Societies of Tropical Africa: A Selective Study.* London: Oxford University Press, 1962.

Jaquot, A. *et al. Linguistic Survey of the Northern Bantu Borderland.* London: International African Institute, 1956 (4 vols.).

Oliver, Roland. "The Problem of the Bantu Expansion." *J. Afr. Hist.* VII, 3 (1966) 361–376.

Ottenburgh, S. and P. Ottenburgh (eds.). *Cultures and Societies of Africa.* New York, 1960.

Reader, D. H. "A Survey of Categories of Economic Activity Among the Peoples of Africa." *Africa* **34** (1964) 28–45.

Smith, T. E. and J. G. C. Blacker. *Population Characteristics of the Commonwealth Countries of Tropical Africa.* London: Athlone Press, 1963.

Spencer, J. (ed.). *Language in Africa.* London, 1963.

Texas University. *International Population Census Bibliography. Africa.* Austin: Bureau of Business Research, University of Texas, 1965.

Tucker, A. M. and M. A. Bryan. *The Non-Bantu Languages of North-Eastern Africa.* London: Oxford University Press, 1956.

Periodicals:

Africa.
African Abstracts.
Population.
Population Index.
Population Studies.
Southwest Journal of Anthropology.

8. THE PLAGUES OF AFRICA

Buxton, P. A. *Trypanosomiasis in East Africa.* London: H.M.S.O., 1948.

May, J. M. (ed.). *The Ecology of Disease.* New York, 1958.

May, J. M. (ed.). *Studies in Disease Ecology.* New York, 1961.

May, J. M. *The Ecology of Malnutrition in the French Speaking Countries of West Africa and Madagascar.* New York: Hafner, 1968.

Nash, T. A. M. *Tsetse Flies in British West Africa.* London: H.M.S.O., 1948.

Prothero, R. Mansell. "A Geographer with the World Health Organisation." *Geog. J.* **128** (1962) 479–493.

Terjung, Werner H. "Bi-monthly Physiological Climates and Annual Stresses and Regimes of Africa. *Geog. Ann.* **50A** (1968) 173–192.

9. TRANSPORTATION

Day, John R. *Railways of Southern Africa.* London: Arthur Barker, 1963.

Hawkins, E. K. *Roads and Road Transport in an Underdeveloped Country: A Case Study of Uganda.* London: H.M.S.O., 1962.

Hoyle, B. S. and D. Hilling. *Seaports and Development in Tropical Africa.* London: Macmillan, 1970.

Leubuscher, Charlotte. *The West African Shipping Trade, 1909–1959.* Leyden: A. W. Sythoff, 1963.

O'Connor, A. M. *Railways and Development in Uganda.* Nairobi: Oxford University Press, 1965.

Taafe, Edward J. *et al.* "Transport Development in Underdeveloped Countries: A Comparative Analysis." *Geog. Rev.* **53** (1963) 503–529.

10. EGYPT AND THE NILE

Berry, L. and A. J. Whiteman. "The Nile in the Sudan." *Geog. J.* 134 (1968) 1–37.

Brander, Bruce. *The River Nile.* Washington D.C.: National Geographic Society (Special Publication No. 2), 1966.

Butzer, K. W. and C. L. Hansen. *Desert and River in Nubia: Geomorphology and Prehistoric Environments at the Aswan Reservoir.* Madison: University of Wisconsin Press, 1968.

Collins, R. O. and R. L. Tignor. *Egypt and the Sudan.* Prentice Hall, 1967.

Eshag, E. and M. A. Kamal. "Agrarian Reform in the U.A.R. *Bull. Oxford Inst. Econ. and Stats.* **30,** 2 (1968).

Farnie, D. A. *East and West of Suez — the Suez Canal in History, 1854–1956.* Oxford: Clarendon, 1969.

Frood, A. McKie. "The Aswan High Dam and the Egyptian Economy." *In* R. W. Steel and R. Lawton. *Liverpool Essays in Geography.* 1967.

Haupert, John S. "The United Arab Republic." *Focus* XIX, 7, March 1969.

Holz, R. K. "Man-Made Landforms in the Nile Valley." *Geog. Rev.* April, 1969, 253–269.

Holz, R. K. "The Aswan High Dam." *Professional Geographer,* **20,** 4 (1968) 230–237.

Kinross, J. B. *Between Two Seas: the Creation of the Suez Canal.* London: Murray, 1968.

Mansfield, Peter. *Nasser's Egypt.* Harmondsworth: Penguin, 1965.

Saab, G. S. *The Egyptian Agrarian Reform.* London: Oxford University Press, 1967.

Said, Rushi. *The Geology of Egypt.* Amsterdam: Elsevier, 1962.

Wilber, D. N. (ed.). *The United Arab Republic — Egypt, its People, its Security, its Culture.* New York: Taplinger, 1969.

Atlas:

Atlas of Egypt. El Giza: Survey of Egypt, 1928.

Periodical:

Bulletin. Societe de Geographie d'Egypt.

11. MEDITERRANEAN AFRICA

Ashford, D. E. "Rural Mobilisation in North Africa." *J. Modern African Studies,* **7,** 2 (1969) 187–202.

Awad, Hassan. "Morocco's Expanding Towns." *Geog. J.* **130** (1964) 49–64.

Becker, M. C. "Quo Vadis Tunis?" *Tijd. Econ. Soc. Geog.* **60** (1969).

Beyen, J. W. and P. E. Booz. *The Economic Development of Morocco.* London: Oxford University Press, 1968.

Clarke, J. I. "Summer Nomadism in Tunisia." *Econ. Geog.* **31** (1955) 157–167.

Clarke, J. I. "Studies of Semi-Nomadism in North Africa." *Econ. Geog.* **35** (1959) 95–108.

Duwaji, G. *Economic Development in Tunisia.* New York: Praeger, 1967.

Harrison, Robert S. "Tunisia." *Focus,* XIX, January 1969.

International Bank for Reconstruction and Development. *The Economic Development of Morocco.* Baltimore: The Johns Hopkins Press, 1966.

Mikesell, Marim W. "Algeria." *Focus,* XI, 6, February 1961.

Mikesell, M. W. *Northern Morocco. A Cultural Geography.* University of California Pubs. in Geography No. 14. University of California Press, 1961.

Monteil, V. *Morocco.* New York: Viking Press, 1964.

Pawera, J. C. *Algeria's Infrastructure: An Economic Survey of Transportation, Communication and Energy Resources.* New York: Praeger, 1964.

Reyner, A. S. "Morocco's International Boundaries." *J. Mod. African Studies,* **1** (1963) 313–326.

Robinson, G. W. S. "Ceuta and Melilla: Spain's Plazas de Soberania." *Geography,* **43** (1958) 266–269.

Yousseff, A. Ben. *Les Populations du Maghreb.* Bordeaux: Faculte du Droit, 1965.

Zartman, I. William. "Morocco." *Focus,* XV, 6, February 1965.

Atlases:

A. Bernard and R. de Flotte de Roquevaire. *Atlas d'Algerie et de Tunisie.* Paris: Emile Larosse, 1923–1933.

Atlas du Maroc. Rabat: Comité de Géographie du Maroc, 1955 (with texts).

Periodicals:

Annales Algeriennes de Géographie.

Mediterranée.

Cahiers du C.E.R.E.S., Serie Géographique. Tunis: Centre d'Etudes et des Recherches Economique et Sociales.

Revue de Géographie du Maroc. (formerly *Revue du Geographie Marocaine* and *Les Notes Marocaines*).

Revue Tunisienne de Sciences Sociales.

Les Cahiers de Tunisie.

Travaux de l'Institut Scientifique Cherifien.

12. THE SAHARA AND THE SAHARAN STATES

Barr, F. T. (ed.). *Geology and Archaeology of Northern Cyrenaica, Libya.* Tripoli: Petroleum Exploration Society of Libya, 1968.

Blake, G. H. *Misurata: A Market Town in Libya.* Durham: Department of Geography, University of Durham, 1968.

Blunsum, T. *Libya: the Country and its People.* Queen Anne Press, 1968.

Briggs, Lloyd Cabot. *The Living Races of the Saharan Desert.* (*Pap. Peabody*

Mus. Archael. -Ethnol., Harvard University), Vol. 28, No. 2. Cambridge: 1958.

Doyel, W. W. and F. J. Maguire. *Ground-Water Resources of the Benghazi Area*. Washington D.C.: U.S. Geological Survey, 1964.

Eagleton, W. "The Islamic Republic of Mauritania." *Middle East Journal* **19,** 1 (1965).

Gautier, Émile-Felix. *Sahara: the Great Desert*. New York: Columbia University Press, 1935 (trans. D. F. Mayhew).

Gerteiny, A. G. *Mauritania*. New York: Praeger, 1967.

Grove, A. T. and A. Warren. "Quaternary Landforms and Climate on the South Side of the Sahara. *Geog. J.* **134** (1968) 194–208.

Harrison, Robert S. "Migrants in the City of Tripoli, Libya." *Geog. Rev.* **57** (1967) 397–423.

Hartley, R. G. and J. M. Norris. "Demographic Regions in Libya: A Principal Components Analysis of Economic and Demographic Variables." *Tijds. Econ. Soc. Geog.* **60** (1969) 221–227.

Heitmann, G. "Libya: An Analysis of the Oil Economy." *J. Modern African Studies,* **7,** 2 (1969) 249–263.

Hernandez-Pacheco, Eduardo *et al. El Sahara Español, Estudio Geologico, Geografico y Botanico*. Madrid: Instituto de Estudios Africanos, 1949.

Meigs, Peveril. "Outlook for Arid North Africa: the Sahara." *Focus V,* 4 (1945).

Moseley, F. and P. K. Cruse. "Exploitation of the Main Water Table of North-Eastern Libya. *Roy. Engin. J.* **83** (1969) 12–23.

Norris, H. T. "The Wind of Change in the Western Sahara." *Geog. J.* **130** (1964) 1–14.

Norwich, J. J. *Sahara*. London: Longman, 1968.

Petroleum Exploration Society of Libya. *First Sahara Symposium,* 1963.

Thomas, B. E. *Trade Routes of Algeria and the Sahara*. Berkeley: University of California Press, 1957.

Williams, J. J. and E. Klitzch. (eds.). *South-Central Libya and Northern Chad. A Guidebook to the Geology and Prehistory*. Tripoli: Petroleum Exploration Society, 1966.

Zartman, I. W. "The Politics of Boundaries in North and West Africa." *J. Mod. African Studies,* **3** (1965) 155–173.

Periodical:

Institute des Recherches Sahariennes de l'Universite d'Alger: *Monographies Regionales; Travaux de l'Institute de Recherche Sahariennes.*

13. WEST AFRICA

Bawden, M. G. and P. Tuley *The Land Resources of Southern Sardanna and Southern Adamawa Provinces, Northern Nigeria*. Tolworth, U.K.: Land Resources Div.; Dir. Overseas Surveys, 1966.

Boateng, E. A. *A Geography of Ghana*. London: Cambridge University Press, 1966 (2nd Ed.).

Buchanan, K. M. and J. C. Pugh. *Land and People in Nigeria*. London: University of London Press, 1958.

Church, R. J. Harrison. "Problems of the Development of the Dry Zone of West Africa." *Geog. J.* **127** (1961) 187–204.

Church, R. J. Harrison. "Guinea." *Focus,* XVII, 7, March 1967.

Church, R. J. Harrison. "Urban Problems and Economic Development in West Africa." *J. Mod. Afr. Studies.* **5** (1967) 511–520.

Church, R. J. Harrison. "The Niger Republic." *Focus,* XVI, 1, September 1965.

Church, R. J. Harrison. "Senegal." *Focus,* XV, 1, September 1964.

Church, R. J. Harrison. "Some Problems of Regional Economic Development in West Africa." *Econ. Geog.* **45** (1969) 53–62.

Clarke, J. I. *Sierra Leone in Maps.* London: University of London Press, 1966.

Coppock, J. T. "Agricultural Developments in Nigeria." *J. Tropical Geog.* **23** (1966) 1–18.

Dickson, K. B. *A Historical Geography of Ghana.* London: Cambridge University Press, 1969.

Dickson, K. B. "Background to the Problem of Economic Development in Northern Ghana." *Ann. Assoc. Amer. Geogr.* **58** (1968) 686–696.

Floyd, Barry. *Eastern Nigeria: A Geographical Review.* London: Macmillan, 1969.

Floyd, Barry. "Nigeria." *Focus,* XV, 2, October 1964.

Forde, Enid R. *The Population of Ghana: A Study of the Spatial Relationships of its Socio-Cultural and Economic Characteristics.* Northwestern University Studies in Geography, **15** (1968).

Fyfe, Christopher and Eldred Jones (eds.). *Freetown; A Symposium.* Freetown: Sierra Leone University Press, 1968.

Gallais, Jean. *Le Delta Interieur du Niger. Etude de Géographie Regionale.* Dakar: I.F.A.N., 1967 (2 Vols).

Gleave, M. B. and H. P. White. "The West African Middle Belt. Environmental Fact or Geographer's Fiction?" *Geog. Rev.* **59** (1969) 123–129.

Gould, Peter R. *Transportation in Ghana.* Evanston: Northwestern University Press, 1960.

Gusten, Rolf. *Studies in the Staple Food Economy of Western Nigeria.* Munich: Weltforum Verlag, 1968.

Hill, Polly. *The Migrant Cocoa-Farmers of Southern Ghana.* London: Cambridge University Press, 1963.

Hilling, D. *Tema: the Geography of a New Port. Geography,* **51** (1960) 111–125.

Hilton, T. E. "Ivory Coast." *Focus,* XVI, 2 October 1965.

Hilton, T. E. "Mali." *Focus,* XVIII, 1, September 1967.

Hilton, T. E. "The Volta Resettlement Project." *J. Tropical Geog.* **24** (1967) 12–21.

Hodder, B. W. "Rural Periodic Day Markets in Part of Yorubaland, Western Nigeria." *Trans. Inst. Brit. Geo* **29** (1961) 149–159.

Hunter, John M. "The Social Roots of Dispersed Settlement in Northern Ghana." *Ann. Assoc. Amer. Geog.* **57** (1967) 338–349.

Hunter, John M. "Seasonal Hunger in a Part of the West African Savanna: A Survey of Body-Weights in North-East Ghana." *Trans. Inst. Brit. Geog.* **41** (1967) 167–185.

Hunter, John M. "Population Pressure in a Part of the West African Savanna: A Study of Nangodi, Northeast Ghana." *Ann. Ass. Amer. Geog.* **57** (1967) 101–114.

Johnston, Bruce F. *The Staple Food Economies of Western Tropical Africa.* Stanford: Ford Research Institute, 1958.

Kuper, Hilda (ed.). *Urbanization and Migration in West Africa.* Berkeley: University of California Press, 1965.

Lawrence, A. W. *Trade Castles and Forts of West Africa*. London: Cape, 1963.

Lloyd, P. C. *et al.* (eds.). *The City of Ibadan*. London: Cambridge University Press, 1967.

Mabogunje, A. L. *Urbanization in Nigeria*. London: London University Press, 1968.

Melamid, Alexander. "The Geography of the Algerian Petroleum Industry." *Econ. Geog.* **44** (1968) 37–56.

Mortimore, M. J. and J. Wilson. *Land and People in the Kano Close-settled Zone*. Zaria, Nigeria: Department of Geography, Ahmadu Bello University, 1965.

Moss, R. P. "Land Use, Vegetation and Soil Factors in South-West Nigeria: A New Approach." *Pacific Viewpoint* **9** (1968) 107–127.

Ojo, G. T. Afolabi. *Yoruba Culture, a Geographical Analysis*. London: University of London Press, 1966.

Oluwasanmi, H. A. *et al. Uboma: A Socio-Economic and Nutritional Survey of a Rural Community in Eastern Nigeria*. Bude; Cornwall: Geographical Pubs. Ltd., 1966 (World Land Use Survey).

Peterec, Richard J. *Dakar and West African Economic Development*. New York: Columbia University Press, 1967.

Simpson, E. S. "Electricity Production in Nigeria." *Econ. Geog.* **45** (1969) 239–257.

Southorn, Lady. *The Gambia*. London: Allen and Unwin, 1952.

Swindell, Kenneth. "Iron Ore Mining in West Africa." *Econ. Geog.* **43** (1967) 333–346.

Thomas, Benjamin E. *Transportation and Physical Geography in West Africa*. Washington: National Academy of Sciences, 1960.

Thompson, Virginia and Richard Adloff. *French West Africa*. London: Allen and Unwin, 1958.

Udo, R. K. "Sixty Years of Plantation Agriculture in Southern Nigeria." *Econ. Geog.* **41** (1965) 356–368.

Udo, R. K. *Geographical Regions of Nigeria*. London: Heinenann, 1970.

Wells, F. A. and W. A. Warmington. *Studies in Industrialization: Nigeria and the Cameroons*. London: Oxford University Press, 1962.

White, H. P. "Dahomey: the Geographical Basis of an African State." *Tijds. Econ. Soc. Geog.* **57** (1966) 61–67.

Wills, J. Brian (ed.). *Agriculture and Land Use in Ghana*. London: Oxford University Press, 1962.

Atlases:

Atlas of the Gold Coast. Accra: Gold Coast Survey, 1945.
Atlas of Sierra Leone. Freetown: Survey and Lands Department, 1953.

Periodicals:

Bulletin. *Ghana Geographical Association.*
Nigerian Geographical Journal.
Occasional Papers, Department of Geography, Ahmadu Bello University, Zaria, Nigeria.
Sierra Leone Geographical Journal.
Sierra Leone Studies.
Bulletin de l' Institute Fondamental d'Afrique Noire
    (formerly de l'Institute Français).
Journal of the West African Science Association.
The Nigerian Field.

14. THE SUDAN

Amin, M. A. "The Khashm el Girba Irrigation Scheme." *Professional Geographer,* **30,** 3 (1969) 150–152.

Barbour, K. M. "Population Shifts and Changes in the Sudan Since 1898." *M.E.S.,* January 1966.

Barbour, K. M. "North and South in Sudan: A Study in Human Contrasts." *Ann. Assoc. Amer. Geog.* **54** (1964) 209–226.

Davies, H. R. J. "Nomadism in the Sudan: Aspects of the Problem and Suggested Lines for its Solution." *Tid. v. Econ. En. Soc. Gy.* September/October, 1966.

El-Bushra, El-Sayed. "The Factors Affecting Settlement Distribution in the Sudan." *Geog. Ann.* **49B** (1967) 10–24.

Hill, R. L. *A Bibliography of the Anglo-Egyptian Sudan.* London: Oxford University Press, 1939.

Hill, R. L. *Sudan Transport. A History of Railway, Marine and River Services in the Republic of Sudan.* London: Oxford University Press, 1965.

Holt, P. M. *A Modern History of the Sudan.* London: Weidenfeld and Nicolson, 1967.

Lebon, J. H. G. "The Land and Water Use Survey of North-Central Kordofan (1961–66)." *Geog. J.* **134** (1968) 546–550.

Lee, D. R. "The Location of Land-Use Types: The Nile Valley in Northern Sudan." *Econ. Geog.,* January 1970, 53–62.

Oliver, J. "Port Sudan: The Study of its Growth and Functions." *Tijds. Econ. Soc. Geog.* **57** (1966) 54–61.

Randell, J. R. *Patterns of Settlement in the Manaqil Extension.* Sudan Notes and Records, 1966.

Randell, J. R. "The Sudan." *Focus,* XVII, 1, September 1966.

Reed, W. *Red Sea Fisheries of Sudan,* Khartoum: Govt. Printer, 1964.

Shinnie, P. L. *Meroe: A Civilization of the Sudan.* London: Thames and Hudson, 1967.

Whiteman, A. J. "Formation of the Red Sea Depression." *Geol. Mag.* **105** (1968) 231–246.

Periodicals:

Geographical Magazine. Khartoum University Geographical Society.
Sudan Notes and Records.

15. ETHIOPIA AND THE HORN OF AFRICA

Abdul-Haggag Y. *A Contribution to the Physiography of Northern Ethiopia.* London: Athlone Press, 1961.

Doresse, J. *Ethiopia.* London, 1959.

Hemming, C. F. "The Vegetation of the Northern Region of the Somali Republic." *Proc. Linn. Soc. Lond.* **177,** 2 (1966) 173–248.

Horvath, Ronald J. "Towns in Ethiopia." *Erdkunde* **22** (1968) 42–51.

Horvath, Ronald J. "Von Thunen's Isolated State and the Area around Addis Ababa, Ethiopia." *Ann. Assoc. Amer. Geogr.* **59** (1969) 308–323.

Huffnagel, H. P. *Agriculture in Ethiopia*. Rome: FAO, 1961.

Karp, Mark. *The Economics of Trusteeship in Somalia*. Boston: Boston University Press, 1960.

Lewis, I. M. *Peoples of the Horn of Africa: Somali, Afar and Saho*. London: International African Institute, 1955.

Lewis, I. M. *A Pastoral Democracy*. London: Oxford University Press, 1961.

Lewis, I. M. *The Modern History of Somaliland*. London: Weidenfeld and Nicolson, 1965.

Lipsky, G. A. *Ethiopia: Its People, its Society, its Culture*. New Haven, 1962.

Mohr, Paul A. "The Ethiopian Rift System." *Bull. Geophys. Observatory, U. Coll.*, Addis Ababa. **3** (1962) 33–62.

Mohr, Paul A. *The Geology of Ethiopia*. Addis Ababa: University College of Addis Ababa Press, n.d. (about 1964).

Pallister, J. W. "Notes on the Geomorphology of the Northern Region, Somali Republic." *Geog. J.* **129** (1963) 184–7.

Pankhurst, R. *An Introduction to the Economic History of Ethiopia*. London, 1961.

Pankhurst, R. *Ethiopia: A Cultural History*. London, 1959.

Shack, William A. *The Gurage. A People of the Ensete Culture*. London: Oxford University Press, 1966.

Sommer, John W. "Ethiopia." *Focus*, XV, 8, April 1965.

Thompson, Virginia and R. Adloff. *Djibouti and the Horn of Africa*. Stanford: Stanford University Press, 1968.

Ullendorff, E. *The Ethiopians*. London: Oxford University Press, 1960.

Atlas:

Mesfin Wolde Mariam. *A Preliminary Atlas of Ethiopia*. Addis Ababa, 1962.

Periodicals:

Bulletin of the Geophysical Observatory. University College of Addis Ababa.
Ethiopian Geographical Journal.
Ethiopian Observer.
Journal of Ethiopian Studies.

16. EQUATORIAL AFRICA

Academie Royale des Sciences d'Outre-Mer. *Livre Blanc*. Brussels: 1963 (3 vols.).

Ardener, E., S. Ardener, and W. A. Warmington. *Plantation and Village in the Cameroons*. London: Oxford University Press, 1960.

Bederman, S. H. "Plantation Agriculture in Victoria Division, West Cameroon. An Historical Introduction." *Geography*, **51** (1966) 349–360.

Belgian Congo and Ruanda-Urundi Information and Public Relations Office. *Belgian Congo*. Brussels: Inforcongo, 1960 (2 vols.).

Billard, Piere. *Le Cameroun Federal*. Tome 2: *Essai de Géographie Humaine et Economique*. London: Imprimerie des Beaux-Arts, Tixer et Fils, 1968. Tome 1: *Essai de Géographie Physique*.

Clarke, John I. Aerial Photograph of Yaounde Cameroon. *Erde*, **98** (1967) 1–4.

Clarke, John I. "Cameroon." *Focus*, XVI, 7, March 1966.

Clarke, John I. Aerial Photograph of Douala, Cameroun. *Erde*, **99** (1968) 205–208.

Hance, William A. and I. S. van Dongen. "Matadi, Focus of Belgian African Transport." *Ann. Assoc. Amer. Geog.* (March 1958) 41–72.

Hilling, D. "The Changing Economy of Gabon: Development in a New African Republic." *Geography,* **48** (1963) 155–165.

Hoskyns, C. *The Congo Since Independence.* London: Oxford University Press, 1965.

Miracle, M. P. *Agriculture in the Congo Basin.* Madison: University of Wisconsin Press, 1967.

Patten, George P. "Gabon." *Focus,* XII, 2, October 1961.

Patten, George P. "Republic of the Congo (Brazzaville)." *Focus,* XIII, 2, October 1962.

Robert, M. *Le Congo Physique.* Liege, 1946 (3rd Ed.).

Sautter, G. *De l'Atlantique an Fleure Congo: Une Géographie du Sous-Peuplement (Republique du Congo, Republique Gabonaise).* Paris: Mouton, 1966.

Slade, R. *The Belgian Congo.* London: Oxford University Press, 1960.

Thompson, Virginia and R. Adloff. *The Emerging States of French Equatorial Africa.* Stanford: Stanford University Press, 1960.

Traveller's Guide to the Belgian Congo and Ruanda-Urundi. Brussels: Tourist Bureau for the Belgian Congo and Ruanda-Urundi, 1956 (2nd Ed.).

Trézenem, Edouard. *L'Afrique Equatorial Française.* Paris: Societe d'Editions Géographiques. Maritimes et Coloniales, 1955.

Vennetier, P. *Pointe-Noire et la Façade Maritime du Congo-Brazzaille.* Paris: ORSTOM, 1968.

Ziéglé, Henri. *Afrique Equatoriale Française.* Paris: Editions Berger-Levrault, 1952.

Atlases:

Atlas du Cameroun. Yaounde: Institute de Recherches Scientifique du Cameroun, 1956.

Atlas General du Congo et du Ruanda Urundi. Brussels: Institut Royal Colonial Belge, 1948.

Periodicals:

Bulletin de l'Institut de Recherches Scientifiques au Congo (Brazzaville).

17. EAST AFRICA

African Land Development in Kenya, 1946–1962. Nairobi: Ministry of Agriculture, 1962.

Alexander, Charles S. "Beach Ridges in Northeastern Tanzania." *Geog. Rev.* **59** (1969) 104–122.

Altschul, D. Robert. *The Arrangement and Dimensions of Rural Settlements of the Northeast Coastal Zone of Tanganyika, Pangani District.* Urbana: Department of Geography, University of Illinois, 1967.

Berry, L. (ed.) *Tanzania in Maps.* London: University of London Press, 1971.

Bishop, Walter W. and A. F. Trendall. "Erosion Surfaces, Tectonics and Volcanic Activity in Uganda. *Quart. J. Geol. Soc. London,* **122** (1966) 385–420.

Brooke, Clarke. "Types of Food Shortages in Tanzania." *Geog. Rev.* **57** (1967) 333–357.

Doornkamp, John C. "The Nature, Correlation and Ages of the Erosion Surfaces of Southern Uganda." *Geog. Ann.* **50A** (1968) 151–161.

Doornkamp, J. C. and P. H. Temple. "Surface, Drainage and Tectonic Instability in Part of Southern Uganda." *Geog. J.* **132** (1966) 238–252.

East Africa Royal Commission 1953–1955. *Report.* London: H.M.S.O., 1955.

Fuggles-Couchman, N. R. *Agricultural Change in Tanganyika. 1945–1960.* Stanford: Ford Research Institute, 1964.

Gillman, C. "A Vegetation Types Map of Tanganyika Territory." *Geog. Rev.* **39**, 1 (1949) 7–37.

Gillman, C. "A Population Map of Tanganyika Territory." *Geog. Rev.* **26**, 3 (1936) 353–375.

Hall, S. A. and B. W. Langlands. *Uganda Atlas of Disease Distribution.* Occ. Papers, Department of Geography, Makerere University, Coll. 12 (1968).

Harlow, Vincent and E. M. Chilver. *History of East Africa, Vol. II.* Oxford: Clarendon, 1965.

Hoyle, B. S. *The Seaports of East Africa: A Geographical Study.* Nairobi: East Africa Publ. Ho. 1967.

Jatzold, Ralph and E. Baum. *The Kilombero Valley.* Munich: Weltforum Verlag, 1968.

Jensen, S. *Regional Economic Atlas, Mainland Tanzania.* Dar es Salaam: Bureau of Resource Assessments and Land Use Planning, 1968.

Knight, David B. "Botswana." *Focus,* XX, 3, November 1969.

Langdale-Brown, I. *et al. The Vegetation of Uganda and its Bearing on Land-Use.* Entebbe: Govt. Printer, 1964.

Leurquin, P. P. *Agricultural Change in Ruanda-Urundi 1945–1960.* Stanford: Ford Research Institute, 1963.

Masefield, G. B. *Agricultural Change in Uganda 1945–1960.* Stanford: Ford Research Institute, 1962.

McMaster, David N. *A Subsistence Crop Geography of Uganda.* World Land Use Survey Occ. Papers No. 2. Bude: Geographical Publications, 1962.

McMaster, David N. "The Colonial District Town in Uganda." *In Urbanization and its Problems. Essays in Honour of E. W. Gilbet.* Oxford: Blackwell, 1968.

McMaster, David N. "Uganda." *Focus,* XIV, 5, January 1964.

Melamid, Alexander. "Economic Aspects of the Kenya-Somali Boundary Dispute." *Scope* (New York) **1** (1964)1964) 1–7.

Millman, Rodger. "Kenya's 'Tierra Templada'" *Scot. Geog. Mag.* **84** (1968) 185–195.

Morgan, W. T. W. and N. Manfred Shaffer. *Population of Kenya: Density and Distribution.* Nairobi: Oxford University Press, 1966.

Morgan, W. T. W. "The Role of Temperate Crops in the Kenya Highlands." *Acta Geog.* **20** (1968) 273–278.

Morgan, W. T. W. "Urbanization in Kenya: Origins and Trends." *Trans. Inst. Brit. Geogr.* **46** (1969) 167–178.

Ojany, F. F. "The Physique of Kenya: A Contribution in Landscape Analysis." *Ann. Ass. Amer. Geog.* **56** (1966) 183–196.

Ojany, Francis F. "The Mound Topography of the Thika and Athi Plains of Kenya: A Problem of Origin." *Erdkunde.* **22** (1968) 269–275.

Ojany, Francis. "The Inselbergs of Eastern Kenya with Special Reference to the Ukambani Area." *Z. Geomorphol.* **13** (1969) 196–206.

Oliver, Roland and Gervase Mathew. *History of East Africa. Vol. I.* Oxford: Clarendon, 1963.

Ruthenberg, Hans. *African Agricultural Production Development Policy in Kenya 1952–1965*. Berlin: Springer-Verlag, 1966.

Sorrenson, M. P. K. *Land Reform in the Kikuyu Country*. Nairobi: Oxford University Press, 1967.

Sorrenson, M. P. K. *Origins of European Settlement in Kenya*. Nairobi: Oxford University Press, 1968.

Ruthenberg, Hans. (ed.). *Smallholder Farming and Smallholder Development in Tanzania. Ten case studies*. Munich: Weltforum Verlag, 1968.

Ruthenburg, Hans. *Agricultural Development in Tanganyika*. Berlin: Spinger-Verlag, 1964.

Soja, Edward W. *The Geography of Modernization in Kenya: A Spatial Analysis of Social, Economic and Political Change*. Syracuse, N.Y.: Syracuse University Press, 1968.

Tanzania Ministry of Information. *Tanzania Today: A Portrait of the United Republic*. Nairobi: University Press of Africa, 1968.

Temple, Paul H. "Further Observations on the Glaciers of the Ruwenzori." *Geog. Ann.* **50A** (1968) 136–150.

UNESCO. *Report of the Upper Mantle Committee (UNESCO Seminar on the East African Rift System, Nairobi, 12–17 April, 1965*. Nairobi: University College, University of East Africa, 1965.

Whitton, John B. "The Landforms of the Central Ruwenzori, East Africa." *Geog. J.* **132** (1966) 32–42.

Atlases:

Atlas of Kenya.
Atlas of Tanzania
Atlas of Uganda.

Periodicals:

Azania.
East African Geographical Review.
Occasional Papers. Department of Geography, Makerere University College.
Proceedings of the East African Academy.
Tanganyika Notes and Record.
Uganda Journal.

18. THE SOUTHERN SAVANNAS

Abshire, David M. and Michael A. Samuels (eds.). *Portuguese Africa: A Handbook*. New York: Praeger, 1969.

Brown, Peter and A. Young. *The Physical Environment of Central Malawi with Special Reference to Soils and Agriculture*. Zomba: Govt. Printer, 1965.

Chilcote, Ronald H. *Portuguese Africa*. London: Prentice Hall, 1963.

Cole, Monica. "Vegetation and Geomorphology in Northern Rhodesia: An Aspect of the Distribution of the Savanna of Central Africa." *Geog. J.* **129** (1963) 290–310.

Collins, M. O. *Rhodesia: Its Natural Resources and Economic Development.* 1966.

Kay, George. *Rhodesia, a Human Geography* London: University of London Press, 1970.

Debenham, Frank. *Report on the Water Resources of the Bechuanaland Protectorate, Northern Rhodesia, The Nyasaland Protectorate, Tanganyika Territory, Kenya and the Uganda Protectorate.* London: H.M.S.O., 1948.

Floyd, B. N. *Changing Patterns of African Land Use in Southern Rhodesia.* Lusaka: Rhodes Livingstone Institute, 1962.

Floyd, B. N. "Land Apportionment in Southern Rhodesia." *Geog. Rev.* October 1962, 566–582.

Gourou, Pierre. "Angola et Moçambique: Etudes de Geographie Regionale." *Rev. Geog. Montreal* 22 (1968) 5–20.

Griffiths, Leuan C. "Zambian Coal: An Example of Strategic Resource Development. *Geog. Rev.* 58 (1968) 538–551.

Guichonnet, Paul. "Le Mozambique: Esquisse Geographique." *Globe* (*Geneva*) 105 (1965) 35–96.

Hamilton, P. "The Changing Pattern of African Land Use in Rhodesia." *In* Whitton, J. B. and P. D Wood. *Essays in Geography for Austin Miller.* Reading University, 1965.

Hance, W. A. and Irene S. van Dongen. "The Port of Lobito and the Benguela Railway." *Geog. Rev.* 46 (1956), 400–487.

Hance, William A. and Irene S. van Dongen. "Lourenço Marques in Delagoa Bay." *Econ. Geog.,* 33 (1957), 238–256.

Hance, William A. and Irene S. Van Dorgen. "Beira, Mozambique Gateway to Central Africa." *Ann. Ass. American Geographers,* 47 (1957), 307–305.

Helen, John A. *Rural Economic Development in Zambia, 1890–1964.* Munich: Weltforum Verlag, 1968.

Hellen, Anthony. "Some Aspects of Land Use and Population in the Ngoni Reserves of Northern Rhodesia." *Erdkunde* 16 (1962) 190–205.

Jack, D. T. *Report on an Economic Survey of Nyasaland, 1958–59.* Salisbury: Govt. Printer.

Kay, George. *A Social Geography of Zambia.* London: University of London Press, 1967.

Kay, George. *Maps of the Distribution and Density of African Population in Zambia.* Lusaka: University of Zambia Institute of Social Research, 1967.

Kay, George. "The Towns of Zambia." *In* Steel, R. W. and R. Lawton. *Liverpool Essays in Geography.* 1967.

Davis, D. Hywel. (ed.) *Zambia in Maps.* London: University of London Press. 1971.

Mendelsohn, F. *The Geology of the Northern Rhodesian Copperbelt.* London: Macdonald, 1961.

Nyasaland, Natural Reserves Department. *The Natural Resources of Nyasaland.* Zambia: Govt. Printer, 1960.

Pelletier, R. A. *Mineral Resources of South-Central Africa.* Cape Town: Oxford University Press, 1964.

Pike, J. G. and G. T. Rimmington, *Malawi. A Geographical Study.* London: Oxford University Press, 1965.

Pollock, N. C. "Irrigation in the Rhodesian Lowveld." *Geog. J.* 134 (1968) 70–77.

Prescott, J. R. V. "Overpopulation and Overstocking in the Native Areas of Matabeleland." *Geog. J.* 127 (1961) 212–225.

Prescott, J. R. V. "Population Distribution in Southern Rhodesia." *Geog. Rev.* 52 (1962) 559–565.

Richards, Audrey I. *Land, Labour and Diet in Northern Rhodesia. An Economic Study of the Bantu tribe.* London: Oxford University Press, 1939.

Roder, Wolf. *The Sabi Valley Irrigation Projects.* Research Papers, Department of Geography, University of Chicago, **99** (1965).

Scudder, Thayer. *The Ecology of the Gwembe Tonga.* Manchester: Manchester University Press, 1962.

Trapnell, Colin G. *The Soils, Vegetation and Agriculture of North-eastern Rhodesia.* Lusaka: Govt. Printer, 1953.

Trapnell, Colin G. and J. N. Clothier, *The Soils, Vegetation and Agricultural Systems of North-western Rhodesia.* Lusaka: Govt. Printer, 1937.

Van Dongen, Irene S. "The Port of Luanda in the Economy of Angola." *Boletime da Sociedade de Geografia de Lisboa,* January–March 1960, 3–43.

Williams, Stuart. *The Distribution of the African Population of Northern Rhodesia.* Lusaka: Rhodes-Livingstone Institute, 1962.

Young, Anthony and P. Brown. *The Physical Environment of Northern Nyasaland with Special Reference to Soils and Agriculture.* Zambia: Govt. Printer, 1962.

Young, A. and P. Brown. *The Physical Environment of Northern Nyasaland with Special Reference to Soils and Agriculture.* Zambia: Govt. Printer, 1962.

Yudelman, Montague. *Africans on the Land.* Cambridge, Mass.: Harvard University Press, 1964.

Atlases:

Atlas of the Federation of Rhodesia and Nyasaland. Salisbury: Federal Department of Trig. and Topo. Surveys, 1960.

Atlas de Mocambique. Lourenço Marques: Empresa Moderna, 1962.

Periodicals:

African Social Research. (Formerly: *Human Problems in Central Africa*).

Memorias. Series B (*Ciencias geograficas-geologicas*). Instututo de Investigacao Cientifica de Moçambique.

The Nyasaland Journal.

The Rhodes Livingstone Museum: Occasional Papers; Communications.

The Zambia Journal.

19. SOUTH AFRICA

Basutoland, Bechuanaland Protectorate and Swaziland. Report of an Economic Survey Mission. London: H.M.S.O., 1960.

Bawden, M. G. and D. M. Carroll. *The Land Resources of Lesotho.* Tolworth: Land Resources Division, Dir. Overseas Surveys, 1968.

Board, C. *et al. The Border Region: Natural Environments and Land Use in the Eastern Cape.* Cape Town: Oxford University Press, 1962.

Boocock, C. "Mineral Resources of the Bechuanaland Protectorate." *Overseas Geol. and Min. Res.* **9** (1964–1965) 369–417.

Brookfield, H. C. "Some Geographical Implications of the Apartheid and Partnership Policies in Southern Africa." *Trans. Inst. Brit. Geogr.* **23** (1957) 225–247.

Clark, J. Desmond. *The Prehistory of Southern Africa.* Harmondsworth: Penguin, 1959.

Coetzee, J. A. "The Transvaal Competitive Area and the Distribution of its

Commercial Seaborne Imports via the Ports of South Africa and Lourenço Marques." *Tijds. Econ. Soc. Geog.* **54** (1963) 186–192.

Daniel, J. B. McI. "Some Government Measures to Improve African Agriculture in Swaziland." *Geog. J.* **132** (1966) 506–515.

Davies, R. J. "The Growth of the Durban Metropolitan Area." *S. A. Geogr. J.* **45** (1963) 15–43.

Davis, D. H. S. (ed.). *Ecological Studies in Southern Africa.* The Hague: W. Junk, 1964.

Davis, D. Hywel. *Land Use in Central Cape Town.* Johannesburg: Longmans, 1965.

Fair, T. J. D., G. Murdock, and H. M. Jones. *Development in Swaziland, a Regional Analysis.* Johannesburg: Witwatersrand Press, 1969.

Grut, Mikael. *Forestry and Forest Industry in South Africa.* Cape Town: Balkema, 1965.

Grove, A. T. "Landforms and Climate Change in the Kalahari and Ngamiland." *Geog. J.* **135** (1969) 191–212.

Henderson, H. J. R. "The Dairying Industry in South Africa." *Trans. Inst. Brit. Geog.* **28** (1960) 237–252.

King, Lester C. *South African Scenery: A Textbook of Geomorphology.* Edinburgh: Oliver & Boyd, 1963 (3rd Ed.).

Logan, Richard F. "South West Africa." *Focus,* XI, 3, November 1960.

Morris, S. S. "Cape Town: Metropolis in the Making." *Town Planning Review* **30** (1969) 102–118.

Namib Desert Research Station. Scientific Papers. Pretoria: Namib Desert Research Association, 1961.

Natal Regional Survey. Cape Town: Oxford University Press, 1951.

Niddrie, David L. "South Africa." *Focus,* XVII, 10, June 1967.

Pollock, N. C. "The Development of Urbanization in Southern Africa." *In Urbanization and its Problems. Essay in Honour of E. W. Gilbert.* Oxford: Blackwell, 1968.

Sabbagh, M. Ernest. "Some Geographical Characteristics of a Plural Society: Apartheid in South Africa." *Geog. Rev.* **58** (1968) 1–28.

Schulze, B. R. *Climate of South Africa. Part 8. General Survey.* Pretoria: Govt. Printer, 1965.

Shaffer, N. Manfred. "The Competitive Position of the Port of Durban." *Northwestern University Studies in Geog.* **8** (1965).

Sillery, A. *The Bechuanaland Protectorate.* New York: Oxford University Press, 1952.

Smit, P. *Lesotho: A Geographical Study.* Pretoria: Africa Institute, 1967.

Talbot, W. J. *Swartland and Sandveld. A Survey of Land Utilization and Soil Erosion in the Western Lowland of the Cape Province.* Cape Town: Oxford University Press, 1947.

Talbot, A. M. and W. J. Talbot. "Economic and Environmental Factors in the Development and Distribution of Viticulture in South Africa." *Wiener G. Schiften* **24/29** (1967) 297–310.

Thornington-Smith, E. *Towards a Plan for the Tugela Basin.* Pietermaritzburg: Town and Regional Planning Commission, Natal, 1960.

Wallman, Sandra. *Take out Hunger. Two Case Studies of Rural Development in Basutoland.* London: Athlone Press, 1969.

Wellington, John H. *South West Africa and its Human Issues.* Oxford: Clarendon, 1967.

Whittington, G. "The Swaziland Railway." *Tijds. Econ. Soc. Geog.* **57** (1966) 68–73.

Wilson, Monica and Leonard Thompson (eds.). *The Oxford History of South Africa. Vol. 1. South Africa to 1870.* Oxford: Clarendon, 1969.

Young, B. A. *Bechuanaland.* London: H.M.S.O., 1966. (The Corona Library).

Young, Bruce S. "High Commission Territories of South Africa." *Focus* XIV, 4, December 1963.

Atlas:

Atlas of the Union of South Africa.

Periodicals:

South African Geographical Journal.
Optima.
South African Journal of Science.

20. AFRICAN SEAS AND ISLANDS

Brookfield, H. C. "Problems of Monoculture and Diversification in a Sugar Island: Mauritius." *Econ. Geog.* **35** (1959) 25–40.

Brookfield, H. C. "Population Distribution in Mauritius." *J. Tropical Geog.* **13** (1959), 1–22.

Chevalier, Louis. *Madagascar; Populations et Resources.* Paris: Presses Universitaires de France, 1952.

Deschamps, H. *Madagascar, Comores, Terres Australes.* Paris: Berger-Levrault, 1951.

Dixey, Frank. "The Geology and Geomorphology of Madagascar, and a Comparison with Eastern Africa." *Quart. J. Geol. Soc. London,* **116** (1960) 255–268.

Hance, William A. "Transportation in Madagascar." *Geog. Rev.* January 1958, 45–68.

Meade, James E. *et al. The Economic and Social Structure of Mauritius.* London: Methuen, 1961.

Minelle, Jean. *L'Agriculture à Madagascar.* Paris: Marcel Riviere, 1959.

Munch, Peter A. *Sociology of Tristan da Cunha.* Oslo: Norske Videnskaps-Akademi, 1945.

Ommaney, F. D. *The Shoals of Capricorn.* London: Longmans, Green, 1952.

Ramdin T. *Mauritius: A Geographical Survey.* London: University Tutorial Press, 1970.

Robequain, C. *Madagascar ét les Bases Dispersées de l'Union Française.* Paris: P.U.F., 1958.

Scott, Robert. *Limuria. The Lesser dependencies of Mauritius.* London: Oxford University Press, 1961.

Toussaint, A. and H. Adolphe. *Bibliography of Mauritius (1502–1954)* Port Louis: Mauritius Archives, 1956.

Wheeler, J. F. G. and F. D. Ommaney. *Report on the Mauritius-Seychelles Fisheries Survey, 1948–1949.* London, 1953.

Atlas:

Atlas de Madagascar.

Periodical:

Madagascar: Revue de Géographie.

Statistical Summary

ALGERIA (El Djazaïria Demokratia Echaabia)

Algeria became an independent republic on July 4, 1962; there are certain special agreements with France.

Area. The more densely settled wilayates (departments) contain 113,883 square miles (295,033 sq.km); the thinly populated Algerian Sahara has an estimated area of 838,315 square miles (2,171,800 sq.km) making a total estimated area of 952,200 square miles (2,466,840 sq.km).

Population. (1966 census) 12,102,000; (mid-1969 UN estimate) 13,349,000.

Towns (1967 estimate). Algiers (Alger, capital) 943,000; Oran 328,000; Constantine 254,000; Annaba 165,000; Sidi-Bel-Abbès 101,000; Mostaganem 64,000; Sétif 98,000; Tlemcen 80,000; Blida 87,000; Skikda 85,000; Bejaia 63,000; Colomb-Béchar 27,000.

Agriculture. 60 percent of total labor force engaged in agriculture.

Land use 1968	hectares
Arable	6,243,000
Permanent crops	544,000
Permanent meadows and pastures	37,416
Forest	2,424
Irrigated land	270,000

Crops (*hectares*)

	1948/52	1961/65	1970
Wheat	1,597,000	1,969,000	2,150,000
Barley	1,166,000	810,000	688,000
Grapes (table and wine)	393,000	348,000	306,000 (1969)

Production, metric tons

Dates	(98,000)	(113,000)	(85,000) (1969)
Figs (fresh)	(97,000)	(56,000)	(45,000) (1969)
Figs (dried)	(29,000)	(8,000)	(8,000) (1969)

Livestock (1969/70). Horses 125,000; mules 195,000; asses 310,000; camels 170,000; cattle 870,000; sheep 7,400,000; goats 2,200,000; pigs 6,000.

Mineral production (1965) (*metric tons*). Iron ore 2,998,000; phosphate rock 420,700; zinc 420,000; crude petroleum (1970) 45,880,000.

Trade.

	1960	1968
Imports	624,531 million fr.	4022 million dinars
	($1249 million)	($804 million)
	(mainly from France, USA, W. Germany, Italy)	
Exports	194,654 million fr.	4097 million dinars
	($389 million)	($820 million)
	(mainly to France, West Germany, Italy)	

Chief exports: crude petroleum, wine, natural gas, fruit.

Currency. Dinar (DA) roughly at par with the French franc.

ANGOLA (Portuguese West Africa)

A Portuguese colony.

Area. 481,351 square miles (1,246,700 sq.km), including the detached tract of Cabinda.

Population. (1960 census) 4,830,449; (mid-1969 UN estimate) 5,430,000.

Towns. S. Paulo de Luanda (capital) (1960), 225,000. Future capital: Huambo (Nova Lisboa).

Agriculture. 82 percent of total labor force engaged in agriculture.

Land use 1953	hectares
Arable and permanent crops	900,000
Permanent meadows and pastures	29,000,000
Forest	43,200,000

Crops (*hectares*)

	1948/52	1961/65	1970
Maize	400,000	516,000	530,000
Wheat	14,000	15,000	20,000
Cassava	94,000	111,000	120,000 (1969)
Sugar cane	9,000	14,000	14,000
Cotton	46,000	38,000	70,000
Sisal	42,000	69,000	70,000

Production, metric tons

Coffee	(49,900)	(185,000)	(198,000)
Palm kernels	(11,100)	(18,900)	(14,000)
Palm oil	(35,800)	(38,000)	(32,000)

There is also production of tobacco and cocoa beans.

Livestock (1969/70). Horses 1,000; asses 4,000; cattle 2,171,000; sheep 7,400,000; goats 769,000; pigs 319,000.

Mineral production (1969). Diamonds 2.02 million carats; iron ore 5.5 million metric tons; salt 80,181 metric tons; crude petroleum (1970) from Cabinda 4.7 million metric tons.

Trade.

	1960	1968
Imports	3,767,864,000 escudos	8,844,820 escudos
	($130 million)	($311.4 million)
	(mainly from Portugal, USA, West Germany, UK)	
Exports	3,587,428,000 escudos	7,796,360,000 escudos
	($123 million)	($274.5 million)

(mainly to Portugal, USA, Netherlands, West Germany, Japan)

Chief exports: coffee beans, diamonds, iron ore, crude petroleum.

Currency. As in Portugal: the escudo, divided into 100 centavos.

THE AFARS AND THE ISSAS, FRENCH TERRITORY OF
(Territoire francais des Afars et des Issas)

An oversea territory of France represented in Paris by 1 deputy in each of the National Assembly and the Senate. At a referendum on March 19, 1967, the majority of the electorate voted for association with France rather than for independence.

Area. 8,490 square miles (22,000 sq.km).

Population (mid-1969 UN estimate). 91,000.

Towns. Djibouti (capital) (1961) 41,200; (1967 estimate) 62,000

Agriculture.

Land use	*hectares*
Arable (1958)	1,000
Permanent meadows and pastures (1963)	244,000
Forest (1963)	8,000

Livestock (1969/70). Asses 3,000; camels 22,000; cattle 16,000; sheep 92,000; goats 540,000.

Mineral production. None. There are probably reserves of gypsum, mica, amethyst, and sulphur.

Trade.

	1966	1970
Imports	6038 million Djibouti fr.	8195 million Djibouti fr.
	($28 million)	($38 million)
Exports	565 million Djibouti fr.	817 million Djibouti fr.
	($2.6 million)	($3.8 million)

Chief exports: hides and cattle; coffee in transit from Ethiopia.

Currency. Since March 17, 1949: the Djibouti franc, divided into 100 centimes.

BOTSWANA

An independent republic within the Commonwealth since 30 September, 1966; formerly Bechuanaland, a British protectorate.

Area. About 222,000 square miles (575,000 sq.km).

Population. (1964 census) 543,105; (mid-1969 UN estimate) 629,000.

Towns (1964). Gaberone (capital) 14,000; Lobatsi 10,000; Francistown 13,000; Kanye 37,000; Serowe 37,000; Molepolole 32,000.

Agriculture. Percentage of labor force engaged in agriculture not recorded.

Land use 1969	*hectares*
Arable	427,000
Permanent crops	1,000
Permanent meadows and pastures	39,508,000
Forest	958,000
Irrigated land	2,000

Crops (*hectares*)

	1948/52	1961/65	1970
Maize	9,000	4,000	30,000
Sorghum	81,000	103,000	122,000

Livestock (1969/70). Horses 14,000; asses 44,000; cattle 1,481,000; sheep 418,000; goats 1,152,000; pigs 8,000.

Mineral production. Gold, silver; manganese ore (1964) 23,041 short tons; asbestos (1964) 1,774 short tons.

Trade. No data. Chief exports (1966) meat and meat products, livestock, hides, and skins.

Currency. As in the Republic of South Africa: the rand (R), divided into 100 cents, since February 14,1961.

BURUNDI

An independent state since July 1, 1962, and a republic since November 28, 1966. Formerly (as Urundi) linked with Ruanda (Rwanda) as mandated, later UN trust, territory, administered by Belgium.

Area. 10,747 square miles (27,834 sq.km).

Population. (1959 census) 2,213,280; (mid-1969 UN estimate) 3,475,000.

Towns. (1969 estimate). Bujumbura (capital) 100,000; Gitega 10,000.

Agriculture. 95 percent of total labor force engaged in agriculture.

Land use 1969	*hectares*
Arable	1,087,000
Permanent crops	160,000
Permanent meadows and pastures	435,000
Forest	69,000
Irrigated land (1966)	28,000

Crops (*hectares*)

	1948/52	1961/65	1970
Cassava	130,000	73,000	86,000 (1969)
Maize	81,000	107,000	145,000
Yams/sweet potatoes	97,000	92,000	117,000
Millet/sorghum	40,000	31,000	33,000
Groundnuts	5,000	6,000	11,000
Cotton, lint	7,000	11,000	10,000
Coffee (*production, metric tons*)	(7,000)	(12,500)	(22,000)

Plantation tea production is increasing.

Livestock (1969/70). Cattle 670,000; sheep 235,000; goats 470,000; pigs 23,000.

Mineral production.   There are cassiterite, kaolin, and gold reserves.

Trade.

1969

Imports   1,652.1 million Burundi fr. ($19.1 million)
[mainly from Belgium/Luxembourg, Japan, West Germany, Tanzania, USA, UK, Zaire (Congo(Kinshasa))]

Exports   1,235.4 million Burundi fr. ($14 million)
(mainly to Belgium/Luxembourg, USA).

Chief exports (1969): coffee, raw cotton.

Currency.   Burundi franc, divided into 100 centimes.

CAMEROUN (République Fédérale du Cameroun)

A republic since January 1, 1960, when the trusteeship territory administered by France on behalf of the United Nations became fully independent; increased in area in February 1961 when the southern part of British Cameroons voted to join the Republic in preference to joining Nigeria. Prior to World War I, a German colony (Kamerun).

Area.   Total area of Federal Republic: 183,570 square miles (475,440 sq.km).

Population.   (mid-1965 UN estimate) 5,229,000; (mid-1969 UN estimate) 5,680,000.

Towns (1969 estimate).   Yaoundé (capital) 130,000; Douala 210,000; Nkongsamba 50,000; Maroua 32,000; Edéa 15,000.

Agriculture.   84 percent of total labor force engaged in agriculture.

Land use 1969	*hectares*
Arable	6,722,000
Permanent crops	578,000
Permanent meadows and pastures	8,300,000
Forest	30,000,000

Crops (*hectares*)

	1948/52	1961/65	1970
Millet/sorghum	654,000	454,000	470,000
Maize	210,000	272,000	370,000
Cassava	96,000	108,000	215,000
Groundnuts	130,000	134,000	199,000
Cotton, lint	6,000	75,000	100,000

Production, metric tons

	1948/52	1961/65	1970
Coffee	(9,200)	(51,400)	(88,000)
Cocoa beans	(52,300)	(81,200)	(115,000)
Palm kernels	(32,500)	(37,200)	(52,000)
Palm oil	(21,500)	(42,500)	(60,000)

Livestock (1969/70). Horses 24,000; asses 58,000; cattle 2,100,000; sheep 1,700,000; goats 2,200,000; pigs 390,000.

Mineral production (1965). Aluminum 51,000 metric tons; gold 1,454 troy ozs.

Trade.

	1965	1968
Imports	33,299 million CFA fr.	46,765 million CFA fr.
	($121 million)	($170 million)
	[mainly from France (nearly 50%); some from West Germany, USA, UK]	
Exports	29,330 million CFA fr.	46,818 million CFA fr.
	($106.6 million)	($170.2 million)
	(mainly to France, Netherlands, West Germany, USA)	

Chief exports (1968): cocoa beans and butter, coffee, aluminum, raw cotton, bananas, groundnuts, palm nuts, and kernels.

Currency. Franc CFA, divided into 100 centimes.

CENTRAL AFRICAN REPUBLIC (République Centrafricaine)

An independent republic since August 13, 1960, and member of the French Community; formerly, as Ubangi Shari, a territory of French Equatorial Africa.

Area. 232,808 square miles (622,980 sq.km).

Population. (census November, 1968) 2,255,536.

Towns. Bangui (capital) 301,793 (in area of préfecture)

Agriculture. 90 percent of total labor force engaged in agriculture. Number of and area covered by agricultural holdings (1960/61): 231,500; 529,700 hectares.

Land use 1968	*hectares*
Arable	5,840,000
Permanent crops	60,000
Permanent meadows and pastures	100,000
Forest	7,400,000

Crops (*hectares*)

	1948/52	1961/65	1970
Cassava	132,000	204,000	200,000 (1969)
Millet and sorghum	54,000	77,000	80,000
Maize	7,000	59,000	50,000
Groundnuts	30,000	77,000	105,000
Cotton	151,000	129,000	120,000
Coffee (*production, metric tons*)	(4,000)	(9,100)	(12,359)

Livestock (1969/70). Asses 1,000; cattle 470,000; sheep 64,000; goats 520,000; pigs 54,000.

Mineral production. Diamonds (1970) 493,605 carats.

Trade.

	1965	1968
Imports	6,770 million fr.CFA ($24.6 million)	8,816 million fr.CFA ($32 million)
	(mainly from France (over 50%), Italy, USA)	
Exports	6,507 million fr.CFA ($23.5 million)	8,816 million fr.CFA ($32 million)
	(mainly to France, USA, Israel)	

Chief exports: diamonds, cotton, coffee.

Currency. Franc CFA, divided into 100 centimes.

CHAD (République du Tchad)

An independent republic since August 11, 1960 and a member of the French Community; formerly a territory of French Equatorial Africa.

Area. 495,740 square miles (1,284,000 sq.km)

Population. (mid-1965 estimate) 3,307,000; (mid-1969 UN estimate) 3,510,000.

Towns. Fort Lamy (capital) (1969 estimate) 132,500.

Agriculture. 92 percent of total labor force engaged in agriculture.

Land use 1968	hectares
Arable and permanent crops	7,000,000
Permanent meadows and pastures	45,000,000
Forest	16,500,000

Crops (*hectares*)

	1948/52	1961/65	1970
Millet and sorghum	1,030,000	1,191,000	1,050,000
Rice	10,000	25,000	33,000
Maize	10,000	14,000	32,000
Groundnuts	100,000	178,000	160,000
Cotton	190,000	304,000	290,000

Livestock (1969/70). Horses 150,000; asses 285,000; camels 370,000; cattle 4,500,000; sheep 1,800,000; goats 2,300,000.

Mineral production. Negligible.

Trade.

	1965	1968
Imports	7,700 million fr.CFA	8,262 million fr.CFA
	($28 million)	($30 million)

(mainly from France, Nigeria, USA)

	1965	1968
Exports	6,722 million fr.CFA	6,824 million fr.CFA
	($24 million)	($24.8 million)

[mainly to France; some to Zaire (Congo(Kinshasa)), Japan, UK]

Chief exports: raw cotton; some fresh meat.

Currency.   Franc CFA, divided into 100 centimes.

CONGO (Republique de Congo)

An independent republic since August 15, 1960, and member of the French Community; formerly a territory of French Equatorial Africa.

Area.   132,430 square miles (342,000 sq.km).

Population.   (mid-1965 UN estimate) 840,000; (mid-1969 UN estimate) 870,000.

Towns.   Brazzaville (capital) (1965) 156,000

Agriculture.   64 percent of total labor force engaged in agriculture.

Land use 1963		*hectares*	
Arable		618,000	
Permanent crops		12,000	
Permanent meadows and pastures		14,300	
Forest		16,250	

Crops (hectares)	1948/52	1961/65	1970
Cassava	70,000	150,000	110,000
Rice	2,000	5,000	4,000
Yams	10,000	10,000	2,000
Maize	6,000	2,000	8,000
Production, metric tons			
Cocoa beans	(200)	(800)	(1,500)
Palm kernels	(8,200)	(7,100)	(3,000)
Palm oil	(4,000)	(6,800)	(5,700)

Livestock (1969/70). Cattle 31,000; sheep 33,000; goats 50,000; pigs 17,000.

Mineral production.   Lead (1965) 12,400 metric tons; gold (1963) 2,951 troy ozs.

Trade.

	1965	1968
Imports	15,974 million fr.CFA	20,605 million fr.CFA
	($58 million)	($74.9 million)

(mainly to West Germany, Netherlands, UK, France)

Exports	11,512 million fr.CFA	12,189 million fr.CFA
	($42 million)	($44.3 million)

(mainly to West Germany, Netherlands, UK, France)

Chief exports: timber, diamonds, veneer sheets.

Currency.   Franc CFA, divided into 100 centimes.

CONGO REPUBLIC (République Democratique du Congo) (*see* ZAIRE REPUBLIC)

DAHOMEY (République du Dahomey)

An independent republic since August 1, 1960, with "special links" with France; formerly a territory of French West Africa.

Area.   44,695 square miles (112,600 sq.km).

Population.   (November 1960 census) 1,934,447; (mid-1969 UN estimate) 2,640,000.

Towns (1965).   Porto Novo (capital), 75,000; Cotonou 111,000; Abomey 42,000; Ouidah 19,600; Parakou 16,300.

Agriculture.   84 percent of total labor force engaged in agriculture.

Land use 1963		hectares	
Arable and under permanent crops		1,546,000	
Permanent meadows and pastures		442,000	
Forest		2,157,000	
Crops (*hectares*)	1948/52	1961/65	1970
Maize	394,000	401,000	420,000
Millet and sorghum	115,000	140,000	135,000
Groundnuts	35,000	75,000	70,000
Production, metric tons			
Palm kernels	(42,200)	(51,100)	(65,000)
Palm oil	(34,000)	(39,000)	(45,000)

Livestock (1969/70). Horses 200; asses 1,000; cattle 570,000; sheep 570,000; goats 600,000; pigs 360,000.

Trade.

	1959	1967
Imports	2,833 million fr.CFA	10,745 million fr.CFA
	($11.3 million)	($39 million)
	(mainly from France and Italy)	
Exports	3,956 million fr.CFA	3,750 million fr.CFA
	($15.8 million)	($13.7 million)
	(mainly to France and The Netherlands)	

Chief exports (1967): palm kernel oil, palm oil, raw cotton, peanuts and oil seeds, fodder.

Currency.   Franc CFA, divided into 100 centimes.

EQUATORIAL GUINEA (Républica de Guinea Ecuatorial)

An independent republic since October 12, 1968; formerly a Spanish colony. Comprises two provinces:
(a) Continental Rio Muni (10,045 square miles: 26,017 sq.km) including adjacent islands, Corisco, Elobey Grande, Elobey Chico (6.56 square miles: 17 sq.km). Population (1960 census) 183,377; (1968 estimate) approximately 230,000; administrative capital Bata (1960) 3,548.

(b) Island of Fernando Póo (785 square miles: 2,034 sq.km) including island of Annobón (6.5 square miles: 17 sq.km). Population (1960 census) 62,612 (including 1,415 in Annobón); (1968 estimate) 70–80,000. Capital (of all republic) Santa Isabel (1960 census) 19,869.

Agriculture.

Land use 1963	hectares
Arable	221,000
Permanent meadows and pastures	104,000
Forest	2,289,000

Crops (hectares)

	1948/52	1961/65	1970
Cassava	20,000	12,000	15,000
Bananas	2,000	3,000	3,000

Production, metric tons

Cocoa beans	(15,900)	(32,100)	(35,000)
Coffee	(26,800)	(141,900)	(220,000)

Livestock (1969/70). Cattle 3,000; sheep 28,000; goats 6,000; pigs 6,000.

Trade.

	1966
Imports	1,278 million peseta ($18 million)
	(more than 50 percent from Spain)
Exports	1,817 million peseta ($25.9)
	(mainly to Spain, some to West Germany)

Chief exports: cocoa, coffee, wood.

Currency.   Peseta, divided into 100 centimos.

ETHIOPIA (Yaityopya Nigusa Nagast Manguist)

A sovereign independent empire state. Emperor Haile Selassie I re-entered, after Italian occupation, in 1941. The former Italian colony of Eritrea became integrated with Ethiopia on November 14, 1962, after a period as an autonomous unit federated with Ethiopia under the Ethiopian crown.

Area.   Approximately 395,000 square miles (1 million sq.km) (Ethiopia 350,000, Eritrea 45,000 square miles).

Population, including Eritrea.   (Official estimate 1962) 21,461,700; (mid-1969 UN estimate) 24,769,000.

Towns.   Addis Ababa (capital) (1967–8 estimate) 644,190; Dire Dawa 50,733; Harar 42,771; Dessie 40,619; Gondar 30,734; Jimma 30,580; Asmara (capital of Eritrea) 178,537.

Agriculture.   88 percent of total labor force engaged in agriculture.

Land use 1968	hectares
Arable and permanent crops	12,900,000
Permanent meadows and pastures	66,000,000
Forest	8,000,000

Irrigated land (1961), Eritrea only	30,000

Crops (*hectares*)

	1948/52	1961/65	1970
Barley	970,000	1,644,000	1,770,000
Wheat	840,000	957,000	1,060,000
Maize	213,000	787,000	865,000
Millet	3,397,000	3,476,000	4,420,000
Sugar cane	negligible	5,000	7,000
Cotton	26,000	32,000	53,000
Sisal	1,000	2,000	3,000
Coffee (*production, metric tons*)	26,800	141,900	220,000

Livestock (1969/70). Horses 1,400,000; mules 1,400,000; asses 3,900,000; camels 960,000; cattle 26,000,000; sheep 12,700,000; goats 12,200,000; pigs 15,000.

Mineral production. Negligible. Salt is produced and there are deposits of potash salts; a placer goldmine produced 956,816 grammes in 1967/8. There is prospecting for oil in progress; natural gas occurs offshore near Massawa.

Trade.

	1964	1968
Imports	E$307.69 million ($123.1 million)	E$432.52 million ($173 million)

(mainly from USA, Italy, West Germany, Japan, UK)

Exports	E$262.52 million ($105 million)	E$258.05 million ($103 million)

[mainly to USA (over 50 percent), West Germany, Saudi Arabia, Italy]

Chief exports: coffee, hides and skins, pulses, sesame seed and other oilseeds.

Currency. The Ethiopian dollar (E$), divided into 100 cents.

GABON (République Gabonaise)

An independent republic since August 17, 1960, and a member of the French Community; formerly a territory of French Equatorial Africa.

Area. 103,348 square miles (267,670 sq.km).

Population. (mid-1965 UN estimate) 463,000; (mid-1969 UN estimate) 485,000.

Towns. Libreville (capital) (1969 estimate) 73,000.

Agriculture. 84 percent of total labor force engaged in agriculture. Number of and area covered by agricultural holdings (1960) 71,395; 124,700 hectares.

Land use 1962	*hectares*
Arable and permanent crops	127,000
Permanent meadows and pastures	5,100,000
Forest	20,000,000

Crops (*hectares*)

	1948/52	1961/65	1970
Cassava	12,000	57,000	58,000

Production, metric tons

Cocoa beans	(2,300)	(3,000)	(4,500)
Coffee	neglibible	(1,400)	(1,200)

Livestock (1969/70). Cattle 5,000; sheep 49,000; goats 53,000; pigs 9,000.

Mineral production. Crude petroleum (1970) 5.57 million metric tons; (1967) manganese ore, 1.1 million metric tons; uranium concentrates 1,452 metric tons; gold 29,157 troy ozs; natural gas 18 million cubic meters.

Trade.

	1964	1968
Imports	13,742 million fr.CFA	15,875 million fr.CFA
	($50 million)	($57.7 million)
	(mainly from France, USA, West Germany)	
Exports	22,253 million fr.CFA	30,714 million fr.CFA
	($80.9 million)	($111.7 million)

(mainly to France, USA, Netherlands Antilles, West Germany)
Chief exports: crude petroleum, timber, and plywood.

Currency. Franc CFA, divided into 100 centimes.

THE GAMBIA

An independent country since February 18, 1965, within the Commonwealth; formerly a British colony and protectorate.

Area. 4,363 square miles (11,300 sq.km)

Population. (1963 census) 315,486; (mid-1969 UN estimate) 357,000.

Towns. Bathurst (capital) (1963) 40,017 (town only: 27,809).

Agriculture. 86 percent of total labor force engaged in agriculture.

Land use 1967	*hectares*
Arable and permanent crops	200,000
Permanent meadows and pastures	400,000
Forest	303,000

Crops (*hectares*)

	1948/52	1961/65	1970
Groundnuts	93,000	131,000	150,000
Millet	52,000	40,000	42,000
Rice	11,000	26,000	32,000

Production, metric tons

Palm kernels	(1,600)	(1,600)	(2,000)
Palm oil	(2,000)	(1,800)	(2,000)

Livestock (1969/70). Asses 4,000; cattle 5,000; sheep 80,000; goats 112,000; pigs 7,000.

Mineral production (1970). None.

Trade.

	1959	1967
Imports	£3,148,308	£7,520,000
	($8.8 million)	($18.05 million)
	(mainly from UK, Japan)	
Exports	£2,956,822	£5,366,000
	($8.3 million)	($12.9 million)

(mainly to UK; some to Netherlands, Portugal, Czechoslovakia)
Chief exports: groundnut oil, groundnuts, fodder.

Currency.   Gambian pound (£), linked with UK£.

GHANA

An independent republic since March 6, 1957, and a member of the Commonwealth; formerly the Gold Coast, a British colony and protectorate.

Area.   92,100 square miles (238,537 sq.km).

Population.   (1970 census, preliminary data) 8,545,561.

Towns (1970).   Accra (capital) 663,880; Kumasi 342,986; Sekondi-Takoradi 61,772; Sekondi 161,071; Koforidua 69,804; Tamale 98,818; Bolgatanga 93,182.

Agriculture.   56 percent of total labor force engaged in agriculture.

Land use 1968	*hectares*
Arable and permanent crops	2,835,000
Forest	12,250,000

Irrigated land (1964)	12,000

Crops (*hectares*)

	1948/52	1961/65	1970
Maize	142,000	193,000	265,000
Rice	20,000	34,000	41,000
Cassava	66,000	127,000	170,000
Groundnuts	55,000	65,000	65,000
Tobacco	negligible	3,000	3,000

Production, metric tons

Cocoa beans	(253,000)	(453,700)	(385,100)
Palm kernels	(6,300)	(15,000)	(35,000)
Palm oil	(30,400)	(39,600)	(55,000)

Livestock (1969/70).   Horses 4,000; asses 23,000; cattle 630,000; sheep 650,000; goats 770,000; pigs 330,000.

Mineral production (1968).   Gold 22,616 kilogrammes; manganese ore 198,000 metric tons; bauxite 280,000 metric tons; diamonds 2,447,000 metric carats.

Trade.

	1961	1968
Imports	£142,735,000	£313,935,000
	($400 million)	($308 million)

(mainly from UK, USA, West Germany, Japan, Netherlands.

Exports	£115,203,000	£309,264,000
	($323 million)	($303.2 million)

(mainly to UK, USA, Netherlands, West Germany,
Japan, USSR, Canada)

Chief exports: cocoa beans; cocoa butter and paste; aluminum (unwrought); timber; diamonds (industrial and some gem); manganese ore, and concentrates.

Currency.   New Cedi (N₡), divided into 100 New Pesewas (NP).

GUINEA (République de Guineé)

An independent republic since October 2, 1958; outside the French Community but has economic and cultural ties with France; formerly a territory of French West Africa.

Area.   95,000 square miles (245,857 sq.km)

Population.   (mid-1965 estimate) 3,500,000; (mid-1969 UN estimate) 3,795,000.

Towns (1964).   Conakry (capital) (1967) 197,000; Kankan 29,100; Kindia 25,000; Siguiri 2,700; Labé 12,500.

Agriculture.   85 percent of total labor force engaged in agriculture.

> *Land use.* Forests covered 1,046,000 hectares in 1963 (no other data available to FAO).
> *Crops* (*hectares*)

	1948/52	1961/65	1970
Cassava	56,000	30,000	32,000
Rice	340,000	258,000	265,000
Groundnuts	31,000	32,000	29,000
Production, metric tons			
Palm kernels	(24,800)	(17,700)	(15,000)
Palm oil	(10,000)	(11,400)	(13,000)

> *Livestock (1969/70).* Horses 1,000; asses 3,000; cattle 1,800,000; sheep 470,000; goats 500,000; pigs 24,000.

Mineral production.   Diamonds (1965) 72,000 metric carats; bauxite (1968) 2,118,000 metric tons; iron ore (1965) 716,000 metric tons.

Trade.

1968–69

Imports	16,100 million Guinea fr. ($66 million)

(mainly from USSR, France, West Germany, UK)

Exports	14,100 million Guinea fr. ($58 million)

(destination: Eastern bloc, France, USA)
Chief export: alumina.

Currency.   The Guinea franc, divided into 100 centimes; on a par with the franc CFA.

IVORY COAST (République de Côte d'Ivoire)

An independent republic since August 7, 1970, with "special relations" with the French Community; formerly a territory of French West Africa.

Area. 124,500 square miles (322,460 sq.km)

Population. (mid-1965 estimate) 3,835,000; (mid-1969 UN estimate) 4,764,000.

Towns (1965/66 estimate). Abidjan (capital) 360,000; Bouaké 85,000; Daloa 35,000; Man 30,000; Korhogo 24,000.

Agriculture. 86 percent of total labor force engaged in agriculture.

Land use 1968	*hectares*
Arable	7,809,000
Permanent crops	1,050,000
Permanent meadows and pastures	8,000,000
Forest	12,000,000

Irrigated land (1969)	17,000

Crops (hectares)

	1948/52	1961/65	1970
Yams and sweet potatoes	169,000	170,000	220,000
Cassava	127,000	197,000	164,000
Groundnuts	34,000	44,000	50,000
Cocoa	152,000	281,000	322,000 (1967/8)
Coffee	190,000	548,000	652,000

(Ivory Coast is the third largest coffee producer in the world)

Production, metric tons

Palm kernels	(8,700)	(17,600)	(24,000)
Palm oil	(6,200)	(24,500)	(500)

Livestock (1969/70). Horses 1,000; asses 1,000; cattle 400,000; sheep 820,000; goats 810,000; pigs 180,000.

Mineral production (1969). Diamonds 202,424 carats; manganese ore 127,050 metric tons.

Trade.

	1959	1968
Imports	28,259 million fr.CFA ($113 million)	75,676 million fr.CFA ($275 million)
	(mainly from France, some from USA)	
Exports	33,821 million fr.CFA ($135 million)	104,890 million fr.CFA ($381 million)

(mainly to France, USA, Netherlands, West Germany)
Chief exports: coffee, cocoa, and timber.

Currency. Franc CFA, divided into 100 centimes.

KENYA

An independent country since December 12, 1963, and a member of the Commonwealth; a republic since December 12, 1964; formerly a British colony and protectorate.

Area. 224,960 square miles (582,600 sq.km); land area 219,790 square miles (569,256 sq.km).

Population. (1962 census) 8,636,263; (1969 census) 10,942,708.

Towns (1969 census). Nairobi (capital) 509,286; Mombasa 246,000; Nakuru 47,800; Kisumu 30,700; Eldoret 16,900.

Agriculture. 88 percent of total labor force engaged in agriculture. Number of and area covered by agricultural holdings (1960) 3,609; 3,128,500 hectares.

Land use 1960	hectares
Arable	1,454,000
Permanent crops	216,000
Permanent meadows and pastures	3,944,000
Forest	2,267,000
Irrigated land (on farms and estates)	14,000

Crops (hectares)

	1948/52	1961/65	1970
Maize	452,000	1,020,000	1,100,000
Wheat	95,000	103,000	165,000
Cotton	21,000	51,000	81,000
Sugar cane	5,000	18,000	26,000
Sisal	93,000	121,000	80,000

Production metric tons

	1948/52	1961/65	1970
Coffee	(10,800)	(39,900)	(48,000)
Tea	(6,000)	(17,400)	(43,000)

Pyrethrum is an important commercial crop of the highlands; coconuts and cashew nuts of the lower lands. Mangroves supply tanning bark.

Livestock (1969/70). Horses 2,000; camels 184,000; cattle 7,850,000; dairy cows 190,000; sheep 7,500,000; goats 6,800,000; pigs 27,000.

Mineral production (1969). Copper 77 long tons; gold (refined) 556,847 grammes; limestone and products 24,904 long tons, soda ash 105,913 long tons, diatomite 2,303 long tons; salt; kaolin; silver; barytes; magnesite.

Trade.

	1949	1968
Imports	£54,123,277	K£114,658,000
	($152 million)	($327 million)

[mainly from UK, West Germany, Iran, Japan, USA;
1968 imports include K£12,342,000 ($35 million)
from Tanzania and Uganda]

Exports   £29,173,704   K£57,488,000
                            ($82 million)   ($164 million)
                    [mainly to UK, West Germany, USA;
               1968 exports include K£26,334,000 ($75 million)
                            to Tanzania and Uganda]

Chief exports: coffee, tea, pyrethrum extract, maize, meat and meat preparations, petroleum products, hides and skins, soda ash; export of fresh fruit is of growing importance.

Currency. Kenya, Tanzania, and Uganda form a trading unit in the East African Economic Community. Apart from a transfer tax there is virtually free trade among them. Each country has its own currency: a shilling, divided into 100 cents; 20 shillings = £1 (East African.) The Kenya shilling, divided into 100 cents, was introduced on September 14, 1966.

LESOTHO

An independent kingdom within the Commonwealth since October 4, 1966; formerly Basutoland, a British protectorate.

Area. 11,716 square miles (30,340 sq.km).

Population. (1966 census) 969,634; (mid-1969 UN estimate) 935,000. In 1966, 97,529 males and 19,744 females were (presumably employed) outside the country.

Towns. Maseru (capital) (1966) 18,000.

Agriculture. Percentage of labor force employed in agriculture not recorded. Number of and area covered by agricultural holdings (1960/61): 161,250; 352,754 hectares.

Land use 1962		*hectares*	
Arable		353,000	
Permanent meadows and pastures		2,495,000	

Crops (hectares)

	1948/52	1961/65	1970
Wheat	49,000	67,000	60,000
Maize	150,000	155,000	80,000
Barley	1,000	4,000	4,000
Sorghum	56,000	65,000	no data

Livestock (1969/70). Horses 63,000; mules 3,000; asses 45,000; cattle 400,000; sheep 1,700,000; goats 930,000; pigs 67,000.

Mineral production. Exploration for diamonds is in progress.

Trade.

	1965	1967
Imports	R17,335,000	R23,800,000
	($24.2 million)	($33.3 million)
Exports	R4,690,000	R4,168,000
	($6.5 million)	($5.8 million)

(most trading is with South Africa)

Chief exports: wool, mohair, diamonds.

Currency. As in the Republic of South Africa: the Rand (R), divided into 100 cents.

LIBERIA

An independent republic constituted July 26,1847.

Area.   About 43,000 square miles (111,000 sq.km).

Population.   (1962 census) 1,016,000; (mid-1969 UN estimate) 1,150,000.

Towns.   Monrovia (capital) (1969 estimate) 100,000.

Agriculture.   80 percent of total labor force engaged in agriculture.

Land use 1964		*hectares*	
Arable and permanent crops		3,850,000	
Permanent meadows and pastures		240,000	
Forest		3,622,000	

Crops (*hectares*)	1948/52	1961/65	1970
Cassava	55,000	55,000	57,000
Rice	261,000	214,000	190,000
Production, metric tons			
Palm kernels	(17,200)	(9,300)	(13,000)
Palm oil	(40,000)	(41,200)	(41,200)
Coffee	(2,000)	(29,000)	(57,000)
Rubber	(31,300)	(43,900)	(64,700)

[The Firestone Plantation rubber planting cover about one million acres (405,000 ha); and B. F. Goodrich & Co. have plantations covering 12,300 acres (4,978 ha)].

Livestock (1969/70). Cattle 28,000; sheep 150,000; goats 139,000; pigs 82,000.

Mineral production.   Iron ore is mined (1969 exports valued at US $137 million) and pelletizing plant is operative. Gold and diamonds occur.

Trade.

	1964	1968
Imports	US$111.1 million	US$106.9 million
	(mainly from USA, West Germany, UK, Japan)	
Exports	US$125.7 million	US$167.5 million
	(mainly to USA, West Germany, Netherlands, Italy, UK, France, Japan)	

Chief exports: iron ore, rubber, industrial diamonds, coffee, palm nuts and kernels, some cocoa beans.

Currency.   US dollar has circulated since 1942 and is used in official accounts. Since 1944 the Liberian dollar, divided into 100 cents, has been at par with the US dollar.

LIBYAN ARAB REPUBLIC (Aljumhuria Al-Arabia Allibya)

A republic was proclaimed on September 8, 1969. Formerly an independent sovereign kingdom, constituted after World War II by Allied Forces from the former Italian territory of Libya; divided into three provinces, Cyrenaica, Tripolitania, and Fezzan, federated in December 1951 as the United Kingdom of Libya with the Amir of Cyrenaica as first hereditary King. Tripoli and Benghazi function as capitals, but a new capital is planned at Al Bayda.

Area. Estimated 679,358 square miles (1,759,540 sq.km).

Population. (1964 census) 1,564,365; (mid-1969 UN estimate) 1,905,000.

Towns (1968). Tripoli (Tarābulus) 247,000 and Benghazi 140,000 are joint capitals.

Agriculture. 60 percent of total labor force estimated to be engaged in agriculture in 1965. Number of and total area covered by agricultural holdings (1960): 145,518; 3,868,728 hectares.

Land use 1969	*hectares*
Arable	2,375,000
Under permanent crops	140,000
Permanent meadows and pastures	1,130,000
Forest	532,000
Irrigated land	145,000

Crops (hectares)

	1948/52	1961/65	1970
Wheat	124,000	149,000	166,000
Barley	354,000	350,000	216,000
Groundnuts	2,000	6,000	5,000
Production, metric tons			
Dates	(34,000)	(36,000)	(55,000)
Olives	(27,000)	(45,000)	(33,000) (1969)
Figs (fresh)	(1,000)	(2,000)	(3,000) (1969)

Livestock (1969/70). Horses 26,000; asses 98,000; camels 163,000; cattle 108,000; sheep 2,163,000; goats 1,234,000.

Mineral production. Libya's output of crude petroleum (159.32 million metric tons in 1970) is the greatest in Africa.

Trade.

	1965	1968
Imports	Libyan £114 million	Libyan £282 million
	($320 million)	($797 million)
	(mainly from Italy, USA, UK)	
Exports	Libyan £282 million	Libyan £668 million
	($797 million)	($1,870.4 million)
	(mainly to West Germany, Italy, UK)	

Chief exports: crude petroleum, groundnuts. Export of oil by the first pipeline to the coast commenced October, 1961.

Currency. The Libyan pound (£) is divided into 1000 millièmes.

MALAWI

An independent member of the Commonwealth since July 6, 1964; a republic since July 6, 1966; formerly Nyasaland, a British protectorate.

Area. 36,324 square miles (94,079 sq.km) excluding inland waters of Lakes Malombe, Chilwa, Chiuta, and that part of Lake Malawi within the national boundary (9,250 square miles: 23,957 sq.km).

Population. (1966 census) 4,039,583; (mid-1969 UN estimate) 4,398,000.

Towns (1966). Zomba (capital) 19,666; Lilongwe (future capital) 19,425; Blantrye 109,461.

Agriculture. 81 percent of total labor force engaged in agriculture.

Land use 1959	*hectares*
Arable	2,590,000
Permanent crops	337,000
Permanent meadows and pastures	596,000
Forest	2,314,000
Irrigated land (1969)	5,000

Crops (hectares)

	1948/52	1961/65	1970
Maize	340,000	809,000	1,000,000
Rice	4,000	5,000	8,000
Cassava	75,000	6,000	5,000
Groundnuts	no data	216,000	200,000
Cotton	26,000	37,000	40,000
Tobacco	53,000	57,000	45,000
Tea	8,000	12,000	15,000

Livestock (1969/70). Cattle 493,000; sheep 82,000; goats 599,000; pigs 142,000.

Mineral production. None

Trade.

	1964	1968
Imports	£14,320,000	£29,044,000
	($35.8 million)	($69.6 million)
	(mainly from UK, Rhodesia, South Africa, USA)	
Exports	£11,504,000	£16,779,000
	($28.7 million)	($40.2 million)

[mainly to UK (over 50 percent), USA, Rhodesia, USA].
Chief exports: tobacco, tea, groundnuts, maize, cassava.

Currency. Until February 15, 1971, £ sterling. On that date decimal currency was introduced: the kwacha, divided into 100 tambala.

MALI (République du Mali)

An independent republic since September 22, 1960; formerly known as French Sudan and part of French West Africa; now has some "special agreements" with France.

Area. 73,000 square miles (1,204,021 sq.km).

Population. (mid-1965 UN estimate) 4,576,000; (mid-1969 UN estimate) 4,831,000.

Towns (1968). Bamako (capital) 182,000; Mopti 33,000; Kayes 29,000; Ségou 31,000; Sikasso 22,000; Timbuktu (Tombouctou) 10,200.

Agriculture.   90 percent of total labor force engaged in agriculture in 1965. Number of and area covered by agricultural holdings (1960): 280,260; 1,220,528 hectares.

Land use 1962	*hectares*
Arable and permanent crops	7,200,000
Permanent meadows and pastures	34,800,000
Forest	4,457,000

Crops (*hectares*)

	1948/52	1961/65	1970
Millet and sorghum	1,268,000	1,173,000	1,000,000
Rice	182,000	178,000	165,000
Groundnuts	172,000	169,000	100,000
Maize	100,000	68,000	72,000
Cotton	33,000	38,000	70,000

Livestock (1969/70). Horses 170,000; asses 540,000; camels 250,000; cattle 5,000,000; sheep 5,900,000; goats 4,900,000; pigs 35,000.

Mineral production.   None

Trade.

	1965	1968
Imports	10,594 million Mali fr.	16,937 million Mali fr.
	($43 million)	($30.8 million)

[mainly from France, USSR, China (mainland), Ivory Coast]

Exports	3,877 million fr.	5,300 million Mali fr.
	($16 million)	($9.8 million)

(mainly to Ivory Coast, France, Senegal, Ghana)

Chief exports (1968): raw cotton, oilseeds and nuts, live animals, fish (salted, dried, smoked), hides, and skins.

Currency.   Mali franc, linked to French franc since March 1968 (MF 100 = 1 French franc), divided into 100 centimes.

MAURITANIA (République Islamique de Mauritanie)

An independent republic since November 28, 1960; formerly a protectorate, later a colony, of French West Africa.

Area.   419,000 square miles (1,030,700 sq.km).

Population.   (1965 UN survey) 1,050,000; (mid-1969 UN estimate) 1,140,000.

Towns (1969 estimate).   Nouakchott (capital) 20,000; Nouadibou 11,000; F'Derik 10,000; Kaédi 10,000; Rosso 8,000; Atar 4,200.

Agriculture.   90 percent of total labor force engaged in agriculture in 1965.

Land use 1964	*hectares*
Arable and permanent crops	263,000
Permanent meadows and pastures	39,250,000
Forest	15,134,000
Irrigated land	3,000

Crops (*hectares*)

	1948/52	1961/65	1970
Millet	75,000	86,000	100,000
Maize	8,000	7,000	7,000

Production, metric tons

Dates	(10,000)	(20,000)	(15,000)

Livestock (1969/70). Horses 23,000; asses 225,000; camels 690,000; cattle 2,600,000; dairy cows 850,000; sheep 2,800,000; goats 2,400,000.

Mineral production. Rich deposits of iron ore and copper are exploited.

Trade.

	1964	1967
Imports	3,879 million fr.CFA ($14 million) (mainly from France, USA)	8,408 million fr.CFA ($30.6 million)
Exports	11,307 million fr.CFA ($41 million)	17,456 million fr.CFA ($50.7 million)

(mainly to UK, France, West Germany, Italy, Belgium–Luxembourg) Chief exports (1967): iron ore; some fish (fresh, salted, dried, smoked).

Currency. Franc CFA, divided into 100 centimes.

MOROCCO (al-Mamlaka al-Maghrebia)

Independent since March 2, 1956, at first a sultanate, later (1957) a kingdom. The monarchy is constitutional and the government includes a cabinet system, a council of ministers, and a single chamber consultative assembly. In 1956 France and Spain relinquished the protectorates which they exercised over the greater part of Morocco; and the powers (including the USA) which exercised control over the Tangier International Zone also restored that territory to the Sultan. The former Spanish province, Ifni, was returned to Morocco on June 30, 1969.

Area. The southeastern borders have not been defined but the area is given officially as 166,000 square miles (500,000 sq.km).

Population. (1961 census) 11,598,070; (mid-1969 UN estimate) 15,030,000.

Towns (1968). Rabat (capital) 410,000; Casablanca 1,250,000; Marrakesh 285,000; Fès 270,000; Tanger 150,000; Meknès 225,000; Oujda 140,000; Tétouan 115,000.

Agriculture. 54 percent of total labor force engaged in agriculture. Number of and area covered by agricultural holdings (1961): 1,106,765; 5,117,000 hectares.

Land use 1966	hectares
Arable	7,462,000
Permanent crops	438,000
Permanent meadows and pastures	7,650,000
Forest	5,359,000
Irrigated land (1965)	265,000

Crops (*hectares*)

	1948/52	1961/65	1970
Wheat	1,287,000	1,578,000	1,940,000
Barley	2,033,000	1,627,000	2,050,000
Maize	518,000	442,000	470,000

Livestock (1969/70). Horses 320,000; asses 960,000; mules 400,000; camels 200,000; cattle 3,600,000; sheep 14,500,000; goats 7,850,000; pigs 10,000.

Mineral production (1969) (*metric tons*). Phosphate rock 12.29 million; coal 482,000; iron ore 742,000; manganese ore 197,750; lead 116,900; crude petroleum 45,000.

Trade.

	1961	1968
Imports	DH 2,257 million	DH 2,847 million
	($451 million)	($580 million)
	(mainly from France, USA, West Germany, Italy, UK)	
Exports	DH 1,731 million	DH 2,290 million
	($346 million)	($458 million)
	(mainly to France, West Germany, UK)	

Chief exports: phosphates, citrus fruits, tomatoes, preserved fish.

Currency. National currency unit introduced in 1959: the dirham (DH), equivalent to 100 French Moroccan francs.

MOZAMBIQUE (MOÇAMBIQUE) (Portuguese East Africa)

A Portuguese colony.

Area. 303,070 square miles (784,961 sq.km).

Population. (1960 census) 6,663,653; (mid-1969 UN estimate) 7,376,000.

Towns. Lourenço Marques (capital) (1960 census) 179,000.

Agriculture. 69 percent of total labor force engaged in agriculture.

Land use 1966	*hectares*
Arable	2,420,000
Permanent crops	280,000
Permanent meadows and pastures	44,000,000
Forest	19,400,000

Crops (*hectares*)

Maize	375,000	409,000	450,000
Cassava	420,000	430,000	430,000
Sugar cane	19,000	32,000	41,000
Coconuts	320,000	383,000	403,000 (1969)
Cotton	263,000	301,000	324,000
Sisal	54,000	55,000	50,000
Tea	7,000	13,000	15,000

Cashew nuts are also a commercial crop.

Livestock (1969/70). Asses 19,000; cattle, 2,050,000; dairy cows 13,000; sheep 210,000; goats 850,000; pigs 230,000.

Mineral production (1968). Gold 0.2 kg; beryl 95 metric tons; bauxite 3,274 metric tons; coal 314,408 metric tons.

Trade.

	1960	1968
Imports	3,646.25 million escudos	6,740.1 million escudos
	($122 million)	($238 million)

(mainly from Portugal, South Africa, UK, West Germany)

Exports	2,099.25 million escudos	4,420.2 million escudos
	($72 million)	($155.6 million)

(mainly to Portugal, India, USA, South Africa)

Chief exports: cashew nuts (fresh, dried and prepared), raw cotton, sugar.

Currency.   Escudo, divided into 100 centavos, as in Portugal.

NIGER (République du Niger)

An independent republic since August 3, 1960, with "special relations" with France; formerly a territory of French West Africa.

Area.   489,200 square miles (1,267,000 sq.km).

Population.   (1968) 3,640,000; (mid-1969 UN estimate) 3,909,000.

Towns.   Niamey (capital) (1968) 70,000.

Agriculture.   96 percent of total labor force engaged in agriculture.

Land use 1969	*hectares*
Arable and permanent crops	12,177,000
Permanent meadows and pastures	2,900,000
Forest	15,600,000
Irrigated land	5,000

Crops (*hectares*)

	1948/52	1961/65	1970
Millet	1,058,000	1,791,000	2,000,000
Groundnuts	123,000	325,000	290,000
Cassava	7,000	17,000	28,000
Cotton	3,000	12,000	14,000

Livestock (1969/70). Horses 160,000; asses 360,000; camels 400,000; cattle 4,300,000; sheep 2,750,000; goats 6,000,000; pigs 23,000.

Mineral production.   Deposits of high-grade uranium ore are mined, production from a processing plant due to commence 1970. Tin ore also mined, salt and natron produced.

Trade.

	1959	1968
Imports	1,787 million fr.CFA	10,237 million fr.CFA
	($7.2 million)	($37 million)

(mainly from France, some from USA)

Exports	2,851 million fr.CFA	9,350 million fr.CFA
	($11.4 million)	($34 million)

(mainly to France and Nigeria)

Chief export: groundnuts.

Currency.   Franc CFA, divided into 100 centimes.

NIGERIA, FEDERATION OF

An independent republic since October 1, 1960, and a member of the Commonwealth; formerly a British colony and protectorate.

Area. 356,669 square miles (approximate) (923,773 sq.km).

Population. (1963 census) 55,653,821; (mid-1969 UN estimate) 65,820,000.

Towns (1963 census). Lagos (Federal Capital Territory) 665,000; Ibadan 800,000; Kano 130,000; Iwo 159,000; Ogbomosho 320,000; Oshogbo 209,000; Ife 130,000; Abeokuta 187,000; Port Harcourt 180,000; Zaria 166,000; Kaduna 150,000.

Agriculture. 80 percent of total labor force engaged in agriculture.

Land use 1961	hectares
Arable and permanent crops	21,795,000
Permanent meadows and pastures	25,800,000
Forest	31,592,000

Irrigated land (1965)   13,000

Crops (*hectares*)

	1948/52	1961/65	1970
Cassava	1,000,000	1,171,000	1,000,000
Millet	3,240,000	3,224,000	3,400,000
Groundnuts	970,000	1,170,000	1,050,000
Cotton	130,000	372,000	420,000
Soybeans	8,000	21,000	14,000
Production, metric tons			
Palm kernels	(371,900)	(418,800)	(250,000)
Palm oil	(422,000)	(521,000)	(480,000)
Cocoa beans	(105,400)	(215,000)	(218,500)

Livestock (1969/70). Horses 335,000; asses 840,000; camels 19,000; cattle 11,550,000; sheep 8,000,000; goats 23,400,000; pigs 820,000.

Mineral production. Crude petroleum (1970) 54,725,000 metric tons; tin (1968) 9,804 metric tons; coal (1967) 95,000 metric tons; gold, columbite, and tantalite are also mined and exported.

Trade.

	1961	1968
Imports	£215,319,000	£193,185,000
	($603 million)	($539 million)
	(mainly from UK, USA, West Germany, Italy)	
Exports	£160,914,000	£206,541,000
	($451 million)	($577 million)

(mainly to UK, Netherlands, West Germany, USA, Italy, France)
Chief exports (1968): cocoa beans, groundnuts, palm kernels, crude petroleum, tin.

Currency. Nigerian pound (£), divided into 20 Nigerian shillings.

PORTUGUESE GUINEA

A Portuguese colony since 1879, incorporates Bijagóoz, an adjacent archipelago, as well as the island of Bolama.

Area.   13,948 square miles (36,125 sq.km).

Population.   (1960 census) 521,336; (mid-1969 UN estimate) 530,000.

Towns.   Bissau is the capital (since 1942) and chief port; Bolama and Cacheu are other ports.

Agriculture.   Number of and area covered by agricultural holdings (1960/61): 86,951; 262,570 hectares (cultivated area only).

Land use 1961	*hectares*		
Arable	235,000		
Permanent crops	28,000		
Forest	1,000		

Crops (hectares)			
	1948/52	1961/65	1970
Rice	73,000	67,000	no data
Cassava	2,000	6,000	6,000
Groundnuts	70,000	90,000	90,000
Production, metric tons			
Palm kernels	(15,400)	(13,000)	(12,000)
Palm oil	(8,000)	(8,000)	(8,000)

Coconuts are also a commercial crop.
Livestock (1969/70). Asses 3,000; cattle 260,000; sheep 64,000; goats 174,000; pigs 113,000.

Mineral production.   None.

Trade.

	1968
Imports	506.6 million escudos ($17.8 million)
Exports	87.5 million escudos ($3 million)
	(most trading is with Portugal)

Currency.   As in Portugal: escudo, divided into 100 centavos.

RHODESIA (Southern Rhodesia)

As Southern Rhodesia a self-governing colony within the Commonwealth from October 1, 1923; part of the Federation of Rhodesia and Nyasalend 1953–63; unilaterally declared independence November 11, 1965 and a republic (judged illegal by the British Government) on March 3, 1970.

Area.   150,820 square miles (390,622 sq.km).

Population.   (1961 census) 3,857,466; (1969 census) 5,090,000, of which 228,580 were European.

Towns (1969 census).   Salisbury (capital) 384,530; Bulawayo 245,590.

Agriculture.   73 percent of total labor force engaged in agriculture. Number of and area covered by agricultural holdings (1960): 430,525; 15,616,763 hectares (European and Asian holdings only).

Land use 1956

	hectares
Arable and permanent crops	1,837,000
Permanent meadows and pastures	4,856,000
Forest	23,570,000

Crops (*hectares*)

	1948/52	1961/65	1970
Maize	405,000	396,000	350,000
Millet and sorghum	297,000	416,000	390,000
Wheat	1,000	1,000	12,000
Groundnuts	50,000	171,000	170,000
Sugar cane	1,000	9,000	11,000
Tobacco	62,000	90,000	47,000
Cotton	4,000	5,000	50,000
Tea	1,000	2,000	3,000

Rice and cassava are important crops and there is increasing cultivation of citrus fruit.

Livestock (1969/70). Horses 6,000; mules 1,000; asses 86,000; cattle 3,900,000; dairy cows 80,000; sheep 450,000; pigs 143,000.

Mineral production (1965). Coal 3,868,300 metric tons; asbestos 1,761,000 metric tons; gold 549,600 ozs; copper 19,800 metric tons; chrome ore 645,500 metric tons.

Trade.

	1965	1969
Imports	£R 119,789,000 ($343 million)	£R 199,426,000 ($557 million)
	[mainly (1965) from UK, South Africa, USA]	
Exports	£R 142,455,000 ($409 million)	£R 226,904,000 ($650.5 million)

[mainly (1965) to Zambia, UK, South Africa, West Germany]
Chief exports (1965): tobacco, asbestos, machinery and transport equipment, copper, meat and meat products, iron and steel, clothing, sugar, electrical energy; and a wide range of miscellaneous manufactured articles.

Currency. Rhodesian pound (£R) (1970), divided into 20 Rhodesian shillings.

RWANDA

An independent republic since July 1, 1962; formerly (as Ruanda) linked with neighboring Burundi as a UN trusteeship territory, administered by Belgium; once part of German East Africa.

Area. 10,166 square miles (26,330 sq.km).

Population. (mid-1969 UN estimate) 3,500,000.

Towns. Kigali (capital) (1969 estimate) 7,000.

Agriculture. 95 percent of total labor force engaged in agriculture.

Land use 1969	hectares
Arable	528,000
Permanent crops	169,000
Permanent meadows and pastures	870,000
Forest	156,000

Irrigated land (1962)	7,000

Crops (hectares)

	1948/52	1961/65	1970
Cassava	14,000	13,000	28,000
Maize	38,000	44,000	42,000
Yams and sweet potatoes	80,000	82,000	61,000
Groundnuts	5,000	4,000	7,000
Coffee (*production, metric tons*)	(4,600)	(8,500)	(13,500)

Livestock (1969/70). Cattle 676,000; sheep 228,000; goats 600,000; pigs 28,000.

Mineral production.   Cassiterite and tungsten are mined and some exported; there are reserves of colombite, tantalite, and beryl, exported in small quantities.

Trade.

1968

Imports   2,245.77 million Rwanda fr. ($22 million approx.)
(mainly from Belgium–Luxembourg, Uganda, Japan, West Germany)

Exports   1,472.41 million Rwanda fr. ($15 million approx.)
(mainly to Belgium–Luxembourg, Uganda; some to UK, France, Kenya)

Chief exports: coffee, tin and tungsten ores, and concentrates.

Currency.   Rwanda franc, divided into 100 centimes; devalued April 12, 1966. Trade data for 1968 calculated at 100.56 Rwanda francs = $1.00.

SENEGAL (République du Sénégal)

An independent republic since August 20, 1960, and a member state of the French Community; formerly a territory of French West Africa.

Area.   76,165 square miles (197,161 sq.km).

Population.   (1965) 3,490,000; (mid-1969 UN estimate) 3,780,000.

Towns (1969 estimate).   Dakar (capital) 474,000; Rufisque 48,300; Kaolack 69,500; Saint Louis 47,900; Thiès 69,000; Ziguinchor 29,000.

Agriculture.   74 percent of total labor force engaged in agriculture.

Land use 1966	hectares
Arable and permanent crops	5,722,000
Permanent meadows and pastures	5,700,000
Forest	5,318,000

Irrigated land	76,000

Crops (*hectares*)

	1948/52	1961/65	1970
Millet	782,000	958,000	1,100,000
Groundnuts	675,000	1,059,000	980,000
Rice	57,000	78,000	90,000
Maize	15,000	39,000	55,000

Livestock (1969/70). Horses 192,000; asses 170,000; camels 30,000; goats 1,570,000; pigs 93,000.

Mineral production (1965). Phosphate rock 1,048,300 metric tons; cement 181,000 metric tons, supplying a major part of the needs of neighboring countries.

Trade.

	1965	1968
Imports	39,568 million fr.CFA ($128 million)	44,527 million fr.CFA ($162 million)
	(mainly from France, Brazil, West Germany)	
Exports	31,712 million fr.CFA ($164 million)	37,369 million fr.CFA ($136 million)
	[mainly to France (nearly 70 percent)]	

Chief exports: groundnuts and groundnut oil, oilseed cake, natural phosphates, cement.

Currency. Franc CFA, divided into 100 centimes.

SIERRA LEONE

An independent country since April 27, 1961, and a member of the Commonwealth; previously a British colony and protectorate.

Area. 27,925 square miles (73,326 sq.km).

Population. (1963 census) 2,183,000; (mid-1969 UN estimate) 2,510,000.

Towns. Freetown (capital) (1968) 163,000.

Agriculture. 75 percent of total labor force engaged in agriculture.

Land use 1964	hectares
Arable	3,612,000
Permanent crops	52,000
Permanent meadows and pastures	2,204,000
Forest	301,000
Irrigated land (1964)	800

Crops (*hectares*)

	1948/52	1961/65	1970
Rice	316,000	273,000	315,000
Maize	8,000	18,000	22,000
Cassava	14,000	20,000	21,000
Production, metric tons			
Palm kernels	(74,300)	(55,000)	(60,000)
Palm oil	(35,000)	(37,000)	(50,000)
Coffee	(600)	(5,300)	(6,300)
Cocoa beans	(1,600)	(3,600)	(5,000)

Livestock (1969/70). Cattle 240,000; sheep 57,000; goats 156,000; pigs 29,000.

Mineral production (1968). Diamonds 2,432,000 metric carats; iron ore (2,535,500 metric tons exported, 1968); bauxite and rutile.

Trade.

	1960	1968
Imports	UK£26,342,213 million	75,459,000 leone
	($74 million)	($94 million)

(mainly from UK, Japan, USA, France, West Germany)

Exports	UK£25,926,801	75,728,000 leone
	($73 million)	($94.6 million)

(mainly to UK, Netherlands, West Germany)

Chief exports: diamonds, iron ore, and concentrates.

Currency. Since August 4, 1964: the leone (Le), divided into 100 cents.

SOMALI DEMOCRATIC REPUBLIC (Al-Jumhouriya As-Somaliya Al-Domocradia)

An independent republic since July 1, 1960, consisting of former Italian Somaliland (a trusteeship territory of the UN administered by Italy from 1950 to 1960) and British Somaliland, a former British protectorate.

Area. About 270,000 square miles (700,000 sq.km).

Population. (mid-1965 UN estimate) 2,500,000; (mid-1969 UN estimate) 2,730,000.

Towns (1969 estimate). Mogadiscio (capital) 100,000; Hargeisa 50,000; Kisimayu 30,000; Berbera 20,000.

Agriculture. 89 percent of total labor force engaged in agriculture, mainly pastoralists.

Land use 1960	*hectares*
Arable and permanent crops	957,000
Permanent meadows and pastures	20,568,000
Forest	14,401,000

Irrigated land (in former Italian Somaliland only, 1960)	165,000

Crops (hectares)

	1948/52	1961/65	1970
Millet and sorghum	77,000	365,000	340,000
Maize	19,000	75,000	75,000
Sesame	12,000	13,000	20,000
Bananas	3,000	11,000	7,000
Sugar cane	3,000	2,000	7,000

Livestock (1969/70). Horses 1,000; mules 20,000; asses 23,000; camels 2,200,000; cattle 2,100,000; sheep 4,600,000; goats 4,800,000; pigs 7,000.

Mineral production. There are known deposits of iron ore, beryl, columbite, and uranium, but as yet no commercial exploitation.

Trade.

	1964	1968
Imports	390,736,000 Somali sh.	339,790,000 Somali sh.
	($55 million)	($48 million)
	(mainly from Italy, Japan, USA, UK, USSR, West Germany)	
Exports	215,697,000 Somali sh.	212,025,000 Somali sh.
	($30.5 million)	($30.3 million)
	(mainly to Southern Yemen, Italy, Iran)	

Chief exports: live animals (including camels), bananas, hides and skins.

Currency. Somali shilling divided into 100 cents.

SOUTH AFRICA, REPUBLIC OF (Republiek van Suid-Afrika)

Became a republic and withdrew from the Commonwealth on March 15, 1961; formerly, as the Union of South Africa (Unie van Suid-Afrika), a self-governing dominion of the Commonwealth.

Area. Total area: 471,445 square miles (1,221,042 sq.km), excluding Walvis Bay.

Province	square miles	sq.km
Cape of Good Hope[1]	278,380	721,004
Natal	33,578	86,967
Transvaal	109,621	283,918
Orange Free State	49,866	129,153

Population.

	1960	1970 census
Europeans or white	3,067,638	3,779,000
Non-Europeans or non-whites	12,773,490	17,503,000
Total	15,841,128	21,282,000

In 1960 the Afrikaans-speaking population numbered 1.79 million, English-speaking 1.15 million, in the white population.

Towns (suburbs excluded: 1968) (white population in parenthesis). Johannesburg 1,364,523 (476,712); Durban 682,910 (184,692); Cape Town 625,740 (200,090); Pretoria 492,577 (261,000); Port Elizabeth 381,227 (118,845); Germiston 197,020 (65,200); Bloemfontein 146,200 (63,200); East London 136,757 (51,570); Pietermaritzburg 112,693 (45,930).

Pretoria is the seat of government, Cape Town the seat of legislature.

Agriculture. 29 percent of total labor force engaged in agriculture. Number of and area covered by agricultural holdings (1960): 10,362; 105,944,935 hectares.

---

[1] Walvis Bay [434 square miles (1,124 sq.km)] is part of Cape Province but is administered by South West Africa.

Land use 1960 (excluding Walvis Bay)

Arable	11,578,000
Permanent crops	480,000
Permanent meadows and pastures (in agricultural holdings)	90,390,000
Forest	4,105,000
Irrigated land	808,000

Crops (*hectares*)

	1948/52	1961/65	1970
Maize	3,228,000	4,186,000	5,200,000
Wheat	928,000	1,197,000	1,300,000
Oats	150,000	290,000	260,000
Barley	45,000	38,000	40,000
Groundnuts	162,000	301,000	395,000
Sugar cane	80,000	120,000	195,000
Sunflowers	120,000	181,000	175,000
Grapes (total)	49,000	67,000	99,000
Cotton	19,000	46,000	81,000
Potatoes	57,000	49,000	70,000
Tobacco	25,000	34,000	45,000

Large quantities of fruits (deciduous and citrus) are produced as well as kaffir corn and some rice.

Livestock (1969/70). Horses 440,000; mules 50,000; asses 290,000; cattle 12,251,000; dairy cows 2,600,000; sheep 39,300,000; goats 5,550,000; pigs 1,230,000.

Mineral production (1968) (*metric tons* unless otherwise specified). Gold 31,086,000 fine ozs (approximately 81 percent of total free world production); silver 3,198,000 fine ozs; asbestos 260,500; chrome ore 1,271,000; coal 56,934,000; copper 146,000; diamonds 7,433,300 carats; iron ore 7,959,000; iron pyrites 648,000; manganese ore 2,675,000; uranium oxide 7,746,000 lb.

Trade (including South West Africa)

	1960	1968
Imports	R1,111,394,912 ($1,556 million)	R1,883,080,000 ($2,633.6 million)

(mainly from UK, USA, West Germany, Japan; from African countries: R120,180,000)

Exports	R789,350,848 ($1,205 million) (gold excluded)	R1,506,300,000 ($2,106.7 million) (gold included)

(mainly to UK, Japan, USA, West Germany; to African countries R248,010,000)

Chief exports: gold, diamonds (rough and polished), maize, fruit and vegetables, wool, copper, iron and steel, petroleum products.

Currency. Since February 14, 1961 the rand (R), divided into 100 cents.

SOUTH WEST AFRICA (Suidwes-Afrika) (Namibia)

A territory administered by the Republic of South Africa. The mandate of the League of Nations, December 17, 1920, was a Class III mandate which laid down that the territory should be governed as an integral part of the territory of the mandatory power. The South African government does not recognize the authority of the United Nations over South West Africa.

Area.   317,836 square miles (823,145 sq.km) including Walvis Bay (434 square miles: 1,124 sq.km).

Population.   (1960 census) 526,004 (73,464 white); (1970 census) 749,000 (90,000 white).

Agriculture.   55 percent of total labor force engaged in agriculture. Number of and area covered by agricultural holdings (1960): 5,358; 61,082,869 hectares.

Land use (including Walvis Bay territory) 1960	*hectares*
Arable	641,000
Permanent crops	1,000
Permanent meadows and pastures	52,906,000
Forest	10,427,000
Irrigated land	4,000

Crops (*hectares*)

	1948/52	1961/65	1970
Millet and sorghum	33,000	42,000	42,000
Maize	13,000	27,000	32,000

Livestock (1969/70). Horses 36,000; mules 4,000; asses 56,000; cattle 2,500,000; sheep 4,000,000; goats 1,700,000; pigs 24,000.

Mineral production.   Alluvial diamonds occur in quantity.

Trade.   Statistics are included in those of the Republic of South Africa. In addition to diamonds, karakul pelts form a valuable and increasing export.

Currency.   As in the Republic of South Africa: since February 14, 1961, the rand (R), divided into 100 cents.

SPANISH TERRITORIES

Spanish West Africa was divided in two in January, 1958: Ifni and Spanish Sahara. Ifni was restored to Morocco on June 30, 1969. The former Spanish colony, Equatorial Guinea, became independent as the Republic of Equatorial Guinea on October 12, 1968. Spanish Sahara and Spanish North Africa continue as Spanish territories.

SPANISH NORTH AFRICA (Alhucemas, Ceuta, Chafarinas, Melilla and Peñón de Vélez in Morocco).

Area.   7,410 acres (3,000 hectares). Population (mid-1969 UN estimate) 164,000.

SPANISH SAHARA

A province consisting of two districts: Sekia El Hamra (31,660 square miles: 82,000 sq.km) and Rio de Oro (71,040 square miles: 184,000 sq.km), totalling 102,680 square miles (266,000 sq.km). Population (mid-1969 UN estimate) 61,000. Capital: El Aaiún, population about 5,000.

Agriculture

Land use 1969
	hectares
Arable	1,000
Permanent meadows and pastures	5,000,000

Livestock (1969/70). Asses (no data); camels 58,000; sheep 18,000; goats 49,000.

Mineral production.   There are rich resources of phosphates.

Trade.   Imports in 1968 estimated to be 210.35 million peseta ($3 million); exports of no account. Trading is mainly with Spain.

SUDAN, THE DEMOCRATIC REPUBLIC OF (Jamhuryat es-Sudan Al Democratia)

A sovereign independent republic since January 1, 1956; formerly a condominium administered jointly by Britain and Egypt under the title Anglo-Egyptian Sudan.

Area.   967,500 square miles (2.5 million sq.km).

Population.   (1955/6 census) 10,262,674; (mid-1969 UN estimate) 15,186,000.

Towns.   El Khartûm (capital) (1967 estimate, includes Omdurmân and Khartûm North) 390,000; Port Sudan (1964 estimate) 57,000; Atbara (1964 estimate) 45,000; Kosti (1964 estimate) 30,000.

Agriculture.   78 percent of total labor force engaged in agriculture.

Land use 1968
	hectares
Arable and permanent crops	7,100,000
Permanent meadows and pastures	24,000,000
Forest	91,500,000
Irrigated land (1967)	711,000

Crops (*hectares*)

	1948/52	1961/65	1970
Sorghum	820,000	1,400,000	1,400,000
Millet	352,000	523,000	700,000
Sesame	158,000	420,000	500,000
Groundnuts	38,000	313,000	385,000
Cotton	187,000	439,000	491,000

Livestock (1969/70). Horses 20,000; mules 1,000; asses 620,000; camels 3,000,000; cattle 13,500,000; sheep 13,000,000; goats 10,050,000; pigs 7,000.

Mineral production.   There is a proven wide variety of minerals, including iron ore, copper, manganese ore; production of gold (1963) 900 troy oz; chromite (1965) 20,500 metric tons; salt pans supply domestic needs and the surplus is exported.

Trade.

	1960	1968
Imports	£S 63,743,828	£S 89,709,000
	($178 million	($256 million)

[mainly from UK, India, Japan, USSR, China (mainland)]

Exports	£S 60,679,266	£S 81,150,000
	($170 million)	($231.9 million)

[mainly to West Germany, Italy, India, UK,
China (mainland), USSR]

Chief exports (1968): raw cotton, oilseeds (groundnut, cotton and sesame), gum arabic, oilseed cake, live animals, cottonseed oil, millet.

Currency. Sudanese pound (£S), divided into 100 piastres and 1,000 millièmes.

SWAZILAND

An independent kingdom since September 6, 1968, within the Commonwealth; formerly a British protectorate.

Area. 6,705 square miles (17,400 sq.km).

Population. (1966 census) 374,571; (mid-1969 UN estimate) 423,000.

Towns. Mbabane (capital) (1966) 14,000; Manzini 16,000.

Agriculture. Agricultural population not recorded.

Land use 1967	*hectares*
Arable	252,000
Permanent crops	2,000
Permanent meadows and pastures	1,268,000
Forest	129,000
Irrigated land	28,000

Crops (hectares)	1948/52	1961/65	1970
Maize	16,000	75,000	90,000
Sorghum	18,000	30,000	32,000
Sugar cane	no data	10,000	12,000
Cotton	1,000	10,000	18,000
Tobacco (*production, metric tons*)	(400)	(200)	(200)

Citrus fruit and pineapples are commercial crops of growing importance.

Livestock (1969/70). Horses 2,000; asses 12,000; cattle 540,000; dairy cows 200,000; sheep 55,000; goats 220,000; pigs 13,000.

Mineral production (1968). Iron ore 2,260,200 short tons; asbestos 42,900 short tons; coal 106,700 short tons.

Trade.

	1970
Imports	R 41,750,000 ($58.4 million)
Exports	R 49,250,000 ($68.9 million)

(most trading is with South Africa, with whom Swaziland has a customs union)

Chief exports: sugar, wood pulp and wood products; iron ore; asbestos.

Currency.   As in the Republic of South Africa: the rand (R), divided into 100 cents.

TANZANIA (United Republic of Tanzania)

Tanganyika was an independent country from May 1, 1961, a republic from December 9, 1962, and a member of the Commonwealth; formerly a UN trusteeship held by Britain; previously part of German East Africa.

Zanzibar, comprising the two islands, Zanzibar and Pemba, off the east coast of Africa became independent on June 24, 1963, the sultanate being replaced by a republic on January 12, 1965; formerly a British protectorate.

On April 26, 1964 Tanyika and Zanzibar united to form the United Republic of Tanganyika and Zanzibar, taking the name Tanzania on October 29, 1964.

Area and Population.
Tanganyika: 362,688 square miles (939,936 sq.km).
　　　　　 (1967 census) 11,776,992
Zanzibar:　 640 square miles (1,658 sq.km)
　　　　　 (1967 census) 190,117
Pemba:　　 380 square miles (984 sq.km)
　　　　　 (1967 census) 164,243
Tanzania:　 (mid-1969 UN estimate) 12,926,000.

Towns (1967 census). Dar es Salaam (capital) 372,515; Zanzibar Town 57,923.

The following statistics refer to Tanzania unless detailed otherwise.

Agriculture.   95 percent of total labor force engaged in agriculture.
In Tanganyika in 1960 there were 1,241 large-scale commercial holdings covering 975,000 hectares.

Land use 1966	*hectares*
Arable	10,734,000
Permanent crops	968,000
Permanent meadows and pastures	44,754,000
Forest	31,074

Irrigated land (Tanganyika only)	40,000

Crops (*hectares*)

	1948/52	1961/65	1970
Millet and sorghum	1,096,000	1,240,000	1,300,000
Maize	262,000	469,000	800,000
Wheat	15,000	34,000	35,000
Cotton	74,000	310,000	470,000
Coconuts	246,000	253,000	300,000
Sisal	210,000	282,000	260,000
Production, metric tons			
Coffee	(14,100)	(31,600)	(54,000)
Copra	(28,200)	(22,500)	(25,000)

Sisal (*Agave sisalana*) is a commercial crop of the mainland;

Zanzibar and Pemba are the largest world suppliers of cloves and clove oil.

Livestock (1969/70). Asses 177,000; cattle 11,000,000; sheep 3,000,000; goats 4,150,000.

Mineral production, mainland only.   Diamonds (1968) 702,000 metric carats; gold (1967) 18,000 troy ozs; tin and salt are also produced.

Trade.

	1965	1968
Imports	Tanganyika $140 million Zanzibar $12 million	Tanzania T£76,583,000 ($217.3 million)

[mainly from UK, Japan, West Germany, Iran; in 1968 imports from Kenya and Uganda totalled T£15,098,000 ($43.1 million)]

Exports	Tanganyika $176 million Zanzibar $11 million	Tanzania T£79,030,000 ($225.8 million)

[mainly to UK, Zambia, India; in 1968 exports to Kenya and Uganda from Tanzania totalled T£4,547,000 ($13 million)]

Chief exports (1968): raw cotton, coffee, petroleum products, sisal, diamonds, cashew nuts; cloves and clove oil are the largest export from Zanzibar and Pemba.

Currency.   Tanzanian shilling, divided into 100 cents (see Kenya).
20 Tanzanian shillings = 1 Tanzanian pound

TOGO (République Togolaise)

An independent republic since April 27, 1960; cooperates with France by convention July 10, 1963; formerly part of German Togoland (1894–1914), later as French Togoland a trusteeship territory under the United Nations.

Area.   21,620 square miles (56,000 sq.km).

Population.   (1955 census) 1,439,772; (mid-1969 UN estimate) 1,955,916.

Towns (1968).   Lomé (capital) 135,000.

Agriculture.   79 percent of total labor force engaged in agriculture. Number of and area covered by agricultural holdings (1961/2: provisional): 217,127; 569,830 hectares.

Land use 1965	*hectares*
Arable	2,113,000
Permanent crops	47,000
Permanent meadows and pastures	200,000
Forest	530,000
Irrigated land (1968)	3,000

Crops (*hectares*)

	1948/52	1961/65	1970
Maize	134,000	157,000	220,000
Cassava	46,000	126,000	151,000
Groundnuts	23,000	40,000	45,000
Cotton	26,000	54,000	62,000
Production, metric tons			
Palm kernels	(9,000)	(12,800)	(16,000)
Palm oil	(2,500)	(1,300)	(2,800)

Coffee and cocoa are also grown in quantity.

Livestock (1969/70). Horses 1,000; asses 1,000; cattle 180,000; sheep 570,000; goats 574,000; pigs 220,000.

Mineral production. Phosphates (production 1968 1,355,000 metric tons) and bauxite have been exploited since 1961. There are iron ore, limestone, and magnesian limestone deposits.

Trade.

	1964	1968
Imports	10,285 million fr.CFA ($37.4 million) (mainly from France, Japan, UK)	11,620 million fr.CFA ($42.4 million)
Exports	7,448 million fr.CFA ($27.8 million) (mainly to France, Netherlands, West Germany)	9,550 million fr.CFA ($34.7 million)

Chief exports: phosphates, cocoa beans, coffee, palm nuts, and kernels.

Currency. Franc CFA, divided into 100 centimes.

TUNISIA (Al-Djoumhouria Attunusia)

An independent republic since June 1, 1959; formerly a French protectorate.

Area. About 63,362 square miles (164,150 sq.km).

Population. (1966 census) 4,457,862; (mid-1969 UN estimate) 4,925,000.

Towns (1966 census). Tunis (capital) 642,384; Sfax 249,991; Bizerta 95,023; Kairouan 82,299; Gabes 76,356; Beja 72,034; Djerba 65,533.

Agriculture. 63 percent of total labor force engaged in agriculture. Number of and area covered by agricultural holdings (1961/2): 325,800; 5,022,000 hectares.

Land use 1961	*hectares*
Arable and permanent crops	4,510,000
Permanent meadows and pastures	3,250,000
Forest	1,240,000
Irrigated land (1968)	80,000

Crops (*hectares*)

	1948/52	1961/65	1970
Wheat	917,000	1,002,000	1,100,000
Barley	590,000	445,000	410,000
Grapes (total)	35,000	46,000	46,000

Production, metric tons

Olives	(211,000)	(311,000)	(125,000)
Figs (fresh)	(13,000)	(20,000)	(20,000) (1969)
Dates	(34,000)	(35,000)	(60,000) (1969)

Livestock (1969/70). Horses 96,000; asses 180,000; mules 59,000; camels 230,000; cattle 610,000; dairy cows 246,000; 3,200,000; goats 460,000; pigs 7,000.

Mineral production (1969) (*metric tons*). Phosphate rock 2,600,000; iron ore 950,000; lead ore 38,000; zinc ore 17,000; crude petroleum 4,220,000.

Trade.

	1963	1968
Imports	93,148,000 dinars	114,044,000 dinars
	($222 million)	($219 million)
	(mainly from France, USA, Italy)	
Exports	52,922,000 dinars	82,829,000 dinars
	($126 million)	($159 million)

(mainly to France, West Germany, Italy, Libya)

Chief exports: petroleum (crude and partly refined), olive oil, phosphates, phosphatic fertilizers, fruit and vegetables, iron ore.

Currency. Since November 1, 1968: the dinar, divided into 1,000 millimes.

UGANDA

An independent country since October 9, 1962, a republic since September 8, 1967, and a member of the Commonwealth; formerly a British protectorate.

Area. 91,134 square miles (236,037 sq.km) including 16,386 square miles (42,440 sq. km) of swamp and water.

Population. (1959 census) 6,610,686; (1969 census) 9,526,000.

Towns. Kampala (capital) (1969 estimate) 80,000: Greater Kampala about 170,000.

Agriculture. 89 percent of total labor force engaged in agriculture. Number of and area covered by agricultural holdings (1963/4): 1,170,921; 3,856,196 hectares.

Land use 1967	*hectares*
Arable	3,772,000
Permanent crops	1,116,000
Permanent meadows and pastures	5,000,000
Forest	9,172,000
Irrigated land	4,000

Crops (*hectares*)

	1948/52	1961/65	1970
Millet and sorghum	558,000	511,000	550,000
Maize	121,000	197,000	300,000
Cotton	624,000	831,000	840,000
Groundnuts	144,000	244,000	250,000
Sugar cane	11,000	18,000	17,000
Castor beans	10,000	5,000	5,000
Tobacco	4,000	7,000	7,000
Sisal	3,000	1,000	1,000
Production, metric tons			
Coffee	(34,700)	(150,900)	(240,000)
Tea	(1,700)	(6,700)	(17,600)

Livestock (1969/70). Asses 14,000; cattle 3,900,000; sheep 760,000; goats 1,680,000; pigs 48,000.

Mineral production (1967). Blister copper 14,392 long tons; tin ore 156.6 long tons; cement (1963) 54,282 long tons.

Trade.

	1960	1968
Imports	£26,030,000	U£43,795,000
	($77 million)	($125 million)

[mainly from UK, West Germany, Japan; imports from Tanzania and Kenya in 1968 totaled U£14,120,000 ($40 million)]

Exports	£41,588,000	U£65,471,000
	($116 million)	($187 million)

[mainly to USA, UK, Japan, Canada, India; exports to Tanzania and Kenya in 1968 totaled U£10,679,000 ($30.5 million)]

Chief exports: coffee, raw cotton, copper, tea.

Currency. Since September 14, 1967: the Uganda shilling, divided into 100 cents; 20 Uganda shillings = one Uganda pound (£). *See* Kenya, currency.

UNITED ARAB REPUBLIC (al-Jumhuria al-Arabia al-Muttahida) (Egypt)

An independent country, and a republic since 1953; from February 1, 1958 to September 28, 1961 linked with Syria as the United Arab Republic; from March 8, 1958 to December 26, 1961 federated with the Kingdom of Yemen as United Arab States; an independent kingdom from 1922 to 1952.

Area. Total: 386,198 square miles (approximately one million sq.km); settled area about 13,500 square miles (35,580 sq.km); marshes and lakes cover about 2,850 square miles (7,381,400 sq.km).

Population. (1966 census) 30,075,858; (mid-1969 UN estimate) 32,500,000.

Towns (1966 census). Cairo (El Qâhira) (capital 4,220,000; Alexandria (El Iskandarîya) 1,801,000; Gîza 571,000; Port Said (Bûr Said) 283,000; Suez (El Suweis) 264,000; Tanta (Gharbîya) 230,000; El Mahalla el Kubra 225,000; El Mansûra 191,000; Imbâbah 182,000;

Subra el Khema 173,000; Asyût 154,000; Zagazig (Sharqîya) 151,000; Damnhûr 146,000; Ismaîlia 144,000; Faiyûm 134,000; Aswan 128,000; El Minyâ 113,000.

Agriculture.   Over 55 percent of total labor force engaged in agriculture. Number of and area covered by agricultural holdings (1960/61): 1,642,160; 2,614,111 hectares.

Land use 1967	*hectares*
Arable	2,725,000
Permanent crops	110,000
Permanent meadows and pastures	nil
Forest	2,000
Irrigated land	2,834,000

Crops (*hectares*)

	1948/52	1961/65	1970
Maize	660,000	678,000	632,000
Wheat	605,000	557,000	548,000
Rice	256,000	348,000	480,000
Cotton	761,000	738,000	685,000

Livestock (1969/70). Horses 63,000; mules 11,000; asses 1,230,000; camels 190,000; buffaloes 1,800,000; cattle 1,760,000; sheep 2,240,000; goats 820,000; pigs 15,000.

Mineral production (1968) (*metric tons*).   Phosphate rock 1,441,000; crude petroleum (1970) 20,755,000; lead and zinc 1,329,000; iron ore 447,000; marine salt 622,000.

Trade.

	1962–3	1968
Imports	£E 344 million	£E 290 million
	($746 million)	($644 million)

(mainly from USSR, France, Romania in 1968)

Exports	£E 198 million	£E 270 million
	($545 million)	($600 million)

(mainly to USSR, India, Czechoslovakia, West Germany in 1968) Chief exports (1968): raw cotton and cotton textiles, rice, mineral products, fruit, and vegetables.

Currency.   Egyptian pound (£E) divided into 100 piastres or 1000 mils.

UPPER VOLTA (République de Haute-Volta)

An independent republic since August 5, 1960, with "special relations" with France; formerly part of French West Africa.

Area.   105,840 square miles (274,122 sq.km).

Population.   (mid-1965 estimate) 4,858,000; (mid-1969 UN estimate) 5,128,000.

Towns.   Ougadougou (capital) 110,000; Bobo-Dioulasso 69,356.

Agriculture.   87 percent of total labor force engaged in agriculture.

Land use 1967   *hectares*
Arable and permanent crops   8,700,000
Permanent meadows and pastures   13,755,000
Forest   2,300,000

Crops (*hectares*)

	1948/52	1961/65	1970
Millet and sorghum	653,000	734,000	680,000
Maize	167,000	159,000	210,000
Rice	12,000	47,000	50,000
Groundnuts	168,000	245,000	206,000
Cotton	99,000	43,000	82,000

Livestock (1969/70). Horses 71,000; asses 180,000; camels 6,000; cattle 28,000; dairy cows 375,000; sheep 1,900,000; goats 2,600,000; pigs 139,000.

Mineral production. Gold (1965) 34,468 troy ozs. Prospecting for manganese and diamonds.

Trade.

	1957	1968
Imports	1,612 million fr.CFA	10,119 million fr.CFA
	($6.4 million)	($36.7 million)
	(mainly from France and Ivory Coast)	
Exports	896 million fr.CFA	5,290 million fr.CFA
	($3.6 million)	($19.2 million)
	(mainly to Ivory Coast, France, Ghana)	

Chief exports: livestock, raw cotton, oilseeds.

Currency.   Franc CFA, divided into 100 centimes.

ZAIRE

As Congo Democratic Republic, or Congo (Kinshasa) an independent republic since June 30, 1960; renamed the Republic of Zaire, October 27, 1971; formerly Belgian Congo, a Belgian colony under a governor-general.

Area.   (estimated) 895,348 square miles (2,345,410 sq.km)

Population (census 1970)   21,637,876.

Towns.   Kinshasa (formerly Léopoldville) (capital) (1970) 1,225,720; Lubumbashi (formerly Elisabethville) (1966) 233,000; Kisangani (formerly Stanleyville) 150,000; Kamanga 141,000; Likasi 102,000.

Agriculture.   69 percent of total force engaged in agriculture.

Land use 1962   *hectares*
Arable and permanent crops   7,200
Permanent meadows and pastures   65,500,000
Forest   129,141,000

Crops (*hectares*)

	1948/52	1961/65	1970
Cassava	655,000	668,000	700,000
Maize	337,000	266,000	330,000
Rice	151,000	102,000	135,000
Groundnuts	250,000	366,000	320,000
Bananas	8,000	15,000	15,000
Cotton	333,000	97,000	100,000
Tea	1,000	11,000	13,000

Production, metric tons

Rubber	(9,800)	(33,600)	(36,000)
Palm kernels	(117,000)	(109,700)	(110,000)
Palm oil	(172,200)	(209,500)	(220,000)
Coffee	(20,500)	(60,000)	(69,000)

Livestock (1969/70). Horses 1,000; cattle 900,000; sheep 570,000; goats 1,600,000; pigs 442,000.

Mineral production (1968). Copper (1969) 362,000 metric tons; cobalt ore 10,394 metric tons; diamonds (industrial and gem, 1967) 12,890,000 metric carats; silver 65 metric tons; tin 7,495 metric tons, manganese ore 187,000 metric tons; zinc 120,000 metric tons. There are also gold, uranium, and iron-ore resources.

Trade.

	1959	1968
Imports	14,994 million fr.	154,789,000 zaïres
	($300 million)	($309.6 million)
	(mainly from Belgium/Luxembourg, USA, Italy, France, West Germany)	
Exports	25,004 million fr.	286,263,000 zaïres
	($500 million)	($572.5 million)
	(mainly to Belgium/Luxembourg, Italy, France, UK, USA, Netherlands)	

Chief exports (1968): copper (over 50% of total exports), diamonds, coffee, cobalt, palm oil.

Currency. Congolese franc (devalued November, 1963), until June 23, 1967. Since that date: the zaïre, divided into 100 makuta (singular: likuta), each likuta being divided into 100 sengi.

ZAMBIA

An independent republic since October 24, 1964, within the Commonwealth; formerly Northern Rhodesia, a British colony; part of the Federation of Rhodesia and Nyasaland 1953–63.

Area. 290,586 square miles (752,262 sq.km).

Population (1966). 3,894,200; (mid-1969 UN estimate) 4,220,000.

Towns (1966). Lusaka (capital) 152,000.

Agriculture. 81 percent of total labor force engaged in agriculture. In 1960 there were 1,467 European holdings of over 10.12 hectares covering an area of 1,721,388 hectares.

Land use 1962	hectares
Arable and permanent crops	4,800,000
Permanent meadows and pastures	33,800,000
Forest	34,000,000

Irrigated land on farms and estates (1963)	2,000

Crops (*hectares*)

	1948/52	1961/65	1970
Millet and sorghum	240,000	315,000	310,000
Maize	425,000	260,000	240,000
Cassava	40,000	48,000	52,000
Groundnuts	47,000	50,000	95,000
Cotton	negligible	1,000	9,000
Tobacco	7,000	10,000	6,000

Livestock (1969/70). Asses 1,000; cattle 1,350,000; sheep 37,000; goats 187,000; pigs 92,000.

Mineral production (1967) (*metric tons*). Copper (blister) 90,500; copper (electrolytic) 588,800; cobalt 1,603,900; manganese 28,000; lead 21,400; zinc 47,800.

Trade.

	1965	1968
Imports	210,742,000 Kwachas	325,173,000 Kwachas
	($294.7 million)	($454.7 million)
	(mainly from South Africa, UK, USA, Rhodesia)	
Exports	380,294,000 Kwachas	544,416,000 Kwachas
	($531.8 million)	($761.4 million)

(mainly to UK, Japan, West Germany, Italy, France)
Chief exports: copper, lead, cobalt metal, maize.

Currency. Since January 16, 1968 decimal currency: the Kwacha (K) divided into 100 ngwee; formerly based on UK £ sterling. (The 1965 trade statistics have been converted to Kwachas for comparability.)

AFRICAN ISLANDS

CANARY ARCHIPELAGO

A group of volcanic islands administered by Spain; since September 21, 1927 divided into two provinces: *Santa Cruz de Tenerife* (comprising the islands of Tenerife, Palma, Gomera and Hierro), area 1,238 square miles (3,208 sq.km), population (1960) 490,655, and *Las Palmas* (comprising islands of Gran Canaria, Lanzarote and Fuerteventura and some small barren islands), area 1,569 square miles (4,065 sq.km), population (1960) 453,793.

CAPE VERDE ISLANDS

Portuguese overseas territory, administered by a governor since 1587 from Praia, the capital. The ten islands and five islets have a total area of 1,557 square miles (4,033 sq.km). Population (December 1960 census) 201,549; (mid-1969 UN estimate) 250,000.

Agriculture.

Land use 1967	hectares
Arable	38,000
Permanent crops	2,000
Forest	1,000

Crops (*hectares*)

	1948/52	1961/65	1970
Maize	30,000	28,000	20,000
Bananas	negligible	negligible	1,000

Coffee of high quality is produced and exported.

Livestock (1969/70). Horses 2,000; mules 2,000; asses 7,000; cattle 16,000; sheep 3,000; goats 21,000; pigs 14,000.

Trade. (1969). Imports totalled 418,8 million escudos ($11.2 million), exports 44.6 million escudos ($1.56 million).

Currency. Escudo, divided into 100 centavos, as in Portugal.

COMORO ARCHIPELAGO (Territoire des Comores)

Since May 9, 1946 the islands of the Comoro archipelago have had administrative autonomy within the French Republic, of which they were formerly a colony; from 1914 to 1946 they were administered from Madagascar (Malagasy).

Area. About 838 square miles (2,170 sq.km).

Population. (1966 census) 248,517; (mid-1969 UN estimate) 275,227.

Towns (1966). Noroni (capital, on Grande Comore) 11,515.

Agriculture.

Land use 1965	hectares
Arable and permanent crops	90,000
Permanent meadows and pastures	15,000
Forest	35,000

Crops include coffee, cloves, sugar cane, vanilla, cocoa beans, sisal, and essential oils. In 1970, 62,000 hectares were devoted to coconuts.

Livestock (1969/70). Sheep 6,000; goats 81,000.

Trade (1969). Imports totalled 2,092 million fr.CFA ($7.6 million), exports 577.9 million fr.CFA ($2.1 million).

Chief exports (1968): vanilla essential oils, copra, cloves.

Currency. Franc CFA, divided into 100 centimes.

FERNANDO PÓO AND ANNOBÓN (*see* Equatorial Guinea)

MADEIRA ARCHIPELAGO

Volcanic islands administered as a district of Portugal. Funchal, the main island, has an area of 307.7 square miles (797,000 sq.km).

Population (1960) 268,937; (mid-1969 UN estimate) 268,700. Cultivable land is scarce; 14,000 hectares are irrigated. Crops include wheat, barley, maize, sugar cane, bananas, and vines. Trade is mainly with Portugal.

MALAGASY (MADAGASCAR) AND DEPENDENCIES
(République Malgache)

An independent republic within the French Community since June 26, 1960; formerly a French colony under a governor-general.

Area.   Approximately 229,233 square miles (594,180 sq.km).

Population.   (January 1, 1967) 6,776,970; (mid-1969 UN estimate) 6,643,000.

Towns (1970).   Tananarive (capital 322,000; Tamatave 50,500; Majunga 43,500; Fianarantsoa 39,500, Diego–Suarez 38,600; Tulear, 34,000.

Agriculture.   84 percent of total labor force engaged in agriculture. Number of and area covered by agricultural holdings (1961/2): 882,000; 917,000 hectares (cultivated area only).

Land use 1968	*hectares*
Arable and permanent crops	2,856,000
Permanent meadows and pastures	34,000,000
Forest	12,470,000
Irrigated land (1966)	620,000

Crops (*hectares*)

	1948/52	1961/65	1970
Rice	615,000	756,000	1,000,000
Cassava	195,000	253,000	260,000
Maize	83,000	99,000	110,000
Groundnuts	16,000	39,000	49,000
Sugar cane	15,000	25,000	22,000
Bananas	11,000	11,000	13,000
Tobacco	6,000	6,000	7,000
Sisal	13,000	18,000	19,000
Coffee (*production, metric tons*)	(32,700)	(52,600)	(50,000)

Livestock (1969/70).   Horses 2,000; cattle 9,800,000; sheep 615,000; goats 780,000; pigs 530,000.

Mineral production (*metric tons*).   Mica (1968) 838; graphite (1968) 16,071; phosphates (1964) 2,020; chrome (1966) 2,383; also ilmenite, zircon, beryl, gold, garnet.

Trade.

	1960	1970
Imports	27,657 million fr.MG ($111 million)	41,936.6 million fr.MG ($152 million)
	[mainly from France (over 50 percent), some from West Germany, USA]	
Exports	18,489 million fr.MG ($74 million)	28,607.9 million fr.MG ($104 million)
	(mainly to France, USA, Réunion)	

Chief exports: coffee, spices, rice, sugar.

Currency. Malagasy franc (MGF), divided into 100 centimes.

MAURITIUS

An independent, monarchical state within the Commonwealth since March 12, 1968; formerly a British colony. Dependencies: Rodrigues, 42 square miles (108.78 sq.km) and other small islands.

Area. 720 square miles (1,843 sq.km).

Population. (1962 census) 681,619, dependencies 19,400; (mid-1969 UN estimate) 870,000.

Towns (1969). Port Louis (capital) 139,300.

Agriculture. Percentage of population engaged in agriculture not recorded.

Land use 1968	*hectares*
Arable and permanent crops	104,000
Permanent meadows and pastures	7,000
Forest	59,000
Irrigated land (1969)	15,000

Crops (*hectares*)

	1948/52	1961/65	1970
Sugar cane	64,000	82,000	80,000
Tea	1,000	2,000	3,000
Piteria fibre			
(*Furcraea gigantea*)	3,000	2,000	1,000

Tobacco also is a commercial crop.
Subsistence crops include cassava and potatoes; and there is widespread onion cultivation.

Livestock (1969/70). Cattle 48,000; dairy cows 20,000; sheep 3,000; goats 67,000; pigs 3,000.

Mineral production. None.

Trade.

	1959	1968
Imports	286,851,725 rupees	421,100,000 rupees
	($60 million)	($75.8 million)

(mainly from UK, Burma, South Africa, West Germany, France)

Exports	282,210,191 rupees	354,000,000 rupees
	($59 million)	($63.75 million)

[mainly to UK (over 50 percent), Canada]
Chief exports: sugar, molasses, tea.

Currency. Mauritius rupee, divided into 100 cents.

LA RÉUNION (ÎLE DE LA REUNION) (Bourbon)

French territory since 1642; an Overseas Department since March 19, 1946.

Area.   968.5 square miles (2,511.6 sq.km).

Population (July 31, 1970).   445,500.

Towns (1970).   St. Denis (capital) 85,992; St. Paul 43,186; St. Pierre 40,364; St. Louis 26,740.

Agriculture.   Percentage of population engaged in agriculture not recorded.

Land use 1966	*hectares*
Arable	62,000
Permanent meadows and pastures	20,000
Forest	51,000

Crops (hectares)

	1948/52	1961/65	1970
Maize	8,000	8,000	10,000
Cassava	1,000	negligible	1,000
Sugar cane	22,000	36,000	43,000

Tobacco, tea, vanilla and essential oil plants are commercial crops.
Livestock (1969/70). Asses 1,000; cattle 42,000; sheep 3,000; goats 17,000; pigs 80,000.

Mineral production.   None.

Trade.

	1960	1968
Imports	12,902 million fr.CFA ($52 million)	31,095 million fr.CFA ($113 million)
	[mainly from France (over 66 percent), Malagasy]	
Exports	8,989 million fr.CFA ($36 million)	11,386 million fr.CFA ($41.5 million)
	(mainly to France)	

Chief exports (1968): sugar, essential oils (of geranium and ylang-ylang), rum.

Currency.   Franc CFA, divided into 100 centimes.

ST. HELENA AND DEPENDENCIES (ASCENSION AND TRISTAN DA CUNHA)

St. Helena: a British colony; area 47 square miles (121.7 sq.km); population (1969) 4,829. Jamestown is the port. Cultivated area 8,000 acres (3,580 hectares).

Dependencies of St. Helena
Ascension: area 34 square miles (88 sq.km); population (1969) 700, and 739 from St. Helena. Cultivated area 10 acres (4 hectares) producing vegetables and fruit.
Tristan da Cunha: one of four in a group of small islands, dependencies of St. Helena since January 12, 1938. The volcano which comprised the island erupted unexpectedly in October, 1961; the population was evacuated, but most returned to the island; 1969 population 271.

SÃO TOMÉ AND PRINCIPE

Islands in the Gulf of Guinea comprising, with other small islands, a Province of Portugal.

Area.   372 square miles (964 sq.km).

Population.   (1960 census) 64,263; (mid-1969 UN estimate) 66,000.

Agriculture.   Arable and permanent crops cover 30,000 hectares. Commercial crops are cocoa, coconuts and products, coffee, palm oil, cinchona bark.

> *Livestock (1969/70).* Cattle 3,060; sheep 2,159; goats 1,027; pigs 3,283.

Trade.

	1969
Imports	224,856,000 escudos ($7.9 million)
Exports	247,199,000 escudos ($8.7 million)
	(trading is with Portugal)

Currency.   As in Portugal: escudo, divided into 100 centavos.

SEYCHELLES ARCHIPELAGO

A separate British colony since November, 1903; formerly, from 1814, a dependency of Mauritius (British).

In 1965 a separate British colony was established, *British Indian Ocean Territory,* comprising the islands of Chagos Archipelago (formerly a dependency of Mauritius), Aldabra, Farquhar, and Des Rochas, with a total area of 31.7 square miles (8,000 hectares). *Seychelles and Dependencies* (British Indian Ocean Territory excluded) comprise some 84 islands and islets; total area estimated to be 107 square miles (277 sq.km). Population (mid-1970) 53,000. Victoria (capital) (1970) 13,000 lies on Mahé, the main island.

Agriculture.

Land use 1967	*hectares*
Arable	1,000
Permanent crops	16,000
Permanent meadows and pastures	400
Forest	5,000

Crops (hectares)

	1948/52	1961/65	1969
Coconuts	53,000	47,000	49,000

Cinammon, vanilla pods, and patchouli (for oil) are other commercial crops; the area devoted to tea is increasing.

Livestock (1969/70). Cattle 4,000; goats 3,000; pigs 5,000.

Trade.

	1964	1968
Imports	15,724,845 rupees ($2.8 million)	33,875,243 rupees ($6.1 million)
	(mainly from UK, Iran, Kenya, Hong Kong, South Africa, Burma, India)	
Exports	8,661,651 rupees ($1.56 million)	16,195,767 rupees ($2.9 million)

(mainly to India, Israel, UK, South Africa, West Germany)
Chief exports: copra, cinnamon bark, and leaf oil, vanilla, patchouli
leaf oil, salted fish.

Currency.   Mauritius rupee, divided into 100 cents.

Sources.
    The Statesman's Year-Book (London: Macmillan).
    Production Yearbook (Rome: Food and Agriculture Organization
    of United Nations).
    Yearbook of International Trade Statistics (New York: United
    Nations).

Explanatory Notes.
1. *Area* refers to total area within the national boundary and includes inland water.
2. *Crops.* Only the principal subsistence crops and the most significant commercial crops have been specified. Data for two five-year
averages (1948/52 and 1961/65) have been included for comparsion
with the data for 1970. The 1970 data are preliminary calculations
made by the Food and Agriculture Organization based on official or
estimated statistics.
3. *Trade* data are the latest valuations available to the United Nations Statistical Office at the time of going to press, and are based on
data supplied by governments for the United Nations *Monthly Bulletin of Statistics* or for the United Nations *Statistical Yearbook*.

Conversion table.

Hectares		Acres
0.405	1	2.471
0.809	2	4.942
1.214	3	7.413
1.619	4	9.884
2.023	5	12.355
2.428	6	14.826
2.833	7	17.297
3.237	8	19.769
3.642	9	22.240
4.047	10	24.711
8.094	20	49.421
12.140	30	74.132
16.187	40	98.842
20.234	50	123.553
24.281	60	148.263
28.328	70	172.974
32.375	80	197.684
36.422	90	222.395
40.469	100	247.105

Estimates of Total and Per Capita Gross National Product at Market Prices

Country	Gross national product at market prices			Per capita gross national product at market prices		
	1963	1966	1967	1963	1966	1967
AFRICA	(Millions of U.S. Dollars)			(U.S. Dollars)		
Algeria	2,743	. . .	. . .	245	. . .	. . .
Angola	358	. . .	. . .	71	. . .	. . .
Botswana	. . .	55	. . .	. . .	96	. . .
Burundi	123	. . .	. . .	40	. . .	. . .
Cameroun	603	. . .	. . .	120	. . .	. . .
Central African Republic	148	. . .	. . .	113	. . .	. . .
Chad	213	. . .	. . .	66	. . .	. . .
Comoro Islands	20	. . .	. . .	96	. . .	. . .
Congo (Brazzaville)	153	. . .	. . .	188	. . .	. . .
Congo, Dem. Rep. (*see* Zaire)						
Dahomey	167	. . .	. . .	75	. . .	. . .
Ethiopia	1,078	1,483	. . .	49	64	. . .
Gabon	138	184	. . .	302	392	. . .
Gambia	26	. . .	. . .	81	. . .	. . .
Ghana	1,667	2,492	2,052	227	314	252
Guinea	333	. . .	. . .	99	. . .	. . .
Ivory Coast	764	1,005	. . .	208	256	. . .
Kenya	898	1,114	1,158	101	116	117
Lesotho	. . .	75	. . .	. . .	88	. . .
Liberia	192	229	. . .	186	210	. . .
Libya	731	1,258	1,535	486	750	883
Madagascar	612	707	737	103	114	116
Malawi	155	203	213	41	50	51
Mali	329	. . .	. . .	75	. . .	. . .
Mauritania	108	. . .	. . .	107	. . .	. . .
Mauritius	213	191	199	303	252	257
Morocco	2,362	2,545	2,706	186	185	191
Mozambique	482	. . .	. . .	71	. . .	. . .
Niger	260	. . .	. . .	81	. . .	. . .
Nigeria	4,163	4,603	. . .	75	77	. . .
Portuguese Guinea	37	. . .	. . .	71	. . .	. . .
Réunion	115	. . .	. . .	310	. . .	. . .
Rhodesia	894	1,004	1,053	223	228	233
Rwanda	117	. . .	. . .	40	. . .	. . .
Senegal	708	811	. . .	213	227	. . .
Sierra Leone	295	. . .	. . .	128	. . .	. . .
Somalia	160	. . .	. . .	69	. . .	. . .
South Africa	9,057	11,968	13,085	470	578	618
Sudan	1,333	. . .	. . .	104	. . .	. . .
Swaziland	. . .	67	. . .	. . .	178	. . .

Estimates of Total and Per Capita Gross National Product at Market Prices (Continued)

Country	Gross national product at market prices			Per capita gross national product at market prices		
	1963	1966	1967	1963	1966	1967
AFRICA	(Millions of U.S. Dollars)			(U.S. Dollars)		
Tanzania, Un. Rep.	708	806	843	65	68	69
Tanganyika	673	806	843	64	70	71
Zanzibar and Pemba	35	. . .	. . .	106	. . .	. . .
Togo	135	. . .	. . .	86	. . .	. . .
Tunisia	942	931	948	226	209	208
Uganda	534	709	754	74	92	95
United Arab Rep.	⁵4,331	⁵5,690	. . .	⁵155	⁵189	. . .
Upper Volta	220	245	. . .	47	49	. . .
Zaire	1,768	1,730	. . .	118	108	. . .
Zambia	532	1,014	1,175	152	265	298
EXAMPLES FROM ASIA						
India	42,251	43,842	. . .	92	88	. . .
Indonesia	8,899	10,649	. . .	89	99	. . .
Japan	65,633	97,477	115,660	684	986	1,158
Pakistan	9,249	13,106	. . .	94	125	. . .
NORTH AMERICA						
Canada	40,134	53,685	57,329	2,121	2,678	2,805
United States	599,705	760,498	803,914	3,166	3,862	4,037
TOTAL FOR AFRICA	**41,100**	. . .	. . .	**140**	. . .	. . .
TOTAL FOR ASIA						
East and South East	**160,200**	. . .	. . .	**164**	. . .	. . .
East and Southeast excl. Japan	*94,600*	. . .	. . .	*110*	. . .	. . .
TOTAL FOR NORTH AMERICA	**640,000**	**814,300**	**861,400**	**3,070**	**3,750**	**3,920**

Source. United Nations Statistical Yearbook.

Climatic Statistics

Recorded at Some Selected Meteorological Stations[1]
(Capital cities in italics)

Station and height above sea level in		Average daily temperature in coldest and hottest month				Relative humidity (percent)		Precipitation			Total annual rainfall	
		Max.		Min.				Average monthly fall in wettest and driest month				
feet:metres		°F	°C	°F	°C	am	pm		ins	mm	ins	mm
ALGERIA												
Algiers	Jan	59	15	49	9	75	66	Dec	5.4	137	30	762
194:59	Aug	85	29	71	22	70	60	Jul	<0.1	<2.5		
Boghari	Jan	49	9	36	2	. . . . . .		Dec	2.3	58	15.9	404
2,986:911	Aug	91	33	68	20	. . . . . .		Jul	0.2	5.1		
Colomb-Béchar	Jan	60	16	35	2	71	41	Nov	0.7	17.8	3.1	79
2,523:769	Jul	104	40	78	26	32	23	Jul	0.0	0.0		
ANGOLA												
Huambo[1]	Jun	80	27	41	5	43	31	Mar	9.8	249	57	1,448
5,577:1,700	Sep	88	31	49	9	47	33	Jul	<0.1	<2.5		
Luanda	Aug	74	23	64	18	84	78	Apr	4.6	117	12.7	323
194:59	Mar	86	30	75	24	79	75	Jul	<0.1	<2.5		
ASCENSION IS.												
Georgetown	Sep	82	28	71	22	67	71	Apr	1.1	30	5.2	132
55:17	Apr	88	31	75	24	67	72	Dec	0.1	2.5		
BOTSWANA												
Francistown	Jun	74	23	41	5	70	70	Jan	4.2	107	17.7	450
3,294:1,004	Oct	90	32	61	16	56	56	Jul	<0.1	<2.5		
CAMEROUN												
Douala	Aug	80	27	71	22	96	84	Jul	29.2	742	158	4,013
26:8	Feb	86	30	74	23	96	75	Jan	1.8	46		
Yaoundé	Aug	80	27	65	18	97	75	Oct	11.6	295	61.2	1,555
2,526:771	Mar	85	29	67	19	97	65	Dec	0.9	23		
CANARY IS.												
Las Palmas	Jan	70	21	58	14	72	71	Nov	2.1	53	8.9	226
20:6	Aug	79	26	70	21	75	76	Jun	<0.1	<2.5		
CAPE VERDE IS.												
Mindelo	Feb	72	22	66	19	67	63	Sep	1.8	46	3.9	99
49:15	Aug	81	27	73	23	74	71	Apr	0.0	0.0		
CENTRAL AFRICAN REPUBLIC												
Bangui	Aug	85	29	69	21	96	72	Jul	8.9	226	60.8	1,544
1270:387	Feb	93	34	70	21	90	49	Dec	0.2	5.1		
CHAD												
Faya[2]	Dec	82	28	55	13	50	28	Aug	0.7	17.8	0.7	17.8
837:255	May	112	44	76	24	39	21	note[3]	0.0	0.0		
Fort Lamy	Sep	91	33	72	22	91	63	Aug	12.6	320	29.3	744
968:295	Apr	107	42	74	23	37	13	note[4]	0.0	0.0		

[1] See map, page 495

Climatic Statistics (Continued)

Station and height above sea level in		Average daily temperature in coldest and hottest month					Relative humidity (percent)		Precipitation Average monthly fall in wettest and driest month			Total annual rainfall	
feet: metres		Max.		Min.									
		°F	°C	°F	°C	am	pm			ins	mm	ins	mm
CONGO (BRAZZAVILLE)													
Brazzaville	Jul	82	28	63	17	86	60	Nov	11.5		290	58	1,473
1,043 : 318	Apr	91	33	71	22	87	65	Jul	<0.1		<2.5		
Loango	Jul	78	26	66	19	86	73	Feb	6.7		17.0	48	1,222
164 : 50	Mar	87	31	75	24	87	74	note[5]	0.0		0.0		
CONGO, DEM. REPUBLIC OF (*see* Zaire Republic)													
DAHOMEY													
Cotonou	Aug	77	25	73	23	88	76	Jun	14.4		366	52.4	1,331
23 : 7	Mar	83	28	79	26	85	69	Dec	0.5		12.7		
Tchaourou	Aug	81	27	69	21	96	80	Jun	8.9		226	44.6	1,133
1,073 : 327	Mar	96	36	73	23	90	51	Jan	<0.1		<2.5		
EQUATORIAL GUINEA													
Santa Isabel	Jul	84	29	69	21	90	90	Jun	11.9		302	70.8	1,798
540 : 165	Apr	89	32	70	21	89	89	Jan	0.2		5.1		
ETHIOPIA													
Addis Ababa	Aug	69	21	50	10	86	72	Aug	11.8		300	48.7	1,237
8,038 : 2,450	May	77	25	50	10	63	43	Dec	0.2		5.1		
Asmara	Dec	71	22	49	9	80	49	Jul	6.7		170	18.4	467
7,628 : 2,325	May	78	26	53	12	69	42	Jan	<0.1		<2.5		
FRENCH TERRITORY OF AFARS and ISSAS													
Djibouti	Jan	84	29	73	23	82	69	Mar	1.0		25	5.1	130
23 : 7	Jul	106	41	87	31	57	43	Jun	<0.1		<2.5		
GABON													
Franceville	Jul	81	27	64	18	95	66	Nov	11.3		287	77.7	1,974
1,398 : 426	Mar	87	31	68	20	97	69	Jul	<0.1		<2.5		
Libreville	Jul	83	28	68	20	85	69	Nov	14.7		373	98.8	2,510
115 : 35	Apr	89	32	73	23	95	75	Jul	0.1		2.5		
GAMBIA													
Bathurst	Aug	85	29	73	23	95	78	Aug	19.7		500	51	1,295
90 : 27	Mar	94	34	63	17	76	29	Mar	<0.1		<2.5		
GHANA													
Accra	Aug	80	27	71	22	97	77	Jun	7.0		178	28.5	724
88 : 27	Mar	88	31	76	24	95	63	Jan	0.6		15.2		
Kumasi	Aug	81	27	69	21	97	79	Jun	7.9		201	55.2	1,402
942 : 287	Mar	91	33	71	22	96	66	Dec	0.8		20		
Tamale	Aug	84	29	71	22	95	74	Sep	8.9		226	41	1,041
635 : 194	Mar	99	37	76	24	62	37	Feb	0.1		2.5		
GUINEA													
Conakry	Aug	82	28	72	22	94	87	Jul	51.1		1,298	169	4,293
23 : 7	Apr	90	32	73	23	83	64	Jan	0.1		2.5		
Kouroussa	Aug	85	29	69	21	95	73	Aug	13.6		345	66.4	1,687
1,217 : 371	Mar	100	38	72	22	72	34	Feb	0.3		7.6		

Climatic Statistics (Continued)

Station and height above sea level in		Average daily temperature in coldest and hottest month				Relative humidity (percent)		Precipitation Average monthly fall in wettest and driest month			Total annual rainfall	
feet: metres		Max.		Min.								
		°F	°C	°F	°C	am	pm			ins	mm	ins	mm
IVORY COAST													
Abidjan	Aug	82	28	71	22	95	79	Jun	19.5	495	77.1	1,958
65:20	Apr	90	32	75	24	93	72	Jan	1.6	41		
KENYA													
Mombasa	Aug	81	27	71	22	76	72	May	12.6	320	47.3	1,201
52:16	Mar	88	31	77	25	77	63	Feb	0.7	17.8		
Nairobi	Jul	69	21	51	11	86	58	Apr	8.3	211	37.7	958
5,971:1,820	Feb	79	26	55	13	74	40	Jul	0.6	15.2		
LIBERIA													
Monrovia	Jul	80	27	72	22	88	83	Jul	39.2	996	202	5,131
75:23	Mar	87	31	74	23	92	77	Jan	1.2	31		
LIBYA													
Benghazi	Jan	63	17	50	10	69	60	Jan	2.6	66	10.5	267
82:25	Jul	84	29	71	22	59	61	Jul	0.1	2.5		
Múrzuch	Jan	67	19	38	3	55	55	Dec	0.2	5.1	0.3	7.6
1,296:395	Jun	108	42	70	21	23	23	note[6]	0.0	0.0		
Tripoli	Jan	61	16	47	8	68	59	Dec	3.7	94	15.1	284
72:22	Aug	86	30	72	22	72	69	Aug	0.1	2.5		
MADAGASCAR													
Tananarive	Jul	68	20	48	9	93	61	Jan	11.8	300	53.4	1,356
4,500:1,372	Nov	81	27	58	14	86	54	Jun	0.3	7.6		
MALAWI													
Zomba	Jul	72	22	53	12	72	61	Jan	12.1	307	52.9	1,344
3,141:957	Nov	85	29	66	19	67	56	Sep	0.2	5.1		
MALI													
Bamako	Aug	87	31	71	22	94	73	Aug	13.7	348	44.1	1,120
1,116:340	Apr	103	39	76	24	63	36	Feb	<0.1	<2.5		
Tombouctou[7]	Jan	87	31	55	13	39	22	Aug	3.2	81	9.1	231
988:302	Jun	109	43	80	27	55	31	Dec	<0.1	<2.5		
MAURITANIA													
Nouakchott	Dec	83	28	56	13	58	34	Aug	4.1	104	6.2	158
69:21	Sep	93	34	75	24	85	59	Jan	<0.1	<2.5		
Tidjika	Jan	82	28	52	11	43	26	Aug	2.1	53	5.8	147
1,312:400	Jun	107	42	78	26	40	25	Jan	0.0	0.0		
MAURITIUS													
Royal Alfred Obs.	Aug	75	24	62	17	85	61	Mar	8.7	221	50.6	1,285
181:55	Jan	86	30	73	23	86	67	Sep	1.4	36		
MOROCCO													
Midelt	Jan	53	12	32	0	73	55	Apr	1.3	33	9	229
5,003:1,525	Jul	93	34	61	16	58	26	Aug	0.3	7.6		
Rabat	Jan	63	17	46	8	89	72	Dec	3.4	86	19.8	503
213:65	Aug	83	28	64	18	91	61	Jul	<0.1	<2.5		

Climatic Statistics (Continued)

Station and height above sea level in		Average daily temperature in coldest and hottest month				Relative humidity (percent)		Precipitation Average monthly fall in wettest and driest month			Total annual rainfall	
feet:metres		Max.		Min.								
		°F	°C	°F	°C	am	pm		ins	mm	ins	mm
MOZAMBIQUE												
Beira	Jul	77	25	61	16	81	65	Jan	10.9	277	59.9	1,522
28:8.5	Jan	89	32	75	24	73	66	Aug	1.1	28		
Chicôa	Jul	86	30	55	13	60	60	Jan	7.8	198	27.4	693
899:274	Nov	100	38	68	20	59	59	Aug	<0.1	<2.5		
Lourenço Marques	Jul	76	24	55	13	71	59	Jan	5.1	130	29.9	760
194:59	Jan	86	30	71	22	72	66	Aug	0.5	12.7		
NIGER												
Agadès	Jan	86	30	50	10	38	17	Aug	3.7	94	6.8	173
1,706:520	May	108	42	76	24	36	18	note[8]	0.0	0.0		
Niamey	Aug	89	32	73	23	91	68	Aug	7.4	188	21.6	551
709:216	Apr	108	42	77	25	37	18	Dec	0.0	0.0		
NIGERIA												
Enugu	Jul	83	28	71	22	92	75	Sep	12.8	325	71.5	1,816
763:233	Mar	92	33	75	24	86	54	Dec	0.5	12.7		
Kano	Jan	86	30	55	13	40	13	Aug	12.2	310	34.2	869
1,533:467	Apr	101	38	75	24	47	14	Dec	0.2	5.1		
Lagos	Aug	82	28	73	23	85	76	Jun	18.1	460	72.3	1,836
10:3	Mar	89	32	78	26	82	72	Dec	1.0	25		
PORTUGUESE GUINEA												
Bolama	Aug	83	28	74	23	86	82	Aug	27.6	701	85.9	2,182
62:19	Apr	91	33	73	23	64	50	Mar	<0.1	<2.5		
RHODESIA												
Salisbury	Jun	70	21	44	7	58	36	Jan	7.7	196	32.6	828
4,831:1,473	Oct	83	28	58	14	43	26	Jul	<0.1	<2.5		
SÃO TOMÉ												
São Tomé	Jul	82	28	69	21	74	70	Mar	5.9	150	38	965
16:4.9	Mar	87	31	73	23	80	76	Jul	<0.1	<2.5		
SENEGAL												
Dakar	Jan	79	26	64	18	71	45	Aug	10	254	21.3	541
131:40	Oct	89	32	76	24	86	65	Apr	<0.1	<2.5		
SEYCHELLES												
Port Victoria	Jul	81	27	75	24	77	76	Jan	15.2	386	92.5	2,350
15:4.6	Apr	86	30	77	25	74	74	Aug	2.7	69		
SIERRA LEONE												
Freetown	Aug	82	28	73	23	91	82	Aug	35.3	897	135	3,429
37:11.3	Apr	87	31	77	25	81	71	Feb	0.1	2.5		
Musaia	Aug	83	28	69	21	90	90	Sep	14.4	366	77.8	1,976
1,181:360	Mar	96	36	67	19	75	75	Dec	0.2	5.1		
SOMALI REPUBLIC												
Mogadiscio	Aug	83	28	73	23	85	80	Jun	3.8	97	16.9	429
39:11.9	Apr	90	32	78	26	78	75	Jan	<0.1	<2.5		

Climatic Statistics (Continued)

Station and height above sea level in		Average daily temperature in coldest and hottest month				Relative humidity (percent)		Average monthly fall in wettest and driest month			Total annual rainfall	
feet:metres		Max.		Min.								
		°F	°C	°F	°C	am	pm		ins	mm	ins	mm
SOUTH AFRICA												
Cape Town	Jul	63	17	45	7	91	67	Jul	3.5	89	20	508
56:17	Feb	79	26	60	16	77	54	Feb	0.3	7.6		
Durban	Jul	72	22	52	11	71	61	Mar	5.1	130	39.7	1,008
16:4.9	Jan	81	27	69	21	79	73	Jul	1.1	28		
Pretoria	Jul	66	19	37	3	72	31	Nov	5.2	132	30.9	785
4,491:1,369	Jan	81	27	60	16	71	47	Aug	0.2	5.1		
SOUTH WEST AFRICA (NAMIBIA)												
Walvis Bay	Sep	66	19	48	9	90	69	Mar	0.3	7.6	0.9	23
24:7.3	Apr	75	24	55	13	89	66	Jun	<0.1	<2.5		
Windhoek	Jul	68	20	43	6	42	18	Mar	3.1	79	14.3	363
5,669:1,728	Jan	85	29	63	17	50	27	Aug	<0.1	<2.5		
SPANISH WEST AFRICA (SAHARA)												
Villa Cisneros	Jan	71	22	56	13	75	51	Sep	1.4	36	3.0	76
35:10.7	Sep	80	27	67	19	89	63	Jun	0.0	0.0		
SUDAN												
Khartoum	Jan	90	32	59	15	37	20	Aug	2.8	71	6.2	158
1,279:390	Jun	106	41	79	26	38	18	Dec	0.0	0.0		
Wau	Aug	89	32	69	21	85	56	Aug	8.2	208	43.3	1,100
1,443:440	Mar	100	38	70	21	48	22	Dec	<0.1	<2.5		
SWAZILAND												
Mbabane	Jun	66	19	42	6	64	64	Jan	10.0	254	55.2	1,402
3,816:1,163	Jan	77	25	59	15	78	78	Jun	0.8	20		
TANZANIA—TANGANYIKA												
Dar es Salaam	Aug	83	28	66	19	84	64	Apr	11.4	290	41.9	1,064
47:14.3	Feb	88	31	77	25	81	74	Aug	1.0	25		
Tabora	Jun	82	28	59	15	67	40	Mar	6.8	173	35	889
4,151:1,265	Oct	90	32	66	19	53	30	Jul	0.0	0.0		
TANZANIA—ZANZIBAR												
Chukwani	Jul	82	28	72	22	87	69	Apr	12.6	320	55.5	1,410
61:18.6	Mar	91	33	77	25	85	72	Jul	1.1	30		
TUNISIA												
Gafsa	Jan	58	14	39	4	79	52	Mar	0.9	23	5.9	150
1,030:314	Jul	101	38	70	21	59	30	Jul	0.1	2.5		
Tunis	Jan	58	14	43	6	83	64	Jan	2.5	64	16.5	419
217:66	Aug	91	33	69	21	72	47	Jul	0.1	2.5		
UGANDA												
Kampala	Jul	77	25	62	17	89	66	Apr	6.9	175	46.2	1,174
4,304:1,312	Jan	83	28	65	18	78	54	Jan	1.8	46		
Lodwar	Aug	92	33	71	22	61	39	Apr	2.4	61	6.1	155
1,660:506	Mar	98	37	76	24	54	33	Jan	<0.1	<2.5		

Climatic Statistics (Continued)

Station and height above sea level in	Average daily tempera-ture in coldest and hottest month					Relative humidity (percent)		Average monthly fall in wettest and driest month			Total annual rainfall	
feet: metres		Max. °F °C		Min. °F °C		am	pm		ins	mm	ins	mm
UNITED ARAB REPUBLIC												
Alexandria	Jan	65	18	51	11	71	61	Dec	2.2	56	7.0	178
105:32	Aug	87	31	74	23	72	68	Jun	<0.1	<2.5		
Aswân	Jan	74	23	50	10	52	29	note[9] <0.1		<2.5	<0.1	<2.5
366:112	Jun	107	42	78	26	26	16	note[10] 0.0		0.0		
Cairo	Jan	65	18	47	8	69	40	note[11] 0.2		5.1	1.1	28
381:116	Jul	96	36	70	21	65	24	note[12] 0.0		0.0		
UPPER VOLTA												
Bobo-Dioulasso	Aug	85	29	70	21	96	75	Aug	12.0	305	46.4	1,179
1,411:430	Mar	101	38	68	20	60	33	Dec	0.0	0.0		
Ouagadougou	Aug	87	31	72	22	81	67	Aug	10.9	277	35.2	894
991:362	Mar	104	40	73	23	39	20	Dec	0.0	0.0		
ZAIRE REPUBLIC												
Kalemie[13]	Jul	82	28	58	14	87	60	Apr	8.4	213	45.4	1,354
2,493:760	Oct	87	31	67	19	89	69	Jul	0.1	2.5		
Kinshasa[14]	Jul	81	27	64	18	93	67	Nov	8.7	221	53.3	1,354
1,066:325	Apr	89	32	71	22	95	70	Jul	0.1	2.5		
Kisangani[15]	Aug	83	28	68	20	97	75	Oct	8.6	218	67.1	1,704
1,370:418	Apr	88	31	70	21	97	68	Jan	2.1	53		
ZAMBIA												
Kasama	Jul	76	24	50	10	61	29	Jan	10.7	272	51.5	1,308
4,544:1,385	Oct	87	31	62	17	44	19	Jun	<0.1	<2.5		
Lusaka	Jun	73	23	50	10	56	32	Jan	9.1	231	32.9	836
4,191:1,277	Oct	88	31	64	18	39	23	Aug	0.0	0.0		

NOTES
1. Nova Lisboa (future capital).
2. Largeau.
3. No rainfall from October to April.
4. No rainfall from November to March.
5. No rainfall from June to August.
6. No rainfall from June to September.
7. Timbuktu.
8. No rainfall from October to February.
9. Rainfall from October to June less than 0.1 in. each month.
10. No rainfall from July to September.
11. Rainfall from December to March 0.2 in. each month.
12. No rainfall in July and August.
13. Albertville.
14. Léopoldville.
15. Stanleyville.

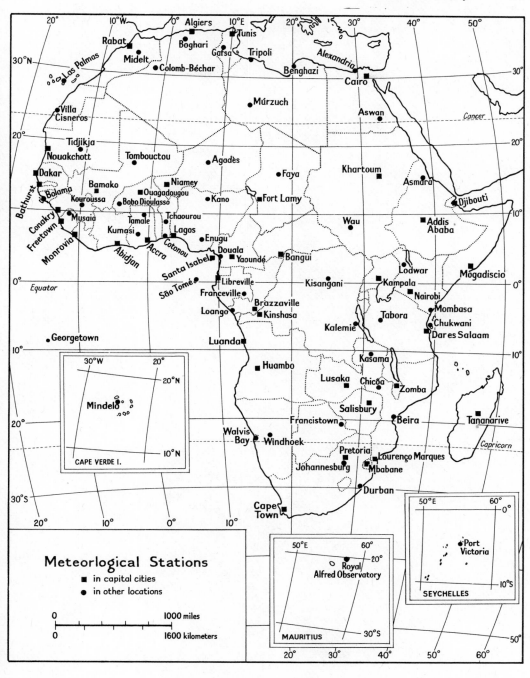

Meteorlogical Stations

- ■ in capital cities
- ● in other locations

0   1000 miles
0   1600 kilometers

CAPE VERDE I.

MAURITIUS

SEYCHELLES

Index

The more important references are shown in bold type; *maps are indicated in italics.*
The Index does not cover the Statistical Summary, the Selected Bibliography, or books listed under the heading "Further Reading."